Expanding the Reach of Education Reforms

Perspectives from Leaders in the Scale-Up of Educational Interventions

Thomas K. Glennan, Jr., Susan J. Bodilly,
Jolene R. Galegher, Kerri A. Kerr

Prepared for the Ford Foundation

 EDUCATION

The research described in this report was conducted by RAND Education for the Ford Foundation.

Library of Congress Cataloging-in-Publication Data

Expanding the reach of education reforms : perspectives from leaders in the scale-up of educational interventions / [edited by] Thomas K. Glennan ... [et al.].
    p. cm.
    "MG-248."
    Includes bibliographical references.
    ISBN 0-8330-3659-9 (pbk.)
    1. School improvement programs—United States. 2. Educational change—United States. 3. Education—Standards—United States. I. Glennan, Thomas Keith, 1935– II. Rand Corporation.

LB2822.82.E94 2004
371.2'00973—dc22

2004016652

The RAND Corporation is a nonprofit research organization providing objective analysis and effective solutions that address the challenges facing the public and private sectors around the world. RAND's publications do not necessarily reflect the opinions of its research clients and sponsors.

RAND® is a registered trademark.

Published 2004 by the RAND Corporation
1700 Main Street, P.O. Box 2138, Santa Monica, CA 90407-2138
1200 South Hayes Street, Arlington, VA 22202-5050
201 North Craig Street, Suite 202, Pittsburgh, PA 15213-1516
RAND URL: http://www.rand.org/
To order RAND documents or to obtain additional information, contact
Distribution Services: Telephone: (310) 451-7002;
Fax: (310) 451-6915; Email: order@rand.org

Preface

The sporadic and often temporary ability to bring innovations in education to scale has long frustrated those interested in improving the performance of K–12 students in America's public schools. In the last two decades, however, developers of educational interventions designed to improve teaching and learning have made some progress toward this goal, with several demonstrating measurable gains in student performance in multiple schools or districts. The purpose of this book is to capture some of the knowledge of these developers, all of whom are leaders in the effort to improve the performance of students in public schools by introducing innovations in curriculum, teaching methods, administrative practices, and funding mechanisms.

This volume grew out of a series of meetings of developers of K–12 reforms convened by RAND Education, a division of the RAND Corporation. The meetings, sponsored by the Ford Foundation, were intended to explore the experiences of the designers of reform efforts, with a particular focus on identifying common problems in scaling up reforms and, if possible, common solutions to them. Developers of 15 different reform efforts contributed chapters. The authors attempt to capture their experiences and the lessons they learned from their efforts to scale up the interventions they had designed and implemented.

Thomas Glennan and Susan Bodily convened the meetings that stimulated these chapters. Along with Jolene Galegher and Kerri Kerr, they helped to shape the final version of the chapters and wrote the introduction and summary.

The contributed chapters were the responsibility of the authors, all of whom are well-known experts in education reform. Their contributions have been reviewed and refined by the editors of this volume, as well as members of the staff in the Publications Department of the RAND Corporation, but the views of education reform presented within each chapter, as well as the data describing the efficacy of the programs they have designed and implemented, are the sole responsibility of the contributing authors.

This book should be of interest to funders of education and education reform efforts, developers of interventions intended to enhance the performance of students at all levels of schooling, legislators, state and federal policymakers, educational researchers, and school authorities interested in supporting efforts to improve teaching and learning in K–12 education.

Dedication

In memory of Tom Glennan, who contributed immeasurably to the development of this book and the field of study it represents. Tom was a wonderful scholar, teacher, and friend, and we are grateful to have had the opportunity to know him and to learn from him.

Contents

CHAPTER SIX

Taking Education Programs to Scale: Lessons from the Field

CHAPTER SEVEN

**Reaching for Coherence in School Reform: The Case of
America's Choice**

CHAPTER ELEVEN

Scaling Up Talent Development High Schools: Lessons Learned from Comprehensive High School Reform

CHAPTER TWELVE

Taking High Schools That Work to Scale: The Evolution of a High School Reform Program

CHAPTER THIRTEEN

The First Few Years of Edison Schools: Ten Lessons in Getting to Scale

CHAPTER FOURTEEN

School Districts as Learning Organizations: A Strategy for Scaling Education Reform

CHAPTER FIFTEEN

Choices and Consequences in the Bay Area School Reform Collaborative: Building the Capacity to Scale Up Whole-School Improvement

Figures

Tables

Acknowledgments

The enterprise that led to the book was prompted by a single important question from Janice Petrovich of the Ford Foundation. Familiar with our previous work as analysts of education reform efforts, she asked us how we would explain the frequent failure of reform efforts to scale up. The Ford Foundation sponsored two meetings at which national leaders in efforts to scale up school reforms were invited to present their ideas and experiences as developers of diverse approaches to education reform. We thank Janice and the foundation for their interest in and support of this work.

The developers—who eventually became the contributors to this volume—responded enthusiastically to our invitation. At each of the two meetings, they provided many worthwhile and insightful contributions, thus helping each other to identify both the common and the unique aspects of their respective efforts and, thereby, contributing to a general understanding of the complexities of scaling up education reforms. The targets of their efforts—particular areas of the curriculum, levels of education, networks of teachers, state education policies—varied widely, but they held in common an intense and enduring commitment to improving the quality of education for all of America's children. We appreciate both their participation in these meetings and their responsiveness to our recommendations as they developed and refined the papers presented here.

Our colleagues Jake Dembosky and Gina Ikemoto supported the meetings by taking notes and conveying the notes quickly and efficiently back to the contributors. Steve Bloodsworth designed the cover; Daniel Sheehan provided preliminary editorial advice, and Phyllis M. Gilmore edited the final version; Carolyn Rowe helped organize production; and John Warren helped organize prepublication marketing. Peter Hoffman, Managing Editor of RAND Publications, answered many important questions about the publication process and, along with other members of the Publications staff, helped us push this book out the door.

The editors thank all these individuals for their help in this effort.

Abbreviations

AED	Academy for Educational Development
ARPANET	Advanced Research Projects Agency Network (precursor to the Internet)
AYP	Adequate Yearly Progress
BASRC	the Bay Area School Reform Collaborative
BAWP	Bay Area Writing Project
BBN	BBN Technologies, a technology oriented R&D company
CCE	Center for Collaborative Education
CCIU	Chester County Intermediate Unit
CES	Coalition of Essential Schools
CFO	chief financial officer
CGI	cognitively guided instruction
CIS	Communities in Schools
CMO	chief marketing officer
CMCD	Consistency Management and Cooperative Discipline
COI	cycle of inquiry
CPRD	Center for Prevention Research and Development
CPRE	Consortium for Policy Research in Education
CSRD	Comprehensive School Reform Demonstration Program
DI	Direct Instruction

HISD	Houston Independent School District
HSTW	High Schools That Work
IFL	Institute for Learning
KERA	Kentucky Education Reform Act
KET	Kentucky Educational Television
KIRIS	Kentucky Instructional Results Information System
LRDC	Learning Research and Development Center (University of Pittsburgh)
MBA	master of business administration
MMGW	Making Middle Grades Work
MTF	mathematical team facilitators
NAS	New American Schools
NCEE	National Center on Education and the Economy
NCLB	No Child Left Behind Act
NIFDI	National Institute for Direct Instruction
NWP	National Writing Project
OERI	Office of Educational Research and Improvement (U.S. Department of Education)
PCA	Pittsburgh Center for the Arts
PBEC	The Public Education and Business Coalition
PG	Project GRAD
R&D	research and development
SAT	Scholastic Aptitude Test
TAAS	Texas Assessment of Academic Skills
TDHS	Talent Development High School
TIMSS	Third International Math and Science Study

CHAPTER ONE

Introduction: Framing the Problem

Susan J. Bodilly, Thomas K. Glennan, Jr.,
Kerri A. Kerr, and Jolene R. Galegher

Fifty years ago, *Brown v. Board of Education* set in motion a series of legislative and judicial efforts to undo the effects of racial segregation, providing opportunities and support for children who had been denied both. Twenty years ago, the publication of *A Nation at Risk* (National Commission on Excellence in Education, 1983) drew attention to the need for reform in all of America's schools to ensure the nation's ability to compete in the international economy. These two forces—pressure to improve the quality of schools for all students and pressure to reduce gaps in access and performance of students—have resulted in both a demand for better approaches to teaching and learning and a supply of interventions intended to build the capacity within our schools to serve all children better.

On the demand side, the nation has given education a high priority, even in the face of economic downturns and international turmoil. Individual states, some on their own and some under pressure from federal leaders, have revamped their standards, their assessment systems, and the incentives they provide to schools to improve their performance. The federal government, through the No Child Left Behind Act of 2001, continues to press for improvements in educational performance within all the many social and ethnic groups in American society and is holding schools accountable for achieving it.

On the supply side, private philanthropists and the federal government have invested heavily in developing and disseminating innovative reforms intended to change the existing practices of teachers and schools. With the help of these investments, organizations external to the school have created interventions to improve curriculum and instruction and to promote stronger teacher collegial interactions in support of better teaching. In this book, we use the terms *designs, reforms, interventions,* and *programs* interchangeably to refer to systems of ideas and activities intended to improve teaching and learning in schools. We refer to the external organizations responsible for these interventions as *providers* or *developers.*

In the past, such external improvement providers often might have helped one or two schools or a few dozen teachers. But, as the nation has demanded systemwide improvements, the education establishment has looked to such providers to implement reforms more rapidly and more extensively than in the past. In addition, recent federal support for school improvement efforts has been made contingent on the ability of the developers and marketers of school improvement services to provide scientific evidence demonstrating the positive effects of their programs. In short, expectations for improvement have risen over the past 20 years, shifting from satisfaction with meeting individual teacher or school needs to demands for improvements "at scale" and with proven effectiveness.

The major challenge states, districts, schools, and teachers now face is building and maintaining the capacity within the newly evolving system to deliver the educational promises of performance-based accountability. The demand for increasing the capacity of states, districts, schools, and teachers for continuous educational improvement on a wide scale is high and insistent.

This moment is fragile; success is not assured. The organizations that supply education improvement services are still young, still working to find better ways to address the problems of large numbers of schools and students. Often, they can provide only limited evidence of their value and have only limited capacity to deliver high-quality services. Further, the capacity of the educational system to use the services is limited; teachers, schools, and school districts have not yet learned how to organize for continuing improvement of instruction and performance on a wide scale (Glennan, 1998; Stringfield and Datnow, 1998).

Thus, it is now opportune to assess what we know about expanding the reach of educational interventions provided by those external to the school and intended to improve the capacity of the existing systems to ensure continuous progress—in particular, reforms designed to improve teaching and learning in the classroom, whether directly or indirectly.

Origins and Purpose of This Book

This book originated with an apparently simple suggestion from the leader of the education program at the Ford Foundation. Several of us at the RAND Corporation had been studying the investments of a number of different foundations in developing education-related interventions intended to increase the capacity of many classes of educators to improve practice. She asked whether we could distill lessons from this work that would help her and other funding executives manage their investments in education reform. In particular, she wanted to determine whether there were lessons to be learned that could significantly increase the likelihood that the products of the investments would find wide use in the education community and would significantly affect student learning.

This book represents a limited inquiry into what the last 20 years of experience reveal about scaling up educational innovations. We used the following principles to shape the boundaries of our inquiry.

First, we defined the topic of interest as specific types of educational improvement efforts—those that attempt to improve the existing practices of the existing teaching staff so as to improve teaching and learning in classrooms—a concept that Wilson (1989) defined as *reform*. Education reform in this sense is distinct from alternative approaches to organizational improvement, such as replacing existing staff, changing the governance structure, or introducing market-based systems.

Second, we focused on reforms from external providers working in a research, development, and demonstration mode with funding from philanthropic or government sponsors. We directed our inquiry into the process of how they spread from their demonstration sites to reach more students, more teachers, and more schools.

Third, our inquiry included models, programs, designs, and interventions with different foci for change, ranging from individual teachers to specific subjects within a school to whole schools and their full curriculum to systems of schools. This definition also included interventions that were highly prescriptive and those that were shaped only by general principles for continuous improvement.

Following our initial conversations with the Ford Foundation, we began the process that led to this book by asking a simple question: Who would know the most about this enterprise? The answer we arrived at was equally simple: the individuals who developed the reforms and have attempted to scale up their programs systematically. Our goal was to engage them in drawing out the practical lessons from their efforts to scale up diverse educational interventions.

This book is a descriptive analysis of the scale-up process, consisting of a collection of reflective essays by leaders of external provider organizations. The essays describe how the providers created interventions and built and sustained organizations and networks that assisted educators, schools, and school districts in implementing the improved practices more systematically than in the past. We asked these leaders to meet with us as a study group to discuss the problems of scale-up as they understood them from their own practical experiences and to identify potentially important issues for further thought. On the basis of this initial meeting, the members of the study group prepared drafts of the essays in this book. The group met again to review and critique one another's essays, after which the authors revised their essays. Working from readings of these essays, reviews of the literature, and the discussions of the study group, RAND staff members wrote this introduction, which provides the context for the contributing chapters, and a final chapter of the book, which analyzes the contributing chapters and provides a set of observations on the scale-up process.

The contributors, all leaders in their field, were asked to participate because they are recognized for achieving at least some success in spreading the programs they developed. The list of possible contributors was quite long, but many were not available to participate because of scheduling and other conflicts. The authors, the programs with which they are associated, the focus of the program, and the number of places using the program as of fall 2003 are listed in Table 1.1.

This is not an evaluation of the interventions associated with the contributors to this book. Others are conducting such evaluations, and as evidence becomes available, it is assembled and distributed by the online What Works Clearinghouse (U.S. Department of Education, undated).

In the remainder of this chapter, we outline the concepts underlying the programs and processes discussed in this book. We begin by describing how the concept of scale in educational improvement evolved, moving from a simplistic replication model to the more-complex view that now prevails. Included in that discussion is a review of the literature of scaling-up educational interventions intended to improve teaching and learning in classrooms, directly or indirectly. We then provide a conceptual framework that includes a specific definition of scale-up and a list of choices facing developers and providers of services. Finally, we introduce the contributed chapters.

Scale-Up in an Earlier Era of Educational Reforms

Significant attempts at widespread instructional reform that were actually evaluated date back to the 1960s. Figure 1.1 provides a picture of the view of the process of scale-up that prevailed in education from the 1960s through the 1970s, which was often referred to as the *replication model*. Based in management science precepts about organizational change, this model envisioned an external provider who would respond to a felt need for change or a performance failure in schooling by developing an idea or sets of ideas for curriculum, instruction, and associated training for teachers intended to improve

Table 1.1
Interventions Included in This Volume[a]

	Description
Cognitively Guided Instruction (CGI)	
Goals	Influence teachers' instructional practices by providing professional development on research-based knowledge about children's mathematical thinking
Grade Levels	K–6
Years in existence	18
Intervention level	Teacher
Discipline	Math
Adopters	
Currently	Approximately 4,000 teachers trained each year[b]
Since inception	More than 20,000 teachers
See	Chapter Two, by Thomas P. Carpenter and Megan L. Franke
National Writing Project (NWP)	
Goals	Improve student writing achievement by improving the teaching of writing in the nation's schools
Grade Levels	K–12
Years in existence	29
Intervention level	Teacher
Disciplines	Writing
Adopters	
Currently	175 NWP sites and 100,000 teacher participants each year
Since inception	More than 2 million teachers
See	Chapter Three, by Joseph P. McDonald, Judy Buchanan, and Richard Sterling
National Institute for Direct Instruction (NIFDI)[c]	
Goals	Accelerate the academic achievement of all students by controlling the characteristics of instruction and relevant variables in the school setting
Grade Levels	K–5
Years in existence	6[d]
Intervention level	School
Disciplines	Reading, language arts, math, cultural literacy
Adopters	
Currently	23 schools[e]
Since inception	57 schools
See	Chapter Four, Siegfried E. Engelmann and Kurt E. Engelmann

Table 1.1—Continued

	Description
Success For All	
Goals	Comprehensively restructure elementary schools serving many at-risk children focusing particularly on language arts curriculum and instruction
Grade Levels	Pre-K–6
Years in existence	15
Intervention level	School
Disciplines	Reading, writing, language arts
Adopters	
Currently	1,500 schools
Since inception	Approximately 1,900 schools
See	Chapter Five, by Robert E. Slavin and Nancy A. Madden
Different Ways of Knowing	
Goals	Work with schools to identify student learning and professional development goals and choose appropriate school improvement strategies and tools to meet school goals
Grade Levels	K–12
Years in existence	14
Intervention level	School
Disciplines	Reading, writing, math, social studies, arts
Adopters	
Currently	101 schools
Since inception	625 schools
See	Chapter Eight, by Linda A. Johannesen
Co-nect	
Goals	Provide professional development services in such areas as curriculum, instruction, technology, and data-driven decisionmaking to help K–12 districts and schools improve student achievement
Grade Levels	K–12
Years in existence	11
Intervention level	School
Disciplines	Literacy, math, science, technology
Adopters	
Currently	225 schools
Since inception	560 schools
See	Chapter Nine, by Bruce Goldberg

Table 1.1—Continued

	Description
Turning Points	
Goals	Assist middle schools with a multiyear, intensive, whole-school reform process to significantly improve teaching, student engagement, and learning
Grade Levels	6–8
Years in existence	4
Intervention level	School
Disciplines	Reading, writing, math, social studies
Adopters	
Currently	68 schools
Since inception	90 schools
See	Chapter Ten, by Dan French and Leah Rugen
Talent Development High School (TDHS)	
Goals	Redesign low-performing high schools using a comprehensive reform model emphasizing organizational and instructional change within an academy approach
Grade Levels	9–12
Years in existence	8
Intervention level	School
Disciplines	Reading, writing, math
Adopters	
Currently	40 schools
Since inception	60 schools
See	Chapter Eleven, by Nettie E. Legters, James M. McPartland, and Robert Balfanz
High Schools That Work (HSTW)	
Goals	Raise the achievement of high school students by providing a combination of challenging academic courses and modern career and technical studies
Grade Levels	9–12
Years in existence	16
Level	School
Disciplines	English, math, science, social studies, career and technical
Adopters	
Currently	More than 1,100 schools
Since inception	Approximately 1,600 schools
See	Chapter Twelve, by Gene Bottoms

Table 1.1—Continued

	Description
Edison Schools	
Goals	Partner with schools and districts to raise student achievement through a business model
	Edison manages all educational, organizational, and management aspects of schooling in partner schools
Grade Levels	K–12
Years in existence	11
Intervention level	School
Disciplines	English language arts, math, science, social studies, foreign language, fine arts, physical fitness and health
Adopters	
Currently	150 schools
Since inception	165 schools
See	Chapter Thirteen, by John E. Chubb
America's Choice	
Goals	Ensure all students are academically successful by creating coherent educational systems focused on instruction and building the capacity of all levels of the system to sustain improvement
Grade Levels	K–12
Years in existence	5
Intervention level	School and district
Disciplines	Reading, writing, language arts, math, science
Adopters	
Currently	466 schools and 133 districts (for districtwide adoption)
Since inception	562 schools
See	Chapter Seven, by Marc Tucker
Project GRAD	
Goals	Improve educational outcomes for students in low-performing schools by providing a comprehensive, coherent model of support, including proven curricular models and community support
Grade Levels	Pre-K–12
Years in existence	10
Intervention level	School and district feeder patterns
Disciplines	Reading, writing, math
Adopters	
Currently	9 school systems
Since inception	10 school systems
See	Chapter Six, by James L. Ketelsen

Table 1.1—Continued

	Description
Institute for Learning (IFL)	
Goals	Partners with school districts to bring about systemwide change in teaching and learning
Grade Levels	K–12
Years in existence	8
Intervention level	District
Disciplines	English, math, science, social studies[g]
Adopters	
Currently	12 districts[g]
Since inception	17 districts
See	Chapter Fourteen, by Thomas K. Glennan, Jr., and Lauren B. Resnick
Bay Area School Reform Collaborative (BASRC)	
Goals	Improve student achievement and narrow achievement gaps through building school-level capacity to engage in a systematic process of continuous improvement
Grade Levels	K–12
Years in existence	8
Intervention level	School and district
Disciplines	N/A
Adopters	
Currently	98 schools and 27 districts (for districtwide change)
Since inception	322 schools
See	Chapter Fifteen, by Merrill Vargo

[a] Information included in this table refers to the status of interventions in 2003 as of the time authors wrote the accompanying chapter.

[b] Numbers of adopters for CGI are estimates due to the grass-roots nature of the organization.

[c] Direct Instruction (DI) was developed in the late 1960s and has been employed in some form by more than 10,000 schools. NIFDI, a not-for-profit corporation founded in 1997, is dedicated to providing school districts with a solid training program and approach for the implementation of DI in districts, schools, and classrooms.

[d] NIFDI has been in existence for 6 years; DI has existed for approximately 35 years.

[e] About 10,000 schools employ DI in some form today.

[f] America's Choice currently contracts with 133 districts for districtwide adoption.

[g] The work of the IFL is intended to apply to all instruction. However, work has focused on literacy, math, or disciplinary literacy, according to the interests of the partner district.

[h] This count includes one consortium of districts.

Figure 1.1
The Replication Model of Scale-Up

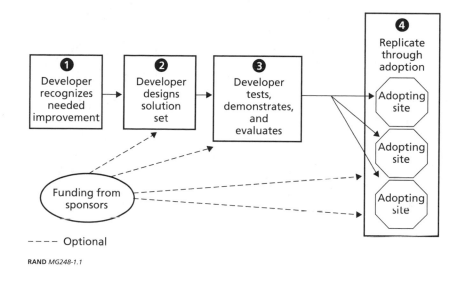

RAND *MG248-1.1*

teaching practices and eventually student performance (steps one and two). This set of ideas would be tested in a specific school or with a group of teachers called a *demonstration site*, then refined and perfected (step three). Sometimes the program would be evaluated to assess its ability to improve test scores or other measures of achievement. It was then assumed that the intervention could be adopted with great fidelity at multiple sites in the same way that had worked in the demonstration site (step four). This transfer was often supported by documented curriculum, pedagogy, and a uniform training regimen. Funders had a role in providing the resources for the development, testing, demonstration, and evaluation and often for expansion of the reform.

In this model, most of the arrows run from left to right because the process was perceived to be a one-way system, with the developers doing something to the educators to ensure adoption in more places by more people. Feedback loops, interactions among the parties, and interactions among sites were not emphasized (Goggin et al., 1990). *Scale* meant quantity—the number of teachers, schools, classrooms, or districts that adopted a reform—and changes in depth of practice in the adopting schools, how long the changes were sustained, or what other changes were needed for sustainability received little attention.

Elmore, writing in *Harvard Educational Review* (1996, p. 1), lamented this view of scale-up, attacking its hollow center:

> The problem of scale in educational innovation can be briefly stated as follows: innovations that require large changes in the core of educational practice seldom penetrate more than a small fraction of American schools and classrooms, and seldom last for very long when they do. By the "core" of educational practice, I mean how teachers understand the nature of knowledge and the student's role in learning, how these ideas about knowledge and learning are manifested in teaching and classwork.

Elmore (1996, p. 21) suggested that this failure to scale up educational interventions "is not so much a failure of a theory of how to reproduce success but the absence of a practical theory that takes account of the institutional complexities that operate on changes in practice."

Throughout the 1970s, in what Goggin et al. (1990) called the first and second waves of implementation studies, evaluators assessed the efficacy of this "cookie cutter" approach and found few new sites that had implemented the design with fidelity (i.e., sites where replication actually occurred). The culminating study was the RAND Change Agent Study (Berman and McLaughlin, 1975), which evaluated several attempts to use the replication model to scale up federal interventions. The study found that implementation in the adopting sites was often rife with departures from the model because of interactions with the institutional setting. The authors coined the term "mutual adaptation" to describe the phenomena of drift away from fidelity to the model.

As a result, some in the education sector began to realize the difficulty of changing the practice of teachers who were embedded in a system of rules and regulations that did not support new practices (Fullan, 1993; Goggin et al., 1990; Tyack and Cuban, 1995). Hierarchical mandates that worked in command structures or the private sector did not appear to work in public education. The market forces that promoted adoption of innovations in the private sector did not operate on schools. Consumption, in the form of attendance, is mandated for those under a certain age, and parents could not select a public school for their children to attend except by choosing a housing location. Public educational institutions were governed by political processes and were administered by entrenched bureaucracies characterized as a system of fragmented centralization prone to seeking legitimacy by remaining the same, not by innovating (Hill and Bonan, 1991; Meyer, Scott, and Strang, 1987; Scott, 1987; Weick, 1976; Wise, 1979). These contextual factors explained some of the inability of interventions to take hold.

Environmental Shifts in the 1980s and 1990s

Nevertheless, the field continued its attempts to bring new practices to scale but in a changing environment. On the demand side, two concerns emerged to prompt a new round of education reforms. Those interested in maintaining a worldwide competitive economic position called for improved educational services for all (National Commission on Excellence in Education, 1983; National Center on Education and the Economy, 1990), while others who focused on the achievement gaps between the white students and minority students called for more targeted improvements (Commission on Work, Family, and Citizenship, 1988; Carnegie Task Force, 1989). These calls for reform galvanized educators to look for ways to improve instructional practices more systematically, often by adopting practices from other countries or based in business (Smith and O'Day, 1990; Chubb and Moe, 1990).

Partly in response to these demands and calls for new approaches, states began to evolve policy strategies involving system reforms that focused on developing high standards, then aligning curriculum, instruction, and assessment with them. The Kentucky Education Reform Act of 1990 was the first such comprehensive state law, followed quickly by similar measures in other states, such as Maryland, Texas, and North Carolina. This push toward a standards-based system was supported by federal funds allocated to states to subsidize the development of goals and standards. At the same time, the role of the district central office was de-emphasized and a greater emphasis was placed on school-level leadership, often called *site-based management* or *decentralization* (Chubb and Moe, 1990). This emphasis on school-level leadership reflected both a growing distrust of central-office bureaucracies, particularly in large urban districts, and the belief then common in the business world that the people closest to the issue were in the best position to make good decisions concerning solutions, so long as standards and expectations were clear.

Finally, growing disillusionment with the role that the federal government played in bringing about desired improvements through its compensatory education programs, especially Title 1, led to significant changes in that program. Starting in 1990s, regulations concerning the use of Title 1 funds were eased, allowing schools with high levels of poverty greater discretion over funding, known as "whole-school status." Finally, in 1997, Congress appropriated funds under the Comprehensive School Reform Demonstration Programs to encourage the adoption of whole-school designs.

On the supply side, in the 1980s, developers created interventions and strategies for implementing these interventions—initially on a modest scale but ultimately in large numbers (Accelerated Learning, Success For All,[1] and the Bay Area Writing Workshop are notable examples of programs that were developed and began to spread at this time). In 1991, the business community founded the New American Schools Development Corporation, which we will refer to by its present name, New American Schools (NAS),[2] to develop "break-the-mold" designs for schools that could be implemented in a wide number of schools throughout the country.

---

[1] See Chapter Five in this volume.

[2] See Chapter Sixteen in this volume.

Throughout the 1990s, other innovations—dealing with specific subjects, whole schools, or even district activities—entered the educational improvement market in response to the growing demands and funding for improvements.

The funding of the design and development work for these interventions was provided largely by private funders and foundations. Until 1997, the federal government provided only a limited amount of funding. For many of the interventions, the initial implementation was also privately funded, but, as the 1990s unfolded and as attempts were made to improve increasingly large numbers of classrooms and schools, an increasing proportion of the funding for the interventions came in the form of fees for the services of the developers who began to provide implementation assistance. The changes in Title 1 mentioned above allowed greater use of federal funds for schools to "buy" the services of external providers. In an important sense, the nation began to see the emergence of a market for external assistance in improving core practices through designs, materials, and support for implementation.

Lessons from the Field

This growth in providers and those attempting reforms resulted in significant evaluative efforts during the 1990s. These evaluative efforts, however, seldom focused on scale as an issue. Rather, they tended to focus on whether adoption improved student outcomes and, in a few cases, on the level of implementation accomplished in specific locales, schools, or groups. Although there are differences between widespread adoption across many teachers and sites and adoption at a single site, we draw on studies of both processes because the results of these investigations point to common issues and, together, capture the current state of knowledge.

In this section, we highlight the factors that researchers (and, to some extent, practitioners) have identified as the most important in determining the success or failure of the implementation and scale-up of educational reforms. These factors are the characteristics of the intervention, school conditions, assistance provided for implementation, and alignment of the policy and infrastructure supports.

Characteristics of the Intervention That Affect Implementation

Researchers hypothesize that the probability that a scale-up effort will be successful is a function of the characteristics of the intervention itself, including comprehensiveness, ambitiousness, and elaboration (Cohen and Ball, 2001; Mazmanian and Sabatier, 1989). The following paragraphs focus on three characteristics of interventions thought to influence implementation: the origin of the reform design relative to adopters, whether the reform is targeted toward specific populations or curricular areas or is implemented broadly across a site, and whether the reform primarily includes structural as opposed to instructional change.

Locus of Development. Nunnery (1998) refers to the locus of development—whether the reform is developed internally by teachers and administrators in a school or externally by a developer—as having major effects on implementation. Both approaches have been associated with successful implementation in specific schools (Crandall and Loucks, 1983; Fullan, 2001). However, there is some evidence that externally developed reforms are easier and less costly to implement and involve fewer risks (Crandall and Loucks, 1983; McLaughlin, 1991; Nunnery, 1998; Stringfield, Millsap, and Herman, 1997). This observation has significant implications for those trying to implement reforms at scale. The easier and less costly it is to implement a design, the more likely it is that dissemination across large numbers of schools or classrooms will be possible.

That a reform has been developed externally does not necessarily mean that teachers and administrators have no role in making key decisions about how the reform will be carried out. Rarely does implementation proceed without some alteration or adaptation of the reform model, regardless of where it was developed. Hence, even external reforms become "co-constructed" at the school and classroom levels, meaning that the form they take in a school is determined by both the actions of developers (and sometimes other external actors, such as state policymakers) and educators within schools (Cuban, 1998; Datnow, Hubbard, and Mehan, 2002; Hubbard and Mehan, 1999; Lytle, 2002). Similarly, Berman and McLaughlin (1978) described the process of "mutual adaptation," whereby teachers alter the reform to fit their students' needs and the local context, while adjusting their own practices to accommodate the requirements of the reform. Cuban (1998) notes that teachers often decide which elements of a given reform to emphasize, incorporating the elements of the model they find useful into classroom practice, while discarding or ignoring the elements they dislike.

Targeted Versus Whole-School Reform. There is some evidence that whole-school reforms might be more effective at improving instructional practice than designs that target a particular segment of the student population, a specific part of the curriculum, or only a few classrooms in a school. In a three-year study of ten types of school reform programs funded under Title 1 of the Elementary and Secondary Education Act, Stringfield and colleagues found that schools using whole-school designs tended to experience greater improvements in instructional practice (and in student achievement) than schools using designs targeted to a segment of the student population (Stringfield, Millsap, and Herman, 1997). In describing the process of scaling up school reform in California, Honig (1994) argued that comprehensive, schoolwide reforms have a greater influence on classroom practice than do piecemeal efforts. Based on their assessment of schools using the Coalition of Essential Schools (CES) model, Muncey and McQuillan (1996, p. 279) learned that

> the more inclusive the reform effort—that is, the more levels in the educational system, participants in that system, and school programs that were brought together—the more likely it has been to endure.

In schools that established programs targeted to certain students or classrooms, tensions developed between CES teachers and those not involved in the reform.

On the other hand, RAND's NAS evaluation reveals how difficult it is to implement and sustain designs on a schoolwide scale. RAND researchers found that, over time, the differences in implementation levels between schools decreased, but the differences *within* schools increased (i.e., in many cases, the design was not being implemented throughout the school). However, among 13 schools that had implemented NAS designs for at least three years, those using the targeted Roots and Wings design had achieved the highest levels of implementation. The researchers attribute this success, in part, to the narrow focus of the design. It addressed the reading curriculum only and was therefore easier to implement (Berends, Bodilly, and Kirby, 2002). The researchers suggest that the high level of assistance provided by the design team and the design's highly specified curriculum and associated materials also made implementation easier. Similarly, Muncey and McQuillan (1996) noted the difficulty that some CES schools experienced maintaining reform practices on a schoolwide basis.

Structure Versus Teacher Knowledge and Curriculum Content. The relative importance of structural or organizational changes versus changes focused on improving teacher knowledge and the content of curricula has been the subject of much debate. In one study of three elementary schools that undertook major restructuring efforts, the researchers found that formal, structural changes—such as altering student groupings in classrooms, establishing team teaching, and giving schools greater discretion over budget and personnel matters—had little impact on actual classroom practice (Elmore, Peterson, and McCarthey, 1996). Muncey and McQuillan (1996) reached a similar conclusion for some of the CES schools they studied, in which significant structural changes (e.g., altering schedules or course offerings, instituting team teaching, providing teachers with more preparation time) did not translate into changes in classroom practice.

In their study of 34 schools in Memphis, Tennessee, that adopted eight NAS designs, Smith and colleagues discovered that, compared to more narrowly focused reforms, designs that require broad changes in the organization or governance of schools before significant changes in teaching practices could be made took longer to implement (Smith, Ross, et al., 1998). In his review of several studies of large-scale reforms, Nunnery (1998) concluded that strategies that call for changes in organization and governance as prerequisites for classroom changes usually fail.

This is not to suggest that structural factors do not matter. For many schools (e.g., those in which teachers have little or no say over the curriculum, scheduling, or similar matters or have few opportunities to provide input into decisionmaking or to seek support from other professionals), restructuring might be a necessary (though perhaps not sufficient) condition for improvement (Fullan, 2001; Sarason, 1990 and 1996). Elmore, Peterson, and McCarthey (1996) pointed out that restructuring has the potential to lead to positive changes in classroom practices, though such changes might or might not materialize. Reviewing the research conducted on reform efforts during the 1970s and 1980s, McLaughlin (1991) noted that the evidence suggested that reforms should attend to both content (e.g., curriculum or specific teaching techniques) and the change process, which usually involves some form of restructuring (e.g., reallocations of decisionmaking authority).

School Factors That Affect Implementation

Other research shows that implementation of changes in curriculum and instruction is only possible if the people involved—namely teachers and principals—are ready, accepting, and have the skills needed.

Teacher Buy-In and Participation. In their assessment of efforts to implement school reforms at scale, Datnow and colleagues note that teacher support is crucial for the success of any reform. If teachers do not support the reform (which usually occurs if the district or principal has imposed it on them), they will often resist it or half-heartedly implement it, with the knowledge that eventually the principal or district staff will probably shift their attention elsewhere (Datnow, Hubbard, and Mehan, 2002).

Chances for success are higher if teacher support comes early, but this is not necessary. There is evidence that teachers who are initially suspicious of or even outright opposed to an initiative can eventually become supportive (McLaughlin, 1991). This shift occurs as a result of their experience instituting elements of the reform in the classroom. In his analysis of several studies of large-scale educational reform efforts, Nunnery (1998) concluded that teacher buy-in is critical to successful implementation, but he also observed that the effectiveness of the intervention has the most influence over whether teachers buy in and gain a sense of ownership over it.

Regardless of whether the reform is developed locally or externally, involving teachers in the selection of the reform raises the likelihood of successful adoption (Berends, Bodilly, and Kirby, 2002; Bodilly et al., 1998; Comer et al., 1996; Cooper, 1998). The widely adopted Success For All program requires a vote of 80 percent approval among the teachers in a given school. Equally important is the inclusion of teachers in planning activities (Comer et al., 1996; Levin, 1998). In their study of large-scale, federally sponsored reform projects, Berman and McLaughlin (1977) discovered that involving teachers in the development of project materials improved the odds of implementation and continuation. Analyzing data from 36 California schools undertaking restructuring initiatives, Olsen and Kirtman (2002) learned that teachers are active, rather than passive, participants of reform, inevitably shaping a given reform initiative and determining how it will look in each classroom. They recommend that teachers should be included in all aspects of the planning and implementation of a reform initiative. Louis and Miles (1990) conducted a large-scale study of urban high schools in the midst of reform initiatives and concluded that broad support for a given reform effort among teachers, and among parents and community members in general, was a necessary condition for successful implementation.

Principal Support and Leadership. Strong leadership of reform efforts on the part of school principals is another important component of successful implementation. As Fullan argues, an important part of the principal's role as school improvement leader is the active management of change from above (e.g., mandates from the district office) and below (requests or demands from teachers). The principal must continually seek resources and support from district staff, while encouraging and monitoring teachers' implementation of reform components (especially within classrooms). In addition, Fullan contends, the principal should seek out new alliances with external organizations, such as reform networks (which can provide much support) and potential funders (Fullan, 1993, 1999, and 2001).

Other research and practical experience supports Fullan's argument concerning the role that principals should assume (Berends, Bodilly, and Kirby, 2002; Bodilly et al., 1998; Desimone, 2000; Finnan et al., 1996). For example, in their multiyear study of the NAS initiative, researchers at RAND found a strong, positive relationship between the quality of principals' leadership and the extent to which schools implemented whole-school designs. Moreover, schools in which teachers perceived their principals to be strong leaders experienced a broader level of implementation within the school (i.e., evidence of reform practices was less likely to be limited to a few classrooms or grade levels) (Berends, Bodilly, and Kirby, 2002). In fact, in cases without strong principal leadership the result is usually failure (Crandall and Loucks, 1983; Desimone, 2000; Fullan, 1999 and 2001; Muncey and McQuillan, 1996).

Assistance Required for Implementation

Much research on the implementation of interventions suggests that specific support is required for implementation and sustainability—in the form of technical assistance, training, and resources.

Assistance Provided by External Developers. Ongoing, intensive support from external design teams strongly affects the level of implementation and likelihood of continuation of educational reforms (Berends, Bodilly, and Kirby, 2002; Bodilly et al., 1998; Comer et al., 1996; Smith, Ross, et al., 1998). This ideally includes an on-site facilitator (either full- or part-time at a given school) who can work closely with teachers, providing assistance or technical support. Such assistance often includes concrete modeling of instructional methods and materials, which some studies suggest is an effective way to help teachers turn knowledge of the model into practice (Berman and McLaughlin, 1977; Bol et al., 1998; Crandall and Loucks, 1983; Nunnery, 1998; Smith, Ross, et al., 1998). The facilitator can either be a member of the external design team or a school staff member trained in the details of the model (Cooper, 1998; Slavin and Madden, 1996).

Several external reform designers have successfully deepened implementation within schools and broadened implementation across large numbers of schools by using regional training facilities or district or regionally based trainers. These facilities are often university-based contractors whose staffs have received training from model developers (Comer et al., 1996; Slavin and Madden, 1996). Further research by Bodilly et al. (1998) indicates that the quality of implementation at scale-up is highly dependent on the support the developers provide to the schools. High-quality support from the developers enables both transformation at a specific site and implementation across many sites.

Assistance Derived from Communication with Other Adopters. Many researchers and practitioners believe that networks of teachers and schools have the potential to be a major source of leverage for scaling up educational reforms (Cooper, Slavin, and Madden, 1998; Fullan, 2001; Honig, 1994; Little, 1993; McLaughlin, 1991). A number of developers have relied heavily on a network approach to disseminate their models, as well as to deepen and sustain efforts at member schools. Prominent examples include Success For All, the Coalition of Essential Schools, the School Development Program, and Edison Schools.[3] Staff in schools linked via a network can draw on each other for support and ideas. Teachers share instructional practices and materials, and administrators share ideas relating to funding, conflict management, and other issues. Under Success For All, teachers and on-site facilitators from different schools in the same area meet regularly to share resources and materials (Cooper, Slavin, and Madden, 1998). Some developers sponsor annual or semiannual conferences at which teachers or administrators gather to share ideas and strategies. Others, such as the School Development Program, have established "demonstration schools" that others can visit to observe the model in practice (Comer et al., 1996).

---

[3] See Chapter Thirteen in this volume.

Assistance from Outside Funders for Developers and Adopters.
The support of outside funders is crucial as well. There is growing
recognition that the conventional funding perspective that schools,
developers, and funders (particularly governments and private foundations) have taken is inadequate. At the adopter level, reforms often
fail to become institutionalized at the school level because district
staff or principals do not reallocate staff or budgets to accommodate
the reform or because they do not begin planning early on the
changes that will be necessary to sustain the initiative (Berman and
McLaughlin, 1978; Crandall and Loucks, 1983; Stringfield, Millsap,
and Herman, 1997). Early planning involves ensuring that the school
has the capacity to carry out the reform over the long term, and this
includes adequate long-term funding (Fullan, 1999; Olsen, 1994;
Smith, Ross, et al., 1998).

Similarly, attributes of the relationship between the funder and
the developer can affect scale-up (Bodilly et al., 1998; Glennan,
1998). Funders tend to target resources to short-term demonstration
projects but fail to provide developers with the support they need to
become financially self-sufficient. Developers usually focus their
energy on creating and implementing model programs but lack a
strategy for building the organizational capacity needed to broaden
and sustain their efforts over the long term (Letts, Ryan, and
Grossman, 1998). Therefore, funders begin to see the developers as a
constant drain on their resources. Often, funders' patience ends
exactly when it is time to move from development to sustained scale-
up. Thus, developing a viable resource stream that slowly, but surely,
moves the developer into a tenable scale-up capacity is a challenge for
both funders and developers.

In recent years, recognition of this problem has grown.
Grossman and his colleagues have argued that funders should develop
a broader view of their responsibilities. In addition to direct financial
support, they should provide other services to their developers—such
as contacts, exposure, advice, and the legitimacy that their patronage
provides, any of which might prove crucial in a scale-up effort (Letts,
Ryan, and Grossman, 1998). In the entrepreneurial fervor of the
1990s, a number of for-profit and not-for-profit firms were estab-

lished to seek out new reform efforts that had the potential for finding a broader market.

Alignment of Policies and Infrastructure in the Operating Environment

Research suggests that the probability of successful implementation is highly dependent on characteristics of the operating environment—the policies, practices, and leadership—that create the environment in which an intervention is implemented (Elmore, 1996; Fullan, 2001; Bodilly et al., 1998). For example, Bodilly et al. (1998); Springfield and Datnow (1998); and Berends et al. (2001) all describe specific barriers in the operating environment of schools and within the teaching profession that prevent scale-up; such barriers include district priorities that conflict with the design emphases of the intervention, union contract clauses limiting time for professional development or opportunities to reassign staff, resource constraints that limit the depth of implementation, significant teacher and student turnover, and fickle leadership.

Barriers Created by Conflicting Mandates. In their study of the NAS initiative, RAND researchers found the alignment of policies and infrastructure between the district, the developers, and the schools to have a significant influence on the extent to which teachers implemented whole-school designs. Of particular significance were the amount of resources provided, the degree of autonomy granted to schools, and the presence or absence of conflicting district mandates (Berends, Bodilly, and Kirby, 2002). In many districts, district staff simultaneously imposed other initiatives or programs on schools that conflicted with the curriculum or instructional practices of the NAS design (Berends, Bodilly, and Kirby, 2002; Berends, Kirby, et al., 2001). Researchers studying efforts to implement the Core Knowledge Sequence at scale also found that the absence of conflicting district mandates aided implementation (Datnow, McHugh et al., 1998; Stringfield, Datnow et al., 2000). A political analysis of school reform by McDermott (2000) helps to explain why districts so often impose multiple and conflicting programs and other mandates on schools (and why states do the same to districts). She notes that district policymakers must respond to diverse constituencies with competing interests and goals. This results in the partial adoption of many reforms rather than the large-scale implementation of a single reform (McDermott, 2000).

Alignment of Standards, Curriculum, and Assessments. Support from districts and states is also often weak and unconnected to school-level reform initiatives in other areas (Honig, 1994). Perhaps nowhere is this more the case than with regard to standards, curriculum, and student assessment systems. The literature contains many examples of district or state standards, curriculum requirements, or testing regimes that are not aligned with the particular reforms that schools are attempting to adopt, often at the behest of the district (Bodilly et al., 1998; Glennan, 1998; Desimone, 2000; Smith, Ross, et al., 1998; Stringfield, Datnow et al., 2000; Stringfield and Ross, 1997). Recognizing that schools must now meet high standards or face significant consequences, many developers are adjusting or tailoring their reform models so that they are aligned with state standards and tests (Bodilly, 2001).

Professional Development Alignment. Support from the district office, including the provision of adequate preparation time and professional development, is equally important, especially if large-scale adoption across a district is to occur. A great deal of existing professional development has little connection to the reforms that schools are adopting (Corcoran, Furhman, and Belcher, 2001; Elmore, 2002; Fullan, 2001; Glennan, 1998; Little, 1993). Although this disconnection rarely spells doom for a reform effort, it does impede implementation and sustainability. Professional development workshops or classes that have little relation to the components of the reform represent lost opportunities. When professional development and reform efforts are aligned (i.e., teachers are trained in the pedagogy, curriculum, and other elements of the reform), teachers receive the training they need to change classroom practices and feel that the district supports their efforts (Bol et al., 1998). One way to ensure alignment is to have external design teams serve as the sole or primary source of professional development.

Elmore (2002) and Fullan (2001) emphasize the need for motivation to support widespread changes in practice and discuss such general solutions as the development of strong organizational and professional incentives that encourage teachers and other school leaders to develop a sense of ownership of the problems within the school and dedicate themselves to appropriate interventions. For some interventions, development of such professional incentive infrastructures are part of the strategy for successful scale-up.

Higher-Level Policy Alignment. Implementation may also be affected by the policy context in place during the implementation of a reform model. Aside from the modest number of schools always interested in innovation and improvement, the market for interventions leading to improved teaching and learning is, to a great degree, shaped by public policy. And the degree to which that market changes or fluctuates due to the influence of changing policies affects the implementation and sustainability of various interventions (Berends, Chun, et al., 2002; Glennan, 1998). For example, the federal government has recently played a strong role in creating a market for whole-school designs by funding the Comprehensive School Reform Demonstration program and changing the regulations regarding the use of Title 1 "schoolwide funds." State standards and accountability regimes have also encouraged teachers and schools to seek the means to improve their practice.

Interaction to Obtain Alignment. The RAND NAS study offered a unique perspective on the scale-up process. Unlike other studies described here, this was not a straightforward evaluation of outcomes. Rather, it documented the unfolding process as the developers interacted with teachers, schools, districts, and states. Bodilly (2001) traced the pathway that the NAS developers followed as they responded to some of the above factors. The report provides evidence of significant changes to designs over time as developers attempted to ensure a market for their product. Many of the NAS teams continuously reworked their designs and their implementation strategies to match changes in state policies, changes in demand from implementing sites, unique adaptations required by implementing sites, or the changing funding picture. In this instance, it was not just the sites doing the adaptation; rather, the developers changed the interventions to adapt them to the policy environment and the needs of the sites for implementation.

A Conceptual Framework for Scale-Up

This review of the changes and lessons from the past 20 years of attempts to scale up educational reforms leads us to a more accurate understanding of the scale-up process and the criteria that a scale-up effort must meet to be deemed successful.

Process of Scale-Up

Inherent in these lessons from the last several years is a move away from the one-way, replication model of adoption to a model that conceptualizes scale-up as a nonsequential process of interaction, feedback, and adaptation among groups of actors—teachers, providers, schools, and district and state administrators. The lessons from the literature review indicate that the sites, whether they are individual teachers, schools, or systems of schools, are not solely being acted upon. They are active participants in an iterative process. Successful scale-up requires these parties, including the developers, to change not only instructional practices but potentially also policies governing standards, assessments, and accountability; the supporting infrastructure, including incentives for teachers and other actors; funding and resource allocations patterns; and networking arrangements.

Figure 1.2 attempts to capture the essence of this more-complex understanding by expanding the replication model to show what is entailed at each site in terms of the scale-up process and mutual realignments, adaptations, and co-constructions being made. On the left side of the figure, the development process has remained roughly the same, but the right side of the figure differs dramatically from a replication model.

The figure's two-way arrows imply give and take, learning, and adaptation. In addition, with the teacher at the center of the figure

Figure 1.2
The Interactive Process of Scale-Up

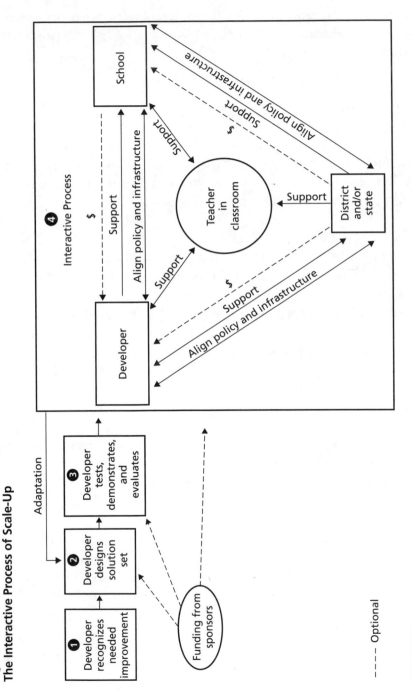

RAND *MG248-1.2*

and some arrows showing "supports," we indicate a move away from a notion of simply adopting a constrained set of practices to one of changing the system to support good teaching practices and good teachers. The mutual-adaptation process shown here encompasses only one site. A scale-up effort would involve this process at many sites, exponentially expanding the challenges to the provider to achieve a successful scale-up as potential negotiations, learning, and responses multiply as sites are added.

Finally, the model is applicable, regardless of the target of the intervention. For example, interventions that provide services to individual teachers emphasize the relationship between the developers and the teachers to a greater extent than relationships between developers and schools or districts, but new teaching methods are doomed to fade if not supported by school- and district-level policies and infrastructure. Similarly, interventions that focus on whole schools emphasize the arrows between the developers and the school but cannot prosper without teacher and district support.

Characteristics of a Successful Scale-Up Effort

The definition of a successful scale-up has changed from replication at a large number of sites or by a large number of teachers to include other important constructs. Coburn (2003, p. 4) articulated this fuller conception of scale, arguing that

> expanding a reform to multiple settings is a necessary, but insufficient condition for scale. That is, scaling up not only requires spread to additional sites, but also consequential change in classrooms, endurance over time, and a shift such that knowledge and authority for the reform is transferred from external organization to teachers, schools, and districts. Thus, I propose a conceptualization of scale comprising four interrelated dimensions: depth, sustainability, spread, and shift in reform ownership.

This more-complex definition of a successful scale-up is now gaining widespread use. We emphasize that it includes four characteristics:

- spread: implementation of reform practices at additional sites or in additional groups within existing sites
- depth: a significant improvement in classroom practice enacted in deep and meaningful ways that influences student performance
- sustainability: policy and infrastructure systems in place to support continued, deep improvement in classroom practice over time
- shift in ownership: transfer of knowledge and authority to sustain the reform to the site, allowing continuous improvement and further scale-up.

The last characteristic of a successful scale-up effort has only recently been articulated. Deep changes in practice will not be sustained over long periods without ownership by teachers and others within the educational system. The faddism prevalent in public-education improvement strategies is testimony to the fact that a shift in ownership seldom takes place. Without this shift in ownership, adopters are permanently reliant on developers to sustain the core practices of the school, a relationship that cannot be, and has not been, sustained financially over the long haul.

These characteristics imply a greater challenge for the providers, districts, schools, and teachers: ensuring that, after the provider has ended its services, the improvement efforts continue. Importantly, the practices will then not be seen as those of the provider but of the teachers or schools.

These characteristics also imply a longer time frame than is often used to assess effects. Under this definition, improved student outcomes within a year or two are not enough, although certainly worth noting. This model of scale-up and the characteristics of success imply a longer view that captures practices and outcomes after the developer has left and the teachers, presumably, have taken on ownership and moved toward continuous improvement.

A Series of Interrelated Developer Activities

The probability of successful scale-up for almost all interventions is a function of carrying out the process shown in Figure 1.2 successfully.

The literature implied a set of decisions or actions that the developer will be forced to make that are strategic in the sense that they interrelate with one another and combine into an overarching scale-up approach. Making a decision or carrying out an action in one task area reduces the freedom of decisionmaking and action for the other tasks. The following are examples of such interrelated tasks:

- develop implementation support
- ensure the quality of implementation
- evaluate and improve the intervention
- obtain financial support
- build organizational capacity
- market the product
- meet local context needs
- sustain the design.

As an intervention is scaled, these tasks are sometimes deliberately or unexpectedly revisited, and the interventions themselves then change (Bodilly, 2001). For example, as a developer moves from creating a strategy for one specific locale to developing one that can be used in many locales, he or she might reconsider certain aspects of the intervention itself—making it more transferable to diverse settings. Alternatively, the developer might recognize that the intervention is not suitable for diverse settings but only for very specific niches. Marketing strategies and materials specific to that niche might then be developed.

The creation of a scale-up strategy requires balancing competing challenges and goals. For example, implementing the intervention in many sites might reduce the assistance the provider can offer teachers and schools. Such a reduction in services could reduce the depth of implementation in succeeding sites. Thus, there appears sometimes to be a trade-off between quantity and quality. Creating great specificity in an intervention at its founding site can ensure greater depth of changed practice there, but that specificity might make the intervention less transferable to other settings. Again, the developer must choose among these trade-offs.

Outline of the Remainder of the Book

All the contributors to this volume are concerned with improving teaching and learning in public school classrooms. They have, however, attacked specific parts of the challenge, targeting different intervention points and using different scale-up strategies. Some of the interventions described here target individuals, usually teachers; others are concerned with specific content areas in schools; others deal with whole schools or school districts.

The editors sought this diversity of approaches, philosophies, and practices. We assert here, and believe the succeeding chapters support, the notion that success at scale often depends on what is being scaled, what basic assumptions developers make about what needs to be improved, and what assumptions they make about their limits and constraints. The diversity of basic assumptions drives the developers to different conceptions of scale-up.

As the ensuing chapters will reveal, each of the developers faced the set of tasks listed above, but each found somewhat different solutions, depending on the focus of the reform effort, the context, and other factors. In short, the what—the challenges of the tasks—were held in common. But the how—the manner of solving them—differed among our contributors. It is the how and the why—the practical solutions—that are the focus of the remainder of this book. The net was cast broadly to avoid drawing lessons from a set of practices that was too small or narrow to reflect the universe of diverse practices in existence.

In ordering the essays, we decided to move roughly from those that deal with improving the teaching skills of individuals to those that focus on programs for entire schools to those intended to influence districts or a collaborative of schools. The order of these essays is fairly arbitrary, and the reader is advised to dip into them as interest dictates. At the beginning of each chapter, we have noted distinctive features of the intervention discussed in the chapter, important observations regarding the scale-up process, or other features that may be of particular interest to particular readers. The following classes of programs are addressed:

- **subject-specific interventions focusing on individual teachers:** Cognitively Guided Instruction (CGI, Chapter Two) and the National Writing Project (NWP, Chapter Three)
- **interventions focusing on the schools:** Direct Instruction (Chapter Four) and Success For All (Chapter Five), Different Ways of Knowing (Chapter Eight), Co-nect (Chapter Nine), Turning Points (Chapter Ten), Talent Development High School (TDHS, Chapter Eleven), High Schools That Work (HSTW, Chapter Twelve), and the Edison Schools Project (Chapter Thirteen)
- **interventions emphasizing clusters of schools:** America's Choice (Chapter Seven), Project GRAD (Chapter Six), the Institute for Learning (IFL, Chapter Fourteen), and the Bay Area School Reform Collaborative (BASRC, Chapter Fifteen).

Dean Millot's essay, the next to last, takes a different approach. Unlike that of the other contributors, his experience is not as a developer or provider but as a senior officer at NAS. Drawing on that experience, he discusses the evolution of the market for the types of interventions described earlier and the actions that funders can take to foster the development and scale-up of reforms.

The final chapter of the book contains the reflections of the editors —an attempt to pull together the lessons the contributing authors have offered. These lessons are, we hope, a further step in the development of the practical theory of scale-up needed to guide school reforms (Elmore, 1996). They provide some advice to foundation and government funders about the needed support for external developers and providers of reform programs to enable their growth to sustainable organizations able to work at scale. The chapter ends with reflections on how the current policy environment might affect the probability of successful scale-ups of improvement efforts.

The book includes two appendixes. The first provides a short biography for each contributor, and the second provides information about each of the interventions discussed in this volume.

References

Berends, M., S. J. Bodilly, and S. N. Kirby, *Facing the Challenges of Whole-School Reform: New American Schools After a Decade*, Santa Monica, Calif.: RAND Corporation, MR-1498-EDU, 2002.

Berends, M., J. Chun, G. Schuyler, S. Stockly, and R. J. Briggs, *Challenges of Conflicting School Reforms: Effects of New American Schools in a High-Poverty District*, Santa Monica, Calif.: RAND Corporation, MR-1483-EDU, 2002.

Berends, M., S. N. Kirby, S. Naftel, and C. J. McKelvey, *Implementation and Performance in New American Schools: Three Years into Scale-Up*, Santa Monica, Calif.: RAND Corporation, MR-1145-EDU, 2001.

Berman, P., and M. W. McLaughlin, *Federal Programs Supporting Educational Change*: Vol. IV, *The Findings in Review*, Santa Monica, Calif.: RAND Corporation, R-1589/4-HEW, 1975.

_____, *Federal Programs Supporting Educational Change*: Vol. VII, *Factors Affecting Implementation and Continuation*, Santa Monica, Calif.: RAND Corporation, R-1589/7-HEW, 1977.

Berman, P., and McLaughlin, M., *Federal Programs Supporting Change*: Vol. VIII, *Implementing and Sustaining Innovations*, Santa Monica, Calif.: Rand Corporation, 1978.

Bodilly, S. J., B. Keltner, S. W. Purnell, R. E. Reichardt, and G. L. Schuyler, *Lessons from New American Schools' Scale-Up Phase: Prospects for Bringing Designs to Multiple Sites*, Santa Monica, Calif.: RAND Corporation, MR-942-NAS, 1998.

_____, *New American Schools' Concept of Break the Mold Designs; How Designs Evolved and Why*, Santa Monica, Calif.: RAND Corporation, MR-1288-NAS, 2001.

Bol, L., J. A. Nunnery, D. L. Lowther, A. P. Dietrich, J. B. Pace, R. S. Anderson, T. C. Bassoppo-Moyo, and Leslie C. Phillipsen, "Inside-In and Outside-In Support for Restructuring: The Effects of Internal and External Support on Change in the New American Schools," *Education and Urban Society*, Vol. 30, No. 3, May 1998, pp. 358–383

Carnegie Task Force on Education of Youth Adolescents, *Turning Points: Preparing American Youth for the 21st Century*, Washington D.C.: Carnegie Council on Adolescent Development, 1989.

Chubb, J., and T. Moe, *Politics, Markets and American Schools*, Washington D.C.: Brookings Institution, 1990.

Coburn, C. E., "Rethinking Scale: Moving Beyond Numbers to Deep and Lasting Change," *Educational Researcher*, Vol. 32, No. 6, 2003, pp. 3–12.

Cohen, D. K. and D. L. Ball, "Making Change: Instruction and Its Improvement," *Phi Delta Kappan*, 2001, Vol. 83, No. 1, pp. 73–77.

Comer, J. P., N. M. Haynes, E. T. Joyner, and M. Ben-Avie, eds., *Rallying the Whole Village: The Comer Process*, New York: Teachers College Press, 1996.

Commission on Work, Family, and Citizenship (also known as the Commission on Youth and America's Future), *The Forgotten Half: Pathways to Success for America's Youth and Young Families*, Washington D.C.: W. T. Grant Foundation, 1988.

Cooper, R., *Socio-Cultural and Within-School Factors that Affect the Quality of Implementation of School-Wide Programs*, Center for Research on the Education of Students Placed at Risk, Report No. 28, December 1998.

Cooper, R., R. E. Slavin, and N. A. Madden, "Success For All: Improving the Quality of Implementation of Whole-School Change Through the Use of a National Reform Network," *Education and Urban Society*, Vol. 30, No. 3, May 1998, pp. 385–408.

Corcoran, T., "Going to Scale: Building Effective Infrastructure," paper presented at New Visions for Spreading School Reform: An Invitational Conference, Portland, Ore., October 1996.

Corcoran, T., S. H. Furhman, and C. L. Belcher, "The District Role in Instructional Improvement," *Phi Delta Kappan*, Vol. 83, No. 1, September 2001.

Crandall, D. P., and S. F. Loucks, *A Roadmap for School Improvement: Executive Summary of the Study of Dissemination Efforts Supporting School Improvement*, Andover, Mass.: The NETWORK, Inc, 1983.

Cuban, L., "How Schools Change Reforms: Redefining Reform Success and Failure," *Teachers College Record*, Vol. 99, No. 3, 1998, pp. 453–477.

Datnow, A., L. Hubbard, and H. Mehan, *Extending Educational Reform From One School to Many*, Educational Change and Development Series, New York: Routledge Falmer, 2002.

Datnow, A., B. McHugh, S. Stringfield, and D. J. Hacker, "Scaling Up the Core Knowledge Sequence," *Education and Urban Society*, Vol. 30, No. 3, May 1998, pp. 409–432.

Desimone, L., *Making Comprehensive School Reform Work*, New York: ERIC Clearinghouse on Urban Education, Urban Diversity Series No. 112, May 2000.

Elmore, R. F., "Getting to Scale with Good Educational Practices," *Harvard Educational Review*, Vol. 66, No. 1, 1996, pp. 1–26.

_____, "The Paradox of Innovation in Education," paper commissioned by Innovations in American Government Program, in A. A. Altshuler and R. D. Behn, eds., *Innovation in American Government: Challenges, Opportunities, and Dilemmas*, Washington, D.C.: Brookings Institution Press, 1997.

_____, *Bridging the Gap Between Standards and Achievement: The Imperative for Professional Development in Education*, Washington, D.C.: The Albert Shanker Institute, 2002.

Elmore, R. F., P. P. Peterson, and S. J. McCarthey, *Restructuring in the Classroom: Teaching, Learning, and School Organization*, San Francisco: Jossey-Bass Publishers, 1996.

Finnan, C., E. St. John, J. McCarthy, and S. Slovacek, eds., *Accelerated Schools in Action: Lessons from the Field*, Thousand Oaks, Calif: Corwin Press, 1996.

Fullan, M., *Change Forces: Probing the Depths of Educational Reform*, Philadelphia: The Falmer Press, 1993.

_____, *Change Forces: The Sequel*, Philadelphia: The Falmer Press, 1999.

_____, *The New Meaning of Educational Change*, 3rd ed., New York: Teachers College Press, 2001.

Glennan, T. K., *New American Schools After Six Years*, Santa Monica, Calif.: RAND Corporation, MR-945-NAS, 1998.

Goggin, M. L., A. O'M Bowman, J. P. Lester, L. J. O'Toole, Jr., *Implementation Theory and Practice Toward a Third Generation*, Glenview, Ill.: Scott, Foresman/Little, Brown Higher Education, 1990.

Hill, P. T., and J. Bonan, *Decentralization and Accountability in Public Education*, Santa Monica, Calif.: RAND Corporation, R-4066, 1991.

Honig, B., "How Can Horace Best Be Helped?" *Phi Delta Kappan*, June 1994, pp. 790-796.

Hubbard, L., and H. Mehan, "Scaling Up an Untracking Program: A Co-Constructed Process," *Journal of Education for Students Placed at Risk*, Vol. 4, No. 1, 1999, pp. 83–100.

Letts, C. W., W. P. Ryan, and A. Grossman, *High Performance Nonprofit Organizations: Managing Upstream for Greater Impact*, New York: John Wiley & Sons, Inc., 1998

Levin, H. M., "Accelerated Schools: A Decade of Evolution," in A. Hargreaves, A. Lieberman, M. Fullan, and D. Hopkins, eds., *International Handbook of Educational Change*, Boston: Kluwer Academic Publishers, 1998.

Little, J. W., "Teachers' Professional Development in a Climate of Educational Reform," *Educational Evaluation and Policy Analysis*, Vol. 15, No. 2, Summer 1993, pp. 129–151.

Louis, K. S., and M. B. Miles, *Improving the Urban High School: What Works and Why*, New York: Teachers College Press, 1990.

Lytle, J. H., "Whole-School Reform from the Inside," *Phi Delta Kappan*, Vol. 84, No. 2, October 2002, pp. 164–167.

Mazmanian, D. A., and P. A. Sabatier, *Implementation and Public Policy*, rev. ed., Lanham, Md.: University Press of America, 1989.

McDermott, K. A., "Barriers to Large-Scale Success of Models for Urban School Reform," *Educational Evaluation and Policy Analysis*, Vol. 22, No. 1, Spring 2000, pp. 83–89.

McLaughlin, M. W., "The RAND Change Agent Study Revisited: Macro Perspectives and Micro Realities," *Educational Researcher*, Vol. 19, 1991, pp. 11–16.

McLaughlin, M. W., and D. Mitra, "Theory-Based Change and Change-Based Theory: Going Deeper and Going Broader," *Journal of Educational Change*, Vol. 2, No. 4, 2001, pp. 301–323.

Meyer, J., W. R. Scott, and D. Strang, "Centralization, Fragmentation, and School District Complexity," *Administrative Science Quarterly*, Vol. 32, 1987, pp. 186–201.

Muncey, D. E., and P. J. McQuillan, *Reform and Resistance in Schools and Classrooms*, New Haven, Conn.: Yale University Press, 1996.

National Center on Education and the Economy, *America's Choice: High Skills or Low Wages!* Rochester, N.Y., 1990.

National Commission on Excellence in Education, *A Nation At Risk: The Imperative for Education Reform*, Washington, D.C., 1983.

Nunnery, J. A., "Reform Ideology and the Locus of Development Problem in Educational Restructuring: Enduring Lessons from Studies of Educational Innovation," *Education and Urban Society*, Vol. 30, No. 3, May 1998, pp. 277–295.

Olsen, L., "Learning Their Lessons," *Education Week*, November 2, 1994.

Olsen, B., and L. Kirtman, "Teacher as Mediator of School Reform: An Examination of Teacher Practice in 36 California Restructuring Schools," *Teachers College Record*, Vol. 104, No. 2, March 2002, pp. 301–324.

Rowan, B., *The Ecology of School Improvement: Notes on the School Improvement Industry in the United States*, Philadelphia: Consortium of Policy Research in Education, 2001.

Sarason, S. B., *The Predictable Failure of Educational Reform: Can We Change Course Before It's Too Late?* San Francisco: Jossey-Bass Publishers, 1990.

_____, *Revisiting "The Culture of the School and the Problem of Change,"* New York: Teachers College Press, 1996.

Scott, R. W., "The Adolescence of Institutional Theory," *Administrative Science Quarterly*, No. 32, 1987, pp. 493–511.

Slavin, R. E., and N. A. Madden, *Lessons Learned in the Dissemination of Success For All*, Baltimore: Johns Hopkins University, November 1996.

Smith, L., S. Ross, M. McNelis, M. Squires, R. Wasson, S. Maxwell, K. Weddle, L. Nath, A. Grehan, and T. Buggey, "The Memphis Restructuring Initiative: Analysis of Activities and Outcomes that Affect Implementation Success," *Education and Urban Society*, Vol. 30, No. 3, May 1998, pp. 296–325.

Smith, M., and J. O'Day, "Systemic School Reform," *Politics of Education Association Yearbook*, 1990, pp. 253–267.

Stringfield, S., A. Datnow, G. Borman, and L. Rachuba, *National Evaluation of Core Knowledge Sequence Implementation*, Final Report, Baltimore: Center for Research on the Education of Students Placed at Risk, Report No. 49, December 2000.

Stringfield, S., and A. Datnow, "Scaling Up School Restructuring Designs in Urban Schools," *Education and Urban Society*, Vol. 30, No. 3, May 1998, pp. 269–276.

Stringfield, S., M. A. Millsap, and R. Herman, *Urban and Suburban/Rural Special Strategies for Educating Disadvantaged Children: Findings and Policy Implications of a Longitudinal Study*, Baltimore: Johns Hopkins University, April 1997.

Stringfield, S., and S. Ross, "A 'Reflection' at Mile Three of a Marathon: The Memphis Restructuring Initiative in Mid-Stride," *School Effectiveness and School Improvement*, Vol. 8, No. 1, 1997, pp. 151–161.

Tyack, D. B., and L. Cuban, *Tinkering Toward Utopia: A Century of Public School Reform*, Cambridge Mass: Harvard Business Press, 1995.

U.S. Department of Education, What Works Clearinghouse, Web site, undated. Online at http://www.w-w-c.org/ (as of June 10, 2004).

Weick, K., "Educational Organizations as Loosely Coupled Systems," *Administrative Science Quarterly*, Vol. 21, March 1976, pp. 1–19.

Wise A., *Legislated Learning*, Berkeley Calif.: University of California Press, 1979.

CHAPTER TWO

Cognitively Guided Instruction:
Challenging the Core of Educational Practice

Thomas P. Carpenter and Megan L. Franke

Carpenter and Franke emphasize the idea that the scale-up of cognitively guided instruction (CGI), a distinctive approach to teaching mathematics in elementary schools, has come about by focusing on changing the practices of communities of teachers rather than on developing organizational infrastructure. Drawing on four case studies, they identify mechanisms that have helped to promote the spread of CGI, all of which emphasize "growth from within," relying primarily on teachers' observations of the success of CGI methods as a motivator for changing practices and on the influence of a cadre of expert teachers who, as their expertise grows, assume responsibility for helping other teachers.[1]

The vision of school mathematics that current reform recommendations (e.g., National Council of Teachers of Mathematics, 2000) offer calls for fundamental changes in what Elmore (1996) calls "the core of educational practice." Elmore conceptualizes the "core" as being the fundamental ways teachers think about the nature of knowledge and as including teachers' and students' roles in teaching and learning. He argues that

---

[1] The research summarized in this chapter was supported in part by grants from the National Science Foundation and from the Department of Education Office of Educational Research and Improvement (OERI) to the National Center for Improving Student Learning and Achievement in Mathematics and Science. (OERI has since become the Institute of Education Sciences.) The opinions expressed in this paper do not necessarily reflect the position, policy, or endorsement of the National Science Foundation, the Department of Education, OERI, or the national center.

> innovations that require large changes in the core of educational practice seldom penetrate more than a small fraction of American schools and classrooms, and seldom last for very long when they do.

The closer an innovation gets to the core, the less likely the innovation will influence teaching and learning on a large scale. Elmore provides a way of conceptualizing the failure to scale up by highlighting the level of change required to affect the core. A great deal of evidence supports Elmore's claims about the difficulty of scaling up educational innovation.

The failure to scale up reforms that have been successful in local (or otherwise limited) contexts is a conundrum. Real reform that addresses the changes in curriculum and teaching that are necessary to teach students meaningful mathematics requires changing the core, but we have had little success in promoting widespread innovation that challenges core conceptions, values, and practices. If we want to bring about changes that make a real difference in the learning of mathematics, we must find ways to overcome the resistance to changes in the core of educational practice. Anything less would fail to address the fundamental problems with mathematics instruction.

We propose that it is possible to scale up innovation that addresses the core of educational practice. To support our contention, we describe specific efforts to scale up one professional development program, CGI (Carpenter, Fennema, and Franke, 1996; Carpenter, Fennema, et al., 1999), that challenges the core of educational practice. In particular, CGI challenges teachers' notions about what students know, how they learn, and what they can accomplish in mathematics. It challenges teachers' ideas about their role in the classroom and how they interact with students. It provides a basis for teachers to listen to students and to talk with each other about their students' mathematical thinking. It engages teachers as learners and provides the opportunity for teachers to see themselves as learning in the context of their practice. Teaching is no longer about covering the curriculum or engaging in activities. It is about learning—learning about the mathematical thinking of one's students and about the practices that will support the development of that thinking. It becomes about learning mathematics. Using CGI, learning becomes what happens in the school, both inside and outside the classroom. Elmore talks about the importance of incentive structures. With CGI, learning (both student learning and teacher learning) is a primary incentive. Although not all teachers may initially see learning as an incentive in itself, many do over time, and it is an incentive that never goes away.

In developing CGI, we did not set out to "scale up" or to affect a large number of schools and teachers. We set out to study what would happen if we shared research-based knowledge about the development of children's mathematical thinking with teachers. From this one systematic study, grass-roots reform, driven by teachers and with multiple models of scaling up, has emerged. In this chapter, we describe four versions of scaling up CGI. We do not propose that the scale-up models we have observed are equal in their effects on teachers and students; neither do we claim that these models will work in all situations. Instead, we provide examples from one long-term ongoing project of how the core can be changed such that the changes are sustained and provide the basis for continued growth.

The Conceptual Basis for Scaling Up

Our work is based on what we know about how people learn, and we have applied these ideas to our conceptions of student learning, teacher learning, and how we think about scaling up. We see "learning, thinking, and knowing [as] relations among people engaged in activity *in, with, and arising from the socially and culturally structured world*" (Lave and Wenger, 1991, p. 67; emphasis in original). Understanding learning as it emerges in activity is paramount, so we look to see how people engage in activity; what the community's practices are; and the role that such elements as tools, artifacts, and participation structures play in the evolving practices. Learning is detectable in members' changing participation in the work of the community. These shifts in participation do not merely mark a change in a participant's activity or behavior. Shifts in participation indicate changing roles and identities—identities linked to new knowledge and skill. Beyond thinking about the shifts in participation and the identities shaped by one's participation, the theories push us to consider the community in which the participation occurs. The norms that are established, the tools and artifacts that exist, and the participants themselves together create the learning space and interact to define the learning that occurs.[2] This conception of learning seems to have significant implications for scaling up. Our notions of scaling up and why it may or may not take hold relate very much to how we view teacher and student learning. We will return to this conception of learning throughout this chapter.

Cognitively Guided Instruction

To understand the particular challenges faced in scaling up a program like CGI, some insight into the goals and details of the program is needed.

CGI is a research-based professional development program that focuses on the development of children's mathematical thinking (Carpenter et al., 1999). The goal, however, is not only to understand student thinking for its own sake but also to provide a context for teachers for developing their own knowledge of mathematics and for reflecting on and revising their teaching practices.

CGI provides teachers with opportunities to engage with research-based knowledge about the development of children's mathematical thinking. This research is synthesized in a book that portrays the development of children's understanding of basic number concepts (Carpenter et al., 1999). The book is supplemented with a series of videos that provide examples of children's strategies for solving key problems and their interactions about their strategies in elementary classrooms. The book and accompanying videos serve to

---

[2] Rogoff (1994, 1997), Wenger (1998), Wertsch (1991, 1998), Greeno and MMAP (1998), Cobb (1999), and Boaler (2001) create the basis for our understanding of these ideas.

define CGI and distinguish it from other professional development programs that focus on students' mathematical thinking.

We neither provide a curriculum for teachers to follow nor specify explicit forms of teaching, grouping students, or interacting with them. Teachers bring knowledge to the task and engage in sense-making around the development of students' mathematical thinking. We saw early on that it was important to take into account how the teachers thought about student thinking in mathematics and to provide ways to connect their new research-based knowledge to what they already understood. Establishing these links between new knowledge and what the teachers already knew made it possible for them to figure out how to implement new approaches in practice.

The first principle of CGI is that fundamental change in teachers' practices can result from understanding and building on their students' mathematical thinking. A related principle is that teachers learn from listening to their students and struggling to understand what they hear. CGI focuses on helping teachers understand the development of children's mathematical thinking by providing a context and support for teachers to construct models of the evolution of children's thinking for specific mathematics concepts and skills. Our goal is not to provide teachers with a static body of knowledge but to help them develop conceptual models of student thinking that they can use for engaging in practical inquiry in their classrooms so that learning becomes generative.

CGI is grounded in research-based knowledge about the development of children's mathematical thinking that provides structure for organizing teachers' understanding. Within this structure, coherent principles relate types of mathematical problems to the strategies that children use to solve them, and the evolution of children's strategies is portrayed as following predictable trajectories. This model of children's thinking is robust, effectively capturing the problem-solving strategies that teachers encounter in their own classrooms.

The Development of Children's Mathematical Thinking

The initial work on CGI focused on the development of basic number concepts, and most of the research on CGI and most attempts to scale it up have focused on this content. When CGI was initially developed, a body of research that provided a consistent and coherent picture of the development of basic number concepts was emerging (Carpenter, 1985; Carpenter et al., 1999; Fuson, 1992).

This research documented that most children enter school with a rich store of informal knowledge and problem-solving strategies that can serve as the basis for developing much of the mathematics of the primary school curriculum. Although older students consistently show deficits in problem solving, young children generally can construct viable solutions to a variety of problems. Building on these intuitive problem-solving strategies not only enhances students' problem-solving abilities but also provides a basis for constructing meaning from the concepts and procedures of addition, subtraction, multiplication, and division.

One principle underlying our model of students' mathematical thinking is that children naturally solve problems posed in real or imaginary contexts by representing the action and relations described in the problems. Thus, to understand how children think about and solve a specific problem, teachers must appreciate the actions and relations that distinguish different types of problems. The following four problems illustrate some of the critical distinctions among problems that result in quite different specific solution strategies:

1. Twelve children were playing on the playground. Five children went home. How many children were left on the playground?
2. Sheryl has 5 dollars. How many more dollars does she need to save to have 12 dollars to buy a basketball?
3. Raymond earned 5 dollars babysitting. When he put it with the money he had already saved, he had 12 dollars. How much money did Raymond have before he earned the money babysitting?

4. Marsha scored 12 points in the class basketball game. Alicia scored 5 points. How many more points did Marsha score than Alicia?

Although all four problems could be solved by subtracting 5 from 12, young children may use quite different strategies to solve them. A first-grade student might solve the first problem using counters by making a collection of 12 counters and taking 5 from it. The same child might solve the second problem by first making a collection of 5 counters, adding counters until the total reached 12, and then counting the number of counters added to figure out the answer. The strategies are quite different, but in each case the strategy directly models the action described in the problem. Thus, an underlying strategy accounts for each strategy and the differences between them.

This underlying strategy is also reflected in the child's response to the remaining two problems. The child would most likely solve the fourth problem by making one collection of 12 counters and another collection of 5 counters, lining them up so that the 5 counters corresponded to 5 of the counters in the collection of 12, and then counting the unmatched counters to calculate the answer. Problem 3 would be quite difficult, and it is likely that the child would not be able to solve it. The difficulty arises because the number of objects in the initial set is the unknown, so the child would have difficulty figuring out where to start. Older children come to recognize the relation between the second and third problem, but younger children generally perceive them as quite different problems.

Over time, children become more flexible and begin to abstract these strategies to make them more efficient. For example, a child who has progressed from the direct-modeling stage illustrated in the above examples might solve the second problem using a counting strategy. In this case, the child would not make the initial set. Instead, she would start counting at 5 and count up to 12, keeping track of the number of counts on her fingers. The answer would be represented by the number of fingers extended as she counted from 5 to 12. Similarly, she might solve the first problem by counting back 5 from 12. In both cases, the strategy corresponds to the action described in the problem, but the representation of the action in the problem is more abstract.

Finally, children move beyond modeling the problem and using related counting strategies to relying directly on number facts. Children do not, however, learn all their number facts at the same time; for an extended period, they may use a core of known facts to generate unknown facts. For example, children often learn doubles (e.g., 6 + 6, 9 + 9) and sums to 10 (e.g., 4 + 6, 8 + 2) earlier than other facts, so they may use this knowledge to generate the answer to the problems above as follows: "Five and 5 is 10 and 2 more is 12, so 5 + 7 is 12. So the answer is 7."

The same progression characterizes the development of basic multiplication and division concepts and addition and subtraction with two- and three-digit numbers. Although multiplication and division are traditionally deferred until children have learned to add and subtract, research shows that, as early as kindergarten, children can successfully apply modeling strategies to learn multiplication and division concepts and skills (Carpenter, Ansell, et al., 1993).

Children extend their strategies to larger numbers by using units of ten to model addition and subtraction involving two- and three-digit numbers. As with problems with smaller numbers, modeling with tens gives way to more symbolic solutions (Carpenter, Franke, et al., 1998; Carpenter, Fennema, et al., 1999; Fuson et al., 1997). For example, a second-grade student might initially solve a problem involving the sum 25 + 37 by modeling the problem using base-ten blocks. She first would represent 25 using 2 ten blocks and 5 one blocks. Then she would make another group of blocks consisting of 3 tens and 7 ones. She might then first combine the ten blocks in the two groups to create a group of 5 ten blocks. Then she may combine the one blocks and find that she has enough for one group of 10 one blocks and 2 left over. She could put the 10 one blocks with the collection of ten blocks to make 6 tens, and together with the remaining 2 ones, would arrive at answer of 62. Another student in the same class may not use the blocks at all, relying instead on a strategy that is essentially an abstraction of what the first student did: "I knew that 2 and 3 is 5, so 20 and 30 is 50. Then I added the 5 and the 7. That's like 5 and 5 is 10, and 2 more. So that's one more 10, so 60 and 2 is 62." Note how similar the abstract strategy is to the description of the solution using base-ten blocks. This strategy also is fundamentally the same as the standard algorithm in which numbers are aligned in columns to facilitate adding ones and tens. The relation between the standard algorithm and representations with concrete materials can, however, be rather opaque, whereas the strategy described above is an abstraction of a more concrete strategy that generally makes sense to children.

The initial CGI research and development focused on the learning of basic number concepts and skills in the primary grades. Recently we have extended this work to show how developing algebraic reasoning throughout elementary school may enhance the learning of arithmetic and smooth the transition to algebra in the middle grades and high school (Carpenter, Franke, and Levi, 2003). Other researchers have extended the work to include basic ideas of fractions (Empson, 1999), geometry (Lehrer et al., 1999), and data analysis (Lehrer and Schauble, 2002).

These efforts have in common a focus on student thinking in specific content domains. This focus includes a fine-grained analysis of the content that plays a pivotal role in understanding student thinking and provides a basis for teachers to learn related mathematical content as they learn about student thinking. The focus may be on student thinking, but that focus provides a context for deepening teachers' knowledge of essential mathematics and for reconceptualizing their practice.

The specificity of the focus is critical. We do not simply provide teachers with general principles about student thinking. We have found that general observations about students constructing their own knowledge, using manipulative materials to develop meaning, and the like are too general to be useful. The details involved in understanding student thinking are essential.

CGI in the Classroom

Although CGI does not provide teachers with instructional materials or specify instructional practices, the professional development materials do include video examples of teachers interacting with students in classrooms. These examples are characterized as ways that some teachers implement knowledge about students' mathematical thinking in their classrooms but are not held up as models to emulate. The teachers in the video examples represent a range of practices, but certain normative practices generally emerge when teachers genuinely engage with the models of children's mathematical thinking described above. Recognizing that children may solve problems in different ways and that the different strategies reflect fundamentally different understandings of the underlying concepts, teachers begin to ask children to explain the strategies they used. Instead of assuming that all students will solve a problem in the same way, teachers expect a range of strategies. Rather than presenting one way to solve a given type of problem, the teacher leads a discussion that becomes an opportunity for students to describe the strategies they used for a given problem. Students learn not by imitating a procedure demonstrated by the teacher but by solving problems themselves and by listening to and comparing one another's problem-solving strategies.

These changes represent fundamental shifts in teachers' epistemology and in their conceptions about mathematics, students, and teaching. Mathematics is no longer a static body of knowledge to be passed on from the teacher to the student. Students do not come to the class as blank slates; they have substantial knowledge worth attending to and building upon. Teaching is not about telling; it is about understanding children's thinking and helping them to build on the concepts and skills that they have already acquired. Decisions about whether a procedure is correct are not based on the authority of the teacher; they depend on the arguments used to justify the procedure.

The Nature of the Professional Development

Consistent with our assumptions about the development of children's mathematical thinking, we recognize that teachers have practical knowledge about students' mathematical thinking that we attend to and attempt to build on. We have found that teachers' experience is consistent with our model of students' thinking, but this knowledge is not well organized and generally has not played a prominent role in teachers' instructional decisions (Carpenter, Fennema, et al., 1988). Our goal is to help teachers focus and build on this initial knowledge.

Our models of the development of children's mathematical thinking provide frames that guide our professional development, but our goal is not to impose them on teachers. Rather, we take them as basic models that we use to help teachers construct and test their own models of students' thinking to guide their instructional practices. Although a leader's guide describes one implementation of CGI (Fennema et al., 1999), professional development based on CGI has taken a number of forms. In all cases, however, it involves the focused and informed study of the development of students' mathematical thinking in specific content domains, and it is grounded in teachers' practice. Professional development may start by considering carefully selected video cases that illustrate critical features of children's mathematical thinking (Fennema et al., 1999) or by having teachers give selected problems to their own students and working collectively to make sense of the responses (Kazemi and Franke, 2002). In both cases, the selection of problems and student work is based on our models of student thinking. In both cases, the most-significant learning takes place as teachers struggle to make sense of their students' strategies for solving problems.

How Change Occurs

The model of the development of children's mathematical thinking described above provides a picture of the trajectory of student learning of basic number ideas but does not account for how or why students progress through the trajectory. That is where the conception of learning we discussed previously comes in. We see student learning in CGI classrooms in terms of their changing participation in the class. CGI classes generally are structured to permit students to discuss alternative strategies for solving problems. At any given time, some students may be using concrete modeling strategies and others more abstract strategies, so levels of participation in the discussion of strategies and the relation among them differ (Carpenter, Ansell, and Levi, 2001). Students' learning is evident in the strategies they present and in their participation in the discussion of relations among strategies. Shifts in participation also reflect changing roles and identities. Over time, students assume responsibility for deciding whether a strategy or answer is correct, whether an explanation is adequate, or whether an argument is valid. Thus, they become learners who can understand mathematics and for whom mathematics should make sense.

In the same way, we conceive of teachers' learning in terms of their participation in their classrooms and in communities of teachers engaged in learning about and implementing CGI. In their classrooms, teachers' roles change from being the source of knowledge and the authority for whether a strategy or answer is right or wrong to participating in a learning community in which everybody's ideas are valued and strategies and answers are validated not by authority but by the warrants for the claims. These changing roles are reflected in changes in the way teachers think of themselves. They come to see themselves not as authorities but as learners and their classrooms as places for their own learning, as well as for learning about students and mathematics.

Teachers' participation in professional development follows related paths. The most-basic level of participation involves getting teachers to give specific problems to their students and to attempt to keep track of how they solve them. When teachers are asked to share the work of their students, they often initially participate in limited ways, sharing only superficial examples of student work. Over time, however, their participation shifts toward much more-detailed discussion of students' strategies and the mathematical thinking the strategies represent. Discussion of students' thinking becomes an important part of teachers' professional lives, and their perceptions of themselves as engaged in inquiry about students' thinking become part of their identities (Franke et al., 2001).

The role of artifacts is important in understanding these shifts in participation for both students and teachers. The problem types illustrated earlier and the descriptions of specific strategies that students use for solving these problems are artifacts that are important for understanding both teachers' classrooms and their participation in professional development. The model of the development of mathematical thinking discussed above provides a framework for understanding the role these artifacts play.

Teacher and Student Outcomes

Our research, as well as that of other investigators, has documented fundamental changes in the knowledge, beliefs, and practice of CGI teachers, and these changes are reflected in the achievements of their students (Carpenter et al., 1989; Fennema et al., 1996; Secada and Brendefur, 2000; Villasenor and Kepner, 1993). Teachers' beliefs became more consistent with the ideas that students construct knowledge and that the teacher's role is to facilitate that construction rather than to demonstrate procedures. Teachers' classroom practices generally evolved toward a focus on student thinking, fostering student invention, solving fewer problems, and providing opportunities to discuss alternative strategies. These changes were reflected in students' problem-solving abilities and in their invention of arithmetic procedures demonstrating understanding of basic number concepts. In spite of a significant shift in emphasis from skills to understanding and problem solving, computational skills were unaffected; spending less time on drills did not reduce students' ability to carry out basic computations. Follow-up studies have demonstrated that teacher change has been sustained years after teachers completed the CGI professional development program and that CGI provided a basis for continued learning and growth (Franke et al., 2001).

Challenges

Perhaps the most critical challenge in implementing CGI is helping teachers attend to the first principles of CGI rather than to its surface features. When they are beginning to implement CGI, teachers often change their practices so that their classrooms look like classrooms in which teachers pose problems and ask how students' solve problems and build on student thinking. The teachers do not demonstrate procedures; students share strategies. Such changes represent progress over traditional teacher-directed instruction, but the adaptations often do not go beyond these surface changes. The changes do not represent changes in the norms and goals of the classroom mathematical practice. In these cases, teachers do not struggle to understand the students' thinking and do not provide the scaffolding that helps students extend their knowledge and adopt more-advanced strategies. They tend to think that the knowledge they have acquired is something that they learned from someone else, not something that they could figure out, adapt, and elaborate. In consequence, they do not engage in inquiry as a regular part of their teaching practice, and their learning does not become generative.

Developing leaders for efforts to scale up CGI embodies the same challenges. To help teachers move beyond the surface features of CGI instruction, leaders must understand the first principles of CGI at a deep level. They must understand that the goal is not to help teachers master a fixed body of knowledge but to help teachers learn in such ways that their learning becomes generative.

Scaling Up

Next, we consider four examples that provide different perspectives on how CGI may be scaled up. The first example is a grass-roots effort involving a group of elementary school teachers working together to learn more about CGI and to engage other teachers in learning about CGI. The next two examples consider how CGI spread through two schools. In one case, the efforts of one teacher were the driving force behind the change; in the other, the principal provided the impetus for creating a community focused on understanding student thinking. These examples might be perceived as representing the efforts of heroic individuals, but neither the teacher nor the principal saw themselves that way. They believed they were simply doing their jobs—providing the best mathematics instruction possible to the students in their schools. The fourth example represents a more-organized effort to scale up in districts served by a center dedicated to supporting professional development in districts throughout the upper Midwest. Together, these examples illustrate how CGI has changed the teaching of mathematics in entire schools and districts and how it has spread to new schools. Underlying the four cases are some consistent themes that we will discuss after we have presented the cases.

Grass Grows in Minnesota

The first example is a grass-roots effort involving a group of elementary school teachers working together to learn more about CGI and to engage other teachers in learning about CGI. "Paul" is one of the leaders of this group; the following account of its progress is based on an extended interview with him.[3]

During the summer of 1993, 22 teachers attended a weeklong teacher academy focused on CGI sponsored by the Minnesota Department of Public Instruction. The principles of CGI and how to apply them in classrooms cannot be fully assimilated in a five-day workshop, and a number of the teachers recognized the need for follow-up support during the school year. They approached the state mathematics supervisor, who was able to make Eisenhower in-service funds available through one of the teachers' districts.[4] Eleven of the

---

[3] We have used pseudonyms for interviewees throughout this chapter to preserve their anonymity.

[4] The Eisenhower Professional Development Program (Title 2 of the Elementary and Secondary Education Act of 1965, as amended) was enacted in 1994 as part of the Improving America's Schools Act of 1994. The Title 2 Program is the largest federal program supporting professional development activities to improve teaching and learning of all students.

original 22 teachers participated in the follow-up sessions during the year. During the following summer, seven of the eleven teachers organized a second summer workshop. Each returning teacher brought two to three additional teachers from his or her school or district. The goal was to create communities within schools and districts for the purpose of discussing children's mathematical thinking.

The program continued to grow within these teachers' schools and districts as the enthusiasm and accomplishments of their students became evident to other teachers. When the teachers who had participated in the CGI workshops reported about their students at local professional meetings, they attracted the attention of teachers outside their districts, and participation began to extend beyond the bounds of the original schools and districts. Currently, a core group of nine teachers is active in helping other teachers learn about CGI, and about 700 teachers throughout Minnesota have participated in programs led by this group. About 300 teachers are enrolled in CGI workshops scheduled to take place in summer 2003. About half are new teachers, and about half are in their second or third year of participation. Although the teachers did not initially have formal district support, four districts have now adopted districtwide programs to scale up CGI.

What is notable about this scaling up effort was that it has had little formal support, organizational infrastructure, or significant infusion of outside resources. Only one of the teacher leaders has had major district financial support. All the other districts have provided tacit support, but none has looked on CGI as a district initiative. The program has grown as a grass-roots effort of teachers working together to learn about, implement, and share something that they believed in.

When we asked Paul what kept the teachers engaged in a program that involved such a major commitment of time and effort, the theme that came up again and again was that it was the students. Participation in CGI helped the teachers see what their students were capable of doing in mathematics, and this motivated them to continue to struggle to learn more:

> Every time I think I have got it, I sit down with a student, and the child puts me in my place. I am so in awe of how my young students think about mathematics. This keeps me going. . . . The students keep me going. [When you can listen and understand what they are thinking, you see that] the mind of a child is awesome.

Before participating in the CGI workshop, Paul had recognized that listening to students was important. He felt he had a lot of ideas but did not really understand how they fit together or what to do with them. CGI gave meaning to what children do. It provided a framework for interpreting student thinking. Paul said that he continues to read other work, but CGI gives him a basis for interpreting it.

Getting teachers to listen to children has been a key factor in motivating new teachers to learn and implement the principles of CGI in their classrooms. A regular feature of the summer school programs in Minnesota has been to involve teachers in work with children. Many of the children do not understand the standard algorithm but show rich informal knowledge. The teachers see children using strategies that the teachers themselves do not initially understand. They see that the children are capable of remarkable insights and are motivated to learn the mathematics and the models of children's thinking that can help them understand the children. The children motivate the teachers and get them to try CGI with their own students.

CGI provides a framework for helping teachers listen to and understand students' thinking, which plays a critical role in keeping teachers engaged in implementing CGI and in engaging new teachers. Teachers do not, however, learn CGI overnight or without support. As the Minnesota teachers were learning CGI, they enlisted the participation of teachers who had been involved with CGI and had a deep understanding of the first principles. As their understanding of CGI grew, they relied less on the participation of outside teachers, although they do continue to have conversations with them via email, telephone, and occasional visits.

By all accounts, it has been critical for the teachers to participate in a network of colleagues they can talk to about children's thinking, and it is important that at least some participants in these conversations have sufficient knowledge of the first principles of CGI to keep the focus on them. Initially, outside experts played this role, but, increasingly, the Minnesota teachers have assumed this role themselves. A critical feature of the success of the program has been that the teacher leaders in Minnesota really understand the goals and substance of CGI.

Administrative and community support has also been important for these teachers. Administrators and parents have been able to see what students are capable of learning and the changes in their learning when they are given the opportunity to build on the intuitive knowledge they bring to instruction. For the most part, administrative support has consisted of letting the teachers assume leadership in implementing CGI, and one of the notable features of their efforts is how they have taken responsibility for the learning of their colleagues. In Paul's words,

> I cannot be an island [with a class that lets students think about mathematics] and then have the kids go back to a traditional class. If I have colleagues around me, it is easier to do my work. And it is motivating to talk to my colleagues [about what they see their children doing].

What a Difference a Teacher Makes

"Lynn" changed the mathematics instruction at her school. She did not do it alone; she had the support of her principal. Neither did she do it quickly. She has been working on it for over three years and sees changing instructional techniques in mathematics as an evolving enterprise. Lynn's approach to working with the teachers in her school was modeled after what she learned as a beginning CGI teacher. As she worked with the teachers in her school, Lynn wanted to engage them, get them working together to figure out the details of CGI, and help them see that CGI does not look the same in every classroom. She made herself available because she felt, "CGI is what we should be doing for kids." Currently, Lynn reports that 100 percent of the teachers in her school are engaged, at some level, in CGI.

After describing her experiences in the school where she now works, she described how she had been able to help the school become what she and others speak of as "a CGI school." Lynn learned about CGI as a preservice teacher working with two teachers in North Carolina. When Lynn moved to California, she knew that she wanted to implement the ideas of CGI that she had learned. She is not the only example of a teacher who has moved to a new community and fostered the spread of CGI, and her story exemplifies the kind of difference we see individual teachers making.

Lynn began laying the groundwork for scaling up CGI even before she relocated. The process began as she searched for a new teaching job. She specifically set out to find a school with a principal who would support her efforts to implement CGI. She found a supportive principal during her interview at Weaver Elementary. She reports,

> I was told that I could use CGI as long as I could also pull in the textbook. I felt I could do that, so I spent my first year there doing CGI, and I invited the principal to come and see what we were doing many, many times.

She found that the principal was impressed with what she saw: "She was amazed at the mileage my kids were getting out of the mathematics we were doing." By building a relationship with the principal around CGI and providing evidence from her classroom, Lynn created an ally. The principal began sending teachers into her room, so they could see her mathematics instruction. The principal also tried to get the district involved. She wanted CGI to be implemented throughout her school and the district. The principal and Lynn had little influence on the district at this point. After observing Lynn's classroom, the district mathematics coordinator concluded that she was unique and that CGI worked only because Lynn was doing it. Lynn told us,

> This made me so mad, so mad. I tried to tell her that she should have seen me when I started. I was a . . . . I was a follow the textbook page-by-page person. If I could do it anyone could do it.

However, Lynn was unable to convince the district mathematics coordinator to think about CGI as a possibility for the district. The principal and Lynn did not, however, give up on the district. Instead, the principal invited the district superintendent to visit. Lynn told us, "She was amazed, but she told us she didn't have any money. She told my principal to do something creative and use Weaver as a place where we can show what can happen." So, with few resources but with support from her principal, Lynn set out to work with the teachers at her school around CGI.

The school-based strategy that emerged developed through a series of cycles. Initially, teachers volunteered; later, all teachers participated. Throughout the cycles of CGI work, Lynn and the principal worked together to find ways for the teachers to become intrigued with CGI and to continue to learn about it. The first engagement with teachers began with seven volunteers. These teachers had seen Lynn and her students engaged in CGI and wanted to know more. They agreed to give up five days of their winter vacation to engage with Lynn in CGI professional development. Following the five days, the principal found money to release Lynn one day a month to visit the teachers. They also met once a month after school to talk about CGI and teaching mathematics. Describing the meetings, Lynn said,

> They reminded me of the North Carolina meetings with no money. We all pitched in and helped each other. . . . we talked about what we were all trying and what the students were doing. One time the meeting went on for four hours.

These teachers met together for more than a year, and they, along with Lynn, now help promote CGI in the school.

The experiences of the first cycle of CGI teachers at Weaver further convinced the principal that CGI could spread throughout the school. The teachers showed her what their students could do in mathematics, and the parents began to request CGI teachers for their children. The principal and Lynn discussed a plan for engaging all of the teachers at the school in CGI. The principal began by having teachers not involved in CGI visit the classrooms of those doing CGI. Lynn felt that many of the teachers already recognized that the math program was not meeting the needs of their students. They [the teachers] knew we needed to do something. For the most part, we were a young . . . a very young staff and that helped. When we started listening to the students, we saw the successes. Teachers [from the first group] left the professional development saying that it was the best professional development that they ever had.

For the second cycle of professional development, the principal arranged compensation days for the teachers and Lynn; every teacher participated. When we asked Lynn why she thought teachers were willing to participate in CGI, she said that

> Probably the most valuable piece was that it was something, they could go back and really find meaning in mathematics. . . . CGI meets our kids' needs, they can see that. . . . They said they saw how to use manipulatives. They have seen and heard about using manipulatives for years, and now they really see how they can use them. The teachers told me that they now understand what the kids are doing. They had felt before that they didn't know what they knew about them.

She admits that some teachers were reluctant. One teacher told Lynn that she did not think she would be able to write the word problems to pose to her students. Another teacher had been teaching for a long time and already had an established way of teaching mathematics. Lynn helped them by explaining that CGI did not need to look the way that it did in her class. She tried to get them to see that they could listen to their students in many different ways and that they could "get started on it slowly." The principal helped by requiring all teachers, even those who were tenured, to teach a CGI lesson as one of the three lessons she observed during the year.

The first group of teachers is now in its third year. Another school in the district is ready to begin to implement CGI, and it wants full training. The teachers who started three years ago are hesitant to do the professional development. They feel that they still have a lot to learn. Lynn understands that fully and has encouraged the teachers to help; she is convincing them that they can continue learning as they work with other teachers. She is hopeful. She sees

CGI building within the district, and she has a growing core of teachers to work with her in expanding CGI.

From the Inside Out

Another approach to scaling up CGI has been to work within the school structure. Crestview Elementary School is a multitrack, year-round school with approximately 1,300 students and 40 teachers. The school draws from a low-income community of new immigrants, and most students speak Spanish as their native language. Our work at Crestview brought together teachers, administrators, and our professional development team to focus on understanding the development of students' mathematical thinking. We worked together for three years, with each of the participants evolving in the ways they participated and the roles they took on. The work has led to a number of changes within the school. First, the focus on student thinking and the inquiry around it continues four years after the professional development team left. Further, teachers and administrators have stated that focusing on children's mathematical thinking has changed their mathematical work: Collaboration exists where none existed before; teachers' practices have changed; and students are demonstrating more mathematical understanding (Franke and Kazemi, 2001; Franke et al., 2001; Kazemi, 1999).

The teachers and administrators at Crestview and the professional development team engaged in monthly work group meetings. Prior to each meeting, all participating teachers posed the same mathematical problem to their students and brought their students' work to a cross-grade-level meeting.[5] A major goal for the professional development was to encourage teachers to come together to make sense of their students' mathematical thinking and to make public their private acts of teaching. We wanted to provide teachers a forum in which to develop relationships and create a community of

---

[5] Our intent was to create space, as Wenger describes, for teachers to share, challenge, and create ideas about the development of children's mathematical thinking. Our work groups were intended to be a place, as Lave (1996) and Cochran-Smith and Lytle (1999) describe, where teachers can shape their identities and take on a "stance."

practice that was not separate from their classrooms and reflected the interactions and identities developed there. Not only were the participants learning about the details of children's mathematical thinking, they were also creating communities of inquiry.

During the work group meetings, participants reported the range of strategies their students had used for the problem they had posed, ranked the strategies in terms of mathematical sophistication, and talked about implications. At each meeting, the teachers were asked to respond in writing to the same set of questions for reflection about their students' work and classroom practices. Between the meetings, we visited each classroom at least once and also spent time within the school (at lunch and talking in the halls). We also met regularly with the principal.

By the end of the first year, all but a few teachers participated regularly in the professional development. At the end of the second year, the professional development team and the principal invited teachers to lead the work groups. At the same time, the principal found money to hire one of the teachers as a half-time mathematics specialist. In the third year, the Mathematics Team Facilitators (MTFs, their name for themselves) led the work groups. We provided support to the MTFs, as did the principal and the mathematics specialist. The work groups continue today, four years after we moved out of facilitating the groups.

Adapting Teacher Evaluation. The leadership practices of the principal, "Karen," were central. She invited us to work in the school and supported our participation in the community. She attended to the learning trajectories of the teachers, was a full participant in the professional development, and kept the district at bay while we struggled together. Karen's evaluation of teachers exemplifies the role she played in supporting innovation, as well as her ability to align her practices with the goals and norms of CGI. During our first year of work together, Karen decided to use students' mathematical work as the basis for "evaluating" her teachers. Rather than observing in their classrooms and documenting pedagogical practice, Karen asked the teachers to discuss their students' mathematical work with her. When asked why she had made this change, Karen replied,

> I was dissatisfied with observation because I found that anybody could do anything for an hour, no matter what they were doing on a daily basis. And little of what I saw or we talked about ever got to how the students were doing. . . . The biggest thing that focusing on student work accomplishes is that it tunes us into student work, it sets the tone that we use student work to talk about teaching, all decisions in the classroom are based on what you see in the student work, not how the lesson goes.

The teachers brought Karen examples of their students' mathematical work three times during the year. Karen asked the teacher to describe the student's thinking, what the teacher thought it meant, and how the teacher would respond to it. Karen would ask questions that pushed the teachers to detail the student thinking and to think about what the student work told them (or did not tell them) about a student's understanding. She would talk with the teacher about what they would do next with a particular student.

In a concrete, highly visible way, Karen showed the teachers that she valued knowing about student thinking and that she wanted all the teachers in the school to be able to talk about it, no matter what other classroom decisions they made. Karen supported the teachers in thinking about themselves as people who understood student thinking. The ritual of evaluation and supervision continues but as a practice focused around students' mathematical thinking and aligned with the professional development. The principal took an existing structure and adapted it, drawing on the substance of the professional development.

Spreading the Core from the School to the District. As the teachers increased their knowledge of students' mathematical thinking and refined their identities as teachers who could determine how to teach mathematics and explain their choices, they not only began to talk with each other more but also joined in broader discussions outside the school. One way in which this broader discussion occurred was through participation in the district's mathematics curriculum committee. During the second year of our work together, three teachers volunteered to serve on the districtwide curriculum committee. The teachers' experiences with the committee began as the district rolled out its new mathematics standards. The Crestview teachers were struck by the long list of skills for each grade level. They were surprised that these standards were introduced to the teachers on the same day that William Schmidt, National Research Coordinator for the Third International Mathematics and Science Study (Mullis, et al., 1998), came to talk to the district about how U.S. schools approach mathematics teaching by teaching many skills each year rather than by going deeply into a few areas:

> We heard Schmidt, the guy from the [Third International Math and Science Study], talk about the problems with math education in America on our opening day and came to the committee the next week asking how we could make changes in accordance with the findings he presented. I and a few others were determined not to let such an opportunity for change pass us by. We felt that the district would support this radical change . . . after all, they invited Schmidt to speak to us! We realized that we were trashing 3 years work by the committee but knew that it was the only way we could fix the problem with math achievement.

At the first meeting of the mathematics curriculum committee, the Crestview teachers proposed that the district standards be rethought. Surprisingly (to the teachers, the principal, and us), the superintendent and the rest of the committee agreed that the standards should be revisited. The Crestview teachers on the curriculum committee took the lead. They ended up not only convincing the curriculum committee to adopt their form of the standards but also convincing the superintendent and the school board. While the process was challenging, the teachers were excited about their ability to argue their case. They had evidence from their classrooms and research they had collected indicating that their new version of the standards would be more helpful to teachers and a better fit for the development of their students' mathematical thinking. The district has now adopted the Crestview teachers' version of the standards.

Building Capacity Within. At the end of the second year, the research team planned to move out of the work group leadership role. The principal took the lead. She worked out a way to release one teacher half-time to provide leadership in mathematics. She quickly realized, however, that one teacher could not take this on alone. The principal came to us with the idea of recruiting a group of teachers within the school who might be interested in taking on leadership roles. Eight to ten teachers met and discussed what their role might look like and what they might work to accomplish. One member of the research team offered to meet monthly with the leadership team to support their work.

The leadership team decided enough school support existed to continue the work group meetings, so each teacher or pair of teachers from the leadership team became responsible for facilitating each work group. The leadership group discussed possible strategies for what to do during the work group meetings. They created a plan to cover the next few meetings and began their work groups. Through the work of the MTFs, the mathematics leadership in the school became shared. The MTFs used their meetings with the leadership team as a way to push their own learning. They viewed their participation in the leadership team as a learning opportunity—an opportunity they thought all teachers needed. So, at the end of a year of their leadership, they proposed that the leadership rotate the following year so that all teachers could take on the role at some point in the year.

Crestview evolved from a school focused on mathematics drill and practice to one focused on developing the mathematical understanding of its students in ways that brought together skills, problem-solving, and understanding. Every person at Crestview participated, and all continue to see themselves as learners. Many structures had to change to engage in CGI at Crestview, and many participants played roles in making sure the necessary structures were put in place when needed. We found learning occurring throughout the school. We saw all participants evolving in the ways they interacted in the professional development, their classrooms, in the hallways with their colleagues, and in the leadership roles they took on.

What remained constant was the focus on the details of students' mathematical thinking. Karen used it in her adaptation of supervision, the teachers used it in their revision of new district standards; the MTFs used it to design the work group meetings; and the teachers used it as they argued points of view with their colleagues inside and outside of the work group setting. However, not only the knowledge or the language around student thinking came out, but also the ways those involved engaged in discussion, used student thinking as evidence to argue their case, and conceived of themselves not as having answers but as having a vision supported by evidence. Becoming learners changed the ways they engaged in their work—in the classroom, as supervisors, and as teachers outside the classroom.

The Kudzu of School Reform

The fourth case describes the program for scaling up implemented by the Upper-Midwest Comprehensive Regional Assistance Center. This center's efforts are aimed at widespread implementation of CGI within participating schools and districts. The long-range goal is to build an infrastructure for scaling up within each of the participating districts. Achieving this goal involves preparing teachers and other district personnel to become leaders in providing professional development and engaging teachers throughout the district in implementing CGI. Although this process involves developing leadership within the district and handing off the responsibility for providing professional development, it is not exactly a training-of-trainers model. Teachers, not professional development providers, are the linchpin of the effort and shifting participation.

To illustrate the work of the center, we focus on the work with one district in Dearborn, Michigan. Dearborn is a city of about 100,000 in the Detroit metropolitan area. It has one of the largest Arabic-speaking populations in the United States, and about 35 percent of the students in the Dearborn Public School District are classified as English language learners. Dearborn sent a group of 17 teachers and administrators to the initial CGI summer institute and has been expanding the program throughout the district in the years since.

The metaphors used to think about problems often drive the actions taken to solve them. Recommendations for changing schooling are commonly based on a metaphor that portrays school systems as large machines with specified inputs and outputs. Based on this metaphor, schools are changed by changing the inputs (the curriculum, materials, and other resources available for instruction), changing the process by which the resources are used (changing instruction), or by more carefully monitoring the output (setting standards and instituting high-stakes assessment). The work of the Comprehensive Center is based on a different metaphor the center's director, Walter Secada, articulated when the CGI scale-up effort was initiated. Rather than conceiving of school systems as machines with inputs and outputs, he proposed thinking of school systems in ecological terms (Secada, 2000, p. 2.):

> We think of the CC-VI [Comprehensive Center-Region VI] work with individual schools as *seeding* change. We strategically introduce new ways of teaching mathematics, support teachers and their schools in implementing those ideas, then depend on the system's own internal mechanisms to help spread the innovation—while still lending our support. The Comprehensive Center assumes that professional development will affect the balance of a school's ecosystem and that forces from within the system will act to strike a new balance. Our goal is to help create the conditions for that balance—a balance in which the introduced species can survive and eventually spread throughout the system.

In much the same way that a new organism may enter an ecosystem, establish a foothold, then expand within the environment, the Comprehensive Center introduced CGI into the schools by initially working with a few teachers. When these teachers (and their students) thrived, CGI expanded gradually but steadily throughout the district.

Districts were invited to send teams of two or three teachers and one instructional leader (a principal, a mathematics specialist, a Title 1 coordinator, etc.) to an initial five-day summer institute, at which they learned the basic principles of CGI. The Comprehensive Center limited participation to teams of teachers, so that the teachers would have one another's support when they returned to their classrooms. The inclusion of an instructional leader was intended to produce broad support for the teachers, and the Comprehensive Center insisted on written commitments from principals that the teachers would be encouraged to try out the ideas they had learned in the institute.

When the teachers returned to their classrooms the following year, they met to discuss their observations about students in their own classrooms and how they were adapting instruction to build on what they were learning about their students. It is one thing to learn about children's thinking in the abstract, and it is another for teachers to see it with their own students. It was this experience that convinced them.

When asked what motivated them to implement CGI and to work to encourage other teachers to implement it, the teachers uniformly responded: "It's the kids!" One teacher elaborated:

> I looked at my students one day, and I was in awe of their ability. I couldn't believe what they did. And I didn't teach them anything. . . . It's [all about] understanding, and they were!

Another teacher talked about the remarkable things she was observing in her lowest-achieving students:

> With traditional math, I would have thought, "This kid can't do it. This kid, maybe, has learning problems." But they have their own ways to figure things out. If we allow them to do that, then we can see their growth.

A third teacher commented that she was still skeptical after watching videotapes of children solving problems in the summer institute. She asked: "Do they know my kids?" When she began asking her students to solve these problems, the level of thinking they exhibited amazed her. She commented that when her first-graders would solve a complex problem using thinking that she had believed impossible: "I'd be so excited. I'd say, 'Go tell Miss T. I don't care what she is doing over there! Just disturb her!" (Brendefur and Foster, 2000, p. 20).

As this last quote indicates, another important factor in nurturing these teachers was the support of their colleagues. The teachers met monthly to share stories of students, write problems, and support one another. They would spend two or three hours sharing, and they were "so excited to share what we started to see [in students]." (Brendefur and Foster, 2000, p. 20).

Full-scale implementation of the principles of CGI often requires teachers to radically change their practices and the ways that they interact with students; not surprisingly, these changes challenge many teachers. Although all teachers used ideas of CGI at some level, three patterns of participation were observed in the teachers' implementation of CGI during the first year: For some teachers, the problem-solving portrayed in the CGI institute was a supplement to their traditional mathematics instruction; some teachers supplemented CGI with traditional instruction; and some teachers adopted CGI as the primary means of instruction.

Although not all participants of the summer institute radically changed their teaching practices overnight, the changes that did occur began to attract the attention of other teachers. The "infectious enthusiasm of the first group of teachers" and the accomplishments and enthusiasm of these teachers' students attracted the attention of their colleagues (Secada, 2000, p. 2). One colleague commented,

> I observed a classroom of one of the teachers who went [to the CGI institute] the first year, and it was just unbelievable! I couldn't believe the types of problems the students were solving successfully and the strategies they were coming up with. And when I saw that, it really was an incentive for me to come [to an institute].

During this first year, CGI was encouraged to grow because it made measurable differences in student learning. The Comprehensive Center provided research-based evidence that students were learning more, and this evidence reinforced administrators' commitment to supporting the teachers' efforts to spread CGI throughout the district.

The following summer, another cohort of Dearborn teachers attended the introductory CGI institute, and five teachers, a principal, and a resource teacher from the first cohort attended an advanced institute to prepare to lead CGI professional development. Currently, with the support of the Comprehensive Center, this group is providing professional development for other teachers in the district. Furthermore, by making presentations at local and national meetings, these teachers are sowing the seeds for CGI to spread beyond the district. One of the interesting byproducts of this approach to scaling up has been the level of professionalism it has produced in the teachers. Many of the teachers are not only concerned with continuing to improve their own practice but are also assuming responsibility for helping other teachers improve.

Conclusions

One lesson learned from these stories is that, for the most part, CGI has not scaled up by changing the organizational structure of the school, by top-down efforts to implement CGI by school administrators, or through continuing implementation or the infusion of resources by outside agents. In the cases we have seen, CGI has scaled up because the teachers and administrators engaged in it felt that it made a difference in students' learning of mathematics, their enthusiasm for learning mathematics, and their conceptions of themselves as learners of mathematics. Seeing the remarkable mathematical achievements of their students has driven teachers (and their students) to become the primary movers in scaling up CGI.

Scaling Up as Participation

In much the same way as we have characterized the learning of students and teachers participating in CGI professional development, we think of scaling up in terms of shifts in participation. As we reflect on notions of participation, four issues emerge that help us better understand scaling up. First, if we see learning as participation, we must take into account the importance of relationships. Second, some participants in the learning must possess the knowledge, skills, and identities that reflect and represent full participation. Third, artifacts need to be available to support participation around the core ideas within and outside the professional development community. Fourth, teachers need opportunities to engage in legitimate peripheral participation.

Importance of Relationships. Relationships played a central role in the success of each of our scale-up examples. Rather than thinking about CGI as something passed on to someone, CGI was seen as something engaged in with another person. Here, those engaged in CGI purposely developed relationships with others that supported the work of CGI. For example, at Crestview, the professional development team worked to develop relationships not only with the teachers but also with the principal and other school staff members. The developers became members of the school community and shared in the lives of the teachers and the principal. The principal became a part of the work—not an outsider. She engaged with the teachers in the work group and talked informally with them about their students' mathematical thinking. In addition, she used her more-formal role to continue to support the development of CGI by changing her evaluation practice and by encouraging different levels of participation in and out of the classroom. In the case of the Comprehensive Center, the administrators also participated in the professional development and had to agree to support the implementation of CGI at their sites. The professional developers worked to create formal and informal relationships with teachers; the teachers were invited back in the years following their initial professional development to work again with the professional development staff. These relationships allowed each participant to gain an understanding of the core of CGI so that they could carve out a role to support the ongoing development of CGI.

Drawing on Expertise. Building a cadre of teachers who understand CGI is critical to scaling up. The purpose of building the cadre is not simply to provide others with CGI professional developers. The purpose is to create communities with teachers who can share expertise and support the learning of the group. Knowledgeable teachers with existing identities as CGI teachers can begin to define full participation. The teachers who understand CGI provide the basis for redefining the norms and goals of the communities they participate in. These teachers can ask questions–challenging each other and their students in ways different from those of an outside professional developer. How the more-expert teachers choose to participate in learning CGI provides a way for dialogue to begin, student thinking to be shared, and stances and practices to be articulated. Thinking about the cadre of knowledgeable CGI teachers this way changes how we think about working with teachers who want to participate. Rather than starting with all teachers, we see the benefit of working with teachers who want to participate and are interested in learning about CGI.

One could argue that working with teachers who want to participate is easy—we are reaching the reachable teachers. The examples we shared all began this way, but none ended there. In each example, the teacher or teachers who had developed expertise worked in communities to assist other teachers and administrators. The goal was to build the capacity to make a difference. We saw this in the case of Lynn, as she pulled in more and more teachers until all the teachers are participating and as a core of teachers began to engage a new school. Or, we saw it in the case of Paul, as he engaged more and more teachers and they began to engage other teachers in their districts. This growing core is essential to scaling up. We do not see expert teachers in CGI as becoming isolated from their colleagues; we see them as teachers who can form the new core.

Building the core does not necessarily work in all scaling up endeavors. We see it working to support the development of CGI because CGI engages teachers in learning about their students' mathematical thinking in ways that enable teachers to see that they themselves will always have more to learn. Even the experienced, knowledgeable CGI teachers see themselves as continuing to learn with their colleagues, and in that way, they can continue to share and learn together, thus removing the basis for isolation.

As teachers develop CGI expertise, a shift in their identities as professionals occurs. Although some CGI teachers do not perceive themselves as participating in a broader community, many of them do. They see their role as not just learning about CGI to improve their own instruction; they also begin to assume responsibility for helping other teachers learn about student thinking. One of the ways that they begin to participate in a broader community is by inviting other teachers into their classrooms or by sharing their students' work with them. Although many teachers are at first intimidated by the thought of leading professional development for other teachers while they are still trying to figure CGI out for themselves, a number will begin to lead professional development efforts. In fact, most of the professional development for CGI is now led by elementary classroom teachers.

Developing Artifacts and Tools That Support Learning. CGI provides artifacts that transcend the different aspects of a teacher's practice and allow learning to occur as different participants engage with those artifacts. The types of problems and strategies are artifacts that can be elaborated in different settings and that can provide the basis for developing a common language and reestablishing norms. The teachers at Crestview posed the monthly problems that became objects of discussion and reflection throughout the school: in classrooms with students, in the hallways with other teachers and the principal, and in work group settings with their colleagues and the professional development team. The CGI teachers that Paul engages with have ways of talking with each other around student work—a common language that is supported by the trajectories of strategies shared in CGI. Paul and other teachers share with each other what surprises them about their students' strategies and, in doing so, elaborate on each other's understanding. In each of these examples, CGI provides artifacts that can be used, elaborated on, and restructured in ways that define and trace participation. These artifacts provide outward signs of how people are participating and allow participants to make explicit shifts in their interactions with students, other teachers, administrators, and professional development staff.

Legitimate Peripheral Participation. A unique feature of CGI and other programs that focus on students' thinking is that they afford opportunities for different levels of participation. Teachers need not buy into it all at once. They can participate in legitimately peripheral ways by giving students relevant problems, by beginning to talk to students about how they solved problems, and the like. Even if the teachers do not entirely understand what their students tell them and cannot successfully provide the scaffolding for their students' responses to help them build on what they know, the teachers are engaged in practices that represent an important step toward understanding and building on student thinking.

Teachers are neither expected to be "CGI teachers" after the initial professional development, nor are they expected to have developed the same understandings or ways of teaching CGI. The teachers that Paul worked with developed over many years. Some of the teachers were seen as full participants and some as participating less actively, but all were seen as participants. Lynn specifically talked about teachers who were not quite ready to participate and described her strategies for engaging them. She knew she needed to get them started and help them see that everyone can participate at different levels. This perspective held true for those doing the professional development or leading the effort: The leaders also saw themselves as participating at different levels. In each case, teacher leaders saw themselves as learners. So, everyone involved in learning about CGI was seen as learning, and learning took on different forms and different trajectories for the various participants. Teachers were not required to buy in completely from day one. Not only was it not required, but teachers who did not buy in helped the groups' learning. The legitimate peripheral participation afforded by CGI allows time and space for teachers to acquire the knowledge and skills they need to move toward fuller participation.

Struggles in Scaling Up

This chapter has portrayed four different scale-up efforts that have been successful in different ways. Our goal has been to show an alternative vision of scaling up—one that is driven by ideas that make a difference in teachers' and students' lives rather than by changes in the organizational structures of schooling. It would be false to leave the impression, however, that implementing CGI has not involved struggles or that scale-up efforts have met with universal success with all teachers or in all situations. Drawing on the agricultural metaphor discussed earlier, if the seeds of change are not nourished, they do not flourish.

For CGI to develop and spread, the environment has to support it. It takes time for teachers to learn CGI, and it takes a community that supports teachers as they learn about their students' mathematical thinking. Some of our colleagues have worked in situations in which teachers were not provided the opportunity to form communities that engaged in inquiry about student thinking. In one large school district, the administration supported initial CGI institutes but provided little opportunity for the teachers to engage with one another afterward. Most of the teachers were in different schools and had little opportunity to talk with one another or to share their struggles and successes with other teachers in their own schools or throughout the district. Many of the teachers in the institute bought into the basic tenets of CGI and made some remarkable changes in their own classes, but because these teachers tended to be isolated from one another and from other teachers who might have learned from their experiences, there were few effects beyond the initial cadre of teachers.

Making It Work

We have outlined what CGI affords, the opportunities it can create for changing the core of schooling, and the potential for scaling up. Describing what CGI affords, however, is different from describing what happens in schools. The affordances play out in different environments in different ways, so we must attend to the particulars of how CGI evolves within a particular environment. The stories we have told about the ways in which CGI has evolved demonstrate that CGI in and of itself does not lead to successful scaling up. It requires those involved to recognize and develop an understanding of the principles driving CGI and to create mechanisms for the principles to lead to continued learning. It requires knowledge and skills of individuals to drive the work and a constant focus on the principles of the development of students' mathematical thinking.

References

Boaler, J., "Opening the Dimensions of Mathematical Capability: The Development of Knowledge, Practice, and Identity in Mathematics Classrooms," paper presented at the North American Chapter of Psychology of Mathematics Education, Snowbird, Utah, 2001.

Brendefur, J. L., and S. E. Foster, "Dearborn, Michigan: A System Changes," *Cognitively Guided Instruction and Systemic Reform: The Newsletter of the Comprehensive Center—Region VI*, Vol. 5, No. 2, Fall 2000, pp. 20–23.

Carpenter, T. P., "Learning to Add and Subtract: An Exercise in Problem Solving," in E. A. Silver, ed., *Teaching and Learning Mathematical Problem Solving: Multiple Research Perspectives*, Hillsdale, N.J.: Erlbaum, 1985, pp. 17–40.

Carpenter, T. P., E. Ansell, M. L. Franke, E. Fennema, and L. Weisbeck, "Models of Problem Solving: A Study of Kindergarten Children's Problem-Solving Processes," *Journal for Research in Mathematics Education*, Vol. 24, No. 5, 1993, pp. 428–441.

Carpenter, T. P., E. Ansell, and L. Levi, "An Alternative Conception of Teaching for Understanding: Case Studies of Two First-Grade Mathematics Classes," in T. Wood, B. S. Nelson, and J. Warfield, eds., *Beyond Classical Pedagogy in Elementary Mathematics: The Nature of Facilitative Teaching*, Mahwah, N.J.: Erlbaum, 2001, pp. 27–46.

Carpenter, T. P., E. Fennema, and M. L. Franke, "Cognitively Guided Instruction: A Knowledge Base for Reform in Primary Mathematics Instruction," *The Elementary School Journal*, Vol. 97, No. 1, 1996, pp. 3–20.

Carpenter, T. P., E. Fennema, M. L. Franke, L. W. Levi, and S. B. Empson, *Children's Mathematics: Cognitively Guided Instruction*, Portsmouth, N.H.: Heinemann, 1999.

Carpenter, T. P., E. Fennema, P. L. Peterson, and D. A. Carey, "Teachers' Pedagogical Content Knowledge of Student's Problem Solving in Elementary Arithmetic," *Journal for Research in Mathematics Education*, Vol. 19, 1988, pp. 385–401.

Carpenter, T. P., E. Fennema, P. L. Peterson, C. P. Chiang, and M. Loef, "Using Knowledge of Children's Mathematics Thinking in Classroom

Teaching: An Experimental Study," *American Educational Research Journal*, Vol. 26, No. 4, 1989, pp. 499–531.

Carpenter, T. P., M. L. Franke, V. R. Jacobs, and E. Fennema, "A Longitudinal Study of Invention and Understanding in Children's Multidigit Addition and Subtraction," *Journal for Research in Mathematics Education*, Vol. 29, No. 1, 1998, pp. 3–20.

Carpenter, T. P., M. L. Franke, and L. Levi, *Thinking Mathematically: Integrating Arithmetic and Algebra in the Elementary School*, Portsmouth, N.H.: Heinemann, 2003.

Cobb, P., "Individual and Collective Mathematical Development: The Case of Statistical Data Analysis," *Mathematical Thinking and Learning*, Vol. 1, 1999, pp. 5–43.

Cochran-Smith, M., and S. Lytle, "Relationships of Knowledge and Practice: Teacher Learning in Communities," in A. Iran-Nejad and D. Pearson, eds., *Review of Research in Education*, Washington, D.C.: American Educational Research Association, Vol. 24, 1999, pp. 209–346.

Elmore, R. F., "Getting to Scale with Successful Educational Practice," in S. Furhman and J. O'Day, eds., *Rewards and Reform: Creating Educational Incentives That Work*, San Francisco: Jossey Bass Publishers, 1996, pp. 294–329.

Empson, S. B., "Equal Sharing and Shared Meaning: The Development of Fraction Concepts in a First-Grade Classroom," *Cognition and Instruction*, Vol. 17, No. 3, 1999, pp. 283–342.

Fennema, E., T. P. Carpenter, M. L. Franke, L. Levi, V. Jacobs, and S. Empson. "Learning to Use Children's Thinking in Mathematics Instruction: A Longitudinal Study," *Journal for Research in Mathematics Education*, Vol. 27, No. 4, 1996, pp. 403–434.

Fennema, E., T. P. Carpenter, L. Levi, M. L. Franke, and S. B. Empson, Children's *Mathematics: A Guide for Workshop Leaders*, Portsmouth, N.H.: Heinemann, 1999.

Franke, M. L., and Kazemi, E., "Teaching as Learning Within a Community of Practice: Characterizing Generative Growth," in T. Wood, B. S. Nelson, and J. Warfield, eds., *Beyond Classical Pedagogy in Elementary Mathematics: The Nature of Facilitative Teaching*, Mahwah, N.J.: Erlbaum, 2001, pp. 27–46.

Franke, M. L., T. P. Carpenter, L. Levi, and E. Fennema, "Capturing Teachers' Generative Growth: A Follow-Up Study of Professional Development in Mathematics," *American Educational Research Journal*, Vol. 38, 2001, pp. 653–689.

Fuson, K. C., "Research on Whole Number Addition and Subtraction," in D. Grouws, ed., *Handbook of Research on Mathematics Teaching and Learning*, New York: Macmillan, 1992.

Fuson, K. C., D. Wearne, J. Hiebert, P. Human, H. Murray, A. Olivier, T. P. Carpenter, and E. Fennema, "Children's Conceptual Structures for Mulitdigit Numbers and Methods of Multidigit Addition and Subtraction," *Journal for Research in Mathematics Education*, Vol. 28, 1997, pp. 130–162.

Greeno, J. G., and the Middle School Mathematics Through Applications Project, "The Situativity of Knowing, Learning, and Research," *American Psychologist*, Vol. 53, 1998, pp. 5–26.

Kazemi, E., *Teacher Learning Within Communities of Practice: Using Students' Mathematical Thinking to Guide Teacher Inquiry*, dissertation, Los Angeles: The University of California, 1999.

Kazemi, E., and M. Franke, *Using Student Work to Support Professional Development in Elementary Mathematics*, Seattle: University of Washington, Center for the Study of Teaching and Policy, 2002.

Lave, J., "Teaching, as Learning, in Practice," *Mind, Culture, and Activity*, Vol. 3, 1996, pp. 149–164.

Lave, J., and W. Wenger, *Situated Learning: Legitimate Peripheral Participation*, Cambridge, England: Cambridge University Press, 1991.

Lehrer, R., C. Jacobson, V. Kemeny, and D. Strom, "Building on Children's Intuition to Develop Mathematical Understanding of Space," in E. Fennema and T. A. Romberg, eds., *Mathematics Classrooms that Promote Understanding*, Mahwah, N.J.: Erlbaum, 1999, pp. 63–88.

Lehrer, R., and L. Schauble, eds., *Real Data in the Classroom: Expanding Children's Understanding of Mathematics and Science*, New York: Teachers College Press, 2002.

Mullis, I. V. S., M. O. Martin, A. E. Beaton, E. J. Gonzalez, D. L. Kelly, and T. A. Smith, *Mathematics and Science Achievement in the Final Year of Secondary School*, Chestnut Hill, Mass.: Boston College, 1998.

National Council of Teachers of Mathematics, *Principles and Standards for School Mathematics*, Reston, Va.: NCTM, 2000.

Rogoff, B., "Developing Understanding of the Idea of Communities of Learners," *Mind, Culture, and Activity*, Vol. 1, 1994, pp. 209–229.

_____, "Evaluating Development in the Process of Participation: Theory, Methods, and Practice Building on Each Other," in E. Amsel and A. Renninger, eds., *Change and Development: Issues of Theory, Application, and Method*, Mahwah, N.J.: Erlbaum, 1997, pp. 265–285.

Secada, W. G., and J. L. Brendefur, "CGI Student Achievement in Region VI: Evaluation Findings," *Cognitively Guided Instruction and Systemic Reform: The Newsletter of the Comprehensive Center—Region VI*, Vol. 5, No. 2, Insert, 2000.

Villasenor, A., and H. S. Kepner, "Arithmetic from a Problem-Solving Perspective: An Urban Implementation," *Journal for Research in Mathematics Education*, Vol. 24, No. 1, 1993, pp. 62–69.

Wenger, E., *Communities of Practice: Learning, Meaning, and Identity*, Cambridge, England: Cambridge University Press, 1998.

Wertsch, J. V., *Voices of the Mind: A Sociocultural Approach to Mediated Action*, Cambridge, Mass.: Harvard University Press, 1991.

_____, *Mind as Action*, New York: Oxford University Press, 1998.

CHAPTER THREE

The National Writing Project: Scaling Up and Scaling Down

Joseph P. McDonald, Judy Buchanan, and Richard Sterling

McDonald, Buchanan, and Sterling introduce the interesting notion of "scaling up by scaling down," by which they mean that, to succeed in a new environment, a reform that is spreading geographically must also challenge and, eventually, penetrate habitual practice in new contexts. To achieve this penetration, the National Writing Project (NWP) focuses on professional development and professional networks for writing teachers. NWP promoted both spread and depth of change through its "improvement infrastructure," a system made up of three elements: an annual review process, the development of specialized cross-site networks, and a commitment to both internal, site-based, practitioner-directed research and external, national, and independent research as a means of learning from experience.

Scaling up educational reform necessarily involves taking risks. This is, first of all, because new investments are required. To scale up their reforms, reformers must raise new resources and decide on an investment strategy. They must then hope that the investment strategy, and the quantity and quality of the resources raised and invested, will be sufficient to create a proportional effect—that a reform effective in three settings, for example, will be effective in nine, ninety, or nine hundred. Many reformers accept this challenge because, by definition, they are risk-defiant. They have already challenged the status quo. They accept it also because they want to protect their original investment. They know that reforms that do not scale up—reforms that stay bound to only one or a few contexts—are, in the end, anomalies rather than reforms.

Risk-taking also plays another role in the scaling up of educational reform, a role often overlooked. Reform at any scale puts practitioners' ordinary beliefs and habits at risk. This is its fundamental dynamic. It aims to displace conventional beliefs and habits with new ones, but old beliefs and habits may be deeply ingrained, tacitly held, comfortable, even useful for reasons the reformers might not appreciate. They are, therefore, very difficult to displace. Working to displace ordinary practice, persuading many teachers in many places that they must risk change, and building the capacity for improved practice is what scaling *down* is all about

In a discussion of theory-based reform and problems of change, Stokes et al. (1997) argue that the word *scale* in the context of educational reform must be understood in two different but complementary senses. First is the *spread* across numbers of different contexts: states, districts, schools, classrooms. This is the sense of the word captured in the phrase "scaling up reform." Second is the *penetration* of actual practice in these contexts. Following Elmore (1996) and McDonald (1996), we use the phrase *scaling down* to indicate the process whereby a spreading reform challenges habitual practice in the new contexts and habitual practice yields to new ways of working.

At the heart of educational reform, we believe, is the challenge of encouraging practitioners, at all levels, to face the risk of undergoing real change. It is a challenge that does not go away when the reform is scaled up. Fullan (1999) puts it well in saying that large-scale reform involves "the development of local capacity thousands of times over" (p. 66). For this reason, scaling up reform involves preparation for risk-taking thousands of times over. Individual teachers, administrators, and community members must be willing to confront their own values and beliefs. Many must be persuaded to invest cognitively and emotionally in new values and beliefs. To persuade these individuals, reformers must be prepared to provide opportunities and support. They may also need to displace some of their own beliefs and habits. For example, they may be forced to recognize that reform is ultimately personal, rather than merely technical, and that its usual targets—namely teachers—must also be regarded as its ultimate agents. To explain this paradox, Stokes (2002) offers an apt analogy:

> A minister can't make a person have faith, and a therapist can't make a person develop self-knowledge; rather the person makes the leap of faith required for both, and that can actualize the change with the help of the right supports.

Without the right supports, people are unlikely to take risks; we may find enthusiasm for reform but are not likely to find much real change. Existing beliefs and habits of practice may be merely amended—glossed over—rather than being displaced. Consider, for example, Cohen's (1990) now classic encounter with Mrs. Oublier, the California teacher who claimed that statewide mathematics reforms had transformed her teaching. As Cohen watched her teach, however, he discerned only a patina of change—one more likely to confuse her students than to equip them with deeper mathematical understanding.

In its noun form, the French verb *oublier* (to forget) can mean an overlooked person or thing. It is not surprising that, in trying to scale up reform across an entire state, what may be overlooked is the depth of support and intensity of effort required to change the tacit beliefs and everyday habits of individual teachers, such as Mrs. Oublier. More generally, what may be overlooked in the rush to instill new beliefs and habits is the problem of unlearning the old ones. Unlearning is required, as Gardner (1991) points out, because an established conception is likely to trump a new conception unless deliberately challenged. Such deliberate challenge must be at the heart of reform, or the reform will fail.

In this chapter, we explore this perspective on the scaling up of reform by considering the work and organizational history of the National Writing Project (NWP). NWP developed over the course of 25 years, from one site in 1973–1974, the Bay Area Writing Project (BAWP) at the University of California, Berkeley, to a steadily growing network of 175 local sites in all 50 states, the District of Columbia, Puerto Rico, and the U.S. Virgin Islands. In this chapter, we consider scale in both its meanings: the development and spread of the network and its capacity to penetrate and challenge tacit beliefs and everyday habits in the teaching of writing.

The NWP Design

Scaling up occurs continually in all layers of the NWP organization. New sites are added each year through an application process that establishes local leadership and programming that follows the NWP model. Existing sites—each a local school-university partnership—continue to grow as new groups of experienced K–12 teachers join four- or five-week invitational institutes every summer at every site and as new opportunities for professional development are designed and launched in partnership with local schools and districts. NWP also designs and conducts national programs to engage sites in exploring salient issues and to amplify and extend their work across the network. The goal of these efforts is to ensure that, eventually, a local writing project site will be within reach of every teacher in the nation.

Meanwhile, scaling down also occurs across all layers of NWP. New teachers must come to terms with the rigorous practices at the heart of NWP involvement, and veteran NWP teachers must continue to integrate these practices into their professional lives: writing, sharing writing, opening up one's practice of teaching writing to peer review, and learning to become a teacher of teachers. Nationally, NWP works to strengthen and deepen the efforts of local sites by requiring them to raise at least half their own funding, open their own practices and theories of action to peer review, identify local needs and interests and build strategies to address them, and examine the influence of their work on teachers and students, modifying these efforts as needed to achieve success.

Indeed, scaling up *and* scaling down are at the heart of NWP's theory of action, as Lieberman and Wood (2003, pp. 100–101) suggest in their recent study of two writing project sites:

> On the face of it, the NWP strategy appears to be directed toward changing teachers one at a time, a strategy that would have limited impact on the teaching of writing and on the profession as a whole. This characterization masks a far more complex strategy, involving strategies of change and professional development both for individuals and for communities within a network context.

Teachers come to the invitational as individuals, but most go home as members of a community. They fulfill their responsibilities as community members by becoming [teacher consultants] and facilitating professional development for others in their profession, creating new ties and relationships. Rather than a strategy for changing teachers one by one, the NWP has launched a far more complex undertaking involving both individual and collective learning.

Mission and Principles

NWP's mission is to improve the teaching of writing and thus improve learning in the nation's schools. Underpinning the mission are big ideas—core principles that serve as the foundation of the NWP model. Among them are the following:

- Writing can and should be taught, not just assigned, at every level of schooling.
- Teachers of writing must write.
- Effective professional development programs provide frequent opportunities for teachers to examine research and practice together systematically.
- Teachers at every level—from kindergarten to college—are the agents of reform; universities and schools are ideal partners for investing together in that reform.
- Although there is no single right approach to teaching writing, some practices are more effective than others, and a research-informed community of practice is in the best position to design and develop a comprehensive writing program.

Getting to scale with these principles is the work of local writing project sites across the country, assisted by a national network deliberately designed with these principles in mind.

Writing Project Sites

NWP exists within and across multiple layers of authority and activity. At one layer are writing project sites housed on university campuses. These sites are designed to be robust professional and social communities that occupy an intermediary or "third space," neither wholly of the university nor wholly of the school districts (Eidman-Aadahl, 1996; Lieberman and Grolnick, 1996).

In addition to providing the core principles that govern site-level work, NWP also prescribes elements of each site's design—even as it leaves other elements to local invention. The prescribed elements include a four- or five-week invitational institute for approximately 25 teachers each summer. This institute has certain required features: participation across all grade levels; readings that involve research, theory, and practice in the teaching of writing; scheduled time for each teacher to present from his or her own practice of teaching writing; and time for each teacher to write several extended pieces during the five-week period. Another prescribed element of local site design is the establishment of a professional community of writers and teachers of writers, in which teachers network and learn from each other through a series of programs.

A third prescribed element is the provision of continuing professional-education programs for other teachers in the local area. These programs are collaboratively designed with schools and districts and are conducted wholly or in part by veteran NWP teachers, known as teacher-consultants. In 2001–02, local writing project sites, with an average of 70 experienced teacher-consultants each, conducted more than 3,000 in-service workshops for teachers, schools, and districts. Many of these workshops reflect the efforts of collaborating schools and districts to integrate the teaching of writing with comprehensive reforms of curriculum and classroom practice and to enhance the achievement of all students, with special emphasis on those most in need.

From One Site to Many Sites

In 1976, California state funding became available to support scaling up the first writing project site, BAWP, to a network of 13 additional sites. A key leadership decision at this time was to expand as a network of autonomous sites and to use what was learned by developing BAWP to support the establishment of these new sites. This early decision can be understood as the first attempt to scale up by scaling down to the creation of autonomous local sites able to adapt to local strengths and challenges and to build local capacity.

From 1977 through 1987, NWP leaders described the project as an expanding network. Both private foundation funding and support from the National Endowment for the Humanities provided "seed money" to support new sites across the country. During this decade, procedures for establishing and mentoring new sites were developed. These included requiring matching funds from local sites and providing support to new sites through visits by experienced NWP directors. By 1987, NWP had expanded to 166 local sites, functioning autonomously in a loosely connected national network.

After this rapid expansion, significant change occurred at every level of the NWP organization—demonstrating that getting to scale is hardly a linear process. The size and diversity of the network produced a range of new problems, issues, and knowledge that the network responded to through a variety of new strategies and structures. In 1991, NWP received federal funding to support its mission. This funding, in turn, provided the opportunity to address new issues of scale. The federal funding carried the same matching requirement as earlier funding for site development had but also occasioned the development of a rigorous annual peer-review process, described below. This annual review has come to be for site development what the summer institute is for teacher development: a crucial mechanism for scaling down.

In the review process, a group of 50 writing project directors and lead teacher-consultants read and review the proposals submitted for renewed funding. Reviewers attend in detail to the basic model of the summer invitational institute, school year in-service programs, continuity programs for teachers in the local service area, and development of teacher leadership at the site. All these components are deemed essential to ensuring the health of a writing project site. This annual process has strengthened the capacity of knowledgeable site directors and teacher-consultants to provide strategies and approaches for other sites in circumstances similar to their own and enforced a strong sense of lateral accountability in the network. The insights and support of this group of peers are important resources, helping the network as a whole solve the real dilemmas of implementing work at individual sites.

Site leaders facing challenges in implementing the model are supported through a program of technical assistance coordinated by the NWP national office and planned jointly by national and local leaders. If the site cannot make necessary changes after significant technical assistance has been provided, it loses its funding. On average, NWP closes three sites a year.

Indeed, the work of the past decade across the network—now 175 sites and growing—has been as much centered on scaling down as on scaling up. That is, it has focused on challenging and supporting new and existing sites so that they can respond locally to increasing demands for their expertise and can use that expertise to challenge and support teachers. The requirement for matching funds helps ensure that sites grow in proportion to their capacity to work in local schools and districts because schools and districts are often the source of these matching funds. The match requirement also builds a sense of local ownership and control even as it ensures the success of the local project in addressing local needs and interests. These requirements help ensure that those who encourage teachers to take risks are not too distant from the work, that they know well how much they are asking, and that they do so in a way that is locally sensitive and therefore potentially more effective.

An Improvement Infrastructure

NWP has been designed over time as if it had been following the 25/75 rule Fullan proposed for managing large-scale change efforts: "Twenty-five percent of the solution is having good directional ideas; seventy-five percent is figuring out how to get there in one local context after another" (Fullan, 2001, p. 268). In the case of NWP, local contexts cover an extraordinary range: Juneau, Alaska; The Bronx, New York; Starkville, Mississippi; and Stillwater, Oklahoma, are only a few of the hundreds of communities served by writing project sites. Much more than cultural diversity can be found in this sample mix, though accounting for the cultural diversity alone is critical. Diversity of policy environments, of system structures, of traditions in teacher preparation and continuing professional development, of curricular constraints, and of experience in school-university partnerships are all present.

Such variation makes achieving the 25/75 mix of good ideas and adaptation to local contexts that Fullan (2001) described a challenge. Can an overarching direction survive intact given this degree of geographic, political, and cultural diversity and, at the same time, avoid seeming distant and bureaucratic? How much adaptation is possible before the adaptation threatens the reform's theory of action and before the mission and its effects become impossible to discern?

In managing this dilemma, the NWP hallmark has been to attend to the knowledge of practice that practice itself generates—not just the practice of teachers but also of sites and of cross-site projects. All the components of the NWP network aim to build and support local, sustainable, professional communities focused on improvement in the teaching of writing. The strategy is to combine local and cross-network perspectives, to integrate direction-setting with continual adaptation, and thus to focus all the benefits of scale—resources, varied expertise and perspective, stability, and reputation—on improving teaching and learning locally. St. John (2002) calls the NWP network an "improvement infrastructure."

The following subsections describe the three key components of this improvement infrastructure, each of which involves implicit risk-taking.

Funding Match and Annual Reviews. As mentioned above, local writing project sites apply to NWP for federal funds to support the basic elements of the model—the invitational summer institute and local teacher networking. Sites must match these funds at a one-to-one rate by developing contracts with schools and districts to provide in-service professional development. One result of the matching requirement is that sites must interpret the core principles and tailor the model to serve local interests. This requires designs and efforts that are locally responsive and therefore locally valued.

All sites are held accountable for the use of funds they receive by means of a rigorous annual review that other site directors as well as national staff conduct. The review combines examination of site activities using NWP's principles as its basis, mentoring of directors by highly regarded peers, and strategic financial planning. The review does not focus only on problem-finding, although the process may reveal serious problems. It also focuses on collaboratively solving whatever problems are found—big or small—and on tapping the resources of the network as a whole to do so.

Specialized Cross-Site Networks. Another component of the overall NWP design is specialized cross-site networks that focus on particular dimensions of practice and thereby generate new directions as needed. For example, an Urban Sites Network and a Rural Sites Network are up and running, in addition to networks focused on the work of teaching writing to English language learners and of supporting teacher inquiry communities. These networks were created in response to needs expressed by site directors and teacher-consultants who gather regularly in regional and national meetings of NWP.

The Rural Sites Network, for example, was first conceived during a breakout session of a 1992 meeting of site directors. Ann Dobie, a rural site director, recalls the meeting in her contribution to NWP founder James Gray's memoir (2000, p. 121):

> [We] talked of serving large areas that make it hard to attract teachers to summer institutes, maintain continuity programs, and provide in-service workshops. [We] agreed that cultural differences sometimes make rural school authorities suspicious of university personnel and reluctant to change, and [we] recognized that [we] serve multicultural populations, including the poor, who live in situations different from those found in inner cities. We realized, with surprise bordering on shock, that we were talking about problems and strengths we had thought were ours alone.

The risk-taking implicit in encouraging the development of networks within networks is that they might prove divisive, that focus of direction might be compromised, and that traditions might be challenged. The benefit, however, is in protecting and supporting diversity and in learning from it, even as the scale of the overall organization grows.

Research. Another component of the overall NWP network design involves research—both internal, site-based, practitioner-directed research and external, national, and independent research. The risk in undertaking research of either kind is that it may show weaknesses, be they in theories of action, in fidelity of implementation, or in impact and effectiveness. The benefit is, of course, that such data either will point to new directions for change and improvement or will substantiate the effort, leading to continued support.

Tracking local effects, and using them as a check on wishful thinking, has been a tradition of the writing project since BAWP's first summer institute. In the early 1990s, internal research suggested there were underserved districts and schools within reach of writing project sites in many locations across the country. The Urban Sites Network was the first cross-site network to focus on this issue. This recognition broadened to include rural sites as well, and the desire to develop new approaches to address this service gap prompted the design of Project Outreach, now in its eighth year. Sites participating in Project Outreach work with local teacher-leaders in previously underserved districts and schools to develop strategies to meet the needs of teachers in these schools for professional development in the teaching of writing.

External and national studies also provide the network with important data and opportunities for reflection. For instance, a three-year study by the Academy for Educational Development (AED) (Fancsali and Silverstein, 2002) traced NWP's influence on student achievement in writing in 36 classrooms across five states. Its data sources included teacher-generated assignments and corresponding student writing samples, as well as student writing produced in response to timed writing prompts. First, the findings of this study indicate a high degree of alignment between the practices NWP advocates and the effects on teacher behavior and student performance. Compared to the classes of other teachers (i.e., not involved in the writing project) practicing in similar contexts and conditions, NWP teachers spent more instructional time on writing than did a comparable national sample of teachers and were more likely to use research-based practices that they had learned in their NWP experiences. Moreover, most of their students reached high levels of rhetorical effectiveness, organizational coherence, and control of conventions on timed assessments of persuasive writing, as well as on classroom assignments.

Specifically, the study included baseline and follow-up writing prompts administered to measure students' writing achievement and progress from fall to spring in the 1999–00, 2000–01, and 2001–02 school years. To allow for analysis of change over time and to control for measurement effects, such as the difficulty of the prompts, the researchers used a counterbalanced design in which students were asked to respond to one prompt in the fall (baseline) and one prompt in the spring (follow-up). Each version of the prompt was administered in both the fall and spring, with approximately half of the students responding to each prompt at each administration. Thus, all students wrote to both prompts. The writing prompts used in the study assessed similar writing skills because they asked students to write a persuasive letter to someone they knew. Their writing was scored on two separate aspects of writing: rhetorical effectiveness and writing conventions. The pattern of student improvement in writing remained consistent across all three years of the study.

In response to these timed writing prompts during the 2001–02 school year, for example, 82 percent of third-graders and 85 percent of fourth-graders reached adequate or strong achievement of effectiveness in persuasive writing by their second assessment. This represents an increase of 16 percent and 6 percent of the third- and fourth-graders, respectively. Overall, 60 percent of third-graders and 49 percent of fourth-graders demonstrated an improvement in rhetorical effectiveness from baseline to follow-up. The percentage of students reaching strong achievement more than doubled from baseline to follow-up, and the percentage scoring only limited achievement dropped by nearly one-third. By their second assessment, most third-graders (72 percent) and fourth-graders (78 percent) also demonstrated general or clear control of the writing conventions of usage, mechanics, and spelling, an increase of 17 percent and 6 percent of the third- and fourth-graders, respectively. Overall, 51 percent of third-graders and 45 percent of fourth-graders demonstrated an improvement in use of conventions from baseline to follow-up.

AED staff also surveyed and interviewed all NWP teachers in years one and two of the study about their participation in writing project staff development and its influence on them professionally. Teachers reported that the writing project caused them to change their teaching practices. NWP teachers were likely to spend much more time on writing instruction than most fourth-grade teachers across the country, and 75 percent of the teachers in the study reported that the writing project provided them with new information, including useful ideas based on research.

Teachers at each writing project site evaluate their local invitational institute experience every summer, providing another national measure of effectiveness. Follow-up studies aimed at assessing the influence of professional development on classroom practices include a large-scale survey of NWP teachers one year after completing the summer institute. Recent findings, based on reports of improved practice and perceived benefit for students, suggest that the impact is substantial. For example, at all grade levels, almost 90 percent of the teachers reported that their students better understand the qualities of good writing and the value of writing for both discovery and communication. Moreover, 80 percent of the participants reported that their students can better explain in writing what they are thinking and learning in the different subjects they (the teachers) teach, and 79 percent of the teachers said that their students have a better grasp of writing conventions and editing skills (St. John, 2002).

Lieberman and Wood (2003) looked in depth at two local writing project sites, one serving a major metropolitan area and one serving a broad geographic area encompassing rural, suburban, and urban districts. The researchers traced the influence of the invitational summer institute on a sample of teachers through observations of their practice. They concluded that the teachers had expanded their teaching repertoires as a result of their network experience and had become more adept at matching teaching strategies with individual student needs in these varied communities.

A Culture of Risk-Taking

To appreciate the *scale* of NWP's scaling up, it helps to have a picture of the state of teacher education in the early 1970s with respect to the teaching of writing. Keith Caldwell, a member of the first BAWP summer institute, recalls the terrain he faced as a teacher-consultant:

> I was moved to ask the first fifty groups I worked with in California and around the country one question: Which university or other institution of higher learning taught you how to teach writing? In no case, did any teacher—from Maine to Arizona or New York to Los Angeles—raise a hand. None, zero, zilch. Not one person could tell me where they had been taught to teach kids to write, to do the job they were hired to do and were doing. No department of education, anywhere, had taught them. We had an entire nation being taught by untrained teachers who had nowhere to go to get trained to teach writing. (quoted in Gray, 2000, p. 23.)

Others in the education community had also noticed and responded to the problem. Researchers Emig (1971) and Britton (1975) and teachers Moffett (1968) and Macrorie (1970) were devising a theoretical and practical framework for the teaching of writing. It would direct attention to the *process* of writing, as well as to its products, reconceptualizing writing as a mode of learning rather than merely a modality for reporting learning.

Indeed, this confluence of new research, professional experimentation, and a shift in public attitude in the 1970s created the same kinds of opportunity with respect to writing instruction that a similar confluence in the early 1990s created for school reform. The problem then was how to overcome contrary beliefs and habits among practitioners, how to encourage them to risk disruption to their practice by seeing the opportunity beyond the risk, and how to enlist the best among them in the creation and dissemination of new practices.

In his memoir of the early years of NWP's development, Gray (2000) recalls how casually the project's initiation rite—participation in the invitational summer institute—came to be founded on risk-taking. A former high school teacher turned Berkeley teacher educator, Gray began meeting regularly with Bill Brandt, a professor of rhetoric at the University of California, Berkeley, and Albert "Cap" Lavin, a high school English teacher, to plan BAWP. "What would this Bay Area Writing Project be and do?" they asked themselves. Hitting first on the idea of a summer institute, they casually brainstormed what teachers would do in it. "We ought to have them write," Gray recalls one of his colleagues saying. This "offhand remark," as he terms it, became a defining feature of the five-week summer institute (Gray, 2000, p. 48).

Asking teachers of writing to dare to be writers themselves may seem an obvious design feature for a writing project. But it was then, as it is now, quite novel for discipline-based teacher education programs to design for actual practice of the discipline. Indeed, Gray's recollection suggests that it was not at first obvious to him and his early writing project colleagues that writing was a *necessary* feature of what they were planning—that one could not think deeply about the teaching of writing without engaging in writing.

The reason for this lag in perception may be that writing appears to be a simpler process than it actually is. Writing is most often encountered in its finished form—when we are reading it as edited and published. Even professional writers who stray from the work for a couple of days or a week may forget how tortuous and challenging a task it is to make words read smoothly, to combine them to build sense and argument. However, professional writers are accustomed to the paradox and soon settle back into the struggle. Those who may be accustomed to engaging only in casual workplace or personal writing may think whenever they take on the risk of more substantial writing that it is only they who struggle and that writing remains for others as simple as it looks in its finished form.

Since that first summer in the Bay Area in 1974, teachers have been writing at local writing project sites and sharing their writing with their kindergarten through university peers in their own institutes. Five years ago, NWP began a new online phase of this work with the launch of a summer "e-anthology," a forum in which teachers in summer institutes across the country post their writing and receive responses from colleagues. In summer 2002, 1,089 teachers at 70 local writing project sites participated in this electronic exchange.

Writing as an activity, rather than as a topic or product, also plays a role in all NWP meetings and workshops. This activity is essential because the challenges of writing are easy to underestimate and misapprehend absent fresh experience of them. One cannot teach writing in sensible ways, or teach others to do so, without understanding these challenges. Thus, asking NWP network members to risk putting pen to paper or fingers to keyboard again and again—as a ritual of membership—is also a strategy to ensure that the scale-up is genuine, and not, as in the case of Mrs. Oublier, something spurious.

Neither is the act of writing the sole risk writing project teachers must face in their summer institutes and throughout their participation in the network. The summer institute and other network gatherings ask them to share drafts of their writing in peer response groups where critical feedback is defined as helpful. They are also asked to share examples of their teaching practices with each other, again with the expectation of both critique and support, and on the basis of an overall understanding that the network is fundamentally an organization of teachers teaching teachers. The teachers also draw on outsiders' perspectives on the teaching of writing; this practice involves yet another risk—opening one's practice to the insights of outside experts by reading and discussing texts.

In facing the first two risks, writing and sharing, teachers experience the relief and exhilaration that come from discovering that they too are writers and that writing is difficult for everyone—though no harder for themselves. In the process, they become open to the equally risky step of sharing their teaching of writing and of opening themselves up to both collegial critique and collegial learning. Finally, in a context made safe by mutual support, mutual risk-taking, and an experience of mutual benefit, they face the fourth risk, which is to open their minds to views about teaching writing proposed by outside experts.

Lieberman and Wood (2003) suggest that what makes all four risks so risky, and so beneficial in terms of teacher growth, is that they turn what are in ordinary professional practice private acts—writing, teaching, learning—into public performances. These performances, in turn, create the mechanism for challenging and extending the learning of other practitioners. Thus, they challenge ordinary practice even as they provide a context for new practice.

Organizational Risk-Taking

As suggested above in identifying the implicit risks attached to components of the NWP network design, risk-taking in NWP goes well beyond the four risks introduced to teachers at their first summer institute. It plays a role in the theories, strategic designs, and practices of the organization at all levels.

Looking at two additional central features of NWP will help to explore this idea further: First, it is a network, and, second, the network is composed of school-university partnerships. Both features carry great risk organizationally, as many reform-minded organizations have discovered. Why, then, has NWP constructed itself in this way?

With regard to networking, the answer is quite simple. The reason BAWP attracted funding and other support to scale up in the first place was because of networking—elemental, word-of-mouth networking. Gray (2000, pp. 112–113) quotes from a report Paul B. Diederich of the Educational Testing Service wrote following a visit to BAWP in one of its early years:

> I could not estimate how many meetings, workshops, and cooperative projects of English teachers I have participated in over the past forty years, but I know that the usual attitude is one of polite skepticism interspersed with strong opposition. I seldom get the idea that these teachers are going to do something about the ideas expressed in these meetings. But here in the Bay Area you have a large group of intelligent and well-informed teachers whose attitude toward BAWP methods of training and rejuvenating teachers are wildly enthusiastic. They are not only applying the ideas they have picked up in their own teaching but are also eager to spread the word. . . . I have been getting bits and pieces of information about the Bay Area project ever since it started, even though no article has been published about it that gave the whole picture of what it is about. The basic ideas

about the project that reached me by word of mouth seemed so practical and attractive that I have long wanted to get a close look.

Diederich sensed that a possible movement was under way, and Gray and his colleagues sensed that what a movement needs to keep moving and growing is a network. An organizationally tighter entity might threaten the momentum; something looser might dissipate the energy. In the introduction to *The Tipping Point* (2000, p. 5), Gladwell asks, "How does a thirty-dollar pair of shoes go from a handful of downtown Manhattan hipsters and designers to every mall in America in the space of two years?" Of course, the reform of writing instruction is different from the resurgence of Hush Puppies—for all kinds of reasons, including the complexity of the task and the importance of the outcome. Still, one should not underestimate the potential for educational reform of unofficial connectors and implementers and the contagion of ideas that work.

Of course, Gray and his colleagues might have taken a different and less-risky direction. Instead of becoming a network in its own right, NWP might have become merely a BAWP outreach program, providing help to other organizations in other places seeking to start their own writing programs, each in its own image. Early on, BAWP did do some consulting of this kind (Gray, 2000). Alternatively, at the other end of an organizational continuum, NWP might have become a strict franchise operation, making no allowances for local contexts and conditions.

Either of these designs would have been less risky because each would have dealt more definitively than a network can with the dilemma of fidelity and adaptation. The first would have dealt with the dilemma by denying the desirability of fidelity: "Let a thousand flowers bloom." The second would have dealt with it by denying the desirability of significant degrees of adaptation: the "McDonald's solution." By contrast, a network design strives for both fidelity and adaptation, then tries to manage the tension between them with principled conversation, collaborative decisionmaking, the development of a strong culture (in lieu of a tight structure), and a balanced effort to draw on both local and national expertise (Lieberman and Grolnick, 1996).

This is demanding work. What makes it even more demanding (and risky) in the case of NWP is that it is a network of school-university partnerships. Lieberman and Wood (2003) detail the challenges involved in maintaining school-university partnerships. Among them are the tendencies of universities to disparage practitioner-generated knowledge, to regard the teaching of writing anywhere—including the university—as low-status work, to consider even long-standing field-focused projects as marginal to the university's business, and to discount—in the form of tenure and promotion decisions—the work of building and maintaining such projects. Comparable challenges originate on the school side of the relationship. For example, many districts and schools seem incapable of investing in long-term instructional improvement or in long-term external relationships. A combination of "policy churn" (Hess, 1999) and unstable leadership preclude both.

Despite these challenges, NWP was founded as and remains a school-university partnership because the reform of writing instruction necessarily involves schools and universities. NWP draws on research, proceeds through teacher education, and aims to influence teaching practice and student learning across virtually all subjects from preschool to graduate school. It has had to face the risks involved in spanning educational boundaries. At the same time, it tries to turn these risks to advantage. That is, it encourages local sites to embrace their marginality, to define themselves as intermediary organizations—neither wholly of the university nor wholly of the school districts with which they work. Indeed, sites whose directors have regular faculty appointments usually have codirectors whose roots are in the K–12 system. As borderland organizations, writing project sites enjoy a certain amount of license as catalysts for change that would be impossible if their identity were less ambiguous (McDonald, McLaughlin, and Corcoran, 2000). They employ resources NWP has raised, in addition to those they raise themselves, and these resources give them clout. They are presumed free of the ordinary institutional interests and political pressures that might affect them were they entirely part of or dependent on either the university that gives them a home or the schools that give them work.

Like many other "irregular organizations," writing project sites cross boundaries to inspire vision; to focus change; to lend support for change efforts; and, at least implicitly, to apply pressure for change (McDonald, McLaughlin, and Corcoran, 2000).

Practices of Scaling Down

The approach to reform that we have explored above in the NWP experience addresses the problem of ensuring that, as a reform extends its reach, it also attends to depth. It presumes that depth requires individual practitioners to face real risks that challenge their beliefs and habits to bring important benefits to their students. How exactly does scaling down work? What are its practices? What must reformers learn to do if they wish to work in this way? We conclude this chapter with five principles that respond to these questions. Drawn from nearly 30 years of NWP experience, these principles contribute to what we hope will be an ongoing effort by researchers, reformers, and practitioners to explore further what we have begun to explore in this chapter.

Design for Teachers at the Center

Throughout his memoir about NWP, James Gray makes a point of portraying the writing project as an effort by teachers to educate themselves. It is a countercultural notion in education to think that the center of reform invention should be further down the organizational chart than reformers often place it. Yet research on high-performing organizations in other sectors of the economy has long suggested that the best ideas for change come from those closest to the problem (Applebaum et al., 2000).

The focus on teachers as agents of reform does not mean, however, that teachers should educate themselves without benefit of others' expertise. In NWP's version of scaling down, teachers filter others' expertise through their own experience, but the status of their own experience as a potential source of insight is equal to that of outside experts. This is why teachers in the summer institutes not only read research about the teaching of writing but also share with each other their own expertise in the teaching of writing. They do so within a learning context deliberately designed to value perspectives from both sources.

Beyond the summer institute, NWP's reliance on teacher-consultants as the principal agents of reform ensures that perspectives from classroom practice continue to inform professional development efforts. Lieberman and Wood (2003, p. 7) note that site directors and veteran teacher-consultants "remain consciously faithful to the highly participatory, teacher-centered design" that James Gray and the first cohort of 25 teachers in the Bay Area originally developed for their summer institute.

Associate Risk with Growth

As is true in other fields, scaling down in education presumes that significant change requires more than just direction and support. It also requires a significant shift in thinking and new insights on the part of the learner. To support practitioners in their efforts to take risks, and thus help their students gain the benefits, the NWP approach cultivates and designs for a "sense of mutual commitment" (Elmore, 1996) within a professional community of practice (McLaughlin and Talbert, 2001). Local sites design programs to improve the teaching of writing through a support system for local teachers and schools. Turning ordinary professional practices into public acts requires an ongoing improvement infrastructure focused on this goal. In NWP, all the risk-taking—from writing in the summer institute to managing the "third space" of a school-university partnership—is manifestly associated with the task at hand.

Pay Attention to Social Practices

In analyzing obstacles to urban school reform, Payne and Kaba (2001, p. 12) argue that reforms often fail for want of attention to social practices. They proceed as if it does not matter, for example, that a school's parents, teachers, and administrators all distrust each other; that racial tensions abound but go unaddressed; that a "happy talk" culture pervades relationships and insulates problems from notice and attention; or even, as the authors say, that the whole place is in a state of "collective depression."

Scaling down must involve dealing with whatever dynamics are evident in the places where the reform aims to take hold. For this reason, scaling up must design for such involvement. In planning to take reforms to scale, reformers must organize resources such that local implementers can draw on a larger pool of expertise in dealing with social problems. Their designs must encourage identifying, discussing, and addressing social challenges. Their theories of reform must be sensitive to the influence of social customs on efforts to implement reform, particularly those associated with region, race, ethnicity, gender, and social class.

In NWP, specialized cross-site networks and national programs have played a crucial role in developing the capacity of the organization to understand and respond to social practices affecting its work.

Expect Perturbations

In work with complex systems, whether they are information systems or reform organizations, people often forget that it is in the nature of such systems to break down regularly—to become "perturbed."

In NWP, the expectation of perturbations starts in the summer institute's writing activities, where teachers of writing come to terms with the fact that writing is inescapably messy. They learn that writers not only expect perturbations, they know that perturbations alert them to crucial issues of meaning and organization. To a writer, something not working is not a sign of disaster but of opportunity. Teachers of writing, therefore, must design learning environments that respect writing's natural way of signaling opportunity. Much the same can be said of reformers—they must design reform environments that stay alert to novel challenges and transform them into learning opportunities.

The measure of success in scaling up should not be "smooth running." A better measure involves the degree to which reformers can identify perturbations without defensiveness. Such a measure would reveal the resourcefulness of reformers in building an improvement infrastructure, as St. John (2002) suggests.

Design for Lateral Accountability

We are accustomed to thinking of accountability exclusively in top-down terms, but the actual demands of many current reforms, including those NWP advocates, cannot be mandated, inspected, or enforced in the usual ways. That is because, as argued throughout this chapter, practitioners' beliefs and habits are involved. Meeting the demands of reform requires a system and culture of accountability that also runs laterally because peers are in the best position to know which beliefs and habits are in place, which need to be challenged, and which need to be reinforced as a foundation for change.

McDonald et al. (2003) describe a different kind of workplace for educators:

> This is one where the power to assess outcomes and to take action to improve them is distributed throughout the organization, and where the people who do the work are able, willing, and even eager—in consultation with their colleagues—to make changes as needed in order to make the work more effective.

Getting there, these authors claim, requires investing in the development of distributed facilitative leadership (Schwarz, 1994). This is the capacity at all levels of an educational organization to help colleagues inquire into the effects of their own work, to lead discussions about what they find, and to organize efforts to take action as needed to change these effects.

At both micro and macro levels, NWP was designed with distributed leadership in mind. Exemplifying this at one level is the lateral accountability of the summer institute and of site networking, where teachers share and critique each other's writing and teaching practices. Exemplifying it at another level are the annual site reviews, in which directors of sites examine and critique each other's work in light of common principles and aspirations, and the national programs during which local leaders pose and solve problems together.

Each of these mechanisms requires pursuing and managing risk, scaling up and scaling down.

Conclusions

Practitioners take risks and persevere with them because they are powerfully motivated to do what they know to be best for their students. The writing project model is consciously designed with this in mind. At this writing, we may be entering a new era in understanding the importance of writing and the teaching of writing. With the introduction of writing on the two national college admissions exams—the ACT Assessment in 2004 and the Scholastic Aptitude Test in 2005—the stakes involved in learning to write well will increase significantly. Opportunities to take the teaching of writing to scale also bring new risks, of course. Scaling up the teaching of writing in America's schools and classrooms requires steady work across all levels of schooling. It will require the efforts of everyone in the educational system—administrators, teachers, parents, students—an effort that is well worth the risk.

References

Applebaum, E., T. Bailey, P. Berg, and A. L. Kalleberg, *Manufacturing Advantage: Why High-Performance Work Systems Pay Off*, Ithaca, N.Y.: ILR Press, 2000.

Britton, J. N., *The Development of Writing Abilities*, London: Macmillan, 1975.

Cohen, D. K., "Revolution in One Classroom: The Case of Mrs. Oublier," *Educational Evaluation and Policy Analysis*, Vol. 12, No. 3, 1990, pp. 311–330.

Elmore, R., "Getting to Scale with Good Educational Practice," *Harvard Educational Review*, Vol. 66, No. 1, 1996, pp. 1–26.

Eidman-Aadahl, E., "My Third Spaces: From Sharkey's to the Urban Sites Network," in National Writing Project Urban Sites Network, *Cityscapes:*

Eight Views from the Urban Classroom, Berkeley, Calif.: National Writing Project, 1996.

Emig, J. A., *The Composing Processes of Twelfth Graders*, Urbana, Ill.: National Council of Teachers of English, 1971.

Fancsali, C., and S. Silverstein, *National Writing Project Final Evaluation Report*, New York: Academy for Educational Development, 2002.

Fullan, M., *Change Forces: The Sequel*, Philadelphia: Falmer Press, 1999.

_____, *The New Meaning of Educational Change*, New York: Teachers College Press, 2001.

Gardner, H., *The Unschooled Mind: How Children Think and How Schools Should Teach*, New York: Basic Books, 1991.

Gladwell, M., *The Tipping Point: How Little Things Can Make a Big Difference*, Boston: Little, Brown, and Company, 2000.

Gray, J., *Teachers at the Center: A Memoir of the Early Years of the National Writing Project*, Berkeley, Calif.: National Writing Project, 2000.

Hess, F. M., *Spinning Wheels: The Politics of Urban School Reform*, Washington, D.C.: The Brookings Institution Press, 1999.

Lieberman, A., and D. Wood, *Inside the National Writing Project: Connecting Network Learning and Classroom Teaching*, New York: Teachers College Press, 2003.

Lieberman, A., and M. Grolnick, "Networks and Reform in American Education," *Teachers College Record*, Vol. 98, No. 1, 1996, pp. 7–45.

Macrorie, K., *Telling Writing*, New York: Hayden, 1970.

McDonald, J. P., *Redesigning School: Lessons for the Twenty-First Century*, San Francisco: Jossey Bass, 1996.

McDonald, J. P., N. Mohr, A. Dichter, and E. C. McDonald, *The Power of Protocols: Educator's Guide to Better Practice*, New York: Teachers College Press, 2003.

McDonald, J. P., M. W. McLaughlin, and T. Corcoran, "Agents of Reform: The Role and Function of Intermediary Organizations," paper presented at the Annual Meeting of the American Educational Research Association, New Orleans, 2000.

McLaughlin, M. W., and J. Talbert, *Professional Communities and the Work of High School Teaching*, Chicago: University of Chicago Press, 2001.

Moffett, J., *Teaching the Universe of Discourse*, Boston: Houghton Mifflin, 1968.

Payne, C. M., and M. Kaba, "So Much Reform, so Little Change: Building-Level Obstacles to Urban School Reform," unpublished manuscript, 2001.

St. John, M., "The Improvement Infrastructure: The Missing Link, or Why We Are Always Worried About 'Sustainability,'" paper presented at TERC Conference on Sustainability, 2002.

Schwarz, R. M., *The Skilled Facilitator*, San Francisco: Jossey Bass, 1994.

Stokes, L. M., N. E. Sato, M. W. McLaughlin, and J. E. Talbert, "Theory-Based Reform and Problems of Change: Contexts that Matter for Teachers' Learning and Community," final report to the Mellon Foundation, R97-7, August 31, 1997.

Stokes, L. M., personal communication, December 3, 2002.

CHAPTER FOUR

Impediments to Scaling Up Effective Comprehensive School Reform Models

Siegfried E. Engelmann and Kurt E. Engelmann

Siegfried and Kurt Engelmann describe organizational obstacles that often arise in efforts to scale up educational reforms, as well as the advantages and disadvantages of models for diffusing innovations throughout a school system. They also offer an important distinction between minimal- and extensive-requirements models of school reform, observing that models that specify numerous requirements are likely to be more difficult to implement but are also more likely to be effective in improving student performance. They challenge school districts to treat reform efforts as information-gathering enterprises, honoring the specifications of extensive-requirements models of change as a means of obtaining an accurate view of the effectiveness of such reforms.

Scaling up involves growth, and any growing organization encounters various impediments as a function of its growth. More people must be recruited, trained, and deployed. Procedures for internal and external communication must be modified. The expanded activities must be funded, which means that the organization must secure additional financial resources. Changes in basic political interactions, public relations, and the organization's goals or structures may also function as impediments to growth.

This chapter does not address these issues—they are growing pains of any organization. Rather, the chapter focuses on impediments unique to organizations that provide services to schools and school districts that have a serious need for models of how to reverse school failure. This chapter focuses on three central issues of scaling up comprehensive reform "designs" or models:

- the relationship between the characteristics of a design and the ease of scaling up the design
- patterns of scaling up and their relative efficiency and economy, with an emphasis on the model-cluster pattern of scaling up
- obstacles inherent in many school districts, especially large urban districts, that hinder the dissemination and implementation of effective models of school reform.

Our identification of these issues grows out of our experience in implementing the Direct Instruction (DI) model of comprehensive school reform.

DI is based on the assumption that controlling the characteristics of instruction and relevant variables in the school setting can greatly accelerate academic achievement. This acceleration is needed most in failed schools, in which high numbers of students perform in the first quartile. DI assumes that even very low-performing children are capable of learning if the instruction is appropriate. The model further assumes that unsatisfactory performance is a direct effect of inadequate teaching.

Compared to traditional programs, the DI model is designed to teach more in the same amount of time. All instructional materials for reading, language, math, spelling, and cultural literacy are specified as required components of the model. These programs, which are commercially available through SRA/McGraw-Hill, are designed to accelerate the performance of children through efficiency, economy, and clarity of presentation. Exercises are scripted so that teachers use effective wording and can present tasks at a relatively high rate. Each program is designed to introduce only a small amount of new material each lesson (about 10 percent of the lesson) with the rest of the lesson continuing the teaching introduced in the previous two lessons and reviewing or applying all the material that children are assumed to have mastered. Each lesson has six to ten ongoing topics that are combined to create increasingly complex applications. The criterion for presenting the material successfully is that, at the end of each lesson, all children are expected to have mastered everything in the current lesson.

The model also requires practices that increase the likelihood that the curricular materials will be used effectively to accelerate student performance by requiring all teachers to participate in the program, providing extensive preservice and in-service training on specific skills and content, and specifying schedules for subjects that provide sufficient daily exposure to the topics being studied. Further, the model specifies grouping children homogeneously, collecting data on student performance, implementing schoolwide management and reinforcement procedures, and using a problem-identification and problem-solution approach.

The basic DI model has undergone extensive evaluation, and, in various meta-analyses, it has been found to be one of the few models for which there is ample evidence of effectiveness—for all populations and socioeconomic levels (Adams and Engelmann, 1996; Borman et al., 2002). In the Follow Through evaluation, the DI model was most successful in all subjects tested (reading, language, math, and spelling), in both basic and cognitive skills (Stebbins et al., 1977). DI also produced the most positive affective outcomes, with DI children having more positive self-images than the children in any other model (Engelmann et al., 1988; Stebbins et al., 1977). The effectiveness of DI has been verified through a variety of other studies addressing a broad range of skills.[1]

Assumptions About the Context and Nature of Scaling Up Comprehensive School Reform Models

The three central issues of scaling up rest on assumptions about models and designs of comprehensive school reform. First, scaling up assumes a model that consists of a stable set of specified or implied practices. As the model is used in an increasing number of schools, the core aspects of the model do not change. Peripheral aspects of the

---

[1] See, for example, Gersten and Keating (1987); Gersten, Keating, and Becker (1988); Carlson et al. (2002). Adams and Engelmann (1996) contains an extensive bibliography of studies on DI.

design may be modified or added to in response to feedback, but the core of the design remains stable.

Second, the logic of schoolwide reform is that schools have been identified as failed schools solely on the basis of student performance. The only possible evidence that a reform model is successful, therefore, is improved student performance. The teachers and administration of the school have not been successful in teaching academic skills—reading, language, math, science, writing. The model may approach this problem either directly or indirectly. Regardless of how circuitous or direct the model is, the test of the model's effectiveness must be referenced to student success. Observations in the classrooms in which the model has been implemented must disclose that the teachers are teaching age-appropriate academic skills and that the students are learning these skills. Certainly, improved standardized test scores imply that the interactions have changed, but nothing more indirect than standardized test scores would be relevant to whether the model is a model of relevant reform or simply of doing things a different way.

Third, not addressing the classroom as the locus of reform implies that at-risk students are incapable of improving unless something that has nothing to do with the classroom changes. This is a serious philosophical indictment of the students' presumed capabilities. Enlisting the parents, the business community, and other possible influences is certainly an option, so long as these activities are not simply ends in themselves but lead to observable improvements in student performance in the classroom. That teachers now collaborate and discuss instructional matters is interesting but irrelevant. If classroom interactions do not change in ways that make it obvious that students are learning more in less time, the model is not effectively addressing the problems that spawned the need for models.

Perhaps the most fundamental question is whether models that fail to produce evidence of consistent improvement of student performance *should* be scaled up. It would seem contradictory to scale up any model that does not meet the fundamental requirement of achieving schoolwide *reform* and instead simply produces changes in school-related activities or personnel.

Problems in Scaling Up as a Function of the Demands of the Model

The context and problems of scaling up a reform model are greatly influenced by the design of the model. Different designs have different implications for patterns of scaling up, degrees of resistance from the district, and types of training practices needed for successful implementation.

Each demand that requires the school to do something it is not already doing and that some staff members would not like to do serves as a basis for the school to reject the model. If a model has only one or two such requirements, there would be only one or two possible reasons for the school to reject the model, which means that the "palatability" of the model would be relatively high. In contrast, if a model has 30 such requirements, a school would be far more likely to reject the model.

We can illustrate this relationship with two extreme models for reforming at-risk schools. Let us say that one, called the minimal-requirements model, is based on the proposition that teachers know how to improve student performance and that empowering the teacher with more resources will enable them to improve student performance. The model gives each teacher and the principal in the school a fairly large sum of money. The teachers are required to answer a series of simple questions, attend three motivational sessions, "spend the money wisely," and fill out an end-of-year summary of how the money was spent and its effects on the school.

The other model, called the extensive-requirements model, addresses all details of how students, teachers, and principals in the failed school interact—what they do and how and when they do it. No detail of the school's delivery system for academic learning remains unchanged. Furthermore, under the extensive-requirements model, student progress is monitored extensively, and serious attempts are made to ensure that all school practices are congruent with the specifications of the model.

The minimal- and extensive-requirements models differ considerably on five critical variables that influence the potential for scaling up: training, time required for implementation, effective patterns of scaling up, compatibility with classroom practices, and compatibility with district practices.

The Minimal-Requirements Model

The minimal-requirements model has a much greater potential for scaling up for the following reasons.

Training. A very large segment of the available population could serve as "trainers" or facilitators to implement the model. Trainers would only have to demonstrate to school staff how to fill out an end-of-year summary form, how to contact the sponsor, and similar details.

Time Required for Implementation. The criteria for full implementation of the model at a school could be met within one year. If all the teachers accept the money, attend the sessions, and fill out the end-of-year report, the model is fully implemented by the end of the year. (The criterion of using the money wisely is general enough that the teachers could meet it by doing almost anything short of activities that are clearly illegal or immoral.)

Effective Patterns of Scaling Up. Various patterns of diffusing a minimal-requirements model would be possible because the performance of each implemented school would have little relationship to neighboring schools. Implementing the model in a particular pattern would not be important because various patterns would be equally effective. The geographic proximity of implemented schools would make very little difference. Training could occur remotely through phone, video, or the Internet. The model could be implemented in single schools in a large district as easily as in clusters.

Model Compatibility with Classroom Practices. A minimal-requirements model would be compatible with any instructional or management procedure the teachers currently use. Because the model does not demand any type of uniformity or teacher-student achievement, nothing would require teachers to change the way they teach, group students for instruction, or coordinate the practices and curricula from one classroom to the next. The teachers could either do things the way they always have or do them in a different way.

Compatibility of the Model with District Practices. A minimal-requirements model would be compatible with a full range of district standards, guidelines, and policies. The model would not affect any of the interactions between schools and the central administration. Whatever instructional requirements had been in place before the introduction of the model could remain in place. The model could readily accommodate any requirement of the district and the presiding teachers' union.

In summary, training time and requirements for the minimal-requirements model would be slight, both for trainers and teachers. The model could be fully implemented in a single school year and effectively diffused through various patterns, and the model has a very slight potential for creating conflict with teachers, principals, or districts.

The Extensive-Requirements Model

The extensive-requirements model is the antipode of the minimal-requirements model with respect to all issues relevant to scaling up.

Training. A very small segment of the available population could serve as "trainers" or facilitators for the model. A trainer would have to be familiar with the various provisions of the model. Because an extensive-requirements model covers a vast range of details and requires performance and monitoring with respect to each detail, the population of potential trainers is very small. Even teachers who have taught the required programs for years could not become trainers until they learned how to train and monitor others, which involves identifying various implementation problems and providing effective solutions.

Time Required for Implementation. Extensive-requirements models could not be fully implemented in less than two years and might require as much as five or six years, because teaching teachers to do just about everything in a new way requires extensive professional development. The implementation would occur in stages, so the teachers and principals would be required to implement only some aspects of the model this year and some the next, until full implementation is achieved. Such staging is both efficient and practical. The teachers will learn only so much during a school year. If they have to learn three new basic curricular sequences (one for reading, one for language, and one for math) and all the related behaviors, many teachers would become overwhelmed. Also, it would be difficult to find the in-service time necessary to bring them up to performance standards. (The greater the amount of school time devoted to in-service, the less time the teachers are working in the classroom, so the less the model is actually being implemented.)

Effective Patterns of Scaling Up. Savings in training time and gains in effectiveness are implied by particular diffusion patterns. For the extensive-requirements model, any possible savings are attractive because of the time and cost of implementation. Implementing the model in a geographical cluster of schools could permit efficient staging of the implementation. First, the model would be implemented in a few of the schools. Then one or more of these schools would serve as a training and dissemination center. Selected teachers from the centers would serve as training assistants or coaches in neighboring schools where the model is being implemented. Particularly great savings would be realized during the first two years of implementation at the neighboring schools.

In contrast to the minimal-requirements model, the sponsors of extensive-requirements models would prefer not to implement the model in isolation. When the model is implemented in single, isolated schools, the potential for efficient expansion is limited. Implementation of the model in the tenth geographically remote school would require as much time and effort as in the first. For rural schools and small districts, isolated implementations may be the only option. The greatest savings are possible in large urban districts.

Model Compatibility with Classroom Practices. An extensive-requirements model would probably be incompatible with a wide range of instructional and management procedures that teachers currently use. The model would specify exactly what teachers teach, exactly how they teach it, the daily schedule for teaching, the management practices they follow, the way they group students for instruction, and the records they keep about student performance.

This endeavor generates a litany of possible conflicts. Some teachers may prefer using their current instructional materials; some may prefer a different schedule for teaching various subjects; some may prefer a different method of interacting with the students, a different grouping format, or a different method of assessing the students; and some may have a different philosophy about the role of the teacher and how children learn best. A list of related problems would be generated by the new role of the principal.

Compatibility of the Model with District Practices. Although the extensive-requirements model may not be in serious conflict with the standards, guidelines, and practices of a smaller district, it would certainly conflict with those of a larger district. The larger district, which has the greatest need for reform and the greatest potential for savings with respect to patterns of implementation, typically has guidelines and standards in addition to those the state imposes. A simple rule for predicting conflict is that the more details the model addresses, the greater the potential for conflict. All details are controlled under the extensive-requirements model; therefore, the chances of the model being perfectly compatible with all district guidelines are effectively zero.

For instance, the district has its own provisions for professional development, which its guidelines articulate. At best, the content and practices of the district's professional development will not be greatly at odds with the content the model requires. However, the more time teachers spend in the course the district provides, the less time they have to learn the specific requirements of the extensive-requirements model. More probably, however, the district practices will conflict with many details of the model. Teachers engaged in such programs of professional development will, understandably, either become confused or assume that there are options when, according to the model, there are none. This is only one of a very large number of possible conflicts between model specifications and the specifications of the central administration—from the deployment of aides to the specific instructional sequences.

So, if the extensive-requirements model is to be fully implemented in a district, some sort of waiver from district guidelines is needed. Without such a waiver, the model will certainly fail because the principal and teachers will be placed in the position of following both the district guidelines and incompatible model guidelines. Therefore, without a waiver that the district and the schools both honor, uniform implementation of the model is impossible.

Effective Models

Models with extensive requirements can be divided into those guided by effectiveness and those guided by more-arbitrary criteria. The effective extensive-requirements models demand that all features of instruction that have been demonstrated to make a difference in the performance of students be controlled to produce a positive effect on performance. The model would therefore control the design of the curricular materials, the sequence of topics and lessons, how the material is delivered to the students, the type of student responses that occur during instruction, the reinforcement and correction practices teachers use, the grouping of students for instruction, the daily schedule of instruction, schoolwide disciplinary practices, the records of student mastery in the various instructional sequences, the procedures for using data to identify and respond to problems of student performance, and how the school celebrates academic success. The role of the principal would change to support the basic changes in teacher-student interaction.

The model the National Institute for Direct Instruction (NIFDI) sponsors has been shown to be effective in accelerating the performance of all students. The model requires procedures that are not used in most failed schools, and all teachers in the school are required to use these procedures. The model designates instructional programs that are explicit, systematic, direct, and precise. Coordinated schedules are established for the teaching of all subjects. Training focuses on how to use these programs—the presentation behavior and corrections that teachers are to exhibit in the classroom. NIFDI requires homogeneous grouping of students for instruction and regrouping students as many as four times a year to ensure that students are placed appropriately in the program sequence.

The model establishes precise expectations in the form of projections of lessons completed at mastery for every group of students in each subject area. Progress is monitored through direct observations, performance on in-program tests, records of the number of lessons each group completes each week, and weekly conference calls when the NIFDI consultant is not on site. The calls are used to identify possible problems (based on data reports) and to review the effects of remedies applied to previously identified problems.

Implementation Versus Stability

A site may implement NIFDI in two years. Judgments about the quality of implementation are based primarily on classroom observations, which are used to answer a series of questions: Are the students placed properly in the instructional sequence? Is the teacher following the schedule and presenting material appropriately (wording, pacing, correction, praise, review)? Is the classroom set up appropriately? Has the teacher posted data regarding student performance? Are the data consistent with the projections for the various instructional groups and subjects?

The NIFDI model may be well *implemented* after two years, but it will not be *stabilized* until about the sixth year of implementation. The site is stabilized when all teachers are projected to teach about the same instructional sequence next year that they taught during the current year. It takes five or six years for this to occur in Grade 5 of a K–5 school.

During each of the preceding years, the material that is taught changes because the performance of continuing students entering every grade increases annually. During the first year, the fifth-grade teacher may have very few students placed in the fifth level of the reading program, many in the third level, and some in a corrective-reading sequence. In the second year of implementation, most of the incoming fifth-graders will be a year ahead of the previous year's students. There will be a larger number in the fourth and fifth levels of the program. By the sixth year, no continuing students (those who started the program in kindergarten) will be in corrective reading, and very few will be below the sixth level of the program. Many will be out of the sixth level and in the final step of the sequence—studying history from a seventh-grade text.

Misinterpreted Data as an Impediment

The misinterpretation of performance data can seriously impede scale-up of NIFDI or any other model that requires a substantial amount of time for implementing the model and stabilize a site. As mentioned above, fully stabilizing an effective site requires about six years in a K–5 school—the time it takes for the first students to pass through the program sequence from kindergarten through Grade 5. If the model is evaluated on the basis of the performance of fifth-graders after two years of implementation, the gains will not be impressive because the fifth-graders would have gone only through Grades 4 and 5 in the model, not kindergarten through Grade 5. The principal, teachers, or central administrators who observe the trends may conclude that the program works in the lower grades but not in the upper grades. They may choose to maintain the model in the primary grades but use other material and approaches for the upper grades. By modifying the sequence, they will likely still show some gains in student performance, but their approach would not produce the results that they would have produced by following the instructional sequence of the effective model. The only way the district can discover this relationship is to fully implement the model for five or six years.

The absolute number of sites implemented could be used to greatly distort data on site effectiveness. If a model developer is able to identify a dozen or more successful schools that use a particular model, the data may be compelling to a district, even if the model has a less-than-chance potential of achieving such gains. Let us say that three of five schools that use an extensive-requirements model are successful and that one of 40 schools that use the minimal-requirements model is successful. If the extensive-requirements model has been implemented in 30 sites, 18 would be successful. In contrast, if the minimal-requirements model has been implemented in

1,000 sites, 25 would be successful. If the ratio of successful sites to total sites is not considered, the minimal-requirements model would appear to be more successful than the extensive-requirements model. It would certainly be able to produce more data on effectiveness. However, its apparent effectiveness is simply an indirect function of its ease of implementation and potential for adoption.

Fidelity of Implementation and Potential for Scaling Up

Acceptance of a model that has the potential to be uniformly effective could be increased and its potential for rapid scaling up could be improved by lowering its standards in several different ways. For instance, more negotiation about the curricula and procedures could be allowed. Partial implementations that involve only some of the components of the model could be permitted, or it could use trainers who are not fully trained.

Although any of these approaches would make implementation easier, the data they generate would not provide realistic information to decisionmakers about how to turn failed schools around. These approaches are problematic in at least three ways. First, schools in which the model is poorly implemented do not provide great benefits to the children and teachers. The implemented model would create some improvement (with great variability from one site to the next). However, the typical school would not serve all students and could not, therefore, provide a model for effective practices. Second, schools in which the model is poorly implemented do not present any compelling reason for a school to follow the tenets of the model. If the gains are modest, they could be achieved by a number of models. Third, these schools do not provide the district with data about what can be done. The rational district would have no inducement to make the changes in district policy necessary to follow the model closely unless it was evident that great gains are achieved only by schools that follow the model closely and that adhering to the model is manageable.

Patterns of Scaling Up and Their Relative Efficiency

As discussed above, the most efficient method of scaling up an extensive-requirements model is through model clusters, which allow schools to maintain a high degree of fidelity to the model at lower overall costs.

Model Clusters

Implementing an extensive-requirements model in clusters of schools is an efficient means of both scaling up and accommodating the high mobility that plagues high-poverty schools (25 percent per year and higher). When the first flight of students in an isolated model school passes through the program sequence from K–5, fifth-graders in the school will be performing as many as three grade levels above students from neighboring schools. Special provisions are required to accommodate incoming students because their performance levels are so much lower than those of continuing students. If the design is implemented in a geographic cluster of schools, however, a considerable proportion of students new to any of the schools will be transfers from other schools implementing the model. Placing these students in the instructional sequence is therefore simple.

Another reason for adopting the model-cluster pattern of scaling up is related to the fact that the extensive-requirements model is constrained by the relatively large amount of time needed to train trainers. With the model-cluster pattern, sites in which the model is fully implemented serve as training and dissemination centers. Teachers and on-site coordinators from schools in which the model is to be implemented are assigned to the model school within the district. This practice simplifies training and also provides teachers from schools that are new to the model with demonstrations of how classrooms are organized and how the program functions. Providing instruction through training and dissemination centers requires only about a quarter the time required to implement the model in isolated schools.

To increase efficiency, the model would be implemented in new schools largely through local coaches with the assistance of the model developer. If the district does not permit a model school to function as a dissemination center, implementation of the model in other schools would proceed more slowly, simply because teachers and principals from these schools would not have people to model how the program was supposed to work. They would have to learn from negative examples instead of positive ones.

With advanced training of local coaches, the district could become virtually self-sufficient in training new teachers and implementing the model in new schools. The district would have to recruit a project director, who would assume management functions previously provided by the model sponsor, and institutionalize the positions of coach and project director. During this period, the sponsor's role would be reduced to overseeing the implementation effort and identifying problems of fidelity in implementation.

Difficulties in Establishing Fully Implemented Model Schools

The time required to establish fully implemented and stabilized schools can create problems. The reason is that the gains in student performance tend to show up first in the grades in which students are closer to the norm. On such measures as reading level, the farthest a student could be below the norm at the end of Grade 1 is about one year. The farthest a fifth-grader could be behind is five years. If the students have historically progressed at the rate of 0.6 year gain per school year, they will perform on average around the third-grade level by the time they complete Grade 5. Given that attaining growth of much more than one year for each year students are in an effective program is unlikely, the pattern of improvement will show up first in kindergarten and Grade 1, then Grade 2, then Grade 3, and so forth. At the end of the first year, students in kindergarten and Grade 1 may show substantial gains over previous performance. The next year, the pattern will change because the first-graders, who have gained one year's worth of skills, will start on the Grade 2 level of the program.

The domino effect continues, a grade at a time. However, observers often misinterpret the progress by assuming that the difficulty of stabilizing the various grades is equal. After the second year, they may observe that children in the beginning grades have improved greatly, but fourth- and fifth-graders are still behind even though they had been in the program for two years. Observers may conclude that the program does not work well with students in Grades 3 and above and may modify the program in a way that dilutes its effects. They may retain the instructional sequence for the primary grades and do something else in Grades 3–5. The remedy for this misconception about the data is to provide the site with information both about the anticipated trends and the reasons they will emerge.

A related impediment to implementing the model fully is what may be called "premature elucidation." Often, school staff members and administrators see students perform better than they had historically after implementing the model for one or two years. Administrators identify some of the features of the design and conclude that they understand how the gains were achieved. They may modify or eliminate aspects of the design they do not consider crucial for student success.

If student performance remains the same or increases, these administrators will feel justified in having modified the design. The increase in student performance may be attributed to the new regime, even though it is actually the result of the model's implementation with earlier cohorts of students. In any case, staff members and administrators do not receive information on how inappropriate the modifications are because they do not receive information on how well the students would have performed if the modification had not been introduced.

Special Challenges of Large School Districts

One of the most serious problems of implementing an effective model in the larger district is to carry out the implementation in such a way that the model is not viewed as a foreign body at odds with the district. The potential for such a perception originates in the conflict between procedures that are effective with students and procedures the district guidelines and standards mandate. If waivers are not provided and honored, the schools in which the model is implemented will be subject to the district guidelines. At least some guidelines will be inconsistent with the specific provisions of an effective model. For instance, a district's rules for behavior management may be reasonable but very general. The rules for behavior management that the teacher follows in an effective model may be very specific. Implementing the district guidelines or presenting general training to the teachers would then be a relative waste of time because the specific training the teacher receives covers everything the general presentation covers but references behavior management procedures to the specific details of the various instructional programs and activities of the model.

If the school follows the district guidelines for test preparation, professional development, and the scheduling of curricular events, the schools will not perform as well as they would have if they had followed the specific guidelines of an effective model. This assertion is based on the fact that the district guidelines have never been demonstrated to be highly effective, but the guidelines of the model have. If a school ignores the district guidelines and is highly successful, it will not be seen as a product of the design's procedures. Rather, it will be viewed as a joint product of the design and the district test-preparation program, professional development, and curricular requirements. Schools that follow this joint formula will tend to fail.

These problems are serious, both because they preempt the district from discovering the model's potential and because data from the school constrained by the district guidelines will show only what the model does when constrained by those guidelines. The district's position is, in the broadest sense, paradoxical. In the past, the district has failed. Even if it has adopted new guidelines, it has no basis for undaunted confidence that they will work. Various guidelines adopted in the past have never worked. Yet, the district often remains staunch in requiring models to follow the current guidelines. From the standpoint of simple probability, any model capable of achieving great improvements in teacher and student performance will tend to fail if its implementation is attenuated by the district requirements.

The most productive way for an effective model to work in a district, therefore, is for implementers to receive a waiver from the district guidelines. The waiver indicates that the design implementer will be responsible for teaching all the skills needed for the students to perform well on the achievement tests, including the state test. In the political world of school districts, such waivers are difficult to obtain because they seem to suggest that the model implementers have no respect for the district's guidelines. However, the district needs to learn at least one effective formula for achieving accelerated performance of at-risk students. The best way to obtain information about what results are achievable and what structures and support are needed to achieve them is to implement effective models fully, then to evaluate them.

Specific Problems with District Guidelines

District guidelines have three characteristics that may create problems in implementing effective school reform models: Some function as a curriculum, some support laxity, and some tend to require work on material that is of only peripheral importance to accelerating student performance.

Guidelines as Curriculum. Guidelines function as a curriculum when they specify a pedagogical process rather than learning outcomes that are reasonable for a particular grade and subject. A process is implied by every standard or guideline that requires schools to teach something before it would be taught in an effective program sequence. Such processes may override sensible instructional sequences. For instance, if the district (or state) guidelines call for teaching the fractions 1/2, 1/3, and 1/4 in kindergarten, the guidelines are not serving as standards but as a curriculum. The teachers are now required to follow this curriculum even though it does not represent a sensible way to introduce fractions or a sensible time to do so. The guidelines do not indicate an outcome that is important for going into Grade 1 or even Grade 2, yet they are very specific about what is to be taught. The guidelines fail to recognize not only that teaching fractions in kindergarten is unwise but also that this sequence of fractions will probably reinforce misconceptions about what fractions are and how they are related to the counting numbers.

There are many other examples of guidelines that function as curricula. For instance, if the guidelines require students to work on a particular type of word problem in fourth-grade math, even though it is doubtful that they have the math skills necessary to solve such problems, teachers must now somehow teach these skills. The idiom of "writing as a process" is reasonable in some ways, but the steps the district may require are certainly not the only set of steps that will lead to good writing. Furthermore, not all the writing the students do should be of the form that involves note-taking, first draft, revision, and publishing. Successful programs that emphasize students' writing more and writing in a way that yields better first-draft material should not be forced into the Procrustean "writing process" mold.

Lax Standards. The second type of failure is created by guidelines that are too lax in that they do not require performance on a skill until long after it would have been taught in a reasonable instructional sequence. The curricular sequence is affected far less by lax specifications than by guidelines that act as a curriculum, but the credibility of the sequence is still challenged. Lax standards provide justification to teachers for not following the specifications of a validated sequence. For instance, districts may adopt the guideline, "Read by Grade 3." NIFDI has consistently demonstrated that if a reading sequence is properly implemented in kindergarten, virtually all at-risk students with the exception of the profoundly retarded and the very frequently absent will read by the end of the year. No program that purports to be a model of reform should have a standard less demanding than "Read by Grade 1."

Guidelines That Stress Peripheral Skills. Guidelines that stress peripheral skills create two problems. First, because they do not test key skills, they suggest that these skills are not important. Second, they test skills of questionable value, thereby implying that these skills are important. For instance, math tests—both standardized achievement tests and district- or state-created tests—tend not to test math skills that are absolute prerequisites for higher math and, instead, tend to test trivial skills and applications.

For example, one of the skills essential for higher math is facility at writing and rewriting equations. This skill is not included in many tests. Instead, tests typically present problem types that students have not learned how to express as equations. Much of what is tested is inconsequential from the standpoint of mathematics. Blueprints, graphs, and virtually anything that has numbers are treated as legitimate math items. Certainly, students should learn this material, but most of it is not really legitimate math content and should not replace legitimate math content.

The main problem with guidelines that stress peripheral skills is that teachers become reluctant to follow an effective program because much of what is taught in the program is not tested. Understandably, the teachers are likely to see the program, not the guidelines, as problematic.

Educating the District
One of the great difficulties in implementing an effective reform design is to educate district-level administrators on specific details of the model. Often, there is no clear channel of authority within the larger district, which means that it is difficult to identify the administrators who should become informed about the model. Attempts to communicate with the school board prove abortive in larger districts because the board does not have provisions for directing the administration in curricular or instructional matters. There is no decision-maker within the district who has clear responsibility for the school in which the model is being implemented. It may be that the superintendent in charge of elementary education has more power than the superintendent in charge of reading instruction, the regional superintendent, or the head of the office of accountability. In practice, however, the responsibilities are not clearly delineated. The school may be bombarded by input from all of these administrators, plus, possibly, the head of English as a Second Language instruction, the Title 1 coordinator, the school's probation officer, the state's probation officer, and the director of special education.

There is little likelihood that model implementers can communicate effectively with the sources of all these inputs and inform those who provide directives to the school about how the program is designed and why they should subordinate their guidelines to those of the model. Even if the district agrees to a waiver, however, it is often not honored, largely because it is not part of the district's organizational structure or patterns of interaction with schools. The result is continual input from the district that conflicts with the requirements of the model.

For example, NIFDI dropped all its schools in one large urban district because there was no probability of fully implementing the model in them. NIFDI had an agreement that specified that the district would not introduce practices that conflicted with the model's requirements; however, the conflicts were legion. The district had adopted the policy (which is now thankfully rescinded) that students were to be instructed only in "grade level" material. If the children were in Grade 3, all instruction had to be provided with third-grade material, even though a large percentage of the students transferring into Grade 3 read on the first-grade level. In one school that had a fairly large population of non–English-speaking children, the ESL director prevented NIFDI from installing a sensible English language program in kindergarten and Grade 1 and insisted on using a program that basically taught Spanish. Neither the principal nor the teachers in any of the schools understood that they were to follow the requirements of the NIFDI program. They responded to the NIFDI implementation managers as sources of possible ideas, not as trainers. For them, the true orders came through the regional educational officer and other district administrators.

Although the results that were achieved in the schools NIFDI worked with were far better than the average of the at-risk schools in the district, the district was not learning anything significant about what could be achieved with a coordinated effort. NIFDI was providing a service for some of the students and teachers in that locale, but the model would have been far more productive in a place with the potential to support the implementation.

In another large district, NIFDI found itself at odds with the district about the kind of preparation needed for the state test (which is horrible and fortunately is being rescinded). NIFDI's position was that the students would be farther ahead if the teachers did not follow the district guidelines about providing extensive "test prep" instruction (daily, from October through March) but used the time to move students farther through the NIFDI curricular sequences. Because of this and other conflicts, the NIFDI model was implemented in varying degrees of fidelity in the schools—from one that basically followed none of the district guidelines about curricula or training to those that tried to follow all of them. The performance data in the fifth and sixth year of the implementation confirmed the correlation between following the model and improving student performance. The school that followed the NIFDI guidelines most faithfully was originally one of the very lowest performing schools in the district. The mean reading scores of the school's fifth-graders on the 1998 reading portion of the Comprehensive Test of Basic Skills (CTBS) was at the 14th percentile. Three years later, the mean Grade 5 reading score was at the 67th percentile, one of the highest scores in the district. The school also had a larger percentage of fifth-graders passing the state test than any of the other NIFDI sites—all of which started higher than this school.

The tragedy is that the district does not view this school as a model of what is possible. The district has made little attempt to learn from this implementation. Although it is a supreme exemplar of what is achievable and although the district has never seen a school achieve a turnaround of this magnitude, the school serves more as a political thorn than as an indicator of the result of implementing effective guidelines for accelerating at-risk students.

Nested Responsibilities

The problem of diverse and often inconsistent inputs to the school implies that the larger district needs an organizational overhaul if it is to support and scale up effective models in a way that does not seriously compromise their integrity. The organizational design would simply funnel all inputs to the school through one central administrator. This administrator could be in charge of perhaps six schools. The administrator's job would be to facilitate the implementation of the model by responding to problems of implementation in a timely manner and ensuring that all inputs are consistent with the model but not in violation of relevant board or union requirements. The administrator would have the arbitrament of reassigning teachers and aides, deploying and training full-time substitutes, providing time for preservice and in-service training, coordinating efforts of the various departments of accountability, elementary education, and so on, as well as overriding or adjusting any requirements from these departments that are inconsistent with the requirements of the model and the board's agreement with the model.

Timely Remedies

The slow pace of responses to problems is pandemic in larger districts. This delay is particularly devastating during the first two years of the implementation because the patterns established during these years tend to persist. One of the more predictable problems is the teacher who receives training but does not follow classroom assignments. In October, the problem may be identified and noted as one that, if not solved, will result in the children being far below the end-of-year performance level projected for them. According to our experiences in working with more than 20 large school districts, the problem typically will not be addressed during the current school year without a central administrator who has the power to effect some form of solution, and the chances of it being addressed at the beginning of the next school year are less than 50 percent.

These and similar problems are not easily solved on the school level, even if the principal tries to solve them in a timely way. For example, the principal's only practical solution to high absenteeism of teachers on Monday is to regroup students and do the best that can be done. The typical solution for the teacher who is not following assignments is to have the coordinator or another teacher teach her groups, creating a domino effect that reduces the capacity of the school and the coordinator to respond to other problems.

The central administrator could solve this problem in far more direct and effective ways. These remedies would be timely, which is particularly important for students who are already seriously behind their peers.

Consistent Inputs to Schools

All district inputs to the school would be screened by the central administrator. Those that are clearly inconsistent with the model would be vetoed; those of questionable compatibility would be discussed with the model sponsor. Any requirements of the model that seem to be unreasonable would be negotiated. The principal would have regularly scheduled meetings or conference calls with the central administrator and model sponsor to discuss implementation problems and progress.

The central administration that had provisions for implementing reform models with fidelity would have ongoing data about the relationship of the schools' compliance with the model and teacher-student performance. This information is essential for districts to make informed decisions about which models to support, what type of support is needed, and the benefits and relative cost of their full implementation.

Conclusions

An extensive-requirements model that has the potential to produce uniform acceleration of students is something of an island of "extropy" surrounded by entropic forces that compromise its implementation. If it is successful, it differs from what districts and schools do now. It is not global but is specific enough to ensure that teachers know exactly what they are expected to do and that what they do works with the students. The success of the model depends on a coordinated effort, which means that unless all teachers play their roles, the potential gains will not be realized. If even a third of the teachers in K–2 "do their own thing," for instance, the implementation will show only modest gains in student performance. The model achieves acceleration not through magic but through careful control of all the school-related variables that affect student performance. The use of time is maximized to make the school environment effective— not nervous, impatient, or hectic, just very effective.

Teachers who participate in this model must be trained, and often retrained, in how to present material and how to correct and interact with students. This training probably should have occurred while the teachers were in college, but, in most cases, it did not. So if it is to occur, the model must provide for it as part of the implementation process. In the same way that teachers must be trained, trainers must first be effective teachers and then receive training on how to work effectively with teachers.

In part, the impediments that an effective model encounters result because the model is different, because the model requires hard work, and because it has strict performance standards for teachers. The most serious problem, however, is the resistance of larger school districts to approaching the adoption of the model as an information-gathering enterprise. The district is failing, which provides strong evidence that it does not have either the structures or procedures necessary to be effective with at-risk students. A model that has the potential to accelerate the performance of all students will provide the district with the information it needs on at least one way to be effective. For the district to receive this information, however, the district must recognize the requirements of the model and honor them. Unless the district assumes that, under the model, school performance will be worse than it is currently, the district should have no trouble with the idea of waiving requirements that are inconsistent with the model and implementing it thoroughly enough to evaluate it. If the evaluation reveals that the gains are only slight or are not correlated with the degree to which the model was implemented in the schools, the district could scrap or modify the model. If the gains are unparalleled, however, the most compelling implication is that the district should make the changes necessary to expand the model.

Within any district that views a model developer not as a vendor but as a partner who has a system that works, the problems of increasing the scale of an intervention in a reasonable period without compromising the model are solvable. The predictable decay that occurs in well-implemented schools that are not closely monitored shows that no systematic solutions will occur until districts recognize what is involved in achieving uniform acceleration of students and therefore what must be done to institutionalize the practices so that the system has built-in monitoring and remedies for problems.

In the absence of these provisions, any model that has the potential to accelerate student performance, particularly in larger cities, will affect only the teachers and students in the schools where the model has been fully implemented. This effect will probably not continue much beyond the period the sponsor works with the schools. In the meantime, the district will continue to specify and implement new guidelines, standards, and rules that may produce modest gains over the current status but will not begin to show what could be achieved with a model that carefully controls the details relevant to teacher-student success.

Ultimately, the most serious impediment to scaling up effective models is the school district's structures and practices. Scaling up would be greatly simplified if districts were organized so they could implement effective models with fidelity. With a responsive district, the model could be implemented in school clusters, and effective training formats could be applied. Most important, effective practices could be identified and institutionalized so the district would gain the capability to train its teachers and closely monitor its schools to ensure that schools not only achieve high levels of student performance but also maintain them. Instead of issuing new standards and guidelines based, for example, on the alleged performance of students in New Zealand (whole language) or England (the open classroom), the district would have ongoing data about what works in its schools and would continue to implement demonstrably effective practices so long as the district is charged with the responsibility of educating at-risk students.

References

Adams, G., and S. Engelmann, *Research on Direct Instruction: 25 Years Beyond DISTAR*, Seattle, Wash.: Educational Achievement Systems, 1996.

Borman, G. D., G. M. Hewes, L. T. Overman, and S. Brown, *Comprehensive School Reform and Student Achievement: A Meta-Analysis*, Baltimore: Center for Research on the Education of Students Placed At Risk (CRESPAR), Technical Report 59, 2002. Online at http://www.csos.jhu.edu/CRESPAR/techReports/Report59.pdf (as of June 14, 2004).

Carlson, C. D., D. J. Francis, L. Latif, S. Priebe, and C. Ferguson, *RITE Program External Evaluation: Executive Summary 2001–2002*, Houston: The Texas Institute for Measurement, Evaluation, and Statistics, August 23, 2002. Online at http://www.hlsr.com/rite/ (as of June 14, 2004).

Engelmann, S., W. C. Becker, D. Carnine, and R. Gersten, "The Direct Instruction Follow-Through Model: Design and Outcomes," *Education and Treatment of Children*, Vol. 11, No. 4, 1988, pp. 303–317.

Gersten, R., and T. Keating, "Long-Term Benefits from Direct Instruction," *Educational Leadership*, Vol. 44, No. 6, 1987, pp. 28–31.

Gersten, R., T. Keating, and W. Becker, "The Continued Impact of the Direct Instruction Model: Longitudinal Studies of Follow-Through Students," *Education and Treatment of Children*, Vol. 11, No. 4, 1988, pp. 318–327.

Stebbins, L. B., R. G. St. Pierre, E. C. Proper, R. B. Anderson, and T. R. Cerva, *A Planned Variation Model: Vol. IV-A, Effects of Follow-Through Models*, Cambridge, Mass.: Abt Associates, 1977.

CHAPTER FIVE

Scaling Up Success For All: Lessons for Policy and Practice

Robert E. Slavin and Nancy A. Madden

As Success For All (SFA) increased the number of schools and districts served, it found ensuring high-quality implementation to be a major challenge. Thus, it shifted its reliance on part-time trainers to introduce and oversee the implementation of its program to full-time, regionally based trainers recruited from outstanding SFA schools, as such individuals can more effectively communicate SFA's goals and methods and can provide more-detailed, comprehensive support to teachers and schools. These staffing requirements are costly, however, and require substantial administrative oversight. Thus, this move and other efforts to expand and improve services prompted SFA to restructure itself, shifting from a program run by faculty and graduate students based in and supported by a university to a fee-for-service model with costs borne, in part, by the schools it serves. To maintain the integrity of such reform programs as SFA, while scaling up their involvement in the high-poverty, low-performing schools where they are most needed, the authors contend that national and state policymakers need to help existing and new reform networks build their training capacity and provide funds to schools to help them with start-up costs.[1]

Never in the history of American education has the potential for fundamental reform been so great. Certain developments have created unprecedented possibilities for change: the bipartisan embrace of ambitious national goals, the restructuring of Title 1 in the No Child Left Behind legislation, the availability of new comprehensive school

[1] This chapter was written under funding from the Institute of Education Sciences, U.S. Department of Education (R-117-D40005). However, any opinions expressed do not necessarily reflect the position or policy of Institute of Education Sciences, and no official endorsement should be inferred.

reform designs for school change, and the growing capacity of many school reform networks. Federal legislation that provides competitive funding to schools to adopt proven, comprehensive reform designs adds both resources and attention to the movement toward school-by-school, standards-based reform. No Child Left Behind, with its strong emphasis on scientifically based research and adoption of well-evaluated programs, adds further resources for school reform based on rigorous research.

However, it is by no means certain that the potential for reform will be realized. Changes will take place, but will these changes actually make a difference in the school success of large numbers of children? For this to happen, the nearly three million teachers in U.S. schools must learn and regularly apply very different and far more effective instructional methods than those they use now. School organization, assessment, grouping, and many other aspects of schooling must change. The systemic changes happening at many levels of government are creating a fast-rising demand for high-quality, sustained professional development, particularly the professional development needed for schools to adopt proven models of school change. Yet the national infrastructure for professional development of this kind is quite limited.

If reform is to produce results, major changes in the structure of professional development are needed. This chapter is intended to shed light on the question of how a national approach to professional development might enable professional development networks to bring proven school change models to scale by describing the lessons we have learned in disseminating Success For All (SFA), a comprehensive reform program designed primarily for high-poverty elementary schools. In the course of disseminating SFA, we have learned a great deal about the process of change, about factors that support and inhibit school-level reform, and about ways of enlisting others in support of our efforts. This chapter describes our experience with dissemination, the strategies we are pursuing, the relative success of various dissemination routes, and the implications of our experiences for public policies.

Success For All

SFA (Slavin and Madden, 2001) was designed to comprehensively restructure elementary schools serving many children who are at risk of failing in school. It emphasizes prevention; early intervention; use of innovative reading, writing, and language arts curricula (and in some schools, math, science, and social studies materials as well); and extensive professional development to help schools start children with success and then build on that foundation throughout the elementary grades.

SFA is a schoolwide program, for students in prekindergarten to sixth grade, that organizes resources to attempt to ensure that virtually every student will reach the third grade on time with adequate basic skills and will build on this basis throughout the elementary grades and that no student will be allowed to "fall between the cracks." Table 5.1 summarizes the main elements of the program.

Research comparing SFA to control schools in 11 districts has consistently shown that SFA has substantial positive effects on student reading achievement throughout the elementary grades (Slavin et al., 1994, 1996; Slavin and Madden, 2000a, 2001; Madden et al., 1993) as well as reducing special education placements and retentions and improving attendance (Slavin et al., 1992, 1996; Slavin and Madden, 2001). A long-term follow-up study found that eighth-graders who formerly attended SFA schools were both reading significantly better than former control students and were far less likely to have been retained or assigned to special education (Borman and Hewes, 2001).

Studies comparing gains on state accountability measures for SFA and other schools have also found that the SFA schools usually gain more than the state or city in which the schools are located. Large-scale evaluations in Texas (Hurley et al., 2001.) and California (Slavin et al., 2002) have found significantly greater gains for SFA than for other state schools, and comparisons in almost all states with ten or more SFA schools find similar patterns (these state-by-state evaluations are listed on the SFA Web site).

Table 5.1
Major Elements of Success for All

Element	Description
A schoolwide curriculum	During reading periods, students are regrouped across age lines so that each reading class contains students at the same reading level. Use of tutors as reading teachers during reading time reduces the size of most reading classes to about 20. The K–1 reading program emphasizes language and comprehension skills, phonics, sound blending, and use of shared stories that students read to one another in pairs. The shared stories combine teacher-read material with phonetically regular student material to teach decoding and comprehension in the context of meaningful, engaging stories. In Grades 2–6, students use novels or basal readers but not workbooks. This program emphasizes cooperative learning activities built around partner reading, identification of main story elements, story summarization, writing, and direct instruction in reading comprehension skills. At all levels, students are required to read books of their own choice for 20 minutes at home each evening. Classroom libraries of trade books are provided for this purpose. Beginning in the second year of implementation, cooperative learning programs in writing and language arts are introduced in Grades K–6.
Tutors	In Grades 1–3, specially trained certified teachers and paraprofessionals work one-to-one with any students who are failing to keep up with their classmates in reading. Tutorial instruction is closely coordinated with regular classroom instruction. It takes place 20 minutes daily during times other than reading periods.
Preschool and kindergarten	The preschool and kindergarten programs in SFA emphasize language development, readiness, and self-concept. Preschools and kindergartens use thematic units, a language development program, and a program called Story Telling and Retelling.
Eight-week assessments	Students in Grades 1–6 are assessed every eight weeks to determine whether they are making adequate progress in reading. This information is used to suggest alternative teaching strategies in the regular classroom, changes in reading group placement, provision of tutoring services, or other means of meeting students' needs.
Family support team	A family support team works in each school to help support parents in ensuring the success of their children, focusing on parent education, parent involvement, attendance, and student behavior. This team is composed of existing or additional staff, such as parent liaisons, social workers, counselors, and vice principals.
Facilitator	A program facilitator works with teachers to help them implement the reading program, manages the eight-week assessments, assists the family support team, makes sure that all staff are communicating with each other, and helps the staff as a whole make certain that every child is making adequate progress.

In all, more than 50 experimental-control comparisons, done by researchers all over the United States, have evaluated the achievement effects of SFA and Roots and Wings. Reviews of this research have concluded that SFA is among the most rigorously and successfully evaluated of all comprehensive reform models (Borman et al., 2003; Herman, 1999; Traub, 1999) and among the most rigorously and successfully evaluated innovative reading programs (Pearson and Stahl, 2002). These evaluations are of great importance in themselves, of course, but are also important for scale-up, as the findings make SFA eligible for funding in funding programs that demand scientifically based evidence of effectiveness.

We have also developed and evaluated programs in mathematics (MathWings) and in social studies and science (WorldLab). In general, schools implement SFA first and then add MathWings and/or WorldLab in subsequent years. Research also shows positive effects of MathWings (Madden, Slavin, and Simons, 2001) and WorldLab (Slavin and Madden, 2000b). Schools that use both reading and math (and/or WorldLab) are often called Roots & Wings schools.

SFA was introduced as a pilot program in one Baltimore elementary school in the 1987–1988 school year. In 1988–1989, it was expanded to a total of five schools in Baltimore and one in Philadelphia. Since then, the number of schools has grown substantially each year. By the 2002–2003 school year, SFA was used in about 1,500 schools in 600 districts in 48 states. The pace of dissemination has slowed from its extraordinary levels in the 1990s, but each year since 1996, more than 100 schools have adopted the SFA reading program. In the peak expansion year of 1999–2000, about 400 schools joined the program. Approximately 170 of these schools also use the MathWings program, and 20 use WorldLab.

Program Characteristics Affecting Dissemination

Several unique characteristics of SFA have an important bearing on the strategies we use in disseminating the program. First, while SFA is always adapted to the needs and resources of each school, there are definite elements common to all. A fully functional SFA school will always implement our kindergarten program and reading program in Grades 1–5 or 1–6, will have at least one tutor for first-graders, and will have a full-time facilitator and a family support team. Other elements, such as preschool and full-day kindergarten, are optional, and schools vary in the number of tutors, the staff time devoted to family support, and other features. Despite this variation, we believe the integrity of the program must be maintained if schools are to produce the results we have found so consistently in our research. The whole school must make a free and informed choice to adopt SFA. In most schools, we require a vote by secret ballot of at least 80 percent. If this is impossible, as in districtwide adoptions, we involve teachers in making the districtwide decision.

When schools or districts make this choice, they are choosing a particular model of reading instruction, a particular use of Title 1 and special education resources, a particular within-school support structure, and so on. Unlike many alternative schoolwide change models, SFA is not reinvented for each school staff. The rationale for this focus on consistency in key elements relates to the program's emphasis on research. We want to be sure that schools are implementing a form of the program that is true to the model that has been evaluated and found to be effective. Further, in the high-poverty schools with which we mainly work, we feel it is essential to have a program that is implemented and making a difference on a broad scale quickly, while the school staff is still willing to give the program a fair trial. A long co-development process risks losing the initial enthusiasm and readiness for change necessary for a staff to fully embrace a new schoolwide program.

SFA requires substantial change in many aspects of curriculum and instruction. It takes time for teachers to learn and perfect new forms of instruction and for facilitators, tutors, family support team members, and principals to learn new roles. Therefore, the program requires a great deal of professional development over an extended period. While the initial training period is only three days for classroom teachers, many follow-up visits from SFA trainers take place each year. Schools usually budget for 26 person-days of training in the first implementation year, 15 in the second, 12 in the third, and 5 to 8 in each subsequent year.

SFA requires that schools invest in tutors, a facilitator, materials, and extensive professional development. Because of the focus of the program and its cost, the program is primarily used in high-poverty schools with substantial Title 1 resources. As of 2002–03, the cost of the program for a school of 500 students averages $75,000 in the first year for materials and training, plus salaries for a facilitator, tutors, and other staff (usually reallocated from other functions). Most SFA schools never have received funds beyond their usual Title 1 allocations, so in one sense the program has no incremental costs, but many schools cannot afford a credible version of the model. While the cost of the program does restrict its use, it also has an important benefit: It increases the likelihood that the school and district will take it seriously and work to see that their investment pays off.

The comprehensiveness, complexity, and cost of SFA have important consequences for dissemination. First, they require the commitment to the program to be long-term, and we must be prepared to be engaged with schools for many years. Second, they require that we maintain a large, highly skilled staff of trainers to work with schools. While we do occasionally use principals, teachers, and facilitators from successful schools in our training programs, the program does not lend itself to an easy "trainer-of-trainers" strategy in which a small staff trains local trainers to work with schools.

Dissemination Staff

Until July 1998, the dissemination of SFA was primarily carried out by our staff at the Center for Research on the Education of Students Placed at Risk at Johns Hopkins University. Since that time, our dissemination has been moved to a separate not-for-profit organization, the Success For All Foundation (SFAF). In spring 2003, our training staff consisted of approximately 200 full-time trainers. Almost all of our trainers are teachers, and almost all have been building facilitators or teachers in SFA schools. The only trainers who are not former teachers are those who focus on family support. Their backgrounds are often in social work or counseling.

The trainers who work for SFAF are organized in 20 regions of the United States, each with an experienced trainer as a regional manager. They are supervised by four area directors. In addition, we have a small number of part-time trainers (some of whom formerly worked for us) in various parts of the country, and we will often ask an especially talented teacher or facilitator to help us with training and follow-up in his or her own area.

In addition to SFAF staff, there is a regional training program for SFA at the University of Memphis. This group, led by Steven Ross and Lana Smith, has conducted research on SFA in districts around the United States. The University of Memphis group has taken responsibility for implementing SFA in Tennessee, Arkansas, Mississippi, and Missouri.

Formerly, WestEd, a federally funded educational laboratory, maintained a regional training program for SFA in most of California, Arizona, Utah, and Nevada. However, problems with this arrangement led to its cancellation in April 1998. Most of the SFA trainers working for WestEd moved to the SFAF, which now serves schools in the former WestEd region. Similarly, a for-profit company in San Francisco, Education Partners (EP), formerly provided training in several Western states, but this arrangement was ended by arbitration in August 2000 (see below).

Dissemination Strategies

Schools first become aware of SFA in a variety of ways. Many articles have been written about the program in educational journals, and our staff has made many presentations at conferences. We have an awareness video and materials, including a book describing the program and its outcomes (Slavin and Madden, 2001). Educators may write for information, call members of our dissemination staff, or otherwise make contact with us. School or district staff may then invite our staff to make awareness presentations. These often take place as part of "effective methods fairs" in which large districts or states invite principals or school teams to learn about many promising models. We encourage schools to send delegations to visit other SFA schools in their region if at all possible. If the awareness presentation evokes interest within the school, school staff will send us a "Preliminary Data Form," which enables us to calculate a price for training and materials. We will negotiate a contract specifying what we, the school, and the district promise to do. The contract makes our intentions and requirements clear.

At some point, a presentation will be made to the whole staff of each interested school. Following opportunities to examine materials, visit other schools, and discuss among themselves, school staff members vote by secret ballot. As noted earlier, we require a positive vote of at least 80 percent of the professional staff. It is rare that we would go through the entire process and then have a vote of less than 80 percent; more often, votes are closer to 100 percent positive. Given the substantial effort to provide information about SFA, the outcome of the vote is rarely in question. Still, the exercise is essential in that it assures teachers that they had a free choice and that the program is supported by the great majority of their colleagues. There are, however, some exceptions to this procedure. In situations in which all teachers apply to work in a given school, there is no vote; instead, teachers are told about the program and understand that by accepting a position they are agreeing to implement SFA. Also, districts adopting SFA districtwide may use alternate means to ensure buy-in, described later on in this chapter.

As soon as a school has decided to adopt the program, planning for implementation begins. A member of the SFAF staff or one of our regional training sites is appointed to serve as the school's lead contact.

A facilitator is then chosen, usually an experienced and respected teacher from the school's own staff. The facilitator position may be new, but increasingly, high-poverty schools have a reading coach or comparable position, and this person becomes the SFA facilitator. The facilitator and the principal attend a week-long training session in one of a few central locations in different parts of the United States, held well in advance of training for the school staff. For example, we hold our main facilitator and principal "new sites" trainings in May, June, and July for schools planning their training for teachers in August. This interval gives the facilitators and principals time to work out issues of staffing, space, finances, ordering and storing materials, and so on. Facilitators may also visit other schools to see the program in action and to get a firsthand view of what facilitators are expected to do.

If a school is planning to begin SFA in September, training will generally take place over a three-day period in August. Additional training is provided later for tutors and for family support staff.

The initial training is typically done by the school's "point trainer," other staff from SFAF or regional training organizations, and (occasionally) adjunct trainers who are facilitators or teachers in existing SFA schools. After initial training, the same staff members will make follow-up visits. A first-year school will typically receive 12 person-days of follow-up—three two-day, two-person visits.

Our main objective during follow-up visits is to strengthen the skills of the building facilitators and principals. We cannot hope to monitor and refine implementations adequately from a distance. Instead, we must rely on the facilitator, as well as the principal and teachers. Our staff members jointly conduct an implementation review, which entails visiting classes; interviewing teachers, family support members, tutors, and others; and looking together at the data on student performance, pacing, attendance, and special education placements. Our trainers model ways of giving feedback to teachers, advise the building facilitators on solving their problems, share perspectives on strengths and weaknesses of the program, and identify goals for individual teachers and for general program implementation. The principal and building facilitator participate in developing these goals and agree to monitor progress toward achieving them. Trainers meet with teachers to provide additional training on such issues as writing, pacing, or classroom management. The trainers respond to questions and discuss issues needing further attention. Later, the trainers complete implementation forms on which they record the quality of implementation and write site reports summarizing what they have seen, noting promises made, issues to be followed up, and ratings of the quality of implementation of each program element.

In general, we are satisfied with our dissemination model. In the regular implementation checks that are part of our follow-up visits, we find more than 90 percent of teachers to be doing an adequate job of implementing the programs, and many teachers are doing inspired teaching, using our materials and methods as a jumping-off point for innovative and exciting instruction. The relative prescriptiveness of the model and the training and follow-up that support it are sometimes perceived to be problematic before implementation begins but are rarely a long-term problem, as teachers and other staff members come to see the flexibility within the program and to see the outcomes for children. In fact, for teachers accustomed to inadequate professional development without the material or human supports necessary to change their teaching on a day-to-day basis, the completeness of SFA, from materials to training to follow-up, is a major plus. The consistent positive findings in evaluations of SFA in its dissemination sites tell us that our model of dissemination is working.

However, while we are confident that the SFA program can be adapted to local circumstances and replicated nationally using the model of dissemination we have evolved, we face constant challenges in providing such an intensive level of service on a broad scale. America has more than 45,000 Title 1 elementary schools. We work in about 1,500 schools, or 3 percent. Our network of schools has been expanding by 100 to 400 schools each year, an enormous rate of growth. Accommodating this growth without compromising quality has required continual restructuring and will continue to do so for the foreseeable future. We still have a long way to go.

Obey-Porter Comprehensive School Reform Demonstration

In 1997, the U.S. Congress allocated $150 million for a new program designed to assist schools in adopting "proven, comprehensive" reform designs. This act is often referred to simply as Obey-Porter after representatives David Obey (D-Wis.) and John Porter (R-Ill.), two of its sponsors. These reform designs provide external assistance to schools to upgrade their curricula, parent involvement approaches, assessments, professional development approaches, and other features. SFA and Roots & Wings were named in the legislation among 17 examples of such comprehensive designs. Schools can apply for three-year grants of at least $50,000 per year to pay the start-up costs of adopting comprehensive designs. Funds were also allocated for labs and state departments of education to help in the awareness and review process (Slavin, 1998).

The Comprehensive School Reform Demonstration program, now simply called Comprehensive School Reform (CSR), has now increased to $310 million annually. CSR is having an important effect on scaling up of SFA. Obviously, it provides funding for schools that might not have been able to afford adequate implementations. More important, perhaps, it raises the profile of such programs as SFA at the policy level. State departments of education, laboratories, and districts are all engaged in disseminating information about comprehensive reform models, and these activities may affect their own involvement in and knowledge about whole-school reform.

Among 4,050 CSR grants made by fall 2002, about 478 grants (11.8 percent) have been made to schools to implement SFA and Roots & Wings. This is the largest number of grants to any program. However, the surprise in the CSR process is that grants are being made to support an enormous array of programs that are neither well-researched nor even comprehensive. Schools have adopted 739 different models. Collectively, the programs rated in the influential American Institutes for Research review (Herman, 1999) as having "strong evidence of positive effects on student achievement" (including SFA) have received only 17.3 percent of CSR grants. Adding programs rated as "promising," the total is still only 25.2 percent of CSR grants. Therefore, almost three-quarters of CSR grants are going to schools adopting programs with limited or no evidence of effectiveness.

Extending Our Reach

As SFA has become a national program, we have had to confront the problem of providing adequate training and follow-up in many widely dispersed locations with very different needs, resources, and circumstances. Early on, we began searching for ways to engage regionally based educators in training or support roles, to extend our training capacity, to reduce travel costs for schools, and to provide schools with trainers who are more familiar with the local scene. For a program as complex as SFA, with such extensive requirements for training and follow-up, it is not simple to train trainers to work in their own areas. As we disseminate SFA, we do not want to compromise the quality or integrity of the model we have developed and researched. It is difficult to train educators who have not been teachers or facilitators in SFA schools, and the need for lengthy follow-up makes it difficult for part-time trainers with other jobs to play a major role in training. With these concerns in mind, however, we have pursued a variety of strategies for building a local and regional capacity for training, follow-up, and support. The following sections discuss our experiences with each.

Regional Training Sites

As noted earlier, we have had three regional training sites for SFA managed by other organizations. Only one of these, at the University of Memphis, is still in operation. The stories of how these sites were established and how other attempts to create regional training sites in other organizations have failed provide an interesting perspective on the possibilities and difficulties of regional training strategies.

Universities. One obvious candidate for regional training sites is universities. This is the route that several other national school reform networks, such as Reading Recovery (Pinnell, DeFord, and Lyons, 1988) and Accelerated Schools (Levin, 1987), have taken. However, SFA does not lend itself as easily as do these other programs to dissemination from universities. Reading Recovery is a tutoring program for at-risk first-graders that provides its training as courses with graduate credit. It therefore fits easily into established structures.

Accelerated Schools emphasizes an organizational development consulting approach that is also familiar to university faculty members (see McCarthy, 1991). In contrast, working with whole schools over extended periods is an unusual activity for university faculty, who are typically too involved with courses, committees, and research to put much time into such activities. With the sole exception of the University of Memphis, no university has attempted to establish a regional training program for SFA.

The success of the University of Memphis regional training site depends on several relatively rare characteristics: the existence of a research center at the university, the unusual motivation and skill of the researchers, and their close relationships with our research center. However, it is important to note that the University of Memphis training site came into being through a traditional university activity, research, and not training per se. In fact, the emphasis of this center is still much more on research than on training. Other attempts to recruit universities to house regional training programs have not worked out.

Education Partners. EP, a for-profit company, was once the largest regional training program for SFA housed in an organization other than our own. Headquartered in San Francisco, EP served approximately 180 schools in the San Francisco Bay area, Oregon, Washington, Idaho, Colorado, and New Mexico. In 1996, EP's president approached us about taking on a training role. At the time, EP was very small and had been in operation for less than two years. EP proposed to carry out dissemination of SFA in a defined region under a stringent set of performance standards, to be monitored by us, that required the company to maintain a high quality of training and implementation at each school it served. It agreed to pay Johns Hopkins University (currently SFAF) a set fee on all revenues. We agreed to EP's proposal as an experiment, to see whether a for-profit organization could do a better job than we could as a not-for-profit entity. Later, when a contract with the Xerox Corporation to do our printing and distribution fell apart in fall 1998, EP bid for and won a contract to broker our printing and fulfillment services as well.

Because EP started out so small, it could design itself solely for the purpose of serving as a training program for SFA. With a few exceptions (such as a more aggressive marketing plan), EP operated much the same way as SFAF does. Although there was an initial plan to expand EP's training territory gradually, this expansion did not occur. Eventually, it became apparent that the company's status as a for-profit organization was incompatible with the goal of extending the reach of SFA. Unlike SFAF, which can invest any operating surpluses into further development and research, EP was obligated to disburse its operating surpluses to its investors. By 1999, it was clear that EP was adding little value to our training or printing efforts and was costing us far more than it would have cost to provide these services directly. SFAF invoked its performance standards under a compulsory arbitration provision of our contract with EP, and, in August 2000, the training contract was terminated. In November 2000, the printing agreement was ended by settlement. Clearly, our experience does not support the idea of subcontracting to for-profit organizations for training services or print brokering.

Educational Laboratories. The regional laboratories would appear to be ideal organizations to become regional training sites for SFA. They are responsible for helping districts in their regions learn about and implement effective programs. In fact, when they were first established in the 1960s, labs were meant to complement the work of national research centers, such as the one at Johns Hopkins, in which SFA was developed and researched. We attempted to engage labs in support of SFA dissemination. We spoke to lab directors and lab communication directors and had various communications with individual labs. However, WestEd, in California, was the only lab to establish a regional training program for SFA. This arrangement was initially successful, but it ultimately did not work out. Part of the problem was in maintaining consistency between Johns Hopkins University–SFAF and WestEd. In many cases, WestEd reinterpreted SFA policies, failed to implement various program elements, or otherwise insisted on its own approaches. These and other problems led to a schism within the WestEd SFA staff, with more than half resigning or threatening to resign during the 1997–98 school year. SFAF took back the region in April 1998.

While our experiences with WestEd and with labs in general do not support the idea of having labs establish their own training programs, labs can be helpful in an awareness and brokering role. In particular, the Obey-Porter Comprehensive School Reform Demonstration, described earlier, provided grants to each lab to help schools and districts in their regions learn about and adopt effective whole-school reform designs. Early on, labs helped states set up awareness activities, such as effective methods fairs, to help schools and districts apply for funding to implement proven designs, including SFA and Roots & Wings.

School Districts. School districts themselves are logical sources of training and follow-up for SFA and other reform models. Many school districts with several schools implementing SFA designate a district coordinator for the program. The district coordinator is intended to serve as a liaison between our staff, the schools, and the central administration. In some districts, this person is expected to learn the program and provide direct support to teachers, facilitators, and other staff, much as our staff does in follow-up visits to schools.

Our experience with district coordinators is that they can be very useful in their liaison function but are less consistently effective in training or follow-up with schools. The need for a liaison is great, especially in large districts. District coordinators help make sure that schools get the resources they need and that district policies are interpreted for the SFA schools. For example, if the district adopts a new reading curriculum, the liaison can help figure out whether SFA schools should simply be exempted from it or whether some attempt should be made to adapt the SFA curriculum to the new guidelines. The district coordinator can act as an advocate for the program within the central office and see that it remains on the district's broader agenda. He or she can provide a single point of contact for our program staff on all issues that go beyond individual schools, from arranging for ordering, duplication, and delivery of materials, to helping with assessments, to keeping our staff aware of changes in district policies.

As important as the liaison role is, our experiences with district coordinators have been mixed. In some districts, district coordinators already have many other responsibilities, and SFA is added to their list with nothing else being removed. Further, assigning a program to a relatively low-ranking central office official can be one way to ensure that a project remains at the periphery of the district's operations (even if it were no one's intention for this to take place). We have found that it is important to maintain close relationships with someone in the district who has line authority (such as the superintendent, assistant superintendent for instruction, or Title 1 director) and not to let the project be seen as "belonging" to a lower-level district coordinator.

Regionally Based Project Staff

As the SFA network has expanded and matured, another means of establishing regional training sites has become dominant. This is the establishment of regional training programs staffed by trainers who are full-time employees of SFAF but remain in their home areas. This arrangement solves several problems. First, we often find staff (usually facilitators) in SFA schools who are outstanding educators, excellent trainers, willing to leave the security of their school district jobs, and eager to travel and work with schools all over the country but not willing or able to move to Baltimore. In our early years, we required most new trainers to relocate to Baltimore but found that a requirement that such unusually able and exceptional people also must be willing to move to Baltimore put a severe constraint on our hiring qualified staff. Having regionally based full-time staff allows us to hire the very best experienced trainers regardless of where they happen to be located.

Second, hiring trainers to serve a region gives us far more control and assurance of fidelity to our program's goals than does engaging regional training sites in universities or other existing agencies, which may have their own agendas and constraints. Otherwise, regionally based SFAF trainers have the same advantages as institutionally based regional training sites. They reduce travel costs to local districts and increase the probability that our training staff will know about and can adapt to local circumstances and needs.

On the other hand, basing SFAF trainers regionally also has several drawbacks. One is that they are often isolated, working from their homes without the informal collegial supports that might be possible in a more centralized organization. Operating far from our center, these trainers cannot routinely attend meetings or keep up easily with the latest information or developments. To deal with this, we hold regular regional and national staff retreats, plus meetings around other functions, to keep everyone on the same wavelength. These meetings have major costs but are essential in a widely distributed organization. Monitoring the performance of regionally based trainers is also problematic. To improve management of the entire system of regional managers and regionally based trainers, we instituted (in 1999) four area offices staffed by experienced trainers who also have management and financial management expertise.

Despite the problems of coordination, we expect to see a continuing increase in regionally based SFAF trainers in the future. In fact, this is the only dissemination model we expect to expand in the coming years.

Networking

Building a national network of SFA schools is one of the most important things we are trying to do (Cooper, Slavin, and Madden, 1998). An isolated school on the frontier of innovation can sometimes hang on for a few years, but systemic and lasting change is far more likely when schools work together as part of a network in which school staff share a common vision and a common language, share ideas and technical assistance, and create an emotional connection and support system. This is the main reason we have an annual conference for experienced sites. At the annual conference, we provide valuable information on new developments and new ideas (most of which we have gotten directly from the schools we work with). We also try to build connections between the experienced schools, so they can share ideas on issues of common interest and build significant relationships with other schools pursuing similar objectives. We also try to create an esprit de corps and an understanding and acceptance of the struggle needed to achieve the goal of success for every child. We have "t-shirt days" and team-building activities that can be as important as the formal sessions. The breaks, when staff from different schools get to know each other and exchange information, may be even more important.

In addition to the national conferences, we try many other techniques for building an effective support network. Our newsletter, *Success Story*, is one example. Our training sessions and the manuals and materials we produce invariably use contributions from experienced SFA schools, making their expertise available to all schools. In particular, our family support and facilitator's manuals are primarily composed of ideas we have received from extraordinary SFA schools, and we revise these and other materials as we learn more from the schools. For example, school staff often modify various materials, forms, and assessments for their own use. We pay attention to these modifications, and if they seem broadly applicable, we use them to revise our materials. Further, through our conversations with participating schools, we learn about specific issues, such as bilingual education, year-round schedules, use of Title 1 funds in non-schoolwide circumstances, use of special education funds to support tutoring, and so on. We can then create connections between schools that have developed useful approaches to these issues and schools that might profit from their experience.

Local Meetings. One of the most common activities of local support networks for SFA is regular meetings of key staff members. Most often it is facilitators or the facilitators and principals together who meet about once a month to discuss common problems and explore ways to help each other. In 1999, we began to introduce a leadership academy program in most areas with a concentration of SFA schools. This is a training course in leadership, but it also serves as a local networking opportunity for principals and facilitators. The benefits of these meetings are similar to the benefits of mentoring, which were discussed earlier. Principals, facilitators, and family support team members learn a great deal from others facing similar problems in similar environments under similar circumstances. Further, regular meetings for the leaders of SFA schools provide routine opportunities for staff to build positive relationships and establish opportunities for other types of mutual assistance.

Some local support networks schedule demonstrations at the host school for the visiting staff from other schools. For example, the host school may have developed a new computer system to help with regrouping, a new thematic unit for preschool or kindergarten, or a family involvement or parent volunteer program they want to show off. The demonstration might take place before or after the meeting.

Local Conferences. Because most school staff must travel great distances to attend our national SFA conferences, few schools send more than one or two people. Because of funding limitations, some schools cannot send anyone. Yet a similar purpose is sometimes served by holding local conferences. These can be scheduled on designated staff-development days so that all staff members can attend. The activities are similar to those of the national conference, with various in-service training, updates, and other sessions and with opportunities for schools to present their accomplishments in a variety of ways. SFAF staff participate, but center stage is reserved for the schools. These conferences provide an opportunity for local networking among entire school staffs that continues to benefit the participants long after the conference has ended.

Organization and Capital

Scaling up a successful school reform model is not only a question of building a strong training corps capable of working nationally. It also involves creating an organization capable of supporting trainers, developing materials and strategies, and carrying out research and awareness activities. This, in turn, requires capital. Many months before school districts pay their bills, any reform organization will need to spend large amounts of money each year on recruiting and training new trainers, developing and printing materials, and other activities. Carrying out these activities requires a line of credit of indefinite duration, over and above whatever funding was necessary to develop and evaluate the program. In recent years, these activities—both creating an efficient organization and securing operating capital—have consumed enormous amounts of our energies.

For ten years, SFA existed as part of Johns Hopkins University. When the program was small, this arrangement worked well. Johns Hopkins took care of most routine business functions, such as payroll, benefits, insurance, and some legal services. It allowed us to run a deficit each spring so long as we had accounts receivable to cover the deficit when schools paid us in the fall.

Separation from Johns Hopkins

By summer 1997, however, it became apparent that this arrangement could no longer work. On our side, the university's salary scales, policies, and practices were constant impediments to growth. We could not hire trainers in the Northeast, for example, because Johns Hopkins' salary scales were much lower than those of northeastern school districts. Similarly, we had difficulty hiring business-related staff, such as accountants, human resources staff, and a finance director, because the university's rates for such staff were half of what commercial businesses were paying. On the university's side, the size and complexity of our operation made managing it difficult and time-consuming, and the university was understandably uncomfortable advancing us ever-larger amounts of capital each spring.

As a result, we decided to separate from the university. We reached agreement with university officials by February 1998 and completed the separation by July 1, 1998, establishing the SFAF as a not-for-profit entity to be responsible for the development and dissemination of SFA and Roots & Wings.

For Profit or Not for Profit?

One of the key issues we had to resolve early was whether to remain a not-for-profit organization. This was a difficult decision. On one hand, it was clear that, as a for-profit, we would have no problem raising capital. Many venture capital firms and individuals courted us heavily. However, several factors led us to favor strongly staying in the not-for-profit world. One was a desire to maintain an institutional ethos that focused on what is best for children, not what is best for profits or investors. Our staff is committed to children and to school reform, and we did not want to undermine this spirit in any way. Another issue involved the public perception of our efforts. Watching the hostile reception in many quarters to EP and other for-profit education reform groups, we wanted to be sure that our program was seen as having unmixed motivations. The American Federation of Teachers and, to a lesser extent, the National Education Association have strongly supported us (and opposed Edison Schools[2]). We did not want to endanger support of that kind. Finally, as a practical matter, we wanted to be certain that any operating profits would go back into development, research, and quality control rather than into dividends paid to investors or into tax payments.

The decision to remain a not-for-profit organization did, however, have serious costs. We found that banks were unwilling to make loans unless we had substantial assets. We secured approximately $5 million in grants and loans from the MacArthur and Ford Foundations, the New Schools Venture Fund, and New American Schools.[3] On the basis of these assets, we obtained a line of credit from a commercial bank. Even with these resources, however, we remain seriously undercapitalized for an organization of our size and rate of growth. For example, we have an annual printing bill of about $15 million, which we must pay many months before school districts begin to pay us. Had we had investors rather than loans, these problems would not have existed. On balance, we are sure we made the right decision and that, in the long run, we will be much stronger as a not-for-profit organization.

In addition to capital needs, we have had to recruit a large corps of people to duplicate all the functions the university had previously fulfilled: finance, accounting, payroll, benefits, insurance, legal services, information technology, space, and so on. These new people had

---

[2] See Chapter Thirteen in this volume

[3] See Chapter Sixteen in this volume.

to be recruited and trained while we were, at the same time, increasing the number of schools we serve by about 50 percent and our total institutional budget by almost 100 percent. As these people have settled in, it has become apparent that we can do a much better job outside the university, having created an organization completely tailored to our needs.

District-Level Failures

In working with high-poverty schools in 600 school districts, it is inevitable that we would encounter failures as well as successes. On a school-by-school basis, not every school achieves the success we seek to attain. Not surprisingly, the key factor in success or failure at the school level is the quality and completeness of implementation (Nunnery et al., 1996). Further, we have occasionally experienced failures on a larger scale, which bear more directly on our scale-up strategies. We try to learn from our failures as well as our successes and adjust our scale-up strategies accordingly.

Two of our most widely publicized failures were almost purely political failures rather than implementation failures. In Baltimore, our original home, a change of superintendents in 1989 put in place one who was openly hostile to outside involvement in the district, most particularly from Johns Hopkins University. Despite substantial and consistent evidence of effectiveness in well-controlled experiments (e.g., Madden et al., 1993), the program was phased out of Baltimore in the mid-1990s. Much later, a change of superintendents in Memphis brought in a superintendent intent on stamping out the accomplishments of his predecessor, Gerry House, who had been named Superintendent of the Year primarily on the basis of bringing into Memphis a variety of reform models, including a large number of SFA schools. As in Baltimore, evaluations had consistently found that SFA had positive effects on achievement tests (e.g., Sanders et al., 2000), but these results were not considered in decisions about continuing SFA.

A key failure in Miami-Dade County,[4] Florida, was partly political but also involved a decision on our part that we later regretted. We had begun in Miami-Dade County on a small scale in 1994. Our initial schools did very well, and an internal evaluation found that SFA schools were making outstanding gains on state assessments in comparison to other Miami schools.

In 1996, the Miami-Dade County Superintendent, Octavio Visiedo, asked us to expand our program in Miami substantially. He created a program for about 40 of the district's highest-poverty elementary schools that included SFA and one of two computer curriculum programs. The nature of the program precluded the voting process that we had long advocated. We resisted this but were finally convinced that the district would do a good job of obtaining buy-in from teachers by treating them as professionals and providing plentiful services and support. In fact, the district did start off this way, but just a few months into the school year the superintendent unexpectedly resigned. The new superintendent reneged on promises to the teachers and to us and provided low levels of training, inadequate tutors, and ambiguous support. As a result, implementation quality, which began at an adequate level, began to erode. An internal evaluation several years into the implementation (Urdegar, 1998) looked at one-year gains (controlling for all the achievement gains from the earlier years) and found that neither SFA nor the CCC and Jostens interventions were making any difference. This evaluation further eroded support for the model. Over a period of years, schools in Miami have gradually dropped out of the program, and the Miami debacle still haunts us throughout Florida and nationally.

The Baltimore, Memphis, and Miami experiences taught us some difficult lessons. First, they reminded us that we play in a rough neighborhood. As long as we remained a small "pilot," we could keep a low profile and continue despite district-level turmoil, but as we became a large presence, our fates could be tied to those of a particular superintendent or other political actors. However, they also influ-

---

[4] In 1997, the name of Dade County was changed to Miami-Dade County. Because our work there spans the time in which the name change was made, we use the newer name.

enced us in maintaining a focus on the principal and school staff—not the district—as the unit of change in school reform. Principals and staffs typically outlast superintendents and are more likely to operate in the interests of children rather than on political bases alone. When change happens in key school leaders, new leaders can maintain the program if the staff as a whole continues to support it.

District-Level Implementations

While our early experiences led us to focus on schools rather than districts, events in recent years have caused us to rethink this strategy and to develop means of working with districts. This new approach has come about primarily through experiences in a few districts that have adopted SFA as their main literacy approach.

Hartford, Connecticut

Perhaps the most interesting districtwide application of SFA is under way in Hartford, Connecticut. In 1998, a new superintendent, Tony Amato, came to Hartford promising to get Hartford off of the bottom rank among Connecticut districts. In collaboration with the Hartford Federation of Teachers, he adopted SFA in all but one of the district's 26 elementary schools and instituted many other reforms directed at enhancing teachers' skills and students' achievement.

Because there was only one reading reform program in the district, the district could support it in ways that other districts could not. Amato himself attended the teacher training and then publicly taught an upper elementary and a first-grade class, communicating "if I can do it, you can do it" to skeptical teachers. He asked his principals to also attend the training and then teach a class from time to time. He aligned many district policies around the requirements of SFA and carefully monitored the eight-week assessments used in the program to gauge the progress of all schools and teachers as a means of obtaining curriculum-based indicators long before the Connecticut Mastery Test scores were available. In combination, these and other interventions led to substantial gains in districtwide performance on the mastery tests, moving Hartford from last to second among Connecticut's seven urban districts.

In fall 2002, Amato left Hartford, and it is too early to tell whether his departure will undermine the district reform strategy. However, during his tenure in this very difficult urban district, Amato created a fascinating model for coherent, integrated change built around research-based reading strategies.

Chancellor's District, New York City

Another districtwide adoption of SFA has also affected our thinking about possibilities of districts being the unit of change. In 1998, New York City Chancellor Rudy Crew created a separate district within the city for schools performing at the very lowest levels. These schools were removed from their community districts and given substantially new staffs and significant resources to move their schools forward. All elementary schools received SFA as part of the initiative. In lieu of a vote, teachers individually applied for their jobs with the understanding that SFA would be used. As in Hartford, schools in the Chancellor's District have made remarkable gains in test scores, and most of the schools have improved enough to escape from the state's list of Schools Under Registration Review. Some of the schools have now been returned to their community districts.

As in Hartford, the Chancellor's District has been able to build its professional development and other strategies around the requirements of SFA. The Chancellor's District has survived two changes of chancellors and two changes of district superintendents and remains robust and well-regarded in New York City and in other urban districts. It is quite expensive, however, requiring far more in extra personnel and release time for training than other SFA schools receive.

Project GRAD

A third model for subdistrict reform is Project GRAD,[5] a national program begun in Houston by former Tenneco chief executive officer

---

[5] See Chapter Six in this volume.

James Ketelsen (see McAdoo, 1998). Begun as a scholarship program for disadvantaged high school students, Project GRAD started in 1999 to work with entire feeder systems of schools leading into its chosen high schools. All elementary schools (and many middle schools) in these feeder systems use SFA. Local Project GRAD staff supplement the training and follow-up provided by SFAF and collaborate with district staff in making each feeder system a district within a district, with its own policies, curricula, and professional development plans. Project GRAD implementations in Houston, Columbus (Ohio), Atlanta, and Los Angeles have all shown substantial gains on state tests. Again, Project GRAD demonstrates the positive effect of subdistrict coherence in ensuring implementation quality, adaptation to local needs, and enhanced outcomes.

The Hartford, Chancellor's District, and Project GRAD experiences, as well as smaller districtwide implementations in Long Branch, New Jersey; Lawrence, Massachusetts; and Galveston, Texas, have given us a vision of how the district can become the unit of change, with appropriate supportive structures. District-level implementations do not generate the same level of initial teacher and principal buy-in that school-by-school implementations do, and we must work to build this commitment over time. However, having a consistent district focus on SFA appears to have advantages that outweigh the disadvantages. In the current environment, which is emphasizing district coherence and control (in contrast to site-based management), we must learn how to take advantage of district coherence in introducing school and classroom change (see Slavin, 2003, for more on district coherence).

Reconciling District Successes and Failures

The previous sections present a paradox. Larger-scale implementations within urban districts have been both major successes and major failures. Of course, the successes are still under way and could become tomorrow's failures.

One possible lesson from our experience with districts or large subdistricts as the focus of reform is simply that, for these arrangements to work, the district must follow through on the opportunity presented by large-scale implementation of SFA. If districts align professional development, curriculum, assessment, and other policies around the requirements of SFA and use the tools that SFA provides (including eight-week assessment data), district coherence can be a strength. If Visiedo had remained in the superintendency in Miami, such policies might have remained in effect. Memphis did a fairly good job of supporting SFA, but at the end it had 19 different comprehensive reform models, too many to support adequately (although the reforms would almost certainly have been swept away anyway for purely political reasons when Gerry House resigned).

District reform is the next frontier in the scaling up of SFA. We have learned a great deal about how to help district leaders create coherence around research-based practices. However, working with whole districts or major subunits of districts also raises the profile of SFA and makes the reform more vulnerable to the shifting tides of district politics that are the bane of school reform, especially in large urban districts.

Lessons Learned

Our experience with the national dissemination of SFA has led us to several conclusions:

- Successful dissemination of a program as comprehensive and complex as SFA requires a combination of two types of assistance to schools. One is a core of talented, dedicated trainers operating from the project's home and/or regional training sites closely coordinated with the project headquarters. The second is a local and national network of schools willing and able to provide technical and emotional support to schools entering the network.

- While other institutions can be helpful in dissemination, we are finding greater success in employing staff from outstanding SFA schools to be full- or part-time trainers. Regional laboratories, other universities, and state departments of education have been helpful in our dissemination efforts, but, with the exception of the University of Memphis, they have not taken major responsibility for disseminating SFA in their regions. District coordinators are very helpful as liaisons between our project, SFA schools, and their central offices. Regionally based trainers on our payroll and staff members in SFA schools who are willing to do some training and follow-up are usually much more effective.
- Quality control is a constant concern. Whatever dissemination strategy we use, constantly checking on the quality of training, implementation, and outcomes is essential. Without it, all programs fade into nothingness.
- To sustain innovations over a long period, the implementing schools must be part of a national network of like-minded schools. To survive the inevitable changes of superintendents, principals, teachers, and district policies, school staffs need to feel that an important group beyond the confines of their district cares about and supports what they are doing.
- District or subdistrict adoptions of SFA can produce outstanding outcomes on a substantial scale if district leaders align their policies and professional development efforts around the model's requirements, but large-scale implementations in urban districts also expose the program to greater political risks.

SFA is the largest comprehensive reform network, but it is only one of many national models of school reform, and it has unique characteristics that may make some dissemination strategies effective and others difficult or ineffective. Other types of programs may find very different strategies to be more effective. However, to the extent that other programs emphasize a strong research base, a well-specified set of materials and procedures, and a comprehensive approach to reform, we believe that our experiences will be a useful guide and will inform policies regarding technical assistance and reform at the local, state, and federal levels.

Policy Implications

Our experiences with the dissemination of SFA have given us some degree of insight into the ways that systemic issues, such as federal, state, and local policies, can promote or inhibit school-by-school reform and have given us some ideas about how these policies might change to support what we and other school-change networks are trying to do.

Substantial positive change in student learning can only come about on a broad scale when major changes take place in the daily interactions of teachers and students. Ideally, we would have a variety of curricula, instructional methods, professional development methods, and school organizational forms for each subject and grade level, each of which has been rigorously researched and evaluated in comparison to traditional practices and found to be effective on valid measures of student achievement. School staffs would be made aware of these effective alternatives and would have the time and resources to learn about them, visit schools using them, see videotapes on them, and ultimately make an informed choice among them. Their exploration of alternatives might be assisted by local "brokers" knowledgeable about effective programs, organizational development, and the change process and aware of local needs, circumstances, and resources (see Slavin, 1997, 1998).

School staffs would control significant resources for materials and professional development and would be able to invest them in the exploration process and in well-developed models supported by national training staffs and local support networks. These national programs would be primarily supported by revenues from schools but would also have seed money for developing awareness and training materials, establishing national networks and regional training sites, and building qualified staffs of trainers and support personnel. Federal and state policies would support the process of school-by-school change by developing and promulgating standards, assessments, and accountability mechanisms likely to encourage school staffs to explore alternative models for change and to invest in professional development. They would push existing resources (such as Title 1 funds) to the school level with a clearly stated expectation that these funds are intended for whole-school reform, not for maintaining current operations or patching around the edges. Some portion of school-change funds would be provided on a competitive basis to schools based on their willingness to engage in whole-school reform and allocate their own resources (especially Title 1 funds) to this purpose. Further, funds would be allocated to outstanding exemplars of school reform methods to compensate them for the costs of serving as demonstration sites, mentoring other schools in their local networks, and participating in local training and follow-up.

The remainder of this chapter discusses the current state of policy support for school-by-school changes and the policy reforms needed to provide this support on a broad scale.

Recommendations

Increase Support for Research and Development of School Change Models

One of the most important deficiencies in the current structure of professional development is a shortage of whole-school reform programs proven in rigorous research to be markedly more effective than traditional instruction and thus ready for national dissemination (see Slavin and Fashola, 1998). Besides SFA, only a few, such as the Comer project (see Cook et al., 1999), Direct Instruction (Adams and Engelmann, 1997),[6] and America's Choice (Supovitz, Poglinco, and Snyder, 2001)[7] have conducted and reported comparisons with traditional methods. Progress has been made on the development of

---

[6] Also see Chapter Four in this volume.

[7] Also see Chapter Seven in this volume.

new school change models; the New American Schools funded seven design teams to develop such models, and the U.S. Department of Education has funded the development of six secondary models, including an SFA middle school design. Only recently has the U.S. Office of Educational Research and Improvement (OERI) begun to fund projects that formally evaluate the outcomes of some of these new designs in comparison to traditional methods.[8]

It is interesting to note that, until fairly recently, the federal involvement in the development, evaluation, and dissemination of these models was minimal. Private foundation and corporate funding was almost entirely responsible for the development and dissemination of all the current CSR models in wide use. SFA benefited from federal funding (its development and evaluation have been part of the work of the Johns Hopkins University's Center for Research on the Education of Students Placed at Risk), but it could not have been successfully developed and evaluated at first without funding from private foundations, especially the Carnegie and Pew Foundations and New American Schools.

There is a need for federal investment in the development of schoolwide change models, in evaluation of these models by their developers, and in third-party evaluations that compare the effects of the models to the effects of traditional methods (see Slavin, 1997; Herman, 1999). Only when we have many successful models with clear and widely accepted evidence of effectiveness will we be able to confidently offer schools an array of choices, each of which may be quite different in philosophy or main elements but each of which is known to be effective under well-specified and replicable conditions of implementation.

Help Proven Professional-Development Networks Build Capacity

The most important limitation on the broad dissemination of SFA is our own capacity to provide high-quality professional development services to a very large number of schools. Our model requires a great

---

[8] OERI has since become the Institute of Education Sciences.

deal of training and follow-up, and any equally ambitious restructuring program that intends to change the daily instructional practices of all teachers would require equally intense training. We can only add so many schools each year without overtaxing the considerable energies of our staff, hiring more trainers than we can train and mentor, or seeing the quality of professional development decline.

Our professional development organization is self-funding; our trainers' salaries are supported by fees we charge schools for their time. However, rapid scale-up has costs. While we train new trainers, we must pay their salaries, fly them to observe schools or training sessions, and so on. Costs for establishing trainers in sites other than the project's home site may be particularly great because these trainers must travel frequently to the home site. No source of funding for these costs exists. By the time a trainer is fully operative and bringing in enough revenue to cover his or her salary, we may have spent more than $50,000. As noted earlier, an even larger problem of scale-up is obtaining a line of credit to cover printing and other cyclical costs.

Training organizations, such as ours, must have access to funds to scale up their operations. Ultimately, such organizations must be self-funding, but they need capitalization as they begin their work and as they engage in significant expansion of their national capacity. As noted earlier, private foundations have largely fulfilled this capitalization function for some projects, including SFA, but if training organizations are to remain in the not-for-profit sector and to operate at significant scale, much more capital must be made available for this purpose by government or donors. Recently, OERI has begun to provide capacity-building funding, and these resources are starting to affect the total availability of reform models substantially.

Provide Resources Earmarked for Adoption of Effective Programs

Serious reform at the school level takes serious funding at the school level. School staffs must have control of resources they can spend only on professional development, especially on adoption of demonstrably effective programs.

School staffs should control professional development funds so that they can choose the development they believe will meet their needs. When they freely select a given program or service provider, they will feel a commitment to that choice, in contrast to the more common case in which teachers resist in-service presentations that they feel do not respond to their needs. A school should be able to purchase services from any provider, including universities; regional laboratories; federal, state, or local technical assistance centers; professional development networks (such as the National Writing Project); or even their own district's staff development office.

The Obey-Porter Comprehensive School Reform Demonstration is making an excellent start in this area, at least as far as whole-school, comprehensive designs are concerned. This initiative is providing modest funding on a competitive basis both to help schools adopt research-based programs and to give them an incentive to use their existing resources (especially Title 1 funds) on programs likely to make a difference in all aspects of school functioning and in student achievement (see Slavin, 1998).

Provide Awareness and Brokering Services to Schools to Support Wise Choices of Professional Development Services

Individual school staffs are poorly placed to select promising or effective programs because they might not be aware of what is available or how to go about obtaining the programs and materials they need.

Providing awareness (and some brokering) of promising programs is one area in which the federal government has played a significant role. National Diffusion Network (NDN) state facilitators organized awareness conferences and helped schools adopt these "validated" programs. However, the evaluation standards were low, and NDN funding was never adequate for providing much more than an informational clearinghouse function (although, even with its limitations, NDN efforts led to thousands of successful adoptions of research-based programs in every state). In 1996, funding for NDN was eliminated.

Far more ambitious outreach to school and district staffs is required to help them assess their needs and make them aware of a range of alternative programs and services available to them. State or federal support might be important in helping establish brokering agencies or individuals, but in a system in which professional development resources are focused at the school level, agencies or individuals providing any professional development services to schools would ultimately have to support themselves on fees from schools. Existing agencies, such as the regional laboratories and regional comprehensive assistance centers, could also play an important role in helping schools make wise choices of professional development services and programs. A process of this kind has been set in motion by the Obey-Porter Comprehensive School Reform Demonstration, which provides funds to labs and state departments of education to increase awareness of proven, comprehensive models.

Provide Funds to Successful Exemplars of Proven Programs to Serve as Demonstration and Training Sites

In disseminating SFA, we have learned how important it is to have schools successfully implementing the program whose staffs are willing to receive visitors and assist neighboring schools in the process of adopting the program. Many of our outstanding schools have put hundreds or thousands of hours into helping other schools start and maintain the program.

However, all this help comes at a price. Many schools can provide only minimal assistance to other schools without overtaxing their staff. Some principals are concerned that if they let their best staff members work to help other schools, they will be hired away. More often, school staffs find that, while their efforts to help other schools bring them recognition and satisfaction, they must limit this activity.

It is unfair and unrealistic to expect that outstanding exemplars of proven programs will work indefinitely as demonstration and training sites without any outside compensation. Resources should be provided to these schools for the real costs of serving as demonstration sites (such as hiring substitutes when staff are elsewhere helping other schools) and to help them see aiding other schools as a part of their responsibilities.

Conclusions

Our experience in the national dissemination of SFA is instructive in many ways. We have discovered that far more schools are eager to make thoroughgoing changes in their instructional programs than we or other national training networks can possibly serve. Policy changes, such as those contained in No Child Left Behind, the Obey-Porter Comprehensive School Reform Demonstration, and state and local systemic reforms, are further motivating schools to seek high-quality, intensive, and extensive professional development services to transform themselves fundamentally. The key limitation in making this change is the limited national capacity to provide schools with well-researched models backed by networks of trainers, demonstration schools, materials, and other resources.

This chapter has focused on our efforts to increase the capacity of our SFA program, enabling it to serve a rapidly expanding network of schools across the United States, and on the policy changes needed to support our network and others in building our nation's capacity for quality professional development. In brief, we have found that our network of schools and our own dedicated staff are the bedrock of a national dissemination strategy and that building on the strengths of this network is the most promising approach to scale-up. Federal, state, and other support to help establish and maintain professional development networks like ours, along with providing money to schools earmarked for professional development, are most likely to create conditions in which schools throughout the United States will focus their energy on exploring alternatives, seeking professional development appropriate to their needs, and engaging in a long-term, thoughtful process of change that results in measurably improved achievement for all children.

References

Adams, G., and S. Engelmann, *Research on Direct Instruction: 25 Years Beyond DISTAR*, Seattle, Wash.: Educational Achievement Systems, 1997.

Borman, G., and G. Hewes, *Long-Term Effects and Cost Effectiveness of Success For All*, Baltimore, Md.: Johns Hopkins University Center for Research on the Education of Students Placed at Risk, 2001.

Borman, G. D., G. M. Hewes, L. T. Overman, and S. Brown, "Comprehensive School Reform and Achievement: A Meta-Analysis," *Review of Educational Research*, Vol. 73, No. 2, 2003, pp. 125–230.

Cook, T. D., F. Habib, M. Phillips, R. A. Setterstein, S. L. Shagle, and S. M. Degirmencioglu, "Comer's School Development Program in Prince George's County, Maryland: A Theory-Based Evaluation," *American Educational Research Journal*, Vol. 36, No. 3, 1999, pp. 543–597.

Cooper, R., R. E. Slavin, and N. A. Madden, "Success For All: Improving the Quality of Implementation of Whole-School Change Through the Use of a National Reform Network," *Education and Urban Society*, Vol. 30, No. 3, 1998, pp. 385–408.

Dianda, M., and J. Flaherty, *Annual Report on Promising Practices and Program Adaptations and Successes*, Los Alamitos, Calif.: Southwest Regional Laboratory, 1994.

Haynes, N. M., ed., *School Development Program: Research Monograph*, New Haven, Conn.: Yale University, 1994.

Herman, R., *An Educator's Guide to Schoolwide Reform*, Arlington, Va.: Educational Research Service, 1999.

Hurley, E. A., A. Chamberlain, R. E. Slavin, and N. A. Madden, "Effects of Success For All on TAAS Reading: A Texas Statewide Evaluation," *Phi Delta Kappan*, Vol. 82, No. 10, 2001, pp. 750–756.

Levin, H. M., "Accelerated Schools for Disadvantaged Students," *Educational Leadership*, Vol. 44, No. 6, 1987, pp. 19–21.

Madden, N. A., R. E. Slavin, N. L. Karweit, L. J. Dolan, and B. A. Wasik, "Success for All: Longitudinal Effects of a Restructuring Program for Inner-City Elementary Schools," *American Educational Research Journal*, Vol. 30, No. 2, 1993, pp. 123–148.

Madden, N. A., R. E. Slavin, and K. Simons, *MathWings: Effects on Student Mathematics Performance*, Baltimore, Md.: Johns Hopkins University Center for Research on the Education of Students Placed at Risk, 2001.

McAdoo, M., "Project GRAD's Strength Is in the Sum of Its Parts," *Ford Foundation Report*, Vol. 29, No. 2, 1998, pp. 8–11.

McCarthy, J., "Accelerated Schools: The Satellite Center Project," paper presented at the annual meeting of the American Educational Research Association, Chicago, Ill., April 1991.

Nunnery, J., S. Ross, L. Smith, R. Slavin, P. Hunter, and J. Stubbs, "An Assessment of Success For All Program Configuration Effects on the Reading Achievement of At-Risk First Grade Students," paper presented at the annual meeting of the American Educational Research Association, New York, April 1996.

Pearson, P. D., and S. Stahl, *Choosing a Reading Program: A Consumer's Guide*, Berkeley, Calif.: University of California, 2002.

Pinnell, G. S., C. A. Lyons, D. E. DeFord, and M. Seltzer, "Comparing Instructional Models for the Literacy Education of High Risk First Graders," *Reading Research Quarterly*, Vol. 29, No. 1, 1994, pp. 8–38.

Pinnell, G. S., D. E. DeFord, and C. A. Lyons, *Reading Recovery: Early Intervention for At-Risk First Graders*, Arlington, Va.: Educational Research Service, 1988.

Sanders, W. L., S. P. Wright, S. M. Ross, and L. W. Wang, *Value-Added Achievement Results for Three Cohorts of Roots & Wings Schools in Memphis: 1995–1999 Outcomes*, Memphis, Tenn.: University of Memphis Center for Research in Educational Policy, 2000.

Slavin, R. E., *Cooperative Learning: Theory, Research, and Practice*, 2nd ed., Boston: Allyn and Bacon, 1995.

_____, "Neverstreaming: Preventing Learning Disabilities," *Educational Leadership*, Vol. 53, No. 5, 1996, pp. 4–7.

_____, "Design Competitions: A Proposal for a New Federal Role in Educational Research and Development," *Educational Researcher*, Vol. 26, No. 1, 1997, pp. 22–28.

_____, "Far and Wide: Developing and Disseminating Research-Based Programs," *American Educator*, Vol. 22, No. 3, 1998, pp. 8–11, 45.

_____, "Converging Reforms: Change Schools? Change Districts? How the Two Approaches Can Work Together," *Education Week*, Vol. 22, No. 25, March 5, 2003, p. 64.

Slavin, R. E., and O. S. Fashola, *Show Me the Evidence: Proven and Promising Programs for America's Schools*, Thousand Oaks, Calif.: Corwin, 1998.

Slavin, R. E., and N. A. Madden, "Research on Achievement Outcomes of Success For All: A Summary and Response to Critics," *Phi Delta Kappan*, Vol. 82, No. 1, 2000a, pp. 38–40, 59–66.

_____, "Roots & Wings: Effects of Whole-School Reform on Student Achievement," *Journal of Education for Students Placed at Risk*, Vol. 5, Nos. 1 and 2, 2000b, pp. 109–136.

_____, eds., *One Million Children: Success For All*, Thousand Oaks, Calif.: Corwin, 2001.

Slavin, R. E., N. A. Madden, A. Cheung, and C. Liang, *Effects of Success For All on SAT-9 Reading: A California Statewide Evaluation*, Baltimore, Md.: Johns Hopkins University Center for Research on the Education of Students Placed at Risk, 2002.

Slavin, R. E., N. A. Madden, L. J. Dolan, and B. A. Wasik, *Every Child, Every School: Success For All*, Newbury Park, Calif.: Corwin, 1996.

Slavin, R. E., N. A. Madden, L. J. Dolan, B. A. Wasik, S. M. Ross, and L. J. Smith, "'Whenever and Wherever We Choose . . .': The Replication of Success For All," *Phi Delta Kappan*, Vol. 75, No. 8, 1994, pp. 639–647.

Slavin, R. E., N. A. Madden, N. L. Karweit, L. Dolan, and B. A. Wasik, *Success For All: A Relentless Approach to Prevention and Early Intervention in Elementary Schools*, Arlington, Va.: Educational Research Service, 1992.

Success For All Foundation, State Reports, Web site, undated. Online at http://www.successforall.net/resource/StateReports.cfm (as of June 29, 2004).

Supovitz, J. A., S. M. Poglinco, and B. A. Snyder, *Moving Mountains: Successes and Challenges of the America's Choice Comprehensive School Reform Design*, Philadelphia: University of Pennsylvania Consortium for Policy Research in Education, 2001.

Traub, J., *Better by Design? A Consumer's Guide to Schoolwide Reform*, Washington, D.C.: Thomas Fordham Foundation, 1999.

Urdegar, S. M., *Evaluation of the Success For All Program, 1997–98*, Miami: Miami-Dade Public Schools, 1998.

CHAPTER SIX

Taking Education Programs to Scale: Lessons from the Field

James L. Ketelsen

Although Project GRAD is supported, in part, by philanthropic organizations, one of its distinctive features is its focus on community involvement as an important component of successful school reform. Now working in more than a dozen cities, Project GRAD requires each new location to form a not-for-profit organization and a board made up of community leaders to provide continuing support for its programs. In the early years of Project GRAD's involvement in a new community, up to 30 percent of operating funds are expected to come from the private sector, individuals, corporations, and foundations. Ketelsen describes the challenges of this approach, which requires significant up-front effort but, he argues, has significant long-term benefits.

Project GRAD is a unique, comprehensive program that has produced—and is continuing to produce—positive and sustainable change in inner-city schools throughout the nation. Established in 1993 as a not-for-profit program, the program is based on the philosophy that children—from prekindergarten through twelfth grade—can be effective learners, regardless of socioeconomic background. We are guided by the belief that any effort to be successful in increasing achievement levels and, ultimately, graduation rates in schools that serve large numbers of children from families of low socioeconomic status must begin with prekindergarten and follow children all the way through high school. The model emphasizes a solid foundation of skills in reading, writing, and math, as well as building self-discipline, providing resources to support at-risk children and their families, and offering them the opportunity to believe that, with scholarship support, the dream of college can become a reality.

A Brief History of Project GRAD

Project GRAD began in 1984 as a college scholarship program in an inner-city, low-performing high school in Houston, Texas. Jefferson Davis High School, located in one of the poorest sections of Houston, had an enrollment of 1,600 children, almost all Hispanic. In the five preceding years, an average of only 174 children per year graduated from the high school, representing about 38 percent of entering ninth-graders. Approximately 20 of the graduates went on to college, representing less than 5 percent of incoming freshman. Average Scholastic Aptitude Test (SAT) scores for the few students who took the test averaged below 800 combined—clearly a discouraging record.

In an effort to turn this situation around, Tenneco, a local corporation and business partner of the school, offered every student in the ninth-grade class of 1988–89 a chance to earn a college scholarship—$1,000 per year for four years, for a total of $4,000. On the surface, the program seemed to work fairly well. In 1992, the first year that students were eligible for the scholarships, 101 students qualified, and 81 entered college—more than four times the average number that had entered college during the years before the scholarship was offered. Although students who graduated from high school were more likely to enroll in college, the lower 60 percent were not helped. They continued to drop out of high school before graduation.

Thus, it became obvious that ninth grade was much too late to have an effect on these children. We came to understand that increasing high school graduation rates and college enrollment rates among inner-city children required working with them throughout their school years, and, out of this understanding, Project GRAD was born. Critical to its design, which was developed during 1992 and 1993, was the idea that maximizing the chances of success required improving schooling in all the schools a child would attend. Project GRAD was launched in the Jefferson Davis feeder system in December 1993 with initial training of some of the teachers in the schools—seven elementary schools and the middle school—that "feed" students to Davis High School.

The feeder system consisted of a total of 7,500 children—88 percent Hispanic and 10 percent African-American. There were 1,600 students in high school; 1,350 in middle school; and 4,550 in seven elementary schools ranging in size from 250–800 students. The various components, to be described later, were introduced throughout 1994–95. The base year is considered to be 1993–94 because none of the Project GRAD curriculum had yet been introduced.

By 1996, it was becoming clear that the program was producing positive results in the Davis feeder system. The proportion of children in Grades 3 through 8 passing the Texas Assessment of Academic Skills (TAAS) had risen from 36 percent in 1994 to 52 percent in 1996 in math and from 55 percent in 1994 to 56 percent in reading. (Note that reading was not introduced until the 1995–96 year.) The number of students graduating from high school had risen from 174 to 209, and the number entering college had reached 117 in the fall of 1995, compared with 20 before Project GRAD started.

After consulting with the Houston Independent School District (HISD), we decided to introduce Project GRAD in a second feeder system—this time in a predominantly African-American area. This feeder system consisted of 12 elementary schools, 2 middle schools, and Jack Yates High School, with a total of 10,000 students—88 percent African-American and 10 percent Hispanic. Our objective was to show that Project GRAD worked as well with African-American children as it did with Hispanic children. So, in 1995–96, we began training teachers in the Yates feeder system.

About this time, we submitted a request for funding to the Ford Foundation, and Ford sent several groups to review our program and its results. After careful examination, they decided Project GRAD was one of the best, if not the best, school reform program they had seen. It was unclear, however, whether the program would scale up—whether it would work outside of Houston.

The Ford Foundation representatives suggested Newark, N.J., as a possible site to test Project GRAD outside its home district. The

Newark schools were not providing inner-city children with an adequate education, and, as a result, the state had taken over the school system and appointed a new superintendent. It was thought that if Project GRAD worked in Newark, it would work anywhere.

So, with funding from the Ford Foundation and the Lucent Technologies Foundation, we began to build capacity to expand outside of Houston. As knowledge of Project GRAD spread, requests began coming in from other cities. Between 1997 and 1999, new Project GRAD programs were launched in Los Angeles, California; Columbus, Ohio; and Nashville, Tennessee. When the superintendent of schools in Newark moved to Atlanta, we were asked to begin a new program there. In each case, Project GRAD was introduced into a single system of feeder schools leading to one high school. These systems ranged in size from 3,500 students in Columbus to 21,000 students in Los Angeles.

The Ford Foundation support has been vital to our expansion and success. The foundation's willingness to support Project GRAD's development—both its capacity to expand nationally and to provide significant start-up support in each new city—has been critical to our success. In addition to providing funding, Ford appointed a senior full-time staff officer to work with the Project GRAD organization. After five years of supporting Project GRAD from within the foundation, this individual became the president of Project GRAD USA, a full-time position.

Without this significant long-term support, it is doubtful that Project GRAD would have attempted a national expansion program. We would have remained active only in the HISD. The role of support from the Ford Foundation illustrates the need for a dedicated supporting organization in almost any successful scale-up of education reform programs.

In the 2002–03 school year, we were operating in ten cities with more than 130,000 children in the program. Additional expansion in Ohio is planned as the State Commissioner of Education wishes to use Project GRAD in several major cities. In 2002–03, work was under way in Akron, Cincinnati, and Columbus; in 2003–04, we will add Lorain, Ohio. To ensure that we can provide adequate help during the start-up phase, as well as adequate training, we have limited expansion to a maximum of four new cities per year. At this writing, we have a small waiting list of cities that want to implement Project GRAD in their schools.

Project GRAD Program Design Elements

Project GRAD was designed to serve children in inner cities, where poverty rates are high and schools often perform poorly. In most of these schools, the students are members of minority groups. Closing the performance gap between students from minority groups and white students is one of our major objectives.

We combine proven curriculum models, significant initial teacher training and ongoing support, and community and parental involvement within a feeder system of schools to improve test scores, graduation rates, and college enrollment rates. Project GRAD involves much of the community—students, teachers, administrators, community volunteers, corporate sponsors, and mentors—to provide a critical mass of intervention and support.

We have already spoken of a feeder system of schools: Project GRAD does not work with one school at a time. A high school and the middle and elementary schools that feed children into that high school make up the "unit" that adopts and implements the Project GRAD program. This unit may range from five to seven schools with 3,000 students to 16 to 20 schools including 20,000 to 25,000 students. The scope of the program—encompassing multiple schools at all levels—means that implementing Project GRAD is a major undertaking, requiring support from the superintendent, school board, and administrators.

A committee made up of the principals of the feeder schools is formed to plan, schedule, monitor, and modify the program for maximum success. Teacher training is at the heart of the initiative. Because of the major effect Project GRAD has on teachers and teaching, we require a vote of teachers with a 70 percent favorable majority in each school before we will undertake the program in a feeder system.

Three programs have been selected to guide the practices of classroom teachers: MOVE IT Math, our math curriculum; Success For All, our reading and writing program[1]; and Consistency Management and Cooperative Discipline (CMCD), our student discipline component. These programs recognize that many inner-city elementary teachers have had little effective training in how to teach math, reading, and writing and how to manage a classroom effectively. To be implemented effectively, the three programs require a total of more than 100 hours of teacher training. Usually, training for only one of these components is scheduled per year. After initial training, these programs are supported by Project GRAD specialists who provide each school with two days of in-school support per week.

Another component of the program involves external problems in the home or community that can hurt a student's performance. Communities in Schools (CIS), a national dropout-prevention program, or an equivalent is used to provide this service. Social workers are assigned to each school—one per elementary school, a team of three or four to middle schools, and four or five to high schools, depending on size. CIS works with the community in dealing with at-risk children. CIS staff are active in building parental involvement, including "Parent Universities" at each school, which provide instruction to parents covering a broad range of activities that can help them support their children in school and expand their own educational achievement. CIS is also responsible for organizing our annual Walk for Success. Volunteers from the community, teachers, and high school students spend one Saturday a year visiting the homes of all new ninth-grade students to ask the parents to sign the Project GRAD covenant, which requires them to support their child in pursuing the Project GRAD scholarship. The walkers also visit the homes of new first- and second-graders and new sixth-graders to

---

[1] See Chapter Five in this volume.

encourage parental support. In some cities, several thousand volunteers turn out to visit thousands of homes.

As previously noted, Project GRAD offers ninth-graders the chance to earn a scholarship to college, usually $1,000 per year for four years. In some cities, larger amounts are offered. The requirements are designed to enlist and retain as many students as possible. Students are required to take a prescribed number of college-preparatory courses, graduate in four years, maintain a 2.5 grade average over the four years, and attend summer institutes during two of their summers in high school. The summer institutes take place at a local college or university, last four to six weeks, and are taught primarily by college professors. These institutes are designed primarily to build confidence and self-esteem in students who generally have not thought of themselves as being able to succeed in college. It provides accelerated teaching or remedial work, depending on the students' needs. Courses in physics, chemistry, advanced mathematics, and so on are offered. The main effort is to get the student thinking about college.

Project GRAD requires each city to form a not-for-profit 501(c)(3) organization for fundraising purposes and to recruit a governing board made up of members from the community, business leaders, school district administrators, local funders, and others. The board is responsible for directing local activities, raising funds, employing a capable executive director, and monitoring and promoting the program. Thus, Project GRAD is not just a program in a school with no external support, but a partnership with the school district that brings together many elements of the community, parents, and school administrators to work toward a common goal: improving education for poorly served, low-income, minority children.

Establishing strong community support through the local 501(c)(3) and having a board made up of respected community leaders are critical to the sustainability of the program, not only from a funding standpoint but also because these individuals and organizations provide support for the program through the inevitable changes in school system leadership and curricula. In Houston, we are working with our third superintendent and the fourth chair of the school board, and each high school principal has changed at least once. Despite these changes, Project GRAD has remained in operation and continues to expand.

Broad community support also helps to minimize the likelihood that program goals and structure will be subverted by the desire to "change for the sake of change" or to adopt "my program." We are a strong voice in the partnership because of our community support and because we contribute significant resources to the schools, both funding and additional high-quality staffing.

The program, including the scholarships, costs $400 to 600 per student per year. The school system is generally expected to and does provide about 25 to 30 percent of the funding at the outset of the program, and we ask it to gradually increase its support to 50 to 75 percent of the cost. The remainder is split roughly 50-50 between private-sector dollars raised from foundations, corporations, and individuals (both nationally and locally) and the public sector (both state and federal funding). At times, city governments also contribute. The school systems, while contributing to the cost of the program, receive significant additional funding. In a system with major participation in Project GRAD, substantial contributions of funding are specifically directed to the program, which is highly effective in addressing its needs.

How Project GRAD Achieves Results

The comprehensiveness of Project GRAD provides many advantages in terms of effectiveness and sustainability. Because the program relies on community support, it has a driving force to maintain, expand, improve, and sustain itself in each city. The local Project GRAD staff receives support to make the program effective and training from Project GRAD USA staff based in Houston.

While Project GRAD requires a school system to make a major commitment, school districts that consider adopting the program recognize that real success requires this kind of comprehensiveness.

Because of the program's broad focus—on both performance and behavior in school and on the links between life in school and life out of school—it has the ability to change the culture of the schools, providing parents and students with hope that attending college is a realistic possibility and, thus, an incentive to stay in school.

The feeder system is one of the key factors contributing to the positive effects and sustainability of Project GRAD. A group of principals work as a team directing the program. When the principal changes, as often happens, the new principal enters a team that is already committed to Project GRAD—making it very difficult to drop the program. So far, this has never happened. The other principals bring the new entrant along into the program. In our first feeder system in Houston, every school has had a new principal, and some have had three or four new principals since the program began. This continuity is much different from what one typically finds in single reform programs in individual schools.

Comparing reform efforts in a feeder system to those carried out in single schools provides strong evidence of greater effects. Consider, for instance, an individual elementary school that employs a program that is successful in improving the performance of its children. When those children move on to a middle school receiving students from several other elementary schools that have not been effective, they often encounter teaching that has been "dumbed down" to address the needs of children from these low-performing schools. By the time the children are in high school, they have lost most, if not all, of the advantage gained. Our program also compares favorably to reform programs aimed at high schools. These high schools receive students working well below grade level from poorly performing elementary and middle schools—creating a demand for remedial programs that drain resources from efforts to improve programs for all students. When we started, only 15 percent of students entering Davis High School passed the state math test. Now, seven years later, the numbers are reversed—only 15 percent of incoming students failed the test. Success of this magnitude builds support for the program and provides the foundation for subsequent success. Everyone wants to be a winner.

The feeder system also provides a means of dealing with the mobility that characterizes low-income, inner-city schools. Virtually all such schools have substantial student turnover, but much of this movement is within a fairly small geographic area. With a feeder system, many elementary students are simply moving from one feeder system school to another and, as a result, can continue to participate in and profit from the program despite having moved to a new school.

The diversity of programs that Project GRAD comprises also contributes to our success. We present the neighborhood schools with a group of programs affecting students, parents, and the community. In addition to the possibility of earning a college scholarship, we improve teaching in basics—reading, writing, and math—allowing all our students to take advantage of the opportunities presented.

To assist school districts considering adopting the program, Project GRAD USA has a team of professionals assigned to work with new cities to provide them with all the information they need, to help them develop community support, to organize tours of schools in cities successfully implementing Project GRAD, and to provide whatever additional help is needed to allow districts to determine whether Project GRAD is right for them. Project GRAD USA also works with cities after they begin to implement the program, providing technical assistance to ensure quality and sustainability.

The services Project GRAD provides include five days per week of consultant support for the three classroom components in every school. The consultants work with teachers, analyze results with principals, and, in effect, provide whatever it takes to make the programs effective for that school. Experience has shown that, without support of this kind, the effects of reform programs decrease rapidly with time. Training of new teachers every year, for example, is an important form of support. Given the turnover of teachers in the inner city, a reform program without a new teacher training program would be gone in three years.

The individual components interact to enhance the effects of each of the programs. An obvious example: Stronger readers are likely to have more success with "word problems" in math. The classroom management program, which builds self-discipline in students and involves them as a part of classroom management, greatly reduces discipline problems. Teachers indicate that they have more than an additional half-hour of teaching time daily because they spend less time on discipline, thus allowing more-effective instruction in all courses. The scholarship program, of course, provides a direct incentive to students in high school, but, because more students are going on to college, the entire feeder system benefits from higher expectations.

When an inner-city teacher looks at her class and thinks, "More than half of these kids will drop out before completing high school, and most of the others will graduate with very low basic skills," the teacher is less likely to be motivated to teach at a high level than if he or she were teaching a class in which 80 percent or more will graduate from high school, with more than half of them going on to college. Better counseling, mentoring, and increased parental involvement all enhance motivation.

The easiest and strongest way for Project GRAD to scale up is to expand into additional feeder systems in school systems or cities in which the program is already successful. The broad community and school district support have already been developed, so the difficult task of building this support has already been accomplished. Because the program is data driven and its outcomes are measurable, the progress we have made strongly motivates teachers and administrators to support the program and spread it to additional feeder systems. The improvement makes them all winners. We began with one feeder of 7,500 students in Houston and spent our first three years proving the program worked in that system. After eight years, we were in five feeders, with 51,000 students. More recently, we have added a new feeder system almost every year.

The Effects of Project GRAD to Date

The key ingredient needed to spur scale-up and to support sustainability is performance. If the program can demonstrate measurable results in meaningful areas, others will be interested in replicating the program. Project GRAD is very much a data-driven program, and, in Houston, it has had strong success in each successive feeder system and has been implemented long enough in three of them to provide meaningful data. In other cities, early observations regarding our programs are positive, but they have not been operating long enough to generate similar data.

The Houston experience is tracked in three feeder systems— Davis with a base year prior to start-up in 1993–94, Yates with a base year of 1995–96, and Wheatley with a base year of 1998–99. These three systems have about 28,000 students, more than 98 percent of whom are either Hispanic or African-American. Of these students, about half are Hispanic, and half are African-American. More than 90 percent qualify for free or reduced-price lunches. Before the project's scholarship program began, the three high schools were sending a total of 75 students per year to college. In 2002, 280 students from the three schools entered either a four-year university or college or a community college, an increase of 273 percent. In 2001, scholarships were first granted in Wheatley High School. We therefore expect a significant increase in college enrollment rates in 2003 as the program gains greater support. To date, an average of 50 percent of the graduates of Davis High School have gone on to higher education—the annual range varying from a low of 40 percent to a high of 59 percent. Davis graduates have enrolled in Bowdoin College, Cornell, Princeton, Columbia, Colgate, Drexel, George Washington, Duke, and the University of Virginia and—closer to home—Rice, Texas A&M, and the University of Texas in Austin, as well as the University of Houston. Across the Project GRAD sites in the three Houston high schools, 1,500 children have entered college. It is too early to assess college graduation rates, since many students take six to eight years to complete their degrees, but the early returns indicate retention and graduation rates above the national average for Hispanics.

Of students from the first three high school graduation classes that entered college, 42 percent of Hispanic students have graduated—much higher than the national average of 26 percent.

High school graduation has increased at Davis from 174 per year (38 percent of incoming ninth-graders) prior to the scholarship program to more than 313 in 2003 (80 percent of incoming ninth-graders). The rate of graduation is also improving at the other two high schools, although not yet as much because the programs are newer. It is noteworthy that, during the same period, there has been no increase in high school graduation rates in other HISD high schools.

From the very first year, we have been externally evaluated. Therefore, we have results comparing cohorts of students who did or did not participate in Project GRAD. For instance, over a three-year period, students who began kindergarten in the Davis system the same year that Project GRAD started outperformed a comparison cohort for three consecutive years in mathematics and two consecutive years in reading (Opuni, 1998).

In addition to these evaluation results, participation in Project GRAD has helped to improve performance on standardized tests. The TAAS, the state criterion-referenced exam, is given annually for math and reading in Grades 3 through 8 and in Grade 10. Students are required to pass the tenth-grade test to graduate. In Grades 3 and 4, where appropriate, students not yet literate in English were tested in Spanish. All students, except a small percentage of special education students, are tested. The results that follow include all students not enrolled in special education programs—amounting to more than 90 percent of all students. Table 6.1 shows the passing rates, for each level, in the base year for each feeder system and in 2002, the most recent year for which data are available.

The elementary school scores on TAAS may understate the true extent of the progress we have made. Because of their socioeconomic background, inner-city children start school quite far behind. It takes all of kindergarten and the five grades to get them where they need to

Table 6.1
TAAS Passing Rates, 1994 and 2002

Feeder System	Math		Reading	
Davis feeder, year	1994	2002	1994	2002
Elementary schools (%)	44	92	63	87
Middle school (%)	28	85	45	82
Davis High School (%)	42	81	51	85
Yates feeder, year	1996	2002	1996	2002
Elementary schools (%)	70	89	74	88
Middle school (%)	47	85	78	85
Yates High School (%)	25	82	63	93
Wheatley feeder, year	1999	2002	1999	2002
Elementary schools (%)	64	92	69	88
Middle school (%)	75	95	76	93
Wheatley High School (%)	83	89	84	89

NOTE: Data are for the base year in each school and for the most recent year available for all.

be. We therefore put a great deal of emphasis on the fifth-grade results, which indicate readiness for middle school. The percentage passing TAAS increases each year from third to fifth grade. Passing rates for fifth graders are shown in Table 6.2.

The TAAS results allow us to see how the performance gap between minority and white students has closed in Project GRAD schools. The ethnic breakdown of scores for 2002 is not yet available, so the data described here are from 2001. In fifth-grade math, 96 percent of Hispanic students passed TAAS (Davis is 88 percent Hispanic.), compared with 93 percent in the state of Texas and 95 percent in HISD. The passing rate for white students in the state of Texas is 97 percent. The difference between the Hispanic students at Davis and all white students in Texas is now only 1 percentage point, when it had been 25 percentage points in 1999—a clear demonstration of the progress we have made.

Similarly, in the Jack Yates feeder system, which is 88 percent African-American, the 2001 TAAS results for the African-American students in fifth-grade math showed that 96 percent passed compared

Table 6.2
TTAAS Passing Rate for Fifth-Graders

Feeder System	Math		Reading	
Year	1994	2002	1994	2002
Davis feeder (%)	52	97	63	90
Year	1996	2002	1996	2002
Yates feeder (%)	73	97	84	90
Year	1999	2002	1999	2002
Wheatley feeder (%)	73	98	64	93

with 89 percent for African-Americans in the state of Texas and 94 percent for African-Americans in the HISD. A comparison of the pass rate for Yates African-American students in math (96 percent) to that for white students in the state of Texas again (97 percent) shows the progress we have made in closing the gap.

If we move from the state's criterion-referenced test to a national norm-referenced test (e.g., the Stanford-9) to assess our progress, we also see significant improvements. In Grades 1 through 5, mathematics scores increased from 39 percent of students scoring at or above the national 50th percentile in 1999, the first year the test was given, to 58 percent in 2002. These figures include students in Grades 1 through 5 in all three feeder systems—approximately 8,600 students.

Another reason to focus on elementary test scores is that these students have had the majority of their education in the Project GRAD curriculum. Students in high school and middle school were well along in their schooling before Project GRAD was introduced. Hence, the results do not fully reflect what can be accomplished. The true test of the Project GRAD program will be in 2007, when the first class in the Davis feeder system that has had Project GRAD from kindergarten graduates from high school.

While we concentrate on test results, we are also mindful of other data that indicate additional improvements brought about by the program. For example, discipline-related referrals to the principals' offices decreased by 74 percent by the end of the fourth year of implementation of the CMCD program. Further, an estimated 3.7

weeks of instructional time was added to the 1999–00 school year in Yates's feeder elementary schools as a result of the reduction in discipline problems associated with three years of implementation of CMCD.

The success of a program and the ability to document it are fundamental to the issues of scale-up and sustainability. Thus, we regard the data presented above as evidence indicating that efforts to expand Project GRAD are both worthwhile and likely to be fruitful.

Challenges in Scaling Up Project GRAD

The easiest and strongest way for Project GRAD to scale up is to expand into additional feeder systems in school systems or cities in which the program is already successful. The broad community and school district support has already been developed, so this difficult part of the program has already been done, but, of course, these resources are not available when we move into a new city.

In fact, the major challenge in scaling up Project GRAD is developing a broad base of initial support and funding at new sites. We definitely need strong support in the community and the school system before embarking on the program, and obtaining this support is sometimes difficult. This difficulty has not, however, slowed our expansion so far. We have the capacity to add three to four new cities per year, depending on the size of the initial feeder systems, and we have always had more cities interested in starting the program than we have capacity to handle.

The program requires funding of $400–600 per year per student in the feeder system. Generally, the school system contributes 25 to 40 percent, but the private sector needs to raise scholarship money before we start and, in some cities, this is difficult.

It has also sometimes been difficult to get the 70 percent favorable vote from teachers in each school in a proposed feeder system, even when the administration strongly favors the program. Most often, this reluctance to participate comes from elementary school teachers who feel they are currently doing a good job even though more than half of their students are not graduating from high school. They do not consider themselves accountable for student performance; instead, elementary test scores or grades are considered adequate for the "type of student" they are serving.

Changing the way reading, writing, and mathematics are taught is a significant challenge for many teachers and schools, and selling teachers, some of whom have been on the job for 15 to 20 years, on the idea of change is not easy. In light of this reluctance to change, it is somewhat surprising that we have expanded as fast as we have, but, most often, this reluctance is overcome by school district and community support.

Related to this need for support both within the school and in the community is our experience in a city in which we did not stick to our basic game plan. We went into the city with only one partner (a university) willing to provide administrative and leadership support. The initial funding came from a source outside the city but close to the university. This effort differed from our usual program in that it lacked broad support within the community, did not have a supporting 501(c)(3) organization and board of directors, and did not have a full-time executive director devoted to the operation, although the university did offer quality leadership and commitment. The school system was not involved in the initial planning and agreed to participate only after extensive negotiations. To add to the problem, shortly after we began, a new superintendent was appointed. Without the broad base of support that we typically build, it was easy for the new superintendent to reduce support for the program. Although parts of the program are continuing under the auspices of the university, we jointly decided to sever our relationship because the program was not true to our requirements. The lessons are obvious. We need to stick to our program design, working only in cities or school systems that provide the support and organizational structure we need to succeed.

Funding Concepts and Their Effects on Scale-Up

We operate with a suggested breakdown of funding requirements from various sources. Each city ends up with some variation of this suggested breakdown. Our recommended guideline in the starting years is a minimum of 30 percent of funds from the school district. The remaining funds would be generated as follows:

- 30 percent of funds from the private sector, individuals, foundations, or corporations
- 10 percent from state programs that provide funding through grants
- 30 percent from the federal government.

Over time, school districts are expected to pick up a higher percentage of the costs—reaching more than 50 percent. Project GRAD USA is generally responsible for generating the support from the federal budget. Project GRAD USA also raises some national funding from the private sector—foundations and corporations—which is then passed down to the various cities on a pro-rata basis.

Obviously, the need for a district to contribute a minimum of about $150 (30 percent of $500) per student in the program can be an obstacle to adopting the program. If one considers, however, that average spending is more than $6,000 per student per year, $150 is an increase of only 2.5 percent. The $350 per student generated from other funders makes the program very attractive to most school systems, particularly after they have studied it, visited schools where it is being implemented, and seen the data that reveal the gains districts have achieved by adopting Project GRAD.

The local funding requirements emphasize the need for strong leadership from the private sector in the community. If this leadership does not include potential funders or entrée to funders, the community will usually be unable to provide adequate support for the program and therefore should not embark on it.

The scholarship component, in particular, requires private-sector funding that is secure long into the future. A pledge is made to ninth-graders that they can earn a scholarship, which is paid out over their four years of college. Thus, the first year's scholars receive money more than seven years after initiation of the program. This requires an endowment or partial endowment before the program begins.

The question has been raised about whether any program that relies on external funding for an indefinite period is truly sustainable. At this point, most private funders are of a mind that they will fund the start-up of a program but want to see it reach a point at which it is self-sustaining. A corollary argument is that a school system that is unwilling to provide 100 percent of the cost of the program within a limited number of years after embarking on it really does not value the program and will not succeed in the long run. Further, critics contend that it is the responsibility of government and the school system to provide a sound education for all children and that programs that solicit funding—especially from public sources other than those specifically dedicated to schooling—constitute double taxation. Finally, some doubt that such efforts are worthwhile, pointing out that, as a society, we have been dealing with failing inner-city schools—devoting ever more financial resources—for more than 30 years and have little to show for our efforts.

Project GRAD rejects all these arguments. First, we believe that most Americans agree that providing every child with an education that will ensure that he or she has the opportunity to be successful should be a high societal priority. It would be wonderful if this result could be achieved with only modest increases in spending, but few programs that require only modest additional funding have produced well-documented positive results. Thus, a more-intensive and more-comprehensive approach is needed to meet this high-priority goal.

Compared to non–Project GRAD schools, participating schools have achieved documented success in the key areas of increased high school graduation rates, college entrance rates, and college graduation rates, as well as increased test scores. The need, the results, and the costs and benefits all suggest that the program should be funded indefinitely in amounts that allow it to grow as fast as it can without reducing the quality of services or performance outcomes in response to the appearance of "customers" who desire its admittedly subsidized service.

Widespread support for such programs has not yet appeared in the educational arena, but experience in other areas of society indicates that continued funding for an enterprise of this sort is not unusual. No one suggests that museums, hospitals, or the United Way should only be supported for a limited period and then be self-supporting. It should not be seen as radical to expect continued long-term funding of a successful school reform program for low-performing, inner-city, primarily minority students if the program continues to produce positive results. Potential funders—foundations, corporations, and individuals—should be willing to understand and undertake this challenge.

The argument that these results should be obtainable through taxation is also inconsistent with our practices with regard to other social problems. Consider, for instance, the problems that the United Way and the agencies it supports try to address. In almost every case, there is a government-funded program aimed at solving the same problem—be it housing, food, or health. In these areas, we do not object to the idea that, because the government aid is insufficient to solve the problem, it is both acceptable and desirable for private philanthropic organizations to "fill in the gap" and to be supported by private contributions indefinitely—so long as they make progress toward solving the problem. We argue that inner-city education reform should be regarded in the same way. Private funding and support will be required to solve the problems of low-performing schools, and, until those problems are solved, private money should be available to meet this need. Finally, it is hard to understand the argument that private dollars should be available indefinitely for charter schools and vouchers but should not be available for public inner-city school reform if such programs are demonstrated to be successful. Such a stance seems to indicate a mind-set against public education, a position that we doubt is shared by most U.S. citizens.

It may very well be that, over an extended period, many private sources of funding will fall by the wayside, but it is equally possible that some will continue and that the school system will bear a larger part of the cost as success is more widely documented. It may also be true that a larger portion of the funding will come from the federal and state governments.

Until proven otherwise, we plan to continue to rely on funding from outside the school system to provide leverage in bringing about systemic change for the better in inner-city schools. The program is dedicated to doing what it takes to reach the goal of providing all children with a solid education so they can fulfill their dreams.

Final Observations on Scaling Up Project GRAD

As the preceding discussion indicates, Project GRAD has been adopted in numerous location and thousands of students have profited from this program. We have developed a system for implementing the program in new locations that involves a complex set of procedures and services, involving community members, school administrators, teachers, Project GRAD staff members, parents, and students. In almost all instances, this approach has been successful, as demonstrated by the effects of our program on student performance and by the continuing demand to establish the program at new sites.

Despite the growth of our enterprise, however, we have found few shortcuts in expanding the reach of our program and ensuring the quality of implementation in new sites. In each locale, we have undertaken the challenging work of developing community support; recruiting funders; training teachers to use the required curriculum; and assessing our results through external evaluations, the use of standardized tests, and observations regarding rates of high school completion and college enrollment. Although we have a national office and a dedicated, full-time leader, the day-to-day, on-the-ground work of implementing Project GRAD must be carried out by the social workers, consultants, and teacher trainers and must be repeated in each school system that adopts our program.

Thus, the primary lessons to be drawn from our experience are, first, that we succeed when we are clear about our goals and when we follow the procedures that we have found to be successful in one location after another. Second, there is no substitute for local leadership and broad acceptance of and support for our program in the communities we serve. Project GRAD is, in some locations, still a very new program, but we anticipate that these lessons will remain valid as we continue to develop and expand the program and as we measure our effectiveness over time and across sites.

Reference

Opuni, K., *Project GRAD Program Evaluation Report*, Houston, Tex.: Houston Independent School District, 1998.

CHAPTER SEVEN

Reaching for Coherence in School Reform: The Case of America's Choice

Marc Tucker

Marc Tucker describes the long history of his organization's efforts to develop, implement, expand, and evaluate educational interventions— informed by observations of the superior performance of schools in other countries, by models of organizational change drawn from corporate experience, and by experience. At the heart of his essay—and his ideas about scaling up reform—is the concept of coherence. He argues that scaling up school reform involves a systematic approach, beginning with the establishment of standards and aligning teacher training and professional development, curriculum frameworks designed to help students meet standards, and assessments that determine whether they have done so. Building the capacity to achieve these goals, he contends, will require coherence in policies and practices from the school through the district to the state.[1]

Since the early 1980s, education policy in the United States has increasingly focused on student performance. Driven by the disap-

---

[1] This chapter distills more than a decade of the experience of everyone involved in the elementary and secondary education program of the National Center on Education and the Economy. I assume responsibility for any errors of fact or interpretation to be found here, but whatever credit is due us must be shared with all my colleagues. I regret that I cannot name everyone who has been involved in this enterprise, but I must recognize my colleagues Judy Codding and Peter Hill, with whom I have worked most closely on the issues treated here, and Phil Daro, whose legacy with respect to the design of our curriculum and professional development strategies will be with us for a long time. Thanks, too, to Judy Codding, Tom Corcoran, and Peter Hill for their helpful comments on this chapter. Finally, I want to acknowledge my debt to Tom Glennan, who many years ago made it possible for me to indulge my interest in building the capacity of educational organizations. From that time right up to his recent death, Tom's thoughtful questioning improved my work at every turn.

pearance of jobs for young people with low skills, rising demand for access to college, reports revealing the poor performance of U.S. students in international comparisons of educational achievement, and the disgust of legislators when increases in funding for the public schools failed to lead to significant improvement in student achievement, policymakers have been demanding much greater accountability for student performance. In the past, both state and federal legislators tended to defer to educators and local decisionmakers, but now state and federal policymakers are setting clear standards for student performance and expecting the profession and local boards of education to do whatever is necessary to make sure students meet them.

New state and federal policies call for improving student achievement at both the top and bottom of the performance distribution. For the first time in U.S. history, schools and the agencies that support them are being called on to raise the top tier of student performance and to narrow the distance between the top performers and the worst performers substantially.

The penalties for failure are unprecedented. Now, for the first time, students can be denied a high school diploma if they fail to meet high standards. Younger students can be denied promotion to the next grade if they fail to perform at stipulated levels. The sanctions for failure to make real progress are no less consequential for school faculties and district central office staff.

The No Child Left Behind Act of 2001 exemplifies the public mood. Under the terms of the act, if a school has not made satisfactory progress for five years in a row, the state must take the school over, recruit a private contractor to run it, or convert it to a charter school. If a school district has not made satisfactory progress for two years in a row, the state must withhold funds, institute new curricula, replace district personnel, remove schools from the district's jurisdiction, appoint a trustee to run the district, abolish the district, or restructure it.

Given these requirements, we must ask what capacity low-performing schools possess to help their students meet these new standards. What capacity do the district offices and state departments of education have to help the schools? Holding schools, districts, and state agencies responsible for improving student performance will produce little if they do not have or cannot rapidly develop the capacity to do the job. Denying students the credentials they need to get a job or continue their education is immoral if the institutions on which they depend cannot provide the services they need to meet the standards. Capacity is the central question evoked by the standards and accountability movement.

Perhaps the framers of the No Child Left Behind Act and its near relatives believe that educators have always known how to improve student performance and were just waiting for someone to put more pressure on them to do it, but I doubt that. I think they know that most educators have been doing their best and simply do not know how to get better results within current resource and organizational constraints. Few, if any, large city systems have been able to produce sustained high achievement for large numbers of children from low-income families. The same is true for rural areas serving low-income children. In fact, much the same is true for individual schools. This observation holds true not just for regular public schools but also for schools supported by vouchers or charter arrangements.

So the most important questions facing American education today are what, exactly, it will take to produce the transformation in student performance that the new policies call for and who will help these agencies if they lack the capacity to do it themselves? These are the questions that this chapter addresses.

The National Center on Education and the Economy (NCEE) was founded in 1988 to develop the tools, designs, professional development programs, and technical assistance that schools, districts, and states would need to meet the challenges described above. This chapter chronicles what the organization has learned about how to do that and how we have used what we have learned to get better at our work. I argue, perhaps not surprisingly, that third-party organizations, such as ours, will prove to be important in raising student achievement across the nation in the beginning of the 21st century. In that sense, then, this paper addresses two kinds of capacity: first, the capacity of schools, districts, and states to respond to the challenge of raising student achievement dramatically and, second, the capacity of such external organizations as the NCEE to help them reach that goal.

First, I share our analysis of the systems other nations use to produce consistently high levels of student achievement at scale. Chief among the attributes of these systems are coherence; well-functioning, highly integrated systems (especially instructional systems); and explicit designs for the systems. I then offer a theory to guide the development of such systems in the United States. I hope to show that no attempt to build capacity at scale directed only at the school level can succeed and that the only systems that will succeed are those that are coherent from the school through the district to the state, in much the same way that such systems are coherent in nations with more-successful education programs.

Second, I describe our early experience in trying to help districts and states develop the capacity to improve student achievement and some lessons we learned from that experience.

Third, I identify the kinds of tools that anyone who aims to build top-to-bottom capacity in educational systems will need. I argue that only sustained professional development tightly connected to school designs and aligned with standards-based instructional systems will alter classroom practice sufficiently to improve student performance in low-performing schools throughout the United States. In this section, I also argue that approaches that use only professional development and technical-assistance strategies are bound to fail and that major new investment in the development of coherent instructional systems is the necessary, though not sufficient, condition for success.

Fourth, I explain how these resources can be deployed by a third-party provider to build the capacities of schools, districts, and states so they can meet whatever challenges arise without depending on external organizations in the future. The immediate aim of this capacity-building approach is to enable the district or state to take over from external providers the task of supporting schools implementing whole-school reforms. The larger purpose is to build the capacity of the state or district to support high-performance schools throughout the district or state, with all that entails, whether or not each school thinks of itself as implementing a particular model of reform. I also show why alignment of structures and systems from the school to the state is a necessary condition for sustaining high performance at scale.

Fifth, I discuss the advantages of having third-party organizations available to provide the assistance that schools, districts, and even states need to turn our education system around. I argue not that it is impossible for schools, districts, and states to do the job by themselves but rather that these institutions are more likely to succeed with outside assistance than by going it alone.

Last, I point out the limits on educational reform posed by factors that are very nearly unique to the United States, chief among them the enormous inequalities in income that have come to characterize our economy and our unwillingness as a nation to provide the resources to our schools and communities to deal effectively with the consequences of poverty for our children.

The Need for Coherent Systems to Drive Up Educational Performance

We should begin by asking whether the job can be done at all. Consider the task the nation faces: In a nutshell, we must figure out how to help schools, districts, and states educate students to a much higher level of performance without substantially increasing the cost. That sounds impossible. What makes us think they can do it?

Years ago, a small group of us set out to create an organization that could help build the capacity to respond to the challenge just described. We were under no illusion about the enormity of the challenge but were optimistic that we could meet it for two reasons. First, a clear precedent existed for an entire sector restructuring itself to meet such a challenge. In the late 1970s and early 1980s, the U.S. business community had met a similar challenge from abroad. Second, other countries were substantially outperforming the United States in education, so we believed that using them as a benchmark would allow us to learn a great deal that would help meet the challenge at home.

If Business Could Do It . . .

In the early 1980s, American businesses had to confront the reality that manufacturers in other countries were producing higher-quality goods that took much less time to get to market and at much lower cost. Many firms went out of business as a result, but many others survived and grew stronger. Some did so by sending their production to countries in which wage rates and other operating costs were lower, but others kept production here. They redesigned the way they did almost everything and learned that they could compete and win in the new environment.

In no small measure, the resurgence of the U.S. economy stemmed from the willingness of American business to reinvent itself and to profit as it did so from the methods of its most successful competitors. We were convinced that the United States could do the same thing in the field of education. Report after report showed that students from other nations outperformed U.S. students. Since 1998, when our organization was founded, we have visited 17 nations on four continents, some of them many times, in an attempt to understand what accounts for their superior results.

Benchmarking the Best

Many businesses that succeeded in this time of testing began by trying to understand the practices of their newly effective overseas competitors. They did not copy them slavishly, but they did everything they could to learn from them. We thought that this technique, which worked so well for business, might work equally well in education. Not least among the advantages of this sort of benchmarking is the ability to see what it takes to make these approaches work, not in a hothouse environment, but at scale, in this case the scale of an entire nation.

The first of our trips to other nations took place in 1989, with visits to Germany, Sweden, Denmark, Ireland, Singapore, and Japan. All these countries had education systems that were outperforming our own. We found it fascinating that, different as these countries are, they share an important set of features that could easily account for their superior performance.

First, they had instructional systems that could properly be called systems. The list is now familiar: clear standards; high-quality examinations designed to assess whether the standards had been met; curriculum frameworks specifying what topics and concepts were to be taught at each grade level; a standard required curriculum (with very few electives), typically though the ninth or tenth year of school; instructional materials that fit the curriculum frameworks; and training designed to prepare teachers to impart the official curriculum successfully.

No less important, in most of these countries, public policy and private commitments combined to ensure that most students had access to high minimum standards of nutrition, health care, housing, and other services. If income transfer programs did not solve these problems in the family unit, the government provided the municipality or the schools the resources needed to address them. Coordination between education authorities and other units of municipal government was much closer than in the United States. Differences in resources for education among jurisdictions within the nation were smaller. The national education authority was stronger in these nations than were our education authorities at either the state or local level, and the authority of the local level (i.e., the school district) was much weaker.

When we compared these characteristics with prevailing practice in the United States, the differences were striking and illuminating. The United States had no standards for student performance, much less common standards for all students. Our teachers abhorred the idea of teaching to the test, whereas teachers in the other nations could not conceive of examinations not being used to assess whether a student had mastered the official curriculum (which was, of course, what the teacher was teaching). Because no official curriculum frameworks existed in the United States, publishers of instructional materials were forced to issue books reflecting the diverse preferences of the members of the textbook selection committees of states and districts.

Consequently, our texts treated a great range of topics at a very shallow level. In the absence of standards and curriculum frameworks, the texts had come to define the curriculum, with each teacher making his or her selection of the topics to be studied, often on the grounds of comfort with that topic. Schools of education rarely offered coherent programs to aspiring teachers, much less programs that would systematically prepare them to teach to state standards (if any such standards existed), because our traditions of academic freedom leave professors more or less free to teach what they wish to teach.

Thus the curriculum for teacher education was unhinged from the curriculum of the schools, and the school curriculum was unhinged from any standards the students were meant to achieve. As a result, tests could not be designed to measure students' performance in relation to agreed-upon standards. It became patently obvious that neither the United States nor any of its school systems had anything that could realistically be called an instructional system with parts that fit together in a harmonious whole.

Furthermore, in most of these other countries, all students had strong incentives to take tough courses and work hard in school because the standards applied to everyone and led to real consequences for the students. Students who did not meet high academic standards were denied entrance to university. Students who did not meet vocational standards were denied access to all but the least desirable jobs. In the United States, access to many jobs required no more than seventh- or eighth-grade literacy, and access to most postsecondary institutions required no more than that.

It is important to acknowledge both the strengths and limitations of this analysis. I argue here that the nations of the world have been conducting a great natural experiment and that those that have chosen to use the system I have described have been able to produce much higher levels of achievement than the U.S. system has, along the whole distribution of student performance. That is a strong argument for adapting the system they have developed for use in this country, especially since nothing else we have tried has worked very well.

We need to acknowledge, however, that the results we get, while better than we have had, may not be as impressive as the results these other nations have gotten because the distribution of income in the United States is more unequal than in any other country we have studied. Whereas students in the other countries typically have access to decent housing and good medical care, students in the United States are not guaranteed the rights to these basic necessities. Poverty looms much larger in this country as a problem that affects student performance than in most of the countries we visited. Poverty affects everything from the ability of students to read the printed page (because they need eyeglasses) to the vocabulary spoken at home to the amount of time that parents are available to their children—all important determinants of academic achievement over which the school has no control. None of these conditions are major impediments to achieving school goals as long as the aim of schooling is to sort the student population into groups of those who will succeed and those who will not, but they become enormous problems when the aim is getting all students to meet high standards.

I would argue, therefore, that we have no choice but to emulate nations that have a superior record in educating their students, and we should expect to improve our performance by doing so. We should not, however, expect to meet or beat their record as long as we lead the world—or, at least the developed nations—in income inequality and fail to take adequate measures to protect our children from the consequences of that inequality by providing them with adequate nutrition, health care, housing, and preschool education.

Among the frequently voiced objections I have heard to the idea of adapting the education policies and practices of other countries to the needs of the United States is the assertion that, "They are homogeneous, and we are extremely diverse." That is true. We are the most diverse large nation on earth in terms of racial, ethnic, and religious background. But the second most diverse large nation on earth is Australia, a nation that scored high on the most recent large-scale international comparative study of educational achievement, the Organisation for Economic Cooperation and Development Programme for International Student Assessment. Racial prejudice is clearly a problem in the United States, but we cannot claim that it is impossible for us to match the performance of the better-performing nations because of our diversity.

A Small, Underdeveloped Country Trumps the Best of the Best

Perhaps the most interesting example of the phenomenon I am describing is Singapore. Most Americans know Singapore as the tiny island nation that puts people in jail for throwing chewing gum on the sidewalk, but students of education policy know Singapore as the nation whose education system was somehow transformed, in less than 20 years, from that of a backwater Third World country into one of the most successful education systems in the world. In the first administration of the Third International Mathematics and Science Study, Singapore was among the top performers, beating out many highly developed countries in mathematics and science, both in math and science literacy and in advanced math and science.

Not only did students from Singapore beat our Advanced Placement students, but the bottom 15 percent of Singaporean students performed above the median of all students tested worldwide. Their bottom 15 percent outperformed our bottom half. These youngsters come from families that have emigrated mainly from India and Malaysia and occupy the lowest social ranks in Singapore (and are often referred to as the "sweepers"). Singapore's ability to educate these students to a world-class standard is especially important in light of what was said earlier about the unique challenges facing educators in the United States.

We visited Singapore to find out how this result was achieved. We saw very little that we would describe as a real pedagogical innovation, but the curriculum was well crafted; the teaching was well executed; and, most important, it all fit together. The Singaporean design was notable for its coherence. It was as if it had been consciously engineered so that all its pieces were connected in such a way that each element reinforced the others, and each piece was of very high quality. There are at least three secrets to the Singaporean success story in education. The first involves people—Singapore assigns its best teachers to the students who need them most, and these teachers work with their students as many hours a week as it takes to help them succeed. The other two secrets are benchmarking and design, and they are intimately related.

About two decades ago, a new minister of education was appointed in Singapore. Determined to upgrade the system radically, he did something characteristically Singaporean: He created a team to benchmark best education practices worldwide. The team was expected not only to identify the best practices but also to sift through them carefully, selecting those that could be used in the design of a comprehensive system that would suit Singapore. They did not want effective pieces of an education system; they wanted a coherent, effective system. And they got it.

Systems, Coherence, and Design

These three elements—system, coherence, and design—are essential to my argument. They are in fact three ways of expressing the same idea. Systems, when they work properly, are by definition coherent, but coherent systems do not just happen. They must be designed. If we want high student performance across the board, at scale, the watchwords must be coherence, system, and design.

The idea of coherence is worth lingering over for a moment. In the late 1990s, I spent an afternoon with my colleague Judy Codding in Singapore's Center for Instructional Technology. We went there because we had heard from the people in their schools how valuable the products of this center were. Imagine my amazement when I realized that the center was producing only videotape and had not yet begun production of any software. Even the video was hardly revolutionary. It was, in fact, a little dull by my standards, but the reason for the enthusiasm of the teachers we had met was immediately clear. The video was closely tied to the standard curriculum. Because it portrayed visually parts of the standard curriculum that were hard for students to visualize unaided—sometimes using graphics and sometimes using other kinds of visual images (e.g., slow motion photography)—the teachers thought it added value to the curriculum, and they could use it with a minimum of training.

This stands in contrast to most of the software produced for U.S. classrooms. Some of it is imaginative and engaging, but the material that is most imaginative and engaging is the least likely to fit with the texts that the teacher uses as a framework for daily lessons and even less likely to fit into the state accountability framework. Indeed, it is almost impossible for national software producers to make products that fit because there are simply too many texts and too many standards. On paper, of course, their software matches all standards and all texts. In reality, it matches nothing. So the humble videotape in Singapore turns out to be much more valuable to the Singaporean teacher than much more sophisticated and expensive technology is to the American teacher.

This example points to problems that occur with many educational products—books, videos, and software. It hardly matters whether we consider hastily developed materials from little-known publishers or carefully evaluated, research-based products created by government-financed developers. If, when the product reaches real classrooms, it is used not the way the developer intended and the controlled research design contemplated but is cropped and trimmed, pushed and pulled, taken apart and reassembled until it is compatible with existing texts and fits the budget, the time, the testing regime, the accountability scheme, and the training of the teacher, it will bear little resemblance to the innovation its originators intended. The Singaporean video worked because it fit the framework of time, schedule, curriculum, texts, ancillary materials, and all the rest in Singaporean classrooms.

Real coherence goes far beyond the formalistic alignment of standards, curriculum, and assessment. It is what you get when culture and all the formal elements, great and small, of the environment are in harmony with each other. It is what happens when classroom discipline reflects the moral stance of the district. It is what happens when the reading level of the texts in all the subjects in the curriculum correlates with the actual reading level of the students. It is what happens when the school makes sure the parents know what standards the students are expected to meet, how their children are doing, and what they can do to help where their help is most needed. It is what happens when the master schedule is set up so that student time is allocated to the tasks on which they are furthest behind and so that teacher time is allocated to the students who need the most help. Finally, it is what happens when tests or examinations are designed to assess whether students learned what they were supposed to learn from the courses they took, which were in turn derived from a curriculum that is referenced to the standards they are supposed to meet. It is a matter of making sure that every aspect of the school's functioning is organized to advance its stated purposes.

Such a system most emphatically does not entail lockstep curriculum or education by state *diktat*. It has to do with form. There are symphonies by Mozart and symphonies by Shostakovich. They are both recognizable as symphonies, but no one would confuse the composers when listening to them. It is form that distinguishes them. Within the form, great variation is possible. Without form, cacophony is inevitable.

No one would suggest that because both Mozart and Shostakovich obeyed the rules defining what a symphony is that they were "paint-by-number" composers. Like these two composers, Singaporean teachers also operate within a certain form (the form defined by the Singaporean standards and curriculum framework) but have a great deal of latitude to decide how they are going to teach the material in their syllabus, just as Mozart and Shostakovich produced very different pieces within the same symphonic form. I am suggesting here that form—or structure—makes fine teaching possible on a sustained, widespread basis. It also enables the production of instructional materials that will yield excellent results, day in and day out, in classrooms organized as the creators of the materials envisioned when they constructed them. Structure permits students to move from school to school and district to district without becoming utterly lost. Coherence of this kind is not an innovation, such as a new method of teaching reading. It is a necessary condition.

Based on what we learned from the countries we studied, we can confidently say that achieving high student performance across the board is impossible unless a highly coherent instructional system is in place. It is also important to ensure that the management and organization of the education system, right down to the schools and right up to the top, are configured to support the standards, curriculum, and assessments on which the instructional system is based. It is no less important to ensure that the incentives for both students and faculty reinforce the goals of the instructional system.

Our research in other countries tells us that coherence does not happen by accident. Neither is it the product of professional development, even the best professional development. Professional development does not by itself produce coherent systems of instructional materials. It does not link incentives to goals. It does not create forms of governance and school organization that are aligned with the structure of sound instructional systems. Coherence is, instead, the result of conscious design. Each element of the education system must be designed to support and reinforce the others, and all must be designed to support the goal of high achievement for all students.

Whose Capacity—To Do What?

In other nations, responsibility for the performance of the whole system rests with the ministry of education. In the United States, no agency of government has assumed (or been assigned) the responsibilities typically under the purview of the ministries of education in other countries. Such ministries are responsible for setting student performance standards, developing national examinations matched to the standards, defining a national curriculum for the first ten grades (including frameworks specifying the topics and concepts to be taught at each grade level in each subject), ensuring that all texts and other instructional materials are keyed to the official curriculum, defining school-leaving standards that also function as university entrance standards, guaranteeing that all teachers are trained to teach the official curriculum, and providing high-quality training and technical assistance to schools that fail to serve their students well. It is, in short, the ministry that is the "keeper of the design."

State Departments of Education: The Juxtaposition of Constitutional Authority and Political Weakness. In every state of the United States, constitutional responsibility for elementary and secondary education rests with the state, not the school district or the school. So one would expect the state departments of education to perform the functions that, in other countries, are performed by ministries of education. Although some states have strong state departments of education, most state departments are weak when measured against the ministries of education in other countries. This is no accident. Suspicion of government has long been an element of U.S. political tradition, and that suspicion grows in proportion to the distance between the seat of government and the citizens who are affected by its policies. It is nowhere stronger than in the arena of education. Added to this basic distrust of government as the overseer of education is evidence that, in many states, the wealthier, more powerful school districts have seen it as in their interest to keep the formal powers of the state department of education weak and its staff small and badly paid. For all these reasons, our state departments of education have largely been restricted to getting state and federal funds to the districts and performing certain narrowly prescribed regulatory functions. Historically, no state department of education has been responsible for the full range of functions that ministries of education typically perform.

This is changing. In the last few years, with the advent of the standards movement, many state departments of education have been inching toward actually using the powers they were granted in the Constitution, rather than delegating them to others, but they are new at it and typically lack the funds, personnel, and experience they need to do it well.

School Districts: The Seat of Political Power in Education. In our system of education, the real power has, up to now, resided at the district level. It is the district that hires, fires, and often assigns and promotes the school faculty. It is the district that controls the school funds and, to a large degree, the school curriculum. But, despite their high degree of effective control over the school, districts do not function like ministries of education. They have rarely set explicit standards for student performance, established assessment systems for measuring student performance against the standards, built curriculum frameworks to specify what topics and concepts will be taught, ensured the development of instructional materials matched to a standard curriculum, or created programs to train the teachers to teach a district curriculum. Even when school districts have done these things, they rarely do them in harmony. The capacity of school districts, even very large ones, to perform the functions just described as well as they are performed by the ministries of most developed nations is almost nonexistent.

The Schools: Overtaxed Teachers Amid Controlled Chaos. Now consider the school. Some education reformers insist that the teachers' professional responsibility includes developing their own standards, building their own assessments, creating their own curriculum frameworks, writing their own instructional materials, and designing all the instruction they offer their students. This approach is akin to expecting physicians to develop their own pharmaceuticals. We know of no nation in the world that has managed to create a successful education system this way. Teaching, when well done, is a demanding, exhausting job. The functions just described are very expensive and time-consuming. To expect teachers to do it all is to expect teachers to do more than is humanly possible.

In the majority of American schools, the pieces simply do not fit together, and the teachers in these schools can do very little about it. American educators have rarely seen this as a problem. The faculties of many U.S. schools are accustomed to a kind of controlled chaos. For them, it is unremarkable that the tests they use do not match the state standards, that the textbooks do not match the tests, and that teachers are given credit for professional education unrelated to the needs of the school. U.S. schools are the setting for a constant stream of improvement projects, many of which owe their existence to the enthusiasms of individual teachers, most of which can be expected to work at cross purposes to one another, and few of which are expected to be elements of a concerted, multifaceted, multiyear plan to improve performance at that school. The irony is that low-performing schools are likely to be the setting for still more such special projects and programs, still more helping agents from outside the schools, and still more nostrums, each of which contends with the others for the time and attention of an already beleaguered staff. In a situation of this sort, only the strongest of leaders can impose order on what has become the antithesis of a coherent program. In our experience, poor leadership and controlled chaos are the defining characteristics of low-performing schools. They go hand in hand.

It is not difficult to find schools that are more successful than the average in even the worst districts. They tend to be the work of renegade principals marching to their own drummers. Sooner or later, these unusually talented and driven individuals tire, and, when they do, their schools inevitably revert, in the hands of ordinary, mortal principals, to the relative chaos and unexciting performance of most of the schools around them. The reality is that schools, let alone districts, are in no position to perform the functions of a ministry of education. It has to be done at a higher level; if it is not done at a higher level, nothing that is done at the school level will last very long.

Building Capacity to Operate a Coherent System at Scale: The Story of the America's Choice School Design

In 1992, a new organization, New American Schools (NAS),[2] invited groups to come forward with ideas for "break the mold" designs for schools. We decided to respond to this announcement because we emphatically agreed that design held the key to superior school performance. The NAS announcement, however, was based on the premise that schools could succeed without making significant changes in the districts of which they are a part. This conception of the problem, we thought, ignored the reality that districts and states hold the key to school performance because they establish the rules, set the culture, and control the resources for the schools. We submitted a proposal to provide services to districts and states intended to enable them to field a team of senior people in the district or state department of education that we would train to develop and support a process of comprehensive school reform.

The emphasis in our proposal was on the word *comprehensive*. Our conception of what that word meant was summarized in a kind

---

[2] See Chapter Sixteen in this volume.

of litany, as follows: (1) Without explicit student performance standards, there would be no target to shoot at, and without measures of performance against those standards, the standards would be useless; but (2) if no change in instruction occurred, there would be no reason for student performance to change, so we would have to attend to the curriculum and other aspects of the learning environment; but (3) if the management and organization of the school did not focus on student performance, every attempt to improve performance would be defeated; but (4) even if all these things happened inside the school, students who come to school hungry, who have no home, and who, in other ways, lack essential supports and services will not learn; and, finally, (5) if we fail to engage parents and the community, the whole effort will fail. We called these five premises our design tasks because each of these arenas required a carefully thought-through design, and all the designs needed to be welded together into an integrated, coherent system.

We thought that we could help the teams that the districts and states assembled develop good designs and implement them in each of these areas by identifying "best-of-breed" organizations in each area to deliver the professional development and technical assistance the districts and states needed. So, we reached out to such organizations as the Learning Research and Development Center (LRDC) at the University of Pittsburgh to partner with us on curriculum, the Xerox Corporation to partner with us on leadership and management, Apple Computer to partner with us on technology, and the Center for the Study of Social Policy to partner with us to help schools make the right connections with the social service system.

The reviewers NAS assembled were kind enough to overlook the fact that we had written a proposal that did not conform to the criteria specified in the request for proposals, and we won the largest contract they awarded. New York City, Pittsburgh, Rochester (N.Y.), San Diego, Vermont, Washington State, Kentucky, and other cities and states joined with us, naming teams to be trained and committing to a standards-based approach to comprehensive reform.

Focusing on School Design

Unfortunately, this approach failed to produce the effects on student performance we were seeking. In retrospect, it is difficult to imagine what made us believe we could effect major changes in the schools in a large district by instituting a program of intensive professional development involving a half-dozen senior people in the central office. All we had to offer them were general principles. We had no instructional system, no school designs, and no blueprint that would enable them to make order out of chaos. We did not then know that we would need all these things and much more to succeed. We did know that we were making very little difference in student perform-ance, and we knew by then that we would have to get much closer to the schools to affect student performance. By then, mostly because of our continuing visits to other nations, we were beginning to appreci-ate the power of the idea of coherence in the school program.

So, when the Obey-Porter legislation—establishing the Com-prehensive School Reform Demonstration program—was passed,[3] we created the America's Choice School Design. Building on our experi-ence with the program we had been running and what we had learned in our wide-ranging research on effective education systems abroad, we created designs for elementary, middle, K–8, and high schools.

To some, it might have looked as though we had abandoned our earlier stance and decided that the path to raising student achieve-ment on a larger scale was to go school by school, more or less ignoring the district and state levels of government and administra-tion, but that was not the case. We were still convinced that the winning approach would have to be comprehensive and systemic, and we still believed that only the states and districts could create the conditions for widespread improvement of student performance in the schools.

---

[3] The sponsors of this legislation were representatives David Obey (D-Wis.) and John Porter (R-Ill.).

What We Learned from Round One

We had, however, learned a great deal from these early efforts. First, we learned that we had too many partners. Each of the partners mentioned earlier, although a powerhouse in its own domain, had its own view of the world, its own methods, and its own organizational needs. We had been busy, it turned out, substituting one form of incoherence for another. The idea that the districts and states needed to build coherent systems of instruction, management, organization, and so on was right, but we were not helping them by simply pointing them toward a set of organizations with expertise in these fields because they did not have the capacity to put it all together, with or without our help. It was as if we had given them plans for a new house and a catalogue of preferred vendors of materials and services. They needed a general contractor.

Second, we learned that, although all the design tasks are important, those that constitute the instructional system are the most important because the ability of the teachers to get students to meet high standards depends absolutely on the quality of the instructional system. American teachers, especially in low-performing schools, need and cannot make much progress without a fully specified instructional system, including the design, the standards, the assessments, the instructional materials, and all the training and professional development needed to make the system work. All these elements must be worked out before attempting to implement the system in schools. To our surprise, the curriculum materials available on the American market for this purpose were not suitable for use in a standards-based system. Although publishers of texts and other instructional systems claim that their materials are correlated with the standards students are expected to achieve, we discovered, for reasons that will be made clear below, that the existing materials would not do the job. New systems of instructional materials, designed expressly for this purpose, would be needed. We concluded that neither we nor our education partners would succeed unless we made a multiyear, multimillion-dollar commitment to standards-based curriculum development.

Third, we had the wrong business model for going to scale. When we got our first contract from NAS, we reserved a substantial portion of the money to share with district and state partners, on the theory that, just as we had expenses in connection with the work, so would they, and it was only fair to share our resources with them. This model cannot, however, be scaled up. As the number of schools using the model rises, the money available to pay for the schools to use it will run out, no matter how big the pot is. On the other hand, if the schools and districts must pay for the services they get and feel that they are receiving good value for their money, there is no limit to the number of schools that can be served. So, when we created the America's Choice School Design, we changed the business model. Henceforth, we would seek foundation and government funds for research and development and would charge our school, district, and state customers the full cost of delivering the training, professional development, and technical assistance needed to implement the designs. We were poised to go to scale.

Another point should be made here. We had learned that, as with all the "soft" money that schools get, they were happy to have it as long as it lasted, but, because they assumed it would go away, they did not build any plans around it or reshape any of their operations around it. Paying for the work turned out to be a surefire way to ensure that our efforts would come to naught. Almost instantly, our relationship with our customers changed. When we instituted the new policy of making our customers pay for the services they received, a few who had gotten used to our paying for everything became disenchanted and left. Most of our former customers made the transition without complaint, some saying they had expected this change years ago. New customers simply assumed they would have to pay and were thus not surprised by this requirement. Most important, we discovered that our hunch was right. Once our customers had to pay for the services, they had to justify the cost to themselves and to those who paid the bills and, consequently, were much more likely to make the changes needed to implement the designs fully because the people paying the bills wanted to see results. As soon as our customers started to pay for what they had formerly gotten for free, implementation improved markedly.

The fourth problem we had encountered in our work with the districts and states was that we were too far from the schools to affect student achievement. This was actually a complex issue. The states and districts saw the problem as lack of capacity, all right, but not their lack of capacity. They thought the lack of capacity was in the schools. So, while the states and districts were happy to participate in the professional development we offered and to accept our technical assistance, they did not, by and large, think that they needed to change the way they organized and managed themselves. Also, the people we were working with, although highly placed, were not typically line managers, and it was the line managers who called the tune in the district or state. In addition, they were too far away from the schools, with too many links in the chain between them and teachers who could directly influence student achievement.

Finally, the argument we could make for radical changes in the way the state or district did its work was far too weak—it was logical but abstract, hardly the stuff that drives bold changes.

The last point is very important. Educators, at every level, are justifiably suspicious of people who try to sell them ideas. They are even suspicious of educational research results. But they are not suspicious of what they can see with their own eyes. Teachers dragged into our program by their colleagues become enthusiasts not because of what we say to them in our professional development programs but because, when they use the tools we give them in the ways that we suggest, they see students doing things they never thought the students could do. Principals become believers when their most-experienced, hard-bitten teachers tell them that the performance of their students exceeds anything they have seen in 30 years on the job. Likewise, school board members and superintendents throw their weight behind our work when they walk into classrooms and are stunned by the work they see students doing. Data on student performance from independent, objective, third-party researchers and evaluators is absolutely vital, but there is no substitute for seeing high-quality student work over and over again, especially from students from whom the least has always been expected.

To get this result, we realized we had to work directly with schools. It is all very well, we discovered, to provide professional development to district-level staff, and even to school principals, on the basis of "what the research says." If the presentation is done well, the audience will be polite and even enthusiastic, but enthusiasm disappears when the time comes for action because, no matter how provocative and interesting the presentations and materials, practicing educators are rarely convinced that a new approach will work when the chips are down. If this is true in general, it is doubly true of low-performing schools, which are the schools we are most concerned about. We had to demonstrate, in the schools, that we had what it takes for schools to improve student performance dramatically. Then, and only then, would we have the legitimacy to walk into a district office or state department of education as consultants on what it would take to go to scale districtwide or statewide. We had to prove ourselves, and we had to do it at scale—in lots of schools in lots of places.

Building Capacity at Every Level: From School to State

Our aims had not changed at all, but our strategies for achieving them had changed greatly. In a nutshell, our original conception of what it would take to build capacity into the system to sustain widespread improvement in student performance was decidedly anemic. None of this should have surprised us, given what we knew about other countries that had experienced more success.

If the question is whether one gets greatest leverage at the state, district, or local level, the answer is that one can begin anywhere, but, to get strong effects at scale, the system must be coherent and aligned from the school to the state. For historical reasons, none of these—school, district, or state—has, by itself, the capacity to make that happen. For us, then, the sensible place to begin was with designs that could be used at the school level to produce results, in the form of test scores and student work, that would give us the credibility we needed to work at all three levels. We set out to do just that.

A Note on Philosophy

We will describe below what we learned about the kinds of tools needed to build the capacity we think necessary. First, however, we need to take a step to one side, as it were, to discuss the philosophical stance from which we approach this work.

We take it as given that the goal of schooling is to educate students so that they not only have the basic skills—new and old—but who can be said to be deeply thoughtful, widely knowledgeable, highly skilled, committed to doing what is both right and good, and able to enjoy fully the highest achievements of human creative effort. We want people who can think for themselves, who can both lead and follow, and who can cope well when confronted with the unexpected. We hope to produce graduates who are tolerant, understand the roots of our freedoms, are prepared to take part in the political life of our nation, are willing and able to contribute actively to their communities, and who have what it takes to be good parents and form strong families.

We believe that an education that has aims of this sort—education that places great value on thinking, creativity, and ethical and moral action—cannot be provided through instruction of a mechanical sort or by teachers simply doing what they have been told to do. This description of what we want for our students clearly requires a thinking curriculum, and it says a great deal about what we expect of teachers.

I say this because the nature of the education one values and one's conception of what it means to be a teacher profoundly affect the approach that one chooses for building capacity in educational institutions for raising student performance at scale. A curriculum that is truly a thinking curriculum demands well-thought-out standards and assessments that reward student work that demonstrates a thorough command and deep understanding of the concepts of each discipline. Building capacity among school faculties is a different task if one believes that teachers must determine what to teach at any given moment and how to teach it rather than that teachers must follow a detailed script as they make their way through the school day.

None of this is said invidiously. People for whom we have great respect hold different views on these issues, but the views I have shared here color everything we do, as well as the way we interpret our experience.

The Tools Needed for Building Capacity

More than a decade of experience tells us that anyone who wants to develop the capacity of any level of government to raise student achievement steadily and on a broad scale to internationally benchmarked standards will need to have the following tools.

Instructional Systems

The first trips we took to Germany, Denmark, Sweden, Ireland, Japan, and Singapore were organized as part of the research program of the Commission on the Skills of the American Workforce, created by the NCEE in 1989. That research program convinced us that coherent, standards-based instructional systems had been the key to success for nations that outperformed the United States in education.

The kind of standards and examinations that attracted our attention are epitomized by the International General Secondary Curriculum Examinations offered by Cambridge University in the United Kingdom. These examinations, based on the current British standards and prescribed curriculum, are taken in about 140 nations around the globe, including Singapore. They are set to syllabi that are deeply thoughtful and, while explicit, still give teachers enough latitude to choose where they will go deep and where they will go broad. We would wager that any teacher in the United States, given a chance to review these syllabi, would agree that they constitute a curriculum well worth teaching and that any student who mastered such a curriculum would be justified in thinking himself or herself well educated. The final score is not based solely on the score on the end-of-course examination but also on what the Cambridge people call course work, scores the teacher assigns to student work according to guidelines in the syllabus. These scores are monitored by the examiners at Cambridge, to ensure that all are anchored to the same scale.

The examinations are not multiple-choice, machine-scored tests. They require extensive writing. Because they are set to a particular syllabus, they assume that the student has read particular books, investigated particular topics, and studied particular concepts and issues. After each year's examination is completed, the exam and examples of passing papers are released.

With such a system, students and teachers have a very good idea of what topics and concepts need to be taught. They know which books must be read, and they know what they will be examined on. It is possible to prepare, and effort pays off. The standard is clear, but one cannot prepare for the test by memorizing the answers to particular questions, because no one knows what the questions on a particular test will be. The only way to prepare is to master the curriculum thoroughly. No test I have seen in the United States approaches the quality of the Cambridge University examinations or their counterparts in other nations we have visited.

When the work of the commission was completed, I asked Lauren Resnick and her staff at LRDC to join with NCEE to create a program to develop academic performance standards and standards-referenced examinations that could be used in the United States to produce results like those we had seen in Europe and Asia. The result was the New Standards consortium, a program of research and development on standards and testing involving our two organizations, a half-dozen big cities, and more than 20 states, funded by The Pew Charitable Trusts, the John D. and Catherine T. MacArthur Foundation, the Atlantic Philanthropic Foundation, and the U.S. Department of Education's Office of Educational Research and Improvement.[4]

The work of New Standards continues, but its first phase ended with the production of a set of performance standards in English language arts, mathematics, science, and applied learning for Grades 4,

---

[4] This organization has since become the Institute of Education Sciences.

8, and 10 and a set of standards-referenced examinations in English language arts and mathematics, published by Harcourt Educational Measurement, for Grades 4, 8, and 10. Following the first phase, we created a set of grade-by-grade standards in speaking, listening, reading, and writing for the primary grades. Another version of these standards was then created for English language learners. Science examinations matching the standards for middle school and high school are forthcoming. These New Standards products represented a clean break with U.S. practice with respect to both standards and testing.

Before New Standards began, virtually all standards in the United States, to the extent that standards existed, were content standards. That is, they consisted of narrative statements about what students should know and be able to do. When we were assembling our math team, two people, one a middle school mathematics teacher and the other a professor of graduate mathematics at a major university, looked at a section of the National Council of Teachers of Mathematics standards for school mathematics. Simultaneously, each of them observed, "That is what I teach in my classroom." Clearly, they did not teach the same mathematics. They reacted as they did because of the necessarily abstract nature of the content standards.

Standards-based education aims to get all students to a high level of performance. Doing this is impossible if neither the student nor the teacher has a clear conception of what that standard of performance is. The distinct contribution of New Standards to the development of standards-based assessment was the idea of creating performance measures that include examples of high-quality student work as a way of demonstrating exactly what students should be trying to achieve and how they should be evaluated. The standards we developed consist not only of narrative statements of what students should know and be able to do but also of examples of student work that meets the standards, with commentary about each that points out specific aspects of the work that meet specific standards and parts of standards. The Australians had used student work to provide occasional illustrations of their standards, but New Standards took this idea one step further by creating a structure for the standards with student work at the center.

The student work in the standards was produced in response to a specific task. The standards describe the assignment and the conditions under which the students worked. The New Standards reference examinations are based, at their core, on the sort of tasks that were developed to help students meet the standards. Thus, the standards and the examinations are seamlessly aligned; the examinations reflect the kind of curriculum needed to enable the students to succeed on the examinations. The examinations themselves include short-answer, multiple-choice questions, but they also include a requirement to respond to complex tasks or assignments with long, written answers. All this stands in sharp contrast to the kinds of standards and tests in wide use then and now in the states and school districts. Most state standards are still content standards, not performance standards. Thus, most state standards are not very useful to teachers developing curriculum or to teachers and students trying to understand how good is good enough. Many states continue to use relatively inexpensive forms of fill-in-the blank tests that, far from reflecting the kind of curriculum that would get students to high standards, encourage preparing for the test in ways that effectively destroy good curriculum.

Teachers elsewhere in the developed world are mystified when told that American teachers deem it unprofessional to teach to the test. They cannot conceive of tests that are unhinged from any particular curriculum. Neither can they conceive of tests of writing that fail to require a student to provide an extended writing sample. In these countries, tests are examinations, of the sort described above, designed to assess the degree to which the student has mastered the curriculum the teacher is teaching. The student provides extensive written responses to questions in the examination, and the written tests are frequently supplemented by oral examinations, often administered by the student's teacher and a teacher from another school. It is impossible to beat the test by memorizing answers. The student must really know the material. On the American scene, the closest thing to this kind of test is the Advanced Placement test, which costs roughly ten to twenty times as much as the typical American test.

More than $40 million was invested in the development of the initial set of New Standards products. This is one indication that development of sound, internationally benchmarked standards and tests is very expensive, beyond the means of almost all districts and most states. The research we have done in other nations shows conclusively, however, that a standards-based system of education simply cannot be run successfully without high-quality standards and examinations.

We involved 600 teachers around the nation (identified by the departments of education as the best in their states) in the work of New Standards. The effect of this innovation on students and teachers when the teachers tried the assessment tasks was electric. Students said to their teachers, "Oh, now I know what you want me to do. I can do that!" Teachers saw their students doing things they never thought the students could do. Eventually, teachers learned to post the standards in their classrooms, along with the work of their students. Students internalized the standards and rubrics used for judging their work. They could explain in which respects their work met the standards and where it fell short and could talk about what they needed to do to ensure that their work would meet the standards. Teachers began to talk about the work that their students were producing and asking each other how they were able to get their students to produce this or that. Their practice, and their efforts to improve their practice, began to revolve around the standards and the work. Suddenly, student work had become the focal point for the efforts of both student and teacher, the effect of which was to orient teachers toward improving their professional practice as never before.

There was just one problem. The teachers in this group of 600 kept telling us they could not find any curriculum materials they could use to get their students to the standards. Lauren Resnick, codirector of New Standards, thought the teachers were simply unaware of the existence of the materials that would do the job. Under this theory, our job was simply to find the materials and point the teachers in the right direction.

Others of us were not so sure. The team from the NCEE decided to put it to the test, asking subject-matter experts for their recommendations for the best materials to support a curriculum intended to get students to internationally benchmarked standards, such as those the New Standards consortium had developed. Nothing the experts found fit the criteria. The teachers, it turned out, were right. The reason we could not assemble a powerful standards-based curriculum from available materials involves the nature of the American market for instructional materials. Other nations, as mentioned earlier, have, over the years, developed curriculum frameworks to match their standards. These frameworks specify, at a minimum, which topics and concepts are to be taught at each grade level in each subject in the required curriculum.

The best of these frameworks are carefully drawn, in the following way. First, the standards specify what the students must know and be able to do at the end of their basic education (not, by the way, at every grade). The framers then work back from that endpoint to determine what must be learned to produce that outcome. Each topic and concept necessary to achieve the standard is arrayed in the logical order in which it must be taught, so everything prerequisite to something else comes before that topic or concept. Only what is essential to this set of building blocks is included. The curriculum specified in the most powerful of these frameworks is carefully balanced among skills and knowledge, concepts, and problem-solving or applications. In nations that possess such frameworks, closely tied to their standards and to their assessment systems, publishers of instructional materials would not dream of producing materials that did not match the framework because they would have no customers.

In the United States, however, we have rarely had such frameworks at any level of our education system. Consequently, publishers of educational materials have been forced to develop texts and other materials that would appeal to the widest possible audience, and the only way to do that has been to poll representative teachers' committees throughout the nation, asking them what they would like to see in the texts. Since no common framework exists, the answers cover an enormous range of topics, subjects, concepts, authors, and so on. To avoid losing sales, the publisher must somehow get it all in there. The result is an enormous collection of the biggest, most expensive textbooks in the world. But inside these texts, each topic and concept is treated only briefly and superficially.

The curriculum materials funded by the National Science Foundation generally go deeper and pay more attention to concepts than do the more traditional materials. Even with these materials, however, it remains difficult to decide what standards have been used to shape any given section of the materials and still more difficult to bring to the surface the relevant concepts. In the American experience, Advanced Placement courses come closest to the model we are describing, but they nonetheless lack some of the important features of the Cambridge examination system courses and, in any event, are offered to only a minority of American students.

We discovered these problems with teaching materials in the United States when we tried to understand what explained the observation that teachers could find no materials to help their students meet the standards. Not long after we did that research, the results of the Third International Math and Science Study were released. According to the authors of that study, the single most important explanation for the poor performance of American students was the character of the American curriculum, which the authors characterized as "a mile wide and an inch deep."

The observation of the 600 teachers who could not find materials that could get their students to the standards could not have been more important. The $40 million that New Standards had spent on getting the standards and examinations right was not enough. NCEE committed to spending whatever time and money would be needed to design a curriculum for its America's Choice School Design program and to create the necessary materials in English language arts and mathematics. We did that because we knew that the schools in our network could not hope to duplicate the performance of the best-performing countries unless our country had a matched system of standards, instructional materials, and assessments equal to the best in the world. To build the capacity to get the job done, we would have to build the curriculum materials because no commercial publisher could afford to do so until someone had shown that the investment would pay off. We assumed that it would cost the NCEE at least as

much to do this as it had cost New Standards to build its performance standards and reference examinations, but we believed we had
no choice.

We will not describe our curriculum development program in
detail here, but it is important to make clear that we are not simply
discussing the development of a text series in each subject. The aim is
to put together a whole instructional system, a system designed to get
students to the standards no matter where they start. To do that, we
have had to start with the standards, develop a curriculum framework
of the kind already described, and derive a set of instructional materials from the framework, grade by grade. To make the materials as
powerful as possible, we have built them to fit a specified set of classroom rituals and routines, generic activities that occur in an expected
order as the class proceeds. In the process, we have embedded assessments that match the standards and the New Standards Reference
Examinations in the curriculum, and we have designed professional
development for teachers to match the instructional materials for the
students.

A curriculum designed to begin when a student is in kindergarten and to bring that student up to a college-ready standard by the
end of tenth grade (that is the specification for the America's Choice
School Design) will be more demanding than 80 or 90 percent of
American school curricula. So most American students are well
behind where our framework says they should be when they begin
our curriculum.

We therefore must have a set of safety-net programs—double-
period courses at key intervals, tutoring programs, summer school
programs, and so on—intimately tied to the curriculum that can help
students who are several grade levels behind catch up as quickly as
possible. An associated system is needed to assess the performance of
each student at frequent intervals against the standards and to signal
to the teacher which students are falling behind in which areas, so the
teacher can invoke the safety-net features that a student needs—and
only these features—as soon as the student needs them. We are in the
process of building all this now. It is expensive, difficult, and time-
consuming. The research literature needed to accomplish it is full of

holes, a legacy of the lack of attention the United States has paid in recent decades to the curricular needs of students who fall behind.

All these components and more need to be designed as parts of a single integrated and coherent instructional system. This idea sometimes makes American teachers uneasy because they conjure an image of lessons scripted by someone in a remote office somewhere. It is the system, not the lessons, that needs to be fully designed. One need only look at the Cambridge syllabi and exams or the actual operation of a Japanese or Danish classroom to see almost instantly that the system assumes a high degree of professionalism on the part of the teacher and gives the teacher a great deal of discretion in deciding how to meet the needs of individual students. A syllabus—if it is the right kind of syllabus—is not a script. In the field of medicine, in which no one would dream of scripting the behavior of physicians or questioning their professional standing, physicians are not, as I pointed out before, expected to invent their own pharmaceuticals, create their own procedures, invent their own standards of practice, and so on. What the physician is expected to do is bring expertise and experience to bear on the diagnosis of the problem an individual patient presents, and, on the basis of that diagnosis, to formulate a course of treatment, correcting along the way to take account of developments as they unfold. We expect a teacher to perform in a perfectly analogous way. To make that work, however, we needed to formulate a set of school designs to create the structures within which the teacher can succeed.

School Designs

The school designs we created are described in detail elsewhere.[5] The short description here should, however, give the reader a sense of their key features.

All the schools in the network are asked to use the New Standards Performance Standards and the New Standards Reference Examinations. When we developed the standards, few states had their

---

[5] This information is available on the NCEE Web site.

own standards. Now all but one does. We explain to the schools that join our network that we expect them to use the New Standards Performance Standards as extensions of their state standards. Once our performance standards have been aligned to the state standards, our standards can be used to set performance expectations with respect to the state content standards. Students take both their own state examinations and the New Standards Reference Examinations. We have carefully designed the report forms for the reference examinations so they provide feedback keyed to the standards, making them useful for diagnostic purposes.

Teachers in our program learn how to organize their classrooms to be standards-based. With respect to the physical aspects of the classroom, this means, among many other things, hanging on the walls of the classroom the relevant standards, the rubrics for judging student work against the standards, the work of students in the class that meets the standards, and other work that is coming along. At a deeper level, it means communicating to all the expectation that they will reach the standards, helping students to internalize the standards, allocating time and other resources in relation to what is needed to get the class to meet the standards, selecting instructional materials based on the standards, and much more.

The English language arts curriculum and the mathematics curriculum are built around the materials we are producing, which are, in turn, matched to the standards and the examinations. We have designed these courses for students making steady progress toward the standards, grade by grade, but we have also designed double-period courses at key points in the grade sequence to enable students who are behind by several grade levels to catch up. These courses focus on essential concepts, skills, and knowledge, omitting everything that is extraneous. Thus, rather than remedial courses, they are actually accelerated courses.

All courses are built around a set of rituals and routines, of which some are common to all mathematics courses and others are common to all English language arts courses. In English, these routines include tasks that small groups can usefully accomplish while the teacher is working with individuals and small groups. Once the students learn the routines in the first grade, they discover that they simply continue through the grades, so the students know what to expect when they advance through the grades, and their new teachers need not spend months acclimating their students to a unique way of doing things.

The routines include a standard sequence of activities in each class for each subject. The rituals include standard activities. For example, one of the activities in the mathematics program is the "Say Why" ritual, in which the students are asked to say why a particular fact in mathematics is true or why a particular procedure works. This ritual establishes an expectation that they will understand not only what to do but also why it works, and it also provides students with the opportunity to practice explaining the mathematics behind what they are doing.

The designs address many aspects of school organization, including the idea of having teachers follow groups of students through the grades, a system of advisement, a "house" system for breaking up large schools into smaller units so teachers will know their students, and approaches to developing schools' master schedules that facilitate the use of the safety-net system.

The America's Choice School Designs include a Planning for Results system that helps school faculty develop plans for school operations based on careful analysis of data on student performance and other key indicators. Planning for Results also includes disciplined approaches for establishing goals and targets and for searching for better ways to accomplish the goals and reach the targets. The Planning for Results system is built on an analytical structure that facilitates the development of nested targets at the student, class, grade, school, and district levels.

The designs also stipulate a distributed leadership structure for the school that ensures that individuals on the leadership team take personal responsibility for the functions vital to improving student performance. Because these are defined roles in the school, we can design the training for the people who occupy these roles with confidence that someone in the school has been assigned to do the work they are being trained for. Parent and community engagement play an important part in the designs, as do student discipline and student advisement.

America's Choice School Designs exist for elementary schools, middle schools, and high schools. The elementary design clearly distinguishes the primary grades from the upper elementary grades and includes elements in the primary curriculum and organizational design intended to ensure that all students emerge from the primary grades reading and writing well. The high school design sharply distinguishes the lower-division years from the upper-division years. Students in the lower division (Grades 9 and 10) study a standard curriculum intended to ensure that, by the time the students leave the lower division, they have the skills needed to enter college without remediation in mathematics, reading, or writing. When the students have met that standard, they can proceed to an upper-division program (Grades 11 and 12) that offers several different versions of "early college" or can go directly to community college or to technical college, if they want a technical education, in their upper secondary years. Thus, all students in the America's Choice system are prepared for college.

Schools are more than collections of structures, procedures, and tools. They are also lively cultures—places with their own values, relationships, and ways of doing things that are just as important as the formal system in shaping the quality of students' lives and the education they get. Thus, parts of the designs are intended to address these aspects of the school, too.

We noted above our commitment to the view that teachers, to be successful, must be treated as professionals, people whose work depends on professional judgment that only the person on the spot can exercise. Nevertheless, our experience has been that the faculties of the schools with which we work are constantly pressing us to make the design and its requirements increasingly detailed. They want us to fill in the blanks wherever possible. The more troubled the school, the more likely this is to be true.

When we ask school people what they value most about the work we do together, the answer is very consistent: The design has brought order and coherence to our school. They tell us that, while many of the things they do now are things they were doing before, the tasks are much more productive now and make much more educational sense because they now operate in ways that tend to reinforce, rather than conflict with, each other. With this structure in place, the teachers can see what they need to prune from their curriculum and their processes and what is missing. They tell us that, when they are done "dropping and adding," the sum of the parts is more than the whole, whereas, before, it was less. By their testimony, design is empowering.

The people who use our design use it in the same way that composers use a musical form, as a structure that makes it possible for them to compose something much more powerful than they could otherwise have done. Nothing is more empowering than the feeling that one is effective in one's work. The designs create the kinds of structures that, in other countries, ministries of education would provide. As we noted at the outset of this chapter, such structures can make schools very effective indeed, so it should not surprise us that the schools welcome the structure these designs provide.

That, of course, begs the question of how detailed the designs should be and how insistent we should be that the designs be implemented faithfully in all cases. We will return to these questions below, when we discuss how districts and states use the designs.

Cascading Blended Professional Development Systems, the "Corporate University," and Responsive Technical Assistance

Clearly, our design would be of no value unless the schools we worked with could be trained to implement it well.

Some years ago, when I was trying to understand how the best American firms were developing their own capacities to respond to the competitive onslaught from Japan and the "Asian Tigers," I focused on the way David Kearns, Xerox's chief executive officer at the time, had rescued the firm from the brink of disaster.

Kearns began by sending teams of engineers to Japan to see how the Japanese had succeeded in cutting costs, reducing cycle time, and raising product quality, all at the same time. In time, Xerox perfected this process of benchmarking and made it a part of the Xerox corporate culture. As soon as the reports started filtering back to headquarters, Kearns put together a top team to drive reforms within the company. The team consisted of a handpicked staff of senior officers and a consulting firm they had engaged. The team focused on a small core of procedures and methods that they wanted to diffuse through the entire organization, worldwide. The message from headquarters needed to be heard in every nook and cranny of this far-flung organization.

The answer was training. Using a system that has since come to be called "the training cascade," the team that Kearns had appointed to devise their strategy trained Kearns and the rest of the top team at headquarters. That team, including Kearns, then trained the people who reported to them, and so on down the line, until the people at the lowest rungs on every ladder had been reached. This training was not conceived as a static, "one size fits all" operation. Because the training included constant measurement of results against goals and standards—as well as a host of search behaviors to find better ways of doing things, including benchmarking—the cascade was dynamic. Each layer in the organization was empowered to find better ways of doing things within the larger framework that the new strategy created, and the strategy itself was constantly under review. Each layer and business unit became a learning community.

To create a training system that could operate at scale, we needed our own version of the training cascade. Initially, when we had fewer than 50 schools in our network, our national staff delivered all the services to the schools. Thus the school leaders received much of their training from the people who had developed the standards, assessments, and instructional materials. With the very rapid subsequent growth of the network, we realized that this system would no longer work. Travel costs were dominating our budget, and the growing travel burden was destroying our staff.

We then made two decisions. First, we decided to decentralize delivery of services and professional development and established six regional offices for these two purposes. Each office would be headed by a regional director and would include a business manager, support staff, and a group of senior professionals who would collectively be responsible for providing all the training and technical assistance our customers needed. These professionals typically play double roles: They are both technical specialists and cluster leaders. As specialists, they are responsible for delivering training and technical assistance in literacy and English language arts, mathematics, or leadership. As cluster leaders, they have lead responsibility for eight to ten schools and call on specialists in the two areas outside their own subject-matter expertise.

At the time, the number of schools in our network was doubling every year. We had no choice but to decentralize service delivery. We were determined to maintain the quality of the services we delivered, but doing so was an enormous challenge. Given our rate of growth, most of the people delivering services were, of necessity, people who had not been on our staff very long, and the decentralization of service delivery meant that central office staff would no longer be able to monitor the quality and consistency of our professional development and technical assistance daily. As a result, we were concerned that, as time went on, each regional office would modify the original professional development curriculum to the point that it was unrecognizable and that, rather than an "America's Choice" way of doing things, there would be six idiosyncratic ways of doing things.

To prevent such departures from our goals and procedures, we borrowed a page from the playbook of the successful American firms of the 1980s. Facing similar problems, they created corporate universities to ensure that their corporate strategies were reflected in the leadership training given to every layer of management in the firm. Following this example, we established what we called our "National College"—our own corporate university—with the mission of training our regional service-delivery staff to a standard that the National College would set. When the National College was fully up and running, no member of our regional service delivery staff would be permitted to provide services without supervision unless that person had completed the National College program and been certified as having met our standards.

The certification program takes almost ten months to complete. The first step is an intensive three-week "boot camp." Classes start at

8:00 a.m. and end at 9:30 p.m. Participants study the school designs for a week and their own specialty for two weeks. Performance assessments are administered at the end of week one and week three. In the next phase, participants serve under a mentor in the field, usually a regional director, implementing a carefully designed individual professional development plan. In the last phase, the candidates present a portfolio of their accomplishments in the field and are formally examined in an assessment-center format, primarily using performance tests. This certification program represents an enormous investment for the National Center, but we believe that our capacity to provide a high-quality program depends on it.

About a year after we established the National College and began the multiyear process of implementing its design, we learned from the Consortium for Policy Research in Education (CPRE) evaluation team that just under half the teachers in the America's Choice schools had changed their teaching as a result of our work. The CPRE team congratulated us, saying that we had made more progress in changing teacher behavior than most external training and technical assistance providers do in the time we had had, but we were deeply disappointed and determined to improve our record.

We responded by greatly intensifying our professional development program. Our general approach, of course, is to focus the whole professional development program on the acquisition of the skills and knowledge needed to implement the design. We have a very catholic view of that goal—ranging from exposure to the theories of Clausewitz on strategy and the views of Vygotsky on learning theory to the specific features of our Planning for Results system and the steps needed to implement our primary literacy program. Here, too, the theme is coherence. Although the professional development program is wide ranging, every aspect of it focuses on enabling the faculty to raise student performance in the context of the plan that they have agreed to use for that purpose.

The America's Choice School Design calls for the designation of certain key people on the school leadership team to play defined roles. In addition to the principal, these include literacy coaches, math coaches, design coaches, and a person whose task is to engage parents and the community in the life of the school. Most of the professional development program is directed to the members of this team. The program consists of a series of institutes and workshops, supplemented by regular meetings of teams of faculty members at every grade level within and across subject-matter specialties, a network of principals led by the America's Choice regional director, and regular direct coaching of the principal and other members of the leadership team by the cluster leader. All these activities are designed and scheduled throughout the year in such a way as to ensure that the professional development is continuous and logically sequenced.

Our signature is the use of the apprenticeship approach to professional development: We provide the participants with a tool; model its use; let them use it with supervision; and, critiquing their performance along the way, gradually withdraw our support until they are fully competent to use the new tool or procedure without further support. This continues for years in iterative cycles as the "apprentices" go deeper and deeper into the substance of the work, becoming increasingly skilled with each cycle.

This approach was developed to raise the skill levels of teachers in the schools in which we work. Of course, although many people beyond the members of the leadership team are directly involved in the process just described, we cannot work directly with each teacher in this way. As a result, we have had to depend on the people we have trained to pass on their skills to the other members of the faculty.

Thus, we established a protocol for rolling out the program schoolwide. The unfolding of our primary literacy program illustrates this procedure. The literacy coach in the school (a full-time position we require the school to establish) attends an extended institute at which he or she has a chance to understand the principles involved, observe experts modeling the expected behavior, ask questions, and try some things out. When the coach returns to the school, he or she is expected to choose a classroom that will become a model for literacy teaching in the whole school and to work with the teacher in that classroom so that the teaching comes to exemplify the America's Choice approach. The coach is then expected to do the same thing, classroom by classroom, covering up to ten classrooms. If the school wants to cover more classrooms, it must designate more literacy coaches.

The model classroom becomes a place where teachers, singly and in groups, can observe the new practices. Working with the coach, these teachers implement every aspect of the literacy design. Classroom by classroom and grade by grade, all the literacy classrooms are eventually brought up to standard. In addition to working individually with the teachers responsible for literacy instruction, the literacy coach is responsible for leading regular meetings in which these teachers continue their professional development and collectively reflect on and address problems of practice arising in their work. The literacy coaches are trained to serve as coaches to individual teachers and to lead these collegial faculty meetings. We provide protocols for both.

An analogue of this procedure for school principals is the focused walk, a procedure that the principal can use as a guide to inspecting the whole school or a single classroom, focusing as he or she does so on a particular aspect of the design and its implementation. We provide the principal with a protocol for the focused walk, thereby ensuring that it is a carefully considered activity that not only enables the principal to gather a great deal of information quickly but also to provide coaching to the faculty that is relevant, insightful, and useful.

Gradually, we have come to see that what is needed is a set of protocols of this sort for a number of actors that encompass a wide range of activities; these protocols must be related to one another, so that, collectively, they provide a structure for the leadership team to use as they draw the separate threads of design implementation together into one coherent activity.

While all this has been going on, we have begun to explore the use of a very different—and complementary—approach to improving the depth of implementation in our schools: the use of blended professional development systems combining face-to-face and e-learning approaches to professional education.

Among the tools we use in our e-learning programs are videos of exemplary practices, simulations, cases, games, videos of national and international experts talking to the participants, and journaling software. Given the problem we set out to solve—unacceptable levels of implementation—e-learning in conjunction with face-to-face delivery has the potential for getting directly to classroom teachers with a powerful product—the quality of which does not degrade as one goes to scale.

The value of e-learning, when used by itself, may seem questionable, but as one of several strategies used to deliver professional development programs, it may offer not only a way to enhance the reach of our implementation effort but also substantial financial benefits. Because the size of the investment in developing the materials is unrelated to the size of the group using them, the cost of developing and delivering instruction per person served decreases as the scale of endeavor increases.

Quality Control

During the first four years of the America's Choice School Design, the size of the network more than doubled each year. In the fifth year, we reduced that growth rate to allow us to institute a series of measures designed to ensure that we could maintain the quality of our services when we resume rapid growth.

Quality has been an overriding concern from the day we began the program. It was the dominant motivation for creating the certification program for our employees that I described above. If the people delivering the program to the field have not been well trained, nothing else we do will ensure quality. At the foundation of any modern quality-control system is the idea of building in quality from the beginning.

We also have other means of monitoring the fidelity with which the design is being implemented and distributing the results of the analyses to the people who need to act on them. As I mentioned earlier, when we started our program, we engaged CPRE both to evaluate the outcomes for students and to obtain feedback on the way the program was being implemented in the field. In several places in this chapter, I have described ways in which the feedback from CPRE revealed weaknesses in the design or in our delivery, which we fixed as soon as possible. CPRE surveys school leaders and faculty about the frequency, completeness, and responsiveness of the services they have received and their satisfaction with the services. In addition, Peter Hill, our director of research and development, working with other members of our staff, has developed a detailed set of rubrics for judging the extent of implementation of the design, which has become the basis for our own regular surveys of every school in the network. We use these surveys both to identify problems in specific schools and as the basis for correlating changes in student achievement with variations in the degree of implementation of specific features of the design. Finally, we use systematic "focus walks" through the schools, sometimes led by senior staff members from our central office, to provide feedback to the schools and our staff on the quality of implementation in specific schools in the network. Some of these techniques are borrowed from the education inspection services of the countries we have researched; others are based on industrial quality-control systems that businesses in this country use. The "focus walks" are based on the work of District 2 in New York City.

An account of this sort may create the illusion that our design, like a self-winding toy set down on the floor, will, once put in place, operate as planned without further intervention, but that is not so. It is difficult work, being done in real schools and communities with real people and real politics of the very local variety. We have had to give up on some schools whose faculties were unwilling to make the effort, once they understood the scope of the work that had to be done. We have lost supportive superintendents, whose replacements wanted to make their own marks by introducing their own ideas, which were incompatible with ours. Our schools have sometimes had to drop out for lack of money. Sometimes, teacher turnover has been so great that our professional development efforts have simply trained teachers to work in other schools, and we have been unable to train their replacements fast enough. Good principals have sometimes been followed by others who simply lacked the leadership abilities to hold their schools together. Some schools have taken longer to get their act together than others—and so on. The design is not self-winding; results do not automatically follow from its introduction within a school. But the record shows that when it is faithfully implemented, student performance improves markedly.

Building Capacity at the School, District, and State Levels

Clearly, we believe in our designs. That belief is amply validated by the reports we have received from our external evaluator, CPRE, which show that, in the districts CPRE studied, in which all or a substantial fraction of the elementary schools in the district are America's Choice schools, students are achieving at levels significantly above control schools. The very rapid growth of our network validates these reports. As of this writing, we were just shy of 500 schools in the network.

That is not the end of the story. If it were the end, we would judge success simply by the number of schools implementing our design and the extent of implementation in each school, but such a judgment would beg a whole series of questions, such as these: Do we believe that schools can be successful only if they implement our design? Do we believe that schools that change the design over time will necessarily fail? Do we believe that schools can implement the design successfully, irrespective of the actions that their districts and states take and the policies they put in place? In short, do we believe that faithful implementation of the design is the one essential to success and that schools are free to implement the design if they wish?

Actually, we do not believe any of these things. In this section, I distinguish between implementation of the design as an objective and building capacity as an objective and share our ideas about how the two might be related. I begin by describing how our ideas about capacity building within the school have evolved and then discuss what it might mean to work with districts and entire states to help them build their capacities to help schools raise student achievement.

Building Capacity at the School Level

When we began our school design work, we worked almost exclusively with individual schools. We adopted a three-year implementation cycle for elementary, middle, and K–8 schools and a five-year implementation period for high schools.

We quickly realized that this was a mistake. At the beginning of the second implementation year for Cohort 1 schools, it was apparent that some of the schools had not made enough progress during the first year to profit from the training scheduled for the second year. Thus, we reconceived the implementation period; rather than treating it as having a predetermined, fixed length, we began to treat it as a progression though stages of implementation. We developed rubrics for deciding when a particular stage would be complete. The idea was to allow a school to move to a subsequent phase only when the standards for the preceding one had been met. Thus was born, for us, the idea of standards-based implementation.

This plan, however, has proven quite difficult to implement. The schools in our network resist being "held back" because they have not met our standards. Only when the principal has left and been replaced, along with a significant part of the faculty, has it proven possible to do as we had planned.

The three-year period for implementation of the elementary and middle school designs was chosen because the Obey-Porter legislation, which made comprehensive school reform a federal program, funded programs for a period of three years. In our experience, however, three years has proven to be insufficient to implement the design and achieve the results we are seeking. Now, we tell the elementary, middle, and K–8 schools that they can expect the implementation period to last five years. We have not, in fact, stretched out our implementation design. What has happened is that we now realize that it takes, on average, three years to get all the pieces in place, but it is often five years before the whole design is institutionalized and its various pieces operate together to produce the desired effects. This is the difference between superficial implementation and deep implementation, implementation not of the parts alone but of all the parts together, working in harmony in a coherent system.

We also had to adjust our implementation design in other ways. We noticed, for example, that some schools were not ready to begin at the beginning. More precisely, some high schools were not ready to begin implementation of the design as we had conceived it. As is the practice for other organizations doing similar work, we had asked that schools interested in joining our network make sure that a comfortable majority of the faculty indicated interest in joining our network, but it became increasingly clear that this agreement did not mean much. It was usually treated on a pro forma basis, and few faculty members really understood what it would mean to sign up for our design. When, after we had been working with them for several months, they began to understand the degree to which implementation of the design would increase the demands on them and the extent to which it would call for them to change their established routine, some schools, almost all of them high schools, decided they really did not want to be on board after all. We concluded that these schools did not have the capacity to begin our program at the point we had planned as the beginning. That is tantamount to saying that they did not have the capacity to begin to build their capacity.

These were often very large high schools whose faculty members were demoralized and in various stages of chaos, distrustful of outsiders and of each other. We therefore devised a program that did not entail a long-term commitment from either party but that would enable us to work in a focused way on a specific problem—typically poor reading ability—that had proven intractable and that underlay many of the other problems the school faced. We reasoned that, if the faculty saw that, by working with us, they could make progress on such a problem, perhaps they would have the confidence to take the next step. By that time, they would also know enough about our design and the way we work to make a more-informed choice about adopting our design and committing years of their time to implementing it in their school. Thus was born the idea of building the capacity of a school to work on its capacity problems.

Some problems also occurred at the other end of the process—when the school had come to the end of the implementation period and the program was over. That is how we thought about it but not how the schools that joined our network thought about it. When the first cohort of elementary, middle, and K–8 schools came to the end of the three-year implementation period, most wanted to continue. "But there is no more," we said. "But it is very important for us to remain part of your network," they said. So we worked out a package for our alumni schools that includes attendance at our national conferences, which are organized as intensive professional development sessions that most of the schools in our network attend. Conference attendees exchange craft knowledge, hear experts from all over the world, learn about new developments in our design and development work, have access to continuing technical assistance and to new products unavailable to the general public, have the opportunity to send new hires to our training programs, and so on.

These schools knew that it would be vital to their sustained success to stay connected to our community, to entertain critical assessments of their operations from friends who understand what they are trying to achieve, and to have access to the new products our development team was creating. They saw themselves as moving to a new stage in their relationship with us, not as ending their relationship because their capacities had been built. They had no such static idea of capacity, and they were, of course, right. We realized that our own idea of going to scale had to include our alumni, as well as those who were in the process of initially implementing the design.

What emerges from this story is the idea of capacity-building as a continuum—a journey that necessarily takes longer for some schools than others, a journey that never really ends. Our design now assumes that stance at its core. We advocate serious school planning based on careful analysis of student performance against explicit standards. We advocate benchmarking best practices and the widest possible search for the practices most likely to address the problems that analysis of the data reveals. We also advocate a host of approaches to continuous, focused learning on the part of the faculty, entirely directed at improving the performance of the school and the students. Taken together, this is a formula for perpetual learning, perpetual capacity-building, and perpetual evolution.

Following this set of procedures long enough inevitably leads the faculty to adopt ideas, curriculum, techniques, and approaches not contemplated in our design. That will be just fine. In fact, it will be entirely consistent with the ethos of the design. When the school has developed the capacity to function at a high level, it will need less structure and prescription than it needs when its capacity is low and it is in relative chaos.

If that is so, then why are we so insistent that our schools fully implement the design in the first place? For the same reason that a seasoned composer can deviate from standard musical forms and still produce a masterpiece and that the developing composer deviates from the same forms at his peril. Many fine schools in this country do not need our design or anyone else's design to do a good job for their students, but a larger number of schools absolutely requires a good design to become competent organizations with the capacity to educate their students to high levels.

Here it is necessary to make a subtle point. In our opinion, all schools and society as a whole benefit from having the kind of structure that good ministries of education provide—the kinds of standards, examination systems, curriculum frameworks, instructional materials, and incentive and accountability systems described above. This is the sea in which all schools swim in a nation whose schools generally are performing at high levels.

Our design incorporates all that and goes a good deal further with respect to the detail of the requirements in each of these categories. We do that because most of the schools that we work with need that level of structure—call it the complete design level—to build their own capacities to the point where they can stand on their own and produce consistently high student performance.

This distinction between the ministry of education level and the complete design level—between the policy structure and the operational structure—will turn out to be very important in the next subsection, in which the idea of capacity-building as it plays out in districts and states is discussed.

Building Capacity at the District and State Levels

Early in the development of the America's Choice network, our long-standing conviction that districts matter was confirmed. Even in our first year, some districts decided to enroll all or almost all their schools in our network. Others decided over time to enroll ever-increasing proportions of their schools in the network; in still other districts, only a small proportion of the schools was enrolled. Thus, from the beginning, we could see what difference it makes to have a greater or lesser share of the schools in a district enrolled in our program. As one might expect, it makes a big difference. The schools using our design do better when the people in the central office embrace the design and find ways to support it in their schools.

Consider the situation in which, let us say, three schools in a district of 60 schools are part of the America's Choice network. That district has its own standards and its own views about how standards should be used. The same is true of assessments and of instructional materials and techniques. Those in the central office have views and policies on all these things and have a schedule of professional development offerings that they expect schools to take advantage of that are related to the preferences of the central office staff on all these points.

Of course, the America's Choice design requires implementation of an instructional system that is unlikely to be aligned with the preferences of the central office. Any school adopting our design is therefore immediately placed in a difficult position. Even if the central office is not hostile to the elements of our design, leaders of the school will likely remain in a constant state of tension with the central office on a host of issues arising from the conflict between the dictates of the design and the preferences of the central office. In this situation, the central office staff has little incentive to support the design. They have their own agenda, and the success of schools released from any obligation to live with that agenda could undermine their authority elsewhere in the system, without redounding to their credit at all.

Now consider the situation in which the top leadership of the district decides to adopt such a design as ours, not necessarily as the exclusive instructional approach to the used in the district (an issue to which I will return in a moment) but as the dominant one. When this happens, the senior people in curriculum, assessment, and professional development have, we hope, been consulted. They are among the leaders in figuring out how to implement the design in their district. The success of the design is their success, and they take both pride and credit for its successful implementation. Their departments actively try to figure out how the New Standards Performance Standards can be used to supplement and extend their standards in a useful way, how the New Standards Reference Examinations can be used to complement their assessment system, how our implementation schedule can be integrated with the district events calendar, and how their professional development facilities and calendar can support our design for professional development. The schools are no longer forced to choose between the dictates of our design and what the central office wants them to do. Our design is their design.

This difference has been idealized to make a point, but the difference is dramatic. When the district has made a conscious choice to build a substantial portion of its program around our design, the personal stakes for the actors change greatly. When a substantial portion of the schools in a district is using our design, the success of the leaders of the district is tied to our success. It is no less true that our success is tied to their success. Thus, it becomes in the interest of both our team and theirs to cooperate to ensure the success of the program. Little wonder, then, that we achieve greater success in that circumstance than when the program is ours but not theirs.

It is important to note, however, that we are more successful in districts where we have a substantial number of schools not just because the interpersonal dynamics are more favorable but also because they result in much more coherence in the instructional system and in the overall environment in which the schools work. Thus, we return here to the theme with which we began. Coherence, though not sufficient, is nevertheless the sine qua non—the single most important factor—in making broad gains in student achievement possible. The way to get the coherence that really matters is to have coherence between the broad framework being used at the district level and the designs being used at the school level.

In this context, let us return to look at the kind of coherence one typically finds in a well-run ministry of education vis à vis the kind of coherence that comes with a detailed operational design.

In the situation just described, the district provides policy coherence for all the actors in the district. The schools in the district using the design get high levels of operational coherence. Notice that I wrote, "the schools that are using the design." Thus, not all schools are using the design—neither do they need to. That is the key to building capacity at the district level.

The story of our interaction with one large district will illustrate the point. The story begins with the new superintendent having read a book that Judy Codding and I wrote on standards-based education (Tucker and Codding, 1998). On the basis of reading the book and a visit with us, he decided to adopt our approach as the top-level strategy for his district.

He suggested, and we quickly agreed, that the best way to begin would be for us to make a full-dress presentation to his board. It went very badly. In retrospect, and with much more experience behind us, it is now clear why. Large jurisdictions—big county or city education systems or states—are comfortable contracting with vendors for specific, limited tasks that they have designated but are very uneasy about establishing partnerships with outside organizations of the sort being suggested. To do that, as they see it, runs the risk of being perceived as ceding responsibility and authority. The larger the entity, the less likely they are to do that.

The superintendent suggested we start with a representative mix of 14 volunteer schools (out of more than 160), some led by highly respected principals, who, if they became enthusiastic, would carry the message to every corner of the district. The result was much as he had predicted. Student performance rose in enough schools to attract the attention of school people throughout the district. Word spread quickly. Many of the America's Choice schools attracted a steady stream of visitors. Some of the visitors started to implement features of the America's Choice design on their own. Soon, schools from across the county were coming to the central office and the board, asking to be part of the next expansion round. They included some of both the top performers and the lowest-performing schools. It was the system talking and not the vendor, and the people in the central office were much more interested in listening.

In the following year, close to 50 new schools in that county joined our network and began implementing the design. A close relationship developed between our senior staff and the top staff in the district, as we worked together to support the schools using the designs and to iron out a myriad of problems in the process that, sooner or later, engaged almost every corner of this large district's central office.

Several years earlier, we had developed a district-level service to match our school-level service. We offered to assist districts with the development of modern accountability systems, data-based central-office planning systems, decentralized resource-allocation and budgeting systems, management-development systems, customer-satisfaction systems, and many other aspects of a modern system of management based on the advances made by American business during the 1980s. The idea was to install in the central office all the systems needed to support standards-based education in the schools.

The team we assembled to do this had actually done it, on the ground, in a district that, as a result, became a magnet for visitors from all over the Northern Hemisphere. In the end, however, we had no takers. School districts, it turned out, did not want to be told how to manage themselves. Superintendents felt that this is what they were hired to do, and their boards agreed. Bringing in another outfit to coach them is perceived as a sign of inadequacy. Again, the larger the district, the more likely this is to be true.

We learned from that. In the district whose story was just told, we did not offer to advise the district on any of these matters. It would have been pointless in any case because the superintendent was at least as conversant with modern management practices as we were and was making steady progress on that front. Instead, we engaged in a constant conversation with him and with the top members of his team about what was needed operationally to make the designs work in the schools that had joined our network. They brought ideas to that table, and so did we. It was a genuine collaboration. That collaboration steadily built more coherence into the whole system, particularly from the standpoint of instruction. In the process, here and in the other districts where we had all or a large fraction of the schools, we learned a great deal about how to organize and manage central office functions to support the process of steady districtwide improvement.

Throughout this period, we involved key people from the central office and their area administrative offices in the training we were providing to their schools. The superintendent was constantly visiting the America's Choice schools in his district and highlighting their achievements. While his support for our program produced a backlash among advocates of other approaches, it also sent a clear message indicating that the central office would support schools that chose to adopt the America's Choice design, although we felt, and the superintendent agreed, that it would be a mistake to require schools that did not want to use the design to do so.

The distinction between the schools implementing the design and those that were not was becoming blurred. At the district's request, we provided early leadership training to all the schools in the district that were not part of our network, and the faculties of these schools imported many features of the design. It was natural for the district leadership to want to continue the work we had begun, and that interest led to our training and providing office space in our regional office for cluster leaders nominated by the district. The future was clear. More and more, our mission in that district was to focus on increasing the capacity of the central office staff to support the design-based reform in all their schools.

What does it mean to support design-based reform in a situation in which many schools are implementing the whole design and others are implementing it selectively? As discussed above, the lowest-performing schools are most likely to be the most chaotic and to have the greatest need for structure and coherence. Put another way, these schools have the greatest need for a fully specified, fully supported school design. When laying out a capacity-building plan for a whole district, it is important to keep this in mind.

The designs we created were not intended to serve only low-performing schools and low-performing students. To the contrary, our goal was to create designs for schools we would be happy to send our own children to. As a matter of implementation design, however, we have always focused first on low-performing schools. This is because they are the most in need of help and because no message travels through a district faster than the message that previously low-performing schools are achieving at higher levels than schools thought to be performing well.

As close collaboration with a district proceeds, and the relationship deepens, the way the whole district operates will more fully reflect the principles behind the design. Moreover, the design will metamorphose as the district makes the design its own over the years. The result will be a district whose policies are coherent and consistent with the design. The district will include among its schools some that are fully implementing such a design as ours and some that may have found their own way to operating procedures consistent with the principles that inform the design but do not represent a faithful implementation of it. The help we provide to a district is not intended to enable that district to turn every one of its schools into members of our network. Instead, we aim to help them use the principles underlying our design to create a context in which all their schools can be successful, whether or not they are faithfully implementing our design. Clearly, what I am describing is a capacity-building process—one that applies to a large district, not a single school.

All the considerations related above cropped up again when we received a call from the top officials in a southern state in late spring 2001. The legislature had just passed a comprehensive school reform bill that required the state, among other things, to identify low-performing schools and provide substantial assistance to any school asking for it. The state recognized that it lacked the capacity to provide the kind of aid that the legislation required and instituted a search for an organization that could provide it. That search led to us and our design.

The issue for both the state and for us was capacity—ours. We eventually figured out how we could meet both their needs and the obligations we had to existing customers, albeit with an extraordinary effort on the part of our staff. We satisfied the representatives who visited us in our offices that we could and would do what they needed to have done. Over the ensuing year, both we and the senior state staff worked hard, with good will and great success, to establish and maintain a close, collegial relationship in the face of enormous pressures to meet the needs of the schools and districts, respond to a deteriorating state budget picture, and meet the expectations of the governor and his staff.

From the day the relationship was initiated, the state representatives made clear that they wanted us to build their capacity to render all necessary services as quickly as possible. For that reason, they wanted us to use professional staff members of their regional education service agencies to deliver most of the services to the schools rather than our own employees. We applauded their desire to own the program and assume its management as soon as possible, but we wanted to make sure that the program would be delivered at the standard of quality we had set.

Eventually, we worked out an agreement. We would continue to work directly with the first cohort of schools in the state all the way through the multiyear, multiphase process required to implement the design fully. We would train and certify the regional education service-agency staff delivering the program and a number of key state officials as providers of professional development and technical assistance. We would license the state to use our designs in their schools, provided that only certified trainers delivered the service, provided that the ratio between trainers and schools remained the same as it is in our regular program, and provided that a quality-assurance process was in place to track implementation and ensure that schools were dropped from the program if they were not making a concerted effort to implement the program. All through the implementation process, we planned our work and executed the implementation plan in close collaboration with senior state staff.

We look back on our year of experience with this state and see that it has illuminated the issues of increasing scale and building capacity in fascinating ways. The whole effort has been a capacity-building effort in that we have, from the start, trained central and regional state staff to provide the training, professional development, and technical assistance needed to implement our program on a very large scale. Regional and state officials from this state formed a substantial proportion of the participants at the "boot camp" described above—the first step in our certification program. We recently received the data from our first year's effort in this state, which show that the America's Choice schools are closing the gap with the schools in the state that have not been designated low-performing. The outlines of a system for building capacity for going to scale are now clear, and we can no doubt improve the strategy as we gain more experience.

Since the day we opened our doors in 1989, NCEE has worked closely with governors' offices, state legislatures, senior staff in state departments of education, and central office staff in large school districts. Our experience during the last four years has greatly enriched our understanding of the practical issues involved in raising student performance in a standards-based, accountability-driven environment. That experience, combined with our research on the effectiveness of education systems in more than 17 other nations, has convinced us of the importance of working at every level of the system, from the schoolhouse to the statehouse, to help educators, policymakers, and system managers build high-quality, fully coherent standards and accountability systems that include all the necessary safety nets, one of which would be the assistance program for low-performing programs, based on our America's Choice School Design.

The Case for Third-Party Assistance

One could argue that the large districts and states we are working with do not need any help from us. Surely, the lessons we have learned could be appropriated by a large school district or a state directly, and the large district or state could do everything we have done to create highly coherent systems for their schools and take them to scale.

To me, however, that seems unlikely. I know of no state or district that could have mounted a decade-long program of international research of the kind we have conducted or could have sustained—

year in and year out—a program of instructional systems development essentially free of political pressure and costing tens of millions of dollars. Fewer than a half-dozen states or cities could have assembled the staff that we have been able to assemble, from every corner of the country and abroad, to do the many kinds of work that we have done, including research; design; development of standards, assessments, and instructional materials; evaluation; professional development; and technical assistance.

In the business world, the closest analogue to our role is that of a large international business consulting firm. Like us, such firms conduct research and development on a large, international scale. Like us, they benchmark best practices worldwide and build proprietary designs, protocols, systems, training products, and other tools for their staff and their clients. They also invest large sums in these activities, spreading the cost across their whole client base, as we do. Like a large consulting firm, we can create an environment that will attract highly capable, very experienced people by offering them the opportunity to make changes on a large scale, to learn constantly, and to have enormous leverage at scale on an education system that badly needs what they have to offer.

We are not alone. Other organizations do the kind of work that we do. More are needed, and more resources are needed both to create new organizations and to sustain and nurture existing ones. If we are right and the need for high-quality, highly coherent instructional systems and school designs is urgent, the country would be well served if a number of organizations developed and offered such systems from among which schools, districts, and states could choose.

Putting Coherent Systems in Perspective

The argument of this chapter can be summarized as follows. The most serious problem American education faces is that our educational institutions lack the capacity to meet the challenge of improving student achievement greatly. The place to look for solutions is the policies and practices of nations that have been much more successful than we have been at educating their students to high standards and at narrowing the gap between their best and worst students. Looking at these nations, one finds standards-based systems of education, the most striking feature of which is coherence—coherence with respect to how every aspect of school functioning reinforces the others. With a consistent approach from the classroom to the statehouse, policies and practices reflect the same conception of means and ends and therefore reinforce each other. By contrast, the education system in the United States is characterized by relative incoherence—programs, policies, and practices that, more often than not, clash and collide with one another, vitiating whatever success they might have had individually.

This does not mean that the character of the components of the instructional system and the leadership, management, and organizational systems that surround it have no bearing on the nature and extent of educational achievement of students. Some standards and some tests narrow the curriculum and omit much of great value. For instance, some management and organizational systems lead to more-equitable outcomes than others. These are very important matters, but, in our experience, no nation has produced high performance at scale that does not demonstrate substantial coherence.

The national systems of education that achieve the best results appear to be characterized by thoughtfully conceived and quite coherent instructional systems that are the result of large investments over long periods. These coherent instructional systems are in turn embedded in coherent policy and operational systems that are generally consistent with the instructional systems.

These points are summarized in Figure 7.1. Clearly, both policy and practice should aim to move our states and the schools in them from the lower-left corner of the graphic to the upper-right corner. The most efficient and practical way for the states, districts and schools in this country to do this is to take advantage of the experience of other nations that have had greater success than we have had and to create designs that capture that experience, adapted for use in the United States. Third-party organizations can facilitate this process

Figure 7.1
Coherence Matrix

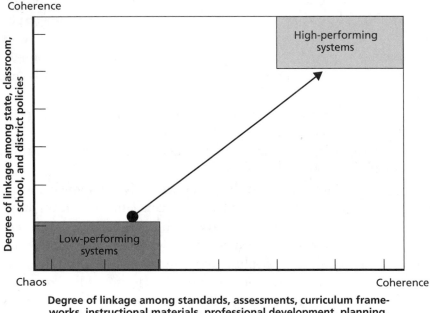

Degree of linkage among standards, assessments, curriculum frameworks, instructional materials, professional development, planning,
leadership, management, scheduling, budgeting, and organization.

RAND *MG248-7.1*

much as established management consulting firms do in the business
world, providing the tools and the training needed to enable firms to
catch up to and overtake their competitors.

A lifetime of work in this field has persuaded me of the strength
of this argument, but it is, nonetheless, important to put that argument in perspective. Above, I observed that income inequalities in
this country—and our unwillingness as a nation to provide the
resources our schools and communities need to deal with the problems children bring to school as a result of such inequalities—will
always act as a brake on what the schools can achieve. We dream of
what will never be if we hope for schools that can, by themselves,
completely overcome the problems that poor nutrition, poor health,

lack of stimulation in the early years, parents who use hard drugs, homelessness, and abandonment pose for children.

Our willingness for many decades to write off the problems of low-performing students has left another set of legacies that schools in other developed countries do not face to the same degree. The most glaring example is the large fraction of secondary school students who cannot read fluently. We cannot solve this problem by copying solutions developed in other developed nations because the nations we have studied do not have such problems. We do not know very much about the solution to this problem because we have invested very little in research on it over the years. We are on our own, and we have a long way to go to develop effective, affordable solutions to many of the problems that result from many years of neglect.

It is also important to be clear that producing a more-coherent education system will not address all the issues of capacity with which this chapter began. Much has been said in this chapter, for example, about what can be accomplished with sensibly conceived professional development. Few, if any, other developed nations, however, expect their schools to produce world-class results and then flood them with teachers holding "emergency" certificates who have no formal qualifications to teach their subjects. There are limits to what professional development—or any of the capacity-building strategies discussed here—can accomplish when school staff members lack the minimum qualifications to teach.

More could be said in the same vein. I do not want to claim too much. I strongly believe that the capacity of our educational institutions is the greatest difficulty we face and that building coherent systems of the kind I have described within and among those institutions is the best hope we have for raising student achievement across the board. But there are other problems that also need to be addressed. If we do not face them and solve them, they will continue to limit the success we can achieve by pursuing the strategies suggested here.

References

National Center on Education and the Economy, Web site, 2003. Online at http://www.ncee.org/ (as of July 2, 2004).

Tucker, M. S., and J. B. Codding, *Standards for Our Schools: How to Set Them, Measure Them, and Reach Them*, San Francisco: Jossey-Bass, 1998.

CHAPTER EIGHT

A Different Way of Growing

Linda A. Johannesen

The origins and growth of Different Ways of Knowing reflect an unusual mix of idealism and hard-headed business experience on the part of its founders; substantial growth in a single state over a five-year period; and, more recently, efforts to respond to market opportunities created by the availability of Comprehensive School Reform funds. The author notes that its current scale-up strategy, developed over many years of practical experience, relies on introducing a three-phase strategy to potential client schools. Focused on planning, implementation, and evaluation, this model is intended to help schools become more-effective consumers of professional development services. More generally, Johannesen argues, future efforts to scale up school reforms depend on the availability of funding not only for such popular programs as libraries but also for the less-glamorous activity of conducting research that will help to refine both designs for school reform and the processes of implementing them in multiple sites.

Different Ways of Knowing was launched in 1989, a watershed year for the standards movement in the United States. That year, the first-ever national standards in a subject area were released (in mathematics), and experts in every discipline and state were busy setting standards in key subject areas. President George H. W. Bush and the 50 governors met in Charlottesville, Virginia, at the first National Education Summit to discuss objectives for improving the quality of education and achieving common national goals. Meanwhile, the Kentucky Supreme Court declared the state's K–12 education system to be unconstitutional and ordered the state's general assembly to create and enact into law a new system characterized by equity and quality. The ensuing Kentucky Education Reform Act (KERA), announced in 1990, would become a national model for reengineering state statutes to establish standards and accountability systems to ensure that all students had the prospect of performing at a high level.

While leaders were busy congratulating themselves on their progress in setting standards and determining how to measure them, they paid scant attention to the resources and supports needed to help educators raise standards and expectations in their classrooms. The policy efforts—in the words of education researcher Paul Hill—came down from on high, like virga, the wisps of precipitation that evaporate before they hit the ground (Bleich, 1995). The Different Ways of Knowing design addressed a glaring need to increase teacher expertise and to provide standards-based tools and services to be used in the classroom to ensure that all students have access to rich course content through approaches to teaching and learning that address individual student needs and learning styles.

In this chapter, I first explain the key elements of the Different Ways of Knowing design, discuss the rationale underlying the program, and describe how the program came to exist. Next, I discuss a major phase of the scale-up of Different Ways of Knowing—our implementation of the program in hundreds of elementary schools in Kentucky, which came about as a result of a change in state law demanding comprehensive school improvement. In this discussion, I provide both research results demonstrating the effectiveness of Different Ways of Knowing as a system for improving student performance and an overview of the lessons we learned about whole-school reform through our efforts in Kentucky. Subsequently, I describe the further expansion of our school and district partnerships and the resulting adaptations in our funding, staffing, and ways of relating to teachers, schools, and districts. I consider the challenges of school reform under the No Child Left Behind (NCLB) Act and the need for continued financial support for research on the effectiveness of tools and services used by schools not meeting their adequate yearly progress (AYP) goals. Finally, I describe how the Galef Institute has continued to adapt its school and district partnerships to thrive as an educational consulting business and school improvement organization.

Development and Implementation of the Different Ways of Knowing Design Through 1998

Different Ways of Knowing was developed by the Galef Institute (Johannesen, 1995, 2003) and integrates important research on how children learn best (Slavin, 1988; Resnick, 1987; Bransford, 1979; Bransford, Brown, and Cocking, 1999; Langer and Smith-Burke, 1982; Bereiter and Scardamalia, 1987; Levine, 1992) with expanded theories of intelligence and learning (Sternberg, 1985; Gardner, 1983; 1993) and a model of adult and organizational change that relies on coaching for breakthroughs, rather than incremental improvements, in teaching.

Different Ways of Knowing Design Elements

The Different Ways of Knowing design specifies seven activities that are essential elements of high-performing schools, as described in the paragraphs below.

Planning Standards-Based Curriculum, Assessment, and Instruction Linked to Essential Questions and Generative Big Ideas. The Different Ways of Knowing design recognizes the importance of careful planning. Successful schools are places where teachers and students have clear and high expectations for learning. Different Ways of Knowing brings standards to life inside classrooms with strategies and tools for effective planning routines, such as analyzing and bundling key concepts and higher-order thinking skills inside standards, thus linking learning goals to meaningful summative and formative assessments, as well as daily instructional routines (Wiggins and McTighe, 1998; Erickson, 2001). Intentional planning can be seen as teachers work independently and in groups to deconstruct their own content standards, identify the essential generalizations that we call *big ideas*, and then flip the generalizations into compelling "building questions" that will be used to guide daily instruction and ensure that each day's learning is connected to the next. Principals and district leaders communicate the importance of standards-based planning and visit classrooms to show support.

Supporting Classroom Teaching and Learning That Generate Student Inquiry and Self-Directed Learning. Through the Different Ways of Knowing tools and strategies, teachers develop expertise in engaging diverse learners in rigorous content and scaffolding inquiry-driven instruction. Teachers model critical thinking, questioning, and reflection so that students become self-directed learners. Teachers hold all students accountable for self-management, group management, and self-directed learning by consistently creating the expectation that students will produce work that meets high standards. Classroom management strategies, such as flexible and cooperative student groupings, sustain motivation and effort (Resnick, 1989, 1995; Stipeck, 1998; Johannesen, 1995, 2003; Costa and Kallick, 2000a, b, c, d; Britton, 1993; Anderson and Kosslyn, 1984; Sternberg, 1985; Piaget, 1971; Klatzky, 1980). This progressive teaching is visible in classrooms as students use the processes and skills of a discipline along with content knowledge to understand the practical, real-world applications of the discipline while teachers give students time to think through problems and show how they value understanding and meaning over getting the "right" answer. When asked, students can describe what they are learning, why they are learning it, and where they are in the learning process. Leaders support the process by observing lessons and by providing feedback and suggestions for additional strategies.

Accessing Expert Strategies in Reading, Writing, and Mathematics to Close the Gap Between Developing and Successful Learners. Teacher quality and the repertoire of instructional expertise can strengthen students' literacy. Similarly, access to expert strategies for developing skills in reading, writing, and mathematics can help teachers become more effective. Different Ways of Knowing provides coaching and tools for modeling research-validated expert strategies that help students deepen their understanding across the curriculum and enable them to become powerful communicators (Beck et al., 1997; Johannesen, 1995, 2003; Resnick, 1989; Lightfoot and Martin, 1988). Different Ways of Knowing teachers develop an understanding of the six "thinking strategies":

- making connections (i.e., forming schemas)
- questioning
- drawing inferences
- visualizing, synthesizing
- determining importance.

They then integrate these strategies into curriculum planning and instruction. Teachers analyze and discuss student work in relation to the students' use of the "thinking strategies" and plan next steps for instruction. This approach is visible in the use of flexible grouping, in the time provided for students to practice thinking strategies, and in the use of multiple means of communication.

Integrating the Visual, Performing, Literary, and Media Arts in the Service of Learning for Understanding in All Subjects. Different Ways of Knowing's arts-in-learning strategies and tools provide all students with access to rigorous curriculum content through their natural wonder and curiosity for learning. The Different Ways of Knowing instructional model integrates the visual, performing, literary, and media arts into the teaching and learning of mathematics, science, history and social studies, and English and language arts. In the elementary grades, students use multiple symbol systems to explore and expand their prior knowledge, conceptions, and biases. Later, teachers and students and use the arts to accelerate and deepen conceptual understandings through metaphor and analogy while students actively construct their own concept maps. As summative assessment projects, the arts provide students with multiple ways of "Showing You Know," thus representing their new, integrated knowledge through, for example, drama and the visual arts. The arts provide schools with a powerful way to link what is intrinsically motivating to students with extrinsic motivators, such as a good report card. When instruction is organized correctly and when the arts are used well inside classrooms, student motivation, engagement, and effort increase. And it is sustained effort in the development of expertise that makes the difference. (Gee, 2000; Gardner, 1983, 1993, 1994; Catterall, 1995; Sarason, 1999; Gilligan, 1983; Jenkins, 1969.)

Honoring Home Languages and Cultures and Developing Partnerships for Learning. Families matter. So does collaboration around a shared vision of student success. Different Ways of Knowing strategies and tools help to develop a caring school culture supporting all stakeholders (Epstein et al., 1997; Mapp, 2003; Comer, 1984; Mandler, 1975). Different Ways of Knowing provides teachers with curriculum-based strategies and tools to link families to student learning in meaningful and culturally congruent ways. Teachers and families implement strategies for celebrating and honoring cultural heritages; expressing cross-generational voices; and using community assets, such as museums, to enhance academic goals. They provide project-based learning experiences that invite family participation and encourage community members to share their knowledge and experiences with students to expand and deepen specific content. These efforts lead to increased volunteerism and family participation in the educational process in school and at home. Leaders encourage this process by linking schools to arts and cultural organizations, bringing added learning experiences to students, and establishing and promoting family-involved learning projects and events (including celebrations of student learning).

Providing Instructional Leadership That Creates the Conditions Necessary for a High-Performing School Community. The role of school leaders is to create the environment, provide the resources, and reflect the attitudes and beliefs of a high-performing learning community. Different Ways of Knowing strategies and tools help school stakeholders create these conditions by using data effectively to ensure quarterly and yearly progress (Schmoker, 1999). The entire school community collaborates in designing the work of the school; shares responsibility for data-driven decisionmaking; and conducts reflective, professional dialogue using the Norms of Collaborative Work, a system of principles designed to promote sharing of ideas, experiences, and outcomes. This emphasis can be seen in the way time is organized to provide for common planning; facilitate small learning communities; and encourage teacher dialogue about lessons, strategies, and support to ensure student success and continuous improvement. The principal takes the role of instructional leader as his or her first priority and mentors other staff to take on responsibilities to develop a system for shared leadership.

Committing to a Theory of Change That Depends on Individual and Organizational Transformation. In the context NCLB has created, districts and schools that have chronically failed to make yearly progress need to do more than develop a "school improvement plan." Many schools that receive federal funding targeted for "schoolwide improvement plans" often achieve only incremental improvements over long periods, rather than the needed breakthroughs in teaching, learning, and achievement. Too often, stakeholders continue to rely on prior knowledge and experience—what worked in the past—to create their plans, their future. For the past five years, with $3 million in federal capacity-building grants, Galef has designed and tested a Coaches Course of Study, applying the "Dispositions of the Artist" and the distinctions of "Coaching for Breakthroughs in Teaching and Learning" to embed knowledge of how students learn best and the related teaching skills into an adult learning model that has a chance of being institutionalized.

The Artistry of Teaching: Learning as "Doing"

In *The Conduct of Life*, Ralph Waldo Emerson (1860) wrote, "Our chief want in life is somebody who shall make us do what we can." More recently, Sir Ken Robinson (2001, pp. 114–115), author and educator, wrote that

> being creative involves doing something. People are not creative in the abstract; they are creative in something—in mathematics, in engineering, in writing, in music, in business, in whatever. You could not be creative unless you were actually doing something. In this respect, creativity is different from imagination.

Thus, the real artistry in teaching is less the charismatic lecturer, transmitting his knowledge to students, and more the teacher who creates the conditions and introduces enough content to get the students "doing"—creating, questioning, and constructing meaning. Toward this goal, Different Ways of Knowing is unique in the attention the design pays to helping teachers understand the interaction between standards-based teaching, the social nature of learning, creativity as doing, and the roles that the arts can play in helping students learn content and construct meaning.

Learning Through the Arts

The Galef Institute supports math, English, science, and social studies and history teachers in integrating music, the visual arts, media arts, dance, and drama to increase their effectiveness in standards-based instruction. Arts integration has made a dramatic difference in the learning and achievement of students whose teachers have participated in the initiative (Catterall, 1995; Catterall, Dreyfus, and DeJarnette, 1995).

How have teachers made the shift in their practice? First, teachers must experience "learning concepts and skills through the arts" themselves, label what they have learned, and articulate the value of the arts. Second, teachers benefit from access to exemplary lessons and units that begin with their content standards, include assessments in the standards, and show the scaffolded instruction by which the arts are integrated into the teaching and learning. Third, teachers benefit greatly from coteaching exemplary arts-integration lessons with an experienced educator or external coach, videotaping the lesson, and analyzing the student work. Different Ways of Knowing teachers are introduced to a framework for thoughtful and intentional arts integration with standards-based teaching and learning to deepen learning in math, reading and writing, science, and history and social studies. Also, elementary teachers and teams of secondary school teachers learn the power of arts integration in problem-solving and in exhibitions of learning in which connections across disciplines and multiple representations of ideas are important tools. Although previous scientific research on the use of the arts in learning has been limited, the Different Ways of Knowing design was inspired, in part, by the early research and publications of David Perkins (1994), Denny Palmer Wolfe and Dana Balick (1999), and Elliot Eisner (1991). The Different Ways of Knowing pedagogical framework (Johannesen, 1995, 2003) allows practitioners and experts to develop and test tools and protocols for teaching and learning in and across subjects. For example, practitioners use and adapt the "Arts Integration Lesson Plan Template" for developing their own lesson plans; the template follows the natural cycle of learning: Coming to Know (processes of integrating prior and new knowledge), Showing You Know (products of learning; assessments), and Knowing You Know (student self-assessment).

Testing the Theory of Learning and Theory of Change

In 1987, the institute's cofounder, Bronya Galef, expressed her conviction that the power of the imagination and the role of the arts were being lost in formal education. Andrew Galef was curious about this hypothesis and used his experience as a "turnaround specialist" in business, offering the education team "lessons learned" as a guide during our formative years. These lessons translated into crucial design constraints for the development and testing of the Different Ways of Knowing model. Mr. Galef required that Different Ways of Knowing model be independently evaluated from the very start; thus, the first study was launched in 1991. Other design constraints were that the model would demonstrate "context validity" by succeeding in areas other than its home base in Los Angeles; that the design would not rely on a theory of change that depends on "charismatic principals"; and that its efficacy would be measured the same way schools measure performance—using state student achievement assessments—and not through institute-designed tests, portfolios of student work, or in-class exams developed by teachers.

The first external evaluation of Different Ways of Knowing was a three-year, scientifically based study by James Catterall of the University of California at Los Angeles that followed 1,000 students in four urban school districts in California and Massachusetts (Catterall, 1995). Tracking this cohort over time, the study found that the Different Ways of Knowing students demonstrated, among other increases, significant gains in vocabulary, comprehension, and other measures of language arts—an increase of about 8 percentiles on the Iowa Test of Basic Skills for each year of participation. Comparing participants and nonparticipants in the same grade, Different Ways of Knowing students scored higher on written tests of social sciences knowledge, and their grade-point averages were higher by one-half point. They also showed increased cognitive engagement and intrinsic interest in the humanities; showed increased levels of achievement and motivation over time, as opposed to the patterns of eroding motivation for nonparticipants; and increased the time spent engaged in complex creative thinking. Teachers increased their use of the visual arts, drama, music, and movement to promote learning and spent more time facilitating student learning as opposed to lecturing (Catterall, 1995). Other comparisons of the performance of students enrolled in Different Ways of Knowing Schools in Kentucky have indicated that their performance is superior to that of other students on statewide assessments (Petrosko, 1997). More detail regarding these studies is provided below. (See "Evaluation of Kentucky Demonstration Sites," later in this chapter.)

Expansion of Different Ways of Knowing in Kentucky

In addition to the constraints described above, Andrew Galef specified that a critical measure of success would be the response from two key markets: schools and potential funders. First, schools would have to value Different Ways of Knowing enough to purchase its products and services with school funds. Second, foundations and government agencies would have to demonstrate willingness to invest funds in the design to enhance and accelerate the institute's capacity to expand and scale up access to Different Ways of Knowing's products and services.

To maintain quality control and make the best use of our financial resources, we have carefully managed the expansion of Different Ways of Knowing. For example, whenever the staff of educators would suggest hiring a pubic relations specialist, Andrew Galef would ask us to reconsider, reminding us that most new businesses fail—not because of the inadequacies of their products but because of poorly managed growth. In our case, we were uncertain about our capacity to serve a rapidly expanding market while providing high-quality services. Despite this uncertainty, however, there was one request to expand our implementation that we could not turn down. This request, from the Kentucky Department of Education, resulted in a dramatic scale-up effort in a single state: The number of Kentucky school partners grew dramatically from 50 pilot classrooms in 25 elementary schools in 1993–94 to thousands of classrooms in more than 300 elementary and middle schools by 1998.

As Table 8.1 shows, the number of schools using the Different Ways of Knowing design expanded greatly as the result of specific changes in Kentucky's school reform law.

For us, winning the opportunity to help implement the changes specified in the new law was like winning the Kentucky Derby. Two factors helped win the race: First, the law required a massive state investment in significant changes in the structure of elementary schools, which the Different Ways of Knowing program was especially well equipped to implement. Second, the new standards-based approach created a new kind of customer, one who asked the types of questions Different Ways of Knowing could answer. The questions about the design that Kentucky educators and policymakers raised reflected a higher level of focus and inquiry, with building-level administrators and practitioners seeking greater understanding of standards-based planning and increasing internal capacity, rather than simply seeking guidance on what programs to purchase and what workshops to provide.

KERA mandated a comprehensive overhaul of the state's K–12 educational system. It called for rigorous content standards that changed the statewide conversation about reform but also for equalized funding, high-stakes performance-based assessments, professional

Table 8.1
Chronology of the Different Ways of Knowing Kentucky Scale-Up

1993–94	Kentucky Department of Education pilot in 50 classrooms
May 1994	Galef Institute–Kentucky Collaborative opens its doors
1994–95	167 schools participate in program, including 24 formal research sites
1995–96	287 schools participate in program
1996–97	319 schools participate
1997–98	331 schools participate in program
July 1998	Collaborative for Teaching and Learning, Inc., opens its doors

development, and technology for student learning. Most important for the Different Ways of Knowing design, the law required a mandatory nongraded primary program that most schools had no idea how to implement. These "continuous progress" classrooms grouped students in Grades 1, 2, and 3 together rather than assigning them to separate classrooms.

The Galef Institute opened its Louisville office, the Galef Institute–Kentucky Collaborative for Teaching and Learning in 1994 and established a statewide advisory board that initially brought together leaders of 30 organizations. This board included leaders in higher education; heads of teachers' unions; cultural, civic, and media organizations; and arts and humanities councils. This board provided Different Ways of Knowing great legitimacy and support, identifying this work as an exemplary approach to helping teachers achieve the requirements of the state law. For example, the *Lexington Herald-Leader*, a Knight Ridder newspaper, donated a column in which educators wrote about best practices on a regular basis. Kentucky Educational Television (KET) provided programming that portrayed Different Ways of Knowing as an innovative system that would support state legislation and policy. The advisory board helped ensure that the state's regional education resource teams, which were assisting failing schools, were trained in Different Ways of Knowing as a way of supporting standards-based practices.

As a result, the Different Ways of Knowing curriculum materials, professional development opportunities, and the images of classroom practices seen on KET became, in Kentucky elementary grades, synonymous with the quality practices the state wanted to see in classrooms. The Kentucky team became a reliable local resource, given further credibility through the leadership of Linda Hargan, who left her position as a policymaker at the Kentucky Department of Education to become a policy implementer.

In the pilot period, before full-time instructional coaches were hired, the institute staff and experienced teachers from other sites worked collaboratively with the Kentucky Department of Education to train teachers at the state's eight former regional service centers. Later, training was delivered to the more than 300 schools in two ways. For the 75 schools that trained their entire faculties, Different Ways of Knowing precepts and practices were articulated in full-day workshops held over four to six days during the school year and in the summer, most frequently at the school. Most schools sent teams of six to twelve teachers to a central regional location for training. All training sessions were followed by school-based coaching services at the school and in classrooms.

In the Different Ways of Knowing Design, schools are supported by teams of expert coaches, rather than individual consultants. The team includes experts in standards-based teaching and learning and in arts education and arts integration. The Kentucky Arts Council supported this work, developing an application form and helping select a roster of nearly 40 artists and arts educators from around the state. Representatives from the Arts Council, KET, the Kentucky Center for the Arts in Louisville, the Jefferson County Cultural Consortium, and other agencies screened applications and chose eight to ten artists in each discipline (music, visual arts, drama, and dance).

Since its early days, the Different Ways of Knowing design has almost always employed full time instructional coaches, who are assigned by geographic region and work primarily out of their homes. Typically, these are master teachers—many of whom were early Different Ways of Knowing teachers—whose classrooms demonstrated teaching and learning consistent with the program's goals and methods and, in Kentucky, with the standards and practices the state was trying to develop in all elementary schools. The Galef-Kentucky collaborative brought the teachers together every six weeks for professional development. In many cases, school districts loaned teachers to participate as consultants to the collaborative. The group reimbursed the districts for two or three years of the teachers' time. The districts recognized that the experience would further develop the teachers' skills and knowledge and that their expertise would ultimately benefit the district.

In 1998, Kentucky colleagues took steps to make Different Ways of Knowing a permanent part of the school reform landscape in Kentucky by forging crucial links with teacher-education programs. Through a grant from the John S. and James L. Knight Foundation,

Different Ways of Knowing training and curriculum, instruction, and assessment modules were presented to students pursuing master of arts in teaching degrees as part of preservice training at the University of Louisville, Murray State University, and Eastern Kentucky University. At these institutions, instructional methods classes incorporated the Different Ways of Knowing orientation training into their curricula. Trainees had the opportunity to review and practice with Different Ways of Knowing modules and to conduct their internships in Different Ways of Knowing classrooms. In this way, Different Ways of Knowing introduced active learning, not only to the trainees but also to their professors, who would incorporate these methods into the training of future teachers.

By 1998, representatives at the Kentucky Department of Education informally stated that so many elementary teachers in Kentucky had developed solid classroom practices with the support of Different Ways of Knowing that they would continue using these practices even if the legislation went away and performance assessments and accountability were abolished. The state's education leaders clearly believed that elementary schools had dug themselves out of the deep hole they had been in, that elementary teachers were doing a better job, and that Different Ways of Knowing had made a difference throughout the state.

In 1998, the staff and advisory board of the Galef Institute–Kentucky Collaborative for Teaching and Learning became its own Kentucky-based nonprofit organization, called the Collaborative for Teaching and Learning, with Linda Hargan as its executive director. Currently, the collaborative and the Galef Institute have a business relationship in which the collaborative has the right to market Different Ways of Knowing within Kentucky and Missouri and is responsible for the implementation and feedback loop of its work.

Evaluation of Kentucky Demonstration Sites

The intersection of Different Ways of Knowing and Kentucky education reform was well documented by Policy Studies Associates, Inc. (1997) and is integrated in the discussion below. Because of its reliance on soft money from key funders and fees from schools and districts, the Galef Institute had to build a case for the model and demonstrate positive results. Continued funding of research enabled us to obtain much-needed evidence of success that was crucial in maintaining confidence in Different Ways of Knowing work. At the beginning of the Kentucky scale-up, the Knight Foundation awarded a $1 million grant to the Galef-Kentucky collaborative to study the effects of Different Ways of Knowing on teaching practices and student learning in 24 Different Ways of Knowing demonstration schools over a two-year period. These schools were chosen because they possessed characteristics that made them representative of schools across the state.

Researchers Ric Hovda, Diane Kyle, and Joseph Petrosko of the University of Louisville conducted two separate evaluation studies (Hovda and Kyle, 1997; Petrosko, 1997), and an additional grant from the National Endowment for the Arts enabled Cecilia Wang and David Sogin at the University of Kentucky to examine the effects of integrating Different Ways of Knowing's arts component into instruction (Wang and Sogin, 1996). This research demonstrated that Different Ways of Knowing influenced teaching and learning in Kentucky's classrooms in a number of ways, as described below:

- **Different Ways of Knowing changed knowledge, beliefs, and attitudes about how young children learn.** Teachers reported that their involvement with Different Ways of Knowing gave them greater confidence, made it easier for them to handle and adapt to change, and taught them to be more flexible in their teaching. Teachers also indicated that they came to appreciate students' unique talents and diverse ways of learning, believed more strongly in the value of the arts in learning, and recognized that active learning increases student engagement and motivation. More than seven out of ten principals saw Different Ways of Knowing as instrumental in enabling teachers to integrate the arts, validate their existing belief that subjects should be integrated, and build confidence in using integrated learning strategies.

- **Different Ways of Knowing changed teachers' instructional practices to accommodate differences in students' learning styles and strengths.** Student-centered teaching and learning practices—which encourage students to take an active role in learning—are at the heart of Kentucky's primary program. Trained classroom observers reported that, in a statewide sample of elementary schools, a higher percentage of teachers in research and development (R&D) sites implemented the student-centered teaching and learning components of Kentucky's primary program as they were intended to be used than did teachers in the other schools. The research findings suggest that use of Different Ways of Knowing has accelerated the implementation of student-centered practices in Kentucky, regardless of whether teachers began to use Different Ways of Knowing in the first or the second year that it was introduced to the state. Large percentages of teachers said that they had made significant changes in their instructional practices since they began using Different Ways of Knowing. Changes included integrating social studies with other subjects, using more hands-on learning activities, making greater use of fine arts, and engaging students in more group activities. Teachers noted that, because of Different Ways of Knowing, they incorporated more writing opportunities for students into their language arts instruction. Only about one-third of teachers indicated that they were, for the most part, "already teaching this way." These teachers suggested that, rather than changing their practices, Different Ways of Knowing affirmed many of the practices they were already using in their classrooms. In addition, more than nine in ten teachers reported that, as a result of Different Ways of Knowing, the school community became more involved in the arts and increased support for arts activities. Not only did the arts enhance the atmosphere of individual classrooms, but they also created an air of excitement and student involvement in learning throughout the school. Teachers in some schools expressed a desire for even more collaboration with music and art teachers, as well as with other school specialists.

- **Students in Different Ways of Knowing schools compared favorably on the Kentucky Instructional Results Information System (KIRIS) assessments with students in schools that did not use the Different Ways of Knowing approach.** As shown in Figure 8.1, the performance of Different Ways of Knowing students on the Kentucky state test compared favorably to the performance of other fourth-grade students throughout the state. The Different Ways of Knowing students showed
  - increased gains over two years in reading (7 percent), arts and humanities (7 percent), math (25 percent), science (7 percent), and social studies (10 percent) compared to other schools in the state
  - greater involvement in their classrooms and more interest in their schoolwork
  - greater eagerness to participate in learning and to show what they know
  - expanded use of "multiple intelligences" strategies.

Remarking on indicators of student achievement beyond test scores, many teachers in the research demonstration schools using Different Ways of Knowing noted improvements that their students had made in specific skills or content knowledge. Students, they said, were better able to link their learning to real-life situations. They also worked better in groups, asked more thought-provoking questions, improved their writing, exhibited better research skills, and retained more information.

Most teachers agreed that integrating the arts into instruction added a new dimension to their teaching. Students appeared to be responding to the program with increased achievement, more interest in and enthusiasm for learning, and improved self-confidence. This was especially true for students who had difficulty learning in the past.

Four out of five principals offered examples of how Different Ways of Knowing contributed to making their schools learning communities. Most often, they mentioned that the model provided

Figure 8.1
KIRIS Index Point Gains over Two Years

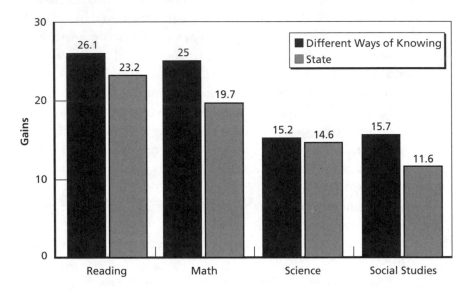

SOURCE: Petrosko et al. (1998).
RAND *MG248-8.1*

both the curriculum and the faculty with a "common thread" or
"common ground." Some principals went so far as to extend this
description to parents and/or the community. Eighty-two percent of
the principals agreed that Different Ways of Knowing contributed to
improved student achievement, citing improved KIRIS scores,
increased writing ability, deeper knowledge of subjects, and improved
speaking skills.

These Kentucky results show that Different Ways of Knowing
can help schools attain their goals for improvement. The program
met teachers' professional needs, improved students' attitudes toward
school, and may have contributed to improved student achievement.
Teachers in research demonstration schools acquired new instructional skills, changing their instructional practices in accordance with
the Kentucky primary program. In fact, the data show that Different
Ways of Knowing teachers implemented almost all the components
of the Kentucky Primary Program at higher levels than teachers in the

state sample. Teachers' own accounts indicate that Different Ways of Knowing helped them teach in ways appropriate to students' varying levels of development.

Chronology and Lessons Learned from Expansion Before 1998

The success of our expansion up to 1998 was the result of developing a multifaceted design that appealed to educators as a tool to raise student performance and integrate the arts into standards-based teaching and learning and as a catalyst to spark school-based teacher development and renewal. The success of the design was also the result of an evolving business strategy, flexible delivery structures suitable to partner states and districts, and an ability to adapt to and take advantage of new circumstances, including dramatic shifts in state and federal policy. The business instincts of the program's founders and suggestions from partner sites led the Galef Institute to recognize that, if the program was to grow and thrive, it needed to bolster its relationships with school districts and create a new delivery model that could serve more schools in relatively contiguous locations.

The original design—used during the early phase of development from 1993 to 1998, when a dramatic influx of federal dollars supported expansion—provided schools with robust services and tools. District partnerships—including San Francisco and Rosemead, California; Seattle, Washington; and Pittsburgh and Penn Hills, Pennsylvania—identified several schools within a single district to work with Different Ways of Knowing as a cohort for at least three years. This structure allowed teachers and administrators to benefit from one another's expertise and provided sufficient resources to hire a local team of Different Ways of Knowing coaches to work with the national team. Each partnership was supported by public and private funding.

Schools in these early partnerships purchased Different Ways of Knowing because they sought a combination of best practices and reliable relationships with program developers to help implement the new methods. RAND's 1998 report on New American Schools

(NAS)[1] design implementations noted similar reasons for acquiring the NAS designs (Glennan, 1998). A second RAND report indicated that the level of implementation achieved depended on the design selection process, school climate, design and team characteristics, school structure and site factors, and district and institutional factors (Bodilly et al., 1998).

Successfully implementing this design required genuine, on-the-ground data regarding programs and political clout to get things done. For example, to facilitate the work with the San Francisco Unified School District (Peterson et al., 1999), the Different Ways of Knowing coordinator was a teacher on special assignment, housed at the district office. In western Pennsylvania, where Different Ways of Knowing was supported by the Heinz Endowment and the Grable Family Foundation, Different Ways of Knowing worked collaboratively with the Pittsburgh Public Schools (i.e., the district) and several of its elementary schools, as well as with the neighboring Penn Hills School District and its schools. After several years in the region, Different Ways of Knowing staff was invited to develop a unique regional partnership with the Pittsburgh Center for the Arts (PCA), a highly respected institution that works with families, communities, and schools. As our regional community partner, PCA became a local training site and coordinating agency. Because PCA's education program and philosophy were well aligned with Different Ways of Knowing, the center participated in local fundraising for the schools. PCA also housed a Different Ways of Knowing local artist-educator coach and coordinator and provided local office space, machinery, and supplies.

Different Ways of Knowing staff members develop close working relationships with district leaders to understand their distinctions and to align the services closely with the professional development needs of districts. Developers of the model also realized that teachers and principals, like the students they serve, are more effective when they are active participants in constructing their own learning. As

---

[1] See Chapter Sixteen in this volume.

Milbrey McLaughlin and others note, effective school improvement efforts must shift professional development away from the dominant mode of "direct teaching" to a broader conception of teacher learning that provides opportunities to discuss, think about, try out, and hone new practices (McLaughlin and Oberman, 1996).

The Different Ways of Knowing approach to professional development also calls for a conception of teachers as career-long learners, so its professional development design evolved naturally to provide teachers with multiple opportunities and multiple settings for the complex task of learning and unlearning, trying out ideas, talking through ideas with one another, using protocols to provide feedback, and constantly adapting their practices.

Later, Different Ways of Knowing incorporated new knowledge about the link between student achievement, the learning of individual school employees, and improvements in the capacity of the organization to solve problems and renew itself (Sparks and Hirsh, 1997). Different Ways of Knowing initially allowed teacher teams to implement the design and found that the effects were consistently more positive when the faculty created and committed to a common set of goals and benchmarks for student progress. As Datnow, Hubbard, and Mehan (2002) discovered, teacher support is crucial because teachers can ignore or subvert reforms they feel are imposed on them.

Responding to New Demands for School Reform Services After 1998: Building Capacity

In 1997, Congress introduced the Comprehensive School Reform Demonstration Program (CSRD), cosponsored by Representatives David Obey (D-Wis.) and John Porter (R-Ill.), which created new incentives for districts to seek support from school reform models. The legislation made $145 million available to state education agencies to help them assist up to 3,000 schools with grants of $50,000 or more that could be renewed for two years. About $120 million of the initial funding was earmarked for Title 1 schools.

Before the legislation was passed, Different Ways of Knowing staff had to spend much of its own time helping schools identify grants to supplement their own local funding for school improvement. But, under CSRD, schools could now use federal dollars to help fund our tools and professional development services, especially since Different Ways of Knowing was included on the Northwest Regional Education Laboratory's catalog of programs (1998). In addition to this school funding, Different Ways of Knowing also became better positioned to compete for contracts and grants.

One of the most significant challenges in helping Different Ways of Knowing expand was obtaining the funding necessary to ensure quality; train school coaches; support ongoing research and evaluation; develop, manufacture, and print new products; and build necessary working capital. The federal government's two capacity grants to the Galef Institute, totaling $3 million, enabled Different Ways of Knowing to respond to new demand for the program, which required training new coaches well in advance of the time schools signed up and could pay for Different Ways of Knowing.

From 1998 to 2003, Different Ways of Knowing partnered with approximately 200 schools, all funded by CSRD. The chronology of our development as an organization, including the dramatic scale-up that occurred as a result of our work in Kentucky, is shown in Table 8.2. As is indicated in the table, Different Ways of Knowing has, all told, worked in partnership with more than 600 schools in 24 states. In addition to its work in traditional public schools, Different Ways of Knowing has developed a unique set of services and tools in response to invitations from charter schools and currently supports charter schools in Pennsylvania, Texas, Michigan, and California.

Funding for the design shifted from 70-percent private funding in 1998 to 90-percent public funding in 2003, a change that has had both intended and unintended consequences for Different Ways of Knowing.

In 1998, as individual schools and districts with CSRD funding called to inquire about Different Ways of Knowing tools and services, the Galef Institute realized that, because CSRD funds made it possi-

Table 8.2
Chronology of Research, Development, and National Expansion

Year(s)	Program	Total Schools
1989–1994	R&D phase for elementary design (California, Massachusetts, Mississippi)	25
1993	Galef opens Kentucky training center	30
1993	Galef launches regional pilots	349
1994–1998	District partnerships (California, Washington, Pennsylvania, Mississippi, Kentucky)	450
1999	First federal capacity-building grant: coaches	500
2000	Middle grades contract with the Office of Educational Research and Improvement (U.S. Department of Education)[a]	550
2001	Second capacity-building grant: tools and protocols for quality control	
	Galef opens regional offices	599
2002	Charter school services: national	605
2004	High school R&D	606

[a]This organization has since become the Institute of Education Sciences.

ble for individual schools to decide which school designs and services to purchase, the existing Different Ways of Knowing cohort model of working with several schools in a district at once would not fit all contexts. Thus, it began the process of developing an expanded reper- toire of implementation tools and quality-control strategies to meet the needs of individual school partners.

For many reasons, teachers and administrators were not always satisfied with the services available. First, states typically made the resources available only to chronically underachieving schools in which the staff did not readily comprehend how to move from focusing on problems to implementing solutions. Before state and federal requirements created pressure for improvement, a sense of urgency for change was lacking in many of these schools, and teachers and other school leaders did not possess the protocols necessary to help them consider new ways to accelerate improvements in perform- ance. Secondly, many administrators and teachers initially misunder- stood the extraordinary funding from CSRD as another punitive measure, primarily because the vast majority of states decided to limit access to these funds to the worst-performing schools, which was not the original intent of the Obey-Porter legislation. Thus, outside of Kentucky, which was primed for our implementation, it took some time to help CSR-funded schools see possibilities in the CSR process. In a handful of extreme cases, a year of constant attitude adjustment was needed for school officials and teachers to recognize their empowerment and to organize for results, rather than viewing them-selves as victims of federal and state or district intrusion. As a result, Different Ways of Knowing realized it needed to develop tools and protocols to address the issue of standards as a way to motivate change and encourage growth.

Not so long ago, only a handful of states, such as Kentucky, Vermont, and Maryland, had their own coherent state assessment systems. Consequently, school-level contracts depended on both school-level leadership and a robust relationship between the school and the district, so that the professional development Different Ways of Knowing provided was linked to system goals and outcomes and so that the Different Ways of Knowing staff could hold themselves accountable for results with students and faculty, rather than making program implementation a goal in itself. Different Ways of Knowing had to champion an agenda focused on accountability and standards long before any system of standards and accountability was in place.

These factors caused Different Ways of Knowing to redesign and expand its repertoire of tools and quality-assurance protocols. The institute recognized that it needed to strengthen its own capacity to serve the lowest-performing schools and to align its services within the larger context of district strategic goals.

An Adaptive Design: Supporting District Policies

Because most urban schools are not independent entities, Different Ways of Knowing is an adaptive design. Lauren Resnick of the Insti-tute for Learning at the University of Pittsburgh uses the phrase "learning communities" to describe the idea that a district is com-posed of multiple communities that might be based on discipline and might focus on a particular grade level, administrative role, or some other attribute linking individuals within and across schools. The

Institute for Learning, a key player in urban school reform, asks districts to value "coherence." One manifestation of the concept of districtwide coherence is the selection of a single reading or mathematics program for all elementary teachers. Thus, Different Ways of Knowing teams that work with schools in large urban districts are required to become expert in district policies, programs, and strategic goals. For example, Galef design teams that have contracts with Los Angeles Unified School District elementary schools focus on enhancing the implementation of the district reading program by providing instructional strategies for second-language learners.

Once a district and schools within the district have agreed to work with Different Ways of Knowing, Galef selects the lead coach, who will manage the quality assurance of the contract. Preimplementation services include data-based, customized planning, in which one-year goals are established and quarterly benchmarks for student, teacher, and administrator progress are defined. To prepare this custom professional development plan, Galef and the district-school team unpack student-, classroom-, and school-level data to create a shared understanding of the data and identify possible implications for the professional development plan. In large urban districts, one goal of the professional development plan is enhancing the school's capacity to implement the district-selected literacy and mathematics programs in ways that meet the unique needs of students, parents, and educators. Meeting these needs helps to engage the community and thus increases the district's capacity to implement a coherent education plan.

Additional Lessons About Scale and Staffing
In the era of increased demand following the passage of CSRD, Different Ways of Knowing also learned other valuable lessons about scale-up and staffing. For instance, because schools have different goals, needs, and populations, Different Ways of Knowing staff made delivery of services more flexible instead of trying to fit all schools to the same Procrustean bed. The design team recognized that a more-effective way of providing support would be for Different Ways of Knowing coaches to work directly with classroom teachers in the first

three years and then with the district's own teacher leaders in the fourth and fifth years as these local experts took over the task of providing direct support to classroom teachers. Different Ways of Knowing found out that sustaining change depends on the stability of leadership and faculty at the school and district. As leadership changes, there are ongoing costs for the professional development and support of new teachers and administrators.

Between 1998 and 2000, the design staff became increasingly conscious of Andrew Galef's early advice about the liabilities of expanding too rapidly. Bigger is not necessarily better. The only way in which economies of scale actually reduced expenses was by reducing nonpersonnel costs, such as printing and travel. The coaching model required ongoing training and intense support in the classroom—the more schools that adopted the program, the more trainers were needed, and the more the program cost.

Different Ways of Knowing management was determined to avoid overexpansion and sought to control growth by marketing only to states in which we had highly skilled coaches and capacity. We determined that controlling our geographic spread by not going to every state fair and marketing everywhere was in our interest as an organization. We also recognized the importance of ensuring an adequate supply of coaches by strengthening retention of coaches and establishing a national faculty of certified coaches.

Management was determined to make the work desirable to quality educators. The notion of establishing a national faculty with real incentives was appealing because our best coaches require less training and can also take on quality-assurance roles to ensure that the implementation meets certain benchmarks, gathers appropriate data from stakeholders, and follows established protocols. Different Ways of Knowing management discovered that it was better and more cost-effective to hire coaches, making them full-time employees of the institute, than to retain a group of part-time consultants. This may seem counterintuitive from a business perspective because of the loss of flexibility associated with a full-time staff and the reduction in the supply of well-qualified applicants. But, in providing a complex school improvement design that includes curricula, professional development, and coaching that costs millions to develop and improve, constant training of the front-line implementers (i.e., the coaches) is essential.

Frequently, only 60 percent of part-time coaches could attend these sessions, creating a need to conduct constant follow-up training. Ultimately, Different Ways of Knowing recognized a need for a dedicated national faculty of coaches, organized regionally, that could be counted on for predictable, reliable scheduling with schools and with the institute to enhance their skills, support and mentor new coaches, keep up to date with new state and federal policies and Different Ways of Knowing products, and receive the six to eight weeks of training necessary to keep up with the best research on adult learning. Also, dedicated staff are more invested in the Different Ways of Knowing model and have proven more effective not only in teaching classroom techniques but also in building support for the model's goals and purposes.

Different Ways of Knowing leaders also recognized that the program could benefit by outsourcing some of its marketing activities. To better serve regional and local schools, Different Ways of Knowing has, in recent years, subcontracted some marketing activities to such organizations as the Kentucky Collaborative for Teaching and Learning; WestEd's Learning Innovation in Massachusetts; and the Pacific Regional Education Lab, where many coaches associated with these organizations have come through Different Ways of Knowing training. With its growing number of charter school clients, Different Ways of Knowing is working with the NAS Education Entrepreneurs Fund to help market the program, vet new schools, and meet the needs of this growing market. Charter school organizers say that the Different Ways of Knowing design helps them gain a competitive edge over private schools, because many parents equate arts-infused learning with the robust, enriched curriculum typically available at private schools.

Cross-Training as a Cultural Norm

The ability to recognize what needs to be done and the willingness to jump in and do it are qualities we seek and attempt to inculcate in

Different Ways of Knowing staff. Everyone—from coaches to senior staff on the business team—knows how to step into conversations with school clients. Equally important, our professional staff members understand that we can all be called in to prepare for a national conference or to respond to sales and promotion requests that help turn leads into prospects and contracts. Staff work together in ad hoc teams and groups using conversation norms and protocols that reflect corporate values that have evolved over years. Before we can sell it, Galef needs to model it and be it.

New Approaches to Commitment: Before the Details Take Over

In recent years, the Galef Institute has found tremendous advantages in launching the partnership planning phase in individual schools with a protocol that reconnects the school stakeholders to a vision of success for all students and educators, one that energizes rather than saps the individuals, and hence the process of intellectual and creative energy. Schools that have been identified as underperforming tend to launch into a planning process with a "what went wrong . . . who went wrong" conversation cycle. Different Ways of Knowing has developed protocols to spark more-productive discourse, encouraging educators to recommit to what is possible for their students and for themselves, imagining a future in which necessary breakthroughs continue to occur. This process provides the much-needed "can do" spirit, especially when a school has been publicly identified as chronically underperforming.

Different Ways of Knowing then works with the school to "unpack" the story of the school from its self-assessment, using various data sets, including student achievement data, professional development histories, district and state policies, and perceptions of strengths and opportunities. The institute also offers schools annual formative evaluation tools and protocols for their own self-study through our collaborative relationship with Professor Steve Ross at the Center for Research in Educational Policy at the University of Memphis. The information helps schools set priorities, establish dialogue, and determine goals, while providing an opportunity for stakeholders to have a greater voice in school improvement. In addition, by disaggregating the data, schools can detect patterns and determine their effectiveness at serving specific populations.

Different Ways of Knowing is in the process of developing a community asset map—a tool for identifying assets in the school and community that can support the partnership goals (including teachers and parents whose artistic talents may have been unknown to the school) and other organizational resources, such as museums and libraries.

New Ways of Working with Schools and Districts: Trust and Verify
Both the process Different Ways of Knowing uses to work with schools and districts and how schools decide on providers have evolved considerably since 1998. Prior to the Obey-Porter legislation, Galef worked in only five states, and participating districts were all supported by private funders, whose support included a full year of planning, school enrollment, and partnership design prior to implementation, as well as continuous funding to support close monitoring of every site's implementation and adaptation. With CSRD, schools and districts decide on their designs in different ways. Whenever possible, Galef continues to use its partnership-building protocols, which include a series of on-site meetings to understand the school's past, present, and envisioned future. Even so, a school's decisionmaking process for using funds is not free of politics. A handful of schools has treated Different Ways of Knowing as a kind of mail-order bride, selected from a group of candidates with great pride and enthusiasm. In some of these cases, Galef chose to build awareness and planning into the first year of services. In one of these cases, we politely asked that the school choose another provider. Thus, Galef has evolved a more-philosophical disposition for defining such concepts as school buy-in, which is captured in the phrase former U.S. President Ronald Reagan was fond of: "trust but verify." And so we do. If the school asks for assistance early on, we provide sessions with protocols for taking a vote or building toward consensus. Either way, we gather data, we trust, and we verify.

With growing experience in implementing comprehensive school reform, and now with NCLB, state and district personnel are increasingly sophisticated consumers of services and more-effective implementation partners because they are focused on results.

New Tools and Benchmarks

Research has shown that the Different Ways of Knowing tools and services produced stronger effects when the entire faculty participated. Thus, from 1998 on, the institute focused its partnership-building efforts exclusively on schoolwide commitments.

In working with these schools, Galef Institute's first key strategy for achieving our growth goals is to focus on establishing benchmarks for rates of improvement. Different Ways of Knowing coaches help determine what constitutes effective implementation and implement tools for identifying where changes need to be made, building a common understanding of success, and taking advantage of unique assets within the community.

Equally important, Different Ways of Knowing has developed an adaptive approach to data-based professional development planning to make schools more-effective consumers of professional development services. The schoolwide professional development plan utilizes the model's design elements, as previously articulated, and engages teachers, site administrators, and other key stakeholders in learning in a variety of instructional settings, including

- **coaching for results:** An interdisciplinary team of coaches provides onsite, job-embedded coaching, direct training, demonstrations, coteaching, and study groups, working with individual teachers, grade-level groups, and departments focused on enhancing and accelerating their literacy, math and science learning, and achievement for students in all demographic groups.
- **school-based institutes:** Teachers, site administrators, specialists, and family and community members use a systematic approach to data-based planning of their curriculum, instruction, and professional development, ensuring alignment with their annual progress goals.

- **leadership team national institutes:** Principals, site administrators, lead teachers, and district leaders strengthen their team capacity to meet the goals of NCLB with a focus on enhancing their leadership skills to accelerate their implementation of school improvement plans. Teacher leaders learn coaching dispositions and skills to accelerate schoolwide best practices.
- **customized professional development workshops, lesson study groups, and practicums:** A series of workshops and other formats focused on standards-based teaching and learning, including lesson study, analysis of student work, and experiential learning environments, deepens teachers' understanding of the construction of knowledge and expands their instructional repertoires for meeting diverse student learning needs.
- **materials, tools, and technology:** Different Ways of Knowing curriculum and instruction modules, multimedia student resource materials, professional publications, and Web-based resources provide a solid infrastructure for developing and sustaining school improvement results for all students identified in NCLB.
- **school self-assessment:** Different Ways of Knowing offers two forms of self assessment. In partnership with Professor Steven Ross of Education Innovation, LLC, we offer schools a Formative Evaluation Toolkit, which includes classroom observations by university-trained individuals. For those schools ready and eager to do their own self-study, we recommend Victoria L. Bernhardt's "The School Portfolio Toolkit" (Bernhardt, 2003a).

In addition, schools completing the multiyear professional development plan can sustain their improved results through involvement in the national network of Different Ways of Knowing schools, continued participation in annual leadership institutes (national and regional), online professional development services, and school-based coaching support for school leadership.

Expansion into Middle Schools

Another type of capacity-building is adapting a program to a new constituency. Although Different Ways of Knowing was originally developed for elementary school students, many educators have expressed interest in adapting the program to students and teachers in the middle grades. The institute began conducting field studies in 1997 in response to demands from middle school teachers and parents in California and Kentucky who noticed that students coming to their classrooms from many Different Ways of Knowing elementary settings had unexpected habits. They found that Different Ways of Knowing students expect to do rigorous research and to express what they had learned in multiple ways. These more-advanced students need different types of middle schools that build on the Different Ways of Knowing methods proven in elementary schools. Finally, in 2001, the institute established a five-year, $13.1 million contract with the U.S. Department of Education to expand the Different Ways of Knowing design into middle schools, adapting it to meet the unique needs of young adolescents.

As a result of this research and an informal assessment of the applicability of the Different Ways of Knowing design for the middle grades that middle grades consultant Joan Lipsitz conducted in 1999, Galef established that the framework for its curriculum tools and professional development designs would use the criteria for high-performing middle schools developed by The National Forum to Accelerate Middle Grades Reform. The criteria require schools to be

- **academically rigorous:** Learning events must be aligned with high standards. Standards are the constant; instructional strategies are variable. Teachers provide the support students need to succeed, with extra help as needed, and students will push the "achievement envelope" and delight themselves with how far they can go with a project. They gain deep understanding of concepts and they develop essential skills and the ability to connect to the real world.
- **developmentally responsive:** Learning events should be personalized to support each student's intellectual, ethical, social,

and physical development. Students work together in small groups and develop mutually respectful relationships. They have access to a wide variety of instructional strategies that foster curiosity, exploration, and creativity. They have opportunities to express themselves, participate in decisionmaking as citizens, and involve their families and community in their learning.

- **socially equitable:** Learning events should give students opportunities to learn about and appreciate their own and others' cultures. Students have equal access in all classrooms to valued knowledge and experiences. They expect high-quality work of themselves and others, as they learn to rely on one another for substantive knowledge undergirding the success of their own performance. They have supportive adults in their daily lives at school. In schools that have achieved social equity, parents and school leaders believe that economic or cultural factors need not place students at risk of school failure.

Challenges Associated with Supporting the Goals of the No Child Left Behind Act

NCLB is now being implemented by each state; thus, such initiatives as Different Ways of Knowing have clear state-by-state guidelines that specify the scope (or kinds) of services most required and organize the limited resources. NCLB creates challenges and opportunities for all intermediary organizations and publishers who provide materials and school improvement services. More than ever, schools not meeting their AYP targets will need strategic support to ensure that all their students and student groups will achieve these new higher standards and to bolster teacher quality to work more effectively with low-income, minority, and special-needs students.

In the context of NCLB, the Galef Institute, with its focus on classroom teaching and learning, is well positioned to respond to the urgent needs of schools. To meet these new requirements of districts and schools, the Galef Institute has become even more flexible and adaptable as a service-centered organization. We have focused on building teams of experts that work with schools to shape, focus, and implement their school improvement plans and help accelerate math, language, and science literacy for different types of students and learners. We have increased our emphasis on developing leadership and introducing systems for change to enhance and accelerate success for all students. The institute has also redoubled its efforts to simultaneously introduce effective standards-based instructional practices that increase student performance for different student groups. But we continually remind our clients that joy and rigor can exist simultaneously, particularly when schools integrate the arts and culture as part of the life of school.

Refining the Implementation of Different Ways of Knowing

In 2003, we introduced a revised scope of services aligned with our new tools and benchmarks to help schools better understand how we work. The services are presented to clients as part of a multiphased implementation process. Each of these phases is described below.

Phase 1: Collaborative Inquiry and Data-Based Professional Development Planning. Schools have a great deal of student- and school-level data. Using Victoria Bernhardt's framework for using data for comprehensive schoolwide improvement (2003b), schools implement a systematic approach to analyzing their data and using it to plan programs and professional development. Different Ways of Knowing also provides schools with the opportunity to document their school improvement processes by working with the Center for the Research in Education Policy at the University of Memphis, using their Formative Evaluation Process for Schoolwide Improvement program, providing baseline data on schoolwide program implementation and school climate. Throughout Phase 1, Different Ways of Knowing coaches collaborate on the development of a "gap analysis" en route to the development of their data-based curriculum, instruction, and professional development plan. Also during this phase, we

- clarify expectations of all stakeholders and organizations involved
- determine roles and responsibilities

- request additional data—e.g., organization charts, attendance, reading program pacing plan, math program pacing plan, calendar (traditional versus year-round), internal leadership structure, anecdotal data about current needs or issues, disaggregated AYP and other standardized data (if we do not already have it), and an enhanced school profile or portfolio.

This planning phase includes formal and informal meetings with school leaders, community leaders and staff, data-based conversations about what is going on in the schools; the implementation of a self-assessment or school audit; and schoolwide content and/or grade-level-specific discussions. Key results and deliverables in this phase include

- establishment of an instructional leadership group
- identification of recommendations for providing customized and specific services
- development of a customized, written plan—including benchmarks—to reach AYP, which is agreed to and signed off on by the principal (and in most cases, the district liaison)
- orientation of school staff.

Phase 2: Implementation of Professional Development Plan. Galef Institute consultants work with stakeholders to enhance and accelerate student learning and achievement through effective implementation of Different Ways of Knowing strategies and tools, as outlined in the seven components of high-performing schools described earlier.

Phase 3: Ongoing Assessment of Impact and Partnership Contract Review. The Galef team and the school team gather and analyze school-, classroom-, and student-level data to assess the effects of the services and to adapt the scope of services for effectiveness.

To enhance its ability to grow to meet new demands, the Galef Institute has repositioned responsibility within the organization to improve quality-control protocols, tighten feedback loops, and strengthen internal training, to make Different Ways of Knowing services as affordable as possible while maintaining quality and to focus our contract deliverables on school results—doing what it takes to accomplish the goals. The national office will continue in an R&D mode of close oversight and documentation of contract fulfillment to learn from each of our participating schools.

To train and support its coaches, the Galef Institute organizes regional coaching institutes and national institutes throughout the year. Through two federally funded grants from the Department of Education, Different Ways of Knowing has developed and tested courses of study and tools for apprentice and master coaches.

Providing Services for New Schools

In response to new school clients, the institute has formally broadened its operation to include New School Services, which are services designed to help community leaders and educators turn their unique visions for public schools into new schools and charter schools with effective operations and learning programs that demonstrate achievement for every child, even in the first year of operation, which is now a mandate under NCLB. To date, the Galef Institute has helped new schools in Grades K–12 in California, Michigan, Pennsylvania, and Texas. Services include overall education planning, professional development, leadership training and coaching, and training of community artists. Other consulting services include personnel selection, fundraising, and brokering services with quality providers of charter school services. If new schools already have a strong infrastructure in place, the institute adapts its tools and services to provide them with an effective approach to teaching and learning that ensures that all students—including nontraditional learners—achieve AYP in the first year. Each school works with a Galef Institute coaching team that supports teachers in using best practices, addressing individual student learning needs, and guiding administrators in leading a process of continuous, data-driven school improvement.

The Future of Schoolwide Reform: Obtaining the Resources to Support Intermediary Organizations

Throughout its history, the institute staff and the national faculty of coaches have worked as an adaptive learning community, documenting the work and changing in response to federal and state legislation and market conditions. Still, Different Ways of Knowing remains true to its theory of learning (represented in its curriculum modules), its theory of change (embedded in a sophisticated coaching model), and its theory of action (embedded in its focus on school-based, job-embedded professional learning for teachers and administrators). As of this writing, Different Ways of Knowing has been invited by charter high schools and by funders of high school reform to expand Different Ways of Knowing to serve small high school communities. We will continue to adapt the original design elements and delivery systems to better serve the needs of educators and school systems under NCLB. The training, ongoing support, and materials that Different Ways of Knowing and similar school designs provide serve as the Velcro between increasing demands for teacher quality and the administrators who must meet these greater expectations. Different Ways of Knowing supports educators in their commitment to increase their effectiveness in the context of today's challenges.

Schools that have partnered with a design or model are not the only ones to have benefited from the movement to scale up schoolwide reform initiatives. The CSR legislation and the explosion of implementation data on CSR have already added value to the national conversation on school improvement and what constitutes a "good enough" school improvement plan. Research has proven school improvement designs to be effective at raising test scores, improving teacher practices, and telling schools and districts where further improvements are needed—provided the schools implement the model rigorously. Different Ways of Knowing has spent millions of dollars on research and on adapting, testing, and refining our program to meet the needs of real contexts and will require millions more. The intellectual capital at the institute is sizable. It remains unclear, however, who values this knowledge enough to protect it.

It is difficult to raise resources that do not go immediately and directly to the classroom, even when they will benefit students in the long run. Everyone wants to fund the coach who sits with a teacher or the book that goes into the hands of a child, but few resources are available to support the groups of educators and applied researchers that develop protocols and tools for coaches and teachers. Still, such R&D is needed to enable schools to cope with current and future challenges. Merck, Lilly, and other pharmaceutical companies create new products by passing costs for R&D and marketing on to the customer. In education, textbook publishers do the same. The developers of school improvement designs cannot, however, front-load a 500-percent markup to pay salaries for technical assistance to coaches or for scientific studies. While the emerging What Works Clearinghouse, established by the Institute of Education Sciences in the U.S. Department of Education, is a strong step forward and a clear proclamation from the government about the vital need for more-carefully controlled studies of outcomes in education, it is still not clear who will provide the "supply side" funds for education research, aside from the math and science initiatives that the National Science Foundation supports. Today, despite a demand for more research, no one seems to be following in the "incubator" tradition of the New American Schools Development Corporation and such visionaries as Andrew Galef, who funded the initial R&D for Different Ways of Knowing.

Different Ways of Knowing has benefited from R&D support to expand its model to reach students in higher grades. The program began in elementary schools, expanded to middle schools, and is now finalizing plans to develop tools and services for prekindergarten settings and small high schools. The real demand for new phases of expansion is in work with schools to meet the needs the NCLB legislation has created.

America's families ache for high-quality K–12 education for their children. Thus, Congress and the White House would be likely to find ample public support for developing and funding a public-private trust that encourages funding for research and infrastructure to make sure schools truly use what works. Education innovators need ongoing support from government and the private sector to identify quality people and ideas, for research, and for infrastructure. The nation needs to develop mechanisms to share the costs of research with school districts. This will enable change agents to focus their energy on R&D activities that can be harnessed to accelerate real results for all our children.

References

Anderson, J., and S. M. Kosslyn, eds., *Tutorials in Learning and Memory*, New York: W. H. Freeman and Company, 1984.

Beck, I. L., M. G. McKeown, R. L. Hamilton, and L. Kucan, *Questioning the Author: An Approach for Enhancing Student Engagement with Text*, Newark, Del.: International Reading Association, 1997.

Bereiter, C., and M. Scardamalia, "An Attainable Version of High Literacy: Approaches to Teaching Higher-Order Skills in Reading and Writing," *Curriculum Inquiry*, Vol. 17, No. 1, 1987, pp. 9–30.

Bernhardt, V. L., The School Portfolio Toolkit, Larchmont, N.Y.: Eye on Education, Inc., 2003a.

———, Using Data to Improve Student Learning, Larchmont, N.Y.: Eye on Education, Inc., 2003b.

Bleich, M., "All Schools Can Learn," *Education Week on the Web*, Vol. 14, June 14, 1995, p. 33.

Bodilly, S., J. B. Keltner, S. W. Purnell, R. E. Reichardt, and G. L. Schuyler, *Lessons from New American Schools' Scale-Up Phase: Prospects for Bringing Designs to Multiple Schools*, Santa Monica, Calif.: RAND Corporation, MR-942-NAS, 1998.

Bransford, J., Human *Cognition: Learning, Understanding, and Remembering*, Belmont, Calif.: Wadsworth Publishing Company, 1979.

Bransford, J., A. L. Brown, and R. R. Cocking, *How People Learn: Brain, Mind, Experience, and School*, Washington, D.C.: National Academy Press, 1999.

Britton, J., *Language and Learning: The Importance of Speech in Children's Development*, 2nd ed., Portsmouth, N.H.: Boynton/Cook Publishers: Heinemann, 1993.

Catterall, J. S., *Different Ways of Knowing: 1991–94 Longitudinal Study of Program Effects on Students and Teachers*, Los Angeles: University of California at Los Angeles, Graduate School of Education and Information Studies, 1995.

Catterall, J. S., J. P. Dreyfus, and K. DeJarnette, *Different Ways of Knowing: Rosemead School District Partnership, 1994–95 Evaluation Report*, Los Angeles: University of California at Los Angeles, Graduate School of Education and Information Studies, 1995.

Comer, J., "Home-School Relationships as They Affect the Academic Success of Children," *Education and Urban Society*, Vol. 16, 1984, pp. 323–337.

Costa, A. L., and B. Kallick, *Activating & Engaging Habits of Mind*, Alexandria, Va.: Association for Supervision and Curriculum Development, 2000a.

———, *Assessing & Reporting on Habits of Mind*, Alexandria, Va.: Association for Supervision and Curriculum Development, 2000b.

———, *Discovering & Exploring Habits of Mind*, Alexandria, Va.: Association for Supervision and Curriculum Development, 2000c.

———, *Integrating & Sustaining Habits of Mind*, Alexandria, Va., Association for Supervision and Curriculum Development, 2000d.

Datnow, A., L. Hubbard, and H. Mehan, *Extending Educational Reform: From One School to Many*, London: Routledge/Falmer, 2002.

Eisner, E. W., *The Enlightened Eye: Qualitative Inquiry and the Enhancement of Educational Practice*, New York: Macmillan Pub. Co., 1991.

Emerson, R. W., *The Conduct of Life*, Cambridge, Mass.: Harvard University Press, [1860] 2003.

Epstein, J. L., M. G. Sanders, B. S. Simon, K. C. Salinas, and N. R. Jansorn, *School, Family, and Community Partnerships: Your Handbook for Action*, Thousand Oaks, Calif.: Corwin Press, 1997.

Erickson, H. L., *Stirring the Head, Heart, and Soul: Redefining Curriculum and Instruction*, Thousand Oaks, Calif.: Corwin Press, 2001.

Gardner, H., *Frames of Mind: The Theory of Multiple Intelligences*, New York: Basic Books, Inc., 1983.

Gardner, H., *Multiple Intelligences: The Theory in Practice*, New York: BasicBooks, 1993.

———, *The Arts and Human Development*, New York: BasicBooks, 1994.

Gee, K., *Visual Arts as a Way of Knowing*, Los Angeles: Galef Institute, and York, Me.: Stenhouse Publishers, 2000.

Gilligan, C., *In a Different Voice*, Cambridge, Mass.: Harvard University Press, 1983.

Glennan, T. K., *New American Schools After Six Years*, Santa Monica, Calif.: RAND Corporation, MR-945-NAS, 1998.

Hill, P., personal communication, 2003.

Hovda, R. A., and D. W. Kyle, *Different Ways of Knowing Study B: Research and Evaluation Project*, Louisville, Ky.: The Galef Institute–Kentucky Collaborative for Teaching and Learning, 1997.

Jenkins, J. F., "A Foundation Course in Art Valuation Project for Young Adolescents," *Art Education*, Vol. 22, No. 1, January 1969, pp. 32–34.

Johannesen, L. A., "Different Ways of Knowing," Los Angeles: The Galef Institute, 1995.

_____, "Different Ways of Knowing," Los Angeles: The Galef Institute, 2003.

Klatzky, R. L., *Human Memory: Structures and Processes*, 2nd ed., New York: W. H. Freeman and Company, 1980.

Langer, J. A., and M. Smith-Burke, eds., *Reader Meets Author: Bridging the Gap: A Psycholinguistic and Sociolinguistic Perspective*, Barksdale, Del.: International Reading Association, 1982.

Levine, M., *A Mind at a Time*, New York: Simon & Schuster, 2002.

Lightfoot, M., and N. Martin, *The Word for Teaching Is Learning: Language and Learning Today*, London: Heinemann Educational Books, 1988.

Mandler, G., *Mind and Body: Psychology of Emotion and Stress*, New York: W. W. Norton & Company, 1975.

Mapp, K., "Having Their Say: Parents Describe Why and How They Are Engaged in Their Children's Learning," *The School Community Journal*, Vol. 13, No. 1, 2003, pp. 35–64.

McLaughlin, M. W., and I. Oberman, *Teacher Learning: New Policies, New Practices*, The Series on School Reform, New York: Teachers College Press, 1996.

Northwest Regional Educational Laboratory, *The Catalogue of School Reform Models*, 1st ed., Portland, Oreg.: Northwest Regional Educational Laboratory, 1998. Online at http://www.nwrel.org/scpd/catalog/about.shtml (as of November 25, 2003).

Perkins, D., *The Intelligent Eye: Learning to Think by Looking at Art*, Los Angeles: Getty Center for Education in the Arts, 1994.

Peterson, J., M. Schwager, M. Crepeau, and K. Curry, *The Galef Institute/WestEd Evaluation Report of San Francisco Unified School District's Implementation of Different Ways of Knowing, 1997–1998*," San Francisco: WestEd, 1999.

Petrosko, J. M., *Different Ways of Knowing Study A: Implementation of Student-Centered Teaching and Learning Practices and Student Assessment Results for Research Demonstration Site (RDS) Schools Participating in Different Ways of Knowing*, Louisville, Ky.: The Galef Institute–Kentucky Collaborative for Teaching and Learning, 1997.

Piaget, J., "The Theory of Stages in Cognitive Development," in D. Green, M. Ford, and G. Flamer, eds., *Measurement and Piaget*, New York: McGraw-Hill, 1971, pp. 1–7.

Policy Studies Associates, Inc., *Different Ways of Knowing: Effects on Elementary Teaching and Learning in Kentucky*, Washington, D.C.: Policy Studies Associates, Inc., 1997.

Resnick, L. B., *Education and Learning to Think*, Washington, D.C.: National Academy Press, 1987.

———, ed., *Knowing, Learning, and Instruction: Essays in Honor of Robert Glaser*, Hillsdale: N.J.: Lawrence Erlbaum Associates, 1989.

———, "From Aptitude to Effort: A New Foundation for Our Schools," *Daedalus*, Vol. 124, No. 4, 1995, pp. 55–62.

Robinson, K., *Out of Our Minds: Learning to Be Creative*, Oxford, United Kingdom: Capstone Publishing, 2001

Sarason, S., *Teaching as a Performing Art*, New York: Teachers College Press, 1999.

Schmoker, M., *Results: The Key to Continuous School Improvement*, 2nd ed., Alexandria, Va.: Association for Supervision and Curriculum Development, 1999.

Slavin, R. E., "Cooperative Learning and Student Achievement," *Educational Leadership*, Vol. 46, No. 2, 1988, pp. 31–33.

Sparks, D., and S. Hirsh, *A New Vision for Staff Development*, Alexandria, Va.: Association for Supervision and Curriculum Development, 1997, pp. 1–17.

Sternberg, R. J., *Human Abilities: An Information-Processing Approach*, New York: W. H. Freeman and Company, 1985.

———, *The Triarchic Mind: A New Theory of Intelligence*, New York: Viking Press, 1988.

Stipeck, D. J., *Motivation to Learn: From Theory to Practice*, Englewood Cliffs, N.J.: Prentice-Hall, 1998.

Wang, C., and D. Sogin, *Different Ways of Knowing Study C: Different Ways of Knowing Arts in Education in Kentucky Schools Research Report*, Louisville, Ky.: The Galef Institute–Kentucky Collaborative for Teaching and Learning, 1996.

Wiggins, G., and J. McTighe, *Understanding by Design*, Alexandria, Va.: Association for Supervision and Curriculum Development, 1998.

Wolfe, D. P., and D. Balick, *Art Works! Interdisciplinary Learning Powered by the Arts*, Portsmouth, N.H.: Heinemann, 1999.

CHAPTER NINE

Co-nect at the Crossroads:
Four Considerations on Getting to Scale

Bruce Goldberg

In his chapter, Goldberg identifies four features of school reform programs that, he argues, make them worthy of being taken to scale: the capacity to improve student performance in a measurable way, the moral desirability of what is taught, the feasibility of implementing an effective and desirable program, and the sustainability of institutional change. Against this backdrop, he discusses recent changes in the environment that governs the supply and demand for school reform services, as well as changes likely to occur in the near future. He describes the efforts of his organization to respond to these environmental shifts, including moves to commoditization and modularization. Contending that adaptability is crucial to the expansion and effectiveness of school reform organizations capable of scaling up the kinds of changes that embody the four features of credible—and creditable—school reforms, he also observes that such organizations are essential for scaling up educational reforms because it is they who can best reconcile policy requirements and economic realities.

Ideas have consequences, and there is, perhaps, no set of ideas more plentiful and more vigorously debated than those that relate to how we might best educate our children. But not all ideas are created equal; both their quality and their consequences can differ dramatically. In the world of educational reform, useful ideas are those that, when effectively implemented, are reliably successful in improving the performance of school children in the near term and are socially and morally desirable in that they provide a foundation for subsequent learning and development. Further, for ideas about school reform to be useful, it must be feasible to implement them in a wide variety of circumstances and locations, and they must provide the basis for sustainable institutional change. It is only these ideas that are worthy of being taken to scale.

In this chapter, I first discuss the current intellectual, political, and economic context of school reform. This discussion provides a foundation for an examination of the four criteria that any school reform program must address: success, desirability, feasibility, and sustainability. The chapter discusses each of these concepts in relation to Co-nect, a school improvement organization I have been associated with for more than a decade. In this analysis, I focus on the importance of adaptability in going to scale—adaptability in the design of reforms, in the efforts of reformers within school systems, and in the positioning of reform organizations within the education reform marketplace.

The Climate and Conditions for Scaling Up

Today's environment for scaling education reforms differs greatly from that of only a few years ago. Important changes have occurred in the intellectual thrust of school reform efforts, in the political context that both supports and constrains school reform, and in the economic environment within which school reform is taking place. Although these changes are interrelated, the distinction is analytically useful in that it draws attention to the diverse levels at which educational reformers must operate: within schools as agents of change in support of specific learning goals, in the political system that shapes educational requirements and allocates resources, and in the larger economy that generates (and limits) both resources for education reform and competition among education reformers.

In terms of the intellectual foundations of educational reform, the key features of the contemporary context are

- a greater focus on content-driven instruction and performance, beginning with literacy and mathematics
- increased emphasis on the importance of individual learners in documenting results and on closing the gap between high-performing and low-performing subpopulations

- a shift from a one-size-fits-all model of school reform to a model employing targeted interventions designed specifically for disadvantaged and poor-performing schools and students.

These changes are based on research documenting a persistent achievement gap between subgroups in the student population and an emerging consensus that the best way to close the gap is to ensure that school change efforts address the variations in how individual students learn specific subject matter.

From the point of view of school reformers, the political context of reform efforts has become increasingly complex as the result of requirements imposed as part of the "standards movement." These changes include

- a shift in focus from evidence of outcomes based on qualitative research to quantitative measures of the effects of interventions
- the emergence of large-scale, high-stakes testing and accountability systems
- a shift from a school-by-school approach to reform to a strategy that necessarily involves districts and states.

Finally, with regard to the economic context of school reform, the key factor is the decline in financial resources available for school reform. The weak economy of the late 1990s and the first few years of this decade has reduced the resources available for school reforms, forcing reformers who want to stay in business to become increasingly efficient and to address their efforts more directly to the demands of the market.

This chapter deals with the lessons learned (and those still being learned) about getting to scale in this environment. As noted above, these lessons are drawn from a particular context: our experience in taking the Co-nect program to scale. Beginning as a comprehensive model school provider in the late 1990s, Co-nect has evolved in new directions over the past decade. We have incorporated elements of the original model, using them in a way that enables us to customize these elements and introduce them at a time that meets the specific needs of individual schools. We have also taken various processes intended to produce change (for example, the implementation of collaborative decisionmaking and the creation of professional communities) and tied these processes to services designed to improve instruction in specific areas, such as early literacy. Finally, we have taken apart some of the interventions our model used and rebuilt them into more substantial and independent interventions so that they function as modules that client schools can use as needed. Underlying this transition is our belief that improving instructional quality through data-informed decisionmaking is essential to improving student results. Thus, since our origin in 1992, Co-nect has grown from a comprehensive school reform design working in two schools to a more broadly focused professional development organization providing a variety of products and services united by this shared focus. By 2002, we were working to improve instructional quality in more than 200 schools in 65 school districts in 30 states.

Table 9.1 provides a general overview of our historical development over the past decade.

Despite this growth (or perhaps because of it), we find ourselves at a crossroads. There are many questions we must address: Where can and do we go from here? As an organization that evolved from a comprehensive school reform service based on a well-defined model, what does getting to scale mean in a rapidly changing environment that demands that services be tailored to the needs of individual students and individual schools? What additional products and services do we need, and what defines their common core? How can we feel confident that what we produce is what is needed and is scalable? Can we do it alone? The contextual shifts cited above have created new realities for education reformers, demanding answers to questions such as these.

Working from our experience and these new realities, I examine four criteria regarding the scale-up of educational reforms: the success of the reform in producing results, the desirability of the actual or potential results, the feasibility of scaling up the intervention, and the sustainability of changes achieved through the intervention.

Table 9.1
Capsule History of Co-nect 1992–2002

Year	Organizational Status	Development Focus	Scale	Measure of Success
1992–1994	Research design team as part of the Educational Technologies Group within BBN Systems & Technologies	Awarded 5-year NAS grant to develop and refine "break the mold" Co-nect design	Co-nect begins in two schools as model provider with focus on project-based learning and technology	Refinement of design and internal team development
1994–1996	Established as Co-nect, a department of BBN Educational Technologies Group	Early development of the exchange, a Web-based portal for teachers. All development internal	Slow growth to about a dozen schools. Development of three-year technical assistance contracts with schools	Implementation of design
1996–1998	Established as independent business unit at BBN	Best practice focus on benchmarks for whole school reform. All development internal	Passage of Obey-Porter Comprehensive School Reform Demonstration Act and rapid growth to 60 schools. Add Co-nectPlus for Co-nect school alumni. Gradual switch from model provider to school-improvement provider	Replication of design incorporating district and state standards
1998–2002	Spun out as independent, venture-backed for-profit corporation, Co-nect, Inc. Gradual focus on developing external partnerships for curriculum content, assessment services, and technology to accompany Co-nect products and services	Exchange-based products: toolbox, diagnostics, knowledge bank, facilitated learning modules. Data-informed decisionmaking. More development resulting from partnerships with other companies and organizations	Rapid growth to 200 schools in 30 states as part of Title 1 Comprehensive School Reform; customization of methodology to school readiness levels; concentration on low-performing and failing schools	Demonstrable improvement in student achievement on specific tests and in specific subject areas

I argue that, although these four considerations are distinct, they are closely related.[1] Indeed, taken together, they might provide the basis for a theory of action regarding the notion of scale. Although individual reforms often embody such theories, we seem, at present, to lack a theory of action about scale itself. The idea that reforms taken *in toto* might benefit from a theory of action is, however, implicit in what follows.

I first outline the relation of scale to success, as indicated by the most important result of reform: student performance. Clearly, judgments about the success of reforms must focus squarely on such results. No longer is it convincing to point to a large number of adherents and advocates of particular interventions to demonstrate success. Evidence of achievement is necessary. But is the evidence now being collected sufficient to validate the goals for which the assessment and accountability systems have been established? Does it ensure that teaching and learning are improving through robust demonstrations of student work? Or is the evidence drawn from a narrower sample of work, circumscribed by norm-referenced, standardized, multiple-choice tests? To ensure that students succeed in a rapidly changing global economy, the tasks on which evidence of achievement is based must reflect at least some of the complexity of what they will need to know and be able to do in that economy.

Following this discussion, I ask what kinds of reforms deserve to be scaled. In so doing, I suggest that we broaden the discussion of results to include not only learning that has already transpired (a necessary condition) but also learning that has yet to occur. Reforms at scale should not only be expected to meet or exceed anticipated gains in learning but should also be expected to encourage learning in the future. Such reforms meet the criterion of desirability. A reform that does not increase the likelihood that students will succeed in the future—that does not provide them with the resources to address new challenges requiring new skills—is not a desirable reform. Getting to

---

[1] These considerations also constitute a set of goals around which a framework of standards for getting to scale might be created.

scale, then, would involve taking into account the likely effects of reforms on the future learning of participating students. Given such concerns, reformers would need not only to define ways to measure current results but also to anticipate how their long-term success might be measured. We will have to not only examine the minimum expectations necessary to ensure knowledge in specific subject areas but also understand and plan to build upon these expectations so that they lead to more complex "project-based" demonstrations of expertise.

Not every reform, desirable or not, can get to scale. A reform might be too unwieldy to enable widespread diffusion or adoption. It might require too many human or financial resources. Or, like a rare orchid, it might be too dependent on particular environmental conditions to implement or cultivate outside a hothouse environment. For educational reforms, the environment includes, among other things, the skills and motivations of those implementing them and the funding required to support them. Although receptivity to a particular reform is not sufficient to judge its success, the degree to which those living the reform believe in and want it is critical in determining whether it will scale. No less important, if funding dries up because the economy declines or priorities shift, even a successful and desirable intervention cannot be taken to scale. In discussing the relationship between scale and feasibility, then, I attempt to unpack some of the conditions that might affect whether a reform can be taken to scale.

Finally, I discuss the notion of sustainability. Here, my perspective differs from what I perceive to be the dominant metaphor underlying strategies for achieving lasting change, a metaphor expressed in the language of mechanical and industrial treatments of change. The context for getting to scale is more complex, and the means by which individual reforms get to scale should be cast in language that portrays reforms as part of a dynamic system in which ideas and organizations interact through a marketplace involving developers, providers, and consumers, each contributing something that exerts a profound effect on the others. Getting to scale, I suggest, is best understood as part of this larger system, one in which reform products and services and the organizations promoting them evolve in an ever-changing marketplace. Moreover, the peculiar nature of this marketplace invites funding agencies, developers, and policymakers to consider whether and how particular interventions and organizations promoting them coevolve. Further, the properties of this marketplace require providers, such as Co-nect, to adapt continuously to circumstances and agents outside their own direct control while maintaining the characteristics that make them unique and valuable.

Scaling Success: Attention to Results

Reforms without results are empty; they provide no justification for efforts to take them to scale. Only recently, however, have scale and results become seriously joined. Up to now, reforms have been disseminated and adopted for many different reasons—clever marketing, the promise of additional funding to adopters, or the perception that they can produce mandated changes with little investment of time and effort. It has also been possible for reforms to approach scale by promulgating principles or processes, which, if faithfully implemented, might help with all sorts of things—faculty morale or student attendance, for instance—but whose precise relation to improved student achievement is tenuous.

No more. Getting to scale now requires reformers to take account of recent changes in our understanding and use of data regarding student performance. In particular, reforms must be fully integrated with developments in the standards and accountability movements. The demand for standards has prompted many states to create tests intended to reflect what students ought to know. These attempts have given rise to a prolonged investigation of the validity of existing testing systems, focusing on whether the tests accurately and adequately represent the content embodied in the state standards, are fair and rigorous, challenge students to think deeply about the content being assessed, and produce results generalizable to other relevant sets of test items. Without subjecting tests to standards related to their use, interpreting their results correctly would be impossible.

These concerns are at the heart of assuring validity. According to the 1999 Standards for Educational and Psychological Testing (American Education Research Association, American Psychological Association, and National Council on Measurement in Education, 1999), *validity* is "the degree to which evidence and theory support the implementation of test scores entailed by proposed uses of tests" (p. 9).

The growth of performance standards and high-stakes testing for students is linked to the establishment of accountability standards for teachers and school administrators. So, in addition to addressing concerns about validity in the interpretation of tests of student performance, states have also had to develop valid systems for assessing accountability. That is, policymakers, researchers, and practitioners have had to determine what kinds of inferences about teachers and schools can be drawn from students' scores. The boundaries of accountability have often been in question: Teachers and principals may be held accountable not only for improving student performance in relation to state standards but also for reducing performance gaps between identifiable subgroups, building public confidence in the school system, and so on. Having established an accountability system, policymakers must determine how to align rewards and sanctions with the goals embodied in the performance standards and accountability models. To ensure that both rewards and sanctions are deserved, policymakers must be confident that changes in student performance flow from the actions of teachers and principals rather than, for example, random fluctuations or sampling error. Out of all of this activity have come suggested standards for accountability systems.[2]

These validity-establishing efforts have, in effect, defined entry requirements for proposed reforms. Reforms that demonstrate results through established assessment and accountability systems are likely to be taken seriously, while those that fail to do so are not.

---

[2] The Center for Research on Evaluation, Standards, and Student Testing in cooperation with the Consortium for Policy Research in Education, has published a full listing of the proposed standards. See Baker et al. (2002).

Results and Measures: Co-nect's Early Years

Ten years ago, the results environment Co-nect inhabited was very different from today's. Established as a New American Schools (NAS)[3] "break-the-mold" design, we were an organization focused on creating a new generation of American schools. Our success was simply a function of making this happen. The more we could influence the design of schools, the more successful we would be. The more schools we could attract to our program, the more effectively we could demonstrate success.

Our design was founded on the premise that school curriculum, instruction, assessment, and organization were intertwined and that to make them more relevant to the changes we perceived occurring in the larger society and economy, each would have to be reconceived. Curriculum would have to be more project-based, instruction more facilitative, assessment more authentic, and the school organization more flexible. Because we believed that the use of technology would be invaluable in bringing this about, we designed computer-based networks in which physically isolated teachers and classrooms could benefit from a shared collaborative culture. A redesigned school would be one whose virtual location was at least as important as its geographical location.

We set out to accomplish this as part of BBN Technologies, a technology-oriented research and development company in Cambridge, Massachusetts. Being housed at BBN minimized our need for outside partnerships because we were able to use the technological developments of the Educational Technologies Department and the larger resources of the company to begin more-intensive work on the design. Beginning in only a very small number of schools also seemed to simplify matters. By 1998, when we became an independent organization, these two factors would play heavily in our ability to get to scale.

---

[3] See Chapter Sixteen in this volume.

Although we expected that our design would eventually demonstrate improved student achievement, we were suspicious of overreliance on traditional standardized measures. Instead, we suggested multiple measures, including the use of performance assessments, portfolios, and projects, or what were often collectively referred to as "alternative assessments." Ten years ago, it was feasible and desirable for a design similar to ours to propose including, as part of its expected results, the effect it would have on the ability of students to work together in teams,[4] the degree to which students would use technology in demonstrating what they know and are able to do, or the degree to which the distinction between in-school and out-of-school learning would become blurred through restructuring of the learning community. These activities and the effects we believed would follow from them seemed as important to us as any proof called for in off-the-shelf, standardized, norm-referenced tests.

Because no one, clear way to define or demonstrate results existed, it was accepted that there would be no one way in which all schools could be held accountable for achieving them. Given some minimal guarantee that their choice was "standards-based," schools were dealt a relatively free hand to choose their own models. In some instances, the district might require a school to choose from a limited set of models; in others, this choice was left largely to the individual school. In either case, the direction policymakers set was one of experimentation. A thousand flowers could bloom.

And they did. The soaring economy of the 1990s brought with it new federal, state, and private funding for schoolwide efforts deemed promising—for the schools and for the organizations that promised them. However, as the standards movement has merged with the accountability movement, student results on established

---

[4] The end of the decade-long standardized Maryland School Performance Assessment Program, which included performance items that had students working in teams, can be considered an early and perhaps unfortunate by-product of the 2001 No Child Left Behind Act (NCLB). Significant, but far fewer, are such states as New Jersey, which are investigating the use of performance assessments that incorporate multiple measures as a means of providing a more fully developed picture of student achievement.

measures are becoming not simply a key determinant of results but, as a practical matter, the only determinant.[5]

High-Stakes Accountability: Unintended Effects

Here, NCLB enters the picture. This law is clearly designed to catalyze progress in closing the all-too-persistent gaps between poorly performing schools and high-achieving schools and between ethnic and socioeconomic subgroups of students who have, historically, performed well and those who have not. One of its key purposes is establishing accountability for results and proof of what works. The logic is fairly straightforward: Results tied to challenging content and high standards for all students are what we want, and it is these results for which students and the providers of services to improve their performance should be held accountable. Holding providers of services accountable will, in turn, motivate schools, districts, and states to incorporate only reforms for which there is strong evidence of effectiveness.

Viewed this way, the federal law is, at least, an indirect attempt to increase the supply of qualified providers to meet the increased demand its accountability provisions will almost certainly trigger. Add to this funding flexibility at the state and district levels, parental choice, and provisions regarding supplemental services for students in failing schools, and the result is a tightly woven set of mutually reinforcing policies and strategies. It is this coherence built upon evidence of effectiveness that NCLB intends to promote.

The advent of these policies and strategies should be good news for those trying to get their reforms to scale, and, on one level, it is. Before the law encouraged this new combination of flexibility and accountability, reforms, good and bad, had been tantamount to fads. They arrived, paraded, and departed on the runway of pedagogical

---

[5] It was really only during in the latter part of the decade that national research initiatives were launched to examine the effects of some of the reform efforts. See, for example, reports compiled by the American Institute for Research (Herman et al., 1999) and the RAND Corporation (Glennan, 1998).

style. Accountability for results and the demand for evidence-based research have helped to alleviate this tendency to adopt the latest educational fashions. Reforms that can show results have a chance at success and longevity; those that cannot will be discarded.

Demonstrating results, however, is not a trivial matter. Part of the difficulty, of course, stems from the many challenges associated with implementing effective reforms in poor-performing schools, but another source of difficulty is the quality of the assessments used to measure performance.[6] Assessments must be relevant to the goals stated in the standards. If what gets measured is what gets taught, it is critical that the assessments measure the kinds of performances we want to measure.

Why is this a worry? First, because the existing state assessments (and the national off-the-shelf tests) do not yet adequately reflect state standards. Neither are they accurate or adequate measures of what students know and can do. Assessment instruments might be getting better, but they do not yet measure student performance satisfactorily. Second, high-stakes accountability systems are premised on reliable and valid assessments. So, if the reforms must demonstrate results, and if the results are based on measures not yet proven to be valid, reformers are in danger of compromising what they know to be good practice simply to demonstrate results.

In particular, paying insufficient attention to these concerns can result in serious and unwanted consequences in three areas: curtailed performance, curricular reductionism, and instructional blindness.

- **Curtailed Performance.** By *curtailed performance*, I mean the propensity for student performance repertoires to shrink when the scope of the assessment items to which students are asked to

---

[6] The implementation of NCLB also involves other unresolved difficulties. For example, as of this writing, it is not yet totally clear how adequate yearly progress (AYP) will play out, given the different sorts of scenarios for measuring AYP among various numbers of individual members constituting subgroups. Neither is it clear how, over multiple years, scenarios exhibiting annual versus "step interval" improvement will meet the criteria specified in the law. These are technical issues that should be resolved over time.

respond narrows. A successful intervention should result in the development of a broader repertoire, not a narrower one. To determine whether a reform effort does, in fact, help expand students' performance repertoires, assessments should be designed to encompass the skills, competencies, and dispositions needed to apply performance standards across a representative sample of tasks, including real-world applications. Avoiding the curtailed-performance effect requires performance measurements that push students toward new problems in new areas, rather than directing their attention to a narrow set of performance criteria.

- **Curricular Reductionism.** Curricular reductionism is the other side of the coin. Curtailed performance limits the range of permissible performances by constructing assessment prompts in a certain way. *Curricular reductionism* refers to the way teachers narrow the curriculum they teach so that it includes only the topics and skills likely to show up on the test. Only a small amount of what is included in a curriculum can be tested. Therefore, when tests are the sole or chief yardstick of accountability, teachers tend to restrict the curriculum and the accompanying instruction to the items being tested. This tendency toward curricular reductionism can compromise the success of reforms intended to broaden the focus of the curriculum (Popham, 2002).

- **Instructional Blindness.** To be fruitful, good assessment should contribute to improved instruction. Assessments ought to inform teachers not only about which students get which items right or wrong but also about the ways in which individual students understand or misunderstand the content domains being assessed. *Instructional blindness* occurs when performance results fail to shed light on the individual differences displayed in what students know and are able to do. Unchecked, it creates impediments to the understanding and treatment of individual students and performance gaps between subpopulations. If the testing and accountability systems emphasize only results for which it is easy and inexpensive to create performance prompts and if the wording of the test items restricts responses, it is not surprising that test results provide limited practical guidance to teachers about ways to help students improve their performance. I will return to this topic when discussing how technology can foster the personalization of learning and the efficient documentation of results.

For Co-nect, these are everyday, real-world problems. We must determine how to prove that what we do with teachers improves test scores yet avoids the temptation to curtail the range of performances we believe necessary to meet standards. We must also determine how to introduce important but neglected parts of the curriculum. Finally, we must determine how to use results to better inform the professional development we provide to teachers. In short, we must avoid becoming a test preparation reform and instead promote the kinds of teaching and learning that not only lead to positive results in the measurement of student performance but also motivate both teachers and students.

One solution to this problem would be simply to do what we have been doing and let the chips fall where they may. But the pressures of time and resources and the increased needs of the schools in which we work make this response unworkable. We need to get results on whatever measures are being used, and we must ensure that we do not harm the standards, the curriculum, or the instruction.

Thus, our program combines training activities, technologies, and content tools to help teachers learn how to "mine and apply" the standards. We help them connect the skills and concepts outlined in the state standards with specific items or prompts in which these skills and concepts are embedded in the state test.

We use three sorts of activities to help establish these relationships. One is directly related to mastery of the skill or concept as it might appear on the test. This we do by using a test-preparation tool that helps teachers understand which specific assessment items point out the need for more or less instructional attention with particular students. A second sort of activity involves analyzing not only the test data (paying special attention to how it can be disaggregated by individual and subgroup) but also examples of student work as gathered through projects, performance assessments, homework assignments, and the like. Finally, to help match the right instructional strategy and tool to the needs reflected in student work, we are in the process of developing a Web-based "teacher toolbox," which contains a number of resources and activities for organizing thinking, lessons, and students. It will help our own professional development experts connect the specific areas in which improvements in student performance are needed with the instructional strategies and resources teachers can use to address those needs. By doing this systematically, we hope to increase the repertoire of skills teachers can use to help students improve their work while maintaining a focus on improving test results.

These are a few ways we address the current limitations of assessment systems, which constitute a very real obstacle to achieving scale, as the development of fair and valid measures proceeds. Together, the three potential adverse consequences of assessment and accountability systems suggested above invite consideration of a minimal standard for getting to scale: To be successful, reforms must do no harm. This is a standard intended for designers of these systems, as well as for developers and implementers of reforms being scaled within them. To meet this standard, we have attempted, first, to ensure that we can adapt our interventions to the existing assessment and accountability systems in which they occur, and, second, to ensure that we do this without abandoning the original core values embodied in our design and for which our original intentions and subsequent research are still valid.

Scaling the Desirable

Reforms, of course, are intended to achieve positive results, but, in some cases, even attaining the modest goal of preventing harm can provide significant benefits. For example, preventing reading difficulties in beginning readers is an important objective of a number of reading programs (including one that I will discuss below, Co-nect's

SafetyNet intervention). When successful, interventions that contain tools for predicting which students are most at risk of failure and measures to prevent failure can be said to have done no harm but also, more importantly, to prevent potential harm from occurring.

Not all reforms, however, are designed to address currently diagnosed problems or shortcomings. They attempt neither to prevent harm nor to undo harm that has been done. Rather, they attempt to address the needs of students who must live in an unpredictable world, a world in which not all situations can be anticipated through rigorous diagnosis and screening. In a very real sense, Co-nect's use of project-based learning is just this sort of reform. This approach is designed to create situations in which the skills needed to meet academic standards are called forth in the context of complex performances and unfamiliar situations that pencil-and-paper tests might not capture easily. That is, an observer can determine whether or not a student understands certain material well enough to meet a particular standard by creating test items to assess performance in relation to the standard and having the student respond. Projects can pose problems that admit of no simple right or wrong answer, complicating the assessment of performance in relation to standards. Whether a student can apply a body of knowledge outside the classroom, in situations that do not involve highly developed measurement systems, may be more revealing than performance on standards-based assessments. How to design the most fitting memorial for the victims of the attacks of September 11, for instance, might require knowledge relevant to standards in mathematics or science, but there is no correct answer to the question.

Often overlooked, but critical to the enterprise of reform, is a key value, a moral purpose, that remains implicit in the work of getting education reforms to scale: ensuring the student's ability to respond to and take advantage of new opportunities and experiences, both as a student and, later, as an adult in a rapidly changing world.

Promoting this ability is as much a value of reforms aimed at pinpointing specific issues that place students at risk of future failure, which is the goal of many reading interventions, as it is of reforms aimed at developing students' abilities to apply what they have learned to complex problems and situations that admit of multiple answers and solutions, which is the goal of much project-based learning. In both classes of reforms, what is important are not only the results that one specifies and aims to achieve in the classroom as a direct result of teaching—results that are typically measured through traditional assessments—but also the results, both positive and negative, that may occur in situations that will arise in the future.

Concern with the ability of students to address new problems is an attribute of reforms that meet the criterion of desirability, of reforms that contribute to what I call "growth through experience," a phrase derived from John Dewey's philosophy. Understanding that not all growth is necessarily desirable (becoming more efficient at criminal activity, for example, is a form of undesirable growth), Dewey (1939, pp. 664–665) raised important questions about the enduring value of growth obtained through the kinds of experiences or work educators provide to students. Ultimately, he left these questions open for each generation of educators to answer for themselves:

> I shall leave you to answer these questions, saying simply that when and *only* when development in a particular line conduces to continuing growth does it answer to the criterion of education as growing.

Reforms that take into account this kind of continuous growth help provide students with the skills they will need to apply the knowledge and problem-solving techniques they learned in school to situations and problems they have not yet experienced. They are sensitive to the ways in which individual students are predisposed to underperforming if left to one-size-fits-all solutions *and* to the ways in which the cognitive tools students acquire as the result of a specific reform help them succeed over time in unique and unforeseen circumstances. Reforms that can accurately predict and preempt reading failure, for example, focus not only on producing positive results but also on preventing negative results. Such reforms could use diverse assessment functions and tools—screening, diagnosis, program monitoring, and external testing, for example—to anticipate whether a student might fail. Reforms that enable teachers to understand and adjust to the continuity of students' experiences over time are those that will help students succeed.

Similarly, interventions that take into account the need to help students acquire the skills to solve new problems—problems that arise after or outside the context of formal instruction and assessment— also serve the moral purpose of ensuring growth through experience. Co-nect's emphasis on project-based learning, for instance, is designed to put students in the position of gathering, organizing, and interpreting data to address problems that are not easy to resolve through the mechanical application of factual knowledge.

Such interventions encourage pedagogies that both personalize learning and individualize instruction. Learning is personalized by assigning appropriate and engaging tasks based on the cognitive and developmental needs of individual students; instruction is individualized by isolating the kinds of instruction particular students need to achieve the goals established. Designing preventive interventions is part of what makes continuous student growth possible. Simply put, to achieve scale, moral purpose, like size, matters.[7]

What is the practical relationship between getting to scale and ensuring continued growth through experience? Certainly, most reformers would say that their enterprises have as a goal—at least an implicit goal—the idea of promoting the ability of students to take what they have learned and apply it to unforeseen circumstances. But if every reform effort makes such claims, does specifying desirability as a criterion for reforms help to distinguish one reform from another? I think so. Consider two related questions relevant to the desirability criterion. First, has the reform or intervention been proven to ensure continued long-term growth in the students for which it is intended? Second, does the reform invite the inclusion of multiple measures against which its success can be evaluated? Only

---

[7] This moral dimension is nicely contrasted in the names of the two most recent Elementary and Secondary Education Acts. The 1994 Act was named "Improving America's Schools." The 2001 Act is "No Child Left Behind." The latter has a clear moral overtone missing in the name of the 1994 act.

the programs of reformers who can answer both questions affirmatively can be said to be desirable.

Interventions that demonstrate increases in student achievement but whose effects fade with time are not conducive to promoting growth through experience. For example, research in the effectiveness of two opposing strategies for dealing with learning-disabled students has shown that exclusive reliance on either "pull-out" or "inclusion" programs often results in similar, undesirable outcomes: Each strategy, when implemented in isolation from the other, fails to deliver long-term improvements in student achievement (Holloway, 2001). That is, each will demonstrate temporary increases in student achievement but fail to sustain that achievement when treated as an exclusive panacea for all students. Such strategies fail to promote the continued ability of students to transform what they know so that they can apply their knowledge to unforeseen circumstances. Thus, they fail to meet the desirability criterion for getting to scale.

More generally, interventions that use only one instructional strategy designed to meet the needs of all at-risk students might also come up short on the desirability criterion. Recent research regarding students who have failed state reading assessments indicates that interventions designed for all students at risk of reading failure often ignore the factors that contribute to failure and, therefore, fail to meet their particular needs (Buly and Valencia, 2002). In part, this is because the programs rely on intervention strategies focused on teaching grade-level standards when "the aim is not to teach the standards, it is to teach the students" (Buly and Valencia, 2002, p. 234).

To help prevent such outcomes, SafetyNet, Co-nect's early literacy program, is designed to assess what each student needs to meet the standards, not how a particular intervention can reach every student who fails to meet the standard. The program does this by placing data-informed decisionmaking at the core of the intervention, not by relying on a particular curriculum or instructional strategy. That is, we have adopted an outcome-driven model that requires continuous assessment of individual student progress. No one intervention can be uniformly appropriate to all cases of reading failure. Reading failure, like growth through experience, "is multifaceted and it is individual" (Buly and Valencia, 2002, p. 232). Related to this concern about getting to the root of individual failure and growth is the use of multiple forms of assessment, including project-based learning. If the results fail to take into account the learning contexts in which assessments matter (both inside and outside school), improvements in performance will also be limited and temporary. Reforms that concentrate exclusively on having students faithfully recapitulate what is already known focus on a necessary, but insufficient, condition in learning new things. Of course, it is impossible to anticipate the full range of demonstrations, performances, and assessments that might be used to measure what is being learned, but this does not mean that the intervention can afford to ignore the attempt.

Environments change; they offer possibilities, opportunities, and dangers that fall outside the well-worn parameters of the known. Organisms attuned, either deliberately or through accident, to these novelties are assured a better chance of survival than those that are not. This "preadaptive" phenomenon, Charles Darwin argued, is responsible for such evolutionary novelties as hearing, the lungs, and flight. If evolution operated by adaptation alone, we would have become extinct long ago. Our capacity to adapt successfully to our environment ensured our existence in the day-to-day struggle to survive. Our capacity for preadaptation enables our survival in the unknown and emerging shape of the future.

The capacity to personalize learning and individualize instruction to engage the unknown, then, is what keeps education reforms from heading down evolutionary blind alleys. These are the characteristics that enable growth through experience. Shepherding this growth is the responsibility of an entire society, not of any specific governmental or private entity. Reformers need to play their part. We cannot consider ourselves successful if, taken as a whole, our reforms fail to prepare individual students adequately for future learning and growth.

The Feasibility of Scale

A reform can get results that matter, but it does not automatically follow that it can get to scale. For that to happen, at least three conditions must be met. First, reformers must ensure that their programs can flourish in soil other than that in which they were first planted. Reforms need to be accessible and doable in many different geographical locations. Reformers need to find ways to customize their programs for different constituencies without fundamentally compromising fidelity to their missions. As with many endeavors at scale, but especially in education, one size does not fit all.

Second, those implementing the reform must embrace it willingly. It must be experienced in a way that helps rather than hinders its implementation. As Michael Fullan (2001, p. 8) has said,

> Neglect of the phenomenology of change—that is, how people actually experience change as distinct from how it might have been intended—is at the heart of the spectacular lack of success of most social reforms.

Third, the reform must be economically viable for those implementing it. Funding is obviously necessary, and, to reach scale, the reform needs to leverage the appropriate resources. As the reform expands within a school, district, or state, it must be planned for and budgeted. Entities implementing the reform must continually monitor their own economic performance and adjust rapidly when and where necessary—contrasting revenue projections and cash flow against expected and actual allocation of fixed and variable costs.

As Co-nect has evolved, we have learned the importance of continuously revisiting these three requirements as they affect both the market we deal with and our internal development and planning. If the reform is not tailored efficiently, excessive costs may drive away customers, undermining the reform organization's capacity to grow or, indeed, its survival. Creating a standardized delivery model may threaten the receptivity of those who willingly embraced it, diminishing the organization's capacity to continue to generate both revenue and results. If the organization grows too quickly—either internally or in the number of schools it serves—it may lose the agility needed to adapt to changing circumstances. In what follows, I focus on two areas that illustrate a few of the lessons we have learned: the customization of our methods for dealing with schools at different levels of readiness and the use of technology in personalizing instruction and delivering actionable data.

Co-nect's Evolution. Co-nect's evolution began with a whole-school reform design and has led us to create a set of interventions that can be assembled in different ways depending on their purpose (see Table 9.1). I have already discussed various elements of the original design, such as project-based learning, as key elements of our response to the requirement for desirability. We continue to believe in the educational significance of project-based learning and real-world application in ensuring continued growth through experience.

What we had not sufficiently realized, however, was the enormous effort and expertise that would be required of us if we were to help teachers and students create the kinds of projects that we originally envisioned. The standards movement, however, began to clarify the necessary conditions and up-front expectations in doing project work. Admittedly, we were somewhat skeptical at first. We saw the introduction of district and state curriculum frameworks as diverting time and energy from the kinds of interdisciplinary projects we embraced. In many respects, we were unwittingly mimicking the behavioral obstacles to change that we confronted repeatedly in the schools and districts in which we worked.

What convinced us that we needed to take a different approach was the evidence—the mixed results on standards-based district and state assessments of students in the schools where we were working. Gradually, we came to understand that not every student and every teacher could immediately embark on the kinds of rich learning experiences we believed to be contained in project-based learning. The standards helped provide a framework not only for learning but also for the kinds of projects that might be most useful in helping demonstrate that learning. If students did not know how to read well, if teachers did not sufficiently understand the mathematics required for students to do the project, mixed results on the local or state assessments would be inevitable. We needed to better understand whether the basic skills of the students were adequate to enable them to take on the more-complex kinds of learning we valued. Results-oriented project-based learning would take more time and expertise on the part of both teachers and students than we initially imagined.

Equally striking was the rapid change in the aggregate composition of the schools with which we were dealing—from a mix of reasonably successful schools with middle-class students to a set of schools in high-poverty, mostly urban areas, in which students were performing poorly. Indeed, the funding stream for the work we did had grown to a sizable river in Title 1 (the CSR legislation) and was clearly targeted to a state's lowest-performing schools. The needs of these schools were far greater than our available capacity, as developers, to serve them. Even though we had developed a number of specific resources to accommodate the many requirements of the CSR legislation, it was soon apparent that, no matter how much we had developed, it would be insufficient.

Many of these schools were dysfunctional. Their problems resembled those of a hospital emergency room more than those of a wellness clinic, and attempts to alter the functioning of the entire school would require a more-deliberate attempt to attack specific conditions within it. We therefore developed specific interventions to deal with subject-matter needs in literacy and math. We included, within our overall service, what we considered to be responsible test preparation. We also developed more-deliberate and generic strategies (such as data-informed decisionmaking) and associated resources to enable the schools to align curriculum with the practical exigencies of state assessments, state- and district-mandated adapted basals, and day-to-day instructional needs.

We were not the only ones who began to focus more explicitly on using data about individual and school-level needs to shape reforms. Districts, too, had begun to conclude that, without specific data regarding what schools needed, school improvement was unworkable. It was no longer desirable for schools to choose models, reforms, and interventions whose motivation and outcomes did not address the problems of the schools directly. Many districts began making the choice for individual classrooms and schools. That is, they began a concerted effort to create districtwide curriculum requirements and other measures that would ensure a more-uniform treatment of the issues their teachers and students faced. At the very least, they reasoned, increased uniformity in requirements might provide a framework for addressing the inordinate amount of student and teacher mobility many of these schools faced.

Transplanting Reforms to New Soil: Standardization and Customization. The discussion above illustrates part of a larger realization. We (as developers) and the districts and schools (as adopters) share a common paradox: Getting to scale requires greater standardization of practice at the same time that it requires greater customization. On the one hand, when teachers are ill-prepared for teaching and when students are ill-prepared for learning, it is crucial to focus on a limited body of knowledge and pedagogical techniques, ideally techniques that research has already demonstrated to be effective. How could this standardization be done in such a way as to provide instruction responsive to the specific needs of individual students and teachers? We understood that learning requires personalization, but we were uncertain about how both standardization and personalization could occur simultaneously.

Co-nect's response has been multifaceted. The cumulative effect of these efforts has transformed our understanding of ourselves as developers and, as I discuss in the next section, what it takes to become sustainable in getting to scale.[8] The first step was to alter our playbook for dealing with our whole schools through our core comprehensive school reform services by creating alternative strategies for schools with distinctly different initial conditions. Some of our client schools were doing well enough on the state tests but needed to motivate their students and teachers further through more-challenging approaches to subject matter. For these schools, the original Co-nect

---

[8] This balance of variety and standardization is also a property of complex adaptive systems. Various types of agents coexist within biological, social, or physical systems that display features of both stability and change within them. See Axelrod and Cohen (2000), pp. 32–61.

design seemed an appropriate fit. We called these schools *design schools*, and, although we modified our understanding of the quality of student work and teaching to be demonstrated, the basic tenets and benchmarks of the Co-nect design remained fairly intact.

However, it was apparent that design schools were rapidly becoming a distinct minority of Co-nect schools. Much more common were the low-performing schools receiving federal funding through CSR. Districts and or states had judged some of these schools to be failing. Others, while not failing, were still performing poorly enough to warrant an altered approach. The former we called *intervention schools*, and the latter *align schools*. For both the intervention and align schools, we adapted the methodologies that, in the past, we had used for all schools regardless of type, creating distinct approaches for each type of school. Intervention schools attempt a limited number of goals over a limited period. These schools focus on content-driven instruction (in literacy and mathematics), data-informed decisionmaking, and peer coaching and mentoring. Align schools include these approaches but add other components, as necessary, that reflect their performance status and allow more time in which to implement them. In short, we had borrowed a page from the larger business community and begun to "mass customize" our services (i.e., making adjustments to suit the needs of particular groups—or masses—of customers). All schools need to demonstrate AYP or face sanctions. How individual schools need to improve, however, varies by situation.

What remains common to all schools is the need for accurate data that enable us and our clients to obtain a working knowledge of their current status and the effects of reform. We have developed a number of methods of ensuring that both we and the client schools and districts we deal with have the necessary data for accurately assessing individual school needs and capabilities to make AYP. These efforts have taken two forms. First, we began to provide potential schools with technical assistance in writing their grant applications. This involvement enabled us to help potential clients better understand their needs prior to engaging them in our services. It makes sense that schools experiencing difficulty in getting results might not understand what is preventing them from improving. Requiring that they identify their problems before they get help intended to improve performance might be counterproductive. An outside organization can often help schools understand their circumstances and prepare for change before they begin to implement reforms.[9]

Second, we began a more-intensive search for technologies that could furnish a more-detailed account of the school's performance and of how individual students were doing or were likely to do on high-stakes tests. We first looked for technologies that would provide a more-accurate and detailed view of how students and subpopulations do on various items that compose their state test. We also sought technologies that can relate this performance to useful instructional resources for teachers. Finally, we have begun to incorporate data warehousing, analysis, and reporting tools into an integrated system that, when deployed, would give a more complete picture of the multiple factors that can contribute to improved performance.[10]

In sum, we have begun to make the changes necessary to deal with greater numbers of schools while providing greater attention to their individual and collective differences. Moreover, we believe we have done this in a way that accommodates the paradoxical need for both greater standardization and greater customization. The proof of the pudding is in the results we are obtaining. Our schools are performing at higher levels—and have maintained this level of performance with greater consistency—than similarly situated schools within the same district.

Embracing Reform. Throughout all these changes, we have continued to believe that all schools can develop into design schools. In fact, we believe that is what all schools want and are working toward.

---

[9] Some states (such as California) now require that schools work with an external evaluator before enlisting specific technical assistance. Problems exist with this approach as well, but they are outside the scope of this chapter.

[10] For example, we have recently (2003) been awarded a three-year U.S. Department of Education grant to develop, with the assistance of a number of organizational partners, a decision-support tool that would correlate student assessment data with data on professional development and classroom practice.

Now, however, we recognize that their route will depend on their initial conditions and capacity. So, for example, we have developed more-intensive training in how to incorporate standards into all forms of student work (including projects), which I described earlier as "mining the standard," and we have developed a process to help teachers align this work with specific assessments and instructional strategies.

Still, we recognize that, for scale to be feasible, the students and teachers who implement the intervention need to embrace it. For our work, this means all schools must find a way to connect what they are being asked to do with an overriding sense of purpose. So, for example, all our schools still participate in various national and local projects in which the potential real-world application of their work is made apparent.

Economics and Funding. Revisions in our basic strategies for implementing comprehensive school reform have caused us to pay greater attention to our capacity to provide new, more-customized services at scale. We have almost doubled the numbers of schools and districts each year since 1996. During that period, we grew from 35 to 90 employees, more than half of whom are located close to the schools and districts they serve. As we add even more mass-customized services, we have adopted more-stringent cost-control measures while seeking a greater range of content and technology to accompany these services. For both these reasons, finding partners became critical to our success. In addition to the costs associated with developing specialized content (in literacy and math, for example), we needed to expend significant resources in time and money to develop the technologies required to incorporate a systematic approach to the use of data in each of our interventions. Going it alone would not only have been more difficult but also counterproductive. It would have taxed our internal capacity to achieve cost efficiencies in the process of creating needed products and services.

I have already mentioned that we began as a unit of BBN Technologies. There, we had enjoyed the benefit of state-of-the-art networking and had been able to draw on the expertise of highly skilled software developers in constructing the early versions of our Internet-based tools for teachers, which are housed on the Co-nect Exchange. Because of these and other resources, we had less need for external partnerships than other providers might have had. After launching ourselves as an independent organization in 1998 and realizing the degree to which we needed to expand and specialize our services while improving their quality, we soon sought more partnerships. It was not that internal development was impossible; it was impractical. Others have invested large amounts of time and money in the very kinds of things we would have had to begin from scratch.[11]

No matter how effective the internal cost-control systems and no matter how useful the partnerships, getting to scale is impossible without a secure funding source. Unlike other sectors of the economy, education funding relies chiefly on an uncertain mix of local, state, and federal revenue negotiated through the political process and parceled out in an often bizarre assortment of budgetary categories.

For us, this diversity of funding sources and mechanisms has created both opportunity and challenge. The opportunity has been for us to ride the CSR wave. As one of the original design teams selected in the 1992 NAS competition,[12] we were able to take advantage of the initial federal funding made available through legislation. It was this original funding that helped make CSR a permanent fixture in Title 1.

Funding sources, however, are not products or services. Because funding remained relatively flat from 2000 through 2003, it appears that, at least for the foreseeable future, there will be a only very small increase in the total pool of potential CSR schools. Undoubtedly, this is a better state of affairs than a complete loss of funding. But because CSR is a three-year program, stable funding means that the available money must be used to support current CSR schools—schools in their second or third year—rather than adding new ones. Part of the

---

[11] What this has meant for our capacity to manage continuity in efforts at scale and what it means for scale in general is a topic I reserve for the next section.

[12] See Chapter One in this volume.

economic challenge for Co-nect—and, I think, for many providers of CSR services—has been to expand the definition and scope of what we do so that funding is accessible through a variety of sources. To attract funding from diverse sources, we have had to disentangle the various components of our work, while ensuring that the resulting modules form a coherent system consistent with the requirements of the district or state for which the modules are intended.

Regardless of the specific way we do this, an important general point can be made. If the nature of the reform is tied to a specific funding stream, changes in political fashion or changes in the economy can prevent the reform from getting to scale. One would like to think that any change in funding is the result of a deliberate and rational process. Unfortunately, this is not always the case. Promising reforms are sometimes abandoned when their funding disappears before they have had sufficient time to iron out the wrinkles that inevitably arise in new, complex enterprises, such as whole-school reform. The lesson for providers attempting to get to scale is important: Tying a specific intervention or reform to a specific funding stream might lead to flailing about in a dry riverbed. Instead, providers should aim for the most general, flexible, and secure budgetary sources. The lesson for policymakers and potential funders trying to determine what investments will be necessary is more complex. They should anticipate and communicate what their exit strategy will be before investing in reforms that are promising for scale-up.[13]

If interventions are to get to scale, they must be feasible. They must be designed so that they can be implemented in a variety of circumstances and conditions. Providers and those implementing the interventions must have the organizational capacity to make this happen. Providers need to understand how to mass-customize resources and services for diverse students, teachers, and schools because needs

---

[13] A recent example of a promising reform that is imperiled as of this writing is Marco Polo, a not-for-profit foundation program implementing an Internet training program that 50 states have adopted but that faces extinction because its benefactor, WorldCom Inc., has filed for bankruptcy.

and skill levels may differ at each of these levels. School districts and states need to balance the specific needs of individual teachers, students, and schools against the economies of scale and efficiency resulting from standardization. If interventions are to get to scale, what is being adopted needs to be embraced by those adopting it. Finally, planning for growth and executing those plans requires the developer, adopter, and funder each to have enough capacity. No one organization can accomplish all this by itself. Developers—as well as schools, districts, and states—need help to build their respective capacities.

Sustaining Reform: Co-nect at the Crossroads

The policy measures that NCLB specifies seem, in at least one respect, familiar. Once again, schools and what goes on in them are being taken seriously. Classrooms have once again emerged as critical partners with the home in effecting change in the lives of America's children. And, as with past periods of reform, districts and states are once again being called on to be more active in determining what goes on in classrooms—from the curriculum taught to the quality of the teachers teaching it to the tests that measure it. What began in 1983 as an economic warning to a nation at risk seems to have come full circle. We began with national goals and state standards, detoured briefly during the 1990s into the realm of local control, and now find ourselves once again driven by national and state educational policy.

One thing is becoming clear: The context for reform has been turned upside down. In the 1990s, state and local governments strained to accommodate a hefty supply of new ideas, strategies, and interventions—along with the abundant tax revenues that helped fuel them. The open marketplace dominated and ushered in a decade of "supply-side" reform. Now, the opposite seems true. Decisions about adopting reforms depend on the perceived fit of the reform with district or state strategies and initiatives. Whether it be federal Reading First funds or CSR funds, the language of models, designs, and innovative content is being replaced with that of scientifically based research, evidence of effectiveness, and consistency and uniformity of practice.

Three factors seem to have converged to help bring about the apparent shift: the decline in the economy (and thus in state and local tax revenue); the demand for bottom-line scrutiny of research-based evidence regarding what has worked (and not) in reducing the achievement gap between high- and low-achieving students; and a pressing need for practical strategies to align curriculum, instruction, and assessment up the chain, from classroom to school to district to state—especially where student mobility is high and teacher quality is low.

Are we then riding yet one more swing of the pendulum back to a period of governmental regulation and activism in education? Yes and no. Yes, in that local, state, and federal agencies are now assuming more control of the ground rules for determining educational success. No, in that, compared to past periods of educational change, this one has some distinctive characteristics. First, the current climate seems to invite a more-disinterested consideration of educational success. The call for scientifically based research might strike some as an ideological wolf in sheep's clothing, a regrettable return to the idolatry of numbers. However, for the first time in many years, there is a shared thirst among the public, researchers, and practitioners for a collaboratively arrived at definition of evidence of success.[14] What matters less is *where* success happens—in public schools, in private schools, in home schooling—than *that* it occurs. Geographies and institutions do not define the boundaries of success.

A second characteristic of this educational shift is the disruptive nature of new technologies. Managing, monitoring, and developing educational resources are not so easy to control and contain these days. The Internet fosters almost instantaneous creation and distribution of resources in a way that no governmental agency or institution

---

[14] We might also be witnessing, as Hirsch (2002) has suggested, a growing regard for better theory on which the evidence is based.

could ever be expected to completely control and manage. Events transpire and are communicated too quickly for the kind of regulations that have governed educational policy in the past. Overhyped as they once might have been, the Internet and the World Wide Web are indispensable features of contemporary life. Their use in classrooms, schools, and homes throughout the country has created a public education space, a virtual commons that was absent just 15 years ago.

New technologies have had an equally disruptive but profound effect on the way in which educators and policymakers keep track of and make sense of the data they generate. Data warehousing technologies now allow even the smallest units of organizations to mine and integrate data from numerous databases, student information systems, human resource systems, financial systems, and the like, allowing everyone from the teacher in the classroom to the governor to make new connections and form new hypotheses about what works and how to improve it.

Whatever the ultimate meaning of the shift, however, getting to scale has meant that providers of products and services have had to adjust to the seemingly obvious fact that the schools they are dealing with are not theirs. In one nontrivial sense, then, it is inappropriate to ask how many schools Co-nect "has." Co-nect has no schools. We are participants in a complex and dynamic marketplace, a space in which public and private meet and in which educational resources are created, used, and monitored. The products and services we bring to this space are interventions whose outcomes are affected by various contingencies and other mediating factors. If we are to survive and scale, it will be because we succeeded in linking the pool of resources we bring to the commons to those of the other institutions and players, private and public, with whom we coexist.

The Dynamics of Getting to Scale

What does all this have to do with charting the route to achieving scale? In discussing the four criteria I identified at the beginning of this chapter, I have sometimes written as if getting to scale was simply an attribute of the intervention being scaled—its conceptual underpinnings, its research base, and the materials and training necessary to implement and evaluate it. In applying the criterion of success, for example, to Co-nect's comprehensive school improvement intervention, getting to scale has meant not how many schools Co-nect has managed to work with or how economically successful the Co-nect organization has been but rather whether the CSR model or design we have employed is able to demonstrate improvement in student achievement.[15] Similarly, in suggesting that desirability is a useful criterion for assessing scale, I have emphasized the degree to which an intervention embodies a moral purpose, best understood as a purpose that promotes growth through experience among the students for whom it is intended. Here again, it was not any particular attribute of Co-nect as an organization that was particularly significant, but rather the kinds of interventions Co-nect has developed and promoted (such as project-based learning or interventions designed to personalize learning).

Feasibility is a different sort of criterion. It takes into account not only the characteristics and measured effects of the reforms but two other factors as well: the overall organizational health of the entities promoting them and the environments in which they are being implemented. Interventions are not Platonic ideals. They cannot achieve scale by themselves. Although they begin as ideas, their successful propagation, refinement, and diffusion depend on organizations, policies, and funding, and their ultimate success lies in their ability to adapt to a variety of school and district conditions. For example, over the past decade, we have learned how to mass-customize our interventions to accommodate the number and variety of changing environments. If we had ignored these changes, we could not have brought to scale the particular interventions we had created.

Because a reform is feasible, however, does not mean it is sustainable. Sustainability requires us to go a step further in understanding what it takes to achieve scale. Sustainability refers to whether

---

[15] This criterion is closely related to what evaluation experts call *construct validity*.

it is possible for reforms to persist over the long run. As a criterion, it asks not only whether the intervention can work but also whether it can work *over time*. A certain paradox exists here: When a reform is sustainable, it disappears from the reform agenda. It does so because the reform is absorbed into the system in which it was introduced. It becomes institutionalized, a taken-for-granted part of the educational landscape. Getting to scale, then, is not only a process; it is also a destination, a state of affairs in which the reform; the places in which it routinely occurs; and the organizations, policies, and economics that support it are working together as a coherent whole.

How are the conditions for institutionalization created so that reforms are sustained and achieve scale? To answer this, we need to go beyond consideration of what makes interventions successful, desirable, or even feasible. We also must take into account the complex interrelationships that constitute the educational marketplace—a space in which promising interventions come to life and evolve, sometimes perishing and sometimes succeeding. We have to consider three factors that enable sustainable reforms to become institutionalized: the interventions that are promoted; the dynamics of the marketplace in which they function; and the strategies and structures of organizations, such as Co-nect, as they seek to survive and grow.

What can be concluded about the complex interrelationships that constitute today's educational marketplace? First, that interventions have become commodities; second, that over the past few years the market has grown to respond more to demand than to supply; and third, that to succeed in today's market, providers need to exercise unprecedented discipline in defining what they do (and do not do) and the best path for them to take in doing it.

The Commoditization of Reform

Commoditization is a clumsy but frequently used term that describes what happens to products as they mature in the marketplace. In many cases, products become commodities and find themselves subject to market conditions characterized by declining prices, lower profit margins, and more competition. Once-unique and expensive products become mainstream. This is what has happened in the computer industry; the banking industry; and, with Starbucks, even the neighborhood coffee shop. It is also taking place in the reform market. Interventions are becoming commoditized.

At first blush, the proposition that reforms are becoming more like commodities might seem counterintuitive. Has the demand for results and evidence, for example, not reduced competition by creating strong barriers to entry in the marketplace? No. In fact, because there is now demand for results, the supply of interventions has increased and hastened commoditization in the market. If there were no standards against which products could be evaluated and reformers could be held accountable, it would be difficult to convince enough schools and districts to purchase services for any reform effort to succeed at scale. Standards and results are the soil from which scale grows. Without these metrics to help schools and districts decide which reforms are worth pursuing, there is only a fragmented market with locally based reforms. A certain math intervention might claim superiority to another math intervention, but, in the absence of uniform standards and an objective means against which one can compare them, no compelling reason exists for a consumer (a school, district, or state) to be more inclined to purchase one rather than the other.

One program might more closely match the philosophy of those purchasing it; the program might be the brainchild of a local consultant, university, or other organization; or the program's brand name might, for historical reasons, be better known. Subjective preference, however, is not a sound basis for getting to scale. This is certainly true with regard to the CSR market. Having arisen in response to market demand for break-the-mold schools, today's CSR products are designed instead to achieve success within the mold. It is not originality in design or preference that is now valuable in the marketplace; it is the ability to efficiently translate design into effectiveness.

Contributing to the phenomenon of commoditization has been a decline in production costs. It is cheaper to produce a reform that meets clear, accepted, and open industry standards than it is to produce innovations in advance of or in the absence of standards because it is easier to reverse-engineer products once the standards become open. This is as true for content and performance standards in education as it is for technical standards in engineering. Although Jack Welch's mantra for success at General Electric, "steal shamelessly," might not be the most felicitous phrase to characterize success in educational reform, there is little doubt that open and clear standards have created a market in which it is easier to borrow strategies that incorporate the appropriate standards from those who once enjoyed almost exclusive access to the market. Why? Because standards-based products must make explicit how they are designed to satisfy the standards. The following quotation, taken from a recent white paper on the effect of commoditization on the information technology industry, could as easily have been written about the education reform industry (Ryder and King, 2002, p. 5):

> An industry standard based marketplace has few if any technical barriers to entry, so the focus of competition shifts from patents and copyrights to implementation quality, time to market, scale, efficiency, and effective marketing.

Who "Owns" the Reform? From Supply to Demand

When markets mature and products become commoditized, supply and demand dynamics also change: The balance of power shifts to the demand side. The market for education reform has experienced a similar change, and many of the reform organizations born and nurtured in the 1990s are now caught in a market driven increasingly by the more clearly expressed needs of consumers rather than by the more vaguely expressed promises of providers. During most of the 1990s, markets were focused on increasing supply. In education, the issue became how to expand the number of developers and providers of interventions. More recently, however, the focus has shifted to demand—how to expand the capacity of schools and districts to intelligently use specific interventions tied to their specific needs.

What a different world the present seems from that of the aggressively entrepreneurial 1990s. That world assumed continuing eras of unprecedented economic growth and technological progress. We conceived the original Co-nect design during this period, taking the initial steps at BBN, a pioneering, research and development–oriented technology company that began to achieve prominence in the 1990s because of its role in the engineering of the ARPANET, the precursor of the Internet. Thus, we were operating at the epicenter of what was to become an Internet earthquake. We developed our Web site, the Co-nect Exchange, earlier than most education groups and relied on BBN scientists for a sense of what future directions the Internet might take through the convergence of voice, video, and data technologies.

The inclusion of the Internet as a fundamental piece of business strategy was an almost unquestioned tenet of planning in the 1990s. Whether through reliance on the Internet, stock options, or "creative" accounting, there seemed to be few obstacles in the way of corporate growth. When consumers' needs were factored into the equation, it was often because the consumers could be aggregated into virtual communities. How well companies were doing with their customers became a function of customer satisfaction, not value added. Many companies boasted about "owning" their customers, and the counting of "eyeballs" on a dot-com's Internet site quickly became the currency in which appraisals of ever-rising company value was computed.

While these excesses were not matched in the education market, clear parallels existed. Policymakers, venture capitalists, and businesses saw the education market as huge, fragmented, inefficient, and ineffective. To get results in this regulated but disjointed system, fresh ideas, technology, and risk-taking entrepreneurs were necessary.

The supply side deserved special attention, and it received it. NAS, a coalition of business groups and policymakers, was formed as an incubator organization to help create and fund organizations to develop a new generation of American schools. Charter school legislation was passed, leading to a new industry of "education management" organizations, and investment companies heralded the financial potential of an untapped education market and funded scores of new educational start-ups. Co-nect and many other reform organizations, both for-profit and not-for-profit, were born, and others were reinvigorated with additional capital for development and expansion.

In the preface to the 1998 congressional bill establishing CSR as a demonstration program, the authors of the bill (representatives David Obey [D-Wis.] and John Porter [R-Ill.]) cited 17 examples of comprehensive school reform model providers—Co-nect among them. Today, the Regional Southwest Educational Development Laboratory's CSR database lists more than 350 model providers that sell and implement CSR services. Vendor supply clearly outdistances CSR demand.

Shifts in the economic and policy environments have combined to alter the relationship between supply and demand. In terms of economics, dramatically less money is now available for purchasing services and products, and less discretionary spending occurs in districts and states than in the 1990s. Because schools and districts have less money to spend for vendor services, they have become more discriminating about where they spend it. As part of the general economic downturn, there is now less money and much less demand for funding new education start-ups. In turn, the loss of venture capital has resulted in the winnowing of venture-funded education companies of the 1990s that failed to demonstrate either financial or educational success.

The transition from strength on the supply side to strength on the demand side also involves the way in which the policy environment has affected accountability. In the earlier section on results, I discussed some of the effects of this relatively new emphasis on accountability but did not mention how the consequences for achieving—or more often not achieving—measurable goals have altered the way educators think about their needs and purchases. The accountability requirements of NCLB have shifted the balance of power in the marketplace from providers to consumers. The demand for proven services, not the relative uniqueness of a particular program or a provider's preexisting strength in the marketplace, is what matters now.

Recently, the answer to the question of who owns the reforms has increasingly become the school or the district. "The school, not the model developer, has to 'own' the reform," writes Edward Gosling, Executive Director of the National Clearinghouse on Comprehensive School Reform, "and the school district must also actively participate in the ownership." The models must "fit with both the district's goals and the particular needs of the individual school" (Gosling, 2003). Building the capacity of the schools and districts has preempted concern over building the capacity of providers.

The Market Position of Organizations and Reform Products That Survive

Interventions are now increasingly commoditized, and the balance of power in the marketplace has been shifting from the supply to the demand side. To survive, providers have had to exercise ever-greater discipline over decisions about what they do and how they do it. We too have changed. Like many companies facing the challenge of survival and growth in tough economic times, we have had to decide which path to take to ensure sustainability.[16]

We have had to evaluate the products and services we offer and determine, based on their associated costs and benefits, whether we should continue to offer all of them. We could focus on taking only some of our present stock of interventions and making them more efficient and less expensive, or we could seek to increase the number and value of our interventions by, for example, expanding into more-specific content areas. We have asked ourselves whether we should introduce breakthrough innovations in features, benefits, or design in current interventions (by using, for instance, various new interactive technologies to deliver them) or should focus more on a specific educational subcomponent, such as assessment or curriculum, creating within this focus a full range of products, services, and materials customized around the specific needs of individual districts and schools.

We had, as I mentioned earlier, already made some decisions. For example, we had decided to offer more cost-efficient versions of products (e.g., Co-nect Tech) that took advantage of an online envi-

---

[16] I have borrowed liberally here from the framework created by a popular business book, *The Discipline of Market Leaders: Choose Your Customers, Narrow Your Focus, Dominate Your Market* (Treacy and Wiersma, 1997).

ronment to enable school-related personnel to guide their colleagues through some of our training. We had also decided that it was important to mass-customize our comprehensive school reform services so that the implementation of our program varied in relation to the needs of the school. This approach required that we adopt a more-consultative posture, becoming a "solutions" organization rather than a traditional product-oriented company. We had to be capable of providing educational solutions to the various and somewhat idiosyncratic problems of particular schools and districts. We had also already begun the process of taking apart pieces of what we were doing in comprehensive school reform, modifying and modularizing certain features—remaking them into stand-alone products.

In short, we had followed all three paths: We had made our interventions more efficient and cost-effective, defined our value to the marketplace in terms of our ability to customize products and services to specific school and district needs, and increased the number and innovative features of services we employed. Although taking each path seemed prudent and even necessary, this strategy now seems simply too difficult to sustain over time. The product development costs entailed in pursuing each path are significant, and following all three provides little or no economy of scale. Each path also places us in a different set of relationships with other players in the education market. Concentrating on a specific intervention and producing a cheaper, more-efficient version of it would limit the number of potential acquirers of the service, narrow our market segment, and place even greater demands on our ability to compete effectively with other, better-financed providers. By focusing on an early literacy intervention, for example, we would face competition from established publishers, thereby putting ourselves at risk by attempting to serve an already saturated market.

Sustainability at Co-nect

Co-nect is, as I have said, at a crossroads. Not only does the marketplace alter the reforms, it also changes the organizations that promote them. No organization, including ours, can continue to be part of the process of institutionalizing sustainable reforms without paying careful attention to the changes taking place in the wider policy and economic environments. Making our own transition to sustainability will force us to decide more deliberately the organizational direction that will ensure our viability and preserve our mission. We need to exercise the kind of discipline that all organizations must exercise to grow. Achieving scale, for example, might well mean that we must abandon some of what we have been doing to advance certain of our interventions so that we can more fully realize what is potentially significant but undeveloped in others. Getting to scale is not only about reforms and how they are implemented; it is also about the decisions made by organizations that design, promote, and evolve alongside the reforms.[17]

A critical part of this process will be to consider what we cannot do (or can no longer do) alone. What will require partnerships with others, and what might these partnerships look like? This is no small matter. Many kinds of partnerships are possible, both in terms of the kinds of organizations and the depth of the relationship the partnership might entail. But this consideration is a natural by-product of the process outlined above. If we are thorough in assessing our strengths and challenges and disciplined enough to act on our conclusions, the needed kinds and depth of partnerships will suggest themselves.[18]

The internal business processes we have begun are conditioned by changes in the wider marketplace: commoditization and the shift

---

[17] In business terms, we must undergo a *product rationalization* process, determining which of our products and services yield the greatest benefit given their costs; how our school and district customers value these products; and how the products fit into management of the larger "supply chain" in which they function. Although the dynamics might differ slightly, the internal organizational process will likely be similar for all organizations—whether for-profit or not-for-profit.

[18] The existence and structure of partnerships may become an important consideration for outside funders, whether they are foundations or venture capitalists. Barring the unlikely event of an intervention growing to self-sustained independence, it will at some point require the addition of components that are not predictable at the time the intervention was originally funded. This expectation of changes the future will inevitably cast on present endeavors is part of what venture capitalists take into account when they talk about "exit" strategies.

from supply to demand. The good news for Co-nect is that reforms cannot get to scale without organizations like ours. We are neither the framework in which reforms are cast nor the one in which they are ultimately judged. We are the connecting links. We make the possible and the desirable feasible. Co-nect and many other reform organizations are integral parts of this larger ecology. Which particular organizations get to scale and which do not is another question.

Sustainability, as a desired outcome of educational reform, grows out of an environment made up of three elements. The first of these is educational policy. Policies provide the context for decisions about what works, who is held accountable for what, and therefore what is deemed more or less important to pursue. Policies are about results, goals, and accountability. They get implemented, however, within a marketplace.

The economic conditions of the marketplace, the second element of the environment that contributes (or not) to sustainability, help condition choices. They give, as William James might have said, "cash value" to the ideas of policy. Economic considerations help frame what is feasible and what is not feasible. They inform the decisions schools and districts make about what they can spend to meet policy goals. When economic prospects are bright, interventions emerge and often grow in relative isolation, but when economic prospects are dim, policy works to hasten the commoditization of the reform in the marketplace and to tip the balance of power to the demand side—to the schools, districts, and states that are implementing the reforms.

The third element of the environment that gives rise to sustainability is the individual and collective strength of outside organizations: the supply side. Provider and developer organizations deliver the resources and services that link the ability to obtain results to the marketplace in which decisions about the allocation of resources are made. For interventions to get to scale, these outside organizations are a collective necessity. Which interventions get to scale depends on the discipline with which each organization can continuously redefine itself as it navigates between the goals of policy and the economic realities of the marketplace.

As of this writing, Co-nect and many other reform organizations are at a crossroads. Conditions have changed and continue to change from what they were a few short years ago. We are adapting to environments that we have not necessarily shaped. Which organizations will be successful? The answer to this question is a bit like Zhou Enlai's response to Henry Kissinger after being asked what he thought of the French Revolution: "It is too early to tell."

Conclusions

Getting to scale, I have argued, requires considering a set of four related criteria: success, desirability, feasibility, and sustainability. Responding to each is necessary; responding to one alone is insufficient. The past decade has seen tremendous gains in our understanding of how best to address the first criterion. Success requires results, and results require evidence. This evidence is most easily and convincingly documented through large-scale assessments and accountability systems. But these systems must be valid and reliable. If the validity of the systems is in doubt, the ability of reforms to attain scale is in doubt. Operating in this environment is difficult for reform efforts, but unavoidable. At the very least, reformers must be committed to doing no harm. However flawed the generally accepted evaluations may be, reformers must still show results and, to be faithful to their goals, must act as though valid assessment and accountability systems were already in place.

Given this commitment, however, we would still need to answer the question of which reforms are worthy of being taken to scale. The answer to that question, I have argued, hinges on whether the reform is successful in promoting and achieving growth through experience. To be desirable at scale, reforms must personalize learning and individualize instruction over time. Co-nect's continued, though selective, emphasis on real-world application through project-based learning is but one means through which this can occur.

To get to scale, reforms must also be feasible. That is, to come to life in the real world, they must contain the internal characteristics that enable them to get to scale. They must be created with economic sophistication so that their growth can be planned and continuously monitored; they must tap into and catalyze the motivation of students and teachers; and they must balance standardization with customization to enable diffusion in differing locales and among different learners—a difficult balance that will seriously try contemporary organizations. These three feasibility conditions are interrelated. Economic planning depends on recognizing that diffusion through standardized delivery is not possible. In education, unlike hamburgers or soft drinks, one size will not fit all. For teachers and students to embrace the reform, they must be able to experience it for themselves. Without this experience, motivation suffers. Finally, the physical means of embracing the reform must be available. Technology represents one way of doing this. It can allow "scaling up by scaling down."

Finally, to be scalable, reforms must be sustainable and manageable so that they evolve and deepen their effects over time. A reform that is sustained eventually becomes institutionalized, a regular way of doing business. On the road to institutionalization, the reforms must inhabit a publicly accessible marketplace that provides constant learning about the results they are getting and enables adjustments and adaptations to the ever-changing policy and economic environments of which they are a part. Today's marketplace is best understood as involving the process of commoditization, a shift in the balance of power from providers and developers to the consumers of their services, and economic pressures on reform organizations to focus exclusively on the aspects of their work that can truly rationalize their future. These conditions might require such organizations as Co-nect to become more adaptable. To survive, our interventions must adjust to new circumstances and new agents. As an organization and as a collection of reforms, we must coevolve with other agents occupying the same marketplace. Getting to scale must, in short, be understood as an evolutionary enterprise.

References

American Education Research Association, American Psychological Association, and National Council on Measurement in Education, *Standards for Educational and Psychological Testing*, Washington, D.C.: American Educational Research Association, 1999.

Axelrod, R., and M. D. Cohen, *Harnessing Complexity: Organizational Implications of a Scientific Frontier*, New York: Basic Books, 2000.

Baker, E. L., R. L. Linn, J. L. Herman, and D. Koretz, "Standards for Educational Accountability Systems," Los Angeles: National Center for Research on Evaluation, Standards, and Student Testing, Policy Brief 5, Winter 2002. Online at http://www.cse.ucla.edu/products/newsletters/polbrf54.pdf (as of November 7, 2000).

Buly, M. R., and S. W. Valencia, "Below the Bar: Profiles of Students who Fail State Reading Assessments," *Educational Evaluation and Policy Analysis*, Vol. 24, No. 3, Fall 2002, pp. 219–232.

Dewey, J., "Philosophy of Experience," in J. Ratner, ed., *Intelligence in the Modern World: John Dewey's Philosophy*, New York: Random House, 1939, pp. 664–665.

Fullan, M., *The New Meaning of Educational Change*, 3rd ed., Toronto: Irwin Publishing Ltd., 2001.

Gawande, A., *Complications: A Surgeon's Notes on an Imperfect Science*, New York: Metropolitan Books, 2002.

Glennan, T. K., *New American Schools After Six Years*, Santa Monica, Calif.: RAND Corporation, MR-945-NAS, 1998.

Gosling, A., "Merging Models: Why the Road to School Reform Is Never Ending," Letter to the Editor, *Education Week*, March 26, 2003. Online at http://www.edweek.net/ew/ (as of November 7, 2003).

Herman, R., D. Aladjem, P. McMahon, E. Masem, I. Mulligan, A. O'Malley, S. Quinones, A. Reeve, and D. Woodruff, *An Educator's Guide to Schoolwide Reform*, Arlington, Va.: Education Research Service, 1999.

Hirsch, E. D., "Classroom Research and Cargo Cults," *Policy Review*, No. 115, October 2002, pp. 51–69. Online at http://www.policyreview.org/OCT02/hirsch.html (as of November 7, 2003).

Holloway, J. H., "Research Link/Inclusion and Students with Learning Disabilities," *Educational Leadership*, Vol. 58, No. 6, March 2001, pp. 86–88.

Popham, W. J., "Seeking Redemption for Our Psychometric Sins," presentation at the 2002 Center for Research on Evaluation, Standards, and Student Testing Conference, Los Angeles, Calif., September 10–11, 2002.

Ryder, C., and C. King, "Commoditization, Standards and the Enterprise," white paper, Union City, Calif.: The Sageza Group, Inc., March 2002.

Treacy, M., and F. Wiersma, *The Discipline of Market Leaders: Choose Your Customers, Narrow Your Focus, Dominate Your Market*, Boulder, Colo.: Perseus Publishing, 1997.

CHAPTER TEN

Scaling Up Turning Points Through Autonomous Regional Centers

Dan French and Leah Rugen

The authors describe a move by the Turning Points organization to ensure successful scale-up of the practices they advocate: the development of a network of regional centers to guide implementation of its program in diverse parts of the nation. Although these centers differ in terms of funding sources, institutional affiliation, and the specific focus of their activities, all have adopted the Turning Points design as part of their respective missions. The network has created systems for shared governance, with accountability based in a system of annual assessments against established benchmarks, national network meetings, regional site visits, and quality reviews of both regional centers and individual schools. The network permits innovation and adaptation to local conditions, while the national center helps to ensure fidelity to the Turning Points principles by providing curriculum guides, professional development, and technical assistance to the regional centers.

Turning Points, a design for comprehensive middle school reform, focuses on creating a professional collaborative culture to improve teaching and learning for every student. The design grew out of a 1989 Carnegie Task Force on Education of Young Adolescents report, Turning Points: Preparing American Youth for the 21st Century. This report presented a set of principles for overhauling middle-grade education. Based on these principles and more than ten years of research and practice in middle schools throughout the United States, the current Turning Points design recognizes the need to strengthen the academic core of middle schools and to establish supportive environments that value adolescents. Coordinated by the Center for Collaborative Education (CCE) and endorsed by the Carnegie Corporation and New American Schools (NAS),[1] Turning Points assists middle schools with intensive, whole-school reform designed to significantly improve teaching, student engagement, and learning.

In this chapter, we describe key elements of the current Turning Points design, provide a brief history that explains the development of the design, and discuss the scale-up strategies we have used, the challenges these strategies present, and how we have addressed them.

The Turning Points Design

Recognizing that each child comes with unique strengths, challenges, and needs, Turning Points teachers have high expectations for all their students and hold a vision that their students will leave middle school able to think creatively; identify and solve complex and meaningful problems; express their passions, strengths, and challenges; communicate and work well with others; lead healthy lives; and be caring citizens of a diverse world. To help students reach these goals, Turning Points middle schools commit to a multiyear, comprehensive process.

Although what happens in their classrooms influences students most directly, a schoolwide culture that is supportive, collaborative, challenging, and equitable magnifies the power of any single classroom strategy. With a schoolwide emphasis on professional collaboration, teachers use the Turning Points principles to create a learning environment that nurtures each student's development and achievement. These principles reflect what has been learned since the publication of the original Turning Points report in 1989 (Jackson and Davis, 2000):

- Teach a curriculum grounded in rigorous, public academic standards for what students should know and be able to do and ensure that it is relevant to the concerns of adolescents and based on how students learn best.

---

[1] See Chapter Sixteen in this volume.

- Use instructional methods designed to prepare all students to achieve high standards and become lifelong learners.
- Staff middle grades schools with teachers who are expert at teaching young adolescents and engage teachers in ongoing, targeted professional development opportunities.
- Organize relationships for learning to create a climate of intellectual development and a caring community of shared educational purpose.
- Govern democratically through direct or representative participation by all school staff members.
- Provide a safe and healthy school environment as part of improving academic performance and developing caring and ethical citizens.
- Involve parents and communities in supporting student learning and healthy development.

To help frame the work with schools, Turning Points has identified core practices that translate the principles into action. Each practice area has tools that help teachers, teams, and whole faculties engage in the work of changing practices schoolwide. These practices, shown in Table 10.1, have been developed and refined through our work with our regional centers and individual schools.

To improve and sustain student learning, Turning Points schools need to use the seven Turning Points principles to create a strong vision of a middle school learning community; focus deeply on improving learning, teaching, and assessment; and create the school culture, structures, and supports that enable all students to perform at high levels and all faculty to engage in continuous professional development and purposeful collaboration. In doing so, schools must embrace the twin goals of equity and excellence—opportunity for every student to succeed at the highest level.

Site-based coaching is a central component of the design. Typically schools receive 30–60 days of coaching per year, depending on their size and available funding. Most commonly, a Turning Points coach will spend several days a month in a school working with a

Table 10.1
Turning Points Core Practices

Practice	Description
Improving Learning, Teaching, and Assessment for All Students	Working collaboratively to set high standards, close the achievement gaps among students, develop curriculum that promotes intellectual inquiry, use a wide range of instructional strategies, and emphasize the teaching of literacy and numeracy.
Building Leadership Capacity and a Professional Collaborative Culture	Creating a democratic school community, fostering skills and practices of strong leadership, establishing regular common planning time, and embedding professional development in the daily life of the school.
Data-Based Inquiry and Decisionmaking	Setting a vision based on the Turning Points principles; collecting and analyzing multiple sources of data to help improve areas that most affect learning, teaching, and assessment; and setting annual measurable goals.
Creating a School Culture to Support High Achievement and Personal Development	Creating structures that promote a culture of high-quality learning and teaching, establishing small learning communities, eliminating tracking, lowering student-teacher ratios, and building parent and community partnerships.
Networking with Like-Minded Schools	Participating in network meetings, summer institutes, and forums and visiting other Turning Points schools.
Developing District Capacity to Support School Change	Building district capacity through collaboration.

wide range of groups and individuals. The coach facilitates teacher team meetings focused on the collaborative practices the Turning Points design identifies—looking at student and teacher work; observing peers; and examining approaches to curriculum, instruction, and assessment. The coach also works with the leadership team to engage the whole faculty in data-based inquiry to develop goals and an action plan for change and consults with school administration regularly to solve problems and develop strategies to cultivate shared leadership with the faculty. An internal facilitator, designated by the school, partners with the coach and shares the work. Gradually, the school builds its own capacity to plan, facilitate, and guide the change process.

Member schools are also provided with resources, including a set of guides (see Table 10.2). A national newsletter called *Conversations* appears twice a year. Each issue focuses on a single Turning Points practice with detailed examples and interviews from Turning Points schools. The guides—a library of ideas and tools—are a starting point for faculty and school teams in changing practice. In a sense, they represent the "curriculum" of the Turning Points design. As with the core practices, we wanted the guides to be collaborative—so, in creating them, we drew from the best work in the field and have refined them using feedback from practitioners. Thus, we developed and presented pilot versions for practitioners in Turning Points schools to review and test, then revised the guides in light of experience. All the guides and the newsletter are available on the Turning Points Web site, which provides information about the Turning Points network and additional resources.

Professional development to support the intensive coaching at each school takes place through a system of regional and national networking opportunities for center and school staff, including network meetings focused on sharing strategies, successes and challenges, regional summer institutes, and a national coaches' institute. The overall goal of the Turning Points network is to teach and support all aspects of the design and to create opportunities for Turning Points faculties to share and critique each other's work. Often, schools in a regional network are paired for "critical friends visits," in which a team from one school visits another and addresses a question that the host school has developed.

In addition to these activities, the design involves a strong emphasis on accountability and assessment. One of our assessment tools, the Self-Study Survey, was part of the original Turning Points program. This tool was developed by Center for Prevention Research and Development (CPRD) at the University of Illinois in collaboration with the Association of Illinois Middle Schools (AIMS)—one of the founding and most active Turning Points sites. The Self-Study Survey addressed all Turning Points principles and domains of best middle school practice. It was designed to be administered to all fac-

Table 10.2
Current Turning Points Guides

Title	Description
At the Turning Point: The Young Adolescent Learner	Provides a foundation for understanding the needs of the young adolescent learner and describes practices, strategies, and tools that can help schools address these needs in a caring and academically challenging environment.
Benchmarks to Becoming a Turning Points School	Specifies rubrics for each of the Turning Points practices with accompanying narratives and guidelines for use.
Guide to Collaborative Culture and Shared Leadership	Describes a set of strategies for effective leadership and school-based professional development.
Guide to Curriculum Development	Defines an approach to curriculum and provides a template for standards-based curriculum planning, a sample plan, and examples of rubrics, criteria, and other assessment tools.
Guide to Data-Based Inquiry and Decision Making	Defines the sequence and steps of this practice and provides accompanying tools and agendas.
Looking Collaboratively at Student and Teacher Work	Presents a set of protocols with discussion and rationale for looking at student work to improve instruction.
School Quality Review	Outlines the process, tools, and strategies of this intensive assessment of a school's progress in implementing Turning Points.
School Structures that Support Learning and Collaboration	Describes strategies for creating small learning communities, grouping students for learning, creating flexible schedules, promoting personalized relationships between adults and students, and allocating resources to support learning.
Teaching Literacy in the Turning Points School	Provides a framework for a middle school literacy model and description of literacy education practices and strategies.

ulty and students annually. The original Turning Points tool, this survey is a key component of the model and has been strengthened by its integration into the broader data-based inquiry process that now characterizes the Turning Points design. This process includes an extensive system of benchmarking, site visits, and the School Quality Review, an in-depth analysis of progress conducted every three to five years.

We will refer to these design elements again in our discussion of how these processes and tools have developed and have been used in the process of scaling up the Turning Points program.

A Brief History of the Turning Points Design

In many ways, the current Turning Points design arose out of a desire to bring the principles specified in the 1989 report to scale and to have a greater influence on "the core of educational practice" (Elmore, 1996) in large numbers of middle schools and districts—particularly those serving high percentages of low-income students and students of color. After the Turning Points report was released, the Carnegie Corporation issued a request for proposals inviting the states to develop programs based on the Turning Points principles. Fifteen states ultimately began Turning Points initiatives. At first, mostly state-level policy documents were produced. After two to three years, Carnegie assessed the initiatives and found that, while the Turning Points report and these early initiatives had helped raise awareness about the need for middle school reform, they had not had a deep influence on school practices, particularly in urban schools and districts. Carnegie also found that much of the positive change was concentrated in suburban areas—bypassing the areas of greatest need.

As a result, Carnegie contracted with CPRD to further study Turning Points schools. The Self-Study Survey described above emerged from this research. The survey designers believed that if schools could be taught to use the survey data to track their own progress and make decisions, they could develop focused plans for improvement. The next five to six years of Turning Points implementation focused on data-based inquiry and decisionmaking using the Self-Study Survey.

The initial data from this work in Illinois and Massachusetts showed significant gains in achievement and trends in improvement of school climate and practice (De Pascale, 1997; Felner et al., 1997). However, in the ninth and final year of funding, Carnegie's analysis concluded that the gains outside of Illinois and Massachusetts were small and that low-income students and students of color were still performing poorly. To address these disappointing results and to ensure the continuation of Turning Points beyond the ten-year funding period, Carnegie turned to the CCE in Boston and proposed that it become the new National Turning Points Center. CCE was charged with developing a more-rigorous and comprehensive model and with affiliating with NAS.

As the national center, CCE brought several strengths to the table. It had been deeply involved in the Massachusetts Turning Points work and in the national conversations about the new direction for Turning Points. As an umbrella organization for several school reform initiatives, CCE was able to draw on an extensive base of knowledge and experience in school reform. For example, the center coordinates the Boston Pilot Schools, a network of 15 public schools each having a level of autonomy much like that of a charter school in matters of budget, staffing, curriculum, governance, and schedule. CCE's work with the Pilot School Network, focused on gaining greater flexibility and autonomy to promote innovation, greatly influenced the Turning Points core practice of Developing District Capacity to Support School Change. It also resulted in the adaptation and implementation of the School Quality Review process.

As a result of its early experience with Turning Points, the CCE lead team concluded that the Self-Study Survey and data-based inquiry were important but not enough. A more-comprehensive array of tools was needed to assist schools with the complexity of adopting a schoolwide reform model. In addition, schools that received regular and consistent external coaching did better than those that did not. Thus, the Turning Points theory of change and scale-up that we developed came to be based, in part, on the premise that schools seeking to transform themselves need substantial support from an external source.

Our early experience with Turning Points, prior to the creation of the NAS design, also taught us that schools working in isolation did not improve as much as those involved in a network of schools engaged in Turning Points reform. But we felt that such a network could not be run effectively from a national office. For the needed support to be effective, credible, and grounded in the local context, we felt it had to be delivered by experienced practitioners in or near the school communities adopting the Turning Points design. We believed a centralized national staff would be unable to deliver the intensive coaching schools required but also that single coaches in diverse geographic areas would not receive the kind of support or oversight they needed.

Thus, a second component of our theory of change involved the creation of networks linked to regional centers that would provide the intensive support individual schools needed as they learned about and attempted to implement the Turning Points model. The regional centers would form a national Turning Points network—coordinated by the national center but with each center remaining independent. Key decisions about the model and the growth of the network would be made through a democratic governance structure. The design assumes that Turning Points regional centers are their own organizational entities, separate from the national center yet affiliated through a collaborative partnership committed to Turning Points reform. CCE's National Turning Points Center would support this relationship by developing design products and providing professional development and technical assistance to regional centers.

The new national Turning Points network was launched in August 1999 with three regional centers: New England (based at CCE); AIMS, based at the University of Illinois; and the Central States Center for School Reform in Kansas City, Missouri, a Coalition of Essential Schools regional center. In January 2000, Turning Points was officially approved as a NAS design—the first added to the NAS portfolio since it began in 1991. For the 2002–2003 school year, eight regional centers served approximately 60 Turning Points schools.

A complete history of the Turning Points program must, eventually, include an answer to the question of whether student performance has improved in the schools that have implemented the Turning Points program. In the next few years, we plan to strengthen our efforts to understand our influence on teacher practice and student learning. At this writing, we lack fully satisfactory answers, but we have collected preliminary data using a mixture of qualitative and quantitative techniques, including coaching logs; case studies of several Turning Points schools; Turning Points self-study data; and a longitudinal database containing demographic information on students and staff, measures of student engagement, ratings of teacher preparation and satisfaction, student achievement data, and information on school practices.

As of this writing, nine studies of the implementation and effects of the Turning Points model have been conducted and disseminated. Three studies are baseline evaluations. Two are case studies of Turning Points schools in Missouri and Illinois. Four are longitudinal studies that have examined changes in Turning Points implementation, school practices, and student achievement over two to five years. In each of these reports, Turning Points schools have attained higher student achievement scores than schools not participating Turning Points. Further, the percentage of improving schools increases with the length of time in the network (Tung and Feldman, 2001; CCE, 2002a, 2002b, 2002c; CPRD, 2001a, 2001b, 2002, 2003; De Pascale, 1997, Felner et al., 1997). A study conducted in 31 Illinois middle schools beginning in 1990 demonstrated that student achievement and other measures of school improvement were positively related to the comprehensiveness of the implementation of the Turning Points principles, as measured by the Self-Study Survey described previously (Felner et al., 1997). In schools that had implemented the Turning Points program comprehensively, student achievement test scores in mathematics and language arts were significantly above the state mean. In addition, as the authors write, "The relationship between a school's level of implementation and its ability to prevent decline or enhance outcomes is even more pronounced in the important case of 'at risk students'" (Felner et al., 1997, p. 549). Teachers also reported that student behavior problems declined significantly, and students reported feeling safer and having higher levels of self-esteem.

An analysis of the effects of Turning Points in five Peoria middle schools in 1998–99 and 1999–00 found that both fifth- and eighth-grade students made significant gains in math, which corresponded to a similar trend in classroom practices as measured by self-study data. Over a two-year period, mathematical skill enhancement practices increased from "several times a month" to "weekly." The percentage of fifth-grade students that met the math standards nearly doubled in 1999–2000. Students in schools where teachers had been working in teams over a longer period had better overall achievement scores. These schools also had fewer students receiving academic warnings and more students meeting or exceeding Illinois state standards.

Measures of student adjustment and self-esteem yielded some unique and positive results. Levels of depression, which typically increase from fifth to eighth grade, actually declined for students in the Peoria middle schools. In addition, eighth-grade Peoria students demonstrated significantly higher levels of academic self-efficacy (i.e., willingness to work hard, belief that their work would lead to positive results, and fewer than average behavior problems) (CPRD, 2001b).

Some of the initial themes emerging from the case studies and coaching studies include the importance of coaching, the importance of the network in creating a sense of common purpose, and the recognition that changing a deeply embedded organizational culture is profoundly challenging (Tung, Ouimette, and Feldman, 2004). We will discuss each of these themes briefly.

The Coach as the Bearer of the Turning Points Vision

The coach is, in many ways, the bearer of the vision. The school relies on the coach to demonstrate how Turning Points can be implemented. The pressures that teachers experience from high-stakes testing, student behavior problems, new curriculum mandates, and so on can overwhelm their ability to participate in Turning Points reform. Given these competing demands, it is critical that the coach make the reform agenda explicit—particularly the role of individual elements of the program in relation to the bigger picture of comprehensive reform. It is also important, however, to find ways to ensure that the reform is not linked solely to the coach. Alleviating dependence on individual coaches involves both local interventions, such as having coaches work in teams, and efforts to strengthen the ties between individual teachers and schools and the regional and national networks.

The Network as the Source of a Common Vision

The Turning Points network of schools—both regional and national—is a vital component of reform. Participation in the network strengthens implementation in individual schools by breaking down isolation, exposing participants to new tools and ideas, and creating a sense of common purpose and vision. Network activities include focused school visits, network meetings to share practices and dilemmas, and summer institutes. Although the benefits of such activities may seem obvious, schools often need to be convinced that participation in network activities is not an added burden or another "initiative" but will instead energize and support their reform efforts.

The Challenge of Changing the Culture of Schools

The initial focus of both schools and coaches in implementing Turning Points is on the core practice of Building a Professional Collaborative Culture. But implementing structural changes and introducing a new vocabulary of practice are, in some cases, easier than changing the organizational culture. For instance, it is easier to create a common planning time than to ensure that conversations during team meetings are productive, and it is easier for teachers to understand and articulate the ideals of new programs than it is to change their practices.

We are, as noted, only beginning to build the infrastructure needed to collect and analyze data from our diverse sites, but even preliminary findings, such as these, help us refine our thinking and practice as we continue to scale up Turning Points reform. In the following section, we describe some of the issues we have faced and the lessons we have learned through our efforts to scale up the Turning Points design through regional networks.

Creating the Turning Points Network of Regional Centers

At the outset of the new Turning Points program in 2000, the risks and challenges of using a regional network, with CCE at the nexus, were clear. A national network of independent regional centers requires a strong foundation of agreed-on principles and practices, as well as shared tools. We were uncertain about whether we would find organizations whose missions were compatible with the goals of Turning Points and whether, even if they shared our vision, such organizations would have the capacity to implement the program and the resolve to persevere in the face of the difficulties that were bound to ensue. We also understood that, inevitably, tension would arise between the goal of implementing Turning Points with fidelity in many schools under the auspices of multiple regional centers and the need to be responsive to local contexts.

Refining the Turning Points Design

The first stage in building a new national Turning Points network involved further developing the Turning Points design, tools, and products. The national center worked to articulate school-based practices that would effectively translate the Turning Points principles into action and to develop accompanying tools. The goal was to develop rich descriptions of best practices, as well as a coherent and consistent set of tools to strengthen and challenge individual sites.

We were helped—and also pushed—in this work by NAS. In 1998, NAS had begun to develop standards for design teams, and Turning Points benefited from being the first to be required to use them in the process of becoming a NAS design. Our work in assembling a portfolio—a collection of evidence of our work as a design team—using the NAS standards of quality enabled us to identify the strengths in what we had already developed and prompted us to articulate missing pieces more clearly. The insistence of NAS on setting targets, schedules, and deadlines also helped us develop the model more quickly than might have been the case without these external requirements. Our goal was to strike an appropriate balance between the clear articulation of the design together with useful supports and the creation of a collaborative network in which member centers had a hand in the development and refinement of the model.

Defining the Criteria and Process for Selecting Regional Centers

It was critical to the success of the model to recruit strong regional centers. Thus, as we moved toward creating the network, we prepared a white paper outlining roles and responsibilities for the national and regional centers, as well as criteria for selecting centers. We wanted the selection of regional centers be a process in which the national and prospective regional centers would work together to assess whether there was a good match. The following criteria and process for selection were developed and have been applied in the recruitment of the current centers.

Selection Criteria: Infrastructure, Capacity, and Commitment. The criteria that guided our discussions with potential regional centers were whether the infrastructure needed to participate effectively in the network was in place and whether centers had the capacity and commitment to do the work.

With regard to infrastructure, we determined that a potential center must be an established nonprofit organization, with federal 501(c)(3) status, or have a confirmed affiliation with such an organization. This stipulation was meant to ensure that the organization would be able to manage its own staffing and finances. In addition, the organization had to demonstrate that it could provide sustained support to Turning Points schools. As indicators of the ability to provide that support, we sought organizations that had an executive director or another salaried person to oversee the organization, an active board of directors, a business manager (if it was managing its own finances), an administrative assistant, and office space and basic equipment (e.g., computers, copier, phones, fax).

In addition to these functional mechanisms, it was important to ensure that potential regional centers had the commitment and capacity needed to initiate and carry through the intricate social and organizational work required to implement the Turning Points design. To gauge these factors, we agreed that a potential center needed an organizational history that reflected its commitment to whole-school change and middle school reform and demonstrated some success in working with schools. In addition, we sought regional partners that were knowledgeable about current state education reform issues, that had experience in providing quality professional development to schools, and that had the capacity to ramp up services to Turning Points schools—improving and expanding the range of services they provided, as well as serving a greater number of schools.

Selection Process. As the National Turning Points Center, the CCE seeks to establish Turning Points regional centers through formal affiliations with organizations in diverse parts of the United States. Prospective regional centers and the national center discuss what we expect of a regional center, the support that regional centers can expect from the national center, and the capacity of the regional center to undertake the work. After a mutual assessment of whether a good fit exists, the prospective organization is either accepted or rejected as a Turning Points regional center. Once a Turning Points regional center has been selected, the national and regional centers develop a memorandum of understanding outlining all expectations and agreements, which representatives of both organizations sign.

This process has created a network of organizations that are diverse in terms of funding sources, institutional affiliation, and the specific focus of their activities (see Table 10.3), but all its organizations have adopted the Turning Points design as part of their respective missions. In regions where schools wanted to implement the Turning Points design but had no compatible organization, we have established CCE satellites, hiring one or two coaches to serve schools in these areas as we develop a center. In the 2002–03 school year, we had such satellites in California, Florida, and Pennsylvania.

Developing a Scale-Up Plan

The support of NAS was instrumental in helping us develop a sound scale-up plan. The plan spelled out a financial formula weighted toward the national center, so that regional centers could more quickly develop financial capacity and self-sufficiency.

Table 10.3
Profile of Current Regional Centers

Center	Responsibilities
The New England Turning Points Center	Serves Turning Points schools in Massachusetts and Vermont; targets low-performing urban districts throughout the region.
The Association of Illinois Middle Schools	Serves clusters of Turning Points schools in approximately 14 districts across Illinois; coordinates a broader network of 114 rural, urban, and suburban middle schools statewide, which may provide opportunities for the expansion of Turning Points in Illinois.
The Central States School Reform Center	Serves schools in Kansas City, Jefferson City, Lexington, and Bolivar, Missouri; began as a Coalition of Essential Schools center but has now integrated Turning Points fully into its mission.
The Public Education and Business Coalition (PEBC)	Supports public schools in Colorado; PEBC's work in literacy became the foundation for the Turning Points model and the Guide to Literacy.
New Visions for Public Education, New York City	Works with public and private sectors to energize teaching and learning and to raise the level of student performance; the largest reform organization dedicated to New York City's public schools.
The Idaho Turning Points Center, University of Idaho School of Education	Focuses on using technology to deliver professional development and gather data on teaming practices to its rural middle schools.
School Leadership Center of Greater New Orleans	Works to develop educators who can lead schools in which teaching and learning are enriched and optimized.
The Principals' Executive Program, University of North Carolina in Chapel Hill	Works to help fulfill the need for strong leadership in the public schools by providing relevant and rigorous professional development to public school administrators.

Each regional center is responsible for raising its own funds and managing its own finances. The national center provides technical assistance to each regional center in these areas. In general, there may be three categories of Turning Points schools:

- Fully implementing schools adopting the Turning Points model for the first time. The national center has built the Turning Points design model at an estimated cost of $50,000 per year for the first three years of a fully implementing school. For this fee, the school receives a comprehensive package of services, including intensive coaching, use of Turning Points guides and materials, the Self-Study Survey, and regional and national network and professional development opportunities.

- Veteran Turning Points schools. Veteran Turning Points schools have already been deeply involved in a Turning Points program similar to that of the current Turning Points design model or have had three years of full implementation services from a regional center. These schools may contract with the regional center for a lesser amount of services (e.g., 10 days of coaching).
- Schools having the capacity to do some of the required work themselves. These schools may be just beginning Turning Points design work but have some capacity to do some of the coaching themselves. In such cases, the regional center may contract to provide a lesser amount of services (e.g., do the Self-Study Survey and provide an agreed on number of days of coaching around standards-based curriculum and looking at student work). However, it is incumbent on the school to demonstrate to the regional center that it has the capacity to do the work that the regional center does not.

The national center is committed to raising a significant percentage of its operating funds through work with Turning Points schools in its own region, as well as through contracts and grants. However, each school with which a regional center works and the individual regional centers ultimately benefit from the work of the national center. Hence, the national center must be able to raise some revenue from each school with which a regional center works. Each Turning Points school pays a small annual fee to the national center. In return, each school receives publications, the opportunity to send a defined number of participants to national network events, and affiliation with the national network.

Although the regional network is the basis of our scale-up strategy, we quickly discovered that market demands would prevent us from relying on it entirely. Because of the rapid expansion of the Comprehensive School Reform Demonstration grant program, we realized that we would have to respond to sites for which we had not yet identified a regional center. For these sites, we established a satellite of the National Turning Points Center with one or more members of the regional staff. Our goal, in such circumstances, was to locate a regional center in each satellite site. As of spring 2003, we have located a regional center, the Chester County Intermediate Unit (CCIU) in southeastern Pennsylvania.

Forging a Collaborative, Accountable Culture Among Diverse Organizations

The decision to create a network of autonomous organizations enabled us both to grow more quickly and to ensure greater quality and innovation in implementation than would have been possible working entirely through a national center. The regional centers provide the capacity to support individuals working in schools and foster collaboration among them, promoting continual feedback, reflection, and examination of practice. If the organization is large enough to have a team of Turning Points coaches, it can use that team to deliver services, thereby obtaining the benefits that come from matching the differing needs of individual schools with the style and strengths of particular coaches.

Although collaboration is the cornerstone of a successful network, effective collaboration is complex, particularly across long distances. Developing the "soft" elements of the network—shared norms, goals, and culture—poses particular challenges. To build effective collaboration and ultimately to ensure quality implementation, the National Turning Points Center focuses on developing structures to provide for shared governance and accountability.

Shared Governance. At the founding network meeting in August 1999, considerable discussion arose about the involvement of the regional centers in important decisions. Thus, a decisionmaking process acknowledging that the decisions that shape the design must be made by those closest to the work was developed. We determined that major decisions governing the Turning Points national network would be made by consensus among the regional centers and the national center.

Who makes decisions? When? The primary governing body is the group of representatives from the centers and partner organizations, including the national center, which convenes three times annually. The group is apprised in advance of major issues to be considered and, when appropriate, given proposals to review. This group may decide that it needs to appoint an executive committee to address important issues that emerge between meetings. An example of a significant decision the Turning Points network has made involved the reformulation of the implementation benchmarks after a year of use. After a discussion of the strengths and weaknesses of the benchmarks at a national network meeting, the participants decided to revise them, incorporating significant changes in structure and language.

What is our operating definition of consensus? We define consensus as a situation in which a significant majority of the group supports a decision and in which every member of the group determines that he or she can, at a minimum, live with a decision. When discussion is particularly contentious, the group conducts some version of a "fist to five" assessment of members' opinions. That is, after a period of discussion, each member holds out an open hand, several fingers, or a closed fist. An open hand expresses a favorable view of a particular decision alternative, a few fingers indicate middling support, and a closed fist indicates strong opposition. If any participant uses the closed fist signal, no decision is made without further discussion. If, after members have aired their points of view, they still cannot reach consensus, the group can either appoint a committee to do further work on the issue and submit another proposal or conduct a vote in which each regional center has one vote, and the national center and the New England center together have two votes. (See below for a discussion of the role of the New England center.)

What is the role of the National Turning Points Center in decisionmaking? The national center has been charged both with leading a democratic network of regional centers and with protecting and enhancing the integrity of the Turning Points model. These two charges should never conflict, because it is through a productive, collaborative network that the design will be strengthened over time.

However, given the unique responsibility the Carnegie Corporation has conferred on the national center and the standards to which NAS holds it, the national center needs to reserve the right to bring a decision, with which it strongly disagrees, to its board of directors for review and possible override. The national center would exercise this right only in an extreme circumstance and has not yet had to do so.

Shared Accountability. Together, the regional and national centers share responsibility with the schools for the influence the Turning Points model has on the "core of educational practice" and thus on student learning. In Turning Points, we use multiple mechanisms to assess and improve the performance of those who are responsible for implementing the design, all of which involve peer review. Some of these mechanisms are formal; others are informal. Whether thinking about schools or centers, it is useful to use Richard Elmore's concept of "external normative structures for practice." According to Elmore (1996, p. 19),

> The important feature in these structures is not their unanimity or consistency which is probably illusory anyway, but the fact that the structures are external to the world in which teachers work . . . .

By establishing external peer review mechanisms, we aim to ensure that performance is assessed by those close enough to the processes in question to understand the issues teachers and schools must address but distant enough to provide relatively unbiased feedback.

School and Regional Center Benchmarks. Our starting point is two sets of benchmarks developed collaboratively, tested, and revised. "Benchmarks to Becoming a Turning Points School" articulates what it means to implement the Turning Points design in a school. "Regional Centers' Benchmarks" defines the qualities of effective external support to schools implementing the design. Benchmarks are only useful insofar as they are the focus for reflection and assessment. Appropriately, both sets of benchmarks are the first of our formal "products" to undergo significant revision as a result of multiple uses in the field.

School Annual Assessments. Every Turning Points school is asked to assess its progress annually, with the help of its coach, using the Turning Points benchmarks. The national center collects the data from these assessments and analyzes them to identify strengths, issues, and challenges the regional center and school network need to explore.

National Network Meetings. Network meetings and follow-up email and phone conversations are major vehicles for sharing work across centers. A Web site and a newly established Web-based forum are creating multiple avenues for communication. As a network, we are developing a norm of public sharing of successes, challenges, and dilemmas. Through these conversations, center staff members develop a shared understanding of what the benchmarks really mean and what evidence of success looks like.

Regional Center Site Visits. Every center has a national center liaison who visits two or three times a year to support the work of the center and facilitate conversations about progress using the regional center benchmarks. The liaison ideally becomes a "critical friend" to the regional center, offering support and ideas, as well as constructive feedback. Should critical needs or weaknesses be identified, the liaison is an important link to the national center.

School Quality Review and Regional Center Affirmation. Turning Points has instituted parallel processes—the School Quality Review and the Regional Center Affirmation—for schools and centers, respectively, to conduct in-depth progress reviews every three to five years. More intensive than the annual assessment, these reviews involve a self-assessment that includes the creation of a portfolio of evidence built around the benchmarks. They culminate in a three-day visit by an external review team made up of national and regional center staff and school colleagues. As of this writing, the New England and Illinois centers and two Turning Points schools, Amherst Regional Middle School in Massachusetts and Eastgate Middle School in Kansas City, Missouri, have undergone reviews.

A Collaborative Culture. While we have made great strides, as we noted above, it is no simple matter to create a culture and practice of collaboration among diverse organizations. Challenges can arise from cultural or stylistic differences between organizations (e.g., regional or local variations may occur in the vocabulary of practice, or the leaders of one center may have a tendency to intellectualize, while others may focus on practical issues), but they also arise from more-profound philosophical differences. Over the past few years, many points of tension have surfaced within the network with regard to our understanding of educational reform. Some of these can be summed up in brief oppositional phrases—"change must be constructivist" (jointly created by the school and center) versus "change must be directed" (led by the regional center); "middle schools have to be understood as unique entities" versus "the lessons of K–12 whole-school reform apply to the middle school as well"; "literacy instruction is a critical component of Turning Points" versus "literacy is a small piece of a much bigger picture."

Framed in terms of a debate between opposing viewpoints, such philosophical differences can be divisive, but it is unlikely that these complex issues can be resolved by edicts from the national center. An overly prescriptive stance is less likely to lead to ownership of ideas and approaches among network participants than is one that fosters constructive exchange and collaborative problem-solving. As a network, we are learning to explore differences in perspectives and to see them as useful ways to advance our thinking about teaching and learning.

Balancing Consistency of the Model with Experimentation and Local Context

Continuous improvement of the model depends on both consistency and innovation. Ideally, the regional centers take agreed-on principles, practices, and tools and make them their own. In the process, they contribute valuable insights, adaptations, and strategies.

As Michael Fullan (2001, p. ix) puts it,

> Grappling with the problem of achieving large-scale reform grounded in local leadership has become the new challenge— overtaking the false choice between local innovation and macro, superficial reform.

The new Turning Points network has shed some light on how to approach this challenge. By agreeing on fundamental elements of the design that every regional center must focus on and building the strengths of each center, Turning Points has gone a long way toward achieving a balance that will lead to deeper reform. A key aspect of this balance involves allowing and sharing different entry points to the work.

We strive as much as possible to focus discussion, collaboration, and decisionmaking on the Turning Points work with schools and on the goal of improving student learning. Doing this means tapping into the particular strengths and perspectives of each new regional center. It also means ensuring that "business" is kept to a minimum in network meetings and that a large share of each agenda is devoted to sharing successes, challenges, and new ideas in implementation.

A major example of this focus can be seen in the development of the "Turning Points Guide to Teaching Literacy." We began with the expertise of the Colorado Turning Points Center, PEBC, and a book called Mosaic of Thought (Keene and Zimmermann, 1997). Adding the perspectives of coaches from the different sites, the guide went through numerous revisions and reviews during several network meetings and summer institutes. The final product distills teaching strategies that are still being tested, refined, and revised. Another key example of a new tool arising from the network is "At the Turning Point: The Young Adolescent Learner." This guide was not originally on the national center's work plan, but several network members felt it was a critical piece and contributed a great deal of the thinking that led to its development. Still another example of how value is created in the network is the development of our assessment strategies, which we based on AIMS's deep experience using the Self-Study Survey as a tool for data-based inquiry. An important challenge for the network is ensuring that it captures all the iterations a particular practice or tool goes through as coaches apply it and uses the experiences to improve the model.

If success rides on implementation, implementation depends, to a greater or lesser extent, on effective coaching. A consuming focus of the network of Turning Points regional centers has been developing a shared and continually evolving understanding of coaching. To address this issue, we have developed a conceptual framework for the work of the coach in Turning Points schools. An annual four-day coaches' institute provides a structure for giving new coaches an overview of the design and a set of tools for engaging in the work. It also allows the national network to develop a common language and set of ideas for Turning Points coaching that cut across the regional centers. Returning coaches participate in leadership roles and in small group workshops and discussions that allow them to stretch and deepen their thinking.

The coaches' institute is both a beginning point for professional development of new coaches within each regional center and across the national network and a refresher for more-experienced coaches. The national center tries to ensure that, through network meetings, email, and newsletter forums, lessons about coaching are continually documented and shared. Some examples of how different centers have shared innovations in coaching include the teamed approach to coaching, which AIMS developed, in which several different staff members serve unique roles in the school (e.g., whole-school staff development, working with teacher teams, principal coaching); PEBC's work developing a clear, effective role for the in-house facilitator, a member of the school's faculty who has been relieved of regular duties to do the coaching; and the Idaho Center's work on what it means to work across a huge rural territory—linking coaches and schools through technology. Some innovations will work only in the local context in which they are developed, but all, as part of the national conversation, inform shared understanding of what effective coaching looks like.

A Closer Look at the Development of One Center

The development of the New England Turning Points Center over the last three years illustrates the balance between consistency and innovation in implementation that we strive for, as well as the value of the network in informing a center's practice. In many ways, the new Turning Points design was shaped by the early experiences of CCE staff in trying to implement Turning Points during the Carnegie Corporation's state-level initiative. We began working with too many schools and too few coaches. In thinking about a more-comprehensive model, we knew we wanted to work more intensively and directly with whole faculties. So, having had lots of early experience with what did not work, we used that experience to inform the Turning Points guides, the coaching model, and the structure of the regional network.

With the establishment of the national network of regional centers, the New England center began using the guides, the coaching model, and the set of services and also began participating in national conversations about progress and challenges. As the New England coaches used the Turning Points guides, they also informed the development of new tools, including "Teaching Literacy in the Turning Points School." Despite some staff turnover, each year saw a stronger, more-experienced team of coaches and deeper work on implementing the Turning Points design.

In spring 2001, the New England center became the first center to undergo the Regional Center Affirmation. Over a three-month period, the New England team compiled a portfolio of evidence of their work in implementing Turning Points. Using the Turning Points regional center benchmarks, a team of colleagues from other regional centers conducted a three-day site visit and inquiry into the center's work, including school visits and interviews with faculty members and principals, interviews with coaches and other center staff, and a review of the center's portfolio. Although the site visitors commended the New England center's work and recommended that it be "affirmed" as a Turning Points regional center, their report also raised several questions and noted areas that might be strengthened. Both areas needing to be strengthened involved coaching. The site visitors recommended that the center look closely at the ways in which coaches were supported and examine the coaching model and workload. In this way, the affirmation process is an example of lateral accountability—a process that leads to further reflection and revision of practice.

As a result of feedback from the review team, the New England center made several significant changes. First, it took a serious look at the coaching model and the number of schools each coach served. In the two school years since the affirmation, coaches have been working with fewer schools and, when possible, working in pairs. Next, the center considered how to strengthen the documentation of work at each school and decided that, at a minimum, each coach would write a midyear update on progress and a year-end final report that would be shared with schools, as well as with Turning Points staff.

Finally, center staff spent several months fleshing out a detailed "roadmap" for Turning Points work in New England. As a starting point, they used the national center's timeline for implementation, and spelled out entry points, questions, and activities in much greater detail. As they write in the introduction to their map:

> This roadmap is meant as a tool for both Turning Points coaches and schools. It is not meant to be the definitive answer to school improvement but to serve as the basis for our work in schools. Certain elements of the roadmap are pivotal (intersections through which all schools must travel), while other elements may be negotiated (the road that each school travels may be different). The goal, however, is for all schools to achieve a vision of excellence for every student.

We see in the experience of the New England center a model of how other centers will enhance the Turning Points design over time. As each center adapts the Turning Points timeline and creates innovations derived from local need and expertise, the design will improve and grow closer to achieving our vision of scale-up and changing the core of teaching and learning.

Looking Ahead: Building on Strengths, Facing New Challenges

Four years after the National Turning Points network began, we are at our strongest—serving more schools and regional centers and having a greater effect on the lives of young adolescents. Looking back, we feel that the scale-up strategy of creating a network of autonomous regional centers was the right choice. Together, our work has achieved greater depth and breadth than would have been possible as a single, centralized organization. The network of regional centers is doing some of its best work, taking a deeper and more critical look at the question of how to help schools change classroom practice. Our network has developed a stronger and more-cohesive culture.

At the same time, we are certainly facing new challenges from the current fiscal environment and the testing culture the No Child Left Behind Act represents. As we move ahead, it will be imperative for us continue to refine our coaching model and approach to professional development to adapt to different contexts and have a greater influence on many more classrooms. Our growth as a network will also enable us to speak with a louder and more compelling voice about the needs and possibilities of middle schools and young adolescent learners.

References

Carnegie Task Force on Education for Young Adults, Turning Points: Preparing American Youth for the 21st Century, New York: Carnegie Corporation of New York, Carnegie Council on Adolescent Development, June 1989.

CCE—See Center for Collaborative Education.

Center for Collaborative Education, Boston Public Schools Turning Points MCAS Analysis, Boston, 2001a.

_____, Turning Points in Action: A Case Study of a Turning Points Middle School, Boston, 2002a.

_____, Turning Points in Action: A Case Study of Eastgate Middle School, Boston, 2002b.

_____, "The Role of External Facilitators in Whole School Reform: Teachers' Perceptions of How Coaches Influence School Change," paper presented at the annual meeting of the American Educational Research Association, New Orleans, La., April 2002c.

Center for Prevention Research and Development, "An Analysis of Self-Study Data from the Boston Turning Points Schools," Champaign, Ill., 2001a. Online at http://www.cprd.uiuc.edu/.

_____, "An Analysis of Self-Study Data from the Peoria Turning Points Schools," Champaign, Ill., 2001b. Online at http://www.cprd.uiuc.edu/ (as of June 24, 2004).

_____, "2001/02 Baseline Analysis of Self-Study Data, Illinois Turning Points Schools," Champaign, Ill., 2002.

_____, "2001/02 Baseline Analysis of Self-Study Data, Massachusetts Turning Points Schools," Champaign, Ill.: 2003.

CPRD—See Center for Prevention Research and Development.

De Pascale, C. A., *Education Reform Restructuring Network: Impact Documentation Report*, Cambridge, Mass.: Data Analysis and Testing Associates, Inc., 1997.

Elmore, R. F., "Getting to Scale with Good Educational Practice," *Harvard Educational Review*, Vol. 66, No. 1., 1996, pp. 1–25.

Felner, R. D., W. J. Anthony, D. T. Kasak, P. Mulhall, S. Brand, and N. Flowers, "The Impact of School Reform for the Middle Years: Longitudinal Study of a Network Engaged in Turning Points–Based Comprehensive School Transformation," *Phi Delta Kappan*, Vol. 78, No. 7, March 1997, pp. 528–550.

Fullan, M., *The New Meaning of Educational Change*, 3rd ed., New York: Teachers College Press, 2001.

Jackson, A., and G. Davis, *Turning Points 2000: Educating Adolescents in the 21st Century*, New York: Teachers College Press, 2000.

Keene, K. O., and S. Zimmermann, *Mosaic of Thought: Teaching Comprehension in a Reader's Workshop*, Portsmouth, N.H.: Heinneman, 1997.

Tung, R., and J. Feldman, "Promoting Whole School Reform: A Closer Look at the Role of External Facilitators," paper presented at the International Congress for School Effectiveness and Improvement, Toronto, Canada, January 2001.

Tung, R, M. Ouimette, and J. Feldman, "The Challenge of Coaching: Providing Cohesion Among Multiple Reform Agendas," paper presented at the annual meeting of the American Educational Research Association, San Diego, Calif., April 2004.

Scaling Up Talent Development High Schools: Lessons Learned from Comprehensive High School Reform

Nettie E. Legters, James M. McPartland, and Robert Balfanz

In this chapter, the authors identify three factors that affect the success of high school reform efforts in individual schools, as well as efforts to scale up these reforms: the features of the reform model, the arrangements with local schools and districts, and the capabilities of the external design team. The Talent Development High School reform model, they argue, provides a well-defined reform framework, supported by extensive planning before implementation, highly specified materials and processes, and technical assistance. The authors discuss strategies for making constructive arrangements with schools and districts, such as requiring buy-in from teachers at new sites, defining funding requirements in advance, and aligning practices with district and state priorities and requirements. They further argue that, to develop the capacity to work effectively with schools and districts, school reform organizations need a well-specified business plan and the ability to manage financial and human resource matters.

Public high schools across the country are under fire for failing to motivate, engage, and provide a high-quality education for the majority of their students. The failure is most evident in large, non-selective high schools, which enroll significant proportions of the nation's poor and minority students. The average student enters these schools almost four years behind grade level in reading and mathematics. These gaps do not narrow in subsequent years and contribute to high course failure, grade retention, and dropout rates (Roderick and Camburn, 1999; Balfanz and Legters, 2004). Low attendance, high suspension rates, and poor learning climates are common features in these schools, and current mandates to institute high-stakes graduation tests have increased concern about the fate of students who attend them.

Over the past decade, our team of researchers, developers, and school-based educators has worked to turn around low-performing high schools in such large cities as Philadelphia, Baltimore, and New York. The reform approach that emerged from this work, called Talent Development High Schools (TDHS), has demonstrated success and is now being expanded to a network of more than 50 large high schools in other districts, including Chattanooga, Chicago, Kansas City, Los Angeles, Newark, New Orleans, and St. Louis. The road to reform—and to developing a reform model—has not been easy. We have described some of the early implementation challenges elsewhere (see Legters et al., 2002). In this chapter, we offer an expanded discussion of these challenges and focus on issues we have encountered recently as we have scaled up our work into a larger and more-diverse group of schools and districts.

We begin by showing how the core components of TDHS emerged in response to major criticisms of public comprehensive high schools. We then discuss challenges we have encountered as we implemented and scaled up the model. In the final section, we examine what might be done to overcome these difficulties. We conclude with a theory of action about high school reform that analyzes the initial conditions that can impede needed organizational and instructional changes and the mediating activities that can accompany the recommended reforms to neutralize or overcome the initial impediments.

What Is Wrong with Comprehensive High Schools, and Why Are They So Difficult to Change?

Over the past two decades, calls to overhaul our nation's comprehensive high schools have intensified. A series of studies and national reports released in the 1980s identified many shortcomings in the organizational, curricular, and instructional practices of traditional comprehensive public high schools (Boyer, 1983; Carnegie Forum,

1986; Goodlad, 1984; Oakes, 1985; Powell, Farrar, and Cohen, 1985; Sizer, 1984). In 1996, the National Association of Secondary School Principals (NASSP), with support from the Carnegie Foundation for the Advancement of Teaching, released *Breaking Ranks*, the final report of its Commission on the Restructuring of the American High School (NASSP, 1996). *Breaking Ranks* heralded what has now become a national movement to rethink and restructure education in public high schools.

Table 11.1 summarizes the major critiques of comprehensive high schools and the reform principles and specific strategies that have emerged in response.

High schools are often criticized because their large size and the resulting tendency toward impersonal, bureaucratic organization interfere with the development of close personal relationships between students and teachers. Research on the characteristics and needs of adolescents and the properties of effective learning organizations shows that caring, supportive relationships are important to students' motivation, engagement in school, social behavior, and academic success and that these relationships are most critical for at-risk students. Hence, a key goal of the current high school reform movement is personalizing high schools by converting them into smaller units or by creating new, smaller schools that encourage closer connections between students and adults.

High schools have also been criticized for breeding apathy. Students experience the high school curriculum and learning activities as boring and largely irrelevant to their lives or anything they imagine doing in the wider world. Research has shown that this sense of apathy and irrelevance is linked to several features of high schools. The organization of content into academic subject-area departments and traditional teacher-centered pedagogy, for example, make it difficult for teachers and students to move beyond fragmented learning experiences to apply knowledge to real-world problems. Infusion of information-age technologies, multicultural materials and perspec-

Table 11.1

Challenges Comprehensive Public High Schools Face, Common Reform Principles Addressing the Challenges, and Specific Reform Strategies

Challenge	Reform Principle	Strategies
Anonymity The large size and organizational structure of most high schools make it difficult for students and adults to know one another well.	**Personalization** High schools become caring and supportive places where students and adults know one another well.	Small learning communities Schools-within-a-school Smaller schools Interdisciplinary teaming Advisories and mentors School, family, and community partnerships
Apathy High school curriculum is viewed as dry, boring, and unrelated to students' lives or futures; as preparing only a select few students for college; and as doing little to prepare students for success in our changing economy and society.	**Relevance** High school curricula prepare all students for two- or four-year college and careers. Curriculum and instruction are designed to engage and motivate diverse learners.	Career themes, clusters, or academies Integration of academic and career curricula Cooperative, contextual, and constructivist teaching methods Applied, field-based, hands-on projects and activities Integration of computer and telecommunications technology Work-based learning (job shadowing, internships)
	High Standards High schools eliminate tracking and hold all students to high academic standards.	Common core curriculum that prepares and certifies all students for postsecondary education End-of-course and high school graduation exams
Diversity The cultural and linguistic diversity of high school students has increased. In addition, students differ in levels of preparation for high school and in styles of thinking and learning.	**Flexibility** High schools provide multiple and varied learning opportunities to promote success for all students, investing time and resources to meet the needs of individual students.	Expanded repertoire of instructional approaches Extended class periods, school days, and school year Extra help to students who need it through catch-up courses and summer or after-hours school programs Opportunities to learn study skills and social skills to promote success in high school work in life

SOURCE: Legters, Balfanz, and McPartland (2002).

tives, critical thinking, and links to life beyond the walls of the class-room and school are typically lacking in most comprehensive high schools.

High schools also have traditionally had different expectations for different students based on prior academic performance. Some students are tracked into high standards, college-preparatory courses, while weaker students take watered-down courses that do little to prepare them for college or careers. The perennial equity concerns of this system have been amplified by a changing economy that offers few living-wage opportunities for students unprepared for postsecondary training. Reform principles that have emerged in response to these problems include expecting all students to achieve in a core set of courses that, taken together, constitute a college-preparatory curriculum of high-standards courses. Relevance also has become a core aim of high school reformers, with a focus on more interdisciplinary, applied, career-focused, and multicultural content and pedagogy.

Finally, comprehensive high schools have been faulted for expecting students with extremely diverse backgrounds and abilities to succeed in a rigid, bureaucratic environment that does little to build on their individual strengths or address their unique needs. Tracking, the traditional approach to managing differences in preparation or perceived ability has generated a highly unequal system of opportunities for learning, with deleterious consequences for the majority of students who fall outside the college-bound stream. Researchers have come to agree that high schools should be more flexible organizations, oriented toward the needs of individual students. Strategies include encouraging instructional techniques designed to reach a greater number of students (e.g., cooperative learning, hands-on kinesthetic activities, projects) and reorganizing time and resources to provide students with multiple opportunities for success.

As we have noted elsewhere, the increasing amount of intellectual activity and practical experimentation around high school reform over the past decade demonstrated a striking level of convergence around the core reform approaches described above (Legters, Balfanz, and McPartland, 2002; Legters et al., 2002). Translating these principles into action that improves failing high schools in a comprehensive and sustained way is, however, a formidable task.

High school is often viewed as the most difficult educational level to change. The sheer size of most high schools—typically more than 1,000 students and more than 100 staff members—presents a major challenge to whole-school reform efforts, especially those that embrace participatory and inclusive approaches to the change process. The traditional organization of high schools into subject-area departments led by department heads presents a more-complex structure of power and authority than is found in the lower grades. Departmental organization also has supported the tendency for high school teachers to identify themselves as subject-matter specialists first and teachers of children second, working against reformers' efforts to institute more personalized relationships and learning environments. Professional development opportunities for high school teachers typically reinforce high school teachers' primary identification as content specialists.

High schools are complex in other ways. In any given high school, numerous programs may be operating simultaneously, each of which serves only a small subset of the student population. Magnet programs serve academically advanced students; dropout prevention programs serve at-risk students; career or technical programs serve another subgroup; and special education programs serve the growing number of students identified as being in need of such services. These programs typically have their own mandates, space, staff, funding streams, and interest groups, and these differences in requirements and in the views of the various constituencies can undermine comprehensive reforms designed to institute major changes across the entire school.

A final challenge to reforming high schools is the lack of public consensus on the purpose of high school and what high school graduates should know and be able to do. Current moves to link receipt of a high school diploma to performance on high-stakes tests have been criticized for narrowing the focus of high school by overemphasizing academic content at the expense of social, athletic, and civic activities that motivate and engage many students and develop skills viewed as equally important to future success.

Large, nonselective, *urban* high schools present additional challenges, including high teacher and administrator turnover, resource-poor environments, and high-need student populations that demand constant attention, leaving little time or energy for planning, implementing, and sustaining reforms. Recent evidence shows that more than half of the entering students never graduate from hundreds of large, nonselective high schools in the nation's major urban districts (Balfanz and Legters, 2001). Problems with the learning environment are obvious to any visitor; half-empty classrooms or disorderly conditions in the halls and stairways are common. Attendance rates in many nonselective urban high schools are typically less than 75 percent, with from 50 percent to 75 percent of students missing more than a month of school during the year. Urban high schools are also typically located in large districts, where multiple mandates, changing leadership, union politics, and bureaucratic inertia thwart reforms (Hess, 1999).

The Talent Development Response

Reforming large, comprehensive high schools is indeed challenging. It is not, however, impossible. The TDHS program emerged in the mid-1990s in response to critiques of comprehensive high schools and as a practical effort to operationalize the broader vision for reform set forth in *Breaking Ranks*. TDHS was first developed and implemented in 1994 through a partnership between researchers at Johns Hopkins University and education practitioners at Patterson High School in Baltimore (see Legters, et al., 2002 for the Patterson case study and the early history of TDHS). The model calls for specific changes in school organization, detailed revisions to classroom instructional activities, and local support systems for the administrators and teachers undertaking the reforms. As such, TDHS embodies many of the research-based reform strategies designed to achieve high standards, personalization, relevance, and flexibility in high schools, as outlined in the third column of Table 11.1.

Organizational Reforms. The organizational reforms involve establishing several self-contained academy units within the school to create curriculum choices that will engage student interests and to foster positive adult-student relationships that will develop caring and respect. These reforms include the following:

- A Ninth Grade Success Academy set up as a separate, self-contained unit for the transition grade into high school, with a common planning time for teams of six teachers; each team serves the same 150 students. These planning sessions focus on individual attendance, discipline, and course passing. Daily attendance is emphasized by publicizing this goal, offering incentives, reaching out to absent students by telephone, and offering opportunities to make up missed work. An extensive career awareness program accompanies the ninth-grade curriculum, so students can select the program they will pursue in the following three years. This awareness program helps students understand their strengths and interests and provides information about career-related opportunities available at their school.

- Multiple career academies established as separate, self-contained units covering Grades 10 through 12, each with a common core college-preparatory curriculum blended with a selected career theme and pathways of elective courses and work experiences related to that theme. Each career academy enrolls about 300 students, which is small enough to permit all students and teachers to know each other as individuals and large enough to support a self-contained faculty with at least two instructors in each major subject. These units are intended to counter the problems of anonymity and apathy at many large high schools by offering a personalized learning environment focused on students' own career strengths and interests. The academies permit students to become engaged in the topics that interest them and encourage the development of a passion for learning.

- An on-site alternative program for the short-term placement of students with serious discipline problems, called the Twilight School, conducted each day after regular school hours. Students assigned to this unit are given smaller classes and extra counseling while earning course credits to develop the coping skills needed to return to the regular day program and be successful. Rather than suspending and transferring highly troubled students, the Twilight School provides a last chance to work out the adjustments needed to make it through a demanding high school program. The Twilight School is also used as a transitional experience for students entering from the juvenile justice system or as suspensions from other high schools, who might otherwise be a source of discipline problems at the school.

Instructional Reforms. These organizational changes are only the first step in high school reform. Even though significant improvements in school climate, student attendance, and promotion rates can be expected from a well-implemented new structure of self-contained academies with strong interpersonal and outreach programs, major changes in instructional practice are needed to address the problems of poor student preparation in literacy and mathematics. Hence, TDHS includes the following:

- Extra instructional time in literacy and mathematics in a 4x4 schedule of extended class periods. Four 90-minute daily classes are scheduled in two 18-week terms. This schedule permits students who need it to receive two years (or a double dose) of instruction in one year by taking literacy and math courses both terms.
- A new "acceleration curriculum" is offered to narrow and, gradually, close student achievement gaps in literacy and mathematics. In the first term of extended class periods, new materials and approaches based on students' current reading levels are used to appeal to young adults while focusing on the real higher-order skill gaps. In reading, the emphasis is on fluency and comprehension rather than word attack and isolated skill drills, which most students do not need, even though the approaches of many large commercial publishers cover these extensively. Classroom approaches follow daily routines of teachers modeling "read aloud–think aloud" examples, short lessons of direct

instruction in using comprehension strategies or recognizing the writer's craft, cooperative learning teams for partner reading and guided comprehension discussions, and self-selected readings from the classroom library of fiction, nonfiction, and audiotape books. In mathematics, the focus is on building skills and self-confidence in reasoning and problem-solving, with mental math, manipulables, and student team discussions that commercial catch-up offerings do not often feature. In ninth grade, the TDHS first-term course features prealgebra units; in tenth grade, it focuses on geometry foundations; and, in eleventh grade, it aims at readiness for Algebra II.

In the second term of each year of the acceleration curriculum, the district's own English and math syllabus is used and is supplemented by TDHS materials to continue the emphasis on comprehension and reasoning.

Student study skills and social skills are developed to facilitate high school learning experiences, such as cooperative learning teams, long-term projects, and research initiatives. In ninth grade, a first-term freshman seminar covers study skills, such as note-taking, memory aids, and preparation for different types of tests; such social skills as team roles and relationships and dealing with authority and peer encounters; and information retrieval strategies using the library and the Internet. This course also provides opportunities for students to become more aware of their strengths and interests as they relate to careers, thus preparing the students to select the upper-grade academy that they will attend. A continuation of study and social skills training is built into all upper-grade courses.

Technical Assistance and Professional Development. TDHS provides multiple forms and levels of support to schools implementing the reforms. Organizational reforms are supported by an on-site organizational facilitator, who leads the school through an inclusive and intensive year-long planning process. This facilitator provides on-site expertise in academy organization, staffing, scheduling, facilities changes, data management, and teaming and helps school leaders work through site-specific implementation challenges throughout the planning and first several implementation years. TDHS also installs an extensive teacher support system to facilitate the instructional reforms. This support consists not only of initial and regular follow-up workshops but also of intensive, school-based technical assistance to each teacher. Each week, new methods and materials are reviewed, and teachers receive classroom-based coaching to ensure strong implementation.

Evidence of Effectiveness. TDHS has documented the implementation and effects of the program in its partner schools. This research, using research designs involving matched control groups and comparisons of performance before and after implementation of the design, shows that intensive and sustained implementation of Talent Development reforms can result in impressive gains in attendance, achievement, course completion, grade promotion, and graduation. TDHS schools have

- increased daily attendance from an average of 60 to 65 percent to an average of approximately 85 percent
- doubled the number of students whose daily attendance is 90 percent or higher, a critical correlate with course passing
- improved school climates, as measured by student and teacher reports and significant declines in suspensions, arrests, and vandalism
- produced gains of two grades in math and reading for one year of instruction for at least half the students participating in TDHS catch-up courses
- increased course completion rates from 10 to 30 percentage points, even in subjects not supported by direct TDHS curriculum intervention
- increased promotion rates by 10 to 30 percent.

The class of 2003 saw the first two cohorts of students to experience four full years of full implementation of TDHS reforms in two high schools in Philadelphia—Edison and Strawberry Mansion. Edison succeeded in increasing the number of graduates by more than 60 percent; at Strawberry Mansion, the number of graduates in 2003 was *double* the number of graduates before the reforms. Neither school experienced any significant changes in enrollment during that period. These findings support our theory that the national problem of undereducated poor and minority youth is solvable if the appropriate organizational reforms, curricular tools, support for both teachers and students, and the financial resources needed to implement these changes are brought to bear in the schools that need them most (see Philadelphia Education Fund, 2000, 2001, 2002, 2003; Kemple and Herlihy, 2004; and the Web site of the Center for Social Organization of Schools, undated, for articles and reports documenting TDHS research results).

Challenges to Implementing and Scaling Up TDHS

Since its inception a decade ago, TDHS has encountered many implementation and scale-up challenges. The following subsections detail difficulties we have faced in implementing the organizational, instructional, and professional development components of the model and then turn to challenges specifically related to scale-up efforts.

Barriers to the Implementation of Organizational Reforms

Impediments to organizational reforms in high schools can involve logistics (building and scheduling issues) and authority structures (shifts of power and responsibilities).

Logistics. The usual division of physical space in a large high school is by subject-matter departments. The science department and its associated labs will be in one section of the building; the business department and its office machines and computer labs in another; and the English, math, social studies, and languages departments each in its own area of the building. Teachers in contiguous classrooms usually cover the same subject for different grades and course offerings, and a department chair in the subject with released time from some or all teaching duties will have an office nearby. Music, art, and physical education each follow a similar pattern. Guidance counselors are also usually grouped together in a centralized suite of offices.

The wall-to-wall academy structure that the TDHS model calls for creates several self-contained interdisciplinary academies within the school. Each separate academy must have classrooms for each core subject (English, math, social studies, and science) and selected elective courses. Each academy must also include offices for the academy principal and other support staff and for its own guidance counselors. If possible, science and computer labs are also relocated to each separate academy. The only remaining schoolwide areas are the cafeteria, auditorium, physical education facilities, and library–media center, all of which are scheduled for use at separate times for student groups from the separate academies. The ideal academy structure also uses different entrances for each academy and has walls with doors to separate space on any floor used by more than one academy.

Thus, an academy structure involves major relocations of teachers' classrooms, administrators' and guidance offices, and student entrances and traffic patterns. Some direct expense may be involved, such as the construction of new dividers and doors or the installation of utilities for science and computer labs. The more serious impediment to change, however, typically derives from the opposition of those who object to being moved from a favorite classroom or away from colleagues in the same department.

Assigning students and teachers to courses and class locations within separate academies that incorporate student choice can be a major implementation challenge. In a traditionally organized comprehensive high school, schedulers have a wider range of options for creating individual student schedules because they work with a seven- or eight-period day that offers multiple sections of the same courses. TDHS and other reform models now call for schedulers to balance class sizes and place students in appropriate courses within the constraints of separate academy boundaries and a four-period day. Further constraints are created by the requirement of common planning time for teacher teams in each academy. We have found that many schedulers trained in traditionally organized schools have tremendous difficulty understanding and adjusting to the demands of the new structure. In more than one school, the scheduler greatly weakened a potentially strong academy structure to protect interests or privileges of influential teachers or programs or was not technically capable of creating a true academy schedule.

Teacher preparation has posed another difficult aspect of staffing and scheduling teachers in the new structure. Moving a school from a departmentalized structure to an academy structure requires that more teachers be able to teach upper-level core academic courses so that each academy may offer these courses. In a typical comprehensive high school, for example, a number of math teachers may have experience teaching basic algebra and geometry, but fewer may have experience teaching advanced algebra or calculus (especially in low-performing high schools, in which only a fraction of ninth-graders reach the eleventh and twelfth grades). Offering the entire college-required course sequence in math in each academy, therefore, has created demands for the development of content knowledge, which high schools adopting TDHS and our technical assistance providers have struggled to meet. Moving to the four-period day and an academy structure also slightly increases the number of core content-area teachers across the board, and schools have had to petition the district for additional teachers to support the reforms. We discuss additional challenges related to teacher preparation later (see "Barriers to Implementing Instructional Reforms," below).

Authority Structures. Reorganizing a school into self-contained academies requires a major delegation of authority by the principal of the entire school to the separate academy principals, a shift away from the influence of department chairs, and the expectation that teachers will work together in interdisciplinary teams and academy groupings. Each change raises different challenges, activates different power interests or conflicts, and requires different interpersonal skills and experiences.

In a traditionally organized high school, decisionmaking is centralized in the office of the principal, with particular administrative and instructional tasks typically delegated to assistant principals and department heads, respectively. In a high school organized into multiple schools-within-a-school or academies, the principal must delegate not just particular tasks but the entire principal function for a smaller part of the school to the academy principals while maintaining oversight of activities and decisions that affect the entire school. The academy principals must have authority over key disciplinary policies and staff management in their units. This new authority structure means the school principal must empower each academy principal and hold him or her accountable for a well-managed and successful program, even though ultimate responsibility for the school success still rests with the school principal.

Most principals have not been trained in the kind of facilitative leadership style that this type of structure requires. It also has been extremely challenging for each school to determine exactly which issues it should address, which tasks it should carry out, and which should be the academy-level decisions and which require the involvement of the leadership cabinet and the school principal. Moreover, academy principals (typically drawn from the pool of existing assistant principals or, less often, from teacher leaders working toward administrative credentials) have varied widely in their abilities to run their own academies. This variation can make it difficult for principals to consistently entrust authority and decisionmaking to the academies.

Shifting the authority of department chairs vis-à-vis academy leaders to strengthen the academy authorities is both a technical challenge and a social implementation challenge. Districts do not typically have an "academy principal" position, so the district bureaucracy must often be negotiated to institute the new position and gain board certification. More difficult is redefining the department chair position, especially because the new organization typically calls on department chairs to teach more classes than they have been accustomed to teaching. The most difficult change for department chairs under the new academy organization is the distribution of subject-area teachers throughout the building, which greatly diminishes the role of the department chair in providing daily supervision to subject-area teachers.

TDHS calls for high school teachers to shift away from their traditional orientation—subject-matter expertise and maintaining high standards in their fields—toward a student orientation—doing what it takes to promote the success of every student in the academy.

Under the organizational reforms, teachers are expected to work more often in interdisciplinary teams and to assume more direct responsibility for improving student attendance, discipline, and course passing. Teachers themselves telephone absent students and set up incentive programs to recognize and reward good attendance. Teachers are expected to deal with student misbehavior, including holding team meetings with offending students and their parents and working with individual students to shape their behavior in positive ways. Teachers are also expected to be present in the halls outside their classrooms to urge students to move deliberately and be on time to their next destination, rather than leaving the whole job of supervising student movement to adult hall monitors or school administrators. Some schools also look to teachers to help monitor cafeteria periods, checking color-coded student identification cards for the proper lunch period and otherwise helping to manage the lunch break. Teachers are also expected to have individual meetings with students at report card times and to reach out to students having difficulties, providing extra help and counseling.

We have encountered union objections in some districts and schools to these expanded roles. In one of our most-disappointing encounters, a district-level union official reminded teachers in one faculty meeting that the contract protected their planning time for individual purposes and that they should not use any of this time to meet in their teacher teams. Individual teachers have also cited the contract agreement in their refusal to go beyond instructional activities within their own classrooms, because they believe other functionaries should be provided for any duties that go beyond a teacher's instructional services. Once, a large number of teachers got up to leave a planning meeting on the precise minute for meeting durations stipulated in the contract.

Barriers to Implementing Instructional Reforms

Barriers to instructional reforms can include student academic weaknesses (not realizing and dealing with poor student preparation for high standards academic work), poor teacher preparation (lack of content expertise, classroom management skills, or readiness for active learning pedagogies), and agendas and directives from district and state officials that distract from real classroom instructional innovations (the need to prepare students for a required minimum competency test, district selection of texts and syllabi that conflict with reform recommendations, and turf battles with middle management curriculum and instruction officials).

Poor Student Preparation. As we have noted, in most of the large nonselective high schools that we work with, the average entering ninth-grader is between three and four years below grade level in reading and math skills. At the same time, most district policies now require all high school students to be provided a high-standards, college-preparatory curriculum in the core academic subjects. The TDHS model confronts this juxtaposition of weak preparation and high standards by increasing instructional time, thereby enabling students to succeed in demanding academic courses, and by adding carefully designed catch-up courses to narrow skill gaps.

Teachers and curriculum supervisors are often unaware of students' actual academic levels; are in denial about the large percentage of students that need massive assistance to catch up; or are satisfied to succeed with only the students who are adequately prepared, failing all others in the core academic courses. Sometimes, teachers and administrators do not understand the kinds of student deficits that need attention—fluency and comprehension rather than decoding and word attack in reading and intermediate arithmetic and reasoning strategies rather than drill and practice in applying formulas and algorithms in math—and so make unwise investments in remedial materials that miss the mark and bore students.

TDHS catch-up courses are sometimes opposed or rejected by district curriculum supervisors and high school teachers as "too easy for our students" when their comprehension and problem-solving deficits are not appreciated or because they have other, competing remedial materials that assume different student needs and use other instructional approaches.

Teacher Preparation. Serious obstacles to instructional reforms often arise because significant numbers of inexperienced teachers are on the staffs of many high-poverty, low-performing high schools.

They may not be fully certified or may be assigned to subjects in which they are poorly trained or have no training at all. Many of these teachers will struggle to teach and are destined to leave teaching within a short period. In some high-poverty schools, experienced teachers also have weak classroom management skills or are weak in content knowledge. These weak teachers, both novice and experienced, will require a great deal of help in basic teaching skills before they can begin to tackle instructional innovations that require confidence and resourcefulness.

But as Elmore (1996) and others have discussed, reforms are problematic for *all* teachers as they change classroom instruction to actively involve students in their own learning and focus on higher-order competencies, such as comprehension strategies, critical thinking, reasoning with evidence, and taking initiative to formulate problems in mathematical terms. The TDHS instructional interventions focus on teaching for understanding and higher-order competencies. As an example of instructional reforms that challenge teachers, TDHS approaches to developing the reading comprehension skills of high school students include teacher modeling of different comprehension strategies. A teacher will provide a "read aloud and think aloud" oral presentation where a literacy passage is read with regular pauses to say what is going through the reader's mind as he or she interacts with the text. At different points, the comprehension strategies will include relating the content to one's own experiences, predicting what may come next, figuring out an unknown word from the context of the passage, or noticing a writer's use of particular formats or literary devices to provide interest and meaning. Such teacher modeling requires great skill and practice, without which students might hear theatric oral reading but miss the regular think-aloud pauses that demonstrate comprehension strategies.

Thus, barriers to scaling up TDHS instructional reforms include both knowledge and experience gaps that some poorly prepared teachers in high-poverty high schools have and the challenges all teachers face in teaching for understanding and higher-order competencies.

State and District Factors. A principal function of state education departments and school district leadership is to establish performance standards, the assessments to measure them, and the related curriculum guidelines. Any new instructional interventions must be coordinated and aligned with these factors. Depending on the jurisdiction and officials involved, the coordination and alignment may be a straightforward exercise of documenting the connection between the instructional interventions and the standards, assessments, and guidelines or may be a major conflict over allocation of instructional time and choice of curriculum materials and pedagogical approaches.

Any instructional reform must address the preparation of students for the state or district tests required for student promotion or graduation. The interruption of instructional reforms while students are drilled on test items is a potential threat to the success of the reforms. Classroom teachers face competing pressures, from supervisors focusing on test preparation about the allocation of time and instruction and from reform agents focusing on instructional innovation and improvement.

We have experienced both accommodation and conflict with state and district standards and testing requirements. In several schools in which required state minimum competency tests were scheduled during the first term, we were able to incorporate some regular practice on test items and to apply some of our lessons to test formats, without jeopardizing the focus of the TDHS first-term catch-up course. However, even when adjustments are made in the TDHS instructional sequences to allow modest time for test preparation or to incorporate testing formats into the TDHS materials, conflicts between the goals of department chairs and TDHS peer coaches may still exist. There are pressures from the chairs to focus entirely on preparing students for these tests and to halt all other instruction. Because department chairs contribute to the teachers' evaluations, their influence frequently outweighs that of TDHS coaches unless the school principal offers direct intervention and clear guidelines. In the same district, an English department chair in one school threatened retribution to any teacher who pursued the TDHS curriculum instead of devoting several weeks of class time to test-item practice.

Similarly, we have experienced extremes of reaction from middle-management curriculum and instruction officials about introducing TDHS acceleration courses in the first term, before the district's own second-term courses. In some districts, the curriculum and instruction official in search of effective reading and mathematics catch-up approaches has welcomed TDHS and set up an evaluation design to compare its effectiveness with those of other approaches, but we have also experienced strong resistance from similarly placed officials in other districts that are committed to other commercially available remediation courses and are unwilling to experiment further. We have often been unable to change these decisions even when the commercial materials focus on decoding skills in English and on drill and practice of formulas in math, which national research panels have found to be inappropriate for most teenage learners. Materials may have been purchased, and teacher-training sessions based on these materials may already have been conducted. For TDHS to be successful in these situations, waivers from district remedial materials and training need to be obtained, or the district approaches need to be focused on the small numbers of students who need decoding or other low-level instruction in a "triple dose" arrangement that also retains the TDHS catch-up courses.

Barriers to Implementing TDHS Technical Assistance and Professional Development Supports

We have encountered several major barriers to implementing the technical support we have found necessary for strong implementation of TDHS reforms, including pressure to move quickly; cost; perceived need; the presence of multiple, preexisting reforms; and staff turnover.

Pressure to Move Quickly. TDHS is a whole-school reform approach that requires the awareness, buy-in, and active participation of the entire school staff in planning and implementation. It also requires addressing the many details of staffing, scheduling, facilities changes, and professional development. For these reasons, we have found that schools that invest in a year or more of awareness-building and planning under the guidance of an on-site TDHS organizational facilitator have much stronger implementations than schools that attempt to circumvent or hurry those steps. Unfortunately, real and perceived pressures from state reconstitution orders, district mandates, and funding agency timelines have interfered with our ability to convince schools to commit to a full planning year. While we acknowledge and make every effort to contribute to the momentum for reform such pressures can generate, our approach of "controlled haste" is at times overrun by reactive efforts that do more to alleviate immediate pressure than to help schools and students in the long run.

Cost. Full implementation support from TDHS includes an on-site team of one organizational facilitator and three instructional coaches (typically 0.5 full-time-equivalent employees per school); off-site training; technical assistance from facilitators based at Johns Hopkins University; curriculum materials; and fees covering data collection, analysis, and regular feedback. On average, a high school of 2,000 students would need about $250,000 per year to cover the TDHS curricular materials, technical assistance, and the on-site support team. Schools may incur additional expenses in moving to a 4x4 block schedule, paying teachers' professional development stipends, and in reconfiguring the school building to support an academy structure. A school of this size typically operates on an annual budget of $8 million to 12 million, so the costs of TDHS reforms usually total less than 5 percent of overall expenses. However, our experience has been that schools are often hard-pressed to come up with any additional funding without guidance. A number of federal multiyear funding sources allow a school to apply for support for some or all TDHS reform costs, including Comprehensive School Reform (CSR), Small Learning Communities in High Schools, and Title 1 from federal agencies, as well as state and private high school programs, such as those funded by the Bill and Melinda Gates Foundation and the Carnegie Foundation. The funds, however, are not always available in a given year for a given school and can fall short of the costs of reform, placing pressure on schools to find additional funds or to attempt to make compromises that can undermine the whole-school reform effort. Federal Title 1 money, a consistent source of reform funding for elementary schools, is typically scarce in high schools.

Perceived Need. Because working with external reform organizations requires such a deep commitment of time and resources, it is tempting for local districts that obtain new funding for high school reform from CSR or other sources to retain all the funds for their own staff to attempt changes rather than to invest in a partnership with an external team, such as TDHS. Not only do districts believe they can implement ambitious reforms themselves, but they also doubt that external "vendors" are worth the cost, especially when the cost is considerable. So we get inquiries about purchasing only selected curriculum materials, perhaps with a bit of training as would occur with textbook publishers, or inquiries about contracting for only a day or two of technical assistance during the district's regularly scheduled professional development days with no further follow-up in classrooms or later in the year. To be sure, some localities need much less external assistance than others, and some schools make important additions to the TDHS reforms through their own inventions (see the scale-up discussion later in this chapter). But our experience suggests that turning around a large, troubled high school in high-poverty areas with the TDHS model requires both a major commitment from the local staff and substantial on-site technical assistance from skilled TDHS facilitators.

Multiple Reforms. Some conditions can weaken the prospects for both organizational reforms and instructional reforms. Such conditions are not peculiar to high schools and can include the existence of several reform components from different sources at the same school and the inevitable turnover in leadership or key staff.

Many schools and districts will try reform components from outside sources, especially if they come with external grant support tied to some innovation. Indeed, some principals are constantly seeking added resources and never turn down any offer of help. However, when multiple initiatives are expected to coexist at a school for the same specific purpose, such as improving student writing, they can get in each other's way and confuse the teachers involved. Such conflicts can worsen when access to free professional development time or other resources is involved. The main idea of comprehensive school reforms is replacing uncoordinated piecemeal changes with a package of mutually supportive improvements that operate synergistically, so multiple uncoordinated activities can distract from an effective reform plan.

Staff Turnover. Staff turnover primarily affects the sustainability of reforms as newcomers replace the initiators of the school changes. When the turnover is in leadership positions, the continuation of key components of the reform may be at issue if the replacement personnel are not well versed in the changes or have different ideas about reforms. When the turnover is of teachers in courses using instructional innovations, the new teachers will require the training and support services necessary to recreate the recommended classroom activities.

General Implementation Barriers

In addition to the problems noted above, we have also encountered more-general difficulties that add to the challenges of implementing different components of TDHS. These include social inertia (preoccupation with daily problems and lack of an alternative vision) and deep-seated beliefs about the sorting function of high school that reinforce the status quo, no matter how detrimental to students.

Social Inertia. The traditional organization of high school— a hierarchical authority structure, departmental fiefdoms, specialists for every problem, and punitive responses for problematic student behavior—often stays in place because the administrators are so busy managing the daily challenges of large high-poverty schools that there is no time, vision, or hope for major changes. Just "keeping the lid on" such potential problems as student fights, assaults on teachers, on-site drug abuse, and other serious misbehaviors is often viewed as the major job of school leaders.

Even the stark reality that less than half of the ninth-graders at many schools ever reach twelfth grade and graduate fails to penetrate the educators' perception of the need for major reform. A simple comparison of the sizes of the twelfth grade and of the ninth grade should make the case. Often, however, teachers and school leaders contend that, until reforms at the elementary and middle grades have major effects or until promotion to high school without prerequisite skills is withheld, the current high school outcomes are about as good as can be expected.

According to this view, improvements come from trying harder with the usual approaches. Increasing security forces, suspending or transferring more troublemakers, requiring daily lesson plans and after-school, teacher-led coaching classes are parts of this traditional litany. Often, school leaders do not understand or accept the idea that coping with problems of student anonymity, apathy, low achievement, and faculty frustration and complacency with current conditions will require major restructuring of the large departmentalized high school. Combating this lack of energy and vision has been an ongoing implementation challenge.

Sorting Function of High Schools. Staff members' deep-seated beliefs in the sorting function of high school and confusion about what constitutes tracking have also presented challenges in implementing the TDHS program. Students are constantly being sorted by the grading system for promotion credits. To be sure, teachers feel some responsibility to try to reach all students and to allow students to make up failed credits. But even when large numbers of students in high-poverty schools fail courses, are held back to repeat a grade, and eventually drop out, these outcomes are accepted as the natural consequence of poorly prepared students entering the school's evaluation and sorting process. That teachers and administrators can and should take steps to enable all students to succeed flies in the face of what many view as one of teachers' central roles: to evaluate and pass or fail students.

Ironically, the ultimate "sorting" function is often acceptable at the same time that policies "tracking" students into different classes to address diverse needs are abhorrent, even when a new type of tracking means the flexibility of scheduling time and resources to give all students a decent chance to reach high standards. Research supports the elimination of tracking that withholds a high-standards college-preparatory curriculum from some students who might typically receive only watered-down business math instead of algebra or consumer English instead of Shakespeare and Steinbeck (McPartland and Schneider, 1996). However, some schools have also rejected the TDHS approach of extending time in core courses to give carefully focused catch-up instruction in the first term and a high-standards common curriculum in the second term, considering this to be unacceptable "tracking."

We need a more-sophisticated definition of tracking, in which tracking involves offering a common core curriculum designed to help all students achieve high standards, along with opportunities for extra time and extra help that will make the sorting function obsolete (Boykin, 1996). The pejorative use of the term *tracking* should be reserved for cases in which different programs of study are assigned to different categories of students, not for cases in which all students are given the same high-standards curriculum but some are offered more time and more expert help to be successful. We also need to evaluate approaches that can offset the stigma associated with providing extra help to students and to be sure that the teachers who provide this help are well prepared.

Challenges to Scaling Up TDHS

In the course of scaling TDHS up beyond the initial sites in Baltimore and Philadelphia, we have not only encountered many of the same implementation challenges identified above but faced additional challenges as well. We have encountered challenges in two broad areas: pressures to adapt our model in response to the needs and desires of a more-diverse set of schools and our own capacity to provide technical assistance to schools far from our home base in Baltimore while sustaining quality implementation in initial sites.

Necessary Compromises. Scaling TDHS up has meant working with high schools that differ from our initial sites in terms of student demographics, overall school climate, level of academic achievement, and external pressure to reform. As a consequence, we have been challenged to adapt our model to match local school conditions. Some of these adaptations have helped us expand and extend our ability to serve different types of schools. For example, schools with large Spanish-speaking student populations have pushed us to translate many of our curriculum materials. Work with schools that use different types of schedules (such as the year-round schools in Los Angeles and schools using an A/B instead of a 4x4 structure for extended periods) has encouraged creative thinking about how to accommodate these arrangements.[1]

Other requests for adaptations have been more difficult to work through. These include requests to implement only parts of the model and requests to phase in different components. We have struggled mightily to learn from our experience and figure out for ourselves what constitutes a "creative adaptation" that will actually help the school and what should be avoided as a "fatal mutation" that a school might prefer simply to avoid the pain and commitment that deep change requires.

For example, a number of schools have approached us desiring to implement only the ninth-grade academy component of TDHS. Depending on the school, we have had to determine whether such a move is advisable. Our experience tells us that implementing only a ninth-grade program without organizational and instructional reforms for upper-grade students only delays course failure and dropout problems to the tenth grade. Convincing schools to adopt the full program, however, is difficult, especially in schools that do not have the severe dropout problems and political pressure to reform our initial sites had and that have special magnet or other programs that may be threatened by upper-grade reforms. Other schools want to implement the organizational reforms but not the instructional components. These schools tend either to be schools with smaller proportions of students below grade level that maintain the view that, at the classroom level, course failures are largely the responsibility of students or to be schools in denial about the extent to which their students are poorly prepared for high school work. Our experience indicates that, in the main, implementing organizational reforms without

---

[1] The 4x4 schedule divides the year into two terms, with students taking a different set of classes in each. An A/B schedule, however, divides the week. A student would take certain classes on A days and different classes on B days. The specific number and length of classes and which days are A and which B will vary.

curriculum innovations or coaching support rarely achieves much effect in the classroom, but we have explored implementing the catch-up curriculum for subgroups of students in schools where many students enter at or above grade level.

Other schools have wanted to implement our catch-up curriculum but have not wanted to adopt the organizational changes needed to enhance personalization. We have found that the academy and team organization is important to improving attendance and that our catch-up curriculum is of little value if students are not attending regularly. On the other hand, it may be possible that a small high school with a stable climate and good student attendance does not need an academy structure but still requires TDHS instructional improvements to close achievement gaps.

Compromises we have seen that had unfortunate consequences include not ensuring that all teacher team members have a common daily planning period, not giving teacher team leaders some relief from teaching, not having separate entrances for each academy, and using department chairs as curriculum coaches instead of nonsupervisory peers. These experiences make us reluctant to depart from requiring full implementation of the comprehensive reform components of the TDHS model unless we have fully explored the matter both among ourselves and with the school.

Likewise, we discourage phasing reform components in over multiple years because early participants may be resented for receiving special privileges; momentum may decline if early improvements are seen as sufficient; or the opposition of initial skeptics to change may build as the inevitable problems associated with change arise. Our experience indicates it is far better to spend a full planning year to implement the entire model, so everyone at the school is involved and so that the multiplier effects of all components can be achieved. We have also found, however, that issues of funding or the timing of decisions can make phasing in changes the best plan, but some sequences are not as feasible as others.

Some local circumstances may require deviations from the ideal of implementing the entire set of comprehensive TDHS reforms at the same time, following a full planning year. For example, a high school might decide at midyear to embrace TDHS reforms and consider several alternative schedules for planning and implementation. One alternative is to use the remaining half-year and the following full year for planning. This approach, however, risks losing the momentum for reform because too much time passes between initial expressions of interest and the implementation of changes. Funding sources may also require immediate rather than delayed implementation. Another alternative is to accelerate the planning period in the remaining half-year and open with the full TDHS model the following fall. This approach may, however, result in underdeveloped career academies with weak faculty commitments. The other alternatives involve planning to phase in some but not all TDHS components in the fall, with continued planning for the remaining components in the following year. An acceptable phase-in might be starting a ninth-grade academy with catch-up courses and the 4x4 block schedule in the first implementation year and adding the career academies the following year.

Ordinarily, it is not good to phase in separate career academies in different years because it is nearly impossible to partially reorganize the building to replace departmental wings with some self-contained interdisciplinary academy units. Phasing in academies also invites unwanted status distinctions that usually will favor the early entries. Likewise, a phased reorganization of career academies by grade level also seems unworkable in creating the required self-contained spaces for academies. We have never seen a process involving starting career academies only for tenth-graders, with other upper-level students mixed together outside of academies, be successful. Because the space changes required for academies cannot be delayed, older students must be brought into the academy structure along with younger students, if only because, given the reallocation of space, there would be no place in the school building to hold their classes outside the academies.

Sometimes a high school will already have one or two "pocket" career academies for some students and will seek to adopt the TDHS model of wall-to-wall career academies for all students (Stern, Dayton, and Raby, 1988). However, the existing academies rarely have self-contained contiguous space for both the academic and elective courses that students in the same academy take. So, a planning process is needed to develop the entire array of career academies, each with its own self-contained space.

Another local circumstance requiring TDHS modification is a shortage of full funding with a school proposal pending, which means that schools cannot pay for curricular materials or coaching. In such cases, partial implementation of the academy structures may be planned to improve climate and attendance, with the instructional reforms to follow when full funding is obtained. Because student achievement is not expected to rise with only organizational reforms (Kemple, 2001), we urge schools to rework their budgets to find internal funds for curriculum materials and coaches, so delay of the instructional reforms becomes a last resort.

Capacities of the External Team. Our early experiences implementing TDHS taught us that comprehensive reform in high schools requires substantial on-site technical assistance, extensive curriculum materials, and sustained relationships with partner schools. As a result, our team has faced many scale-up challenges, most of which involve staffing and financial considerations.

Staffing. The TDHS model depends on a well-trained staff of TDHS facilitators to help implement the recommended reforms in each locality. We cannot rely on the existing high school leaders and staff to learn enough about TDHS organizational and instructional reforms at our national meetings and from our printed manuals to implement the program thoroughly on their own. The organizational reforms need regular, expert, on-site guidance for carefully scheduling and staffing the academy structure and using the team planning times and local data to address issues of student attendance, discipline, and course completion. The instructional reforms must have expert TDHS facilitators as coaches regularly in the classrooms to assist teachers with the new materials and approaches in English, math, and freshman seminar. Before a partnership with a new school begins, we must recruit, train, and relocate a team made up of an organizational facilitator, who begins in the planning year, and two or three instructional facilitators, who are added for the first implementation year.

It takes at least two months to train an organizational or instructional facilitator to be thoroughly versed in the TDHS reforms for which they will be responsible. This is usually accomplished by working side by side in schools or classrooms with expert TDHS facilitators and by receiving training in the content of TDHS courses or approaches from experienced university staff members. Sometimes, we have been able to recruit an administrator or faculty member from an existing TDHS who has managed or taught TDHS reforms and who is interested in becoming a facilitator and moving to a district in which a new TDHS partnership is forming. Locating, training, and relocating these teams and assuring their quality from a distance have been the central challenges of scaling up.

Finances. Research to develop and evaluate the TDHS model has been supported by large federal grants and contracts that, in the beginning, also covered major portions of the implementation costs for the initial pilot sites. The process of scaling up to new sites cannot, however, rely on subsidies to cover planning or operating costs. Instead, fee-for-service arrangements with new sites can only be made when payments from schools or their districts are sufficient to cover the actual costs of materials, services from staff, and the management of scale-up operations. Establishing a price structure that covered our costs and was reasonable for schools has also been a challenging aspect of our development.

School districts, as cash customers for materials and services, are often notoriously slow in paying their bills. Districts can often take six to twelve months after receiving the actual curriculum or staff services before finally paying the invoices. For a while, the university was paying the salaries of the technical assistance staff and for the printing of materials, which payments from the receiving school systems later reimbursed. As the volume of business has grown, however, we have had to explore alternative sources to maintain an adequate cash flow, including private foundations, loans from commercial agencies, and the New American Schools program.[2]

---

[2] See Chapter Sixteen in this volume.

We have also required capital to cover the costs we incur before being able charge fees for services to school districts. These expenses include the costs of developing technical assistance staff (described above) and of awareness-building activities in new districts. The awareness activities we provide schools and districts before they vote or make final commitments can be a significant start-up cost. When potential schools are known from the outset, awareness activities involve providing written materials on TDHS reforms and results, sending TDHS representatives for local awareness and question-and-answer sessions, and hosting visits to existing TDHS sites. When a large district is interested in nominating schools that do not yet know about TDHS, or when a major division of opinion exists at an interested school, it may be necessary to relocate a TDHS organizational facilitator to the district for several weeks or months to oversee the awareness process and represent the TDHS model locally.

Meeting the Challenges

What can be done to anticipate and overcome the barriers that have made high school reform in both individual sites and at scale so difficult? Our experiences in scaling up the TDHS model, both successful and unsuccessful, indicate that three broad factors make a difference: the features of the reform model itself, the arrangements with the local districts and schools, and the capabilities of the external design team.

Features of the Reform Model

Several features of the TDHS reform model help schools overcome inertia and resistance to the deep changes required to achieve the ambitious goals of establishing safe and serious learning environments, increasing student promotion and graduation rates so they trend toward 100 percent, and closing major skill gaps by the time of graduation.

The Model Is Comprehensive. Although the heart of any approach to improving student learning is the classroom instructional component, innovative curriculum materials and lessons cannot be very successful if student absenteeism is high, if the school climate is chaotic, or if teachers are unwilling or unable to use the classroom innovations. Similarly, organizational reforms that establish a personalized learning environment of caring and respect among students and teachers may produce better student attendance and serious academic expectations but will not likely raise achievement levels if classroom instruction remains unchanged. No combination of promising organizational and instructional reforms will be effective unless teachers and administrators are prepared and committed to putting them in place. The TDHS model enables high schools to undertake all three components of comprehensive reform.

The Underlying Reform Framework and Rationale Are Clear. Experienced teachers and administrators may not be ready for the major reform components of the TDHS model and for the changes in their roles and responsibilities because they have been through previous so-called reforms that did not really change much or because they do not believe great strides are possible with their students. A clear rationale for why the recommended reforms can work can address these staff attitudes and get them ready for changes in their own jobs and relationships.

The rationale for the TDHS model begins with awareness that the true dimensions of the problems of low-performing high schools require major changes in key aspects of the school organization and climate, as well as in classroom activities. Trying harder with the same structures and methods will not be enough to turn around a very troubled high school. The TDHS reforms are aimed at replacing student anonymity with a personalized learning environment, attacking student apathy with a choice of programs to match student interests and goals, and addressing student diversity with flexibility in time and resources, so that all individuals have a chance to succeed in a high-standards curriculum.

Important new elements of the TDHS framework include providing students with opportunities to develop both their academic and personal career-related talents and requiring teachers to work in collegial groups responsible for each student's academic growth, adjustment to high school, and personal growth. All these components are rooted in research on adolescent development, effective organizations, and optimal instructional approaches and materials for diverse groups of high school-age youth.

The Model Provides for Awareness-Building to Promote School-wide Buy-In and Partnership Development. TDHS incorporates a standard and substantial awareness-building process to build commitment and buy-in from the staff and to either negotiate local adaptations or screen out sites having barriers to reform that are currently too high.

The process begins by informing school leaders and all the staff about the key organizational and instructional changes required, as well as the conceptual and practical rationale for these changes. Ample opportunity is given for leaders and staff to ask questions about adapting the reforms to local conditions and how the reforms will affect their everyday roles and responsibilities. The awareness stage also usually involves local school representatives visiting successful existing TDHS sites—often the most powerful tool to converting the skeptics. TDHS staff members also make several presentations, ending with question-and-answer sessions, at local school staff assemblies and smaller departmental meetings. Often, instructional materials and organizational manuals are made available, and an entire school day is set aside for local staff to inspect the materials with TDHS staff being available for questions. Sometimes, a local newsletter is issued a number of times with question-and-answer sections about the recommended reforms.

The teachers' union should also be intimately involved during the awareness period before a faculty vote. The reforms must adhere to all aspects of negotiated agreements. Therefore, we must determine how recommended changes fit with stipulations for teacher instructional assignments and planning time. The shift to a schedule of extended class periods with interdisciplinary teacher teams for assisting a shared set of students needs to be reconciled with contract regulations. Usually, common planning time for teacher teams can be worked into the weekly schedule because extended periods can cover both individual teacher preparations and common team activities.

Increased duties to improve student attendance or school climate can be made voluntary for teachers, with the expectation that most teachers will be interested in working together for better conditions at the schools and in continuing these efforts when they pay off. We have received strong support for TDHS reforms from the national offices of the American Federation of Teachers and the National Education Association, which helps us deal with local collective bargaining representatives during the awareness phase in selected high schools.

The awareness-building process typically culminates in a secret-ballot faculty vote on whether to approve or disapprove a TDHS partnership. Sometimes the failure to reach an agreed-on threshold (e.g., 70 percent) indicates an underlying disconnect between district or school leadership and the teaching faculty or their union at the site or some other serious problems that further information-sharing and negotiation are not likely to overcome.

With a successful vote, the school is ready to move into the planning year, during which the reforms are tailored to local priorities and conditions so that activities in the implementation year that follows will be based on staff input—an important element in producing the buy-in needed for successful reform.

The Planning Year Promotes Acceptance of Reform and Allows Development of Local Adaptations. The planning year usually follows a month-by-month schedule of discussions and decisions beginning in September and ending in June; if necessary, however, a more-compact planning schedule can be used. The decisions focus on choosing the themes and locations for the career academies at the school; assigning teachers and students to each academy, including the ninth-grade academy; and initial training in such changes as block scheduling or working in teams to improve attendance and discipline. The planning year is managed by a school-level steering committee and guided by a TDHS organizational facilitator from Johns Hopkins University. A published technical assistance manual, *Creating a Talent Development High School: The Planning Process* (Legters and Morrison, 1999), outlines the planning-year steps and schedules.

A well-executed planning year helps overcome resistance to reforms by engaging all the school's leadership and staff in extensive discussion and decisionmaking and provides time for staff to collaborate to resolve many of the technical issues of staffing and scheduling that can make or break implementation efforts. We have built local decision points into the planning year that allow the school leadership and staff to put their own stamp on how TDHS will look at their site. The reform decisions for the local participants primarily concern the themes and pathways for the career academies and the criteria used to assign students to the first-term catch-up courses.

The TDHS model determines the number of career academies based on enrollment. The desired size of each upper-grade career academy is about 300 students, large enough for two teachers in each major subject and small enough for a personalized learning environment in which most adults and students will know each other. Thus, dividing the total number of students in grades 10 through 12 by 300 and rounding off the result yields the number of career academies. The career themes and course pathways for each academy should be developed by the school staff, starting with strong programs they want to retain and taking the local labor market and business partner opportunities into account, while ensuring that students have a wide variety of choices. Other worthwhile topics for staff discussion and decisionmaking include building location and decor, nomination and recruitment of business or community partners, and promotional materials to attract students to each academy. Having the school staff make the various decisions should develop a strong sense of ownership and pride, as well as a sense of momentum and anticipation for successful implementation. Faculty assignments to each academy should account for individual preferences and special talents or interests.

Policies and processes for assigning students to the TDHS catch-up literacy or math courses may also be a topic for staff discussion. Many TDHS sites put all students in these classes because they are poorly prepared and can profit from the fluency and comprehension emphases of the literacy offerings or the reasoning and problem-solving focus of the math courses. Sometimes there is differentiation of materials within a diverse classroom, with a few students using higher-level reading materials covering the same competencies as the rest of the class. However, some school enroll both large numbers of students who need remediation and large numbers who are on grade level or above and can move on to advanced placement courses. In such cases, some classes of top achievers would not be assigned to the catch-up term that precedes the high-standards courses for all. Instead, the time that would otherwise be devoted to the catch-up class would be available for advanced placement, more foreign languages, or other electives. TDHS does not withhold the high-standards college-preparatory courses from any student in English, math, or science, but some students with poor preparation will be given extra time and extra help to succeed. Based on accurate data on the achievement levels of the incoming freshman class, a school faculty can help decide how time and extra help will be incorporated into their program.

The faculty can revisit other decisions during the planning year, such as consistent school discipline rules and consequences for misbehavior, student uniforms, and junior and senior class activities during the year. Involving staff members in such decisions during the planning process may also strengthen their commitment to a strong implementation of the main TDHS reforms. Celebrations marking milestones along the way and an off-site retreat before school opens also help to boost the enthusiasm of teachers and increase the energy they are willing to invest in implementing the model.

Reforms Are Supported by Highly Specified Materials and Processes. The quality and comprehensiveness of TDHS instructional materials contribute greatly to the likelihood that the instructional interventions will be implemented as intended. Materials that provide complete descriptions of daily learning activities, along with overheads and handouts to be used each day, are much more likely to result in classroom improvements than are more general materials that state the learning objectives and provide broad pedagogic suggestions, such as "use cooperative learning teams" (Ball and Cohen, 2001). High-quality, detailed materials that are easy to follow are especially important both for novice teachers and for those who are not well prepared in the subject they are teaching.

Some critics of highly specified instructional materials are concerned that they will appear insulting to the professional standing and judgment of well-qualified teachers, but the TDHS materials do not go so far as to provide exact word-for-word scripts, which may be the most off-putting form of specified materials. The TDHS materials also leave room for enhanced lesson components for individual teachers to introduce after the core recommended learning activities are complete and offer some suggestions about further directions for teacher initiative to support the particular goal of a lesson.

Organizational reforms also need to be laid out in great detail, providing enough information to guide space allocations, staff loading charts, and scheduling decisions. We have developed technical assistance manuals (such as the planning-year guide) that offer details on how to take advantage of common planning time, how to schedule self-contained academy staff, how to conduct attendance improvement drives, and other "craft knowledge" for making the organizational reforms work well. The TDHS model includes numerous information and training modules to make the organizational recommendations explicit. We have found that explicit blueprints for academy arrangements and specific directions for staffing and scheduling from the TDHS external team can avoid mistakes and weaknesses in implementation.

The Model Requires Technical Assistance with Regular Follow-Ups. One of the most powerful features of TDHS for promoting high-quality implementation is the technical assistance schools receive as they plan and implement the reforms. The on-site organizational facilitator helps school leaders overcome inertia and reform fatigue, moves the reforms forward by working with school leaders on analyzing and presenting data, facilitates awareness-building and planning-year activities, and serves as constant support for the principal and leadership team while they work simultaneously on reform and on running the school. Organizational facilitators are trained in technical aspects of converting large schools into multiple small learning communities, such as staffing and scheduling, and can coordinate further assistance from TDHS experts as needed. Organizational facilitators also provide ongoing training for academy leaders, team leaders, teacher teams, and the entire staff on practices that promote effective collaboration and relationships with students.

Components of the TDHS instructional interventions for reading, writing, and mathematics demand that teachers have a thorough command of the subjects and be able to be spontaneous in the classroom. The quality of the teacher training and the follow-up support are essential determinants of how strong the implementations of classroom instructional reforms will be, especially when the innovations require unusual teacher resourcefulness and responsiveness in classroom interactions. Accordingly, the TDHS model provides multiple levels of teacher training and support for the instructional innovations.

Training begins with two or three full days of workshops for teachers in each subject, usually at the end of the summer before the classroom implementations begin in the fall term. These workshops are conducted by senior university staff, usually former teachers of the innovative courses, who are expert in the TDHS approaches to either English or math. In addition to discussion of the needs and rationale for the TDHS instruction interventions in the particular subject, these workshops create a simulated classroom in which the teachers assume the role of students and the workshop leader conducts model lessons using the key TDHS pedagogical innovations. Workshop participants watch videos of actual classrooms participating in the recommended instructional approaches and discuss them in terms of teacher behaviors, student reactions, and learning outcomes to further prepare for implementation of the new TDHS activities in their own classrooms.

While the workshops provide a good foundation for teachers, the follow-up activities remain important as teachers work with students in their own classrooms. The TDHS model provides expert peer coaches to help teachers implement the new instructional approaches in their classrooms. These coaches are experienced teachers with strong reputations for classroom effectiveness who have become expert in the TDHS instructional innovations as the result of previous classroom experience or extensive training. One full-time coach in English and one coach in math are typically assigned to two high schools, so they work for two and one-half days per week at each site and with five to ten different teachers per location. Each participating teacher can expect to be visited about twice per week, depending on individual needs and desires. The coaches will model or coteach a lesson, make sure all materials and equipment are available, discuss the elements that worked best or presented difficulties in different lessons, and otherwise troubleshoot, all to ensure strong classroom implementation. The coaches never evaluate teachers, either formally or informally, or report any individual teacher's strengths or weaknesses to supervisors or authorities. Confidentiality is needed to establish trust between the coach and the classroom teachers. Sometimes, private ratings of teachers are used in research evaluations of instructional impacts, but these ratings never reveal an individual's identity and are never shared outside the research team.

Another form of support for teachers is the visits university-based TDHS instructional specialists, often the same people who provided the initial workshops, make to the school during the term. These visits involve refresher workshops, usually held in two-hour meetings after school, to review the upcoming units and to refine some of the key pedagogical approaches. The visits also include sessions with the local peer coaches to review the progress of participating teachers and to plan corrective actions when needed.

The cost of the multilevel training and support system for teachers can be considerable because it includes the salaries of the full-time coaches and teacher stipends for workshops participation, as well as fees for the services of university TDHS staff. Presenting the recommended learning activities is so demanding, however, that the risk of weak classroom implementation is great if teachers do not receive the full range of training and follow-up coaching. These risks are almost certain to be large in most high-poverty nonselective high schools with many new or poorly prepared teachers.

Networks of Specialists Support Peer Networks. TDHS strengthens its technical assistance by engaging participants in peer networks that promote productive exchanges of ideas and experiences. Our national TDHS Principals Network gives school principals from TDHS sites a chance to learn from their peers about decentralizing authority, practical examples of reform decisions to be made or avoided, strategies on budget reallocations, and the benefits of implementing a comprehensive model in which each component enhances the other. We bring together TDHS principals from across the nation in an annual meeting and also hold monthly districtwide or regional meetings for principals.

Networks of academy leaders and ninth-grade team leaders have also proven themselves useful for sharing practical ideas, strengthening role performances, and sustaining the reform spirit for the individuals filling these important roles. Again, we convene an annual meeting for people in these positions, as well as providing more-frequent local gatherings.

As described earlier, scheduling can make or break TDHS organizational reforms. Thus, a talented scheduling expert is needed to create the student, staff, and space assignments for a structure of separate, self-contained academies. The TDHS program conducts annual workshops for schedulers to provide networking opportunities and provides training manuals and technical assistance focused on scheduling issues to individual schools.

The Model Provides for Sustainability. To retain and strengthen the positive changes, reforms must also account for the inevitable turnover of school leadership and staff. TDHS addresses sustainability in several ways.

Key TDHS reforms are part of the formal structure of the school's organization and will naturally stay in place unless some authority consciously uproots them. The academy structure involves the very architecture of the building, with location of classrooms for all major subjects in each academy, offices for academy leaders and staff, physical barriers between academies, and separate entrances and traffic patterns. All this can be returned to a departmental wing structure in a single large building but not without conscious effort.

The TDHS model creates multiple levels of leadership, including several academy principals and teacher team leaders. This leadership structure ensures that a complete turnover of leadership is unlikely and that some experienced reformers will remain from year to year.

Recruiting the TDHS curriculum coaches for the district and training them to be expert in the innovative curriculum and methods also builds local capacity. The TDHS program also encourages our partnership high schools to identify a lead teacher in each subject. These teachers can become additional coaches or be available to help train new teachers about how to offer TDHS courses or use TDHS supplemental materials. A regular summer training routine is maintained for new staff.

TDHS also conducts national workshops each year at which new leadership or staff from TDHS sites can become well informed to sustain TDHS improvements. We also expect most TDHS sites to retain a formal partnership with our university operations, to receive annual feedback reports and regular TDHS newsletters, and to have regular contact with a TDHS liaison. The TDHS model continues to develop new materials every year, including materials for catch-up courses for the upper grades. Plans are now being made to add TDHS materials in science and social studies, as well as for blended units in core academic subjects that integrate career applications for different career academy themes. We expect that high schools that have successfully implemented original TDHS reforms and curriculum will be interested in continuing the partnership and will add the new materials as they become available.

Arrangements with the Local Systems and Partners

In the course of scaling up reforms to new locations, we have found that investing in up-front negotiation and planning with the school, district, and other local partners can overcome some implementation barriers. Important steps include identifying promising sites, securing funding for the proposed changes, aligning reform programs and activities with district goals and priorities, and developing partnerships with local education funds and similar entities.

The Model Requires Buy-In from New Sites. A general question in scale-up strategies is whether the identification of promising sites for such ambitious comprehensive high school reforms as TDHS begins at the district or school level. We have found not only that strong buy-in from a high school's leadership and faculty is essential to strong implementations but also that a district can either support or impede the recommended changes in important ways. Early on, a new school must demonstrate its seriousness about reform and its commitment to the key changes; the district's officials must at least be willing not to interfere with the key reform provisions and, preferably, be willing to support them actively.

While particular high schools or district officials often take the initiative to contact our headquarters, there is certainly no guarantee that a strong commitment to change will follow. For example, the availability of federal and state funds through CSR or other competitions will often tempt local grant writers to submit proposals for the money without really strong school commitments to undertake anything beyond superficial changes while claiming adherence to a specific model, such as TDHS. The identification of promising sites should therefore quickly lead to opportunities for local educators to become aware of the reforms the TDHS model requires.

The size of a local district will often determine the strategy we use to identify initial sites. We consider a potential "hub district" to be one with several large, nonselective high schools having serious student dropout and low-achievement problems. In such a district, our ideal strategy is to identify two schools with strong readiness for reform as initial demonstration sites in the district, with others to follow when these initial sites prove successful. This approach allows us to invest initial technical assistance in the district within our capacity to recruit, train, and relocate expert TDHS facilitators and, later, to increase our local staff as the number of sites expands. Our staffing capacities would ordinarily be stretched too far if we began with more than one team in a new district, hence our desire to begin with two schools.

Once the first pair of schools has been established, we can draw on staff from the original schools to serve as the next wave of technical assistance facilitators for additional high schools. The initial demonstration sites are invaluable for orienting staff from new schools and answering their questions about how TDHS reforms would work for them. This strategy of using the first sites as demonstration sites, with phased expansion to other schools in the district, has been successful for in establishing the TDHS model in Philadelphia and Newark, and New Orleans, New York, St. Louis, and other districts are currently pursuing it.

We have found that getting started in new sites is easiest when the initiative for a potential partnership comes from the leadership of a particular high school. Usually, the initial interest is tied to information associated with federal or state funding opportunities to address serious school problems, and the school leadership has already done some research that links particular TDHS components with the needs of their school. Launching the program at a new site is more difficult when a third party, such as a school or district grant writer or high school reform official, initially identifies an underperforming school as a potential candidate for TDHS reforms. In these cases, we must start from scratch to convince the local high school administrators and faculty that the TDHS model could be the vehicle for them to greatly improve their learning environment and student outcomes. We have learned that histories or reputations can sour next steps in partnerships that local third parties have initiated and that such cases may require more-intensive awareness-building activities at the school site.

When a district has only one or two schools and is not close to similar districts with which it could form a "regional hub," our scale-up strategy obviously does not involve demonstration sites, with the program spreading across the district later. The next steps are the same, however, because a strong local commitment needs to be established before we will be willing to train and relocate a team of expert TDHS facilitators.

Funding Requirements Are Defined at the Outset. Before the planning year begins, we work out the funding requirements with the local district for our partnership. We have found that being clear about the costs at the outset facilitates implementation. Costs fall into four categories. First, an annual fee covers regular liaison with a university contact and the yearly evaluation and feedback prepared for each school. Trends in surveys of a school's students and faculty are reported on implementation progress and climate outcomes. School records are reviewed for trends on student attendance, promotion, completion, disciplinary removals, and achievement test results. Second, curriculum materials are purchased for the catch-up courses in literacy and math at multiple grade levels, for the freshman seminar, and for supplementary TDHS curriculum materials that accompany the district's own course offerings and texts. Third, the on-site technical assistance from university facilitators has daily fees and travel costs and may involve 40 or 50 days per year. Fourth, the local four-person team of half-time organizational and instructional coaches must be budgeted.

We support schools and districts in finding the resources necessary to implement TDHS. Some cost categories may be covered by shifting local accounts: The school's book allotment may be assigned to pay for some TDHS materials, and local coaches may be paid by eliminating some existing department chairs or other positions. Others may be covered by grant funding, as mentioned earlier. Before we agree to provide a letter of support for a proposal, we will assist with the proposal budget so that it covers all the required costs for TDHS curriculum materials and technical assistance. Once the local funding is secure, we will enter into a memorandum of understanding and a formal contract that specifies the services and materials to be provided and their costs and payment schedule.

Elements of the TDHS Model Are Aligned with District and State Reform Priorities, Standards, and Assessments. As described above, school districts and state education departments will have their own curriculum guides, performance standards, testing schedules, and reform programs that may or may not coincide with the instructional interventions TDHS or other external models are recommending to the selected high schools. Usually, a supervisory hierarchy extends into individual schools in the persons of department chairs or other local staff authorities to see that the district or state directives are followed. Also, professional development days are scheduled for teachers during the school year, but these may focus entirely on specific state or district reform programs, leaving no time for training in external reforms. District curriculum and instruction authorities make textbook and syllabus decisions for remedial and core curriculum activities that may coincide or conflict with external reforms.

Establishing collegial relationships with state and district officials from the outset, rather than waiting for problems to emerge, can avoid turf battles and work out reasonable allocations of time and professional development opportunities for district needs and reform goals. Early discussions can also address any other reforms and their representatives that might also be at an emerging TDHS site, to avoid clashes over multiple partnership goals and activities by giving priority to the comprehensive reform model or by carefully coordinating activities in a common subject or area. Professional development time that the district has already scheduled is extremely valuable because using these for training will not impose added costs for teacher stipends. Thus, we try to arrange release time for selected teachers during district professional development sessions for workshops in TDHS instructional reforms. At some sites, we also have succeeded in negotiating additional release time for school staff members for collaborative planning, which is especially valuable during the planning year.

We also take time to sit with local curriculum coordinators to review TDHS curriculum collectively and to take the steps necessary to ensure alignment with district and state standards and assessments. Because the core of our curriculum offerings are catch-up courses that supplement rather than replace traditional requirements in math and English, alignment is typically not difficult. However, our curriculum developers have written some new materials and helped schools choose certain novels or units to accommodate local standards.

Partnerships with Local Education Organizations Are Established. In some cases, developing partnerships with local education organizations, such as public education funds, has helped overcome implementation and scale-up barriers. The primary example is our partnership with the Philadelphia Education Fund (PEF), which has helped educate us about the reform history and landscape in the district, secure funding, and establish a base for coaching and facilitating staff. PEF also has supported expansion and sustained implementation of TDHS in Philadelphia by analyzing data and producing research reports and by helping us negotiate district politics in a period of major leadership and policy change. We are developing similar partnerships with other education funds in Chattanooga and Baltimore that are coordinating large districtwide grants for high school reform from the Carnegie and Gates foundations and have worked with intermediary organizations in New York, New Orleans, Kansas City, and elsewhere. We have learned that such partnerships, when handled in a clear, up-front manner can reduce the inevitable tensions and be a major facilitating factor in scaling up TDHS reforms.

Model Provider Capacity

Scaling up TDHS has required us to shift our organization from a small, exclusively grant-driven research and development operation to one that supports the reality of a growing service business. Having learned from other groups that had undergone a similar transformation (e.g., Success For All[3]), we took several steps to support our growth while maintaining quality service to schools.

A Well-Specified Business Plan Was Created. With some help from business consultants familiar with comprehensive school reform finances, we developed a business plan for the TDHS scale-up activities. It established a price structure for TDHS curriculum materials, daily technical assistance fees for on-site services, and charges for evaluation and liaison activities from TDHS headquarters. The plan was based on conservative projections of the growth in the number of partnership schools over the next few years and the size of the TDHS scale-up staff to serve the expected schools. Hence, the business plan helped us articulate our costs and forced us to develop a clearer sense of what responsible scale-up might look like.

The business plan also has helped clarify levels of start-up capital we need to cover awareness-building and training costs so that we can establish and fulfill partnerships with new districts. Articulating these needs has helped us seek external federal and foundation grants for these start-up costs. Eventually, we will build these costs into our fee structures as overhead, so new partnership schools will, in effect, pro-

---

[3] See Chapter Five in this volume.

vide reimbursements for early awareness visits and training of the facilitators they use.

New Organization. In addition to our Research Division and our Materials and Curriculum Development Division, we have established three additional divisions within the TDHS program. Staff members from the New Schools Development Division do everything necessary to develop new partnerships with schools and districts, including making presentations at state design fairs, following up on inquiries, conducting awareness sessions, and negotiating contracts with school and district leaders. The Implementation and Support Division manages all aspects of TDHS implementation, including developing multiyear implementation plans and staffing, training, materials distribution, and technical assistance to partner sites. The Finance and Human Resources Division manages all contracts, payroll, and other financial matters and interfaces with Johns Hopkins University Human Resources. A TDHS management team, consisting of directors of each division and the overall program director, meets weekly to troubleshoot and coordinate efforts.

Unlike other models, TDHS has remained within Johns Hopkins University. The existing university human resources and procurement apparatus is used for personnel benefits, salary administration, purchasing, legal, and insurance services. Otherwise, we would have had to establish separate units and staff for these functions and pay to establish a separate nonprofit organization legally and operationally. TDHS continues to obtain federal and foundation support for developing and evaluating additional components of the reform model. According to the business plan, the three new aforementioned units are, however, expected to become self-sustaining through fees for service over the next several years.

It Is Not Too Late for Reforms in High Schools

Large numbers of American high schools with concentrations of high-poverty students are in dire straits. More than half their students drop out; student achievement levels fall far below the minimum needed for postsecondary success or decent-paying jobs; the schools are chaotic; and many teachers have low expectations. It is not, however, necessary to wait until elementary and middle grade reforms have produced more students who are well prepared to enter high school to effect change. High school reform efforts that match the magnitude of the problems with a "no-excuses and no-compromises" stance for major reorganizations of the school structures and *thorough* redesigns of classroom activities and professional development systems can succeed. We have shown that the comprehensive TDHS model—when its organizational, instructional, and teacher-support reforms are well implemented—can bring impressive improvements to school climate and student outcomes (Legters et al., 2002).

The question this chapter has addressed is how strong implementations of the demanding TDHS reforms can be replicated in the face of initial conditions that prevent many high schools from being ready or able to make powerful changes.

The best way to be successful with a reform model is to screen for unfavorable conditions and work only with schools in which reform readiness seems assured. Indeed, if we do not obtain a large favorable vote from the faculty, our TDHS team will no longer try to form a partnership and will walk away from the school. In general, however, we do not shy away from very troubled high schools; instead, we engage in a series of mediation activities to head off or address serious initial problems. This chapter has discussed three broad categories of mediating factors: features of the reform model, arrangements with the local district and schools, and the capacities of the external team.

We have listed several major barriers to reorganizing high schools into self-contained academy structures with a team approach to improving school climate and students' attendance and discipline. The possible impediments include the logistical demands of relocating classrooms and offices and of scheduling the separate academy units, the authority challenges of decentralization and teaming, and the cultural inertia of blaming others and lacking a new vision.

The TDHS program approaches these threats to reform with an extensive planning year to engage the faculty and adapt the academy structure to local conditions. Administrators become familiar with a decentralized management structure by observing successful TDHS sites and participating in networks of educators with similar roles and responsibilities. Union representatives and local faculty learn how a teaming approach can serve student needs and improve the working conditions by visiting other schools, studying reports, and attending workshops. Each of the academy units and teacher teams are given time to personalize their groups and to build their spirit for reform. A local team of well-trained TDHS organizational and instructional facilitators keeps the reforms moving forward and getting stronger as time goes on.

Other specific impediments to providing effective classroom instruction to meet high standards in the face of diverse student needs include very poorly prepared students with weak attendance habits, chaotic school climates, too many inexperienced or poorly prepared teachers with high turnover, intrusive state or district directives for use of time and professional development, and rigid course assignments. The TDHS responses to these conditions begin with a comprehensive model that creates a desirable climate and attendance conditions for learning, with specific curriculum materials aimed at the true student deficiencies for both inexperienced and veteran teachers. In addition, an extensive multitiered training and support system is provided for teachers, including continuing in-class coaching from peers. The planning year allows a school's faculty to understand the true needs for the recommended instructional innovations and to commit to their potential for student growth. Taking the time to work with state, district, and school officials also helps to align the TDHS innovations with required tests and learning standards and to avoid conflicts over time and training allotments for different reform and learning goals.

Our experiences with implementing the TDHS model in large, high-poverty high schools have made us optimistic about the prospects for transforming significant numbers of low-achieving schools with weak learning environments. At the same time, we have come to understand that this job will require very strong reform models; great patience and persistence in gaining the commitments of the local educators who must make the changes; and significant resources for the planning, training, and expert follow-ups needed for powerful implementations.

We can now confidently predict that even the most-troubled high schools can develop safe and serious climates for learning, in which students can accelerate their achievement growth to close gaps in literacy and math by the time they graduate. Our current evidence is still based on a few schools, in which the TDHS model has been well-implemented for several years, and on projections of the continuation of our student achievement trends from the early grades with innovative materials in the hands of competent teachers. Careful research will continue, including third-party evaluations, to further evaluate the influence of the TDHS model on learning environments and student outcomes to build stronger evidence and understanding of how much can really be accomplished under these demanding high school reforms.

It is clear, however, that a very powerful reform model is essential for dealing with the poor preparation of most students and many teachers in high-poverty high schools. The model should transform both the organizational structures to create personalized relationships for improved student attendance and positive overall expectations and the classroom instructional practices to offer flexible time and carefully aimed extra-help curriculum for narrowing achievement gaps. The process of reform should activate the commitments and energies of the local educators as they adapt reforms to local strengths and receive regular expert support for the recommended changes.

Major additional resources are required to pay the on-site facilitators and curriculum coaches, who are critical for keeping the reform components on track, and the added local staff to head up the academy structure and teacher teams, as well as for purchasing the new curriculum materials for the first-term transition courses and the supplementary materials for the second-term district-required courses. Resources are also necessary for building the capacities of the external team, for expert staff ready to work with new partnership schools, and for reliable and cost-efficient management of technical assistance services.

So, although high school reforms will not be easy, quick, or inexpensive, our plan to scale up the TDHS model to reach as many as possible of America's large failing high schools is clear; we are implementing it in an expanding number of schools; and we are confident that, given the necessary resources and conditions described above, we can have a substantial positive influence on the performance of students in these schools.

References

Balfanz, R., and N. E. Legters, "How Many Failing High Schools Are There? Where Are They Located? Who Attends Them?" paper prepared for the Harvard Civil Rights Project and Achieve, Inc., Forum on Dropouts in America, Boston, January 2001.

_____, "Locating the Dropout Crisis: What High Schools Produce the Nation's Dropouts, Where Are They Located, Who Attends Them," in G. Orfield, ed., *Dropouts in America: Confronting the Graduation Rate Crisis*, Boston: Harvard Education Press, 2004.

Ball, D. L., and D. K. Cohen, "Scaling Up Instructional Improvement," Occasional Paper Series, Ann Arbor Mich.: University of Michigan, School of Education, 2001.

Bloom, D., M. Farrell, J. J. Kemple, and N. Verna, *The Family Transition Program*, New York: Manpower Demonstration Research Corporation, 1998.

Boyer, E. L., *High School: A Report on Secondary Education in America*, New York: Harper and Row, 1983.

Boykin, A. W., "Harvesting Talent and Culture: African American Children and Education Reform," in R. Rossi, ed., *Reforming Education for Children and Youth*, New York: Teachers College Press, 1996, pp. 167–202.

Carnegie Corporation Forum on Education and the Economy, Task Force on Teaching as a Profession, *A Nation Prepared: Teachers for the 21st Century*, New York: Carnegie Corporation of New York, 1986.

Center for Social Organization of Schools, Web site, undated. Online at www.csos.jhu.edu (as of June 22, 2004).

Elmore, R., "Getting to Scale with Good Educational Practice," *Harvard Educational Review*, Spring, Vol. 66, No. 1, 1996.

Goodlad, J. I., *A Place Called School: Prospects for the Future*, New York: McGraw-Hill, 1984.

Hess, F. M., *Spinning Wheels: The Politics of Urban School Reform*, Washington, D.C.: Brookings Institution Press, 1999.

Kemple, J. J., *Career Academies: Impacts on Students' Initial Transitions to Post-Secondary Education and Employment*, New York: Manpower Demonstration Research Corporation, December 2001.

Kemple, J. J., and C. Herlihy, *The Talent Development High School Model Impacts on Student Engagement and Performance: Context, Components, and Initial Impacts on Ninth-Grade Students' Engagement and Performance*, New York: Manpower Demonstration Research Corporation, June 2004.

Legters, N. E., and W. F. Morrison, *Creating a Talent Development High School: The Planning Process*, Baltimore, Md.: Center for Research on the Education of Students Placed at Risk, Johns Hopkins University, 1999.

Legters, N. E., R. Balfanz, and J. M. McPartland, "Solutions for Failing High Schools: Converging Visions and Promising Models," paper commissioned by the U.S. Department of Education Office of Vocational and Adult Education, 2002.

Legters, N. E., R. Balfanz, W. J. Jordan, and J. M. McPartland, *Comprehensive Reform for Urban High Schools: A Talent Development Approach*, New York: Teachers College Press, 2002.

McPartland, J. M., and B. Schneider, "Opportunities to Learn and Student Diversity: Prospects and Pitfalls of a Common Core Curriculum," *Sociology of Education*, Extra Issue, 1996, pp. 66–81.

National Association of Secondary School Principals (NASSP), *What the Research Shows: Breaking Rank in Action: Changing an American Institution*, Reston, Va., 1996.

Oakes, J., *Keeping Track: How Schools Structure Inequality*, New Haven: Yale University Press, 1985.

Philadelphia Education Fund, *The Talent Development High School: First-Year Results of the Ninth Grade Success Academy in Two Philadelphia Schools 1999–2000*, Philadelphia, Pa., October, 2000.

_____, *Philadelphia's Talent Development High Schools: Second-Year Results*, 2000–2001, Philadelphia, Pa., October 2001.

_____, *Year Three of the Talent Development Initiative in Philadelphia: Results from Five Schools, 2001–2002*, Philadelphia, Pa., October 2002.

_____, *Year Four of the Talent Development Initiative in Philadelphia: Results from Five Schools, 2002–2003*, Philadelphia, Pa., October 2003.

Powell, A., E. Farrar, and D. Cohen, *The Shopping Mall High School*, New York: Houghton Mifflin, 1985.

Roderick, M., and E. Camburn, "Risk and Recovery from Course Failure in the Early Years of High School," *American Educational Research Journal*, 1999, pp. 303–344.

Sizer, T. R., *Horace's Compromise: The Dilemma of the American High School*, Boston: Houghton Mifflin, 1984.

Stern, D., C. Dayton, and M. Raby, *Career Academies and High School Reform*, Berkeley, Calif.: University of California at Berkeley, December 1998.

Taking High Schools That Work to Scale: The Evolution of a High School Reform Program

Gene Bottoms

As with many school reform programs, the scale-up of High Schools That Work (HSTW) has occurred partly as a result of demand—cities and school districts have invited the organization to work in their schools—and partly as a result of funding increases that have enabled it to expand both the reach and the range of its services. With growth have come refinement and expansion of program elements, diversification of services, and strengthening of organizational capacity. Perhaps the most distinctive aspect of HSTW's growth, however, is its early and continuing focus on influencing state education policies. In addition to dramatically increasing its direct services to schools and school leaders during the more than 20 years of its existence, HSTW has contributed to the scale-up of education reform by working with state education officials to shape the requirements that students and schools must meet and by informing the officials about the resources—both human and material—needed to meet them.

High Schools That Work (HSTW) is the nation's first large-scale effort to engage state education and school district officials, school-level leaders, and teachers in partnerships with students, parents, and the community in efforts to improve the way high school students are prepared for work and further education. HSTW began as an initiative designed to improve high school education for career and technical students in the Southeast and has evolved into a comprehensive reform design for high school students with diverse post-secondary aspirations, as well as for middle school students. This initiative was prompted, in part, by regional concerns about improving the academic achievement of students in the general and career or technical curricula and the related need to have more students develop the ability to continue to learn new jobs in the work setting and to succeed in further study.

Among the leading high school reform efforts, HSTW is unique in its focus on changing state curricular requirements as one of the most important elements of its program. More generally, we are committed to improving public policies governing education. We see our role as developing—through our school reform efforts and our assessment efforts—the information about the relationship among curricular requirements, teaching practices, and school governance needed to make sound policies. Based on our information-gathering and analysis, we are able to present ideas and recommendations to the policymakers who are responsible for state-level decisions governing funding and other aspects of education policy and to the state education officials who are responsible for ensuring that new policies are effectively implemented in the schools.

Thus, our approach to school reform and to scaling up reforms through broad and deep implementation of a comprehensive reform program might be said to be both school-based and policy-based. We believe, on the one hand, that changing practices and improving student performance at the level of schools and districts gives policymakers and leaders in state departments of education a rationale for introducing and supporting policies that will, effectively, require that such programs be broadly implemented. And we believe that, ultimately, broad-scale school change must be policy-driven. The level of commitment and the diverse investments in teacher training, curriculum development, leadership development, and community support at the school and district level are unlikely to be forthcoming unless they are motivated, at least in part, by the need to comply with policy requirements. It is this two-pronged approach that we have taken in scaling up HSTW, and we believe the success of our efforts provides evidence of the value of this approach.

In this chapter, I describe the factors that led to the development of HSTW, the principles that drive it, and how it has evolved over time—both in response to perceived needs and in response to opportunities and requirements present in the policy environment. I then discuss the lessons we have learned through our long experience in school reform efforts and the challenges we see before us.

Linking Career and Technical Education to High School Reform: The Impetus for HTSW

In the mid- to late 1980s, state career and technical leaders, academic leaders, and policymakers in the southeastern states became concerned that neither the students completing a career or technical concentration in high school nor those completing the general track were adequately prepared to be successful in the emerging international, information-centered economy. At that time, about one-third of high school graduates in the states represented on the Southern Regional Education Board (SREB)[1] had, upon leaving high school, finished a career or technical concentration and at least another one-third finished the general track. These graduates completed a steady diet of low-level academic courses that did not provide either the depth of knowledge or the skills needed for a good job in the modern workplace or for further study.

The importance of addressing this issue as a regional concern was first articulated in *The Need for Quality* (SREB, 1981). In that report, SREB challenged states, schools, and colleges to work together to develop higher academic standards and to increase levels of achievement for all students. Just two years later, the National Commission on Excellence in Education, an advisory body to the U.S. Secretary of Education, published a report charging that "the educa-

---

[1] The Southern Regional Education Board (SREB), the nation's first interstate compact for education, was created in 1948. SREB helps government and education leaders work cooperatively to advance education and, in doing so, improve the social and economic life of the region. SREB's 16 member states are Alabama, Arkansas, Delaware, Florida, Georgia, Kentucky, Louisiana, Maryland, Mississippi, North Carolina, Oklahoma, South Carolina, Tennessee, Texas, Virginia, and West Virginia. SREB is governed by a board that consists of the governor of each member state and four people that he or she appoints, including at least one state legislator and at least one educator. SREB is supported by appropriations from its member states and by funds from private companies, foundations, and state and federal agencies.

tional foundations of our society . . . [were] being eroded by a rising tide of mediocrity" (National Commission on Excellence in Education, 1983, p. 1). Almost every state in the nation responded to this report by increasing the number of academic courses required for high school graduation.

This approach had the effect of improving the academic competencies of students enrolled in traditional college-preparatory programs—students who were already likely to graduate from high school and enroll in postsecondary education. State career and technical leaders from the Southeast were, however, disappointed with the response to *A Nation at Risk*. They believed the goals of the reform movement excluded students who did not have access to college-preparatory language arts, mathematics, and science courses and to modern, high-demand, high-quality career and technical studies—a population that, as we have noted, included, up to two-thirds of students of high school age in some states. For many students in general, career, and technical programs, increasing the number of required courses meant another year of repetitive, low-track English, mathematics, science, and rudimentary career or technical courses—an approach unlikely either to reduce the rate at which students dropped out of high school or to improve the skills of those who stayed and graduated.

To address the needs of such students, the SREB Commission for Educational Quality developed a statement arguing that academic skills must become a priority for career, technical, and academic educators. *Ten Recommendations for Improving Secondary Vocational Education* (Commission for Educational Quality, 1985) recommended changes focusing on two major themes. First, the commission argued, career and technical education must become a full partner in efforts to improve the academic skills of high school students. Second, the commission recommended that each state design pilot programs to merge career and technical training with academic education.

Encouraged by the ideas presented in the SREB proposal and passage of the Carl D. Perkins Vocational Education Act of 1984, which was aimed at strengthening the quality of vocational training, a progressive group of state career and technical leaders from the

Southeast approached SREB in late 1985 with the idea of developing a joint effort to implement the recommendations of the SREB commission in their states. They wanted SREB to lead this enterprise.

Phase I: Launching HSTW

Over the next two years, in meetings involving SREB and state career and technical and academic leaders, the SREB-State Vocational Education Consortium was formed. The participants in these meetings defined a strategy for improving high school education that involved connecting state and local policies and resources to school-based efforts to improve curriculum, instruction, and student learning. Out of these discussions came a plan for a multistate network of high schools—called HSTW—to be implemented through a partnership between SREB and the states. This partnership differentiates SREB's efforts in comprehensive school improvement from those of groups that have attempted to influence instructional practices without first gaining the support of policymakers and state departments of education.

In addition to its efforts to improve education through its work with state officials, the consortium set out to provide services designed to improve instructional practice and student achievement to teachers, schools, and districts that states did not have the resources—either financial or human—to develop and deliver such services on their own. Under the HSTW plan, schools in the network would focus on improving education for students in the general track and in career and technical studies. At the outset, it was agreed that each participating state would support at least two pilot sites in pursuit of agreed-on goals. A collaborative effort, with states sharing lessons learned at the various sites, was envisioned. Mechanisms for linking state-level actions to activities in schools are shown in Table 12.1, and states participating in HSTW must agree to undertake each of the listed actions. SREB was to manage the process, facilitate the exchange of information among the states and sites, and conduct evaluations.

Table 12.1
Requirements for State Participation in HSTW

Requirement	Description
Board membership	Name a representative to serve on the HSTW board and identify one or more coordinators to work with HSTW sites in the state
Funding	Allocate discretionary funds to help sites implement their school improvement plans
Technical assistance visits	Conduct technical assistance visits to one-third of the sites annually to help new sites develop and implement action plans for raising student achievement and to recommend ways for existing sites to advance student learning
Staff development	Link staff development to school improvement plans and create opportunities for teachers and administrators to participate in state-sponsored institutes and SREB workshops and conferences
Site support	Support sites participating in the HSTW assessment and help sites use data to improve their action plans
Networking	Foster networking of sites through meetings, visits, and electronic communication
Resource-sharing and problem-solving	Convene the sites regularly to share resources and solve common problems

Core Beliefs Underlying HSTW

Consortium members held in common a set of core beliefs that have served to perpetuate HSTW for almost two decades. The first of these beliefs is the idea that students get smarter by working harder. HSTW is an effort-based high school reform centered on the conviction that almost all students can master higher-level academic content—historically taught to only the best students—if they are given the opportunity to learn that material and are taught in ways that engage them in making the effort to meet solid course standards.

Second, we believed that, to have stability and staying power, HSTW would need to remain focused on a few valid practices that promise to improve the academic achievement of general and career and technical students. SREB, the parent organization for HSTW, is a highly accountable intermediary organization that brings consistency of effort and support to the reform process. It accomplishes its goals by persistently keeping the HSTW school improvement initiative alive and in the public eye despite changes in pedagogical fashion and the political context surrounding education.

Third, we believe that employing a common assessment process is important because it provides an opportunity for SREB, the states, and the schools to compare outcomes and learn from their experiences.

These three ideas underlie the practical goals we have tried to achieve, as well as the school conditions, professional development strategies, instructional practices, and assessment systems that we have defined.

HSTW Goals, Key Practices, and Key Conditions

The consortium had three major goals for its network of high schools. The first was to increase the mathematics, science, and reading achievement of students both in the general track and in career and technical programs to national averages. The second was to integrate the basic content of traditional college-preparatory studies in English, mathematics, and science with career and technical studies by creating conditions (see Table 12.2) that help school principals and teachers carry out certain key practices (see Table 12.3) and by advancing state and local policies and leadership initiatives necessary to sustain a continuous improvement effort for challenging studies in both academic and career and technical studies. Nearly two decades later, these goals remain the cornerstone of the HSTW initiative, and, taking into account minor modifications, we also continue to advocate the conditions and practices designed to enable achievement of those goals. Relying on these principles and practices, HSTW has become the largest high school improvement initiative in the country. In 1987, the HSTW program was implemented at 28 sites in 13 states.[2] There are now more than 1,000 sites in 30 member states, and we have contracts to provide services to an additional 10 states.

---

[2] When HSTW was launched, SREB had 15 member states, 13 of which participated in the program. As noted previously, SREB now has 16 member states, and all participate in HSTW.

Table 12.2
Key Conditions for Accelerating Student Achievement

Condition	Explanation
An organizational structure and process for ensuring that school administrators and teachers are continuously involved in planning strategies to achieve the key practices	Each school needs a clear mission statement to prepare high school students for success in postsecondary education and the workplace.
Leadership from the district and the school to improve curricula, instruction, and student achievement	Each school site should have a leadership team consisting of the principal; the assistant principal; and teacher leaders who support, encourage, and actively participate with the faculty in implementing the key practices.
A commitment from the school board to supporting the school in replacing the general track	Schools should offer a more-demanding academic core and either an academic, a career and technical, or a blended concentration.
A system superintendent and school board members who support school administrators and teachers in carrying out key practices	This commitment includes financial support for instructional materials, time for teachers to meet and plan together, and six to eight days per year of staff development focusing on using the key practices to improve student learning.
A school superintendent and a school board that will allow the high school to adopt a flexible schedule that enables students to earn more credits	The block schedule that HSTW recommends for challenged schools makes it possible for students to earn 32 credits in four years.

The HSTW Change Strategy

Our approach assumes that high school change occurs not through sweeping efforts but in a series of carefully planned small actions that—when successful—build confidence for making more and greater change. We believe that comprehensive reform is based on making a series of changes that involve getting the school mission right: what is taught; how students are taught; what is expected of students; how the school is organized; how teachers relate to students, to each other, and to parents; how the school uses data; how teachers are prepared, selected, and supported; and the quality of school leadership.

Table 12.3
Key Practices for Accelerating Student Achievement

Practice	Description
High expectations	Set higher expectations and get more students to meet them.
Access to career and technical studies	Increase access to intellectually challenging career and technical studies, emphasizing the use of high-level mathematics, science, language arts, and problem-solving skills in the modern workplace and in preparation for continued learning.
Access to academic studies	Increase access to academic studies that teach essential concepts from the college-preparatory curriculum by encouraging students to use academic content and skills to address real-world projects and problems.
A challenging program of study	Require students to complete a challenging program of study with an upgraded academic core and a major.
Work-based learning	Give students and their parents the choice of a system that integrates school-based and work-based learning that spans high school and postsecondary studies and is planned by educators, employers, and employees.
Teachers working together	Create an organization, structure, and schedule that give academic and career and technical teachers the time to plan and deliver integrated instruction aimed at teaching high-level academic and technical content.
Students actively engaged	Get every student involved in rigorous and challenging learning.
Guidance	Involve each student and his or her parents in a guidance and advisement system that ensures the completion of an accelerated program of study with an in-depth academic or career and technical major.
Extra help	Provide a structured system of extra help to enable students who may lack adequate preparation to complete an accelerated program of study that includes high-level academic and technical content.
Keeping score	Use student assessment and program evaluation data to improve continuously the school climate, organization, management, curricula, and instruction to advance student learning and to recognize students who meet both curriculum and performance goals.

Teachers and leaders caught up in the daily struggle to keep a school running do not have time to develop a school improvement framework and to find the resources needed to implement such a framework in their classrooms, but the adoption of a comprehensive school improvement framework allows teachers and other school leaders to fit smaller initiatives into a larger picture, thus creating a "change culture" while avoiding the fragmentation of disconnected projects or the adoption of the fad of the year.

Further, we believe that any significant change will only occur if school and teacher leaders are dissatisfied with the status quo. In too many schools, the adults—teachers, principals, and other school leaders—who are responsible for managing the school and teaching the students operate at a "comfort level" that makes them resistant to change. We argue, therefore, that a set of strategies that helps to identify and articulate sources of dissatisfaction with student achievement levels—as well as, perhaps, dissatisfaction with existing instructional and administrative practices—and provides potential remedies for that dissatisfaction is fundamental to successful school improvement efforts.

Finally, as noted earlier, we believe that enduring school change must, ultimately, be both driven and supported by state education policies. Thus, our change strategy involves diverse and continuing efforts to communicate both the requirements for improving student performance in high school and the results of such efforts to state education officials and policymakers.

Thus, the HSTW consortium began with six initial change strategies built on these basic beliefs: site development workshops, technical assistance visits, summer staff development workshops, continuous data collection, state accountability systems, and communication with policymakers. Although each strategy has been elaborated and refined based on our experience, they remain the basis of our school reform efforts.

Site Development Workshops. All new HSTW sites agree to send a team to a two-day site development workshop. These workshops are intended to help schools begin the journey toward the development of a more-challenging curriculum and improved student performance. Teams are typically made up of about eight people—a representative from the district office (often the assistant superintendent for instruction), the school principal, teachers from the core academic areas (English, math, and science), vocational education teachers, and school counselors. Selection processes vary. In some cases, team members are chosen by district officials; in other cases, they are nominated by a school's faculty senate; and, in other cases, they are self-nominated. Teachers who are selected to participate in the workshop (or who select themselves) tend to be individuals who are passionate about school change, who have demonstrated success in helping low-performing students achieve at higher levels, and who can work effectively with other teachers across disciplinary boundaries. In short, such individuals are respected within their schools and likely to be able to generate enthusiasm for school change efforts among other teachers.

Workshop participants are asked to assemble a profile that captures the performance of their schools. These profiles are based on SAT or ACT scores over a five-year period, high school completion rates, scores on state assessments, and the percentage of students who are required to take remedial courses in postsecondary education. Often, the requirement to assemble this profile reveals that schools do not have the data needed to understand their current circumstances or to provide a baseline for measuring improvement, but a review of the school's master schedule can provide a basic picture of current practices. By explicating the requirements in the courses specified in the schedule, workshop participants can begin to understand their current practices and identify curriculum areas needing changes.

The site development workshop is intended to help teams view their schools through the lens of the HSTW key practices. The workshop leader introduces each key practice, giving a rationale for the practice, a description of strategies that might be used to implement it, and evidence that it can improve student achievement. Then, each school site team is asked to speculate about how they think their students would respond to a number of indicators dealing with the key practice. After completing that exercise, the teams are asked to identify at least three actions they might take at their school that would be likely to lead students to change their perceptions of the school.

Thus, the structure of the workshop provides each team with an opportunity to discuss every key practice in the context of its own school, generate a series of actions, and leave the workshop with 20 to 25 specific actions the members might take to improve their school. They return to the school and repeat the process with the entire faculty and, within three months, complete a three-year site improvement plan. In that plan, the schools identify three to five specific actions they will take the following year to change school and classroom practices and, ultimately, we hope, student achievement. After selecting priority actions, the team examines what will be needed to implement each of the new practices and develops an implementation plan. To oversee the implementation of the site improvement plan, schools are required to form a school improvement committee. When invited to do so, SREB staff comment on these site development and implementation plans. The plans are also reviewed by local school boards and by officials in the state department of education (if the state will be providing at least part of the funding).

As this description indicates, the HSTW program differs from more-prescriptive programs in that it uses the experience of workshop participants to identify needed changes and bases the methods specified for bringing about the changes on the participants' beliefs about what can be accomplished in their schools. That is not to say, however, that identifying needed changes and change strategies is a "free form" activity. Rather, these judgments are tested against HSTW's key conditions and practices, which provide a set of criteria against which the importance and value of ideas for change can be measured. We view the site development workshop as "beginning the journey" toward school improvement in a particular site, a journey that progresses through additional HSTW activities and the analysis of experience over time.

Technical Assistance Visit. Creating a sense that change is needed within the broader school community—that is, among those who did not attend the site development workshop—is accomplished through a three-day external technical assistance visit, followed by a report identifying major challenges and actions that the school needs to take to improve student achievement. Led either by an SREB staff member or by someone from the state staff, the team conducting the technical assistance visit consists of classroom teachers from academic and career and technical areas, guidance counselors, school leaders, parents, and representatives from the business community and from community and technical colleges. These observers draw on the HSTW framework to answer the following questions:

- What is the school presently doing that it should keep doing to improve student achievement?
- What specific plans must teachers and school leaders make to change school and classroom practices to improve student performance?
- What challenges does the school face?
- Why do these challenges exist?
- What can the school do to address the challenges?

Following the visit, the team leader summarizes the answers to these questions orally—generally in a two- to three-hour discussion with school leaders and teachers. The oral report is followed by a 15- to 20-page report that specifies, in very concrete terms, the challenges the school faces and what it must do to address them. The report provides a three-year plan designed to encourage teachers, principals, and other school leaders to think about what they can do to move from an ability-based system to an effort-based system. Equally important, the report gives the school and district leadership teams an externally generated—and therefore both more potent and less threatening—justification to engage the faculty in a deeper discussion about the changes they must make. Local school principals and superintendents give the technical assistance visit high marks because the three-year plan presented in the report subsequent to the visit provides a concrete basis for setting priorities and allocating funds in a way that links identified needs and available resources.

Summer Staff Development Conference. Summer staff development conferences have been held annually since 1987. Attendance has grown consistently since then—from 140 participants at the first conference to more than 7,000 participants in 2003.

People attend the conference in teams from network schools and, increasingly, from schools outside the network. We encourage the principal to be a part of the team, as well as someone from the district office, preferably the superintendent and possibly the director of career and technical education. We also encourage those who are setting up these teams to include a language arts teacher, a mathematics teacher, a science teacher, and a career and technical teacher, as well as a guidance counselor. Finally, we invite staff members from state departments of education who are responsible for HSTW programs to attend, and we provide opportunities for them to meet with school teams from their states.

At the conference, educators from both participating and non-participating schools learn about school and classroom practices believed to have improved student achievement and to have helped implement HSTW key practices and key conditions in network schools. The intent is to share ideas that workshop participants can use to improve practice in their own schools and classrooms, as well as ideas they can use to persuade system, school, and teacher leaders that almost all students can succeed in the rigorous academic core that has, historically, been taught to only the best students. The conference helps participants understand that they are part of a larger network, one of individuals who have worked their way through common problems and, in doing so, have contributed to the success of their students and their schools.

The conference planning committee consists of representatives from each of the participating states. Its members include state education leaders, system leaders, school leaders, teacher leaders from both academic and vocational fields, and guidance counselors. A substantial portion of its time is devoted to examining the most recent data from our network of schools, including the results of a high school faculty survey, the results of student surveys, achievement data, and follow-up data. This analysis helps the committee identify priorities for conference themes, objectives, and topics.

Building on the planning committee's analysis, each conference begins with a presentation that uses data from network schools to show what is working and what is not and to identify gaps in achievement and in implementation of our design. This presentation emphasizes the ideas that our program is data-driven and that if students and teachers come to view their schools more favorably, student performance on achievement exams will improve, as will attendance, graduation rates, and postsecondary education enrollment rates.

Many participants attend preconference sessions on a single topic designed to "go deep." During the conference, simultaneous sessions, typically lasting two hours, are held; these sessions include presentations about outstanding practices, how-to workshops, and sessions for groups of people in similar jobs (e.g., principals, guidance counselors, fifth-grade teachers), termed *job-alike sessions*. In these sessions, participants talk about issues and problems they have encountered as teachers in particular disciplines, as principals, as counselors, as school board members, and the like. In addition to the "successful practices" information-sharing sessions noted above, we hold brief roundtable discussions in which teachers share classroom strategies and materials with other teachers.

Most of these sessions are staffed by school people—teachers, advisors, and principals—which is consistent with our view that generating enthusiasm for change and the willingness to make concrete changes in practice depends, in part, on demonstrating that other similarly situated professionals have met these challenges successfully. In addition, we invite 25 to 30 national experts to serve as workshop leaders and speakers. They make keynote presentations and presentations at theme sessions and conduct hands-on workshop sessions on such topics as small learning communities, classroom management strategies, and new approaches to assessment.

Many superintendents have said that the summer conference is the best staff development investment they can make. They tell us that one of the biggest stumbling blocks they face is getting teachers to believe that almost all students can achieve at high levels. They know, however, that if they send eight, ten, or fifteen people to the summer conference, the participants will come back believing that they can help students achieve at higher levels than seemed possible previously.

Continuous Data Collection. HSTW uses continuous data collection and reports based on benchmarked indicators to keep schools moving toward their goals for student achievement (see SREB, 2002). These data permit teachers and schools to compare their own outcomes to those of schools with similar student populations that are performing at a high level and to consider the results in relationship to the degree to which HSTW's key practices have been implemented in each school. In most instances, these data create a sense of dissatisfaction among teachers in schools that are performing poorly, motivating them to make changes. The results of these analyses also provide school personnel with ideas to improve performance levels and specify strategies that others have already used successfully.

HSTW's common assessment process includes measures of student achievement in reading, mathematics, and science, as measured by exams developed by the Educational Testing Service and referenced to the National Assessment of Educational Progress, student and faculty surveys designed to capture perceptions about high schools, analysis of transcripts to link student performance to the number and types of courses taken in high school, and a follow-up survey one year after graduation to determine the status of former students and to identify ways the high school might have better prepared them for postsecondary pursuits. The assessment is administered every other year. To join the HSTW network and to remain in it, district and school leaders must participate fully in the common assessment. Schools that fail to participate are dropped as active HSTW sites.

The key to the success of SREB's assessment effort is the way the various sources of data are combined and then disaggregated for the sites. Data are organized in the broad themes that correspond to the improvement framework:

- academic achievement and classroom experiences
- high expectations in the classroom
- active engagement of students in the classroom
- availability of extra assistance
- guidance and advisement
- student achievement and courses taken.

Each report provides results on these themes for the school, the entire network, and the top 25 percent of school sites with similar student populations. By using themes associated with the comprehensive improvement framework, HSTW links key practices to a set of performance indicators that reveal improvement (or the lack thereof) in student achievement. In addition to these reports to individual schools, HSTW identifies pacesetter schools and profiles their practices through research briefs and case studies. (These publications are described in more detail below.) Further, SREB organizes one-and-a-half-day visits to pacesetter schools, which enable teachers and school leaders from other schools to discuss the application of HSTW's key conditions and practices with school personnel who have been successful in using them to improve student achievement.

HSTW also conducts a national workshop every two years to help state, school, and school district leaders learn to use the data reports. Of course, not everyone who might profit from these workshops can attend, but state education officials—usually the state-level HSTW coordinators—repeat the workshops in school districts and at individual sites as more school leaders and teachers are engaged in the assessment process. We believe that linking student achievement to students' descriptions of school and classroom practices informs school leaders and teachers about the changes they need to make to further improve student achievement.

State Accountability Systems. SREB and the HSTW consortium advocate state accountability systems that emphasize assessments in core academic subjects. Such an accountability system serves as a reality check for both teachers and students. If the results indicate that a school is not working well for many students, a school improvement design can become a positive force for improving student achievement. Our experience has shown, however, that public reports of test scores, along with sanctions, cannot alone ensure the right changes. Effective action is more likely to occur if school leaders understand school and classroom practices that improve student achievement. Without a deep understanding of practices that work to advance academic achievement, many schools resort to "quick fix" methods, such as a proliferation of worksheets, that may increase student boredom and produce little or no gain in student achievement. Nonetheless, we advocate well-constructed state-level tests as part of our strategy of working toward change through mechanisms that promote linkages between state policies and local practices.

Communication with Policymakers. Beginning with the baseline assessment in 1988, HSTW has prepared annual reports for state policymakers, which are presented at meetings of the SREB Board and at the annual SREB Legislative Work Conference.[3] At the outset, the thrust of these reports was to inform policymakers about how students were actually spending their time in high school and to describe the results of channeling students into college-preparatory, career and technical, and general curricula. Initially, many were unaware that so many students were pursuing the general strand and, as a result, how few were actually being given a chance to pursue a demanding course of study. We were able to demonstrate that students pursuing a vocational education curriculum performed better on standardized tests than did students in the general strand and that, later, as we began to emphasize more-rigorous academic courses for students in career and technical programs, their performance also improved. Further, we used these discussions as a forum to advocate changes in state graduation requirements. Arguing that it was difficult for principals, superintendents, or even local school boards, to establish policies and procedures that would encourage students to pursue a more-demanding course of study, we recommended, instead, state-level changes in the requirements for high school graduation—changes that would both support the efforts of local school officials to implement more-challenging curricula and motivate students to pursue them.

Becoming an HSTW Site

The first schools to enter the HSTW program came in as a result of outreach efforts in the states that had formed the SREB-State Voca-

---

[3] The Legislate Work Conference is an annual meeting sponsored by SREB's Legislative Advisory Council, which comprises state senators and representatives from the 16 SREB states. The attendees include at least two legislators from each state, typically members of the legislative committees responsible for education, as well as other legislators appointed by the governor, the speaker of the house, or the president of the senate. These conferences provide an opportunity for SREB to inform policymakers about what we are learning in our school reform efforts, which, in turn, helps them make well-founded decisions about state education policies.

tional Education Consortium. State departments of vocational education approached schools with, essentially, a request for proposals, inviting them to submit school improvement plans in keeping with HSTW's key practices and conditions. Although any school was eligible to apply, state leaders tended to approach schools that were (1) known to have strong local leadership and, thus, the potential to implement the HSTW program successfully or (2) known to be performing poorly, as measured by graduation rates, test scores, or other indicators that had led the state to designate them as low-performing schools. By encouraging such schools to enter the network during its early stages, we were able to gather information about issues related to implementation and effectiveness in environments where the program had a good chance of succeeding, as well as in environments that presented many challenges.

Although state leaders both invited and encouraged participation in HSTW, entry into the program was entirely voluntary. To build enthusiasm for the program and increase the likelihood of successful implementation, SREB encouraged school or district leaders to orient the faculty to the HSTW design and attempt to develop a consensus regarding their willingness to participate in the program. To support this process, we held one-day orientation conferences at schools that had shown interest in the program. At these conferences, teams of teachers and school leaders learned about the program in considerable detail and, as a result, were able to describe its goals and requirements to their colleagues.

As noted previously, school board approval was required for schools or districts that wished to become members of the HSTW network. Schools and schools systems participating in HSTW agreed to a series of activities (shown in Table 12.4) designed to promote the goals specified by the consortium. During its first five years, HSTW was funded primarily through a $6,000 state membership fee paid to the consortium. The cost of the assessment of student performance was paid by states and local districts.

Table 12.4
Requirements for Becoming an HSTW Site

Requirement	Description
Buy-in	Have site leaders—the superintendent, school board members, the principal, and a core group of teachers—examine HSTW's goals and key practices and decide that the program is viable for the school and the community. Schools or school systems that wish to participate must commit to at least a five-year effort to implement the key practices and to eliminate the general track.
Coordination, monitoring, communication, and integration	Appoint someone to coordinate HSTW action planning, staff development, and technical assistance; coordinate data collection; monitor progress; foster communication; and integrate the HSTW goals and key practices with other school improvement efforts.
Support to staff	Support academic and career and technical teachers with staff development, materials, and time to work together to implement the key practices.
School improvement committee	Organize a school improvement committee consisting of key academic and career and technical teachers and administrators; guidance counselors; and representatives of business, industry, and postsecondary education.
School action plan	Prepare an action plan for implementing the key practices and a site-specific staff development plan to help teachers carry out the action steps.
Participation in assessment	Participate in the HSTW assessment to obtain baseline data and to measure progress in raising student achievement.
Monitoring progress	Use HSTW indicators of progress in working toward a goal of having 85 percent of career-oriented students meet the HSTW achievement goals in reading, mathematics, and science.
Participating in the network	Become an active member of a state and multistate network for sharing information and ideas.
Access to career and technical courses	Give students access to modern career and technical courses, either at the high school, at an area career and technical center, at a college or university, or in a work setting connected to school-based academic and technical studies.
Coaching	Designate staff members to coach all teachers in getting students to use reading, writing, and mathematics across the curriculum to improve achievement in all content areas.

Early Results

Assessments conducted between 1987 and 1992—the initial phase of HSTW—enabled us to determine whether student performance improved in schools that made the changes we advocated. Of the initial 28 HSTW sites, about one-third made significant improvements in student achievement during the first five years. In these schools, reviews of transcripts indicated that the percentage of students completing the HSTW-recommended core curriculum increased significantly, as did the percentage of career and technical teachers emphasizing reading and mathematics. Surveys of students indicated that schools also improved their guidance and advisory activities and increased their efforts to provide extra help to enable students to meet higher course standards. Finally, students reported that their courses were more challenging and that they were asked to make greater effort. The results of the transcript review and the student survey were consistent with the annual reports submitted by the schools and with our informal observations during technical assistance visits. Taken together, these indicators revealed that the schools in which achievement levels improved were the schools that had made the most progress in implementing the HSTW design.

Findings from these early years showed a strong link between the quality of students' high school learning experiences and their achievement. However, although we had achieved a certain measure of success, the number of schools we were then serving was small, leaving unaddressed the needs of many schools and districts in our state network. Further, the discrepancies in levels of implementation of the HSTW program—and the related discrepancies in performance—made us aware that substantial progress could be made in helping schools and school leaders adopt the new practices HSTW advocated. We also recognized that we would need to expand and strengthen our organization to achieve these ends. Thus, the combination of this early success and the needs we observed prompted consortium leaders to seek outside funding to expand the network to a larger number of schools, to provide additional services to more schools, and to build the capacity of our organization.

Phase II: Scaling Up HSTW

The scaling-up of the HSTW initiative began in November 1992 on receipt of a six-year grant from The Wallace Foundation.[4] This grant was specifically intended to enable us to scale up the HSTW program, increasing the number of schools and the number of states included in the HSTW network. In addition, the terms of the grant specified that SREB aim to change the demographic composition of its network schools to be consistent with those of states involved in the HSTW program. This grant opened doors to other foundations, making us less dependent on the state membership fees and assessment fees. Some of these later grants also supported particular aspects of our growth. For instance, a substantial grant from the Whitehead Foundation helped HSTW make the national staff development program (described below) self-sustaining, and a grant from the Pew Charitable Trust Foundation enabled us to hire a specialist in career and technical education to help a subnetwork of schools link work-based learning with the HSTW improvement design.

HSTW was ready to use these new resources effectively because it possessed four essential features necessary for a large scale-up. First, we had a clear set of assumptions about goals, key practices, and conditions that constituted a comprehensive improvement framework for high schools. Second, we had a set of services to help schools implement the framework and a set of ideas about how these services could be expanded. Third, we had a score-keeping system for assessing student achievement and changes in school practices. Finally, HSTW had a means of informing policymakers outside the existing network in the SREB states about school practices that shape, support, and sustain changes and improvements in high schools. Taken together, the activities we undertook during this period, which we describe below, reflect our commitment to promoting school improvement both by working directly with schools and by communicating with state policymakers.

---

[4] Previously known as the Wallace–*Reader's Digest* Funds.

Expanding Organizational Capacity

The grant from the Wallace Foundation was critical to increasing our organizational capacity in several ways. We were able to increase our staff, provide more and better professional development opportunities, and develop publications to inform educators and policymakers about the goals and structure of our program and the services we provide.

Expanding the HSTW Staff. The increase in our resources enabled HSTW to go from one administrative support staff member to three and from two full-time professional staff to six: the program director; a director of research and evaluation; a director of publications and communication; a director of technical assistance; a staff development coordinator; and, as noted earlier, a specialist in career and technical education. The additional staff allowed us to serve more schools. We were able to conduct more site development workshops for new HSTW sites and to lead more technical assistance visits. In addition, the HSTW staff could train state personnel to lead technical assistance visits. Finally, we could assess a larger group of schools and improve the assessment report.

Expanding Professional Development Opportunities. In addition to increasing the number of schools for which we could provide the services that were already part of our repertoire, the expansion of our staff enabled HSTW to provide new professional development opportunities. For instance, in addition to the annual summer staff development networking conference, we instituted a series of national staff development conferences to be held throughout the year. The national staff development workshops are guided by four basic principles.

First, priorities for the national workshops are derived from our assessment data. Beginning with the identification of gaps in school and classroom practices or specific problems in student achievement, we create a list of proposed national workshops each year and present it to the HSTW board, which approves the workshops it believes most likely to benefit local site teams. Second, each workshop focuses on why the proposed practice is valuable to teachers within a given discipline. Third, we insist that schools attend as teams of teachers and school leaders. During the workshop, teams collaborate to determine how to implement the new ideas in their schools. Finally, we ask participants to evaluate each staff development activity to improve future efforts.

Each workshop is built around a planning template. This template helps participating teams generate specific ideas for implementing new practices based on the topic of the workshop and also helps the teams make plans for implementing these ideas in their own classrooms and schools. Like the site development workshops, these national workshops focus on going back to the schools, trying out new ideas, and supporting teachers in their efforts to change their practices.

Expanding HSTW's Communication Capabilities. The Wallace Foundation grant also made it possible for HSTW to produce a series of timely, state-of-the-art publications designed to help teachers, school leaders, and policymakers bridge the gap between research and practice.

Our research briefs present evidence of improving student achievement and concrete actions teachers and leaders can take to promote such achievement in readily understandable language. These briefs demonstrate for state policymakers the impact of the HSTW design on student achievement, and they often recommend actions that policymakers can take to extend these practices to other schools.[5]

A series of best practices publications shows, for each key practice, how the most-improved schools—as measured by the HSTW assessment process and as verified by state achievement data, including state achievement tests, graduation rates, and ACT and SAT scores—implemented that practice. Singling out such exemplary practices helps to build a network of collaborators who see part of their mission as helping others in the network succeed. These guides provide a rationale for a key practice, a brief description of the underlying research supporting it, the best practices from schools in the network, and a set of actions for implementation.

---

[5] These materials are available from HSTW.

Case study reports show how successful schools raised student achievement by providing solid evidence of improvement woven into a story of how they changed school and classroom practices. Case studies offer a credible counterargument to the often self-fulfilling belief many teachers have that many students cannot succeed in a challenging academic curriculum; thus, the studies become powerful tools that help change traditional ways of thinking. These real-life examples build confidence that schools can take risks and succeed in raising student achievement.

The Wallace Foundation grant also enabled us to start a twice-a-year newsletter to provide updated information about network progress and to reinforce network goals and vision.

Increasing the Number of States and Schools

The number of HSTW sites grew from 60 in 1992 to more than 700 in 1997, while the number of states grew from 13 in 1987 to 21 in 1997. The average number of sites per state increased from four in 1992 to 31 in 1997. Six states—Georgia, Kentucky, Louisiana, North Carolina, Virginia, and West Virginia—had more than 40 sites each. This increase was not achieved through marketing or other efforts to publicize our program. Instead, the growth of our network was fueled by a number of processes that—taken together—might be described as a diffusion process. For instance, school people read about our program in both popular (e.g., *Fortune* magazine) and professional sources and contacted their state education leaders about joining the program; SREB presentations to education and business leaders attracted new participants; and state-level directors of career and technical education spoke of their experience with our program to their colleagues, prompting inquiries and subsequent expansion to new sites. In all these ways, "the word got out," prompting new teachers, schools, districts, and states to seek information about and, eventually, come to participate in the HSTW program.

Achieving Demographic Balance

During the initial years of the HSTW program, program leaders felt that they had been more successful in working with rural schools that depended on state education officials for services and support than with urban schools, which tended to have district-like structures and their own professional development programs, curriculum committees, and such. Comparisons of the demographic make-up of schools in the HSTW network with schools in the broader geographic region indicated that urban schools and students who were members of minority groups were underrepresented in the HSTW network. This state of affairs was unsatisfactory to SREB and to our external funders. Thus, in 1997, with support from the Charles Stewart Mott Foundation, we appointed a staff member to lead a network of urban schools and adopted a strategy that treated urban schools more like states or districts. That is, HSTW staff began to work with urban school leaders to carry out site development workshops and provide services geared to the needs of urban schools.[6]

Note that, according to an independent analysis (Bradby, 2004), students in HSTW schools were, by 2001, more likely to qualify for free or reduced-price lunch programs, to be located in urban areas, and to be members of minority groups than were students in the SREB states overall and to students in U.S. schools overall. We had thus, by this time, made substantial progress in extending our program to schools that served students most in need of the kinds of challenges and support embodied in HSTW's key principles.

Developing a Growing Number of Spokespersons

As HSTW expanded the size and diversity of its programs, individuals in schools and districts that had successfully implemented the program and achieved favorable results became "champions" of HSTW. These champions played a valuable role, both inside and outside the network. In various forums—site development workshops, our summer workshops, the annual Legislative Work Conference, and others—they spoke about their experiences with HSTW and the results they had obtained. Their experiences enabled them to challenge other

---

[6] See the discussion of Phase III activities for a fuller description of these efforts.

leaders to examine their traditional beliefs about curriculum and classroom practices for career-oriented students.

In particular, their presentations helped to convince teachers, principals, and school superintendents that "the old ways" were not helping students meet the demands of modern workplaces or adequately preparing them for postsecondary education. They helped to persuade teachers and principals that schools could be turned around, that the results that they had achieved could be achieved in other schools too. These platform presentations were supplemented by visits to "pacesetter schools," which, as noted previously, gave school leaders who were considering adoption of the HSTW program an opportunity to gather information from on-the-ground school leaders about new practices that these pacesetter schools had tried, the consequences of these practices, and follow-up actions these schools undertook to deepen implementation and achieve better results.

Equally important, these spokespersons helped convince policymakers that HSTW's key conditions and practices could be implemented effectively and that, when this was done, positive results could be achieved. By presenting the positive results of their efforts, they helped give policymakers the confidence to raise high school graduation requirements—an undertaking that is sometimes met with skepticism stemming from beliefs that student achievement is, fundamentally, ability-based rather than effort-based and that more-stringent requirements would, therefore, only result in higher failure rates. By demonstrating that students could meet the challenges of a more-demanding curriculum based on assumptions about effort-based learning, HSTW spokespersons were able to inspire an "if they can do it, we can do it" attitude among state education officials and legislators.

Supporting Implementation of the HSTW Program

During this period, we continued to rely on the key practices and key conditions that had been the basis of our enterprise. However, in numerous ways, our understanding of what "deep implementation" required grew, and we could foster such implementation by developing implementation guides, user-friendly materials, and assessment tools. For instance, we produced guides describing strategies that schools could use to provide extra help to high school students and to improve their counseling and guidance services. We also created videotapes about how to close down the general-education strand and about how to integrate academic and career and technical education. And we produced materials describing the development of organizational teams to implement the HSTW design.

More generally, we grew in our own thinking about depth of implementation. We came to see school change as a continuous improvement process involving goal-setting, implementation, assessment, and subsequent refinement of both goals and practices. We attempted to ensure that HSTW would be flexible enough to incorporate best practices and products from other improvement initiatives, looking constantly for ideas that had been invented elsewhere that might help refine our practices and enhance the quality of implementation. Finally, we came to see that one of the chief requirements for achieving deep and lasting change in schools is patience—the recognition that, given our resources and the complexity of the problems we were trying to address, the pace of change might never be as fast as we would like. We learned to celebrate small victories and use them as a basis for demonstrating that attention to implementation would produce results.

Assessing the Phase II Achievements of the HSTW Program

At the conclusion of Phase II, our goals of improving student performance by establishing a more challenging program of study for career and technical students and eliminating the general strand had begun to be realized. Through our annual assessments, we were able to demonstrate to legislators that students who completed the HSTW-recommended curriculum could succeed in demanding academic courses. In a study of performance in schools that were part of our network in both 1996 and 1998, we found that reading scores had improved in 53 percent of the schools; science scores had improved in 82 percent of the schools; and mathematics scores had improved in 85 percent of the schools (Frome, 2001).

This evidence helped to convince policymakers that raising graduation requirements for career and technical students and closing the general strand would not, in fact, result in "leaving students behind" but would, instead, help promote higher levels of achievement. As a consequence, by the mid-1990s, many participating states had taken steps toward closing the general strand and making the HSTW-advocated academic core the basic requirement for high school graduation for all students.

Identifying New Challenges

As we began to achieve the goals we had set for ourselves, we also identified new issues that needed to be addressed.

First, as career and technical education improved, we began to see cases in which career and technical students were outperforming students in the academic track, as indicated by the number of students in each of the two areas who were required to take remedial courses in postsecondary institutions. Students were choosing to complete only the minimum requirements rather than taking full advantage of the opportunities their schools provided. In many instances, students had completed these requirements by the end of the junior year and spent their senior year taking fewer and less-challenging courses. These observations led us to consider how the HSTW curriculum might be adapted to promote higher achievement for all high school students.

Second, as state standards for high school graduation and the kinds of courses taught in high school began to rise, we began to see more students encountering academic difficulties in ninth grade. Thus, we saw a need to provide services to ninth-grade students that would help them succeed in a more challenging curriculum and also to become involved in efforts to enhance the preparation of middle school students for high school.

Third, we began to observe variations in the depth of implementation of our program. In some of the schools in our network, student performance was simply not improving. Closer examination of what was actually occurring in these schools revealed that they had made little progress in implementing the HSTW design. This recognition led us into several related activities: the development of measures of the quality of implementation, the development of site-specific services in schools whose implementation was most problematic, and the development of leadership programs to prepare school leaders to undertake the challenging task of implementing complex reform designed to improve student performance.

Fourth, we understood that we would need to continue our efforts to communicate both the needs and the achievements of schools, teachers, and students to policymakers and state education officials, providing them an information base for legislative and administrative decisions regarding education.

Phase III: Increasing Breadth, Depth, Stability, and Financial Resources

Taken together, the list of concerns described in the previous section provided the foundation for the objectives we set in the late 1990s—the period we refer to as Phase III. These objectives included expanding the HSTW program to include all high school students, smoothing the transition into and out of high school, increasing depth of implementation, and expanding efforts to translate lessons learned into state and local policies. To achieve these substantive objectives, we also set ourselves the objective of obtaining additional funds, both through contracted services and government and foundation grants. We describe our fundraising efforts first because our resource base both enables and constrains the work we are able to do to meet our other objectives.

Obtaining Funds to Maintain and Diversify HSTW

By the late 1990s, the kinds of relationships we had with the schools we serve had become more differentiated, as had the services we provided. We continued to provide our standard services to schools in the SREB state network, but we also continued our efforts, begun in 1997, to establish formal relationships with urban districts, many of which contained a number of challenged schools for which we designed a more-intensive set of site-specific services. And we undertook efforts to implement our school improvement programs in clusters of rural middle and high schools, again providing site-specific services adapted to the needs of the schools.

To provide these new services, while continuing our established programs, we also needed to build the capacity of our own organization. We needed, for instance, a cadre of trainers who could deliver site-specific staff development around critical instructional strategies to build teachers' confidence that they could teach more demanding materials to more students. We needed to develop guides and training materials to deal with the transitions from middle grades to high school and from high school to postsecondary studies. Finally, we needed the capacity to build the leadership skills of school leaders.

Given these new demands, it became apparent that the membership fees states paid to the consortium, the assessment fees schools paid, and the grant support we had received would no longer be sufficient to carry out the activities that we saw as necessary and that our constituencies sought. Thus, we undertook several efforts to find financial support for our projects from both public and private sources.

As a result of these efforts, we received major grants from the Office of Educational Research and Improvement (OERI)[7] in the U.S. Department of Education and from several private foundations—the Edna McConnell Clark Foundation, the Carnegie Corporation of New York, and the Goldman Sachs Foundation, as well as a continuation grant following the initial 1997 grant from the Charles Stewart Mott Foundation and additional support from the Wallace Foundation. In addition, we have obtained contracts to provide school services through the Comprehensive School Reform (CSR) program and through fee-for-service arrangements with several urban school districts. With these resources, we have been able to pursue the objectives described above.

---

[7] This organization has since become the Institute of Education Sciences.

Adapting HSTW to Include All Students

As noted above, our observations regarding patterns of course-taking and performance led us to consider how the HSTW curriculum might be adapted to promote higher achievement by all high school students. Our response to this problem was to develop curricula that would capture the goals and interests of diverse groups of students.

To encourage districts and schools to move further in closing down the general track and to achieve the objective of including all high school students in the HSTW program, we recommended that students complete one of four concentrations (career and technical, mathematics and science, humanities, or blended career and technical and academic) in addition to their core courses in English, mathematics, science, and social studies. Ideally, all the courses in each concentration, as well as the core courses that made up the basic HSTW curriculum, would be taught in a manner that embodied the key practices set forth in our original program description. Following these practices would help ensure that the courses would require students to meet high expectations—that advanced mathematics courses, for instance, actually contained advanced material.

Currently, implementation of these academic concentrations might be said to be in a developmental phase. The concept has been slow to be taken up because there is, as yet, no formal policy structure supporting it. We have, however, begun to see increases in the percentages of students taking math and science courses during the senior year, taking precalculus courses, and taking Advanced Placement courses. Between 2000 and 2002, the percentage of students taking four years of mathematics increased from 61 percent to 65 percent, and the percentage of students taking four years of science increased from 50 percent to 55 percent. Preliminary analyses indicate that enrollment in mathematics and science courses in the senior year is associated with both better performance and a reduction in the percentage of students who must take remedial courses to enter postsecondary education (Educational Testing Service, 2002).

Supporting Transitions to and from High School

Although we had achieved considerable success in improving the achievement of high school students, we began to recognize, as we entered Phase III, that focusing entirely on high schools presented certain problems. In particular, middle school students were often poorly prepared to meet the requirements of the HSTW curriculum, and, even if they had completed the requirements of the curriculum, high school students sometimes found it difficult to meet the demands they encountered in postsecondary school and work environments. Thus, we developed programs to help students make these transitions successfully.

Supporting the Transition to High School. Implementing the changes we believed were needed in the high school curriculum was problematic because many students were leaving the middle grades unprepared to succeed in challenging high school studies. According to the National Assessment of Educational Progress, administered in mathematics and science in 1996 and reading in 1998, almost 50 percent of middle school students in SREB states were performing below the basic level in mathematics and science and approximately 30 percent were performing below the basic level in reading. The problem of poor preparation for high school could also be seen in the high failure rates in Grades 9 and 10. For instance, in 1999, failure rates in three SREB states—Georgia, Texas, and Tennessee—were three to five times higher in Grade 9 than in any other grade.

Thus, SREB is focusing its attention on improving instruction in the sixth, seventh, and eighth grades by aligning the middle grades curriculum and expectations with the standards we want students to meet in high school. In the late 1990s, we initiated the Making Middle Grades Work (MMGW) network. We now have 200 middle grades schools in this network, of which 180 are linked to an HSTW site. We spent two full years planning the middle grades initiative—developing a mission and goals statement, developing a set of key practices and conditions grounded in the research information available on what works to improve student performance in middle schools, and preparing four publications to increase the awareness of policymakers about the middle grades problem. The services we provide these middle grades schools are very similar to the services provided to HSTW sites in the state network. In addition to the middle schools we serve through the SREB network, we are now providing site-specific services through CSR contracts to ten MMGW sites.

Further, we want to modify the ninth grade by identifying the students who are not yet ready for college-preparatory Algebra I and language arts. We advocate providing catch-up instruction aimed at moving these students into the college-preparatory curriculum rather than letting them wander through high school in watered-down courses. As a consequence of this shift in emphasis, which began in the mid- to late 1990s, more than one-third of HSTW sites now provide special transition programs with their feeder middle schools and have modified of their ninth-grade curriculum to include catch-up courses

Supporting Postsecondary Achievement. As more and more career-oriented students go on to further study, the senior year has become a focus of our attention. According to a follow-up study of more than 8,000 high school graduates who completed a career concentration in 2000, almost 80 percent enrolled in some form of further study within 15 months of graduation. Yet, 34 percent of these students were enrolled in one or more remedial or developmental courses.[8] If, however, students had completed the HSTW-recommended curriculum and met HSTW performance goals, the percentage of youths having to take remedial courses decreased to 24 percent. More-detailed analyses indicated that, among students who had completed an English language arts sequence that required them to do a short writing piece each week, only 3 percent had to take a remedial language arts or reading course. Of students who had completed four years of mathematics in high school, fewer than 15 percent had to take one or more remedial mathematics course.

We thus modified our design so that all students—including career-oriented students—spent half their time in core academic sub-

---

[8] Note that even this percentage compares favorably to national averages; in 2002, 42 percent of students entering community colleges were required to take at least one remedial course (Parsad and Lewis, 2003).

jects in their senior year. These courses were to be designed to prepare students for their next step, so that they could go on for further study without having to take remedial courses and could pass employers' exams for good jobs. Increasingly, we find ourselves working with high schools and with community colleges, technical colleges, and traditional four-year colleges to determine what knowledge and skills students must have to avoid having to enroll in remedial writing, mathematics, and language arts courses in college.

To measure progress on the implementation of our emphasis on supporting the transition to postsecondary work and school environments, we rely on reports from technical assistance visits; biennial teacher and student surveys; assessment of seniors in reading, mathematics, and science; and an annual report from schools about their initiatives to prepare students for postsecondary work and education. Over time, we expect wider implementation of the amended HSTW design, thus providing a more challenging senior year for many students and, as a result, improving their adjustment to whatever environments they enter after they graduate.

Deepening the Implementation of Reform

As noted above, we observed that the quality of implementation of the HSTW program was uneven. In many schools, a substantial proportion of students, including some students following a college-preparatory curriculum, were not being taught to high standards. Course titles, after all, are ultimately only labels. What matters is what is actually taught and how it is taught. Our observations indicated that gaps between the apparent content of courses and what was actually being taught were common, especially in urban districts that served populations with high proportions of students living in poverty. Schools in which the HSTW program had been poorly implemented had not developed district or school leadership teams that were capable of engaging the staff in the activities needed to implement a comprehensive school reform program.

To address this problem, we undertook three kinds of activities: creating tools to help teachers and school leaders assess and improve the quality of implementation in their schools; defining and developing site-specific services for challenged schools; and building leadership capacity in states, districts, and schools to support reform activities and assume responsibility for comprehensive improvement.

Deepening Implementation Through Analysis and Planning. To improve the quality of implementation in poorly performing schools, we developed workshops that could be conducted within schools to enable teachers to identify weaknesses in implementation and make "course corrections" designed to strengthen teaching and learning. Based on a set of implementation indicators, teachers can determine whether the actual content of their courses is such that students who mastered the course material would be able to meet or exceed state standards. For instance, to be classified as being taught at the college-preparatory level and in keeping with the HSTW design, an English–language arts course must require (1) a major research paper, (2) reading an assigned book each month, and (3) completing a short writing assignment at least once each month. Similar indicators were defined in other areas of the curriculum. In addition, we developed indicators for assessing the level of integration of academic content and skills into career and technical studies, the quality of worksite learning, the creation of a positive culture of learning for all students, and the provision of timely guidance. Student surveys provide the data for these assessments. In addition, teachers respond to a number of measures designed to indicate the degree to which the school emphasizes the creation of a climate of continuous improvement.

A second workshop helps teachers and other school leaders learn to disaggregate student performance data to determine whether performance differs across student subgroups (e.g., based on race, ethnicity, gender, parental education). These data enable guidance counselors to ensure that students enroll in courses that will help them meet standards, prompt teachers to review their practices to ensure that all students are being held to high standards, and provide information to school administrators about the need for "extra help" programs.

Other efforts to improve implementation at the classroom level include developing small learning communities, which are planned to operate in accordance with HSTW's key practices; encouraging state education officials to visit low-performing schools more frequently so that they can assess the quality of implementation and stress its importance; and emphasizing the importance of deep implementation in the technical assistance visits conducted by HSTW staff.

Deepening Implementation Through Site-Specific Services to Challenged Schools. As with the other schools in our network, HSTW depends on the states to deliver most of the direct technical assistance to challenged schools. Thus, deepening the implementation of the design means getting states to do more to assist HSTW schools in our state networks; providing this assistance is especially important in the schools that face the greatest challenges in meeting the HSTW goals.

To encourage more state-level participation, we are attempting to model a way for states to provide more site-specific services to low-performing schools. This approach would not require states to take over these schools, but it would require building the state's capacity to provide services to them. To help build this capacity, we have added a new group of school improvement consultants to our staff. In most instances, these consultants have previously worked in state departments of education or at one of our middle grades or HSTW sites.

The services we have developed and are working with state and district officials to implement include needs-based action planning, site-specific professional development, site-based technical assistance, and visits from a school improvement consultant. The consultant helps the school use assessment data to determine what is working and what is not working and to specify particular actions to advance student achievement. HSTW works with district leaders including, when necessary, the school board to identify the policies, district support, and resources needed to more fully implement the HSTW design. As school improvement consultants visit districts to work with the school, they discuss with the superintendent what the district office needs to do to support the school.

In addition to these efforts to improve services to challenged schools by expanding the kinds of assistance state departments of education offer, we have also undertaken a number of special initiatives to assist challenged schools in both rural and urban areas, relying on funds obtained through special initiatives or contracts.

Assisting Urban Schools. The first initiative, funded by the Office of Adult and Vocational Education in the U. S. Department of Education, enabled us to assist 25 urban high schools, which we referred to as New American High Schools, in adopting the HSTW design. With the exception of a school in Philadelphia, these schools were all in urban districts in SREB states. Relying on these funds, we were able to provide concentrated services to these school sites for 12 months. When we compared the progress made in implementing the design and the improvement in student achievement at these schools in 2000 to those of schools that had not received the site-specific support, we found that these schools were implementing the HSTW design more deeply and had showed greater improvement in reading, mathematics, and science achievement (MPR Associates and SREB, 2001). While these changes were not dramatic, they were positive.

In 1997, HSTW began to work with a second set of urban districts: Atlanta, Georgia; Savannah, Georgia; Greensboro, North Carolina; Philadelphia, Pennsylvania; Huntsville, Alabama; New Orleans, Louisiana; Nashville, Tennessee; and, later, Jackson, Mississippi, and Little Rock, Arkansas. For this network of urban districts and high schools, the aim is to build district capacity to support high school reform. These districts receive more services than we provide to the HSTW sites in our state network but less-intensive services than those we provide to the New American High Schools, rural sites for which OERI funds our efforts, and the CSR sites.[9]

SREB meets annually with a committee from the district office and school sites from each of the participating urban districts to review what we have accomplished in the past year and to decide what we are going to work on during the coming year. As part of this review, we assess the support the district office has given the school sites, particularly changes in policies that give principals the authority needed to implement the design more fully. In spring 2003, we held

---

[9] We describe the services we provide to the OERI and CSR sites later in this section.

our first meeting with urban superintendents, state legislators, state leaders, and business leaders. Our goal was to identify ways urban communities and the state can work with school districts to improve urban high schools. These discussions help to counter fragmentation by aligning district policies, initiatives, and resources with efforts at the school building level.

Assisting Rural High Schools and Middle Schools. In contrast to schools in urban districts, schools in rural districts often have more-limited resources. They are unlikely to have curriculum specialists, reading experts, and others who can support instructional initiatives, and their faculties are more likely to lack depth in particular subject areas. Because of these and other limitations, rural schools may face particular difficulties in attracting talented, dedicated teachers and principals; further, local culture may not emphasize academic achievement.

To help address these problems, HSTW received a grant from OERI in 1999 to help 80 clusters of rural middle grades and high schools implement our middle grades and high school improvement design. This grant gave us resources to provide on-site technical assistance, coaching, and staff development services to these schools. We worked with 25 school clusters per year and provided them with about 18 months of intensive services.

In this enterprise, we were attempting to determine whether providing concentrated services for a relatively short period would be sufficient to launch reform efforts that local school leaders could sustain. We found that schools having committed leaders who participated in our national and site-specific staff development services and in our leadership development programs could implement the design more fully than could schools that lacked such leadership and that gains in student performance followed. But when existing local leadership was weak or when local leaders were not committed to the program, this short intervention was insufficient to build leadership skills or to bring about the changes in outlook needed to support deep implementation. We also learned, through this experience, the importance of continuity in our own organization. School improvement consultants develop relationships with teachers and principals, and, if these relationships were disrupted, our programs foundered or failed.

Providing Services Through the CSR Program. The fourth network of schools for which we have provided services includes schools that adopted the HSTW design and pay for the services we provide through a CSR grant. We contract with these schools to provide $25,000 to $30,000 of services per year. These include the basic services (the site development workshop, the technical assistance visit, opportunities to attend the national and summer conferences, and so on) and the services of improvement consultants, each of whom works with about 10 sites. The consultants provide these sites with 10 to 15 days of on-site staff development, coaching, and technical assistance annually.

Over a three-year period, achievement levels at some CSR sites rose modestly, but some schools did not improve at all. These schools experienced substantial turnover in district and school leadership during this interval, echoing our observations about the importance of strong local leadership in our OERI-funded work with rural schools.

Supporting Implementation Through Leadership Development. It might be said that SREB has, since the outset, been involved in developing educational leadership through the HSTW and MMGW programs. In recent years, however, our leadership development efforts have become both more explicit and more intense—a result of our convictions about the importance of effective school leaders, convictions that the results of our OERI and CSR projects have strengthened.

Through partnerships with states and districts, HSTW attempts to increase their capacity to support reform activities and assume responsibility for comprehensive improvement. For instance, in 1997, HSTW raised its fee for membership in the SREB consortium by $2,500 and designated that increase to support an annual State Leadership Forum. This forum brings together legislators, state superintendents of schools, members of state boards of education, and state-level directors of career and technical education to examine lessons learned from HSTW and their implications for state leaders, policies, and redirected resources. In each of these day-long meetings, we provide information about what we have learned with regard to a particular topic, as a means of educating both policymakers and education professionals.

As a part of the HSTW urban initiative, we are creating an urban district leadership forum for urban superintendents, members of urban school boards, state legislators, and state superintendents of schools. The purpose of the urban leadership forum is to examine better ways to connect district policies, leadership, and resources to comprehensive school improvement in both middle grades and high schools.

We are also assisting five states in developing state leadership academies focusing on low-performing high schools. These leadership academies will work not only with existing principals but also with a team made up of district officials, aspiring principals, and teacher leaders. Over a three-year period, the team will participate in a series of leadership development efforts organized around a comprehensive school improvement framework. These teams participate in sessions and return to their schools to work on problems—often with some outside coaching and assistance.

Finally, we are working with 11 institutions of higher education to help them identify measures for changing their leadership preparation programs. We contend that the leadership preparation program must be developed in collaboration with local districts and must be aligned to school improvement efforts and that great teachers should be tapped as future school leaders.

Translating Lessons Learned into State Policies

Obviously, we do not have the authority to make policy, but communicating with policymakers and explaining how policy can embody educational goals has, since the outset, been an important part of our work and remains so today. In addition to the State Leadership Forum and the Legislative Work Conference, we make presentations to state boards of education regarding the progress of HSTW sites in their states. In these presentations, we describe what we see as the difference between HSTW schools that have performed well and those that have performed less well, with a view toward helping these officials identify ways to embed in state policies practices that have helped improve performance. We also provide state profiles combining a number of indicators—graduation requirements, course-taking patterns, achievement scores, reports of student experience, and so on—currently and over time, within their state and compared to other SREB states and to the United States as a whole.

As a result of our efforts to inform state policies, seven of the SREB states (Arkansas, Georgia, North Carolina, Oklahoma, South Carolina, Virginia, and West Virginia) brought their high school graduation requirements closer to the HSTW-recommended curriculum in the mid- to late 1990s. As a consequence of these changes in graduation requirements, the proportion of students in these states completing the college-preparatory core has increased, as has the proportion of students taking a rigorous academic core along with their career concentration. In addition, several of these states closed the general track. These policy changes were associated with improvements in student performance. Between 1993 and 2003, scores on college readiness exams (i.e., SAT and ACT) in these states rose at rates equal to or greater than the national average. Further, the proportion of high school students taking these exams increased during this period (Bottoms, 2003).

Achieving Success at Scale: Lessons from the Past and Challenges for the Future

The long-term aim of the HSTW-State Vocational Education Consortium has never been to have every high school in the United States in our network. Rather, it has been to show that high schools can teach almost all students to perform at high levels, as well as to inform policymakers and leaders at the state and local levels that such outcomes are possible and more likely to occur if they are driven, in part, by policies—whether at the state, district, or school level—that both demand and support high achievement.

In attempting to achieve these goals, we have had to address numerous issues in our work with schools, in our own organization, and in our efforts to inform state policies governing education. In this section, I describe lessons we have learned in each of these areas, presenting one key lesson and one key challenge in each area. These are not, of course, the only lessons and challenges that might be discussed, but they are, I believe, of central importance.

Scale-Up Issues in Work with Schools

Our direct work with schools has evolved in many ways as the number of schools we serve has expanded and as our understanding of what it takes to create deep change has grown. Here, I discuss the lessons we have learned regarding the tension between adherence to our core principles and adaptation to new circumstances, as well as the challenge of developing leadership as a means of driving ownership for reform into the core activities of educational institutions.

The Lesson: Adaptation to New Demands and Opportunities Is Needed, but Successful School Reform Requires Commitment to Core Principles. Having begun as a program focused specifically on the needs of high school students in career and technical curricula, we have, over time, broadened our reform efforts. Our programs are now designed to serve all high school students, help middle school students prepare for high school, and help high school graduates make smooth transitions to work or postsecondary education—in many school districts in many states. This expanded focus has been, for the most part, a response to the data on poor performance among high school students regardless of the curriculum they follow, high failure rates among ninth graders, evidence of variation in the content of courses that bear the same name, and so on.

Thus, we have, over time, developed new kinds of relationships with schools (e.g., relationships with urban districts, as opposed to individual schools), site-specific services for low-performing schools, tools designed to help teachers and schools implement our program, and programs to help prepare students for high school and to help them succeed once they have graduated. More generally, we have attempted to tailor our efforts to address the needs we encountered and to offer more-concrete advice about how to achieve the goals we advocated. At the same time, we have refined our techniques for assessing our progress, in terms of both the quality of implementation and the outcomes achieved. As we have done so, we have encouraged bottom-up contributions from teachers and school leaders at all levels, as well as from state education officials and policymakers. We believe that this approach helps build commitment among those who must enact change in their day-to-day work.

Nonetheless, we have, in all cases, held fast to the core beliefs in HSTW as an effort-based reform program, the need to focus on a few valid practices, and the need to create and sustain a common assessment system, as well as commitment to the key conditions and practices and the basic change strategies that characterized our early efforts. Maintaining our commitment to these beliefs, conditions, and practices and continued reliance on these change strategies has brought many advantages. It has allowed us to communicate our goals clearly to diverse audiences, to evaluate new ideas against an established set of criteria, and to assess student performance over time and across settings in relation to a variety of standards, including commercial standardized tests, the multifaceted HSTW assessment program, and state standards.

Adhering to these elements of our enterprise, all the while attempting to adjust our program to the specific needs of students and be responsive to the specific ideas and concerns of teachers and other school leaders, has been a constant challenge and is likely to remain so. Still, our experience has taught us that, without this clarity, it is all too easy for good intentions to fall by the wayside when schools confront the real difficulties of change, and it is much too difficult to achieve the "message discipline" required to inform policy decisions.

The Challenge: Achieving Sustainability and Ownership of Change Through the Development of Strong Local Leaders. Earlier, I described the efforts that we have undertaken to help current and potential school leaders develop leadership skills. Although we have made substantial progress in this area, we believe that we still have much work to do, not only practical work but also a good deal of thinking about how leadership is defined, how leaders are identified and trained, how changes in leadership affect reform efforts, and how leadership is shared among school leaders and school staff. Addressing these issues is essential to sustaining successful reforms and creating ownership of new practices.

We believe that, whether school leadership is viewed from a careerist perspective focused on meeting state standards or a moral perspective focused on helping students succeed, the most-effective local leaders will be those who foster a school culture based on the idea that all students can learn at high levels and that adults are responsible for helping them do so. In such a culture, students would be helped not only to perform well on tests but also to see that their performance is related to a larger purpose: their ability to be happy, successful, prosperous adults who will succeed in postsecondary education, enjoy their work, be able to care for their families, and contribute to the society in which they live. Building such a culture is, we believe, the only way to turn a low-performing school into a school in which students graduate with the kind of academic foundation they need to move with confidence into the next stage of their lives.

To do more than that—to turn good schools into excellent schools—school leaders, state education officials, and policymakers must plan for succession. Too often, district superintendents and, at a higher level, school boards believe that bringing in "new blood" is desirable, that new leaders who are not stuck in old ways of doing things will be able to introduce changes that accelerate the rate of improvement in student performance. In our experience, such changes kill improvement initiatives. The new leader must start anew with the faculty—getting to know them, earning their trust, and inspiring them and helping them adopt new instructional practices. Changing instructional practices is extremely complex and requires the cooperation of multiple actors over periods of years. Newcomers will rarely have the deep knowledge of the local culture needed to move reform forward.

Of course, turnover in leadership positions is inevitable, but given that inevitability and the value of deep knowledge of the individuals that make up the school community and the larger community in which the school exists, there is much to be said for systematic efforts to identify individuals already working within the system. Current principals and other teachers are likely to know which teachers have been successful in helping ordinary—or even failing—students succeed and who will be respected as an instructional leader. In most cases, individuals who want to become principals now select themselves and train themselves, which may produce results that are entirely satisfactory at the individual level, but it is, at best, highly optimistic to assume that such individuals will be available when a new principal is needed. Instead, current school leaders should be working to identify people who are passionate about teaching and learning—people other teachers will follow—and helping them prepare to be school leaders.

The idea that principals must be respected as instructional leaders is more than a political desideratum. For reforms to be sustained and for ownership of new practices to develop, it is a practical necessity because teachers and principals must work as a team. School leadership must, ultimately, be shared with teachers, both those who take on special roles on committees and those whose work as change agents consists entirely of introducing new instructional practices in their own classrooms. The need for teachers to take on such roles and to make such changes requires that principals understand what teachers need to do their work and that teachers see them as having that understanding. Both the understanding and the perception of understanding are more likely to exist if the principal is deeply familiar with the students, the teachers, the parents, and the system within which the individual school is situated.

Scale-Up Issues as a Reform Organization

Within our own organization, we have, as in our work with schools, faced issues involving the value of continuity and the necessity of change, as well as with building our capacity to learn from experience and plan for the future. Once again, we draw one key lesson and identify one key challenge for the future.

The Lesson: Change Takes Time and a Commitment to Measuring Progress. Achieving broad and deep change in educational structures and practices requires efforts on many fronts; among them are curricular reform, professional development, community involvement, and changes in the policies that govern and support education. It requires substantive shifts in what students are taught; how they are taught; what is expected of them; how the school relates to them; and how teachers relate to each other, to students, and to parents.

As change agents, we are still learning how to provide services to schools in manageable bits, so that new ideas can be absorbed and new practices learned, so that teachers and principals take ownership of the change process, and so that they develop the confidence needed to make the next set of changes. On the one hand, we are constantly striving to accelerate the rate of change—the better to serve students now in school and those soon to follow. On the other hand, our experience teaches us that achieving deep, lasting change on a broad scale—for instance, throughout a large district or a state—rarely occurs rapidly.

Despite our now-extensive experience with what we regard as a well-developed reform model and with the many tools, guides, and other specialized services that we have developed, entering a new situation with a fully detailed plan of what to do and how to do it is, we believe, impossible. Our approach requires analysis of the current situation within a school or school system, identification of the changes required, formulation of solutions to the problems identified, and training in how to implement those changes. This approach, which involves incorporating ideas from teachers and local school leaders, requires significant, sometimes delicate, interactions with school personnel, and these interactions take time. Generating the commitment required for deep implementation, leading to the ownership of the change process that contributes to sustainability, demands respect for the people who must implement change and the challenges it presents. Demonstrating this respect helps provide a foundation for commitment to change, but relationships that embody this respectful stance cannot be created overnight.

Further, because the change process is, inevitably, interactive and, therefore, subject to variation across locations and over time, we cannot assume that our involvement necessarily leads to the changes we seek. Both implementation and outcomes must be assessed. Such assessments typically reveal that new practices, even if undertaken with the best intentions in the world and as much support as we can provide, must be refined and strengthened. These assessments and the refinements they entail take time. Meaningful reform is a continuous process. Although some changes should be observable in the short run, expectations of dramatic improvements within a year or so are unrealistic. Reform organizations and those who provide resources for change—both governmental and private funders—must be prepared to take the long view.

The Challenge: Building Organizational Capacity to Sustain Long-Term Change. Begun with a half-time leader and one support staff member, our organization has, over its nearly 20-year life, grown to an enterprise with nearly 60 employees. Our staff is now too large and our activities too varied for any individual to know what everyone else is doing and learning. We are also, most often, too busy doing to take time for reflection and analysis. These facts mean that our organizational memory is dispersed—embedded not only in our databases but also in individual expertise acquired through experience, in the shared wisdom of teams working in the field, and in the complex web of our relationships with school leaders, departments of education, and legislators. Both to keep our existing activities on track and to plan for the future, we need to develop and implement a plan to extract and organize these diverse sources of knowledge about our activities to answer high-level questions about our strategies and procedures.

The following are some examples of the kinds of questions we need to address:

- How (and how well) are the results of the reports that follow our technical assistance visits used?
- What factors influence the depth of implementation of the HSTW practices?
- Are the site-specific services we offer addressing the needs we have identified?
- How can we do a better job of matching coaches with schools?

- What kinds of expertise are we lacking, and how can we best bring that expertise into our organization?

I suspect that we already know the answers to these and other such questions, but we do not know that we know because we have not systematically formulated and attempted to answer them. Doing so, however, is critical to ensuring that we have the capacity to meet the day-to-day challenges of our current work, as well as the capacity to respond to large-scale social and economic changes that call for creative responses from the education community.

Perhaps the greatest challenge we face in sustaining and enhancing our organizational capacity, however, is the upcoming transition in the leadership of our organization. The test of whether we have built the capacity needed to lead and support school reform efforts on a broad scale will be how the organization responds to the challenge of replacing senior leaders. It is tempting to consider recruiting a visionary leader—someone who has demonstrated success in another reform organization. But in keeping with our advice regarding the development of local leadership in schools, we expect to address this issue by identifying people within our organization who understand our culture and have demonstrated that they have the capacity to think through difficult problems, earn the respect of the staff, and communicate effectively with diverse audiences. Our efforts to identify and provide growth opportunities for such individuals are only beginning.

We anticipate establishing a task force to define substantive goals for the future, develop guidance about change strategies that are consistent with those goals, and determine what resources are needed and how to obtain them. An important part of the charge to this body will be ensuring that the organization has leaders who possess the capacity to meet the emerging challenges of education in the 21st century.

Scale-Up Issues in Educational Policy

From the start, we defined communicating with policymakers as one of the key elements of our change strategy. Our experience has convinced us of the validity of this approach and has also led us to believe that policymakers must address one of the most important challenges high schools now face: increasing the percentage of entering students who complete high school.

The Lesson: Policies Influence Performance, and Performance Influences Policy. Without the requirement to meet state standards for graduation, local school leaders do not have the backing to engage teachers in the broad-based change efforts needed to improve student performance. Thus, policies that set high standards for graduation are necessary to motivate the district- and school-level changes required to strengthen the curriculum, implement better teaching methods, and provide students with the support and guidance they need to succeed in their studies and graduate with a sense of purpose and the knowledge and skills they need to carry out that purpose. In addition to their role in establishing standards, policymakers are important to education reform because, through the budget process, they determine, at least in part, what resources schools and districts will have for making changes and what resources state departments of education will have for leading and supporting district- and school-level change efforts. Thus, we see no possibility for achieving and sustaining deep change if improvement goals are not embodied in and supported by policies consistent with improving the quality of education.

We regard policymaking as a continuous improvement process, with ever increasing clarity about what is required of schools, teachers, and students and with tighter links between policy requirements, instruction, assessment, and resource allocations. We work in SREB states, as well as in the other states with HSTW schools, to perfect this alignment. An important component of this process is providing policymakers with data about student performance—not only in their own states but also in other states that have adopted requirements consistent with the HSTW program. We have found, again and again, that there is nothing more likely to persuade policymakers that students in their states should be held to high standards—and that the students can meet the standards—than evidence that students in neighboring states are being held to such standards and are meeting them. Evidence of this sort helps open conversations about the role of state policies in producing such changes. Further, as evidence regarding the effect of changes in policy accumulates, it increases the likelihood that policymakers will be responsive to recommendations on ways to refine policies and to requests for the financial resources needed to achieve policy goals.

The Challenge: Creating Policies to Hold Schools Accountable for Performance *and* Completion. As emphasis on improving student performance to meet state standards has swept the nation, too little attention, we believe, has been paid to the problem of keeping at-risk students in school and providing them with the help they need to graduate. Although scholars differ about how graduation rates should be assessed, a recent report, based on well-specified methods, indicates that only 70 percent of students who entered U.S. public high schools in the 1997–98 academic year earned a diploma in 2001. That unimpressive average obscures the even lower graduation rates of some demographic groups. A bare majority of African Americans (51 percent) and Hispanics (52 percent) earn traditional high school diplomas (Greene and Forster, 2003). Clearly, many students are either underprepared or undermotivated—or both—to succeed in high school.

The current focus on accountability for achievement often leads to drill-oriented instruction that fails to motivate and excite students. The use of this single approach to assessment makes it more difficult to engage teachers in efforts to learn and use the research-based instructional strategies, contextual learning, and hands-on learning that were a centerpiece of our work a decade ago. Students, perhaps especially those least likely to find school engaging and rewarding, are unlikely to derive meaning and a sense of achievement from such assignments. As noted above, our program has undertaken significant efforts to support students in the transition to high school, but we believe more attention must be given to supporting students as they enter and progress through high school—by schools, as well as by policymakers.

State accountability systems must accord equal importance to graduation rates and student performance. If such standards were in place, school leaders and teachers would feel the same pressure to help students stay in school until they graduate that they now feel to help whatever students stay in school perform well on state exams. In fact, improving average performance and retaining students in school until they graduate need not be competing goals. We recently identified 13 high schools in Georgia that had improved performance on the Georgia High School Graduation Test by an average of 15 percent between 1997 and 2002 and that had improved high school completion rates between 1999 and 2002 by an average of 16 percent. Although few, these schools offer lessons about the structure and focus of future high school reform efforts. They establish high expectations, provide extra help for ninth-graders, ensure that all students and their parents have access to sound advice about education and careers, and work hard to connect the classroom to real life through quality career and technical studies (Bottoms and Anthony, 2004).

Focusing only on pushing up the scores on high-stakes tests at the end of high school is a disservice to the many students who leave school before graduating, resulting in an enormous waste of human talent that could be developed to the great advantage of the students, their families, and their communities.

Closing Thoughts

In this chapter, I have described the evolution of HSTW, beginning with the underlying conception of our program as an effort-based reform. To meet high standards, students must be given rigorous assignments that provide meaningful learning experiences, as well as the support and guidance needed to carry out these assignments. Persuading teachers, school leaders, and policymakers of the validity of this assertion; providing services to support implementation of practices consistent with this premise; and informing policymakers about the outcomes of our efforts and the need for their support are the central components of our work. We believe that our key conditions and practices provide the foundation for education that can help all students complete high school with the sense that they have achieved a meaningful goal and are prepared to meet the challenges that lie ahead of them.

Such education can provide the bridge to a good life for all our citizens, enable them to participate in democratic institutions, and sustain our national prosperity. Our students deserve no less. Those who lead our nation, make decisions regarding the allocation of resources for schools, and teach our children must understand the importance of high-quality education for all and commit themselves to providing both the inspiration and the support that students need to succeed.

References

Bottoms, G., presentation to the Southern Regional Education Board's Legislative Work Conference, Charleston, S.C., October 2003.

Bottoms, G,. and S. Anthony, "Raise Academic Standards and Get More Students to Complete High School: How 13 Georgia Schools Did It," research brief, Atlanta, Ga.: Southern Regional Education Board, February 2004, pp. 1–8.

Bradby, D., unpublished manuscript comparing *HSTW* sites in 2000 and over time, Washington, D.C.: MPR Associates, Inc., 2004.

Commission for Educational Quality, *Ten Recommendations for Improving Secondary Vocational Education*, Atlanta, Ga.: Southern Regional Education Board, 1985.

Educational Testing Service, unpublished composite report of experienced High Schools That Work sites participating in the 2002 *HSTW* Assessment, 2002.

Frome, P., *High Schools That Work: Findings from the 1996 and 1998 Assessments*, Research Triangle Park, N.C.: Research Triangle Institute, April 2001. Online at http://www.sreb.org/programs/hstw/Research Reports/RTI_study.pdf (as of July 1, 2004).

Greene, J. P., and G. Forster, "Public High School and Graduation Rates in the United States," working paper, New York: Manhattan Institute for Policy Research, September 2003.

MPR Associates, Inc., and the Southern Regional Education Board, "The Impact of Intensive Services on Practices and Achievement at High Schools That Work Sites," Phase I evaluation report, Alexandria, Va., November 2001.

National Commission on Excellence in Education, *A Nation At Risk: The Imperative for Education Reform*, Washington D.C., 1983.

Parsad, B., and L. Lewis, *Remedial Education at Degree-Granting Postsecondary Institutions in Fall 2000: Statistical Analysis Report*, National Center for Education Statistics, November 2003. Online at http://nces.ed.gov/pubs2004/2004010.pdf (as of July 1, 2004).

Southern Regional Education Board, "Establishing Benchmarks for New and Maturing HSTW Sites," Atlanta, Ga., 2002. Online at http://www.sreb.org/programs/hstw/Assessment/EstablishingBenchmarks.pdf (as of June 28, 2004).

_____, *The Need for Quality*, Atlanta, Ga., 1981.

SREB—see Southern Regional Education Board.

CHAPTER THIRTEEN

The First Few Years of Edison Schools: Ten Lessons in Getting to Scale

John E. Chubb

Edison Schools is unique among the models discussed in this volume in that it has always been a public company that markets school reform services to schools and districts. Thus, its scale-up strategy is, essentially, a business model for attracting and satisfying its customers—a strategy that reflects its key business practices. The elements of the model include standardizing its product; controlling the recruitment and management of personnel; developing systems by providing professional development and support to enable customers to take advantage of its services; establishing accountability systems that permit evaluation of its services and their use in schools; determining the elements of its services needed to maintain the integrity of its programs and that can—or must—be adjusted to meet local variations; and, as with all businesses, balancing the requirements of market growth against organizational requirements with a view toward increasing profitability.

In 1991, media entrepreneur Chris Whittle launched the Edison Project, the precursor to Edison Schools, Inc., with the goal of running perhaps a thousand schools 10 years later. Edison was to be a business, a company that would offer a "world-class" education to students of all backgrounds for the same money spent on students in public schools. Edison aimed to bring many of the qualities of great businesses—research and development, economies of scale, best practices, and efficiency—to public education. Edison also aimed to do many of the same things as the New American Schools reform initiatives.[1] Edison believed in improving schools through comprehensive

---

[1] Both were launched at about the same time. Chapter Sixteen in this volume addresses some aspects of New American Schools.

school reform, "breaking the mold," and starting schools over. Edison was virtually alone at the time as a for-profit organization, intending from the outset to reach sufficient scale to become a viable business.

In 1992, Whittle recruited some of the most prominent figures in education and technology to convert his vision into reality. Benno C. Schmidt left his prominent post as president of Yale University to lead a research and development project supported with $40 million in private capital. Three years later, Edison had completed a comprehensive school design and had settled on an implementation strategy. The company would contract with charter school boards and public school districts to manage new or existing schools according to its design. It would take full responsibility for everything in the school, from curriculum and instruction to hiring and firing, and would be paid whatever local authorities spent on average per pupil in their public schools. Edison would invest its capital up front on all new instructional materials, technology, and training to give the school a fresh start and would be accountable for student achievement. Contracts would run five years, over which time the company stood to earn a profit and a return on its capital if it managed the schools efficiently.

In fall 2002, Edison was operating 150 schools and serving more than 80,000 students in 23 states and the District of Columbia. Edison was operating schools in virtually every major city in the United States and in 50 smaller communities.[2] From 1995 to 2001, Edison Schools grew at an annual rate well in excess of 50 percent. In 2002, however, the rapid expansion slowed. In 2001, Edison served 74,000 students in 135 schools. The following year, these numbers improved by a net of only 10 percent. Edison parted company with a number of its customers during 2002 and added only one new large customer, the School District of Philadelphia, which gave the company 20 schools to run beginning in September 2002. Although the contract was the largest in the company's history, it fell short of investor and company expectations and generated unusual political acrimony. A

---

[2] A current list of schools can be found on the Edison Schools Web site.

publicly traded company since November 1999, Edison saw its stock rise from its initial public offering price of $18.00 per share to more than $38.00 in early 2001, only to plunge in mid-2002 to less than $1.00 per share. As the 2002 school year opened, Edison faced questions about its viability. The company had not yet posted a profit, and its low stock price made it difficult to raise capital.

Some have already opined that Edison has proven the case against private management of public schools (Steffens and Cookson, 2002). Others have suggested that there are simply no meaningful economies of scale in education (Levin, 2001). Business models and market analogies, they argue, have little relevance to education. These conclusions are premature and wrong. Whatever Edison's fate, and I fully expect it to be positive, education can benefit a great deal from such organizations as Edison. The ups and downs that Edison experienced over its first ten years offer straightforward lessons—and considerable hope—for the improvement of public education through comprehensive reform models and third-party interventions.

Lesson One:
Start with a Proven Reform Model—and Standardize It

During its research and development phase, Edison's leaders became convinced of the need for a truly comprehensive approach to school reform. The best schools in the nation and the world were not distinguished by any single curriculum or instructional methodology. They did not subscribe to a particular model of assessment. They certainly had no agreed-on approach to technology. They did, however, seem to have one thing, or set of things, in common: The best schools were organized around a clear mission instead of a collection of classroom objectives; their teachers and administrators worked together instead of in isolation; and the best schools took responsibility for learning—that is, results—as opposed to mere teaching. Great schools, in other words, looked like great organizations in any field of business or not-for-profit endeavor.[3]

This conclusion, as much as any other during the research and development phase of the project, led Edison to embark on the road of whole-school management. Getting great education results requires great schools, and getting great schools requires running them—not just supplying them, training them, or advising them. At the same time, Edison came to believe that such things as best practices in education clearly existed. A well-run school with bad ideas about reading instruction, for example, will not maximize reading achievement. Edison needed to ensure that the schools it hoped to run would follow best practices. Edison also came to believe that if it were going to run a network or system of schools effectively, it would need to identify which best practices it would support. For example, more than one reading program successfully embodies best reading practices. Edison concluded, however, that no reform organization, at least at the outset, could support too many versions of best practices and still support or manage schools effectively. Thus, Edison reached a second critical conclusion: The schools it would aim to manage would adhere to a reform model that was both thoroughly specified and comprehensive.

As a result of these critical preliminary decisions, Edison's research and development project became a process of identifying and integrating best practices in every area of K–12 education. Four design teams competed to create the most promising model; the teams then came together to produce a unified model, *The Edison School Design* (Edison Project, 1994). Lengthy, though somewhat schematic, this document covered every dimension of schooling: organization, calendar, schedules, curriculum, instruction, assessment, career ladders, professional development, supervision, evaluation, compensation, technology, family and community, budgets,

---

[3] This point of view was influenced by the field observations of the original Edison research team, the formal research by myself and Terry Moe, as reflected in Chubb and Moe (1990); the input of business advisors to the project; and the body of education research known as "effective schools." On the Edison school design process, see Chubb (1997).

and more. In short order, Edison also fleshed out the academic program with national curriculum standards and frameworks, organized around each of the model's first four academies, the Readiness Academy, for preschool; the Primary Academy, for Grades K–2; the Elementary Academy, for Grades 3–5; and the Junior Academy, for Grades 6–8. A high school program was published two years later.

The design and academy books provided the blueprints for the first four Edison partnership schools, launched in 1995. The initial plans worked reasonably well. The schools opened as smoothly as might be expected, given that they were starting from scratch. The early academic results were encouraging.[4] The initial plans had their shortcomings—but not the shortcomings the design team expected. The implementation experience of 1995 suggested that Edison had erred in leaving too many of the details of the design for the school site itself to fill in. Edison had worried during the research and development phase about how to strike a balance between site autonomy and accountability: how much management can tell a school to do and still expect the school site to feel responsible for getting results, instead of just following orders. The Edison school design was actually quite specific, prescribing, for example, certain instructional programs, such as Success For All reading—itself a prescriptive reading program.[5] Yet, by the end of the first year, Edison found that schools were hungry for detailed guidance. In 1996, Edison responded with its first implementation guidelines and operating manuals.

Why were schools so anxious for detail? It takes years to affect student achievement in major and lasting ways, but reform cannot survive the wait. Progress needs to be evident early, or the years required to make a major and lasting difference will never come. Teachers lose enthusiasm and patience if the innovations they are asked to implement do not make a noticeable difference quickly. Teachers spend most of their time in their classrooms unsupervised.

---

[4] See various controlled studies of reading achievement in the first Edison schools conducted by Robert Mislevy of the Educational Testing Service and summarized in Chubb (1998). For a more critical view, see American Federation of Teachers (1998).

[5] See Chapter Five in this volume.

They can and will abandon curricula, tools, or methods that do not seem to be helping their students. In time, as described below, teachers are happy to take on creative responsibility. But not in year one. This is perhaps especially true in schools that serve students with serious academic and social needs. Edison's schools serve primarily low-income and low-achieving students. More than 70 percent of the students in Edison's schools are eligible for the federal government's free or reduced-price lunch program. Teachers opening schools to serve students with great needs look for reformers who can help meet this challenge, not reformers who want the teachers and administrators to do all the work. Moreover, veteran teachers have seen many promising reforms come and go. They can be excused if they are somewhat jaded about the prospects for improvement. Reforms need to be very carefully planned; they need to work; and they need to work fast.

Policymakers, particularly elected policymakers, also have short time horizons. The education landscape is littered with reform ideas that were tried—for too little time—and then abandoned when the next attractive idea came along. Think of some of the big ideas that became passing fads over just the last decade: outcomes-based education; school-based management; whole-language instruction; even comprehensive school reform, which has lost some of its steam in recent years. Electoral pressures place a premium on quick fixes: It is difficult to get reelected pleading with voters to "give our education plan a little more time." The two-year average tenure of contemporary urban school superintendents is a measure of this harsh reality.

So Edison detailed and standardized every element of its design, developing more than 100 scheduling models to convert schools of any given size into an Edison organization of academies, houses, and teaching teams. A special report card, the Quarterly Learning Contract, was created to move all schools nationwide to the use of a unified set of curriculum standards. The longer school day (seven to eight hours in all Edison schools) serves not only to enrich the curriculum for students but also to provide teachers an extra period of professional development every day, supported by a prescribed weekly sequence of house meetings. A career ladder provides every school a differentiated staff of lead teachers and curriculum coordinators, as well as regular teachers. Every school executes the same special-education program of "responsible inclusion." Every school also uses such instructional programs with substantial research bases, documented achievement records, and ample prescription as Success For All,[6] Everyday Math developed by the University of Chicago School Mathematics Project, and the science program developed by Biological Sciences Curriculum Study. The execution of every element of the design—these and many more—is guided by standards that track progress from "beginning" to "developing" to "proficient" to "exemplary," the last two meeting or exceeding the standard.

Edison could not have provided the kind of detailed operating guidance in year one that experience made possible as the project began to expand. Yet it seems unlikely that the project could have grown as quickly as it did had standardization not been attractive to the teachers and administrators in the school. The educators working in Edison schools generally welcomed and sometimes even demanded more direction, and the greater direction accelerated subsequent school openings. Scaling up required a model that could produce results quickly and reliably in many different states and communities, and that model, fortuitously, benefited from standardization. It is possible to open a few schools in a hands-on fashion, and the early versions of any model should be done this way. Opening many schools, however, requires standardization. Edison did open many—eight schools in 1996; another 13 in 1997; another 26 in 1998; and, for each of the following three years, at least 50 percent more new schools than the total previously in existence. For many years, educators in Edison schools have spoken knowingly about what is "on-design" or "off-design," a clear indication that they are internalizing the standards. Had these standards not helped to produce sound schools and solid academic gains quickly and reliably, they could not have been developed—and Edison could not have reached scale as smoothly as it did.

---

[6] See Chapter Five in this volume.

Lesson Two:
Hire and Fire Your Own Principals and Teachers

No school reform can succeed without the cooperation of the principals and teachers who must carry it out. This much is obvious. What should policymakers do to ensure cooperation? Public school systems generally rely on authority. School boards, state legislatures, and the U.S. Congress adopt policies and ask their respective administrative arms—school districts, state education departments, and the U.S. Department of Education—to carry them out. Bureaucratic rules and regulations are then promulgated to put the policies into action. Ultimately, district administrators must ensure that principals and teachers carry out the mandated reforms. If the school district is lucky, the reforms will be those that educators have been asking for or perhaps even reforms that educators have been trying to put into law. Frequently, perhaps even normally, school reform is a policymaker reaction to practices in the schools that they, the authorities, want principals and teachers to change. If it is to succeed, reform must often overcome reluctance or even opposition in the schools. Policymakers have the advantage of employing the principals and teachers who need to bring reform about, and, as employees, principals and teachers can be required—and even rewarded—to get the job of change done. But change is really not so easy. The difficulty—and it is a great one—is that principals and teachers will *comply* with reform, that is, follow the letter of the new law, but not dedicate themselves to achieving *results*.[7] Schools can be forced to use a new reading program—as they are all the time, for example—but they cannot be forced to use it effectively.

Comprehensive school reform faces the most daunting implementation challenge because it aims to change so many things in schools and because the "authority" leading the change is not a school district or a public authority at all. Instead, it is merely a reform organization that policymakers have authorized to get a job done.

---

[7] On the unintended consequences of top-down control of schools, see Chubb and Moe (1990).

Edison was dubious about this arrangement from the start. Edison's decision to become an education management organization was predicated on the belief that successful implementation of something as difficult as comprehensive reform required at least as much authority as public school districts had, especially the ability to hire and fire principals and teachers.

Edison actually wanted something more. Edison believes that schools can succeed with a variety of education models, so long as they have certain essentials in place. All the models that New American Schools (the current incarnation of the New American Schools Development Corporation) offers have substantial merit. Edison also believes that different models will better suit the talents, experience, and values of different educators. Educators will do a better job working with a reform model and helping students learn if they are comfortable with or even enthusiastic about the model. Reform has the best chance to succeed, then, when reformers have the authority to carry it out and when educators have the right to choose whether they want to participate in it. Edison therefore asks public authorities for two controls over personnel: the right to hire and fire and the right to seek voluntary participants in its program.

These requests take different forms, depending on the education venue. In charter schools, Edison normally hires the principal jointly with the public charter board. The principal, with Edison's input and oversight, then hires the teachers. The charter board adopts the policies for evaluating, retaining, promoting, and terminating teachers, but Edison can and typically does supply these policies to the board. At this juncture, all but two of Edison's charter schools were opened under Edison's management, so there were no issues of buy-in among existing staff: The original staff members were Edison hires. About one-third of Edison's 150 schools are charters.

In school districts, matters are more complicated. As in charter schools, Edison asks for and usually receives the authority to choose principals, with district participation or sign-off. With a few exceptions, districts have honored this request and have not imposed principals that Edison would prefer not to have. Edison generally also has the authority to choose teachers—or to have its principals choose teachers. Often, these choices must go through district screening processes or, if a collective bargaining agreement is in place, must adhere to seniority rules. In practice, however, these constraints have not posed major problems. The main issue with respect to teacher hiring and firing is voluntary transfer. Edison requests the right to transfer back to the district, without prejudice, anyone that the principal believes is not a good fit with the school. Such transfers are not about performance; there are evaluation procedures for dealing with performance problems. Transfers for fit or compatibility are about providing the school the power to build a staff that buys into a coherent education model and is willing to work together to bring about change. Edison has had mixed success in getting district cooperation with this request. Small districts sometimes cannot honor it because other schools do not always have space to accommodate transfers. In districts with strong unions, the district may not be able to negotiate a waiver from collective bargaining restrictions on such transfers. Edison has, however, been able to secure the power for principals to transfer teachers in perhaps half of its district contracts.

Edison's authority to hire, fire, and transfer, whether circumscribed or not, tends to give rise to informal influence that, taken together with formal power, provides Edison the wherewithal to build and maintain supportive faculties. When Edison is awarded a contract to manage district schools, principals and teachers in them who do not care for Edison's reform model tend to leave voluntarily. Or, if principals and teachers decide they would like to give the design a try for a year, they tend to request new assignments voluntarily if the program is not to their liking. School districts often try to minimize transfers initially by assigning schools to Edison whose teachers or principals have expressed interest in working with Edison. Edison's seven schools in Las Vegas were awarded through such a process. Districts have also assigned Edison their most-troubled schools, in an effort to turn them around, giving principals and teachers no say whatsoever. The district selected the 20 Edison schools in Philadelphia because of their chronic academic failings—and half the principals and teachers opted to leave.

Edison has taken advantage of its personnel authority by organizing national recruitment systems for principals and teachers. Edison recruits principals through national advertising and teachers through a national Web site, as well as through college job fairs, including elite colleges and universities. Recruiting educators who know the Edison design and who want to teach in Edison schools increases initial buy-in to the program and facilitates implementation. Hiring Edison recruits also minimizes the need for Edison to rely on authority to get the job done—even though authority, in the end, is what makes all the other sources of influence possible.

Finally, any organization that wants to get to scale must do a good job at whatever it is promising to get done—helping students achieve in Edison's case—or clients will not buy or use whatever the organization is offering. The power to hire, fire, and transfer is vital to the success of any organization—especially a growing one. A small-scale operation may get results through hands-on management of even the most recalcitrant and empowered employees. A large-scale operation needs to be able to count on employees faithfully acting in the best interest of the organization without a great deal of hand-holding or direct supervision. That kind of commitment does not come without the organization having the ability to decide who works in the organization.

Lesson Three:
Build Effective and Efficient Support Systems

Schools are notoriously poorly supported. Teachers complain that they cannot get supplies. Principals complain that district offices do not answer their phones or return phone calls. The best urban schools in America are often those with the ingenuity to work around the system. There is little agreement how much of every education dollar the education bureaucracy—or the support system—spends, but few argue that the system is either a model of efficiency or effectiveness. The education business has been no better. The schools obtain most educational materials—textbooks, software, and other instructional programs—from publishers, who provide as little training as possible in how to use the materials. The reason for this is that publishing provides a high profit margin, while professional development, which is labor intensive, does not. School districts do not help matters, allocating very few days in the calendar or little of the budget for training.

Comprehensive school reform requires tremendous support. You do not change everything in a school successfully by sending the school piles of materials and a bunch of how-to manuals. You need to provide direct support. As a reform builds to scale, the support needs to be systematized. The first schools with which any reform organization works are likely to receive the close attention and loving care of the founders of the organization. The early support need not be delivered according to any well-thought-out plan. Indeed, the first schools should provide learning experiences from which the support systems are built. As more schools join the reform, however, support systems become vital.

Edison's support system is structured as a classic matrix. Principals and schools are supervised by regional vice presidents of school operations, who are, like principals, responsible for delivering quality in every area of school operations—including student achievement, design implementation, and financial management. The schools and the school operations division are then supported by other divisions that provide specific services. The largest of these is education, which provides curriculum, instruction, assessment, student services, student management, and something Edison calls "student achievement." Others include technology, finance, legal, supply-chain management, and human resources. The structure of the support system is less important than the services it delivers and how the schools' experience them.

The most important service that the system delivers is professional development, for both teachers and principals. Edison provides roughly four weeks of preservice training for every new principal and two weeks of preservice training for every new teacher. We provide this training not only when the school first opens as an Edison school but also for every new principal or teacher. The level of commitment that Edison has made to training has been absolutely critical to taking this organization to scale and maintaining the quality of the schools. During each of the summers of 2001 and 2002, Edison trained 2,000 teachers, primarily in teaching academies held throughout the nation.

Edison also provides education site support. A staff of national curriculum coordinators visits schools both regularly and as needed, directly helping teachers and principals implement the program according to the school's performance standards. The coordinators specialize in reading, writing, math, science, social studies, and special subjects. In addition, a team of student achievement directors is deployed regionally, one director to every eight schools, helping schools plan for high achievement and helping them execute their plans. Edison provides similarly deployed support for technology, student services, and financial management. Vice presidents of regional operations oversee the support system for their schools, ensuring that they get the support they need and that the support is effective.

Having learned that schools need ample and continual support, Edison has also learned that such support must be of the highest possible quality. This goes not only for professional quality, or what one might call effectiveness, but also for efficiency. On the quality side, Edison has found that promoting from within may well be a panacea. By far, the most-effective coordinators, directors, and even part-time trainers are educators who have learned Edison's program by doing it, and doing it successfully, themselves. Many key members of Edison's support system began as teachers or principals in Edison schools, and the numbers increase every year. As Edison scales up, it needs to balance the support system's need for talented insiders against the need for such individuals to stay in their schools. Another key lesson about quality is the need for local applicability, but that will be discussed below.

On the efficiency side of the ledger, schools are hungry for a support system that does all the so-called "little things" right. Delivering everything a school needs to get started—all-new curriculum materials, technology, and school supplies—and delivering everything on time, in the right quantities, and ready for distribution to the right classrooms are huge logistical tasks. Because school systems do not open many new schools in any given year, they rarely have to tackle such tasks. Even so, school systems do not have stellar reputations for keeping schools supplied. Edison supplies more new schools per year than any school system in the United States. Getting this right has been one of the company's toughest operational tasks, but getting it right has earned enormous gratitude and support from educators, who are completely unaccustomed to having all the materials that they need when they need them. On the other hand, when Edison occasionally trips up and fails to get every book to a school on time, it can easily lose the support of teachers, who have often experienced more than their fair share of broken promises from reformers. The same reward-to-risk ratio applies to such services as running conferences, getting bills paid, providing reports, and even answering phone calls and emails. Great organizations put in place the systems to provide quality services, however mundane. Edison has been trying to learn this lesson as rapidly as possible, because it is critical to scaling up. Yet it is a lesson that education reform organizations might not even have on their radar screens until it is too late. Reformers tend to be all about education. Scaling up is about education, of course, but it is also about building an effective and efficient organization.

Lesson Four:
Build Site Capacity

While a support system for comprehensive school reform is vital, no comprehensive reform can hope to grow unless it brings about sustainable change at the school site. The support system can and must provide the guidance and reinforcement without which schools will slip back into the ways of their local school district. Sociologists often observe that schools are products of their environments (Weick, 1976). Without a strong support system providing clear and different direction—without letup—schools will take their cues from their local political, social, and educational environment and gradually return to their local ways, leaving the comprehensive reform behind as just another passing fashion. The support system cannot, however, do it all. A support system that does not nurture and breed effective supporters within every school will not grow to any scale.

School-based support is important for several reasons. First, the improvement of educational practice—that is, bringing about better teaching and learning—is an ongoing task. Teachers improve by trying new ideas, getting immediate feedback, and going back into their classes to try again. Teachers learn from watching other teachers teach. On-the-job training is by far the most important kind of training. For this to happen, schools must have people on staff to provide feedback and coaching every day. Second, no organization can be highly successful unless its own personnel—not external advisors or authorities—take responsibility for results. Third, there are political considerations. For comprehensive reform to take hold and mature, it needs active and reliable support at the school site. Schools lose personnel through normal attrition. Thus, a reform will not be sustained if it depends on the personal influence of key individuals. A comprehensive reform has no chance to scale, for example, if its presence on various campuses stems from the advocacy of a particular principal or cadre of teachers. The reform organization must have a way to maintain enthusiastic support for the reform at the school site even as the cast of characters changes. Finally, there is economics. Public school budgets are not going to cover the cost of a reform strategy that requires enormous external support systems. Philanthropy cannot be the answer either—at least not for permanent school improvement. Economics demands that schools develop the capacity to carry out reforms without a lot of external support.

How has Edison tried to build site capacity? To begin, Edison reorganizes the school. Every teacher is given two periods for professional development every day. One of these periods is reserved for "house team" meetings and the coverage of specific professional development agendas. For example, one day every week is for curriculum training, another is for data analysis, another is for addressing student social and behavioral issues, and another for developing technology skills. The time and agendas for professional development give teachers regular daily opportunities to work with colleagues and get better at what they do. The reorganization also provides for special teacher positions in every school. Lead teachers head house teams and mentor teammates in classroom management and pedagogy. Curriculum coordinators provide site-based training and classroom observation for each of the content areas. Lead teachers and curriculum coordinators are trained by Edison's national system to provide quality on-site support. Edison also sustains them—through monthly conference calls, national and regional meetings, and on-site interactions with Edison's achievement directors and national curriculum coordinators, who are deployed throughout the country. These system personnel work, then, not only to provide direct services to teachers and principals but also to build and maintain the capacity of specialists on every school site to provide expertise locally. Because Edison builds time into the daily schedule for teachers to play these critical roles, the work actually gets done. Moreover, because the site responsibilities are vested in teachers, who are paid stipends for the extra duties, this organizational solution adds no school bureaucracy or cost and is a powerful boost to teacher morale and professionalism.

Lesson Five: Establish Clear and Simple Accountability Systems

A standardized design, an efficient support system, a strategy for developing leadership at every school site—these are all part of the *process* of reforming schools. Ultimately, however, it is not the process that is of greatest interest; it is the results. Are the processes yielding better outcomes for students? Are students achieving more than they would have otherwise?

Over the course of Edison's first decade, it became increasingly easy to get teachers and administrators to be concerned about academic results. As state after state has put extensive testing and accountability systems into place, educators could not help but pay attention to student achievement results. The heightened sense of accountability for test scores can, however, be a double-edged sword for comprehensive school reform. On the one hand, it increases the pressure on local officials to adopt aggressive reforms, such as the comprehensive models, and increases the pressure on educators working within the models to get results. On the other hand, it creates an impatience for results that may cause participants in comprehensive efforts to seek quicker fixes.

Edison has come to believe that the heightened reliance on test scores for accountability can be a major plus for its business, for two reasons. Most obviously, Edison's model is all about helping students, regardless of background, achieve higher standards. If it is successful at that crucial objective, Edison should grow as a reform organization and business. Equally important, Edison has always espoused accountability as a basic organizational principle. All Edison contracts with school districts or charter boards provide for termination if test scores fail to improve. Edison wants to be held strictly accountable for results, but the accountability does not stop there. Edison, in turn, holds its principals strictly accountable for results—and all system personnel as well.

The results that matter, however, are not just test scores. This is where Edison has learned how to dull the dangerous edge of the test-score sword. Edison has developed an accountability system, known as the "five points of accountability," for use throughout its organization. The results that matter to Edison include student achievement, customer satisfaction, design implementation, financial management, and system growth. Each of these outcomes is gauged against specific standards with four levels of possible accomplishment. "Stars" are awarded for each point of accountability. A four-star rating represents exemplary performance; a three-star rating means proficient performance; and so forth. For student achievement, proficient performance means making gains in three quarters of all tested grade levels and subjects, with an average level of gain that will take a school to the upper end of grade-level achievement within five years. For design implementation, a proficient performance requires an average rating of proficient across all Edison school performance standards. For system growth, a proficient performance is based on school attendance at all Edison conferences, as well as other measures of school commitment to the reform organization. Accountability for design implementation and system growth discourages schools from abandoning comprehensive reform and embracing tempting quick fixes for student achievement.

Because Edison controls personnel in its schools, it can use its five points of accountability to reward and motivate performance. Principals and teachers are frequently offered bonuses, which are based on the five points of accountability. Schools receive a weighted average of their star scores on each point of accountability. Student achievement is weighted most heavily, but everything counts. Edison also runs school recognition programs—most prominently, its Four Star Achievement awards—which schools have come to prize.

Edison is fortunate among the comprehensive reform organizations that are able to hold schools accountable for their performance. Reform is ordinarily a voluntary enterprise. Schools sign on to a reform and make their best effort, but few, if any, consequences redound to the school if the effort is inadequate. The reform organization can walk away, of course, but that is not much leverage. Accountability is also critical for scaling up. If a reform organization must micromanage the success of its schools, it will never get to scale; the system costs would be prohibitive. A strong accountability system makes it possible to place much of the responsibility for success on the school instead of the system. That is an efficient organizational solution.

Lesson Six:
Establish Strong Measurement Systems

The organizational mantra goes: "what gets measured gets done, what gets measured well gets done well." Edison has certainly come to see the wisdom of this view. The standards that Edison has developed and the accountability system are useless without strong measures to support them. Edison has therefore invested in developing a number of proprietary measurement tools to support these systems. In education, measurement systems are still in their infancy. The marketplace has not yet provided educators the kinds of measurement tools routinely used in other fields, particularly business. Chris Whittle, Edison's chief executive officer, has frequently observed that modern shipping companies know much more about their packages than schools know about their students. Federal Express can tell a customer the precise location of a package in transit, despite shipping millions of packages a day. A school system may be able to tell a parent where their child is physically, but they will not be able to tell them with much precision where their child is educationally.

Edison has tried to provide its teachers and administrators with a high level of easily accessible and useful information on a regular basis. This effort takes many forms, but two merit special mention. First and most important, Edison has developed a monthly benchmark assessment system. This online tool provides teachers and administrators feedback every month on the achievement of all students as measured against end-of-grade tested state standards. Each month, students take short tests of 20 or so items in reading, language arts, and math in the school's computer lab or on computers in the back of classrooms. Edison has written all test questions to mimic the kinds of questions that students will face on their high-stakes tests. The distribution of items each month reflects the emphasis that the state or national test places on the particular standard, strand, or objective. Teachers and administrators can pull up reports online that show the specific strengths and weaknesses of students, subjects, grade levels, and classrooms. These reports enable teachers to adjust instruction regularly—instead of once a year after high-stakes test results come back. Regional administrators can also quickly identify the schools that need additional support and of what kind.

A second tool is Edison's monthly achievement profile (MAP). Comprehensive school reform is complex. Reform organizations must find ways to help schools cut through the complexity and remember what needs to be done. Edison, like most reform organizations, has thick manuals for teachers and administrators. Realistically, however, this kind of detail needs to serve as a reference resource, not a daily guide. To help administrators and teachers manage the necessary detail, Edison has developed an online tool that tracks the status of design implementation. The MAP provides a one-page summary of such categories as the status of student achievement planning, data analysis, reading and math instruction, teacher training, student discipline, and benchmark scores. Principals and teachers can drill down from the one-page summary to see what has been done or needs to be done to take their reform efforts to proficient levels and beyond. The MAP is populated on a monthly basis by achievement directors and regional and school-based coordinators. The MAP serves as a convenient reminder to school personnel of the requirements of the comprehensive model. It is a useful indicator for principals and support personnel of the assistance the schools need most.

It is inconceivable that a reform of any scale could be managed without a strong measurement system. The stronger the measures, the more the system can depend on school sites to get the work done, and the more strategic the system can be about supporting schools. If measures, and accountability for them, are weak, the system must invest a great deal of time and resources in direct supervision—an imprecise and very costly form of management. Schools welcome strong measures. Schools are empowered by the ability to gauge their progress and take responsibility for it. Systems can scale when the units that constitute them become self-sufficient. Measurement is a critical piece of that process. Important as measurement is, however, public education is a long way from developing the requisite measurement tools. Investing in such tools has been perhaps the most-important expenditure that Edison has made in securing its future.

Lesson Seven:
Get Measurable Results—Fast

When Edison was founded and took shape in the early 1990s, accountability in public education was relatively weak. States were just beginning to develop measurable academic standards. Most states tested for minimum competency. Few states specified any real consequences for schools that performed well or performed poorly on standardized tests. The prevailing attitude among educators was that the tests reflected the achievement of the students, not that of the school.

Edison's goal, like that of many comprehensive reform organizations, was to help students reach high academic standards. Like most serious reformers, Edison believed that meaningful achievement, the kind that lays a foundation for a lifetime of learning—the kind of learning that will show up on any test that may come a person's way—is a product of schoolwide efforts sustained over many years. This belief is even stronger for achievement in places with poor academic performance, deeply rooted in generations of economic and educational need. Edison's reform model tries to strengthen every conceivable area of a school's performance, to envelop teachers and students in a new culture of high achievement.

Because Edison's model is ambitious, Edison asked customers for five-year contracts to ensure time would be available to bring about the tough but requisite changes. In its first years, Edison even cautioned that results would not be immediate, that test scores might even take a step backward for a year while all the changes in the school gelled and took effect. In the early 1990s, such caveats were acceptable to policymakers and gave comfort to teachers and principals. Ten years later, impatience is the name of the game. Every state now has a testing system in place (or under rapid development) that includes high standards, aligned tests, and meaningful consequences. The quality of these systems varies widely, but they are all moving in the same direction. The federal government has accelerated change with the passage of the No Child Left Behind Act of 2001, which mandates testing all students in reading and math at every grade level from three to eight and demands adequate yearly progress. While no state will punish a school for one year of weak results, the branding of a school as a potential failure begins the first year a school slips up. There is no longer much room for a deliberate approach to improvement. Principals and teachers know and fear this, and they are rapidly losing whatever patience they might have had for comprehensive efforts a few years ago.

Edison faces double pressure. Unlike most other comprehensive reform organizations, Edison is interested in a level of control over the reform process that is threatening to those traditionally in control. Individuals and groups, such as teacher unions, who feel their control over the schools will be diminished by Edison's role oppose the outsourcing of school management. Added to this concern with control is Edison's for-profit status, which some oppose for ideological reasons. Taken together, these factors can create strong resistance to Edison's efforts. Edison aims to work cooperatively with all the interests in local schools and often does so successfully. But those who remain opposed to Edison find test scores to be potent weapons on the political battlefield. The opposition regularly tries to attack Edison schools for their academic performance, even if the schools have been open only a year and had been turned over to Edison after generations of academic failure.[8]

Early on, Edison stayed its original course and aimed to produce results as quickly as possible, though not necessarily in the first year. By the late 1990s, politics forced Edison to change course. While Edison did not alter its fundamental design, it added elements to ensure that academic progress registered quickly on official measures. Edison developed a model for student achievement planning that required all schools to employ a set of proven strategies to ensure maximum measurable returns from the design. As part of this effort Edison developed a unique aligning-and-embedding strategy, supported by extensive training, to link its academic design to state testing objectives. We added the position of achievement director to the support system to help schools devise and implement their achievement plans and established the benchmark system to help schools take the guesswork out of teaching students the skills and content they need to demonstrate on high-stakes tests.

The objective of all this effort was to help schools provide students with the kind of education that Edison has always envisioned: deep and enduring. Edison does not believe a comprehensive reform can scale if its academic gains are short-lived. If Edison helps a school bump up its test scores for a year or two, only to see them decline thereafter, Edison will lose its customers. The only way to avoid this outcome is to focus on building strong schools comprehensively,

---

[8] The American Federation of Teachers has published perhaps the most blatant examples of snap judgments. For example, see American Federation of Teachers (2000).

while ensuring that schools get the measurable results that supporters and opponents need to see.

Lesson Eight:
Satisfy Your Customers

Smart businesses work as hard to keep existing customers as they do to attract new customers. Great businesses are famous for high-quality customer service, the kind of attention to customer needs that keeps them coming back for more. Quality customer service simply makes good business sense. It is much cheaper to keep an existing customer than to win over new ones. Yet businesses often get this sensible practice wrong, for many reasons. Sales forces are rewarded for signing new customers. Operating divisions are rewarded for delivering a service on or under a budget. Thus, customers sometimes fail to receive the attention they deserve, but such practices cannot continue indefinitely. A business cannot grow forever—get to scale and beyond—if it loses customers at an appreciable rate.

Edison's record on customer satisfaction has two distinct sides. Parents and teachers constitute one set of customers. Edison has contracted with one of the nation's leading quality management polling firms, Harris Interactive, to measure parent, teacher, and student satisfaction in all its schools every year since Edison schools opened in 1995. The polling data come with thorough analyses of the causes of satisfaction and dissatisfaction in the schools. Principals use the data to improve customer satisfaction. The record of Edison schools in promoting customer satisfaction is excellent. Nearly 90 percent of all parents in Edison schools rate their overall satisfaction with their school an "A" or "B." This level of satisfaction is almost 20 percent higher than the national average in public schools. Indeed, the *New York Times*, no supporter of Edison schools, lauded the schools for their parent satisfaction in a summer 2002 review of Edison's school performance record.[9] Teacher and student satisfaction are also very solid, especially given the tough socioeconomic circumstances in which most Edison schools operate.

The other set of customers consists of the school districts and charter boards that are Edison's bottom-line customers. If Edison's customer satisfaction has generally been stellar at the school level, it has been inadequate at the policymaking level. Even if parents flock to Edison schools and teachers sing their praises, the schools will not have long futures unless the officials who pay the bills like them too. As of fall 2002, Edison still held 45 of the 52 school management contracts it has signed. Maintaining this record will require much greater effort than Edison has expended to date. Edison is probably not alone among comprehensive reform organizations in needing to tend to policymaking customers.

The challenges of satisfying policymakers are many. First, the political composition of boards changes frequently. A board that supports Edison can quickly be replaced by one that does not. Edison experienced this political about-face most visibly with its school in San Francisco. Were it not for the strong support of parents and teachers, the board majority that took over in 2000 would have removed Edison from its school. As it turned out, the board compromised and transferred the school's charter, and the contract with Edison, from the district to the state. Similarly, opponents who may have wanted to prevent a board from signing a contract with Edison may continue to try to build a case against Edison as it operates. Edison experienced, and successfully weathered, such opposition in Peoria, Illinois—again largely through the support of parents and teachers. Edison must also deal with the ambivalence that districts feel when Edison schools succeed. While districts certainly want the best for their students, they sometimes have trouble taking satisfaction in success that a reform organization has produced. Charter boards present their own challenge. After Edison has completed the tough work of getting the school off the ground and performing successfully,

---

[9] The national satisfaction level can be gleaned from the Gallup Poll, which uses the same question wording as Harris. See also Henriques and Steinberg (2002).

boards sometimes develop an interest in running schools themselves. Edison lost its school in Boston after seven years primarily for this reason.

The challenges of keeping customers as the reform organization scales up are not unique to Edison. New reform ideas come along. Decisionmakers change. Any reform idea can fall prey to politics. Edison learned that it is not enough to build a local constituency for its schools. The support of parents and teachers is certainly crucial, and building this support is an important task for any reform organization. Parents and teachers are the day-to-day focus of the reformers. If a reform organization is going to keep its customers, grow to scale, and sustain itself for the long haul, it must pay as much attention to its customers as it did in striking the original deal. At Edison, this attention took an organized form in 2002, when the company created high-level positions for "relationship managers." These individuals are responsible for ensuring that the needs of the ultimate customer are met. This may seem an overly simple solution, but it is also simple for such reform organizations as Edison to overlook the politics that can put their work at peril. Recognizing this necessity and paying close attention to it are important steps in the right direction, steps that any organization with hope for a substantial future must take.

Lesson Nine: Adjust To Local Norms

Schooling is an intensely local enterprise, especially in the United States. In any locale, schooling has to build deep local trust. Parents cannot be expected to turn their children over to institutions that seem remote. American parents have especially strong expectations in this regard. Public schools are locally controlled. Some 15,000 school districts run the public schools across America. Despite the increase in federal and state influence over the last 50 years, the schools are still locally controlled—both in reality and in public mythology.

Local control presents a special challenge for comprehensive reform models. These models have strong and complete views of how schools should function—what they should teach, how they should teach, how they should organize, and obviously much more. These models insist on a high level of fidelity to their reforms. Some of the models—including Edison—have an identity. A school becomes known, for example, as an "Edison school" or a "Success For All school," to cite just two. In running against the grain of local control, comprehensive reforms bring unique strength to local schools. Principals and teachers learn best practices and how to integrate them from organizations with the resources to bring information to schools that they could never acquire on their own. Principals and teachers benefit from the opportunity to interact with and learn from educators across the country, unified by their shared commitment to a particular brand of reform. But comprehensive reform can also cut coarsely across the local grain. Nationalization and standardization can desensitize a school to the need to make local adjustments—educationally, politically, and culturally. To reach national scale, a comprehensive reform must learn how to balance its national standards with diverse local circumstances.

Edison had to learn this lesson in myriad ways. We had to compromise some of our goals for education content. For example, we had to abandon our early views on high standards for secondary science and social science because state standards were often at odds with the views of the national experts and national professional organizations on which Edison relied to build its core curriculum. Edison sometimes had to allow schools to take cues from local experts to prepare for standardized tests. Edison preaches embedded test preparation and actively discourages the isolated variety. However, Edison would lose the support of its teachers, and run the risk of short-term embarrassment, if it failed to let its schools try out the ideas that other local educators were embracing. Local customs all tend to support specific approaches to special education and bilingual education. On the latter, the evidence does not validate any one approach, so we have been open to local variation. On special education, however, we come down solidly behind responsible inclusion—a practice that, while all but dictated by federal law, is resisted by some local districts. Edison's pervasively positive approach to student discipline also meets some amount of local opposition—particularly in certain urban environments, in which police and paraprofessionals have come to play a major role in discipline and in which teachers have won the right to do little beyond their own classrooms.

Reform organizations cannot be blind to the potential value of new ideas wherever they may arise. No organization can afford not to learn, both from its own experience and from the experiences of others. Openness to local problem-solving is a must. At the same time, a reform organization must know what it stands for and must not compromise the integrity of its design. Too much compromise produces educational mush—the very stuff for which comprehensive reforms are supposed to be the antidote. Maintaining integrity is tough in the heavily compromised world of public education, especially in local arenas where the final compromises get struck. If they stick to their guns, national reform organizations risk accusations of inflexibility at best and arrogance at worst. "Who are these outsiders to tell us how to run our schools?" is a refrain that Edison and other national reform organizations must somehow counter. We aim to overcome this resistance by courting local teachers and principals and by building site capacity—by having local educators, not a bunch of "suits" from New York, represent "Edison." Deft compromise is required to make local educators embrace the design as their own, while keeping the elements essential to its success intact. But compromise is essential: No comprehensive reform organization can hope to reach national scale without balancing its interest in promulgating best practices with the local community's interest in controlling its own schools.

Lesson Ten:
Find a Better Balance of Growth, Systems, and Profitability

How fast should a reform grow? This question is central to any education reform organization with a mission beyond its own backyard. The answer may differ somewhat depending on whether the organization is set up on a for-profit or not-for-profit basis, but basic issues are the same regardless of bottom-line economics. No reform can grow to scale unless it gets its basic product—or educational model—correct and then develops the operating systems necessary to replicate the model reliably around the country. Grow too fast, and the model will fail. The first schools can succeed through the tender loving care of the founders. Once hands-on management becomes impossible, however, the reform organization had better have systems in place to support the schools. The schools will fail if more are added to the system than the system is prepared to support.

On the other hand, there is such a thing as growing too slowly. No reform organization can produce results on a large scale without substantial systems, without infrastructure. This infrastructure takes resources to build. Not-for-profit reform organizations rely on philanthropy of one form or another to get started. For-profit organizations, such as Edison, rely on venture capital. In either case, the funds are limited. Investors want to see evidence that the organization can sustain itself with its own revenues. If a reform organization grows too slowly, it will require external capital to fund its operations longer than anyone is likely to be willing to pay. The business calculation, then, is to determine the growth rate that will allow the necessary operating systems to be built, the model to yield good results, and the organization to sustain itself without additional outside funds.

In retrospect, Edison may have chosen to grow too rapidly. Edison's annual growth rate of more than 50 percent from 1995 to 2002 required regular and substantial infusions of outside capital. The capital enabled Edison to build the infrastructure to help its schools achieve substantial success. At the end of 2001, 84 percent of our schools were achieving at higher levels than when they began. Schools were improving their test scores an average of five national percentiles annually on norm-referenced tests and 6 percentage points annually on criterion-referenced tests. These rates of gain exceeded those of any of the 50 largest school systems in America (Henriques and Steinberg, 2002). Not every Edison school was doing well, of course, but the company was fulfilling its education mission more than satisfactorily.

There was, however, one significant problem. Edison had essentially reached scale without being able to pay its own way. The company was not profitable. Without outside capital, it could not make the annual investments necessary to open new schools. This was not a serious problem so long as Edison was growing in excess of 50 percent per year. It was literally only a matter of time until the costs of Edison's infrastructure—only about 14 percent of revenue in fiscal 2002—would fall low enough as a percentage of revenue to yield profits. Infrastructure costs had fallen steadily as a percentage of revenues throughout Edison's existence. With Edison growing at a high rate, investors saw real future value in the company's revenue stream.

Once Edison failed to meet its annual growth targets, as it did in 2002 when a large and widely predicted contract with the School District of Philadelphia came in at less than half its expected size, investors rapidly lost confidence. Edison's stock plunged, and capital for opening new schools became scarce. By fall 2002, Edison had raised the capital necessary to open new schools in Philadelphia and elsewhere, but it was rapidly retooling its business plan. Additional outside capital would be difficult to raise. Future growth would need to be funded from the company's own resources, which would only be available if the company became profitable. Summer 2002 found Edison reorganizing, seeking efficiencies, and aiming to produce operating profits in the 2003 fiscal year. Edison also found itself scrambling to repair a reputation tarnished by its failings as a business.

In retrospect, it is easy to say that Edison should have grown more slowly and sought profitability sooner. Edison's strategy did enable the organization to reach economic scale, to build the systems necessary to operate schools successfully—most often impoverished and previously failing schools. The question, then, is less whether we should have chosen a different road to national scale and more what we do with the scale we have achieved. The lessons that we have learned are all lessons that the company can put and is putting to use at this very instant. They are lessons that not-for-profit, as well as for-profit, organizations can put to effective use. In the end, they suggest that good systems can produce good schools—and that together they can make for good business.

References

American Federation of Teachers, *Student Achievement in Edison Schools: Mixed Results in an Ongoing Enterprise*, Washington, D.C., May 1998.

_____, *Trends in Student Achievement for Edison Schools, Inc.: The Emerging Track Record*, Washington, D.C., October 2000.

Chubb, J. E., "Lessons in School Reform From the Edison Project," in D. Ravitch and J. P. Viteritti, eds., *New Schools for a New Century*, New Haven, Conn.: Yale University Press, 1997, pp. 86–122.

_____, "The Performance of Privately Managed Schools: An Early Look at the Edison Project," in P. E. Peterson and B. C. Hassel, eds., *Learning from School Choice*, Washington, D.C.: Brookings Institution Press, 1998, pp. 213–248.

Chubb, J. E., and T. M. Moe, *Politics, Markets, and America's Schools*, Washington, D.C.: Brookings Institution Press, 1990.

The Edison Project, *Edison School Design*, New York: 1994.

Edison Schools, Web site, undated. Online at http://www.edisonschools.com/home/home.cfm (as of June 24, 2004).

Henriques, D., and J. Steinberg, "Operator of Public Schools in Settlement with S.E.C.," *New York Times*, May 15, 2002, p. C1.

Levin, H. M., "The Bear Market," *Education Matters*, Vol. 1, No. 1, 2001, pp. 6–15.

Steffens, H., and P. J. Cookson, Jr., "Limitations of the Market Model," *Education Week*, Vol. 21, No. 43, 2002, pp. 48, 51.

Weick, K. E., "Education Systems as Loosely Coupled Systems," *Administrative Science Quarterly*, No. 21, 1976, pp. 1–19.

School Districts as Learning Organizations: A Strategy for Scaling Education Reform

Thomas K. Glennan, Jr., and Lauren B. Resnick

Unlike comprehensive school reform models that begin with a single school or even a small set of schools, the work of the Institute for Learning, according to the authors, begins at scale. That is, it begins with the assumption that school districts are both the seat of accountability for school reform and the organizational entities that can control what happens in large numbers of schools—by influencing curriculum, providing professional development opportunities, and establishing performance standards. Thus, the institute's approach to scale-up is both "top down," in that it requires the engagement of high-level school officials, and "bottom up," in that it helps these officials identify the means to improve performance in the schools for which they are responsible. The direct services the institute provides—professional development activities, teaching tools, and systems for measuring outcomes—help to build the organizational capacity schools and districts need to meet performance goals.[1]

The problem addressed in this paper, as in this volume, is how to take ambitious proposals for education reform to scale—that is, how to convert demonstrations of successful models of teaching and learning into normative practices. Put another way, we seek ways of making

[1] Preparation of this chapter was supported by grants from the Ford and Wallace Foundations. While the authors are responsible for what is written, we have drawn upon the expertise of colleagues. The Resident and National Fellows of the Institute for Learning, Rosita Apodaca, Donna DiPrima Bickel, Victoria Bill, Sue Goodwin, Judy Johnston, Patti Magruder, Stephanie McConachie, Sally Mentor-Hay, Donna Micheaux, Annette Seitz, Judith Simmons, Lillie Sipp, and Kathleen McCarthy Young, made important contributions to the conception and writing of this paper. RAND colleagues Gina Ikemoto, Kerri Kerr, and Julie Marsh carried out the fieldwork on which many of the observations attributed to RAND are based.

powerful, high-demand teaching and learning for the full spectrum of young people the rule, rather than an applauded exception.

It is difficult to overestimate the pedagogical and organizational challenges embedded in this goal. Helping teachers within a school implement effective instructional practice is a major challenge, and the idea of doing so across a significant number of schools, with the diverse and changing student and teacher populations found in major urban districts, is daunting.

Teachers and schools operate in an extraordinarily complex environment. They are funded through local, state, and federal sources and are governed by policies promulgated at each of these levels. Until recently, teachers have tended to operate autonomously and have rarely been judged on the performance of their students. Often, they are hired and supervised by administrators whose expertise is managerial and financial rather than instructional. Expectations for the performance of principals and superintendents have rarely focused on providing professional development opportunities and instructional leadership for teachers. Yet, despite the traditionally limited emphasis on instructional leadership among school and district administrators, it is these individuals who have the greatest opportunity to influence day-to-day activities within classrooms.

In this chapter, we describe an approach to school reform based on two premises derived from these observations. First, instruction must be designed to meet the needs of all students; second, educators at all levels of a district—superintendents and their staffs, principals, and teacher leaders—must continually lead and support efforts to improve teaching and, hence, student performance. The second premise is the most distinctive feature of the Institute for Learning (IFL) at the University of Pittsburgh, whose work we analyze in this chapter. We assume that school districts are and will remain both the target of demands for improved performance and the primary agents capable of improving professional practice in the district.

This comprehensive view means the work of the IFL begins at scale. Rather than implementing instructional programs in one or a few schools and, subsequently, trying to implement them at additional sites, the IFL seeks to influence activities throughout a district with the goal of building a vision of and a capacity for continuous improvement of teaching and learning at every level of the district's operation.

Thus, at the outset IFL takes seriously the four dimensions of scale—breadth, depth of implementation, sustainability, and ownership—described by Coburn (2003).[2] IFL's work aims for breadth in that it focuses on all schools within a district. It focuses on depth of implementation by aiming to influence instructional practice in specific subject areas through extensive professional development, by providing diverse teaching tools, and by developing supportive supervisory practice. It focuses on sustainability by attempting to build, within districts and schools, a culture of mutual accountability to support the invention and reinvention of the multiple systems—human resources, curriculum, assessment, and others—necessary for effective instruction. And it focuses on ownership by helping teachers and other school leaders understand how they can continually assess and improve their practice.

Providing High-Quality Education for All Students

Until the late 1980s, few seriously proposed that *all* students—black and brown, as well as white; students from lower, as well as higher, socioeconomic groups; and even many carrying "special education" labels—could be expected to learn demanding intellectual content. The 20th century American schooling system was founded on beliefs about immutable, inherited intelligence that set boundaries on what individuals and groups could learn (Resnick and Fienberg, 1997a, 1997b). Given these beliefs, it made sense to establish schooling policies adapted to individual and group differences by setting different expectations based on family background and entering test scores. These practices seemed consistent with the best scientific knowledge of the day. They also accorded well with an economy that needed

---

[2] See Chapter One in this volume.

many industrial laborers but only a few engineers, religious leaders, or teachers.

The use of schools as sorting machines, however, no longer makes economic sense. A prosperous society now requires an educated workforce at every level of the economic system. The idea that all individuals must receive a high-quality education is important not only because their talents and skills are needed to contribute to our national prosperity but also because only individuals who have had the benefit of a high-quality education will be able to participate fully—to earn wages that enable them to provide a good life for themselves and their families—in an economy in which both the chief inputs and the most important products are information. High-quality education is also needed to maintain a participatory democracy—in particular, to increase the involvement of individuals whose voices have not always been heard in either local or national political discussions.

Thus, we now face a massive social agenda: transforming an education system designed to educate only a few to high levels of performance to one that is organized to teach everyone. Fortunately, the science of learning and intelligence has made it clear that, while there are myriad individual differences, there is no established limit on how much or what kinds of things people are able to learn. Taken together, neuroscience, cognitive science, and social psychology (Neisser, 1998; Bransford, Brown and Cocking, 1999; Perkins, 1995; Resnick and Nelson–Le Gall, 1997) tell us that the capacity for learning is open-ended and that providing opportunities to learn—both through diverse kinds of social experiences and through educational institutions—affects individual capabilities in multiple and complex ways.

Nearly every education reform proposal that has had any serious level of political traction in the past 20 years has addressed the problem of providing a high-quality education to everyone, with the details depending on the experience and perspective of the proposers. State political leaders, acting in national councils and with some federal support, have focused on establishing standards for learning in the nation's schools and, most recently, on establishing accountability systems that make it clear that the expectations being set are intended for all classes of students. This is a very "top-down" approach, but it is not incompatible with—indeed, it is often promoted alongside—a "market-driven" approach that proposes to abandon compliance demands other than test-based performance standards and to allow individual schools to compete for students and the accompanying resources.

The market approach has been applied to public school bureaucracies through such challenges as charter schools, voucher programs, and home schooling. But it has also helped to fuel a movement within the public school system (Ouchi et al., 2003), where it has been joined (sometimes uneasily) with calls for greater community participation in school governance or with the "magnet school" systems that came into being in the 1970s, in part as a response to desegregation requirements. Some funds (e.g., Title 1) today often go almost directly to individual schools, in effect bypassing district offices and thus weakening what remains of old school system bureaucracies.

This situation has, perhaps ironically, given rise to a new form of centralized curriculum and teaching system, embodied in whole-school or comprehensive school reform models that individual schools can choose. When schools make such a choice, they typically contract with an intermediary organization that provides a curriculum, professional development for teachers, and leadership training for principals.[3] In these arrangements, the third-party organizations take over some of the traditional functions of district bureaucracies. However, depending on contracts and local relationships, other functions (e.g., appointment of principals, assignment of teachers, evaluation, budgeting, special education policies) are left untouched, leading sometimes to conflicts and often to difficulty in attributing responsibility for both successes and failures.

---

[3] Several chapters in this volume describe the efforts of such third-party organizations, which can be either nonprofit or for-profit.

The District as the Target of Reform

In this chapter, we describe and analyze an alternative approach to scaling education reform, an approach rooted in a transformation of the school district itself. Its aim is to transform school districts from ineffective bureaucracies that impose requirements and monitor compliance into true learning organizations.[4] By *learning organizations*, we mean organizations that operate to create new capacity for the high levels of intellectual performance demanded today. School districts as learning organizations do this, in our theory, by promoting and rewarding learning among adults in the system, as well as among students. In doing this, we posit that districts will be able to bring quality instruction to scale. By focusing on the creation of organizational capacity, we believe that school districts will be able to ensure that their reform efforts achieve both depth and breadth—that is, that reforms are implemented with fidelity to their stated goals in a high proportion of the district's classrooms.

This seemingly simple and unarguable goal—creating capacity by promoting learning among adults so that they can more effectively create learning opportunities for students—constitutes a major challenge. It calls not only for reviving the school district, rather than dismantling it, but also for redirecting the efforts of the central office. It requires people to behave in ways that are unfamiliar and, at least initially, are also likely to be uncomfortable. The district-as-learning-organization approach to scaling, although different from that of the CSR models in many respects, is similar in that it goes directly to the "technical core" of education (Elmore, 2000). It calls for districts to take positions on curriculum and teaching processes that, for several decades, have been viewed as outside the purview of anyone but individual teachers, yet to exercise these responsibilities in far more collaborative and professionally respectful ways than the bureaucratic systems Tyack (1974) and others have described.

---

[4] Despite the rhetoric of "local control," districts are often acting as local agents of state and federal programs and regulatory offices.

This shift in the locus of control means districts will have to redesign their curriculum and professional development departments—sometimes reinvigorating them by inventing new forms of interaction and collaboration with schools. It means changing the relationships between supervisors and staff members to focus less on evaluation and more on supporting professional learning. It calls for management changes in which budgeting, human resource management, and other operational activities are more clearly focused on optimizing learning than is now typical. Above all, it calls for a focus throughout the organization on what goes on in each classroom.

It is unlikely that many school districts will be able to manage this extensive transformation on their own. They will need the help of third-party organizations, both to formulate plans and to carry them out. IFL was founded specifically to take instructional reform to scale by helping large school districts become learning organizations. In this chapter, we describe IFL's history, its theory of action, and some of its on-the-ground successes and challenges. Against this background, we then raise a number of questions concerning the role of districts in an environment of multiple reform agents, the possibilities for learning within hierarchically structured organizations, and the most-effective ways a third-party organization can help transform school districts.

There have been four important strands in the institute's development up to now, each of which represents an important phase of its learning. The IFL program is best understood through a brief recounting of these phases of its history.

A Design Seminar for Reforming Districts

IFL began on a small scale in summer 1995, when staff from a group of districts, several of which had been associated with the New Standards assessment development program,[5] began meeting to explore the instructional practices needed to help students develop the skills required to meet the New Standards. The institute was constituted as

---

[5] See Chapter Seven in this volume.

a think tank and design center for innovative professional development systems and an educator of core groups of school and district professionals. Located within the Learning Research and Development Center (LRDC) at the University of Pittsburgh, a research center of some renown in both education and the basic sciences of learning, IFL was meant to link research and practice. The institute aimed to convey to educators the best of current knowledge about processes of learning and principles of instruction. Accordingly, in its early years, the work of the institute focused on articulating the forms of teaching and learning called for by the changes in our society and the improved understanding of learning derived from 25 years of research in the cognitive sciences.

The specific language describing these principles was the product of a collaboration involving a group of scholars at LRDC: IFL resident fellows drawn from the world of practice—former teachers, principals, professional development specialists, and central office curriculum specialists—as well as leading staff members from the districts that had joined with the institute in its early years. The institute believed that the resulting principles of learning should guide instruction in modern classrooms (Resnick et al., 2001); these principles formed the core of the institute's engagement with school district (see Table 14.1)

In its early years, the institute built partnerships with the Pittsburgh school district and several smaller nearby districts, as well as with large urban districts in San Diego, California; Philadelphia, Pennsylvania; Boston, Massachusetts; and Kansas City, Missouri and with several community districts in New York City. The institute's resident and district fellows came to constitute a professional learning community dedicated to bringing the principles of learning into action in significant numbers of schools.

The institute's leaders assumed, at first, that district educators would be able to translate knowledge and principles into practice with only minimal on-the-ground assistance from the university-based group. A substantial component of this phase of the institute's activities was a series of national meetings that brought the group

Table 14.1
Core Principles

Principle	Description
Organizing for effort	Everything within the school is organized to support the belief that sustained and directed effort can yield high achievement for all students. High standards are set, and all students are given as much time and expert instruction as they need to meet or exceed the expectations.
Clear expectations	Clear standards of achievement and gauges of students' progress toward those standards offer real incentives for students to work hard and succeed. Descriptive criteria and models that meet the standards are displayed in the schools, and the students refer to these displays to help them analyze and discuss their work.
Fair and credible evaluations	For them to be fair, tests, exams, and classroom assessments must be aligned to the standards of achievement. Further, grading must be done against absolute standards rather than on a curve so that students can clearly see the results of their learning efforts.
Recognition of accomplishment	Clear recognition of authentic student accomplishments is a hallmark of an effort-based school. Progress points are articulated so that, regardless of entering performance level, every student can meet the criteria for accomplishments often enough to be recognized frequently.
Academic rigor in a thinking curriculum	In every subject, at every grade level, instruction and learning must include commitment to a knowledge core, a high demand for thinking, and active use of knowledge.
Accountable talk	Classroom discussions should use evidence that is appropriate to the discipline and follow established norms of good reasoning. Teachers should create the norms and skills of accountable talk in their classrooms.
Socializing intelligence	Intelligence comprises problem-solving and reasoning capabilities along with habits of mind that lead one to use those capabilities regularly. Equally, it is a set of beliefs about one's right and obligation to make sense of the world and one's capacity to figure things out over time. By calling on students to use the skills of intelligent thinking—and by holding them responsible for doing so—educators can "teach" intelligence.
Self-management of learning	Students manage their own learning by evaluating feedback they get from others, by bringing their own knowledge to bear on new learning, by anticipating learning difficulties and apportioning their time accordingly, and by judging their progress toward a learning goal. Learning environments should be designed to model and encourage the regular use of self-management strategies.
Learning as apprenticeship	Learning environments can be organized so that complex thinking is modeled and analyzed in apprenticeship arrangements. Mentoring and coaching will enable students to undertake extended projects and develop presentations of finished work, both in and beyond the classroom.

together for presentations and study. However, the institute also worked with districts to develop demonstration schools, to promote visits between schools in member districts, and to develop protocols and other tools that member districts could use. From the beginning, districts paid a fee to be members of the institute, which entitled them to a specified level of attendees at meetings, consultations, and access to materials.

A Model of a School District as a Learning Organization

From the outset, Community School District 2 in New York City (District 2) had been an active partner in IFL's work, providing some of the most vocal and active district fellows and demonstration school sites. District 2 had achieved significant improvements in learning, particularly literacy, and school leaders from other districts often visited to observe the real-world practices that accorded with the principles of learning. The relationship between IFL and District 2 was cemented when Lauren Resnick (coauthor of this chapter), Mary Kay Stein, and colleagues at the LRDC, together with Harvard researchers Richard Elmore and Deanna Burney, began to study the activities of Anthony Alvarado (superintendent), Elaine Fink (deputy superintendent), and their colleagues in that district with the intent of developing an understanding of a high-performance learning community.

From this research, Resnick and the IFL staff took several important ideas and concepts. First, they judged that the improvement of performance was, in large part, the result of district leadership, including the building principals, making instructional improvement the focus of their work. Second, it seemed clear to them that continuing professional development, which usually took place at the school and frequently could be seen as job-embedded, was essential to the continuing improvement of instruction. Alvarado had reduced his central office staff by eliminating positions unrelated to instruction and used the freed-up resources to support this professional development.

Over time, the study team came to see that District 2 possessed several critical organizational attributes. Throughout the district, one could find *learning communities*. In three case studies in District 2 schools, the team expanded and validated this concept. The most fundamental community was the classroom itself, in which the students *and* the teacher were learners, with the teacher having the responsibility of leading the learning process. District 2 schools also included other types of learning communities. In most schools, for example, the principal and the teachers created a learning community focused on instructional technique, curriculum, and effective ways to engage the community. Other learning communities might center on grade levels or content. Finally, the superintendent, key staff, and the principals formed still another learning community, in which the learning surrounded the effective management of instruction within a school.

Membership in these learning communities frequently overlapped. For example, principals led communities of teachers and were members of communities consisting of principals. The study team came to call these "nested learning communities" to emphasize the idea that each community was embedded within another community. The prevalence of learning communities was seen as contributing to a level of coherence in district instruction that was unusual at a time when public policy emphasized the autonomy of schools, site-based management, and whole-school designs. The social interaction within these communities served to mediate the behavior and learning of students, teachers, and principals. For example, teachers new to a school learned, through interaction within the community, how they were to teach and work within the school.

A related feature of this organizational form was what the high-performance learning community study team came to call *mutual* or *reciprocal* accountability (Elmore, 2000; Spillane, Halverson and Diamond, 2001). In an organization characterized by mutual accountability, individuals understand clearly what they are expected to do—what they are accountable for—and their leaders are responsible for enabling them to meet these expectations. In a school system, mutual accountability means that teachers understand that they are responsible for the performance of their students, and principals understand that they are responsible for ensuring that teachers have the resources and skills needed to succeed with their students. Mutual accountability is an important part of the glue that maintains nested learning communities.

By 1999, IFL was working with a rich set of ideas and theories, including

- the principles of learning
- the role of the principal as a leader of instruction
- nested learning communities
- sustained management focus on instructional improvement
- mutual accountability
- extensive job-related and job-embedded professional development.

A number of tools and protocols were being developed to assist in implementation. These included texts, video examples, case studies built around the principles of learning and a set of processes for building common views of the teaching and learning process organized into what became known as the LearningWalk[SM]—an adaptation of a process we observed in District 2 (Fink and Resnick, 2001). The LearningWalk is an organized walk through hallways and classrooms using the principles of learning to guide observations of the instructional core—how teachers teach, how students learn, what gets taught to whom, and how a school is organized so that effort creates ability. Mutual accountability became a centerpiece of discussions among IFL partners because it embodied a moral commitment to provide the learning opportunities needed for everyone—students, teachers, and instructional leaders—to meet the demands of then-emerging accountability systems.

Principals as Instructional Leaders: Developing Nested Learning Communities

The number of districts involved in IFL work was growing, as was enthusiasm for its ideas within them. Yet it was becoming clear that an intervention focused largely on helping a few district staff members understand how people learn was not sufficient to affect instruction and learning throughout a district. A focus on both the content of learning and the organizational features of the district was needed.

An opportunity to work from the ground up on designs for organizational learning arose when, in 1999, the Providence, Rhode Island, school district hired a new superintendent, Diana Lam. She had recently left San Antonio, Texas, where she had been successful in improving student test scores and had worked to strengthen instructional leadership throughout the district. She had placed "instructional guides" in each school site with the intention that these individuals would supply instructional leadership that principals did not have time to provide. She made improving instruction a major function of her area superintendents.

Shortly before accepting the superintendency in Providence, Lam attended a meeting of school superintendents, organized by the Danforth Foundation, at which she learned about IFL. She especially liked the ideas about effort-based learning, nested learning communities, and instructional leadership from principals that the institute was developing. When she went to Providence, she decided that the institute could probably help her as she developed her broad strategy.

IFL assigned one of its senior resident fellows, Judy Johnston, to organize its work in Providence. Lam asked Johnston to develop an instructional leadership program for all her principals and agreed to participate regularly in LearningWalks and other professional development in Providence, in accord with IFL's emerging design principles for building districtwide nested learning communities.

Johnston began meeting with Providence principals for two and a half days each month. They studied standards and conducted LearningWalks, focusing on identifying instruction consistent with the principle of clear expectations. During the first year, Lam participated in parts of these sessions and led LearningWalks when she visited schools. Her participation sent a clear signal to the principals about her high regard for them and for the work of IFL. As might have been expected, on the whole, the principals reacted positively, and over the next two years, Providence's practice of continuous training of principals as instructional leaders was institutionalized, and the practice was expanded to include assistant principals.

Lam also emphasized literacy and writing across all grade levels. She chose and mandated the use of a balanced literacy program in elementary schools. Drawing on her experience in San Antonio, Lam decided to create a group of literacy coaches who would be assigned to schools to work with individual teachers, as well as a team of teacher-leaders in each school who would, in turn, also work with fellow teachers. By this time, Lam had named Melody Johnson, her deputy in San Antonio, as her deputy in Providence, and the two of them oversaw the process for selecting coaches.

The district turned to the institute for help in training these coaches. Under the leadership of another resident fellow, Donna DiPrima Bickel, Providence became a development site for IFL's emerging program in content-focused coaching (Staub and Bickel, 2003), a professional development program for literacy coaches that focused on applying knowledge of the principles of learning in lesson planning, enactment, and reflection and on the then-new primary literacy standards developed by the New Standards program (Daro, Hampton, and Resnick, 1999). Over three years—one interrupted by a work-to-rule action of the teachers' union, which was finding the frequent presence of administrators in classrooms objectionable—the IFL system of intensively developing the instructional leadership skills of both principals and coaches became standard operating procedure in Providence. In organizational terms, the *system* had learned a new way of behaving (Leavitt and March, 1988). Test scores began to show a modest rise (Togneri and Anderson, 2003) that could be linked roughly to the level of a school's participation in the professional learning opportunities.

The Providence experience had provided IFL's first opportunity to work directly with district leaders to implement its central ideas in all the district's schools. The improved test scores indicated that this approach had helped to bring about positive results, but, equally important, subsequent events demonstrated that the ideas IFL espoused had taken root in the community. In fall 2002, Lam left the district on short notice to become Deputy Chancellor for Instruction in New York City. Her deputy, Melody Johnson, was immediately appointed as superintendent and made clear her commitment to continuing and expanding the programs that had been developed in collaboration with IFL, a demonstration of the degree to which the nested learning community reform had taken root in Providence.

Expanding Learning Initiatives: Districtwide Instructional Programs

The Providence experience provided a model for a new strategy for IFL work in its partner districts. Attention shifted from national seminars focused on the principles of learning to on-the-ground training of principals and others in all the districts. IFL's development of a program for training literacy coaches, first in Providence and then elsewhere, is an example of how such engagement developed. In Providence, however, the focus was mainly on building instructional leadership capacity in literacy, not on implementation of a specific instructional program. The tradition of very local, school- or even teacher-level decisionmaking concerning the "technical core" of teaching was still dominant.

This focus on decentralized decisionmaking has changed rapidly, and several IFL districts have now moved toward districtwide specification of teaching programs in core subjects. The impetus for this movement was growing pressure from state accountability systems, but IFL also supported such efforts because it was becoming increasingly clear that the full power of the nested-learning strategy would depend on having a common instructional program around which professional development at every level of the district system could occur (see Resnick and Glennan, 2002). The move to district instructional systems took different forms in IFL partner districts, as the subsections below describe.

Austin, Texas. After participating in a leadership training program similar to the one in Providence but adapted to a larger district, Austin began to change its operations by reorganizing its central office. The concept of nested learning communities guided Austin's reorganization, which gave more responsibility for instructional leadership to its area superintendents, who were now expected to provide leadership development for principals, to know the instructional practices and capacity of schools in considerable detail, and to support principals in their development of professional learning communities in the schools.

Relying on the Principles of Learning, Austin also developed Web-based instructional planning guides consistent with the Texas state standards for core subject areas in K–12 education for six- to nine-week planning blocks. These guides provide information regarding research-based best practices, including the principles of learning, instructional resources, assessment strategies, and descriptions of student work. In RAND Corporation interviews in spring 2003, principals described the guides as valuable and approved the development and revision process. A minority of the staff was concerned the guides were too structured and overemphasized *what* to teach over *how* to teach. However, on the whole, the new instructional guides seem to be providing a clear foundation for Austin's aggressive efforts to raise the quality of teaching and the achievement of students.

In addition to developing its core instructional program, Austin selected six of its schools with long records of low performance and designated them "blueprint" schools. Outstanding principals from across the district staffed these schools. The principals had considerable latitude to hire teachers, and the process effectively led to reconstitution of three of the schools. The six school principals used many of the institute's tools and consulted with its staff. In particular, they emphasized collaborative planning, and provided the schools with coaches and a corps of substitute teachers to allow the staff time to participate in extensive professional development.

The blueprint schools had considerable initial success, registering substantial gains on state tests. Across the schools, reading scores increased between 13 and 31 percent; mathematics scores increased between 12 and 35 percent (Forgione, 2003). In 2003–04, the district applied the lessons from this experience with other poor-performing schools. Austin's student achievement record is improving across the board as well. Student pass rates in Grades 3–8 and 10 increased between 6 and 16 percent for all student groups reported as part of the Texas state accountability system (Austin Independent School District, 2003; Westbrook and Tousek, 2003).

The Austin experience, then, took IFL a step beyond its efforts in Providence in two ways. First, its efforts to improve instructional quality in Austin could be more focused than they were in Providence because, rather than attempting to improve instructional quality in general—or even in a particular subject area—the goal of the Austin enterprise was to enhance the ability of principals to help teachers use a predetermined curriculum based on the instructional planning guides. Second, aligning these guides with the Texas state standards helped Austin's reform efforts achieve a higher degree of coherence between instruction and assessment.

Los Angeles, California. The Los Angeles Unified School District (LAUSD) is the second largest in the nation, with about 750,000 students. It is divided into 11 local districts, with a superintendent and an array of district staff, including school service directors, who supervise principals; math and literacy specialists; and staff in charge of programs such as Title 1. Given the size of the district and the complexity of these organizational arrangements, LAUSD represents a clear challenge to any effort to achieve education reform on a large scale. Since 1999, the district has chosen to follow a relatively centralized curriculum, first in elementary reading with districtwide adoption of Open Court, a prescriptive reading program, and then with an elementary and middle school math program.

LAUSD initially invited IFL to provide leadership training, based on the principles of learning, to support the district's curriculum initiatives. This work began in winter 2001. The scale of the LAUSD effort precluded direct work with principals, so the institute worked through the local district structures, developing instructional leadership capacity among the school service directors. IFL subsequently also directly trained a group of lead principals, who would assist other principals. Los Angeles IFL fellows were named both in the central office and in the districts; many of these individuals became leaders in LAUSD's efforts to establish nested learning communities. In addition, IFL's district liaison began to spend a half day per month in each local district, tailoring actions to the particular strategies being used in the district.

In spring 2003, LAUSD's program evaluation branch examined the extent to which IFL's leadership development program had taken root after two years of work, focusing particularly on the instructional leadership role of the directors who supervised principals (Cantrell et al., 2003). In three of the local districts, evaluators found that directors were functioning substantially in keeping with IFL concepts, focusing their time with principals on instruction and creating an atmosphere of mutual accountability in their relationships with principals and other staff. In six of the districts, directors were practicing the IFL principles in a partial way, focusing on instruction but doing so in a fashion that was more managerial than collegial. Two of the 11 districts still had not substantially begun to function in accordance with the IFL principles.

Meanwhile, LAUSD also asked the institute to support the district's core curriculum effort directly. This work began with the training of Open Court coach coordinators, using a variant of IFL's Content-Focused Coaching program adapted specifically for use with Open Court. IFL resident fellows and the leaders of the district's reading program worked closely together to adapt the program and create professional development materials for coaches. Next, the institute began to provide training for middle school mathematics coaches using an intensive lesson analysis approach that eventually became the foundation of IFL's Disciplinary Literacy program. The objective of this program is to train cadres of secondary school teacher leaders in four core disciplines: English language arts, mathematics, science, and history. Through all these activities, the institute became increasingly engaged with many aspects of instructional planning and training, even though its direct training efforts represented only a small portion of the vast professional development efforts launched across the district. LAUSD invited IFL to lead or attend most senior management retreats and to be present at weekly meetings of the local superintendents with Superintendent Roy Romer and his lead central staff.

IFL's increasingly close relationship with LAUSD led to its being actively consulted as the district launched, during 2002–03, an aggressive program to establish a core districtwide instructional program in all subjects for elementary and middle schools. The effort, which would eventually encompass all subject areas, began with mathematics. The LAUSD mathematics department created an instructional guide specifying topics that should be taught during each quarter of the school year for each grade and showed which chapters of each of two approved textbooks could be used to teach each one. The selection and sequence of topics were based on a careful staff-led analysis of the California standards. The systematization of the mathematics curriculum and the professional development based on the instructional guides led to a substantial rise in elementary mathematics scores on California's standard tests in spring 2003.

Influenced in part by studies that showed that the urban school districts most successful in meeting accountability standards focused heavily on using student data to guide instructional decisions (Manpower Development and Research Corporation, 2002), LAUSD had decided even before the state test scores came in to establish quarterly assessments geared to the instructional guides. IFL worked closely with central staff through a process of selecting an external provider (the Educational Testing Service) to develop the tests and manage a system of nearly immediate reporting of results to teachers and schools. Results from these interim math assessments first became available in fall 2003. Not surprisingly, given the demographics of the student population and the speed with which the instructional guides and assessments had been introduced to teachers, students did not perform very well in the first two rounds of these assessments.

The effect on the district was electric. Everyone—in both the central office and in the local districts—became focused on how to improve performance. LAUSD asked IFL to help develop an agenda for aligning instruction to the tests (without drilling on the tests themselves); providing additional instruction to students in greatest need; and strengthening the districts' professional development offerings, including substantial revision of the instructional guides. Although the impetus for these activities was the negative outcome of student performance assessments, we see the response to these assessments as positive. LAUSD has resolved to extend the instructional guides and interim assessment approach districtwide. Work in English language arts is under way, and science is following shortly behind.

In Los Angeles, then, IFL demonstrated that it was feasible to adapt its approach to developing instructional leadership to the requirements of a very large district by working within existing district structures and relying on a combination of direct training for local district leaders and lead principals, who could, along with support from IFL's district liaisons, carry these ideas into individual schools. Further, IFL's role in helping to develop the quarterly assessment system, as well as procedures for rapidly reporting assessment results, helped to establish both the importance and the feasibility of collecting and analyzing performance data as a basis for the continuous improvement of instruction.

Denver, Colorado. In the latter part of 2001, when Denver began discussing a partnership with the IFL, it faced a particularly challenging problem. Ninety-five of its 140 schools were on a state watch list for poor performance, and 21 were viewed as failing and subject to being made charter schools. The superintendent, Jerry Wartgow, asked IFL to help turn around a failing district not only by providing training programs but also by placing one of its fellows in Denver as chief academic officer.

The district and IFL did not have the leisure to begin with general capacity building, as had been done elsewhere. Instead, the district focused immediately on marshaling resources to improve elementary and middle school reading and math. By reallocating funds and with some foundation support, the district was able to support extensive coaching, assigning one coach for every 10 teachers. Area superintendents were accountable for implementing the coaching program, which involved substantial training and collaboration among coaches. Training for coaches and principals was built around the specific literacy program that Denver was crafting.

Like Austin, Denver attended to its failing schools with special intensity. The district audited each of the 21 schools in danger of takeover, assessing the capabilities of the building leadership, staff, and program. The district replaced many principals and effectively reconstituted several of the schools. IFL provided additional coaching when needed. At the end of the year, 20 of the 21 schools were no longer on the list of failing schools, and there were promising improvements across the entire district. An independent evaluation revealed an encouraging correlation between the level of improvement of a school and the degree to which it had implemented the district's plan. As in Austin and Los Angeles, student achievement also rose across the board, particularly in literacy (Farr and Yasui, 2003).

The Denver experience demonstrates both the consistency and the flexibility of the IFL approach to school improvement. Facing demands for immediate improvements, IFL adapted its program to focus on specific, short-term instructional outcomes but continued to emphasize building instructional capacity, as opposed to, say, an extensive test preparation program.

Building High-Performance School Districts: A Theory of Action

As the examples presented above suggest, IFL intervention has evolved as the institute has gained experience. We have tried to capture both the lessons of that experience and our growing understanding of what is needed to take deep instructional practice to scale in a theory of action. This theory, first proposed in 2002 (Resnick and Glennan, 2002) and later refined based on the experience recounted here and elsewhere, is, like most such theories, both a group of hypotheses concerning district organizational features needed to achieve the goal of widespread student learning and a proposed set of strategies for developing them.

IFL's theory of action (see Figure 14.1) is framed by the fundamental goal we discussed in the introduction to this chapter: educating America's diverse students to levels once reserved for a privileged minority. Here, we elaborate the elements of this theory and how they are related to each other.

Design Principles for a High-Performance District

Currently, the institute identifies seven district design principles, shown in the center box of Figure 14.1. If these principles are pur-

Figure 14.1
IFL Theory of Action

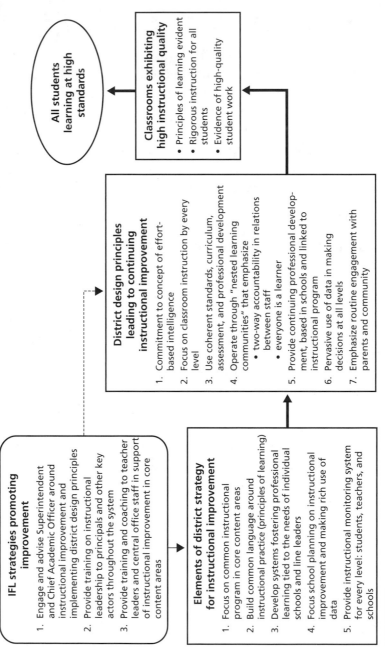

All students learning at high standards

Classrooms exhibiting high instructional quality
- Principles of learning evident
- Rigorous instruction for all students
- Evidence of high-quality student work

District design principles leading to continuing instructional improvement
1. Commitment to concept of effort-based intelligence
2. Focus on classroom instruction by every level
3. Use coherent standards, curriculum, assessment, and professional development
4. Operate through "nested learning communities" that emphasize
   - two-way accountability in relations between staff
   - everyone is a learner
5. Provide continuing professional development, based in schools and linked to instructional program
6. Pervasive use of data in making decisions at all levels
7. Emphasize routine engagement with parents and community

IFL strategies promoting improvement
1. Engage and advise Superintendent and Chief Academic Officer around instructional improvement and implementing district design principles
2. Provide training on instructional leadership to principals and other key actors throughout the system
3. Provide training and coaching to teacher leaders and central office staff in support of instructional improvement in core content areas

Elements of district strategy for instructional improvement
1. Focus on common instructional program in core content areas
2. Build common language around instructional practice (principles of learning)
3. Develop systems fostering professional learning tied to the needs of individual schools and line leaders
4. Focus school planning on instructional improvement and making rich use of data
5. Provide instructional monitoring system for every level: students, teachers, and schools

RAND MG248-14.1

sued, we hypothesize that the organizational units and processes of the district will operate in ways that reinforce one another, producing coherence in district operations and, ultimately, improving instruction and student performance in the district's schools. The keys to this coherence are the nested learning communities based on commitment to learning and improvement, operating with genuine accountability to one another. Here, then, we describe the IFL district design principles.

Commit the District to an Effort-Based Concept of Intelligence and Education. A district's instructional program should be based on commitment to an effort-based concept of intelligence. Initially, many of the staff may need to be asked to suspend their traditional beliefs that aptitude is the major determinant of performance and take on the goal of enabling all students to reach these standards as their core function (Resnick, 1995; Resnick and Nelson–Le Gall, 1997).

Develop a Focus on Instructional Improvement Throughout the District. Commitment to and implementation of high-quality instructional programs require a focus on classroom instruction throughout the district. Personnel at all levels (e.g., principals, area superintendents or supervisors, the superintendent), as well as those in instructional support offices (e.g., curriculum, professional development, mandated programs), should attend, primarily, to instructional leadership, rather than to managerial functions. The emphasis on instructional leadership by line and staff personnel means that administrative activities that intrude into instructional concerns must be carefully scrutinized. Those seen as essential should be managed in ways that support rather than detract from instruction.

Seek Coherence in Standards, Curriculum, Assessment, and Professional Development. Curriculum and assessment should be aligned throughout the district and should focus on a set of clear achievement standards. The district should consider adopting a core instructional program in each subject area. Professional development efforts in each area should focus on that core. The district should carefully study variations in instructional programs and implementation and should gradually incorporate the most-effective variants into each of its core programs.

Create a Culture Emphasizing Continuous Learning and Two-Way Accountability Throughout the District. Any system that emphasizes continuous improvement must emphasize continuous learning on the part of its staff. Schools need to become places of learning for teachers as well as for students, and principals have a primary responsibility for bringing this about. That is, just as teachers are responsible for orchestrating effective learning opportunities for students, principals must be responsible for orchestrating such opportunities for teachers. At the same time, just as students must take advantage of the learning opportunities that teachers provide if they are to achieve, so teachers must take advantage of professional learning opportunities provided and expected in their schools.

Foster Continuing Professional Learning for All Staff. Adult learning should be supported by continuing professional development for all staff, based in schools and embedded in the professionals' jobs. For maximum effect, professional development should be linked to the instructional program actually taught to students.

Base Decisions at All Levels of the District on Data and Analysis. Decisions made at all levels, from classroom to boardroom, should be based on data and analysis. The data should be of multiple types—classroom observation, student work, research products, visits to effective sites, enumeration of the use of resources, and test scores. A culture that emphasizes the use of data rather than reliance on beliefs and professional judgment in making decisions is likely to engage in the continuous learning that is the hallmark of a high-performance district.

Sustain Routine and Continuing Engagement with Parents and Members of the Communities That the School District Serves. Instability in district leadership may undermine the coherence of district operations. At least some instability can be traced to inadequate efforts to engage the community in developing policies and programs. Creating and maintaining such engagement is an extraordinarily difficult task in the highly politicized environment of public schooling, but, if a district is to reach and sustain high performance, routine and continuing involvement with parents and members of the communities that the district serves is essential.

IFL Strategies for Supporting District Improvement

In the preceding section, we described the design principles that, according to our model, districts should implement to improve instruction and student learning. Here we describe what, according to the theory of action, IFL must to do to help launch and, subsequently, support efforts to make these principles the foundation for high-quality instruction and improved student performance throughout the district.

If an IFL-district partnership is to succeed, the time, tools, and expertise of the institute must be used in ways that add significant value to training and policymaking in the district. As we described in the opening section of this chapter, the institute's views on how it can best contribute to a district improvement effort have evolved with experience. It now has a clearer view about how to begin work with a district than it did at the outset. This experienced has led IFL to use three key activities, shown in the box in the upper left corner of Figure 14.1, as it becomes involved with districts.

These activities have three objectives. First, they seek to establish that the institute brings a distinctive improvement initiative that has strong top-level support and is not likely to be another transient reform activity. Second, they seek to create a common language about and focus on instruction. The institute believes that, for improvement to take place, staff must come to share the same views about what constitutes good instruction. The training of the frontline leaders—principals and lead teachers—is intended to begin this process. Third, from the beginning, the goal is to start building capacity within the district to take on and extend this work.

Engage the District Superintendent to Obtain Support for the Broad Institute Vision. Much of the research related to implementation of broad reforms emphasizes the importance of the active support of the superintendent (Bodilly et al., 1998; Berends, Bodilly, and Kirby, 2002; Datnow, Hubbard, and Mehan, 2002). For reforms that target a broad and diverse set of practices, the work of schools and the entire line structure and supporting staff offices must change. If the superintendent does not have both a deep understanding of IFL principles and goals and strong local support, participants will inevitably view IFL's efforts as simply another new program that has been added to the ample array already in place in most urban districts.

The institute seeks the support of the superintendent and his or her immediate subordinates in a number of ways. First, it has worked only with districts that seek its assistance. In virtually all cases, the superintendent has made the approach. Second, unlike reform efforts that rely on external grants, IFL has always charged districts for its services and materials. Districts often pay for the services with funds they have raised externally, but the cost is sufficiently large that the superintendent may also need to seek support from his or her board and perhaps important interests in the district staff.

Third, before they negotiate a relationship with IFL, superintendents and several members of their staffs are invited to institute events to learn more about working with the institute. Once they become institute partners, superintendents are encouraged to attend three day-and-a-half "think tanks," a significant commitment for a busy person. Most do. Superintendents and their deputies are also encouraged to participate in the annual institute retreat, at which staff from each district plan for the coming year. The director of the institute also tries to communicate with the superintendent several additional times each year to discuss issues that either the superintendent or the institute has identified, thus building a personal relationship that provides a framework for the exchange of ideas. Superintendents frequently seek advice from IFL's director or staff members, not only about IFL services but also about general district policies and operations.

Provide Training in the Principles of Learning and Improve the Instructional Leadership Skills at the Building Level. When the institute shifted its strategy to conduct most training within individual districts and to negotiate membership agreements to develop accountability between the institute and its district partners, school principals were the initial target. Much of the training and professional development was intended to help the principals understand the principles of learning, recognize opportunities to apply them in classrooms, and prepare them to help teachers incorporate these principles in their teaching. LearningWalks were an important focus of the effort. All principals were to receive this training, and the districts generally made attendance nominally mandatory. Actual attendance, however, has depended on the degree to which supervisors hold principals accountable for instructional leadership.

Early experience suggested that training only the principals created problems. A significant proportion of the principals lacked the substantive knowledge to use what they were learning. Central office staff felt left out. Teachers were skeptical of the effort, and some assistant principals resented being cut out of any instructional leadership responsibilities. Thus, we have adjusted our practices to make at least part of the training more inclusive.

As the examples presented above indicate, training for instructional leaders has differed across districts, depending on the size of the districts and their preferences. In Providence, a district with about 50 schools, IFL staff and the superintendent trained the principals in the first year. In Austin, which has 107 schools, early training was largely done by the area superintendents trained and coached by IFL staff. In Los Angeles, which has about 800 schools, directors of school services (who are each responsible for supervising principals in about 25 schools) have provided direct training for principals, after having been trained by IFL staff. What is common in these situations, however, is the institute's goal of building capacity for instructional leadership in the administrative line in the district.

We know something of the responses to this effort. In 2001, RAND interviews with and direct feedback from principals in five districts suggested that the training had reached broadly across the district. The language of the institute's program became commonplace. However, many teachers in these districts reported that they did not feel the principals were able to provide good support for their learning. Interviews with district leadership similarly indicated great support for the change in the language and focus associated with the institute's work, but the interviewees were concerned that the content was not reaching into the schools. The institute shared this judgment.

However, interviews two years later suggested that, with time, teachers developed better knowledge of the concepts and used them routinely in discussing their work. What has not yet been adequately studied is the degree to which the concepts actually affected their practice.

Work with Teacher Leaders and Central Office Staff to Create Capacity to Improve Instruction in Core Content Areas. The institute encourages its member districts to focus attention on the districtwide core curriculum, which has meant that it needed to develop strategies to support curriculum implementation. The principles of learning, while broad in their application, take on greater meaning for staff when presented in the context of specific content. However, the institute itself could play only a limited role in direct work with teachers because, in most cases, it was working at a geographical distance from the district. Instead, the institute has focused on developing district capacity to support teachers, both among central office curriculum staff and among teachers themselves. The institute's Content-Focused Coaching (Staub and Bickel, 2003; West and Staub, 2003) and Disciplinary Literacy programs are among tools that districts use to develop strong teachers as instructional leaders. This approach is consistent with the institute's still-evolving emphasis on developing distributed instructional leadership within a district.

District Strategies That Create and Sustain a High-Performance Learning Community

Having described the institute's district design principles and the way it works to develop the capacity for instructional leadership in the administrative line, we turn now to the district-level strategies needed to make effective use of this capacity in implementing the principles. Our analyses and experience have suggested several key strategies that are of special importance to the wide-scale improvement of instruction.

Focus on a Small Number of Core Content Areas. While the institute began its work with a focus on developing understanding and practice around the principles of learning, it now recommends that a district focus initially on one or two core content areas—

normally literacy and mathematics. Moreover, it recommends the adoption of a districtwide curriculum in these subjects. Adopting a common curriculum permits a district to develop a common system of professional development to support the programs across all schools, thus promoting coherence in district operations. Common core programs should also help districts deal with the intradistrict mobility of many urban students. Districts have done this in a variety of ways, as suggested in the reforms in Providence, Denver, and Los Angeles that we described above.

Build Common Language Around Instructional Practice. A common language helps members of an organization communicate effectively with each other. As noted above, the institute typically begins by training principals, other instructional leaders from schools, and key staff in the central office. The training seeks to develop an understanding of the principles of learning as a way to view and assess the quality of instruction. Building on the themes of this training, many IFL districts use the language of the principles of learning as they develop instructional guides, guidance for school improvement planning, and training for content-oriented coaches. Leaders, in talking with district staff, parents, and members of the community may also use this language. This use of a common language helps promote the coherence necessary in a high-performance learning community.

Develop Systems to Foster Professional Learning Tied to the Needs of Individual Schools and Their Staffs. The institute encourages districts to develop multielement systems to support the professional learning of teachers, principals, and other members of the district. Such systems may include extensive use of school-based coaches, as in Denver, Providence, and Los Angeles. If resources to place coaches in each school are unavailable, schools may make use of curriculum specialists from the central office, as in Austin. In both cases, the institute has sometimes provided training and, often, advice on effective means to get professional development to the school level and targeted on problems that the school identifies as important.

The institute emphasizes another means of fostering professional learning that is more difficult to implement: basing the supervision of teachers, principals, and others on the principles of learning and teaching. An area superintendent who is knowledgeable about instruction and regularly meets and does LearningWalks with the principals that he or she supervises, as well as reviewing school improvement plans, fosters the principals' professional learning. Similarly, principals who have learned to recognize effective instructional practice can assist teachers by obtaining appropriate professional development for them.

Numerous principals in IFL districts assist teachers in these ways, and several of the larger districts, such as Austin and Los Angeles, have begun to use area superintendents to assist the principals. The recent New York City reorganization, which clusters schools into groups of 10 or 12, each led by a local instructional superintendent, is intended to focus the supervisors' work on helping principals improve as instructional leaders. This structure is directly based on the institute's concept of nested learning communities. Creating supervisory structures that focus on instruction may be difficult because of the reallocation of resources and roles involved. The new supervisory behaviors they are intended to enable are even harder to bring into being. The supervisors (principals or area superintendents or instructional directors or local area superintendents) are not normally trained to provide such assistance. The explicit or implicit "job description" for these positions may not emphasize these practices. Changing this job to include assisting professional performance and recruiting people capable of effectively providing such assistance is a district responsibility—one it must carry out effectively if the nested learning communities and mutual accountability that, according to our model, underlie significant school improvements are to develop successfully.

Make School Improvement Plans an Effective Instrument of Instructional Improvement. Virtually every school district has a system for school improvement planning. Often these systems are mandated by the state department of education. While the stated intention of all school planning systems is to promote goal-setting and accountability, school improvement plans are commonly used for other purposes, including collecting data for reports to funding sources.

Appropriately used within a system of nested learning communities, school plans can play a significant role. The process for creating them provides an opportunity for teams of school staff to review data, devise instructional strategies to deal with weaknesses, take stock of the school's assets, consider changes in schedules to facilitate better instructional planning, and explore opportunities for professional development. Above all, the planning process can force school teams to choose a limited number of priorities that they really intend to accomplish. In addition, a plan can foster mutual accountability by providing an agenda for conversations among an area superintendent, key central office staff, and the leadership of a school about the instructional program at the school and the resources and strategies needed to improve that program.

The potential value of school plans, as guidelines for action and as vehicles for connecting learning communities, led the institute to devote one of the principals' think tanks to school improvement planning. The think tank engaged about 20 principals, arguably among the best principals in the IFL districts, who were asked to bring their plans and to share them with institute staff. As documents, most of the plans were unimpressive. In most cases, they were constrained by district-prescribed formats, and the analysis of reasons for poor performance was generally shallow. None of these plans considered alternative strategies for improving instructional performance and learning. While plans seeking improvement would be expected to consider investments needed to improve school capacities, such investment was seldom hinted at. Finally, and probably most important, the plans seemed to be static documents covering a single year. They did not normally propose a course of action accompanied by benchmarks extending over several years. They were, at best, tactical rather than strategic documents.

Further exploration suggested, however, that the *written* plans provided little evidence about the activities behind them. At the meeting, the principals were asked to write "stories" about their work. These almost always revealed activities more consistent with the ideas behind nested learning communities than the written plans did. As these outstanding principals described, their schools had often created learning communities to examine student work, standards, and the organization of the school. The work of these groups provided the basis for principals to approach the central office to obtain assistance or resources. The planning and the resulting plans served as starting points for subsequent discussions of progress within the schools. The institute is now working with its partner districts on strategies for making school plans into "living documents" that, although lean in the number of actions they outline, serve as the basis for regular conferencing between teachers and principals or between principals and their supervisors.

Monitoring Instructional Practice and Providing Data Concerning Instruction and Learning to Instructional Leaders. The district design principles specify widespread use of data to support the planning and operations of districts, schools, and classrooms. Such data can often be made available through Web-based information systems. Further, commercial systems are now available that can provide staff with data in usable forms, and many IFL districts have experimented with them. The value of such systems will become increasingly apparent as schools respond to the No Child Left Behind Act, which calls for enhanced accountability systems.

As we have noted, multiple sources of data should be used to monitor instructional practice and student performance. It is all too easy to concentrate on test data. However, data from state accountability systems are normally available only after the students have completed their courses and, even then, provide only a limited picture of a student's capabilities. Thus, these data must be supplemented by information from other sources, including student work and observations of instructional practice. The district can help organize the collection and interpretation of such data. For instance, the district can help school staffs develop the capacity to assess student work and to collect data about instructional practice through LearningWalks, examination of lesson plans, and formal instructional quality assessments. In all its actions, the district should foster a culture of evidence-based decisionmaking.

Lessons from Experience

As we have recounted the history of IFL and described the theory of action it espouses, we have identified some of the lessons that IFL has learned. In this closing section of the chapter, we consider some of the broader lessons learned from eight years of experience helping urban school districts in the daunting task of transforming themselves into learning organizations focused on improved student achievement. We do this in a spirit of reflection. The "hard data" on effectiveness is only now beginning to appear. Meanwhile, however, we can share what we are learning as IFL attempts to function as "outside insiders" within emerging nested learning communities.

Assessing Effectiveness Is Difficult

In these times of accountability for results, an obvious first question is whether IFL's programs are helping more students—especially poor and minority students. This is not a simple question to answer. We have alluded here to promising improvements in student outcomes (particularly at the elementary level), in four of the districts working with the institute. A similar account could be given for other IFL partner districts, especially Columbia, South Carolina, and St. Paul, Minnesota. It is difficult, however, to know how to attribute respon sibility for these gains because the IFL's strategy is to work with and through district leadership rather than as an intervention program whose contributions can be measured separately.

Detailed Research on Effectiveness Is Needed. What is needed now is a program of research examining the various features of the IFL theory of learning, tracing their effects all the way down to student learning. In particular, if classrooms in which student learning has improved significantly embody instructional qualities consistent with the IFL principles of learning—and if the quality of the instruction can be traced to leadership actions and behaviors of the principal, coaches, and lead teachers tied to institute programs—we would be able to make stronger claims about IFL's effectiveness than we can now. The institute is currently attempting to initiate research along these lines in several districts. Moreover, it encourages other organizations to study its partner districts and helps such organizations negotiate research entry in the districts. IFL partner districts are not only cooperating in these efforts but also asking to be objects of inquiry. This openness to evidence is one of the key features of learning organnizations.

Evidence of Penetration of IFL Concepts and District Commitment to IFL Principles Is Promising. In the meantime, there are some indicators of intermediate outcomes. We have already mentioned Los Angeles's internal evaluation of the extent to which local districts within the unified district have implemented the instructional leadership and nested learning activities the institute promotes. RAND, with support from the Hewlett Foundation, is conducting an independent study of districtwide instructional reform in three other IFL districts: Austin, Texas; Providence, Rhode Island; and Springfield, Massachusetts. In its preliminary work, the RAND team has found that the language and concepts introduced by the IFL are widely known and used in professional conversation. District leaders remark on the value of this conceptual vocabulary. In the review of the instructional reforms as a whole, RAND's view is that while many of the reforms are new, they seem to have a reasonable level of coherence and consistency at the rhetorical level. Moreover, all the major districts affiliated with IFL in 2002 renewed that affiliation in 2003, most using general funds to cover institute fees.

Success Depends on Building Partnerships with Districts

The relationship between IFL and its partner districts has been maintained even though the institute does not fit easily into the categories of technical assistance that districts and schools typically purchase. School districts are inundated with vendors—organizations or individuals that provide programs, services, or products needed for school operations or their improvement. Because IFL charges for its services, it is often viewed as "just another vendor."

The institute, however, wants to be viewed as a partner. To be sure, annual agreements specify the services to be delivered, but much of what the institute views as its most important contribution is the advice it provides to district leaders at all levels. In providing this advice, institute staff members seek to help build a culture focused on improvement of student learning, emphasizing continued professional learning—including supervisory activities that assist subordinates to perform effectively—and mutual accountability. Such behaviors do not result from occasional training sessions from outsiders; they require continued discussion with and coaching by trusted partners.

Building Effective Partnerships Requires Multiple Strategies. The institute has tried several strategies to promote the notion of partnership. Its initial and continued engagement with both the superintendent and the deputy or chief academic officer is intended to build this understanding. The IFL director and resident fellows have met frequently with school boards and, in retreat settings, with senior district staff. In some districts, IFL fellows function as members of senior leadership and planning groups. The institute also tries to build a sense of partnership by modeling such partnerships in the execution of its professional development activities. Finally, the institute meets periodically with superintendents and their deputies, with key staff in the central office, and with leading district principals to share experiences and work collectively to improve their own and IFL's strategies.

Despite these efforts, achieving this partnership status is a continuing challenge in education systems accustomed to a succession of short-term programs abandoned in favor of the next idea that comes along. This is particularly true with the teaching staff, which has typically seen new programs come and go with considerable regularity.

"Lethal Mutations" May Undermine Cooperative Construction of Effective Learning Communities

IFL has several tools and procedures that it emphasizes in its work with districts. But tools with the power to build instructional capacity also have the power, if misused, to affect the overall improvement effort adversely.

The most serious examples of such misuse have occurred with the LearningWalk. The institute's intent is that the LearningWalk be used, initially, as a means for district personnel to learn by analyzing a school's instructional practices from the perspective of one or another of the principles of learning. As the use of the LearningWalk evolves in a district, emphasis increases on providing feedback to the school concerning possible improvements in instructional practices. In some districts, LearningWalks involving principals and their supervisors, together with other building leaders, have become a regular means of improving instructional practices.

However, it is easy to imagine such LearningWalks being perceived as, or actually used as, means of evaluating teachers or principals. Indeed, this has happened in many of the districts associated with IFL, sometimes inadvertently and sometimes because a district leader or principal chooses to use the walk in this manner. This generally happens when the concepts of continuous learning and mutual accountability—the heart of the nested learning community concept—are not yet fully understood and when administrators assimilate this fundamentally new (in intent) practice into the evaluative classroom visits they have always made. In several cases, the uproar over this inappropriate use of LearningWalks has seriously set back the IFL program in a district, creating problems with unions and with the teaching staff generally.

While the LearningWalk may be the most common opportunity for lethal mutation of an IFL tool,[6] others—for example, the use of prepackaged "criteria charts" or lists of standards as a way of demonstrating compliance with the IFL principle of clear expectations—also occur. IFL considers the construction of charts listing expectations for outcomes in a class and criteria for students and teachers to judge whether they are meeting the expectations to be an important instructional move. Building such a chart is a means of engaging students in judging their own work. However, if the supervisors of the teachers in a school only emphasize that a chart be visible and if teachers simply pull out an old chart or a chart done by others, the display of the charts becomes merely an act of compliance with perceived school or district mandates. This not only deprives the students of the value of

---

[6] The term *lethal mutations* seems to have been introduced in discussions of education reform by Brown and Campione (1996). It is common in biology.

participating in the creation of charts of expectations but may also breed cynicism within the teaching staff.

There is no foolproof way to prevent lethal mutations. However, as the institute has reviewed its materials and presentations, it has identified tools that are particularly susceptible to misuse and has devoted considerable effort to clarifying the explanations accompanying the tools and to specifying the potential dangers of using them inappropriately. In their district work, IFL staff members now try to devote time to coaching district staff as they use the institute's tools. Perhaps the best means of ensuring effective use of tools, however, is promoting the practice of mutual accountability.

Building District Capacity Requires Multifaceted Changes from Diverse School Personnel

The core goal of IFL is enabling a district to build its capacity to improve the quality of instruction continuously across the entire district. As expressed in the IFL theory of action, district capacity includes the capacity of teachers, teacher leaders, principals, central office staff, and line officials. It also means the capacity of organizations—schools and the central office—to communicate and collaborate. Doing this means reaching lots of people.

Capacity-Building Must Recognize the Existing Capacities of a District. Providence began its work with significant investment in the training of two core groups—the principals and a group of literacy coaches. Providence and the institute hoped that these two groups could learn a good deal about the principles of learning; techniques of instructional leadership; and, in the case of the coaches, coaching strategy and literacy content. With these capacities, the institute hoped that the principals and coaches could, in turn, build the individual and collective capacity of teachers. Others in the central office participated in some of the training but were not directly targeted. RAND interviews with principals, teachers, coaches, district leaders, and IFL staff conducted two years after the effort in Providence began suggested that many of the people trained were either unable or unwilling to take on the tasks that would lead to the extension of teaching capacity throughout the districts.

Those interviewed identified several explanations for this outcome. Some principals lacked underlying knowledge of instruction and content and thus felt uncomfortable engaging teachers on the subject. In some cases, principals had not been relieved of other duties, so they lacked not only time to work with teachers in classroom settings but also time to absorb and study the materials. Many teachers lacked respect for principals as instructional leaders, and they had neither the time nor, in some cases, the motivation to undertake efforts to improve their instructional practice. Many felt they were already incorporating the principles of learning; the more cynical among them thought the initiative and the additional burdens it entailed would soon be replaced by another one. Finally, some interviewees identified an additional hindrance: a shortage of content knowledge among staff members in the central office, who, in some districts, can play important roles in building instructional capacity at the school level.

If these problems arose in the modest-size districts initially associated with IFL, they were far more prevalent in larger districts, such as Los Angeles and Austin. In these settings, a "cascade" of intermediaries was, initially, expected to engage in training down the line until the content and practices reached the teachers. The problems of deteriorating rigor and substance associated with "training the trainer" models were present in abundance. Denver has led the way toward an approach that is less dependent on a cascade of training by providing direct training for significant numbers of lead teachers and coaches. Within the limits of available financial resources, other IFL districts are now moving in that direction as well.

Success Requires IFL and Partner Districts to Make Long-Term Commitments. The institute and its partner districts have approached the problem of building district capacity in several ways. One straightforward and important move is to stay the course. Absorbing and implementing the complex ideas and practices that are a part of the institute's model for effective districts takes time. The results of interviews RAND has recently conducted as part of its research on instructional improvement in Austin, Providence, and Springfield indicate that persistence in fostering incorporation of these ideas and practices can lead to wider understanding and acceptance.

Redefined Organizational Roles May Be Needed to Support Reform Efforts. Individuals in critical instructional leadership roles must be chosen on the basis of their potential to develop the skills necessary to perform those roles. Several districts have gone further, redefining traditional roles and sometimes even reorganizing to facilitate these roles. Perhaps the most significant redefinition is around the role of the individuals that supervise principals—often the area superintendents. In Austin, for example, the role of the area superintendent has shifted to assisting the principals and their key leadership staff to bring about improvement by engaging in LearningWalks and careful review of building level planning.

Creating Professional Networks May Support Capacity-Building Efforts. A third approach to improving teaching involves the development of professional networks of teachers who use IFL ideas and tools as aids to their professional learning. A related strategy is to encourage the development of networks of professionals that cross levels, both in the "line" and the "staff." Such networks are forms of nested learning communities.

Tools Are Needed to Build Districtwide Capacity. It is critical that both the district and the institute pay attention to building capacity throughout the district rather than focusing only on the school-building level. As the preceding discussion indicates, there are diverse mechanisms for creating capacity, but implementing these mechanisms involves many challenges. As one means of addressing this problem, the institute is now developing, with help from the Wallace Foundation, a suite of leadership tools intended to support individuals in leadership roles throughout the instruction-related components of school systems.

Districts Must Allocate Time for Capacity-Building. The difficulty of finding time to do the work is a subject that appears in virtually any discussion about the institute activities that RAND or institute personnel have had with teachers, building leaders, or members of the central office. One element of the problem is that some actors treat institute-related work as simply another effort to be added to the myriad of programs already in place. Rather than replacing current activities, such institute-related activities as professional development, learning to do LearningWalks, participating in study groups about content or instruction, and working with teachers in their classrooms on improving practice all take what is normally perceived to be extra time.

In some schools in any district, the leadership and teachers, if taken by the ideas, will contribute extra time. But, in many schools, most staff will not voluntarily make such contributions, and what is done must happen during the days or hours the district sets aside for professional development. In districts with rigid collective bargaining agreements, the provisions of the agreements constrain both teachers and administrators.

While reluctance to invest time in improvement efforts is sometimes attributed to lack of motivation or even laziness, anyone who has spent much time with either teachers or principals appreciates that most of them work very hard over long hours. In our view, the predominant problem is not unwillingness of individuals to work hard but the inability or unwillingness of the system to redefine roles and jobs in ways that reduce the time spent on activities of marginal importance to instruction and learning so that those playing the roles have time to invest in improvement efforts.

Building Allegiance Requires Demonstration of Effectiveness Over Time. Finding time is a problem any intermediary organization faces in attempting to improve student performance. A district cannot use an external organization's services effectively if the district is unwilling to give up existing ways of doing things. On the other hand, in the absence of clear and persuasive evidence that a new approach to instruction will clearly yield results, most school people will probably resist giving up current practices, even in the face of strong entreaties or mandates from the superintendent or senior staff.

The success of an improvement initiative that, like the institute's, is both new and critically dependent on the work of the district cannot be guaranteed, which reduces the likelihood that teachers and administrators will be willing to shift their activities to make the time necessary to implement it. Rather, the initiative must gradually prove itself to larger and larger proportions of the district staff. This need for an initiative to demonstrate its value over time must be considered in the choice of entry points for districtwide initiatives.

Sustaining the Improvement Effort

The institute's fundamental goal is to help districts initiate a process of continuous improvement in instructional performance that they can and will sustain over time. The institute views key contributors to sustainability as

- a clear vision of effective instruction and effective district operations
- coherence in district instructional practices through alignment of standards, assessment, and instruction
- capacities in the district to assist school personnel to perform effectively
- a culture of mutual accountability throughout the district
- capacity to monitor performance at all levels and make use of the resulting data to improve performance.

The institute's principles of learning and district design principles serve as inputs for its vision. Through its staff and tools, IFL helps develop coherence in instructional practices and helps the districts build and sustain the capacities noted here. Through its advice and modeling, it promotes a culture of reciprocal accountability, and through its efforts to develop and implement systems for data-driven decisionmaking, it helps to promote the capacity to monitor performance as the foundation for continuous improvement.

The process of reaching the desired sustainability in the face of the fiscal and political challenges that any district inevitably faces, however, requires another form of sustainability—the kind required to sustain the effort to make the transition from existing conditions to the capabilities outlined above. While many of the lessons IFL has learned and spelled out in this chapter relate to such efforts, it is important to note briefly some important keys to success in this transition.

Human Resource Policies Must Be Designed to Support Sustainability. One key to sustainability is dealing realistically with the inevitable turnover of personnel in any large urban district. Some of this turnover is sought, as it creates opportunities to place more-qualified people in important roles. Some of it is associated with the institutional context—for example, the movement of new teachers into and out of the profession, the movement of teachers from less-attractive to more-attractive jobs, and retirement. Since the strategy outlined in this chapter involves heavy investments in human capital, human resource policies should be structured to maximize the return on such investments. Moreover, because so much of the success of the system IFL advocates depends on the capacities of school and district staff, attention must be paid to ways in which newcomers to the system are trained and inducted.

Third-Party Organizations Must Collaborate to Provide Meaningful Assistance to School Districts. Another requirement is effective collaboration of the various "third parties" providing assistance to the district. Few if any districts have adequate numbers of properly skilled professional developers in house and must rely on outsiders. Indeed, for many purposes, third-party collaborators have important advantages (Kronley and Handley, 2003). Both the district and the third parties, including IFL, must understand one another's missions and actively pursue effective collaboration.

Expertise in Evaluating and Incorporating New Curriculum and Instruction Is Needed. A third challenge is incorporating new curricular materials and programs, instructional techniques, and various information technologies into the district's program. Improvements are emerging from research and development programs, as well as from studies of professional practice. A strong tension exists between the desire to promote instructional coherence through sustaining and perfecting existing programs and the potential for improvements through the introduction of new programs. Districts need to devise procedures for scanning new program offerings to identify potential improvements and determine whether and how they can contribute to district performance. At the same time, districts must learn to weigh the "transition costs"—in terms of money, staff time, and the threat to the coherence of district practices—against the possible benefits of new programs.

Coordinating and Adapting Policies and Practices of IFL and School Districts Requires Mutual Adjustment. Finally, it is important for both the district and IFL to monitor and adjust their activities continually in light of experience. IFL now does this by regularly convening its key district liaison personnel to review and critique one another's plans and work. The senior leaders of the institute talk regularly with the top district leadership to ensure that its work is effective or to advise them about changes they are considering. In several of the districts, institute staff regularly participate in superintendents' cabinet-level retreats. And, increasingly, IFL encourages external monitoring of the capacity-building effort through formative evaluation.

Closing Thoughts

We have described a complex and evolving program of assistance to school districts attempting to organize themselves as agents for taking effective instruction to scale, especially in urban schools. In choosing to focus on existing school districts as agents of scale-up, IFL has been, until very recently, swimming upstream against a current of opinion that has viewed districts as mostly part of the education problem—not as part of its solution. The institute chose to focus on districts because they are institutions "ready-made" for scale-up. They already exist, charged with the task of raising academic achievement across the demographic spectrum. Many of their functions need to be met by some organization above the level of the individual school, and the institute is betting that transformed urban school districts can perform these functions faster and better than new organizations—such as charter school chains, publishers, or service organizations supporting individual school subscribers—invented expressly for these purposes.

Whether the institute and its district partners win this bet will depend on how quickly and thoroughly the districts can change. The challenge is enormous. Current methods have both inertia and self-interest behind them. Every change in practice called for by the design principles outlined here represents a challenge to someone's way of life. Some theories of institutional development suggest that resistance to change will make it difficult, at best, to succeed in fundamentally transforming school districts.

The institute's focus on organizational learning is its answer to this challenge. We have documented some early and partial successes: Districts, and schools within them, are beginning to behave differently, and students are performing better. Throughout its efforts, IFL itself seeks to model behavior as a learning organization. Its tools and training processes are under constant scrutiny and redevelopment. Research aimed at systematically linking student learning to the nested learning design, to the principles of learning, to instructional leadership, and to district-led instructional initiatives is under way. We believe that, as the efforts of IFL and its partner school districts mature, this research will demonstrate that capacity-building at the district level is an effective—perhaps the most effective—means of providing students and teachers in U.S. schools with the tools and resources they need to perform at a high level.

References

Austin Independent School District, "Austin ISD: Evidence of Continual Progress," information sheet, Austin, Tex., Fall 2003.

Berends, M., S. J. Bodilly, and S. N. Kirby, *Facing the Challenges of Whole-School Reform: New American Schools After a Decade*, Santa Monica, Calif.: RAND Corporation, MR-1498-EDU, 2002.

Bodilly, S. J., B. Keltner, S. W. Purnell, R. E. Reichardt, and G. L. Schuyler, *Lessons from New American Schools' Scale-Up Phase: Prospects for Bringing Designs to Multiple Schools*, Santa Monica, Calif.: RAND Corporation, MR-942-NAS, 1998.

Bransford, J., A. L. Brown, and R. R. Cocking, *How People Learn: Brain, Mind, Experience, and School*, Washington, D.C.: National Academy Press, 1999.

Brown, A. L., and J. C. Campione, "Psychological Theory and the Design of Innovative Learning Environments: On Procedures, Principles and Systems," in L. Schauble and R. Glaser, eds., *Innovations in Learning: New Environments for Education*, Mahwah, N.J.: L. Erlbaum Associates, 1996, pp. 289–328.

Cantrell, S., M. Sithole, D. Patton, J. Mackay, K. Kelly, L. Campos, and J. Borgardt, *IFL Implementation and Instructional Leadership: A Role Study of the Directors of School Services*, Los Angeles: Los Angeles Unified School District, Program Evaluation and Research Branch, Planning, Assessment and Research Division, Publication No. 168. October 16, 2003.

Coburn, C. E., "Rethinking Scale: Moving Beyond Numbers to Deep and Lasting Change," *Educational Researcher*, Vol. 32, No. 6, 2003, pp. 3–12.

Daro, P., S. Hampton, and L. B. Resnick, eds., *Reading and Writing Grade by Grade, New Standards*, Washington, D.C.: National Center on Education and the Economy and Pittsburgh, Pa.: the University of Pittsburgh, 1999.

Datnow, A., L. Hubbard, and H. Mehan, *Extending Educational Reform: From One School to Many*, New York: RoutledgeFalmer, 2002.

Elmore, R. F., *Building a New Structure for School Leadership*, Washington, D.C.: Albert Shanker Institute, 2000.

Farr, B., and E. Yasui, *Evaluation of Denver Public Schools Literacy Program*, Mountain View, Calif.: Farr & Associates, 2003.

Fink, E., and L. Resnick, "Developing Principals as Instructional Leaders," *Phi Delta Kappan*, Vol. 82, No. 8, April 2001, pp. 598–606.

Forgione, P. D., "Intervention for Blueprint/Focus Schools," presentation to IFL meeting, Pittsburgh, Pa., November 14–15, 2003.

Kronley, R. A., and C. Handley, *Reforming Relationships: School Districts, External Organizations, and Systemic Change*, New York and Providence, R.I.: Brown University, Annenberg Institute for School Reform, April 2003.

Leavitt, B., and March, J. G., "Organizational Learning," *Annual Review of Sociology*, No. 14, 1988, pp. 319–340.

Manpower Development and Research Corporation, *Foundations for Success: Case Studies of How Urban School Systems Improve Student Achievement*, Washington, D.C.: Council of Great City Schools, 2002.

Neisser, U., ed., *The Rising Curve: Long-Term Gains in IQ and Related Measures*, Washington, D.C.: American Psychological Association, 1998.

Ouchi, W. G., B. S. Cooper, L. G. Segal, T. DeRoche, C. Brown, and E. Galvin, *The Organization of Primary and Secondary School Systems*, Los Angeles: University of California, Anderson School of Management, 2003.

Perkins, D. N., *Outsmarting IQ: The Emerging Science of Learnable Intelligence*, New York: Free Press, 1995.

Resnick, L. B., "From Aptitude to Effort: A New Foundation for Our Schools," *Daedalus*, No. 124, 1995, pp. 55–62.

Resnick, D. P., and S. E. Fienberg, "Reexamining the Bell Curve," in B. Devlin, S. E. Feinberg, D. P. Resnick, and K. Roeder, eds., *Intelligence, Genes and Success: Scientists Respond to the Bell Curve*, New York: Springer-Verlag, 1997a, pp. 3–18.

———, "Science, Public Policy, and the Bell Curve" in B. Devlin, S. E. Feinberg, D. P. Resnick, and K. Roeder, eds., *Intelligence, Genes and Success: Scientists Respond to the Bell Curve*, New York: Springer-Verlag, 1997b, pp. 327–339.

Resnick, L. B., and T. K. Glennan, "Leadership for Learning: A Theory of Action for Urban School Districts," in A. M. Hightower, M. S. Knapp, J. A. Marsh, and M. W. McLaughlin, eds., *School Districts and Instructional Renewal*, New York: Teachers College Press, 2002, pp. 160–172.

Resnick, L. B., and M. W. Hall, "Learning Organizations for Sustainable Education Reform," *Daedalus*, Vol. 127, No. 4, 1998, pp. 89–118.

Resnick, L. B., M. W. Hall, and Fellows of the Institute for Learning, "The Principles of Learning: Study Tools for Educators," CD-ROM, Pittsburgh, Pa.: University of Pittsburgh, Institute for Learning, Learning Research and Development Center, 2001.

Resnick, L. B., and S. Nelson–Le Gall, "Socializing Intelligence," in L. Smith, J. Dockrell. and P. Tomlinson, eds., *Piaget, Vygotsky and Beyond*, New York: Routledge, 1997, pp. 145–158.

Spillane, J., R. Halverson, and J. Diamond, "Investigating School Leadership Practice: A Distributed Perspective," *Educational Researcher*, Vol. 30, No. 3, April 2001, pp. 23–28..

Staub, F. C., and D. D. Bickel, "Developing Content-Focused Coaching in Elementary Literacy: A Case Study on Designing for Scale," paper presented at European Association for Research on Learning and Instruction, Padova, Italy, August 2003.

Togneri, W., and S. E. Anderson, "Beyond Islands of Excellence: What Districts Can Do to Improve Instruction and Achievement in All Schools," leadership brief, Washington, D.C.: Learning First Alliance, 2003. Online at http://learningfirst.org/publications/districts/ (as of June 24, 2004).

Tyack David B., *The One Best System: A History of American Urban Education*, Cambridge, Mass.: Harvard University Press, 1974.

West, L., and F. C. Staub, *Content-Focused Coaching. Transforming Mathematics Lessons*, Portsmouth, N.H.: Heinemann, 2003.

Westbrook, D., and C. Tousek, *The Austin Blueprint After One Year: A Report to the AISD Board of Trustees*, The Austin Blueprint Initiative, Austin, Tex., September 22, 2003.

Choices and Consequences in the Bay Area School Reform Collaborative: Building the Capacity to Scale Up Whole-School Improvement

Merrill Vargo

Vargo identifies three dimensions of scale: breadth, or broad involvement in and ownership of school reform efforts within the program's ethnically diverse and administratively complex region; depth, or changes in classroom-level teaching and learning; and sustainability, or maintenance of both specific changes and the understanding of school reform as a continuous improvement process. It is, primarily, a focus on the last dimension that has driven the activities of the Bay Area School Reform Collaborative. Recognizing the imperviousness of school culture to deep change and the unreliability of funding for institutional change, the collaborative has focused on building organizational capacity—the capacity to identify internal problems, generate solutions, implement new practices, and assess their outcomes. It is this capacity, she argues, that is essential to sustaining not only particular reforms but also the flexibility to address new challenges and to respond to fluctuations in school financing.

Our nation has never felt more urgency about the task of improving its schools. School reformers have responded by setting very ambitious goals: changing teaching and learning, fostering broad engagement in and ownership of the improvement process, and sustaining these changes over time. These goals reflect a definition of scale that has three dimensions—*depth*, or classroom change; *breadth*, including both broad engagement and broad ownership; and *sustainability*. Success in achieving the goal of scale thus defined has been elusive. Despite decades of hard work and significant investment of resources, the history of scaling up school reform is largely one of failure.

If achieving any one of the three dimensions of scale constitutes a significant challenge, achieving all three seems virtually impossible.

Individual schools often improve and researchers find particular programs or approaches to be effective. But what has been euphemistically called "the complexity of the school environment" seems to prevent even programs that meet the highest standards for proof of effectiveness from being well implemented, widely adopted, adjusted to local conditions in ways that maintain the integrity of the program, broadly owned by those charged with implementing them, or sustained in the face of personnel turnover or budget cuts. The current focus of both state and federal policymakers on improvement efforts aimed at spreading programs that are "research-based" is thus important, but it tells us what ought to be scaled up, not how.

This long history of failure has produced various responses among school reformers, responses that reflect strategic choices—both conscious and unconscious—about what fosters each of the three dimensions of scale and how to prioritize them. That these dimensions are potentially in conflict seems clear. The goal of depth—influencing teaching and learning—often seems to compete with breadth—engaging many teachers, many schools, or many levels of the system. Some reformers place the highest priority on the transformation of teaching, while others seek to build broad engagement first. However, the goal of sustainability is almost always postponed in the interests of the balancing act between the first two. Yet the failure of reformers to sustain successful improvement efforts makes all gains temporary—and thus, in one sense, moot. For this reason, it could be argued that sustainability deserves particular attention.

This chapter describes the Bay Area School Reform Collaborative (BASRC), a San Francisco–based school reform effort. This effort has taken all three dimensions of scale seriously but attempts to pay particular attention to the goal of sustainability. The formation of BASRC was prompted by a challenge to American educators from philanthropist Walter Annenberg, who, in 1993, announced a $500 million gift to support school reform programs throughout the nation. This promise led William Hewlett and the Hewlett Foundation to respond to the opportunity the Annenberg challenge presented by offering $25 million to support the creation of a regional education reform initiative. Annenberg matched the Hewlett grant, funding the creation of BASRC in spring 1995.

In 2001, the Hewlett and Annenberg Foundations, together, granted BASRC another $40 million. These new grants were intended to support continued work with schools, as well as expanded efforts to change school district central offices. This chapter treats the eight-year history of BASRC as data and explores a series of strategic choices BASRC made in its attempt to scale up school reform in the Bay Area. In so doing, I attempt to cast light on two rarely discussed aspects of efforts at scale: the balancing act reformers perform as they make choices among strategies aimed at each of these three dimensions and the trade-offs that result from these choices.

Scaling Up Capacity for Continuous Improvement

State and federal policy is driving much of today's education reform, and policy today places the highest priority on classroom change, the dimension we have called depth. The central strategy is to foster classroom change by identifying "research-based programs" and then employing various tools and policy levers—scripted curricula, a focus on testing and accountability, sanctions for low-performing schools, the adoption of standards, and investment in professional development for teachers and administrators—to encourage the achievement of part, at least, of the second dimension of scale: broad adoption and implementation of such programs. The goals of ownership and sustainability are not specifically addressed. The assumption is that sustainability can be achieved by doing more of the same.

Yet many educators have greeted the promising results—rising test scores and, in a few places, signs of a narrowing achievement gap—with a combination of support for the goals and misgivings about the strategy. Criticism often takes the form of arguments against testing and accountability, and these important tools are worth getting right. But there are deeper issues at stake. An alternative view of the current arsenal of school reform policies takes issue not with tools or strategies but with policymakers' underlying assumptions about what exactly needs to be scaled up. This argument reflects the idea that—especially if the goal of sustainability is taken seriously—the content and the process of changing schools cannot be separated. The *what* that needs to be scaled up is good teaching and learning. But assumptions about both what constitutes good teaching and how to achieve it are intertwined, and both shape strategies for scale.

According to this argument, schools do lack good programs, but they also lack the capacity to engage in an iterative process that includes a systematic investigation of their students' needs, careful analysis of the results they are getting, identification of improvement goals and strategies, and thoughtful implementation of these goals and strategies in ways that balance the need for good implementation of good programs with the needs for ongoing adjustment in response to data about effectiveness. In this view, the real purpose of the currently popular policy levers is or ought to be building the capacity of educators to engage in a systematic process of improvement. This emphasis on scaling up capacity for continuous improvement is particularly important in California. The ability of schools and districts to engage in continuous improvement is arguably the key not only to good implementation of effective curriculum and teaching strategies but also to their ability to respond to California's rapidly changing demographics, policy mandates, and labor market.

BASRC's work reflects a particular view of what, exactly, deserves to be scaled up in public education. For BASRC, good teaching is a challenging activity that requires teachers to make choices and decisions every hour of every day. Wise choices depend on teachers' deep understanding of students, content, pedagogy, and learning. Standards, research-based practices, and even scripted curricula are all reasonable tools for teachers, but they are just that: tools that are or should be part of a teacher's repertoire as he or she attempts to provide or respond to learning opportunities for students. They provide useful, even essential, ways for teachers to manage the complexity of the learning environment, but they can never eliminate this complexity. They are not a substitute for deep understanding. By striving for a deep understanding and becoming actively, intellectually, and emotionally engaged in the process of teaching and in their own and their students' learning, teachers are not only more effective but also provide models for students of what is required of them. This view of teaching sees today's proven program as tomorrow's outmoded practice and hence assumes that, although what needs to be scaled up in schools in the short term may well be particular "research-based" programs, what needs to be scaled up in the long term is a respect for evidence and the capacity for continuous improvement. In this view, it is continuous improvement that is both sustainable and worth sustaining.

Building Capacity in Education Organizations

Policymakers often approach education as though capacity, including capacity for improvement, resided almost exclusively in individuals. This view leads, for example, to the emphasis on requiring schools to hire "highly qualified teachers" but not on requiring them to incorporate time for school-based teacher planning, collaboration, and professional development into school schedules. On a system level, ignoring the role of organizational capacity causes states to invest heavily in creating information management systems to track data for state and federal accountability purposes, but the lack of emphasis on organizational capacity also leads them to underestimate the importance of providing assistance to school districts to create data systems that aim to inform local improvement efforts.

Although it is not central to today's policy debates, the idea that capacity for improvement resides—or can reside—not only in individuals but also in organizations is not new. Organizational change literature focused on the private sector takes that capacity for granted, especially the capacity for improvement, and also assumes that it resides not just in individuals but also in organizations. For example, Cohen and Levinthal (1990) describe what they call "absorptive capacity." Absorptive capacity is, in brief, the ability of an organization to find and put to use new knowledge, and it is regarded as a feature of high-performing private-sector organizations. Others have described organizations as having (or lacking) the skills for "knowledge management." This understanding of organizations as having capacity and, in particular, capacity for improvement should not surprise us: This attribute is an expression of the social dimension of learning.

BASRC focused its work on the school as an important unit of change in large part because it sees the school as not the only, but the crucial, locus of organizational capacity-building in the education system. In this view, systemwide improvement in education can only happen by relying on strategies that support intelligent decisionmaking at multiple levels. The education system is too large, complex, and loosely coupled for anything else to be effective. This is not to say that school districts have no role. Districts, in fact, play a very important role in allocating resources in ways that support improvement, in providing both common assessments, an information management system and data analysis, high-quality instructional materials, access to professional development, and so on (Togneri, 2003).

But schools are still central, and if what matters in school is better teaching and if teachers, by and large, do the best they know how, systematic improvement requires investment in teacher learning. Neither is fostering teacher learning only about improving preservice teacher education or about planning better and better professional development sessions. Rather, it is about reinventing schools to make teacher learning a central part of what they do (Vargo, 1999). Locating teacher learning in schools implies that such learning needs to be based on analysis of patterns of student learning; collective action to identify and implement new strategies, programs, or approaches; and a collaborative effort to engage in a disciplined process of reflecting on results and improving implementation.

This is not to say that teachers can or should invent the new strategies or curriculum they work together to implement. On the contrary, teachers need and have a right to have access to the best that systematic research and knowledge gleaned from practical experience have to offer. But the implementation of appropriate "best practices" in schools is a collective activity that involves teachers working together. Organizational capacity in both schools and school districts includes, most importantly, the capacity to support teachers in taking collective action to improve teaching and learning systematically.

A Focus on Cultural Change

An outsider might predict that educational institutions should be particularly good at learning, yet the opposite seems to be true. Such a program as BASRC, which aims to build organizational capacity in schools, must be based on an assumption about why such capacity is lacking. One explanation is the history and resulting culture of education institutions. In the private sector, organizational culture is recognized as a major contributor to what Apple, Hewlett-Packard, General Electric, or any other firm does and how effectively it does it. In the public sector, though, it is relatively new for either researchers or reformers to pay attention to the culture of educational institutions.

It does not take long, however, to notice that, in contrast to high-performing private-sector organizations, school cultures are notably dysfunctional in ways that constitute barriers to scaling up reform. Researchers have documented many characteristics of school cultures that undercut the ability of educational institutions either to implement proven programs well or to engage in systematic improvement: teacher isolation, a culture of autonomy that interferes with creating a professional learning community or holding educators at any level accountable for improvement, unexamined beliefs about students' capacities, unwarranted respect for tradition, a focus on outward compliance with changing policy mandates, and a reliance on intuition even when it contradicts the data. School cultures do not support the taking of collective action or the engagement in a purposeful process of individual and organizational learning.

But how can an external actor—whether an intermediary organization, such as BASRC, a school district, or a state or federal agency—change school cultures? Here, BASRC made an important assumption: The way to work on values, beliefs, culture, systems, and structures is to begin working right away to institutionalize continuous, results-oriented improvement processes (i.e., raising achievement for all and closing the achievement gap) anchored in disaggregated student achievement data. The realization that culture is an important barrier to change has often frustrated reformers, either because culture has seemed impervious to direct efforts to change it or because changing culture can be dreadfully time-consuming. Most reformers skip culture and jump directly to work on whatever they believe matters, which is, most often, curriculum and instruction. For BASRC, the solution is to do several things at once: Begin to build organizational capacity for continuous improvement and, in so doing, improve curriculum and instruction and also change the important foundational elements of culture, including the values that underlie it and the systems and structures that express it.

Organizational Capacity and Continuous Improvement in Action

Organizations, including education organizations, have (or lack) many important capacities. However, the purpose of this chapter is to explore the interconnections among continuous improvement, organizational capacity, and organizational culture and, in particular, to explore the strategies used by one intermediary organization to build organizational capacity for improvement to achieve that most elusive dimension of scale: sustainability. For the purposes of this chapter, then, *organizational capacity* is the capacity for individuals and groups within an organization to engage in both formal and informal processes to

- identify problems
- establish goals, standards, targets, and measures for improvement
- develop plans
- implement these plans in ways that affect teaching and learning
- collect and analyze data
- adjust plans and implementation efforts as indicated by analysis of the data.

This list is hardly new; in fact, the rhetoric of continuous improvement has been a staple of school improvement efforts for decades. But rhetoric is not reality. Two vignettes—familiar to anyone who has worked in and around schools—illustrate the difference between the reactions of high- and low-capacity schools to performance data.

Analyzing Performance Data in a High-Capacity School

A high-capacity school receives its most-recent test score data. Perhaps the data come in a binder from the district office, a package from the test publisher, or over the Internet via the provider of a Web-based data system. In the high-capacity school, leaders (including, at least, teachers and administrators and, perhaps, parents and students as well) knew these data were coming and knew what questions they were hoping the data would answer. In fact, everyone in the school knows about these questions because they are tied to a professional development program that many or all teachers participate in. Perhaps, for instance, the school has been working on improving reading comprehension.

The leadership team has a regular meeting time, and roles are clear, so everyone knows whose job it is to look at the data and distill the answers to the questions. The data person (probably a teacher with some release time, not the principal) is familiar with the form the data will take and knows which subscores are of particular interest. If the test is a typical norm-referenced test that does a better job of identifying which students are struggling than of diagnosing what they need to learn, this teacher leader has access to data from diagnostic assessments that they will look at next to learn more. If it is a tough budget year, there will be some anxiety because programs or positions will probably have to be eliminated or streamlined. The school's literacy coach is particularly concerned. She has worked hard all year modeling lessons and coaching the upper elementary teachers on a set of instructional practices that all had agreed to implement, and she is hopeful that scores will reflect this hard work. If scores are not up, her position could be eliminated.

There are no secrets about the process. Everyone knows when the data will be shared with the rest of the staff, what decisions the data will inform, who will make these decisions, and how and when they will be made. Underlying all this "data-driven" (or at least data-informed) activity is the assumption that achievement gaps reflect gaps in students' opportunities to learn and that many of these gaps have their source in school structures and teacher practices.

Reacting to Performance in a Low-Capacity School

In the low-capacity school, the picture is different. No one except the principal remembered that the data were coming. He or she spends a late night poring over the numbers. The leadership team does not exist, does not meet regularly, or is occupied with responding to day-to-day crises or district mandates. The only question that anyone can think of about the data is, "Did the scores go up or down?" The principal is anxious about unfavorable coverage by the local paper. No particular decision is necessary because the school operates a host of apparently worthwhile programs that together ensure that no focused improvement effort is under way.

Since teachers view their autonomy as a right, it is guaranteed that no collective action to change classroom practice will be taken because of the scores. In fact, the faculty has little sense of whether they agree or disagree with each other about what good practice looks like, and they have little idea what is going on in each other's classrooms. If the test score news is bad and if the scores are down (or not up enough to meet state targets), there will be some hallway and parking lot talk, but most of it will focus on flaws in the test and how the student population is different from what it used to be.

There are no common assessments beyond the mandated standardized test, so there is no possibility of delving deeper into students' gaps. Even if this school has gotten the word about "data-based decisionmaking," poring over the scores from any one test will do little to suggest corrective actions. If the principal is an activist and creative with the budget, he or she may bring forward a proposal for an add-on test-preparation program.

It is worth noting that the low-capacity school may—and probably does—have strong individuals and good teachers on staff. But, as an organization, the school lacks the values that tell teachers and other school leaders they are collectively responsible for student learning; the culture that supports ongoing learning as part of being a professional; the structures to think and decide together on actions to be taken; and the systems to reinforce connections among program, personnel allocations, and budget. This is the kind of school that causes Richard Elmore and others to observe that "[i]t would be difficult to invent a more dysfunctional organization for a performance-based accountability system" (Elmore 2002, p. 4). Today, low-capacity schools outnumber high-performing schools, and no effective and replicable process exists to transform a low-capacity school into a high-capacity school.

Organizational Capacity and Urban Schools

Neither are low- and high-capacity schools randomly distributed across the landscape. Although organizational capacity is a function of culture and structure, resources also help. Low-wealth schools and urban schools are much less likely to be high-capacity schools than are high-wealth and suburban schools. Ignoring the issue of organizational capacity is, therefore, fraught with consequences for poor children. Organizations with low capacity are less able to respond to new programs and requirements than are those with high capacity. Since the highest-need schools typically have the lowest capacity and since schools with low capacity are most often urban schools that serve poor children, presenting these schools with new programs or requirements is unlikely to produce improvement (Elmore, 2002).

Again, this is not the fault of individuals. Schools serving poor children are beset with a combination of high staff turnover, high levels of regulation, and a high frequency of daily or even hourly crises. They lack exactly the kind of programmatic coherence that yields improvement because they are also often homes for a high number of arguably worthwhile but uncoordinated interventions that, taken together, prevent a focused effort at improvement (Newman et al., 2001). It has become commonplace to note that schools and school districts are "loosely coupled" systems, but it is less widely understood that this is far more true in urban than in suburban systems and that this fact is one cause of the much-talked-about achievement gap.

Of course, some urban schools do succeed in developing organizational capacities that permit them to respond to these challenges and still engage in a process of improving instruction. But because efforts at improvement—especially those that emphasize work to develop teachers' subject-matter expertise—rarely focus on building organizational capacity, implementation of reform in our most challenging schools relies on superhuman efforts by heroic principals and teacher leaders, efforts that by definition cannot be scaled up or even sustained over time. Educators have an oft-noted tendency to debunk rather than believe success stories. Part of the source of this sad reflex is undoubtedly the widespread frustration with policymakers' assumptions that heroic effort can be both replicated and sustained. It cannot.

Given this situation, it should not be surprising that evidence is accumulating that high-poverty and low-performing schools are apparently less likely to respond to the demands of high-stakes accountability systems than are schools that serve less-challenging populations and that have greater organizational capacity. Thus, rather than helping to narrow the achievement gap between high-performing and low-performing schools, high-stakes accountability systems ensure that low-capacity schools will lose ground relative to schools with greater capacity (Elmore, 2001; Hatch, 2000).

The latest wave of reform, despite its many strengths, fails to include strategies to respond to key demands of making change in our most challenged and challenging schools. This situation calls attention to the importance of scaling up organizational capacity within schools. This perspective is of particular importance to an organization like BASRC, whose mission includes a sharpening focus on creating schools that meet the needs of groups of students who have typically been underserved.

A Response: BASRC's History and Approach

From its founding, BASRC's mission was to enhance education quality on a regional scale in the San Francisco Bay Area. The Bay Area is an unusually challenging context in which to undertake broad-scale reform: It is a region characterized not only by great socioeconomic, racial, ethnic, and linguistic diversity but also by what has been called "jurisdictional dissonance." The Bay Area consists of six counties; 118 school districts (some of which feed into each other); and countless cities, towns, and other governmental structures. This context could have prompted a narrower scope, but BASRC's focus on the goal of broad engagement of the education community and on regionwide change was a condition of its initial founding. The interest of the national Annenberg Challenge in reforming urban school districts led the BASRC planners to approach the foundation with the argument that the Bay Area, like New York, Chicago, Philadelphia, and Los Angeles, was a major urban area. Not coincidentally, the six-county region chosen to make this point was also the focus of the William and Flora Hewlett Foundation. The interests of the two foundations converged, and the regional focus was a condition of the grant that resulted in the creation of BASRC.

At the time BASRC was founded, many individuals concerned with school reform felt that reform efforts lacked policy coherence. What came to be called *systemic reform*—a package of reform strategies aimed at creating policy and programmatic coherence—was a response to this view of the problem (Smith and O'Day, 1990). BASRC planners appreciated the partial promise of this approach, but they also saw that the lack of *programmatic* coherence in schools and districts did not entirely originate in a lack of *policy* coherence in Washington or Sacramento but rather was, in part, a local phenomenon. BASRC's founders felt that increased policy coherence could dramatically improve educational outcomes, especially for the children that the current system does not serve well, but also required the development of a coherent, focused, intensive, and coordinated improvement effort at the school level. Thus, one missing ingredient was school capacity to do something in particular: engage in and manage a process of continuous improvement. One result of a systematic improvement effort at the school level would be more-effective implementation of whatever policies or programs were under way.

Equally important, a systematic improvement process would need to lead schools to discontinue programs or processes that were not effective or not appropriate for their students. The inability to discontinue ineffective programs might arguably be one of the most formidable obstacles to the sustained improvement of education. Like many public-sector industries, education funding—especially in states, such as California, where education funding is no longer closely tied to property taxes—is subject to a "boom and bust" funding cycle. For example, beginning in fall 2003, California schools entered a period of large budget reductions resulting from the combination of the demise of the dot-com economy and the state's heavy reliance on income taxes to fund schools. Although the scope of this particular round of reductions is unprecedented, the pattern is all too familiar, and the response of the education system was all too predictable. When tax revenues rise, programs grow and new ones are added. But new programs are not added with the idea of testing out possible approaches. When revenues fall, rather than eliminating the least effective of the last round of new ideas, schools and districts most often rely on a combination of political and budgetary calculations to determine what stays and what goes.

From the outset, BASRC went beyond merely advocating the use of continuous improvement processes in schools and instead made building school-level capacity to engage in a systematic improvement process the focus of its program. There are inherent dangers in what some have called derogatively a "process approach" to reform, and BASRC understood that the continuous improvement process it proposed would have to ensure that schools maintained a focus on students, on learning, and on improving instruction; it would have to have the potential to engage and hold accountable all teachers; and it would have to create an appetite among participating teachers and administrators for information about research-based best practices and ensure that content specialists are there to train teachers in high-quality implementation of instructional programs. If it worked, such a process could help ensure that schools did a thoughtful job of what some call "knowledge management," a concept that includes identifying problems, accessing new ideas, translating ideas into action, and evaluating results. BASRC's work toward classroom-level change, then, would take the form of work to institutionalize a process of continuous improvement in the life of schools. By working on such implementation issues, BASRC would build the capacity of schools to take interventions to scale within their own walls. Thus, BASRC's planners began with an awareness of the challenge of building organizational capacity, an idea about what capacity might look like, and a concept of how to go about fostering it.

BASRC Results

The BASRC network of schools is spread across more than two dozen school districts. Beginning in 1996, BASRC was the subject of a major independent evaluation, led by the Center for Research on the Context of Teaching, which is housed at Stanford University. Evaluation findings released in 2002 summarizing findings from 1996 through 2001 indicated that BASRC schools scored significantly higher than a matched sample of similar schools in terms of improvements on the state-mandated Stanford Achievement Test (SAT-9). This improvement occurred despite imperfect alignment between this test and the goals schools established for their BASRC-supported work. Evaluators also found that gains were greater among schools that had made the most progress in implementing BASRC's "inquiry," or continuous improvement, process. The evaluation linked survey data from teachers, students, and administrators to data about student learning and thereby tested BASRC's hypothesis that its inquiry process would change both student learning and school culture. Findings from this evaluation effort confirm this, strongly suggesting that BASRC was successful in changing school cultures in a number of important ways and that these changes are positively correlated with improvements in student learning (McLaughlin, Talbert, et al., 2002).

Early Strategic Choices and BASRC's View of Scale

As the brief history above suggests, BASRC began its work with a more-explicit commitment to scale than do many school reform efforts or interventions. From the outset, BASRC sought to improve teaching and learning, to foster deep understanding and broad ownership among teachers for new ways of teaching, to engage educators across the San Francisco Bay Area, and to do so in ways that rendered these improvements sustainable over time. It is easy to dismiss the charge to work simultaneously toward the three dimensions of depth, breadth, and sustainability as mere rhetoric, but, in fact, the BASRC planners thought explicitly from the beginning about strategies to work toward each of these three dimensions of scale.

However, BASRC was not unaware of the dismal track record of efforts at large-scale change in education and, for this reason, viewed its work from the beginning as partially experimental. While BASRC's fundamental approach to reform is grounded in research (Fullan, 2001; Little and McLaughlin, 1993), BASRC saw its effort to work toward scale and to build organizational capacity in schools as subject to an iterative process of trial and review. Over the eight years of BASRC's history, these trials took a number of forms. In addition, each of these three dimensions calls for different strategies, and maximizing all three requires a constant balancing act in which the designers of the reform effort recognize and respond to trade-offs and in which each choice both constrains and enables future design decisions.

Reform initiatives typically have life cycles that also shape choices because they dictate which of the three dimensions of scale takes priority at a given moment. BASRC was founded as a five-year initiative. In the early stages of such an effort, the issue of breadth is paramount as the initiative seeks to enlist partners and recruit schools and districts; later, issues of depth take precedence as the initiative strives to ensure results for students. Finally, the focus shifts to sustainability as the initiative winds down or, as was the case with BASRC, transitions to a new phase.

Work on Breadth: Creating a Vision

The first focus of the BASRC planners was a choice on behalf of the goal of breadth. BASRC found itself in a state and region with an active school reform community whose work was set against a backdrop of state leadership that for decades had spawned multiple state-sponsored categorical programs and school reform efforts. Thus, BASRC planners were quick to conclude that, despite BASRC's commitment to fostering classroom-level change, another new curriculum or instructional program was the last thing Bay Area schools needed. As a result, BASRC did not define its goal for classroom change in terms of a particular instructional approach or curriculum. Instead, as both a pragmatic response to political realities and a principled position, BASRC began its work with the collaborative creation of a vision statement that defined its goals for school change in rather broad conceptual terms. The resulting vision statement was a consensus document that attempted to describe a comprehensive picture of changes in what Richard Elmore has called the "technical core" of schooling (Elmore, 2000). BASRC described changing relationships between and among teachers, students, and curriculum as at the heart of its mission but took the inclusive view that strategies to reach the vision might well vary.

The group that created the BASRC vision included representatives of schools, districts, foundations, and school reform organizations. The vision remained a draft, open to revision, for some time, and the highly politicized status of education in California made BASRC and the BASRC vision an important anchor for Bay Area educators. Many participants in the BASRC network were energized to realize that professional consensus and commitment still existed despite political losses and years of what educators felt was chronic "education-bashing" by the press and politicians alike. Thus, though the content of the vision statement itself focused on the dimension of scale that was about classroom change (and the system elements that support this), the process of its creation was a tool for breadth, for engagement of the Bay Area's diverse education community. This early choice constrained later choices in important ways, making it difficult or impossible for BASRC to take on the role of sponsor of any particular instructional program.

Work on Depth: Translating the BASRC Vision into a Set of Criteria

Largely missing from the education policy context in California in the early 1990s were both data regarding student achievement and accountability for results. Given BASRC's goal of scaling up a continuous improvement process that focused on improving teaching and learning, it is thus not surprising that a major focus of BASRC network events in the early years was on helping school people find and use the data or evidence needed to inform a systematic improvement process. However, in the absence of a state-mandated test, BASRC focused its attention on other kinds of data. In so doing, BASRC did what many reform initiatives do: It chose to further articulate or specify selected elements of its program (Cohen and Ball, 1999). BASRC translated its vision statement into a set of "rubrics" that described developmental stages for reforming schools, districts, and support organizations. The rubrics focused discussion on evidence of both student work and adult work. They were also important to the BASRC developers because of their sense that, to be effective, a continuous improvement process needed to be anchored to a set of criteria or standards.

In creating the rubrics, however, BASRC retained its commitment to the goal of breadth, or broad engagement of the Bay Area education community. Network members met first to create rubrics for both school and district work and then, over a period of several years, to review and score school membership portfolios, applications for "leadership school" status, and annual progress reports. These processes were fairly structured, but they also left considerable latitude for professional judgment. Network members included teachers, administrators, parents, foundation program officers, and miscellaneous others who met on equal terms to review documents against the detailed standards that had been produced via BASRC's collaborative process and, ultimately, to make real decisions about the merit of each other's work. One result was a level of conversation about schoolwide issues that, for many educators, felt both new and invigorating. Other results included a surprisingly high level of professional consensus about what constituted high-quality school reform work and surprisingly harsh judgments of the quality of much of the work that was submitted.

BASRC's decision to focus on the review of school-level, rather than classroom-level, work also had consequences. While much research supports the idea that the schoolwide issues that BASRC has lumped into the general concept of school capacity do affect teaching and learning (Little and McLaughlin, 1993), there is a built-in lag between work to build a professional learning community and improvements in student performance. The focus on building organizational capacity in schools was also a better fit with the realities of elementary schools than of large high schools. The high schools that engaged most actively with the BASRC process were those that were able to embrace a schoolwide focus on literacy. Often, though not always, these were smaller high schools in urban settings, schools in which large numbers of students were struggling with reading.

The ability of schools to translate analysis of data and evidence into action depends, of course, on some important external factors, including, most importantly, the supply of appropriate professional development. BASRC assumed that the state of California, which began in 1996 to focus significant resources—far beyond what BASRC could muster—on professional development and instructional materials in reading, would supply this need. This was an attractive solution because BASRC itself lacked the staff resources to provide intensive professional development at the school level.

Over the years, BASRC found that, while its emphasis on building organizational capacity in schools does pay off, professional development resources are still in too short supply. Despite continued high levels of investment from the state, this situation continues to affect many schools negatively. For this reason, BASRC has moved in recent years both to scale up the expertise in literacy of its staff and to form partnerships with organizations that have expertise in teaching reading. BASRC predicted such choices from its founding, arguing that applying the same continuous improvement process to its own work that it advocates for schools would lead, over time, to a weeding out of programs and approaches. BASRC may have begun with an approach that resembled the "let a thousand flowers bloom" branch of reform, but this was only a starting point—not a principled position. Nevertheless, those whose favorite programs were subject to the weeding process were unhappy.

Work on Sustainability: Culture Revisited

Most education interventions have no strategy for sustainability that does not involve perpetuating both a funding stream and their own existence. But BASRC had a built-in theory about sustainability: By defining the problem of school change in terms of the organizational capacity of schools and districts, BASRC put forward both the goal of sustainability and a hypothesis about achieving it. Every observer of schools has marveled at the resiliency of negative school cultures, cultures of isolation and dysfunction that appear to outlast changes in personnel in ways that lead discouraged change agents to ask, at least in private, "Is it something in the water?" While no one expects the needed cultural change to happen overnight, BASRC's idea was that increases in organizational capacity, reinforced by changes in organizational culture, could and would sustain themselves.

Building on the Policy Context: Choices and More Choices

BASRC's goal of scale and focus on organizational capacity-building led to a series of choices, many of which fall into categories that will be familiar to most observers of reform efforts. As stated above, vision-building strategies are typically breadth choices; program-articulation strategies are most often depth choices. The choice to align with influential policy initiatives can serve either purpose, depending on the nature of the policy initiative involved, although policy is probably most frequently effective in the service of broad engagement. In the balancing act that typifies the evolution of many reform efforts, BASRC's breadth choices balanced its depth choices. BASRC chose to build on, rather than to oppose or ignore, the evolving state policy context in California. The corresponding depth choice was to focus on an "inquiry" form of the continuous improvement process and to specify the elements of that process more and more clearly over the years, including at the school, grade, department, and classroom levels. Finally, and most recently, the goal of sustainability has come to the fore, and, in its interests, BASRC has added a new and intensified focus on changing school districts.

All these choices were just that—real choices. There were alternatives; there were dissenters; and each choice had consequences and constrained future choices in important ways. This process of making strategic choices is not unusual. Designers of reform efforts—from school principals to superintendents to state leaders, as well as leaders of intermediary organizations—engage in such choices routinely. But the process of making strategic choices too often remains invisible and unexamined. In the following paragraphs, I describe several areas in which we faced strategic choices, the choices we made, and their consequences for BASRC's activities in the 1990s.

More Work on Breadth: Embracing State Assessments as "Good Enough" Data

Like most intermediaries, BASRC is a relatively small player in a large and highly politicized arena. At the moment of BASRC's founding, the combination of recession and political deadlock in the early 1990s had produced a significant vacuum in state leadership of education. These conditions made the moment ripe for the rise of a regional reform collaborative, but they also meant that the toolkit available to local reformers was limited. California's state testing program had been dismantled and had not been replaced; state leadership was no longer focused on the curriculum improvement efforts of the 1980s; and the implementation of the federal Goals 2000 legislation (Goals 2000: Educate America Act, 1994) had become mired in the state-level political stalemate. Then, several years after the founding of BASRC, the state policy context shifted dramatically as economic recovery coincided with a series of court decisions that ended a long legal battle between the governor's office and an elected state superintendent of public instruction and that consolidated the governor's control of education policy. The results were a new state test; a highly structured California Reading Initiative; and, ultimately, the Public Schools Accountability Act with its new focus on school-level accountability.

BASRC responded by adopting the state's tools and attempting to use them to reinforce its initial focus on data and accountability. There were multiple reasons for this choice. BASRC's lack of hierarchical authority over schools led its leadership to be concerned with retaining the attention of the schools when they faced a new, activist political leadership. Second, the data from the new state test, however imperfect, were useful in offering new insights into patterns of student achievement and especially into the achievement gap between underperforming groups and their largely white and Asian peers.

But the choice to align with the state and use the flawed data from the new test was controversial within the BASRC leadership group and network, and the critics made good points. Inevitably, the California policy toolkit was imperfect. State investments in professional development and other kinds of support for improvement lagged behind its investment in developing standards, adopting tests, and putting accountability measures in place. The tests themselves were imperfectly aligned with state standards and, of course, failed to capture important dimensions of students' intellectual, social, and ethical development. From the point of view of the BASRC network, the state's approach also seemed unlikely to produce large-scale improvement. Even though the approach held schools accountable, state policy shifted professional development resources away from school-based professional development and toward university-based summer institutes. These, by their very nature, routinely failed to reach whole faculties, to tie closely to the curriculum or instructional program of any individual school, or to build organizational capacity within school faculties to engage in the systematic improvement of instruction.

Thus, these new initiatives from the state presented BASRC with a dilemma. Many of the new state policies were wildly unpopular among educators. Some, such as the ballot initiative that placed most of California's English language learners in English-only classrooms, challenged deeply held beliefs. Others, such as the state's effort to revamp the teaching of reading, had a strong foundation in research but were handled in such a heavy-handed, top-down manner that even the many educators who understood the research and supported a change in strategy were turned off. Critics were justified in warning of the dangers of turning "professional development into a tool for control" (Elmore, 2002, p. 12).

As an organization with a strong grass-roots following among teachers and administrators, BASRC could have opted for popularity and the stance of critic. Instead, BASRC took a longer view, arguing that educators could not and should not try to buck the voters of the state and that, just as the charge of public education included teaching all the children, it also included making good educational programs out of all the educational policies that the state adopted. From a pragmatic standpoint, it seemed clear to the BASRC leadership that new state policies were here to stay and that increased accountability was not an inappropriate step for a publicly funded system. In the long term, it seemed that the only way to capture the attention of a critical mass of teachers and administrators—especially within the low-performing schools at the heart of BASRC's mission—was to align BASRC's work with emerging high-stakes state programs. Advocacy groups and many parents were adamant that test results could not be ignored. BASRC's regional (as opposed to national) focus was essential in making its decision to align with the state possible; BASRC could adjust its strategies to respond to a changing state policy context in ways not available to intermediaries seeking to work in several states.

However, there were downsides. The limitations of the state test made it unlikely to prompt deep professional conversation about teaching and learning, yet, in the rush to respond to state-sponsored accountability, local efforts to develop and use assessments that were either more diagnostic or more authentic or both atrophied. Thus, the California context provided BASRC with both important tools and important challenges. BASRC began an effort to build on educators' newfound test- and accountability-driven interest in data, shifting its accountability efforts away from the review of organizational plans and portfolios and, instead, focusing its efforts on what it called the "cycle of inquiry" (COI), an educator-friendly form of continuous improvement relying on data-based decisionmaking.

BASRC's COI became its key tool for school leaders to change teaching and learning. It was also a tool for building organizational capacity: It guided school leaders to focus and manage their change efforts, change school cultures, build professional community among teachers, and foster distributed leadership. Finally, the COI— especially as it came to be articulated at the classroom, grade, or department level—was a tool for depth, helping to ensure that BASRC's reform work had a positive effect on teaching and learning. All this would work together, in BASRC's view, to produce sustainable improvements in student learning.

The choice to refocus this core BASRC strategy on assessment data rather than on more broadly defined evidence of student learning and of school change had mixed consequences. On the one hand, this choice was an effective strategy for promoting the breadth dimension of scale: Teachers and principals saw BASRC and its work as aligned with a state focus that inevitably captured much of their attention. Thus, BASRC escaped being marginalized. The emphasis state accountability measures placed on disaggregated data and the progress of subgroups of students gave BASRC a concrete way to talk about the achievement gap. This was useful, given BASRC's long-standing commitment to improving student achievement for low-performing students, language minority students, and students of color. On the other hand, discussions of standardized test data did not lead to the rich, reflective conversations among teachers that resulted from discussing actual student work, and California's test data were not suggestive, in the way that actual student work or results from more diagnostic assessments can be, of changes in instructional practice. Thus, as often happens, depth was sacrificed for breadth. Yet exactly this limitation created a new appetite for more diagnostic data and for more information about "best practices." The focus on diagnostic data and online data analysis tools is a major new area of emphasis for BASRC today.

Revisiting Depth: Connecting to Classroom-Level Change

Over the years, as the COI process became more and more central to BASRC's program, it also became more and more specific. One source of this increasing specificity was BASRC's growing understanding of what the typical failures were in schools' efforts to engage in continuous improvement. The decision to articulate steps in the process was also controversial, with some members of the BASRC network interpreting BASRC to be making rules rather than spreading helpful information and complaining that, "BASRC is becoming just like the state."

The BASRC COI that resulted differed in several key ways from many data-based decisionmaking processes. The BASRC process begins with a focused set of questions about student achievement and, where standards and aligned assessments are in place, about student achievement of standards. By beginning with a question, BASRC sought to keep the focus on organizational and individual learning rather than on collecting data for compliance purposes.

The BASRC cycle also asks teachers to raise questions, collect data, and think about standards for teacher practice, as well as for student achievement. This focus seemed essential to BASRC, especially in a system that seemed much more focused on standards for children than for adults. BASRC schools have come to think of their inquiry work as organized around a question or set of questions about student achievement (in BASRC jargon, "A" questions) and a related set of questions about teacher practice ("B" questions). The questions evolved over time. BASRC eventually came to describe three stages in the evolution of inquiry questions: an inventory stage, an implementation stage, and an effectiveness stage. These stages apply both to questions about student learning and to questions about teacher practice.

Inventory questions ask, "What's going on?" Any effort at systematic improvement begins here. A typical inventory question about student performance might be, "Which students (or which groups of students) are not reading at grade level (or not meeting our standards)?" An inventory question about teacher practice might be, "What strategies are teachers using now to teach reading comprehension?" Teachers who do not trust their assessments might ask, "What evidence do we have that some students are struggling with reading?" Initially, BASRC staff felt frustrated with such questions, worrying that they stopped short of changing teaching and learning. But BASRC came to see these questions as an important starting place. The question about evidence above, for example, leads to an examination of the quality and reliability of data sources and causes teachers to confront the mismatch between their intuition about what students are learning and the data. Thus, these early questions are necessary—though clearly not sufficient—steps in a continuous improvement process.

In the next stage, questions go deeper. Teachers ask, "What else do we know about the students we have identified?" This stage leads to a focus on diagnostic assessments. Skipping this step is tempting but often leads schools to begin to implement new programs or approaches that, although they appear to align with student needs, are actually off base in important ways. These "what else do we know" questions also need to be asked about teacher practice. At this stage, teachers realize that the inventory data about what strategies are in use is insufficient, and they begin to ask questions about quality: "How well are we implementing the strategies we say we are using?" At this stage, some form of formal standards for teacher practice or a shared picture of excellence in instruction is essential.

Effectiveness questions ask, "How effective is strategy X with our target population?" Such questions are always the goal, and, in the real world of schools, the standards for connecting cause and effect are less rigorous than those in the world of research, so answering them does not seem impossible. Thus, schools often feel a sense of urgency to ask and answer these questions. But without identifying which students and which practices to focus on, and without setting standards for implementation of these practices, it is impossible to know whether improvement efforts are effective.

Finally, since the BASRC inquiry process emphasizes teachers taking collective action, it includes the idea that the cycles of inquiry should lead to the investigation, adoption, and implementation of research-based "best practices" in curriculum and instruction. BASRC's intent in emphasizing a whole-school cycle of inquiry was to provide school leaders with an opportunity, incentive, and a tool with which to choose a schoolwide focus for their improvement efforts. This schoolwide focus laid the groundwork for teachers to engage in the kind of common work that is the foundation for the creation of a professional learning community.

The effects of BASRC's choice to focus on inquiry and data were mixed. School communities that embraced the central idea became comfortable with and wedded to the idea of data and inquiry. Today, some of the BASRC districts express a remarkable degree of consensus, including teachers and administrators and even board members, about the centrality of inquiry to their improvement efforts. The external evaluation of the BASRC program found that the schools that were most advanced in the use of the inquiry process made the largest test score gains (McLaughlin, Gilbert, et al., 2002). Yet BASRC's own analysis raised important questions. Too many schools began with data that were too weak to identify problems, questions that were ill formed or too far from teaching and learning to lead to improvement, or ideas about "best practices" that were too narrow or not grounded in research. Still others continued to see data as primarily a political and accountability tool and merely added BASRC's requirements to a long list. Too often, the schools with the lowest levels of capacity—often the high-poverty urban schools reformers seek to change—were the least able to translate inquiry into classroom change.

Expanding BASRC's Reach

From the beginning, BASRC had the challenge of finding strategies for a relatively small intermediary organization to support a group of schools spread across six counties and more than two dozen school districts. Networks have long been a staple of educational improvement efforts, and BASRC thought of itself as creating a network of schools. Cross-school networks of teachers—often teachers interested in particular subject matters, instructional approaches, or programs—offer individuals social support, peer problem-solving opportunities, and a setting for professional development. Networks are also an attractive component of most efforts to scale up reform in that, in essence, they offer the opportunity to enlist volunteers to support implementation of whatever new program or approach is at issue; thus, networks offer a "multiplier effect," which is always attractive.

But for BASRC, networks were also problematic. Teacher networks are often fueled by the absence of exactly the kinds of school-based professional communities BASRC aims to create. Since teachers' work environments lack a sense of professional community and identity, many turn to networks to supply these. Given its interest in building professional learning communities within schools and school districts, BASRC was emphatically not interested in creating situations in which teachers' sense of professional identify was strongly linked to a cross-school network because such links could siphon off energy from creating in-school networks. Yet BASRC needed network structures to extend the reach of its relatively small staff.

Neither was this the only challenge BASRC faced in designing the work of its network. Another dilemma was that building school-level organizational capacity is a necessary step toward scaling up reform, yet school-level work could come at the expense of work to improve classroom practice. In an effort to work simultaneously on both these important fronts, BASRC built on its view of classroom practice and used it as a guide in designing professional development. In this way, BASRC attempted to both teach and model some aspects of standards-based classroom practice while working at the regional level.

The approach BASRC adopted had advantages. If, as BASRC assumes, changing schools requires building school capacity—including changing school culture, embedding in schools cycles of continuous improvement, and building professional learning communities—an intermediary organization must, to bring about such changes, find a way to work with large segments of school communities and must do so within the confines of regular school schedules. The size of the BASRC network of schools meant that BASRC needed to do this work "from afar." In its search for ways to do this, BASRC viewed its network of more than 100 schools spread across more than two dozen districts as a very large and very diverse classroom of learners.

This metaphor and a set of assumptions about the role of standards in the learning process led BASRC to make a number of assumptions about how it could go about building individual and organizational capacity at scale. First among these assumptions is the idea, familiar to classroom teachers but foreign to most staff development efforts, that students, if given the right scaffolding, can learn things, including things that the teacher (or staff developer or intermediary) does not know, and that this learning can take place without the teacher being present. This assumption, if it could be actualized, gave BASRC the opening to insert professional development activities into life at school, even when BASRC staff were not present. Doing so would require a clear set of standards, a variety of "exemplars" or detailed pictures of work done in response to standards, and multiple opportunities for learners (in this case, teachers and administrators) to put their own and others' work up against these standards and receive feedback. The idea of working with standards in this way—even though it underlies, for example, such models of classroom practice as standards-based practices, project-based learning, and writing workshops—is rarely connected to teacher professional development. Yet it was essential for BASRC's approach to scale.

This approach is far different from the view that says that educators working at school sites already know what they need to know and that what they need is more time, support, and permission to take action on that knowledge. BASRC assumed that site-based educators know some, but far from all, of what they need to know about either the process or the content of their reform work. For improvement to occur, BASRC believes that educators need an incentive to improve; clear standards about what constitutes improvement; access to the best ideas and coaching on their implementation; exemplars of high-quality work; and useful real-time information about results

(Sabel, 1999). Over the years, BASRC has made multiple attempts to provide the right mixture of these ingredients.

In its early years, BASRC took on the challenge of creating the conditions for school communities to engage in new, countercultural capacity-building work, not to engage in an exercise in grant-writing. In the interests of this goal, BASRC invited interested school communities to apply for membership in BASRC and to do so by using actual school reform work to demonstrate that the school shared BASRC's collaboratively developed vision of teaching and learning. To this end, applicant schools and districts prepared portfolios of work that were scored using a set of collaboratively developed rubrics. Exemplars of high-quality entries that reflected such criteria as "a focus on teaching and learning" or "systems to manage the change process" were collected and used as "anchor papers" in the application review process, which was directly modeled on the National Writing Project process for scoring student papers.[1] Anchor papers—or, in this case, portfolios—were widely disseminated. This strategy drew on the work that the state-funded SB 1274 network had done in the early 1990s.

Thus, BASRC used as a change strategy the very tools and processes that constituted the content of its reform effort, giving teachers real-life experience of operating in a standards-based system. The effect for many thoughtful participants was that attending a BASRC portfolio or application-scoring session was far more than an administrative process of scoring applications and instead constituted high-quality professional development about standards-based instructional practice (McLaughlin, Talbert, and Crowe, 1999). Over a period of years, perhaps 500 people, representing schools, districts, foundations, community groups, universities, and nonprofit organizations, worked together in the context of these BASRC-sponsored portfolio-scoring activities. The breadth of this involvement was an important step toward building a regional consensus in the Bay Area about both the goals and the strategies of reform. The activity was popular

---

[1] See Chapter Three in this volume.

enough among educators that two major school districts (Oakland and San Francisco) for a time incorporated school portfolios into their own internal accountability and improvement efforts.

The portfolio experiment was successful in engaging some, but not all, school communities in a shared experience of reflection about their collective improvement efforts. In these engaged schools and districts, the process of collecting and reflecting evidence of work and evaluating it against a set of standards seemed authentic. Other schools treated the production of these documents as one more—in this case extraordinarily complicated—compliance activity. But even in the best of cases, and despite the argument that this kind of structured reflection should reasonably be part of any self-conscious community, the portfolio application process was too artificial, time-consuming, and time-limited to be sustainable for scaling up reform.

The appropriate organizational home for such a peer-based accountability process is probably the school district, and, had the school districts that adopted the process maintained it, it could have been an ongoing strategy not only for scaling up understanding of reform among a broad community of professionals but also for building a sense of internal accountability among education professionals. Interestingly, the districts that currently have internalized some version of BASRC's peer accountability processes are the middle-sized, middle-income urban districts that are common in the Bay Area. But the state's adoption of a high-stakes data-driven accountability system shifted the focus from peer-based to hierarchically based accountability, and the larger districts and BASRC abandoned the school portfolio process.

Working with Districts as a Route to Sustainability: Political Realities and Instructional Priorities

While BASRC began with a focus on building organizational capacity in schools, the goal of sustainability led to the need to build organizational capacity in school district central offices as well. Without district-level support, schools can rarely marshal and almost never sustain a reform focus, especially in the face of rapidly changing state policies or rapidly dwindling resources. Even when schools are succeeding in reform, their efforts can easily be "trumped" by districts (McLaughlin, Talbert, and Crowe, 1999). Although the COI was designed first as a school-based process, districts provide essential ingredients—the standards for both students and adults. Equally important, they can and should provide the assessment system and information management system that gives teachers and administrators the data and information to fuel a continuous improvement process. Similarly, district infrastructure can enable or undercut high-quality school-level professional development.

Admittedly, this is a delicate balance. If the goal is to create a school-level professional learning community, the traditional districtwide staff development day is not an effective strategy. But individual schools will rarely be able to locate and access the high-quality training teachers need. So, both schools and districts have important roles in professional development (Elmore and Burney, 1996; David and Shields, 2001). Finally, in the first phase of BASRC's work, we learned that district-level support for school-to-school learning is an important factor in disseminating reform. BASRC began this phase with a concept that "leadership schools" could develop and carry out leadership roles vis-à-vis other schools that would result in the spread of BASRC reforms. This assumption proved false, except in a few cases in which districts actively assisted schools to develop and carry out such leadership roles (McLaughlin, Gilbert, et al., 2002).

Although districts matter in multiple ways, few districts succeed in leading a sustained reform effort. Most that try fail to navigate between the temptation of top-down mandates and the tendency to use improvement programs as a strategy for managing local politics. Both of these two mistakes are instructive.

The temptation of the top-down mandate is well known in organizations beyond school districts. However, it is particularly dysfunctional in districts, because school systems are so "loosely coupled" and because schools are such masters of the routines of lip service and compliance that leave the core functions of teaching and learning untouched. The top-down strategy continues to be tempting despite its dismal track record in large part because so few other tools seem to be available. It has become a cliché in education reform circles to say that "neither top-down nor bottom-up work." But what tools can districts use to scale up a reform effort that actually penetrates the classroom? Conversely, what strategies are available to school leaders to engage district offices in providing practical, useful support to their schools' improvement efforts? Finally, if the goal is narrowing the achievement gap, are there particular approaches that work? These are the questions BASRC is currently seeking to answer.

Yet no answers to the question of district strategy are helpful unless they also address the challenge of district politics. Districts, of necessity, play both political and instructional roles (David, 2003). Educators often hear the word "political" as an accusation, but the education of the next generation in a democracy is, and ought to be, a political issue. Districts inevitably must marshal human forces; build coalitions among those with competing worldviews and agendas; find (or construct) common ground; allocate scarce resources; and communicate, communicate, communicate. This is a good part of what superintendents must and should do, and this is politics. The many repetitions of the phrase "instructional leadership" have obscured this fact. The challenge for district leaders is not eschewing politics but rather marshaling politics in the interest of improving instruction, especially for low-performing groups of students.

While virtually all districts function in the political realm, a decade or more of various kinds of experiments with site-based decisionmaking has made a district-level focus on instruction seem optional. In contrast with this view, BASRC has taken the position that both research and experience tell us that school improvement requires a long-term focus on improving instruction, that this requires a sustained investment in teachers' learning and in the development of organizational capacity in schools, and that this cannot be accomplished without the district. While some districts encourage or even require such a focused approach to improving instruction, others use multiple reform strategies, programs, and efforts as a strategy for maintaining political coalitions (Hill, 2000). In these districts, what looks like a focus on instruction is not; in fact, political challenges trump instructional priorities. Reformers often advocate for focus and sustained investment without acknowledging the reality of the politicization of public education and districts' real need to manage politics.

In response to the need to help districts manage both instruction and politics, BASRC has recently mounted an effort to coordinate top-down and bottom-up approaches to reform. BASRC's model focuses on building organizational capacity at both the school and district levels. BASRC provides or brokers content-focused professional development on reading, coaching on implementation at both the superintendent and school leadership team levels, and a suite of data analysis and assessment tools. At first glance, the content focus on reading and BASRC's endorsement of particular approaches to data analysis and assessment both appear to be major departures. Yet both represent BASRC's continued effort to provide educators with the tools for engaging in a continuous improvement process and to use the changing policy context as a source of tools for continuous improvement. This long-term focus on the goal of continuous improvement, combined with the flexible approach to particular tools, strategies, and tactics, is a particular strength of intermediary organizations and underlines their potential importance in the education system.

Lessons Learned About Scale

The need to improve schools and to scale up that improvement across three dimensions is urgent. The state and national policy focus on testing and accountability has raised public expectations, and educators and politicians alike will be tempted to continue to set ambitious improvement targets even in the face of budget cuts. Given our current structures and levels of investment in improvement, our prospects for meeting these goals seem bleak. Political pressures may well "solve" the problem by adjusting the goals and measures, but the deeper issues—the underperformance of large groups of students and of the system at large—remain. BASRC bases its work on the assumption that building organizational capacity in schools—the capacity to engage in a systematic process of improving instruction and to focus this process on improving achievement for underperforming groups—is an essential and achievable goal. BASRC's experience suggests a number of lessons about effective work toward this goal. Though these lessons are derived from the experience of an intermediary organization, they also are relevant for policymakers and reform leaders working within the formal education system.

Lesson 1: The balancing act between depth, breadth, and sustainability strategies is not indecision; it is an inescapable part of the work. Too often, critics of reform efforts see the choices reform leaders make as they balance depth strategies with breadth strategies or sustainability strategies as vacillation or even ineptitude when they should see an effort to manage trade-offs. No one strategy yields classroom effects, broad engagement and ownership, *and* sustainability. Rather, what is needed is a toolkit and the flexibility to use it. One result of the quick reflexes of the critics is that reformers themselves are too often not sufficiently conscious of the need to engage in a balancing act. As a result, many find themselves being reactive rather than proactive. Both reformers and the communities that support them—researchers, policymakers, and funders—need to develop conscious strategies to work toward scale.

Lesson 2: The third dimension of scale—sustainability—is not merely about "doing more of the same" but about continuous improvement and cultural change. Sustainability cannot be achieved by being postponed, and neither can it be achieved by the simple strategy of doing more of the same. When the goal of sustainability is understood as being about cultural change and the development of capacity to engage in continuous improvement, it becomes clear that achieving this goal requires strategies that are different in kind from the strategies currently in use—even when it appears that these are effective in achieving the goals of depth and breadth. Such strategies need to be built into reform efforts from the outset.

Lesson 3: Local reform leaders inevitably use state and local policies, mandates, initiatives, and so on as raw materials to build a local reform strategy. Often, policymakers or even their critics speak and act as though all the work of designing the process of educational improvement happens at the state or federal level, with local leaders assigned the task of implementation. This view is false. Policy inevitably provides part, but never all, of the toolkit local reform leaders need. Critics who complain that policy toolkits are incomplete or flawed miss this crucial point.

What is needed is the acknowledgement of the situation and a much-heightened willingness to build the capacities of individual leaders and of local education organizations to design and carry out a reform effort that both uses and supplements the policy toolkit. This does not mean that the quality or completeness of the policy toolkit is unimportant, but local leaders need flexibility and support to engage in this local construction project. Perhaps paradoxically, scale can only happen at the local level. State and federal policymakers would do well to make the effort to view the toolkit they are providing from the vantage point of local leaders and ask themselves whether the tools are sufficiently robust and whether local leaders have been granted sufficient flexibility both to use and to augment them.

Lesson 4: Intermediary organizations can play important roles in scaling up improvement. Although the boom-and-bust funding cycle that results from California's heavy reliance on a very progressive income tax to fund state services is nothing new, schools today face unprecedented budget cuts. History tells us that schools and districts respond to budget cuts in predictable ways. They will "keep the cuts as far from the classroom as possible" and, in the process, systematically dismantle exactly the organizational capacity for improvement that this chapter argues is essential for scaling up reform. Intermediary organizations, which enjoy at least modest protection from political pressure, are arguably the only remaining place to build the infrastructure needed to sustain an improvement process.

The work of improving the nation's schools remains urgent, and it is not clear whether the odds are in favor of the reformers. Large-scale institutional change is rare, even in the private sector, and the public sector faces additional daunting challenges. Even the advocates of school choice, small schools, charter schools, and other market-based models for improvement presuppose that these settings will foster schools' capacity to engage in continuous improvement. All this argues for careful attention to the issues this chapter has raised and to the experience of the many school reform organizations struggling with similar challenges. Without such careful attention, the reform movement only replicates the dysfunctional culture of schools themselves—a culture that fails to engage in systematic experimentation, that is too busy with the "next new thing" to learn from the past, and that neglects to consider the all-important issue of implementation. The stakes for children are too high for these to be acceptable responses.

References

Cohen, D., and D. L. Ball, *Instruction, Capacity, and Improvement*, Philadelphia, Pa.: Consortium for Policy Research in Education, 1999.

Cohen, W., and D. Levinthal, "Absorptive Capacity: A New Perspective on Learning and Innovation," *Administrative Science Quarterly*, Vol. 35, No. 1, 1990 pp. 128–152.

David, J. L., "Mid-Year Progress Report," internal memorandum, San Francisco, Calif.: Bay Area School Reform Collaborative, 2003.

David, J. L., and P. M. Shields, *When Theory Hits Reality: Standards-Based Reform in Urban Districts: Final Narrative Report*, Menlo Park, Calif.: SRI International, August, 2001. Online at http://www.sri.com/policy/cep/pubs/pew/pewfinal.pdf (as of January 12, 2004).

Elmore, R. F., *Building a New Structure for School Leadership*, Washington, D.C.: Albert Shanker Institute, 2000.

_____, "Psychiatrists and Lightbulbs: Educational Accountability and the Problem of Capacity," paper prepared for the annual meeting of the American Educational Research Association, Seattle, Wash., 2001.

_____, *Bridging the Gap Between Standards and Achievement*, Washington, D.C.: Albert Shanker Institute, 2002.

Elmore, R. F., and D. Burney, "Staff Development and Instructional Improvement, Community District 2, New York City," paper prepared for the National Commission on Teaching and America's Future and the Consortium for Policy Research in Education, 1996.

Fullan, M., *The New Meaning of Educational Change*, New York: Teachers College Press, 2001.

Hatch, T., *What Happens When Multiple Improvement Initiatives Collide*, Menlo Park, Calif.: Carnegie Foundation for the Advancement of Teaching, 2000.

Hill, P., *It Takes a City: Getting Serious About School Reform*, Washington, D.C.: Brookings Institution Press, 2000.

Little, J. W., and M. McLaughlin, eds., *Teachers' Work: Individuals, Colleagues, and Contexts*, New York: Teachers College Press, 1993.

McLaughlin, M., S., Gilbert, A. Hightower, J. Husbands, V. Young, and J. Talbert, *Bay Area School Reform Collaborative: Phase I Evaluation*, Stanford, Calif.: Center for Research on the Context of Teaching, 2002.

McLaughlin, M., J. Talbert, and B. Crowe, *Assessing Results: The Bay Area School Reform Collaborative, Year Three*, Stanford, Calif.: Center for Research on the Context of Teaching, 1999.

McLaughlin, M., J. Talbert, B. Crowe, C. Roller White, B. Achinstein, K. Anderson, S. Beese, R. Ebby, J. Goldstein, K. Ikeda, J. Imburg, J., Mishook, K. Moffitt, I. Oberman, M. Wechsler, and J. Zarrow, *Bay Area School Reform Collaborative: Phase One (1996–2001) Evaluation*, Stanford, Calif.: Center for Research on the Context of Teaching, 2002.

Newman, F., B. Smith, E. Allensworth, and A. Bryk, "Instructional Program Coherence: What It Is and Why It Should Guide School Improvement Policy," *Education Evaluation and Policy Analysis*, Vol. 23, 2001, pp. 297–321.

Sabel, C., "USA: Economic Revival and the Prospect of Democratic Renewal," *International Politics and Society*, No. 1, 1999, pp. 95–108.

Smith, M. S., and J. O'Day, "Systemic School Reform," in S. H. Fuhrman and B. Malen, eds., *The Politics of Curriculum and Testing: The 1990 Politics of Education Association Yearbook*, Bristol, Pa.: Falmer, 1990, pp. 233–267.

Togneri, W., "Beyond Islands of Experience: What Districts Can Do to Improve Instruction and Achievement in All Schools," leadership brief, Washington, D.C.: Learning First Alliance, 2003.

Vargo, M., *Improving Teacher Quality: Building Professional Communities in Bay Area Schools*, San Francisco, Calif.: Rockefeller Foundation, unpublished manuscript, 1999.

CHAPTER SIXTEEN

Leveraging the Market to Scale Up School Improvement Programs: A Fee-for-Service Primer for Foundations and Nonprofits

Marc Dean Millot

In this chapter, Dean Millot draws on his experience as a senior staff member at New American Schools—the business-led, nonprofit, nonpartisan organization that provided at least part of the funding for several of the innovations described in previous chapters—to argue that foundations and nonprofits that have funded educational reforms must shift their emphasis from funding the development and preliminary testing of innovations to funding the implementation and long-term operation of reform enterprises now operating in a fee-for-service environment. This shift, he claims, is needed to create sustainable change on a broad scale and will require significant changes in the organizational culture, operations, and strategies for measuring success that have typically characterized philanthropic involvement in school reform.

The growing market for school-improvement services offers an unprecedented opportunity to scale up programs that nonprofits have developed with foundation sponsorship. This chapter examines the relationships between the developers of school-improvement programs and the foundations that support them at a time when the American public school system is increasingly willing to contract with for-profit and nonprofit organizations to improve student performance.

This section will first cover my experience with school-improvement programs. Then, because their financial power permits foundations to write the rules that dominate their relationships with nonprofits and because foundations, as financiers, are ultimately responsible for the value their decisions create, the introduction concludes with a discussion of the influence of philanthropy on student performance over the past decade and the challenges philanthropic organizations face in achieving quality, scale, and sustainability in school improvement today. Much of this chapter is based on the experience of New American Schools (NAS) with organizations known as design teams that were involved in comprehensive school reform.

In the 1990s, long before what we now call venture philanthropy came into vogue, NAS recognized the potential of the market to bring high-quality education programs to a national scale. More important, NAS took advantage of and accelerated the development of the education improvement market—stimulating demand, building supply, advocating changes in government policy, and sponsoring the research required for consumers to make good programmatic choices. This experience offers philanthropy a roadmap to success in the development of a scale-up strategy. The next section of the chapter discusses the evolution of the market in the context of NAS's ten-year experiment applying market principles to the development and dissemination of school-improvement programs.

The next three sections examine (1) why and how foundations and nonprofits should take advantage of the emerging market as a vehicle for scaling up educational programs, (2) the challenges they face in doing so, and (3) the actions needed to realize the potential for social good. Although more research and development (R&D) can always be justified, a much larger portion of philanthropic investment would be better spent scaling up the implementation of programs that have already been developed and tested. Adopting a market-based scale-up strategy requires foundations and their grantees in education to embrace a change in policy, including adopting a fee-for-service revenue model and redirecting philanthropic investments toward the culture and institutions required to take programs to scale.

My Vantage Point

During the 1990s, I worked with a RAND team and NAS on strategic planning. I focused on the problem of taking NAS design-team programs to scale, writing the first memorandum on the problem of making the transition from grant to fee and drafting the memoranda of understanding NAS first employed to bring its designs to scale in major urban districts around the country. In 1997, I joined NAS as its director of design team operations, becoming, in effect, its grants program officer. In 1998, NAS stopped making grants and started making loans, and I became vice president for design team investment, a position analogous to the lead partner in a venture capital firm. In 1999, I formed the $15 million Education Entrepreneurs Fund as the financing and technical assistance arm of NAS and became its first president. Today, I am an independent consultant working with a range of clients to help them operate effectively in the emerging K–12 school-improvement market.

My observations are informed by nearly ten years of direct personal involvement in the transformation of eight original NAS design teams from grant-based research teams to fee-based professional service firms, including Success For All,[1] America's Choice,[2] Audrey Cohen College's Purpose-Centered Education, Co-nect,[3] ATLAS Communities, Urban Learning Centers, Expeditionary Learning Outward Bound, and Modern Red Schoolhouse. These experiences encompassed everything from governance to business planning, from financial planning to financing agreements, from product development to quality control, from market research to the sales process, from costing to pricing, from intellectual property protection to school contracting, and from creating new legal entities to carry on program dissemination to merging providers with other organizations.

---

[1] See Chapter Five in this volume.

[2] See Chapter Seven in this volume.

[3] See Chapter Nine in this volume.

The chapter also describes the lessons of my subsequent experience as the NAS senior manager overseeing the quality review process of providers' programs, services, and organizational capacity that NAS used to decide on affiliations with additional comprehensive school reform organizations. More than a dozen reviews were conducted during my tenure, but NAS acknowledges only successful reviews. Successful reviews included the Accelerated Schools Project/National Center, the Leonard Bernstein Center/Grammy Foundation, the Turning Points/Center for Collaborative Education,[4] the National Institute for Direct Instruction,[5] Different Ways of Knowing/Galef Institute,[6] and Voices of Love and Freedom.

As president of the Education Entrepreneurs Fund, I was responsible for the decision to recommend that our board approve loans, equity investments, or joint ventures with most of the organizations named above, as well as the education technology organizations TeachFirst, LearnNow, and Education Impact Online; Total Education Solutions, a special education services provider; and the standards matching service Align to Achieve offers. The fund also provided technical assistance to such organizations as School Renaissance, the National Council of La Raza Development Fund, and the Middle Start comprehensive school reform model. Finally, my observations are informed by my efforts, as chief operating officer and fund president at NAS, to "walk the talk" by shifting the revenue base of these activities from grant to fee—a task that, in the case of the fund, is well on its way to success.

Philanthropy's Challenge

The tax benefits available to those who establish and support philanthropies are justified, in terms of public policy, because networks of

---

[4] See Chapter Ten in this volume.

[5] See Chapter Four in this volume.

[6] See Chapter Eight in this volume.

private foundations can address certain social problems in certain settings better than government or business can.[7] The prevailing wisdom has been that public education presents such a case. Since 1991, when researchers began to track philanthropic giving for reforming America's public schools, more than $2.5 billion has been donated to the cause. Figure 16.1 illustrates the trends since 1996. What can we say about the social return on that investment? Where has philanthropy worked and where has it not?

Much research on new approaches to teaching and learning has been conducted, including many pilot projects that demonstrate the potential to duplicate the success of these new approaches at multiple schools, and quite a few disadvantaged children have been helped in

Figure 16.1

Spending on K–12 School Improvement: Foundation Grants Versus School Purchases

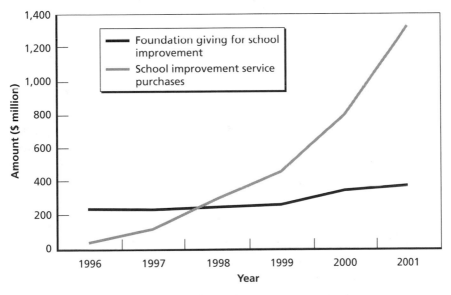

RAND *MG248-16.1*

---

[7] See, for example, Porter and Kramer (1999).

the process. Moreover, philanthropy has created a vast pool of human capital, with real expertise in school improvement. A decade of philanthropy has left the nation with most, if not all, of the programs and expertise necessary to improve public education.

Despite the accumulation of this intellectual capital, the nation has seen marginal improvements in student performance—in a few schools for a brief period. At best, the investment has yielded the rare and too often temporary "islands of excellence"—schools with a brief, shining moment of exemplary practice and performance that usually revert to the norm. Little in the way of improvement seems to stick. Today, there is little dispute among leaders in the field of school reform that the social return on philanthropic investment has been grossly inadequate.

How could philanthropic efforts have had more strategic value? Very simply, by focusing more support on scale-up and long-term viability rather than by disproportionately funding R&D. Unfortunately, few foundation managers have taken responsibility for these vital steps in the process of improving American public education. Consequently, philanthropy's investment in education reform has helped generate knowledge but has been largely ineffectual in improving the nation's schools.

In business terms, philanthropy has had no "exit strategy" for realizing the full value of its investments. Indeed, foundations have approached education improvement from the standpoint of being patrons of science, wherein the success of investment is represented by the publication of research results and subsequent discussion in seminars and academic publications. Although this research adds to the body of knowledge regarding education and becomes available as a basis for additional research, the dissemination strategy amounts, at best, to "print it and they will come."

This R&D paradigm emphasizes dissemination by researchers at the expense of adoption by schools. This approach is suitable to academia, where the goal is knowledge generation, but not to education, where the goal is improving the performance of students. To have a broad and lasting effect, the innovations identified by research efforts must become embedded in the practice of millions of teachers in more than 90,000 schools across the country. It is simply naive to believe that this can be accomplished with an implementation strategy stimulated by publication of research results.

Leaders in philanthropy seem increasingly aware of the shortcomings of their traditional approach to school improvement, a trend exemplified by the frequency with which they ask certain questions: How do we know what works and whether it will work beyond the development site? How can high-quality programs be disseminated to every child who would benefit? How can we ensure that these programs will continue to be effective? Unfortunately, the philanthropic community engages in far more hand-wringing and after-hours discussion on these topics than in taking concrete steps to address the issues and exhibits a tendency to focus on the shortcomings of grantees rather than on the incentive system that philanthropy has created, which has yielded this result.

Out of frustration over the unsatisfactory performance of their programs, many foundations are reexamining their efforts in school reform. Over the past several years, a handful of prominent foundations with a substantial history of engagement in the field have begun to withdraw. A group of newly formed organizations is replacing them. There are, however, few differences in the underlying practices of these organizations that suggest the "new philanthropy" is doing much more than temporarily infusing public education with new money. How this new group will perform any better than the old by employing what is fundamentally the same grant strategy is hard to imagine.

Just as established foundations are struggling to realize a significant social return on their investments in improving public education and are approaching the conclusion that they should leave the field, a decade-long process of changes in government policy is creating an opportunity for philanthropy to see the realization of its investment in ideas, programs, and people. Culminating in the reauthorization of the Elementary and Secondary Education Act as the Bush administration's No Child Left Behind initiative of 2001, this march of federal and state law has outlined clear standards of what students should know and be able to do; called for better alignment of tests to standards; and identified unpleasant consequences for districts, schools, and educators who fail to bring student performance up to standard. These pressures have created a demand for innovation within the public school system.

On the supply side of the equation, alternatives to the traditional means of delivering public education through schools directed by school districts are now more widely available. Additionally, changes in the use of state and federal funds permit and even encourage districts and schools to purchase services aimed at improving teaching and learning. More recently, standards have been developed for scientifically based research that specify the kind of evidence that providers of school-improvement services must present to demonstrate the efficacy of their programs. These standards enable public schools to ensure that the programs they purchase—programs developed with foundation funding—will, in fact, help improve student performance. Taken together, these forces have created a market for school-improvement services that is growing at a remarkable rate, from virtually nothing as recently as 1995 to $1.5 billion in 2002.

How NAS Came to the Fee-For-Service Strategy

Investing in R&D to "Break the Mold"

In 1991, following years of declining student performance in public schools, then-President George H. W. Bush encouraged the nation's top business leaders to support efforts to break the mold of the nation's stagnating education system by adopting the innovative and entrepreneurial spirit of the private sector. Under the stewardship of David Kearns, former chairman of the Xerox Corporation and Deputy Secretary of Education, the New American Schools Development Corporation (NASDC), known since 1998 as New American Schools (NAS), was founded in response to this call.

Shortly after its formation, NASDC invited all interested Americans to design prototypes for a new American school—one that would prepare students to meet the demands of work and citizenship in the next century. Only three constraints were imposed:

- All students must reach world-class standards in core academic subjects.
- All schools must operate at costs comparable to those of current schools, after start-up expenses.
- All designs must address every aspect of school operations directly related to the core functions of teaching and learning.

Within these boundaries, NAS established the guiding principle that still sets it apart: The school designs were to be comprehensive—in sharp contrast to the traditionally piecemeal nature of education reform—and had to be proven to enhance teaching and learning in various settings with diverse student populations.

Before NASDC, schools and school districts often adopted multiple and even competing improvement programs focused on one aspect of teaching and learning. Broader reform initiatives were treated as "add-ons." Good ideas that could have been refined with additional investment were abandoned at the first sign of trouble, as government and philanthropy turned their attention to the next new thing. In short, school reform was a victim of fashion. Under these conditions, even the relatively modest goal of "replication" seemed elusive, and moving to a national scale was simply unthinkable. NASDC, on the other hand, attempted to emphasize high quality, an iterative approach to refining programs, and a balance between flexibility and consistency in implementation. To do this, the corporation adopted high standards for demonstrations of efficacy, invested in the development of initiatives that showed the greatest promise, and made the best programs available as systems that could be implemented in and adapted to a broad range of schools.

NASDC initially selected 11 designs from 686 proposals from school systems, corporations, colleges, universities, think tanks, associations, and foundations. Over the next five years, NASDC granted tens of millions of dollars to each design developer (or *design team,* as they are now called). This competition was managed by a small, relatively young, multidisciplinary staff with the assistance of an advisory board of experienced educators, led by Saul Cooperman, former superintendent of New Jersey's public schools. The RAND Corporation evaluated the designs and the broader NAS strategy.

Toward a Market-Based Dissemination Strategy

In many respects, selecting and developing designs was the easy part for NAS. The greater challenge was enabling the designs to work at a large scale in schools throughout the country. With the developers and education advisory board focused on creating models, the NAS staff turned its attention to disseminating the designs and determining which attributes of the public school system, if any, offered high leverage. In the mid-1990s, NAS encouraged teams to expand the number of schools using designs and began to focus its investment on enhancing the quality of the designs themselves. NAS also began to study ways to ensure that the movement as a whole could be sustained over the long haul.

The first major shift in NAS strategy stemmed from RAND's finding that, as powerful a blueprint for teaching and learning as a design might be, it is not a "do-it-yourself" kit that can be pulled "off the shelf" and "installed." The leaders of NAS initially assumed they would adopt philanthropy's traditional dissemination strategy of publication, but even the modest expansion of the development effort to new schools quickly demonstrated that, because designs are meant to work in schools of varying performance levels, they must be adjusted to the specific needs of the school that adopts them. This process generally requires too much from the faculty of a working school. RAND research and the experience of the developers demonstrated that schools need help to implement and adjust such designs. Who better to help teachers to learn, use, and refine a design than the developers of the designs themselves?

As a result, under NAS President John Anderson, design teams were urged to take on a new role. To accommodate schools' need for direct on-site assistance and to provide that support at scale, teams had to find ways to increase staff and translate their designs and implementation processes into products and services. In essence, they had to harness business concepts and discipline in pursuit of their school reform missions.

Given the NAS objective of reaching every school in need, the cost of this approach to dissemination required design teams to look beyond philanthropy for ways to finance their operations. Schools would have to value the service enough to pay for it themselves. Teams would have to consider schools as clients rather than the beneficiaries of philanthropic generosity. To help the teams make the transition from depending on grants to being viable fee-for-service providers, NAS provided not only financial aid but also consultants in business planning and operations. Eventually, NAS would shift its financing of teams from grants to loans and other forms of investment.

As NAS helped providers of school reform services become more sustainable through the adoption (and adaptation) of modern business practices, it also focused on helping sustain the improvements the designs were making in schools. Research demonstrated that leadership and support from the school district and from state departments of education were critical to success. At the same time, design teams urged NAS to help find their first client schools. To stimulate demand, NAS entered into memoranda of understanding, establishing partnerships with a dozen districts and states—urban, suburban, and rural—to work alongside district staff to determine how to manage specific district functions that can support or inhibit school-level improvements.

NAS strategy involved a deliberate effort to leverage market dynamics on behalf of school reform. The decisions to push design teams into the market and to work with school districts demonstrated NAS support of a wider comprehensive school-improvement approach, wherein whole-school models are only one piece of the puzzle. NAS was moving toward support of comprehensive school reform as a system of reform and of models as instruments of that reform strategy. From this point on, NAS policy was guided by a desire to influence the comprehensive school reform movement by looking for points of leverage that could help shape the comprehensive school reform market. NAS leadership would pay equal attention to supply (represented by teams), demand (represented by schools and districts considering comprehensive school reform as a reform strategy), research (represented in the work of RAND and others), and public policy (represented by the decisions of federal and state legislatures and departments of education). It was a revolutionary attempt to break the mold of a school reform culture based on grants.

By 1995, the staff of NAS, along with its board of directors and the program developers, was committed to a fee-for-service dissemination strategy. NAS was swiftly using up its $100 million–plus war chest, so necessity clearly precipitated this decision. Nevertheless, it must be recognized that the NAS Board of Directors was truly committed to the mission of helping every child meet high standards. "Every child" meant each school and program implementation at each site would require substantial technical assistance costing teams $25,000 to $100,000 per year for three years. This could be achieved only if the public school systems' own resources could be enlisted in the effort. Many involved with NAS felt that, if schools and districts purchased program implementations, they might be more committed to them, and the programs would be more likely to take root.

The innovations NAS set in motion transformed the dissemination, adoption, and support of best practices in teaching and learning and demonstrated how these practices could be in put in place in classrooms across the United States. The promise of this new system to carry on school reform did not go unnoticed. In 1997, led by representatives David Obey (D-Wis.) and John Porter (R-Ill.), Congress added the $150 million Comprehensive School Reform Demonstration (CSRD) program to the U.S. Department of Education's Title 1 budget to support schools implementing the designs NAS affiliates and others had developed. The design teams affiliated with NAS at that time, along with nine other models, were specifically mentioned in the accompanying report as examples of where CSRD program funds could be used. The allocation has received bipartisan support year after year. By 2001, annual funding had reached $260 million.

In 1998, NAS stopped making grants to design teams and began making loans. Again, the decision was precipitated by a pending shortage of money; loans could be recycled and so give more "bang for the buck" than one-time grants. But the option was given impetus by NAS's experience with what has been called "the compliance mentality," the tendency of grantees to meet the letter of the grant but not its spirit. The requirement to repay an investment imposes a discipline on the recipient that vastly increases the chances that the plan on which the investment is based will be realized—mere compliance is no longer an option. At the same time, NAS's interest in repayment provided a strong incentive to strengthen its technical assistance, adding experts in law, finance, and accounting to its stable of consultants.

Social Return on NAS Investment

In terms of quality and scale, and sustainability, the return NAS has produced is without doubt higher than any comparable social investment in K–12 public education. Although quality is the subject of enormous debate in the growing national market for school-improvement services, the best available evidence indicates that the programs NAS has fostered are among the finest available to schools around the nation today. The preponderance of evidence points to the likely success of the programs' NAS sponsors, when school and district factors support design implementation. Over time, design developers have become better at choosing to work only in places that can meet these conditions.

Even if the quality of the outcomes the design teams produce is the subject of much debate, their scale and sustainability are not. Today, these organizations earn over $120 million in revenue from their work with the public schools. They have reached more than 2,000 schools. By both measures, the original NAS design teams continue to grow at a very healthy pace. In most cases, the large majority of their expenses are covered by fees, and the gap between the total cost of their work and their fee earnings continues to close.

Decisionmakers at the school, district, and state levels are increasingly willing to pay for the full costs of education programs— if they can demonstrate real promise of reforming schools and improving student performance. Comprehensive school reform has become the dominant school reform effort in the United States. More than 5,400 public schools, almost 6 percent of the 92,000 public schools in the country, have obtained funds through the federal CSRD program to finance design implementation partnerships with model developers. Annual CSRD appropriations reached $310 million in FY 2002. Thousands more schools have paid for work with comprehensive school reform models from other funding sources. Moreover, while comprehensive school reform providers earned $270 million in FY 2001, RAND estimates that, for every dollar paid to teams, another two to three dollars are spent on teacher training time, substitute teachers, and support for new staff positions. By this reckoning, public schools are now investing some $1 billion annually in the human capital built around some comprehensive school reform designs.

Comprehensive school reform is even part of the charter school movement. NAS-affiliated teams have entered into partnerships with 65 charter schools in the past three years. Comprehensive school reform providers also play an important role in the growing school management sector. Direct Instruction became part of Advantage Schools' curriculum (Advantage became part of Mosaica in 2001), and the programs of former NAS affiliates America's Choice and Success For All were adopted by LearnNow and Edison,[8] respectively.

Today, the technical assistance and loan programs NAS supports are housed within the Education Entrepreneurs Fund, an affiliate of NAS with a $15 million capital pool and a staff of 10, plus consultants and a range of support services. The fund is a nonprofit social investor in for-profit and nonprofit organizations that provide high-quality school-improvement services on a fee-for-service basis to public schools across the United States. The fund provides social entrepreneurs with the following:

- assessments of their program and organization readiness for the school-improvement market
- consulting services to help them build management infrastructure

---

[8] See Chapter Thirteen in this volume.

- investment in the form of lines of credit, term loans, equity funding, and joint venture financing to build implementation capacity
- online services to reduce nonprogrammatic costs, including School Funding Services, a Web-based resource that tracks several billion dollars of federal, state, and private funding sources available for school improvement.

The fund assists and invests in a broad range of educational programs with potential for reaching national scale and financial sustainability. Its new clients include such organizations as Voices of Love and Freedom, a supplemental services provider developing a comprehensive school reform design; the La Raza Development Council's work on charter schools; and Align to Achieve, the nonprofit fee-for-service distribution arm of a standards alignment service developed by Achieve.

Pursuing a Fee-for-Service Dissemination Strategy

Fee-for-service dissemination is a plausible strategy for scaling up promising educational programs on a national basis under certain conditions.

The Program Developer Perspective

For the program developer, the fee-for-service approach certainly merits consideration if it becomes apparent that foundation funding will be insufficient to the task of achieving scale and if the developer is not content either to scale back to the available grant budget or to put the program on the shelf. The higher the cost of program implementation in a school, the more likely it is that foundation funding will fail to match a program's potential for scale. High costs tend to follow programs in which the fidelity, depth, and length of implementation are of great importance and in which specialized knowledge and experience in implementation are critical. These factors also tend to lead the program developer to desire some degree of direct control over the implementation process.

Developers rarely understand the requirements of implementation well enough to spell them out as contract terms. As a result, such programs are rarely licensed successfully for others to implement. The need to control implementation often leads the developer to become the provider of the program, hiring and training consultants and staff to work directly with the schools or teachers. If the developer—now the provider—of school-improvement services is intent on taking the program to national scale, foundation funding may well remain part of the organization's revenue structure, but fees for work in the schools are the only plausible route to achieving the program's full potential.

Developer-providers may also find that the fee-for-service approach plays a role quite apart from underwriting the cost of implementation and enabling dissemination on a national scale. Most who have adopted the approach would agree that the fee-for-service strategy tends to improve the quality and longevity of implementation over the "free" alternative.

Most developers intend their programs to make lasting changes in teaching and learning. To do so, the programs' practices and routines must become deeply embedded in the normal processes of teacher and school operations. They need to become something that teachers and schools "must do" rather than something that is "nice to have." More often than not, programs provided to schools as the result of foundation largesse fail to become "must dos." They may be free, but they are also temporary and are provided alongside whatever practices the school and teachers are expected to follow as a result of tradition or district policy. When the program ends, most teachers return to standard routines and practices. Lacking a mechanism that would help sustain the program or pass it along to others, the few teachers in the school who do embrace it are gradually replaced by those who understand the standard approach.

Regardless of the institution, nothing is more central to policy and practice than the budget. By becoming a part of the budget, a program is on its way to becoming embedded in school operations. As part of the budget, the program's fees are paid, and other resources, such as teacher time, are devoted to maintaining the program at the site. Given the importance (and, given always-limited resources, the difficulty) of budgeting for school reform, a school's willingness to purchase a program says something about its willingness to implement it. The screening-function fees not only help improve a program's overall quality of implementation across all its schools but also helps the provider save time and resources that would be better spent on implementation. The willingness of a school to pay a fee is no guarantee of a program's success, but unwillingness can certainly be taken to mean a lack of commitment to the program and a higher probability of failure.

The Foundation Perspective

Foundations that seek to realize the full potential of their investments in education reform programs face three challenges: quality, scale, and sustainability. Particularly when programs are costly to implement for the reasons discussed above, a fee-for-service dissemination strategy, while no silver bullet, represents a significant advance in meeting each of these challenges over the "free" alternative.

The decision to purchase a program is by no means a perfect measure of its quality, but it is generally a better indicator than any gleaned from giving the program away. Purchases require a far higher level of commitment than does the acceptance of a gift, implying that a cost-benefit analysis and an assessment of the alternative uses of funds lead to a valuation of the proposed program. Particularly when superintendents, principals, and even teachers are becoming personally accountable for student performance, a decision to purchase a program aimed at improving performance is credible evidence of a belief that the program will have that effect. My experience in a market with many fee-for-service and free offerings suggests that, at first, objective evidence of a strong track record is likely to be weak for any program, but, as each program reaches more schools over the next several years, subsequent purchasers are likely to be influenced by the correlation of program implementation with actual student performance in the schools using the program.

Furthermore, as schools shift from being the third-party beneficiaries of foundation grants to the direct purchasers of programs, the quality of the programs simply must improve to meet customer demands. If not, the programs will fail in the market. Just as fee-for-service increases the commitment of schools to the program, so it compels the developer-provider to make the program relevant to the needs of schools. In a perverse way, foundation funding gives developers real freedom from accountability for what happens in the schools where they work. Fee-for-service ensures that providers are accountable to schools for their work in schools.

Developers might be content to pursue R&D for its own sake—many, perhaps most, are today. But private foundations, enjoying the fruits of tax benefits for donations, have an obligation to maximize the social benefit of their investments in R&D. In the case of public education, this obligation translates into a need for foundations to make their best efforts to get promising educational programs to every child who will benefit. For foundations, fee-for-service is the only plausible means of disseminating costly programs on a national scale. It is a viable exit strategy—a way for foundations to realize the full social return on their investment in education reform before they turn their resources to focus on the next social need.

Further, with regard to sustainability, fee-for-service offers providers the continuous revenue stream necessary to support and improve a program and the network of schools using it over time. As long as the program adds value to the schools it serves, it will remain in business to serve them.

Is There a Market?

Whether considered from the perspective of a developer or of a foundation, the adoption of a fee-for-service strategy clearly requires a market with ready, willing, and able customers. As recently as five years ago, the lack of a market for school-improvement services would have rendered this discussion academic. Today, market segments that have to do with the American public school system's core functions of teaching and learning are growing rapidly. While foundation funding has hovered at around $250 million to $300 million per year for some time, purchases of school-improvement services have gone from virtually nothing to well over a billion dollars and continue to increase. Indeed, the effects of market purchases far outweigh foundation giving in school reform.

A superintendent considering how to improve school performance can now draw on a broad array of strategies and providers: in school management, such firms as Edison and Chancellor; in tutoring low-performing students, Sylvan and Kaplan; in districtwide curricular programs, Open Court and the National Writing Project[9]; and in comprehensive school reform, Success For All and Accelerated Schools. Each segment has some larger players, but many for-profits and nonprofits now compete for the school-improvement dollar on the local, regional, and national levels. It is an emerging market, highly fragmented, with poor controls, and with many ill-prepared consumers. Nevertheless, it is moving in the direction of better standards and controls, more useful information, and smarter customers.

The school-improvement market is being driven by the imposition of performance standards by state and federal law. Its rapid growth has been facilitated by the increasing flexibility of federal and state funds to purchase privately developed services to improve student performance. No Child Left Behind epitomizes this trend. This act requires schools to meet annual yearly performance requirements or face corrective action, including parental rights to use the funds that would otherwise go to a failing school for private tutoring. It also institutionalizes CSRD, which provides federal funding for schools to purchase a wide variety of services for school improvement.

As presently deployed—to promote research and publication—foundation funds are becoming marginal to the goal of school improvement, and if they are not already irrelevant, that eventuality is certainly foreseeable. This likely scenario calls into question the future role of philanthropy in education reform and suggests two options. The first—declaring victory, winding down commitments to nonprofit grantees in education, and shifting investment to the next great social problem—is a tack reminiscent of philanthropy's approach to international security at the end of the Cold War. The second—

---

[9] See Chapter Three in this volume.

embracing the market as an exit strategy for investment in education research, ensuring quality in the market by giving nonprofits the means of acquiring significant market share, and seeding the market with the social intermediary institutions required for nonprofits to compete successfully—calls to mind philanthropy's efforts to rebuild international security in the wake of the post–Cold War disorder brought home on September 11, 2001.

Nonprofits that expect to survive and remain relevant to public education have no choice but to adopt a fee-for-service strategy. This course offers little hope of success, however, if foundations choose to leave the field. As the discussion below will make clear, the transition from grant to fee is difficult for all and perhaps even impossible for most nonprofits. Without substantial philanthropic efforts to create for nonprofits the kinds of institutions indispensable to entrepreneurs in the for-profit environment, most nonprofits will not survive in the market. Consequently, the remainder of this chapter assumes that philanthropy adopts the second course

Are Developers Ready for Scale?

The leader of a nonprofit considering scale-up based on a fee-for-service model must ask four questions: Is my program ready to go to scale? Am I prepared for the cultural and functional transformation of my organization? Am I prepared to grow as a leader-manager? Can I finance the strategy?

Program Readiness

No program is ever ready for scale in the sense that nothing more could be done to improve it before it is put in the market. Moreover, no program is ready in the sense that nothing could be improved by taking it to the market. I have yet to see a program that did not improve through the feedback and the demands of paying client schools. Nevertheless, I have yet to see a development team that did not prefer to wait for the next version of a program before taking it to market.

I will write very little about any program's research base. As a result of No Child Left Behind, public oversight agencies are developing standards for the evaluation of educational innovations that will establish a hurdle for the use of public funding to purchase programs. In all likelihood, states will apply the same rules to their own funds. It is generally accepted that third parties should conduct evaluations and ought to be subject to some sort of peer review. More important, developers should be prepared to track the implementation and outcomes of every school that adopts their programs for the purposes of managing implementation and improving service. As a program scales up, the research base needs to scale up as well. If developers fail to assess program outcomes as the program is implemented more widely and is in place longer, they will regret it later.

The future lies with programs that can demonstrate quality on a large scale through sustained improvements in test scores across the majority of their schools. The state of the art around "scientifically based research" remains relatively primitive by the standards of the hard sciences, but organizations that start now with an adaptive management approach based on the best available information will be in the best position to clear an incipient barrier to entry in the market. Those who fail to build the systems to demonstrate performance will eventually be shut out, very possibly by government regulation and certainly by consumer choice.

The assessment of a program's readiness for the market starts with an appreciation of two structural factors. The first is recognition that all but the simplest of programs are packages of interventions in the practice of teaching and learning, together with some appreciation for how each of intervention contributes to changes in practice. At the start, it seems that few developers understand or can really describe their programs as much more than the proverbial "black box"; the mechanism by which their program achieves its results is dimly understood. Yet, developers who appreciate that interventions do interact are more likely to monitor program implementation in ways that give them insights into the program's inner workings. To the extent they do this, developers are more likely to improve their program deliberately over time.

Second is an appreciation that every program is conveyed by some medium and that there is an array of media to choose from. People can help a school implement the program, or developers could rely on printed matter, videos, or tape recordings. Invariably, because publications and other materials alone have proven insufficient for quality implementation, there is a mix. The people chosen can be senior or junior, staff or consultants. Work can be done at the school site; school staff can be taken off site; and, increasingly, schools can have access to rich multimedia experiences online. Teachers can be trained individually, with other teachers of students of about the same age or students who are studying similar subjects, with other teachers from throughout their schools, or with teachers from other schools, other districts, or other states. Use can be made of "800" number phone lines, online help desks, and online or printed responses to frequently asked questions. As with interventions, few developers understand or can explain the cost-benefit assessments that led to the particular mix of media that constitute the program when it first goes to market. If, however, they appreciate that they can choose from diverse media to achieve their program objectives and that there is no reason for that choice to remain fixed, they are more likely to monitor the implementation of their programs in ways that help them work toward an optimal mix of media over time.

An appreciation of these two structural aspects of a program is important because few programs will work exactly the same way in the first paying schools as they did in the development sites or as they will in the next schools that will eventually populate the network. Understanding this likelihood motivates installation of a quality-control system that is really more a system of continuous improvement. At least as important, an appreciation of the somewhat arbitrary nature of the original mix ensures that the model developer will be prepared to modify the program when necessary. My experience suggests that the need for modification will come both early and often.

Organizational Transformation I: Culture First

Nonprofits adopting a fee-for-service strategy for scaling up face substantial challenges. It is not about becoming a business or adopting the values, norms, and routines of profit-maximizing individuals. That would be relatively easy. Adopting the strategy is about internalizing the discipline, tools, routines, and requirements of business and harnessing them in pursuit of the nonprofit's social purpose. Relatively few organizations have done this at all, let alone well, and no formula exists for adopting the dual criteria of success: "mission and margin."

Culture shifts can easily and quickly become culture shock for people in the organization. The move from developer to provider is really the move from "think tank" to "professional services firm." Anyone who has experienced both can say that the work environments have a very different feel. Even if the organization retains a research staff, the sheer size of the services staff will drastically tilt the culture toward the environment of the professional services firm.

In a think tank, like most nonprofits, few staff members worry about generating revenue. In a think tank, researchers conceptualize ideal solutions as viewed by objective observers. Researchers practice a form of noblesse oblige, offering their vision and good works to needy schools for free. Conversely, in a professional service firm, everyone is aware of his or her place in the calculation of the "bottom line." The emphasis is on value—results at a price as perceived by a client, within tight deadlines. Ultimately, client expectations drive the work. One leader of an organization making the transition talked about the changing nature of his relationship with schools "from Santa Claus to used-car salesman."

For most nonprofits, the immediate implication of adopting a fee-for-service strategy is to shift the organization's revenue base from grants to fees. This sounds like a narrow and simple challenge, but in practice it is pervasive and complex. It is pervasive in that it will ultimately change every aspect of the organization. It is complex in that these changes will occur simultaneously and interact in predictably explosive ways.

Fee-for-service implementation implies a significant increase in staff and in the infrastructure required to support that staff. Finance and accounting will grow. The bookkeeper—whose job too often consists of tracking management's financial missteps—will be replaced by a chief financial officer (CFO) who will have a real say in managing the organization's money. People will gradually start talking about "marketing" instead of "finding partners." The organization will hire a consultant or a staff member to develop a brochure and a videotape and to place positive stories about the program in newspapers and education publications with an eye to impressing customers. Eventually, a chief operating officer will be hired to manage a diverse staff and its work in a growing number of schools. The computer and telecommunications infrastructure will become a significant set of costs, and someone will be brought in to manage it. What was once a management team made up of researchers eventually becomes one in which researchers are in the minority.

Nonprofit leaders must expect these changes to precipitate a certain degree of staff turmoil and turnover. Many of the "old guard" are likely to leave, dissatisfied with the presence of new people from business, finance, and marketing; the need to keep timesheets and develop precise cost estimates; the replacement of corporate credit cards with a reimbursement policy; and the more-hectic pace of work. At the same time, a new type of nonprofit staff member will join—many with some experience in the schools, all eager to apply their business, finance, and marketing skills to a social mission they care about passionately. Many of the older staff members will take a pay cut; most of the younger staff will forgo higher-paying opportunities in the for-profit world. Melding the best of the old and the new staffs is the greatest responsibility of the organization's leaders. While it is sad to see old friends go, it is pointless to try to keep them. One should be grateful that they are leaving of their own volition because further reorganization will certainly follow.

Organizational Transformation II: Functional Issues

At its heart, the functional transition from think tank to professional services firm is about role specialization. In an R&D project, great overlap of roles and functions occurs. Someone may be better at spreadsheets or statistics; others will be better at writing first drafts and editing; and others would enjoy interacting with schools or sponsors. Nevertheless, the creative process works best when everyone on the team has some involvement in everything. This approach might work when the organization moves to implementation in a handful of schools, but, as the dissemination grows, the need for role specialization becomes acute.

Members of the original development team will almost certainly resist the move to role specialization. Usually, when all members feel they are responsible for everything, no one is clearly responsible for anything. Management must impose role specialization before something truly important slips through the cracks. Absent the direct attention of leaders, the process will likely take several years.

While role specialization is essential to managing growth, an equally vital function—integration—becomes both more important and more difficult with growth. During development and while the number of schools in which the original developer-provider team is working remains small, all the problems and opportunities that arise in the course of working with schools come to everyone's attention immediately. Solutions are the result of a similarly intimate joint effort. Everyone on staff becomes involved in crisis management. At a small scale, the process of integration is so efficient that no one ever captures the knowledge generated in writing. Staff members capture it in the shared moment, and new staff members receive it as part of the oral history they are exposed to through conversation during their apprenticeship.

This overlap of roles and functions raises another problem that becomes more difficult to manage with growth: quality control. The small-group process of identifying problems, solving them, and then integrating the new knowledge through participation and apprenticeship is an informal yet efficient system of quality control. It works reasonably well as long as implementation staff work in close proximity and in the same schools, meet regularly as a team, add staff from a fairly well-defined and even well-known pool of applicants, and train staff through a close mentor-apprentice relationship.

As too many schools are added for most staffers to appreciate the situation in each school, as staff members are dispersed to serve a geographically distributed network in ways that make regular formal and informal meetings difficult and far less frequent, as the leadership runs out of people they know to fill new positions, and as the number of new staff members outnumbers the veterans, these informal systems simply disappear or disintegrate. Unless they are deliberately replaced with formal systems in anticipation of this collapse, quality will suffer—often dramatically.

The list of formal systems is brief, but the effort to build them is significant.

School Tracking. Implementation and outcomes must be tracked in every school. All who work in the school must provide input on their work in the school—what they did, when they did it, to what effect, and what the issues are that other school staff should understand. Reform program staff members must have access to the data and review it before they visit the school on their own assignments. Test scores and relevant documents must be readily available. Someone needs to ensure that data are entered when they should be and that they accurately reflect the situation at the school.

Personnel. Positions must be well defined, and the sets of skills, training, and experiences that best prepare people for the job should be identified. The education program must be understood well enough to devise a training program. New staff must be trained, and someone needs to ensure that trained staff are implementing the program with fidelity.

Program Improvement. Data on schools and people must be combined and assessed in ways that improve the program by identifying conditions under which the program works well or does not, developing means of identifying such conditions, avoiding schools that have the wrong conditions and changing the conditions or working around them, refining the profile of ideal implementation staff and developing means of improving staff skills, and refining the program itself.

Operations. Work in schools is labor intensive; as the number of schools grows, integrating school scheduling, staff availability, and travel becomes incredibly complex. Someone must "own" the logistics of implementation at scale.

Finance. A grant-maintained nonprofit generally receives revenues from a few grantors—foundations or the government—on time and all at once and more or less controls the timing of disbursements. If cash is tight, researchers can postpone site visits. A fee-for-service operation receives lots of payments from many sources, in small amounts, and generally late, but must provide services and hence must disburse money under contractual obligations. Even if cash is tight, staff members still need to serve their schools. Someone needs to own finance, which is one reason that the CFO in the fee-for-service organization sits at the management table while the finance director in a grant-maintained organization does not.

Marketing. Signing up schools is an expensive process. The costs of travel and materials are the most visible but are only the tip of the iceberg. Leadership, senior management, and implementation staff time is the hidden, largest, and most important cost because the time these people spend finding good partners is time they do not spend running the organization, refining the program, or working in schools. It is important to control these costs and to spend resources wisely, which requires understanding the characteristics of schools at which the program is likely to succeed, focusing on finding them, helping them decide to adopt the program by tailoring it to meet their needs, and helping them find the resources to purchase and implement it.

Legal. Good legal support is vital. Surely, the primary assets of the organization are its people. The importance of these assets is honored, at least in the breach. A second kind of asset—intellectual property—is also very important, yet rarely recognized. Most nonprofits do little to protect it, and the grant policies of foundations generally discourage efforts to protect it—prohibiting the use of patents, copyrights, trademarks, or other legal devices meant to control ownership. Such control, however, is essential to the success of any professional services enterprise. Organizations must protect their materials, the ability of consultants and staff to resell or reuse work the nonprofit has sponsored, and the names of both the organization and the program. Moreover, when the developer becomes a service provider, its work in the schools becomes a matter of contract and liability, not diplomacy and good works, making solid legal advice essential.

Organizational Values. Having described the need for systems, it is equally important to impress on nonprofit leaders the danger of throwing the mission baby out with the bathwater of old organizational practices or attitudes. Moving toward a more-businesslike culture should not be confused with a need to adopt top-down management, pervasive centralization, or endless process. Bureaucracy is not a good business model for professional services. The creative edge and personal autonomy that the very best nonprofit staff members crave—and for which they are willing to forgo the financial advantages of the for-profit world—can be easily stifled by excessive process. What matters is not the extent of procedural controls over staff—although reporting is required—but a pervasive appreciation among staff that finance matters as a means of pursuing the mission and that business concepts are nothing more than tools to help the staff take its educational innovations to more students with greater quality.

This attitude must become as much a part of the values of the new business staff at it was of the old program staff. Leaders would do well to remember the old adage that "those who do not know what to do, do what they know." Business types, as well as program staff, will be entering a new world, and just because this is the way they did it at Amalgamated Materials does not make it right for a new enterprise. Nonprofit leaders must look to the principles and concepts that make up business discipline and apply them to their organizations. A business system should not, however, be mindlessly adopted because a new staff member used it in his or her last job. Instead, nonprofit leaders need to be constantly aware of the need to balance and combine the perspectives of the two groups to create a new culture.

Organizational Transformation III: Leadership Challenges

Perhaps the greatest temptation leaders about to make the transition from grants to fee-for-service face is that of becoming their own CFOs and/or chief marketing officers (CMOs).

The temptation is strong for several reasons. First, the finance and marketing functions are enormously sensitive. The budget is policy, and even small changes in budget allocations go directly to what staff members do in an organization. Change the budget, and you signal changes in policy, status, routines, and image to staff members. Similarly, "marketing" is something nonprofit leaders often think they do not do or, at least, that is what they would prefer their donors to think. Start talking about marketing and you begin to change the world's image of your organization and your staff's self-image. It is understandable that leaders would feel more comfortable controlling these directly, particularly because it is still unlikely that a CFO or CMO will have substantial experience in the schools, and plenty of opportunities for serious missteps remain in this emerging market.

There is also a second, less charitable, explanation for the tendency of nonprofit leaders to keep these functions to themselves: fear. Most nonprofit leaders have been very successful people with real mastery over both the substance and management of their work. Admitting to yourself that you do not know what you need to know about finance and marketing when they are absolutely vital to your success is incredibly difficult. It is equally difficult to give someone else the responsibility for these functions, knowing that that person might have the knowledge and the willingness to trump whatever arguments you might make for some important policy decision. In my experience, a willingness to be vulnerable in this way is a sign of real mastery but is exceedingly rare, and few leaders have proven capable of deliberately making themselves so vulnerable.

Because most leaders are very smart, they correctly assume that they can acquire the necessary skills and expertise on the job. Typically, leaders take between 18 months and two years to learn enough about the CFO and CMO functions to know that they should hire professionals. By this time, they have probably made their own serious missteps and have learned enough about the substance of finance and marketing to feel confident in their ability to manage the new hires. This is not a bad place to be. The problem, however, is the opportunity cost of the "do it yourself" decision. While the leader has spent two years getting an on-the-job MBA in finance and marketing, the program, implementation, and culture have probably failed to get the attention they deserve.

The highest and best use of any leader's time is leading. Many people have marketing and finance expertise in the setting of a growing enterprise. No one knows what the leader knows about the organization and where it needs to go, and these cannot be attended to if the leader is buried in a spreadsheet or out making sales calls. The smartest, best, and bravest leaders hire a CFO and a CMO from the start, or as soon as possible, and stay focused on the big picture.

Organizational Transformation IV: Financing the Enterprise

The financial problem has two parts: achieving the correct mix of fee-for-service and grant revenues for the mature enterprise and determining how to finance the process of scaling up.

Mission requirements should inform the correct mix of fee-for-service and grants. The goal should be to cover the provider's operations budget with fees earned working in schools rather than by grants given directly to the provider. Because schools invest heavily in human capital to implement and maintain the program and must rely on support from the provider, the provider should be able to rely on fees from the client schools to provide that support. If schools leave the network, the provider must be capable of scaling back operations or "plugging" the holes in its revenue stream, perhaps with grants from foundations.

Relying on foundation grants as operating subsidies to make up shortfalls in revenue is, however, impractical. Few foundations support operations, and few providers can become permanent recipients from the local "community chest."[10] Consequently, most foundation grants that "plug" a nonprofit's operating deficits are program-oriented. These plug programs divert the nonprofit from its true focus, divert critical staff resources from the implementation work in school, and leave the organization in deficit when the grant ends.

---

[10] This is the strategy Project GRAD adopted (see Chapter Six in this volume).

To appreciate fully the need for nonprofits to rely on fees, providers need to consider the implications of the propositions they offer schools. If a school adopts the program the provider is offering, the school must, in addition to paying the provider's fee, pay for teacher release time and substitute teachers to allow the staff to adopt the new program. In some cases, the program will also require the school to use the provider's student materials. Moreover, whether the school or the provider understands it at the start or not, school staff turnover alone is likely to force the school to depend on the provider both to implement the program and to sustain implementation. Thus, in an environment of high-stakes accountability, choosing to contract with a service provider is fast becoming a high-stakes decision for a school and its staff.

To justify this commitment, the school must be confident that the provider can meet its obligations—not just in the first year but every year, and not just when the provider serves 25 schools but when it is growing to serve hundreds and then thousands of schools. This confidence is justified only to the extent that the provider can demonstrate sustainability based on fee revenues. A foundation grant that subsidizes a substantial portion of costs may seem attractive to a school in the short run, but when the grant runs out and that school cannot afford to make up the difference, the program will die, wasting the school's investment in human capital (i.e., its own staff) and shortchanging the children who benefit from that program.

Thus, the provider organization must be able to meet its current contractual and future obligations to schools without significant grant funding. In addition to the direct costs of implementation at a site, fees must also cover the indirect costs of operating the organization. Perhaps the only costs that can be reasonably trusted to grants are one-time capital expenses, such as a new headquarters building, or R&D, although in the long run a provider's sustainability depends on the development of new products and services and hence on fees.

The liabilities of relying on grants may, however, be irrelevant to the nonprofit leader, even the nonprofit leader committed to the fee-for-service dissemination strategy. Although the strategy seems valid in theory, such a high reliance on fees cannot work in practice—if by "in practice" we mean "from the start." If anything should be clear from this chapter thus far, it is that, to obtain quality at scale, the provider must build quality for scale before achieving scale. In the market of fee-for-service contracts, however, money generally follows performance rather than preceding it. Providers are typically paid 90 days after they submit a bill for their work in client schools; much longer periods are far too common. New implementation staff must be hired and trained months before new schools sign up to adopt the program. In addition, marketing costs must be recovered. As a practical matter, formal systems of quality assurance must be put in place years before the provider has achieved economies of scale.

In the for-profit environment, this kind of growth is financed through personal resources, investors, and banks. After using personal savings to get a business going, an entrepreneur with a promising idea will seek "angel" investors—wealthy individuals with a taste for risk, expertise in the business, and contacts in the sector. These angels will help the entrepreneur take the new enterprise to venture capital firms. Along with financing, a partner at the firm will help steer the growing company through its next phase of growth and on to maturity through an initial public offering on the stock market, purchase by another firm, or as a privately held company. From there, the firm will have access to private-sector financing in the form of bonds or bank loans. Traveling this road is much harder than this discussion implies, but it is done regularly by thousands of entrepreneurs.

No such path from new idea to maturity exists for social entrepreneurs. The specific sources of for-profit finance are, for the most part, unavailable to the nonprofit entrepreneur, as is the array of technical expertise that surrounds the for-profit investment process. Neither has philanthropy nor government created an analogous route for taking nonprofits to scale.

In this environment, nonprofits must exploit the few sources of capital available. Nonprofit leaders cannot afford to overlook the rare unrestricted grant to help capitalize an expansion of capacity. They must also seek restricted grants intended to tap into the latest trend in education reform among foundations, despite the diversion of effort and the risks of leaving schools without support when the grant ends.

To the extent possible, nonprofits must bootstrap, beg, and bend the rules to ensure their survival.

A few nonprofits will find their way to a foundation practicing venture philanthropy or to such an institution as the Education Entrepreneurs Fund at NAS. Under the venture philanthropy model, nonprofits will receive grants based on the credibility of their business models and the quality of the management teams. As with a venture capital firm, the venture philanthropy foundation will likely place a staff member on the nonprofit's board and help steer them to scale. Unlike the venture philanthropist, the fund will not join the board and will secure its loan with the nonprofit's assets, including its name, its proprietary materials, and its receivables. Apart from financing, the fund will also make a range of consulting and cost-reducing services available to help the enterprise grow. The relative merits of either approach will not be discussed here. Suffice it to say that, given the limited availability of either investment, the nonprofit leader should seek both aggressively and take whichever comes first.

The Role of Foundations in Attaining Scalability

The R&D Paradigm—An Obstacle to School Improvement

Regardless of the underlying quality of their approaches, the majority of school-improvement programs financed through philanthropy have failed to take hold in the schools. This outcome stems, in part, from the lack of access to a mechanism that would permit promising programs to become part of the permanent fabric of public education. Philanthropy, on the whole, has made no concerted effort to identify, foster, and take advantage of mechanisms that might embed their grantees' programs in school operations.

The foundations' dominant role in education reform is financing R&D. For the most part, this approach is quite sensible because philanthropy lacks the resources to take its investments to a national scale through grants. The school system spends $330 billion a year; philanthropy has invested a bit more than $2.5 billion in reform over the past ten years. Absent some strategy for philanthropy to take promising programs to scale, a disproportionate investment in R&D seems somewhat inevitable.

Without doubt, philanthropy has proven highly adept in developing incentives for nonprofits to do research. Over the last decade of school reform, this "R&D paradigm" has been perfected, and many nonprofits operate quite successfully within it. A nonprofit researcher convinces a foundation program officer that an idea for improving student performance has merit. A school is located in which to study, develop, and test this "intervention." A team is assembled to carry out the study. The researchers document the results of the experiment. The results are presented, peer-reviewed, published, disseminated, and discussed and then placed on a shelf in a library or in the files of other researchers. There may, at best, be a follow-on project with a few more schools to demonstrate replicability. The reporting cycle is then repeated. The team breaks up, and the researchers move on. Invariably, these research activities take place in schools with principals who know how to squeeze benefit out of these free, but temporary, resources, and that is usually the extent of the program's direct benefit to teachers and students.

For the most part, the reports and the temporary benefit to the school are all philanthropy has to show for its investment. Once the project ends, the program slowly and inevitably disappears. Few practitioners read the report, and fewer still try to integrate it into their schools. Even fewer have the capacity to implement the program with commitment.

The sustainability of research organizations depends not on sustaining their ideas through action but on sustaining their ability to anticipate the next trend in reform R&D. The quality of the researchers' last report becomes the basis for their next grant. The extent to which the idea can become part of practice and help students is not relevant. Moreover, because what is happening in the school is an experiment, it cannot be central to that school's operation or replace its core processes. Whatever the educational program, the school must continue to perform the routines the district expects. Knowing that the researchers will disappear and that school staff will turn over, no principal can truly rely on the reform activity. The

R&D paradigm is tantamount to an academic exercise; as a means of reforming American public education, it is a dead end.

The researchers use the schools to derive their benefit—publications. The schools use the researchers to derive their benefit—free on-site support. The parties' interests in the experiment coincide, but they do not align. To both, the experiment is a passing phenomenon. As a result, it is easy to conclude that, under the R&D paradigm, the intended beneficiaries of all this investment—the nation's students—rarely benefit from foundation grants for school reform.

A Pathway to Scale Through Systemic Change

The R&D paradigm has survived because neither schools nor the researchers who work in them have been accountable for performance. Until quite recently, schools have felt no material consequences for poor performance, except for the students, who feel the harsh social consequences of a poor education. Similarly, education researchers funded by foundations have not been accountable to schools. Only during the last decade has the United States reached a point at which the combination of standards and testing requirements, indirect competitive threats from charters and vouchers, and direct threats of takeover and reconstitution from the state and federal legislatures shows signs of compelling the accountability of superintendents, principals, and teachers for school performance. We have hardly scratched the surface, but this fast-moving trend of top-to-bottom accountability in the public schools, which No Child Left Behind has accelerated, provides foundations with the vehicle they need to guide their investment in public school reform.

Accountability is forcing a widespread recognition among opinion leaders that the existing methods of reform or improvement have failed to keep up with society's needs. It has also opened the minds of superintendents, district administrators, principals, and teachers to new methods of teaching and learning. Federal and state governments have made great strides in permitting and encouraging districts and schools to use federal and state funding streams to purchase these services for improvement. These factors combine to bring outside service providers into the core teaching and learning operations of schools and school systems. Increasingly, we see ready, willing, and able consumers of school reform services. We now have a market and a means for quality to show itself for all to see, for quality to go to scale, and for ensuring that quality will continue to have an effect.

But with every opportunity comes danger. Like nature, the market abhors a vacuum. Organizations are rushing in to meet demand; among them are various for-profits, new nonprofits, local "mom-and-pop" operations, and publicly traded companies. Some see quality as an important element of their models. A few have no such commitment, while others are well intentioned but objectively without merit. Almost every segment of the growing school reform industry is coming to be dominated by select firms, such as Edison in school management, Sylvan in pull-out programs, and NCS-Pearson in assessment. Only one, comprehensive school reform, is dominated by a nonprofit: Success For All. All these large for-profit firms are driven first and foremost by a commitment to "shareholder value," which translates into a requirement to turn some portion of profits over to the shareholders.

If high quality is what consumers truly want in public education, high quality is what they will get. However, high quality is not the only attribute consumers value in any market, including public education. To gain a glimpse into this point, one need only look at cases in which charter schools with less-than-stellar records of academic performance serve parents who voluntarily send their children, suffering no more from reduced enrollment than do poorly run public schools to which the students are assigned by district fiat. Chartering agencies do not find these charter schools any easier to close than districts or states find reconstitution. Quality counts, but it is only one of several factors contributing to the competitiveness of any educational program.

Likewise, in the absence of a clear standard-bearer of quality, there is certainly reason for concern that competition in the school-improvement market will gradually come to revolve around price and marketing. Here, the nonprofit sector could play an important role.

Because they exist solely to pursue a social purpose, nonprofits could become high-quality standard-bearers in the emerging school-improvement market. Without access to finance, technical assistance, and support services, however, nonprofits will never be able to compete with for-profits well enough to capture and hold the market share necessary for playing this crucial role. Only philanthropy has the resources, flexibility, and local knowledge to meet this need around the country.

Philanthropy at the Crossroads

Markets are preferable to central planning. Until recently, however, the public school system has had more in common with the latter. But markets are not perfect solutions. Indeed, they can do great harm unless certain institutions are in place to protect the public. The most-important institutions are intermediaries that provide the consumer with reliable information on quality, help consumers work with providers, and advance the interests of small providers to enhance competition and choice. So foundations stand at a crossroads. As public education quickly becomes a marketplace, they can yield this social space to for-profits, with all the benefits and risks that offers—much as they did with health care—or they can foster the development of a healthy nonprofit sector.

The former requires no change in behavior, although eventually it spells the end of any meaningful role for nonprofits in public education. For a while, for-profits will continue to reap the fruits of foundation investment in nonprofit research. Eventually, they will conduct their own product development activities, as they do today in textbook publishing.

The latter implies significant changes in the behavior of foundations. Adopting the market as the vehicle for improving quality, increasing scale, and achieving sustainability in public school improvement requires foundations to demand that taking programs to market become a criterion of grantee success. It also means that foundations must recognize the move to the market as the vehicle for nonprofit sustainability and therefore must create and support the intermediary institutions that will give nonprofits an opportunity to thrive in the market.

To accomplish this, foundations must do four things:

- develop program staff with a positive attitude toward the "business" of fee-for-service program dissemination
- change the rules of success for nonprofit engagement with philanthropy
- redirect a substantial portion of giving away from research and toward sustainable dissemination
- invest in the creation of a nonprofit equivalent of the pathway that ensures growth and sustainability in the for-profit world.

Changing Foundation Staff

The R&D culture is more academic than business-oriented. It is no surprise that the foundation staff member working in education reform is more likely to have experience in grant-funded nonprofits, government, and research than in business. Beyond this lack of business experience and expertise, many foundation staff managing education programs are skeptical of the business world and business values in general. Academia disdains commerce. To go even further, some foundation managers have substantial difficulty with the idea that school systems could outsource public education services on a fee-for-service basis without shortchanging children. Many believe that the effort of providers to generate a financial return on their work is at odds with the goal of a high-quality education. This attitude is more or less pronounced, depending on the foundation, but in my experience, it remains the dominant staff perspective in philanthropy today.

If philanthropy is to embrace the market as the vehicle for reaching scale and realizing the potential of its educational investment, foundation leaders must set out deliberately to balance their existing R&D culture by fostering a "venture culture" in their staffs. Foundations need to add people with expertise and experience in the challenges of taking good ideas to scale, maintaining and even improving quality in the process, and building sustainability into service offerings and enterprise finance. Given the nascent state of this process in the nonprofit and foundation worlds, the bulk of this new staff must come from the world of business. Foundations should invest in the capacity of intermediaries rather than build their own venture activities in house, primarily because it is more efficient and because these intermediaries should themselves be required to operate in a market, generating their own income from the providers they serve. Regardless of how they decide to address this question, foundations need a cadre of strong senior managers and staff to champion and manage the fee-for-service strategy.

Nevertheless, nonprofit ventures differ from for-profit ventures in important ways, and the new foundation staff members must be open to this reality. The single most important difference is that, in the for-profit environment, the investee and the investor's representatives speak the same language—business. In the nonprofit world, the investee's first language is and should be social purpose. Just as the investee needs to harness business concepts in pursuit of its mission, so the foundation staff drawn from business needs to put business concepts into terms that make sense to those steeped in the language of social enterprise.

A second important difference is that for-profit start-ups tend to offer their services to business or consumer markets dominated by financial factors. The representatives of the investor community often know more about the broad market than the investee. The education market is about selling to local government, is dominated by politics, and involves the heretofore noncommercial and intensely intimate endeavors of teaching and learning. The investee is likely to know far more about the particulars of this market than the investor. This knowledge differential means that foundation staff must listen carefully to their investees on matters of client attitudes, meet regularly with the customers of school-improvement services, and strive to adjust their functional expertise and professional experiences to this new market.

If nonprofit leaders too often say, "Education is different, so what you're saying doesn't apply to me," people from business too often say "Here's how we did it at Mega-Widget. It was successful, and you should do it too." What foundations need to leverage is not business anecdotes or even business models but business discipline. The tools of analysis and management must be applied to the realm of nonprofits selling services to districts and schools as a means of pursuing their nonprofit mission in education. This requirement creates demand for people who can separate the particular business context in which they honed their skills and gained their expertise from the skills and expertise themselves. It is the skills, rather than the domain-specific knowledge, that have the most value. Foundations need people who have the mind-set of the teacher, the mentor, and the coach.

Changing the Rules of Nonprofit Success

The paradigm of nonprofit success in education R&D was established by philanthropy, and nonprofits have made it work to their benefit. If philanthropy is to take advantage of the market as a means of scaling up programs, foundations need to create some new "rules of the game." The right rules make the right results possible.

Foundation managers must make clear to R&D grantees that the ultimate value of any educational program is how many students actually benefit from it. Foundation willingness to fund the next R&D proposal needs to be conditioned on the grantee's success in taking the last R&D concept to scale and in realizing a stream of revenues from its dissemination activities. Grantees need not disseminate on their own. They might sell their ideas, license them, or partner with other organizations to ensure the ideas' distribution but cannot be permitted to let programs sit on a shelf. The developer must assume some responsibility for the quality of the delivered program, either as provider or by some means of monitoring licensees and partners. The foundation must put into place some means of assessing the quality of services and their educational outcomes. What matters is not dissemination by developers but adoption by schools.

Redirecting Resources

As necessary as rules are to results, they are not sufficient. Foundations cannot establish new criteria for nonprofit success and then sit back and watch it happen. To move nonprofits from the R&D mindset, foundations must also show their grantees a credible route to success in the fee-for-service context. Reduced to its simplest components, this pathway consists of access to investment capital and technical assistance. The capital is required to allow nonprofits to finance the infrastructure necessary to operate at scale before the revenues to support that infrastructure are in hand. The technical assistance is required to help nonprofit leaders make the vast range of changes discussed in this chapter.

The amount of money necessary to create the credible path is not entirely clear, but it is substantial. It must be large enough to demonstrate that philanthropy has made a real shift in direction and to offer a sizable number of nonprofits adequate resources to compete in the market. Assuming that $350 million a year is now devoted to school improvement, anything less than 10 percent ($35 million) would fail the first test, and something like 20 percent ($70 million) is probably required to meet the second. Roughly two-thirds should go to capitalizing nonprofits and the balance to creating the infrastructure of technical support.

Whatever the right number, two factors will strongly affect the total investment required: whether capitalization is made in the form of grants or repayable instruments and whether foundations decide to build their own capacity for investment and technical assistance or invest in such intermediaries as the Education Entrepreneurs Fund. While grants are one-shot cash infusions, such repayable investments as loans can be recycled and applied to new organizations. If every foundation decides to start its own program in house, the overall effort will lack economies of scale, as well as the effects of learning and experience curves. Such effects will tend to improve the efficiency and scale of both investment and technical assistance activities. There is a great need for new social intermediaries but not for every foundation to develop its own venture capital and incubator capacity.

The New Pathway

The nonprofit leader preparing to embark on a transition from grant to fee-for-service is trading a known future for the promise of greater mission effects and self-control in the long run. Just as the schools need to know that the nonprofit provider will be there to serve them, so the nonprofit leader needs to know that those who will help him or her make the transition have substantial expertise, will be in it for the long run, and are no less dependent on their ultimate success.

In the for-profit arena, the investor seeking a financial return is the most important driver on the pathway to growth. If the investee fails, the investor fails and may go out of business. This simple fact ties the two together in a powerful way. Neither can let the other down, and both must be clear about shared expectations from the start. On the investor side, the investee's promise of repayment is powerful evidence of the investee's commitment to the plan for growth. On the investee side, the investor's need for repayment provides some guarantee that the investor will do everything in his or her power to ensure the investee's success.

This basic relationship needs to become a part of the process of taking nonprofits to scale.

Philanthropically financed investors do not need the types of financial returns that venture capitalists expect to effect this relationship with their investees. Moreover, nonprofits cannot grow their way to scale or sustainability without some level of grant financing for initial capitalization. Without the mutual dependence that repayable investments impose, the relationship is most likely to take the form of most grants, in which the grantor lacks both an objective means of influencing grantee action and a real incentive to act in the face of grantee failure. The grantee lacks both the assurance that grantors will have to focus on grantee problems on the grantee's timetable and any incentive to reveal problems the grantor might help solve.

Foundations have extremely limited capacity to perform the investment partner function in house. They are legally committed and culturally attuned to giving away their corpus of funds. Even the small percentage of funds they can disburse in the form of program-related investments lacks the binding repayment obligation of the typical loan. If philanthropy is to benefit from the investment partner relationship in its effort to take an educational program to scale in the market, philanthropy must create or capitalize these intermediary institutions as independent entities and ensure that they also move toward a sustainability model—based here on the financial success of their investments.

Capital is a necessary condition of nonprofit success in the market, but it is not sufficient. Expert technical assistance is also required. Again, what nonprofit leaders require is support from individuals and firms with a shared financial interest in success. The nonprofit leaders need to be confident that the support provided will be there when needed and is based on a deep appreciation of the challenges they face. While volunteers have their place, support functions critical to the success of the nonprofit's transition from grant to fee-for-service need to be performed by paid professionals with an interest in their own reputation for high-quality work.

Conclusions

Philanthropy shaped the conditions that now govern nonprofit success in public school improvement, leading to much innovation. If the vast store of intellectual capital that philanthropic organizations have built over the last decade is to be effective on a national scale, education nonprofits must do the heavy lifting. Their work will be that much more effective if philanthropy changes the rules of success to reflect the value of scale. This change requires that foundation boards and leaders embrace the emerging school-improvement service market, hire senior staff advocates for this approach, direct real financial resources to make a fee-for-service dissemination strategy viable, and invest in the intermediary organizations best positioned to leverage that investment. The NAS experience demonstrates the feasibility and promise of this approach, and foundations should follow the pathway to growth that NAS has established. If they do, their grantees will surely follow, and philanthropy will be able to demonstrate a healthy social return on its considerable investment in school improvement.

Reference

Porter, M. E., and M. R. Kramer, "Philanthropy's New Agenda: Creating Value," *Harvard Business Review*, Vol. 77, No. 6, November–December 1999.

School Funding Services, Web site, Alexandria, Va., undated. Online at http://www.schoolfundingservices.org (as of July 1, 2004).

CHAPTER SEVENTEEN

Summary: Toward a More Systematic Approach to Expanding the Reach of Educational Interventions

Thomas K. Glennan, Jr., Susan J. Bodilly,
Jolene R. Galegher, and Kerri A. Kerr

The contributors to this volume—developers of designs to improve teaching and learning—have described their goals, their methods, and what they learned while trying to scale up their programs. Despite the heterogeneity of the interventions, the diversity in the sites implementing them, and variations in the length of developers' experiences, it is possible to distill some general lessons for producing widespread, deep, and lasting education reform. In this chapter, we identify and describe the lessons derived from our analysis.

First, we return to the conceptualization of scale-up we presented in Chapter One and offer a fuller description of that process. This more-detailed framework captures the experiences our contributors have described and emphasizes the first major lesson we derived from our analysis of their experience: *No matter the target of reform or the design construct, the scale-up process is necessarily iterative and complex and requires the support of multiple actors. This is likely to remain so for the foreseeable future.*

Next, we return to the set of developer activities we identified in the initial chapter. Here, we refer to these activities as core tasks, a term that emphasizes their centrality in the scale-up process. We summarize the approaches the developers used to carry out these tasks, answering the question of how they managed to scale up their improvement ideas. In this discussion, we also identify trends or future challenges they discussed. From this review, we drew a second major lesson: *If scale-up is to succeed, the actors involved—including developers, district officials, school leaders, and teachers—must jointly address a set of known, interconnected tasks, especially aligning policies and infrastructure in coherent ways to sustain practice.*

We reemphasize here that our analysis is descriptive. We do not have the evidence needed to determine which combination of approaches works best. Instead, we describe the tasks that must be performed, specify the roles of diverse actors, and depict the types of solutions now being tried. We also summarize some of the challenges the different contributors reported facing in an ever-changing environment. The final section of this chapter addresses ways to use these lessons.

Further Elaboration of the Scale-Up Process

The essays constituting Chapters Two through Sixteen have led us to a more-detailed conceptualization of the scale-up process that we described in Chapter One (portrayed graphically in Figure 1.2). Illustrated in Figure 17.1, the more-detailed model emphasizes the complexity of the organizational environment in which interactions between students and teachers take place and the need for mutual adjustment—of policies and practices—among the key actors in this environment.

Scale-up assumes that a developer has created a design that supports teachers facing the challenge of helping students achieve at high levels. As noted in the introduction, this is usually done through an iterative process involving the developer and a set of teachers, schools, districts, or states, (as diagrammed in steps 1 to 3 in Figure 1.1). As the essays illustrate, the designs eventually take many forms.

The contributors have described an iterative process of trial and error consonant with research and development efforts in other fields in the development of the intervention itself, the development of the means to scale that intervention, and actual experiences in scale-up. Such trial and error was natural and unavoidable in the 20-year period covered by the cases in this volume. Because there was little codified wisdom to guide these activities, designers and developers had to learn through experience.

Figure 17.1
The Mutual Adaptation Model of Scale-Up

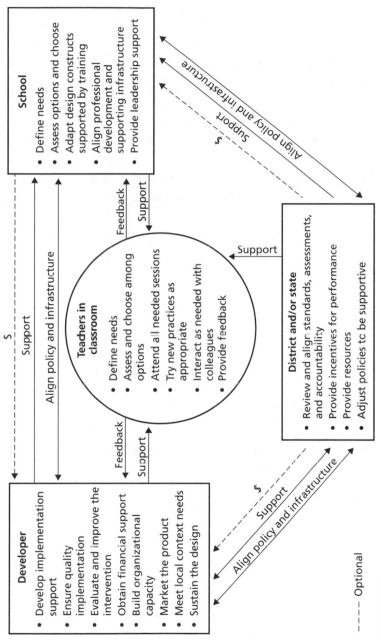

RAND *MG248-17.1*

The essays make clear, however, that some aspects of the trial-and-error process eventually result in codification or solidity in some components of the design. For example, the Co-nect designers spent several years attempting to modify their design for specific sites (see Chapter Nine). They eventually devised a system of three alternative designs intended to fit the needs of schools that differ in terms of existing levels of student performance and the level of external support required to implement the intervention. The Turning Points program has taken a similar three-level customized approach (see Chapter Ten). In another example, the National Writing Project (NWP, see Chapter Three) described a set of quality standards that the regional providers use in a consistent way to ensure high-quality delivery of its program. The Direct Instruction (DI) design concepts and many materials have remained relatively unchanged for several decades (see Chapter Four). Thus, the initial process of trial and error in the demonstration and early scale-up efforts does give way to relatively well-defined sets of processes and products.

The scale-up process involves systematically and significantly changing the practice of teachers in classrooms through interactions among developers, teachers, schools, districts, and other major actors. The evidence the essays present confirms that, after the demonstration stage and after some codification, the process of scale-up, like the process of design and demonstration, is necessarily

- interactive, involving the developers, teachers, schools, and districts in relationships that continue over time
- adaptive, involving reciprocal relationships among the actors and reactions to unfolding situations
- iterative, with continuous reexamination and learning over time
- nonlinear, with the sequence of activities depending, to some extent, on the need for adjustments as the actors adapt to unfolding circumstances.

The contributors describe prolonged interactions and discussions with schools and districts and adaptations among the parties, including funders. In short, these essays confirm the scale-up model we offered in Chapter One, as an iterative process that involves several parties, all engaged in an attempt to change teacher practices in depth and to sustain these changes across many sites and over time.

In addition, our analysis of the essays suggests some of the tasks each of the different parties faces. The developers' core tasks were introduced in Chapter One and are presented again in the developer box in Figure 17.1, but the figure also reveals some of the implied tasks of the other parties. For example, developers provide implementation support and ensure the quality of its delivery; teachers and schools reciprocate by attending the training sessions provided and adapting the design constructs to their sites. Meanwhile, districts might change incentive structures to motivate teachers to make their practices more consistent with the developer's design constructs. While the lists of tasks presented in Figure 17.1 are not exhaustive, especially for the teachers, schools, and district, they highlight both the developers' tasks and the activities of other parties in the process.

The arrows linking the parties emphasize that, even for teacher-focused designs, schools and districts must act in some way to provide a supportive and coherent infrastructure if the new practices are to take root and grow. All the contributors emphasized a process in which "the system" moves toward providing better support for teachers as a means of promoting improved practice. In many cases, such moves entailed ensuring that appropriate resources and infrastructure were available to support implementation of the new practices. The following are examples of some areas that might require attention:

- curriculum and instructional practices and such associated resources as textbooks, libraries, and technology
- the district's human-resource infrastructure, including professional development; policies for hiring, assigning, and retaining teachers; and performance incentives
- governance systems, including realigning decision authority, especially among the teacher, school, and district
- resource allocations
- systems of data collection and accountability.

Throughout the text, but especially in the chapters that emphasized system-level change (e.g., Chapters Seven and Fourteen), the authors underline the importance of having both a coherent set of practices for teaching, learning, and assessment and the associated infrastructure. Without this coherence, changes in classroom practice will not survive. The job of scale-up is not only getting teachers to change their practices but also creating the environment and institutional supports needed for such changes in practice to endure (Elmore, 1996; Fullan, 2001; and Sarason, 1990, 1996). Achieving such coherence is likely to require extensive training, mutual adjustment on many dimensions, and possibly even legislation. Thus, those interested in promoting the scale-up of education reforms must, necessarily, take the long view and emphasize the need for mutual adaptation to support better practice.

In sum, scaling up will continue to require an iterative process of learning by doing. This iterative approach is likely to continue for the foreseeable future. The importance of context and of the interactive learning the many different actors must do to ensure continued improvement means that there is no alternative. Moreover, although current evaluations of some programs might lead to an improvement in the underlying research for building designs, the necessarily limited scope of that research in the near term means that most improvement efforts will continue to begin with the wisdom and knowledge of practitioners, academics, and developers rather than strong scientific findings.

Core Tasks in the Scale-Up Process

Although our conception of scale-up involves many actors, this volume focuses primarily on the role of the developers. Thus, in the remaining sections of this chapter we consider each of the core tasks, describing how the contributors accomplished them. This list of core tasks is primarily meant to capture what the developers whose work is described in this volume have done in implementing reforms, but it can also be useful to potential purchasers of improvement services or potential funders of research, development, and implementation of reform services. The set of core tasks can provide a sort of checklist, enabling purchasers and funders to assess improvement services against a uniform set of criteria.

The core tasks we describe here are the elements of a strategy for achieving the four characteristics of a successful scale-up that we described in Chapter One: spread, depth, sustainability, and ownership. In making choices about the character of their interventions, designers are also making choices about how to work toward these four goals—how to carry out each of the core tasks with a view toward achieving spread, depth, sustainability, and ownership. Like the contributors to this volume, we see the core tasks as being interrelated. For instance, if the design assumes that the only way to establish a high-quality curriculum is for a reform organization to create it and teach the teachers how to use it, the reform is also likely to carefully articulate and execute the necessary support for implementation (e.g., through providing curriculum materials, professional development workshops, and coaching) and to ensure the quality of implementation (e.g., through careful training and monitoring of coaches). On the other hand, the needs of the local context, at least insofar as they involve variations in the curriculum, might receive less attention. Here, then, we describe each core task, keeping in mind that design principles drive decisions about how to carry out particular tasks and that such decisions have implications for the execution of other tasks.

Develop and Provide Support for Implementation

Assuming that the developer has worked with a demonstration site or a group of teachers to move a novel educational practice to a more formal design, scale-up requires developing approaches and tools that enable multiple actors to implement the design at specific sites.

Approaches to Implementation Support. While the importance of specifying and supporting procedures for change at the classroom level might seem obvious, one of the main contributions of this wave of developers has, in fact, been that all have paid attention to the adopters' needs for support in the implementation of new practices. The developers in this volume have chosen to support teachers, principals, and schools directly in the implementation of classroom practice improvements in many different ways:

- **Planning.** Some designs emphasize data-based planning and development of interventions to address needs. These designs provide support for collecting and analyzing data.[1] In addition, several require school-planning teams to review data and create specific plans for improvement.[2]
- **Curriculum and instruction modules, guidelines, or examples.** Several developers specify curriculum and instruction.[3] Others provide curriculum or instructional guidelines, examples, or model units.[4]
- **Professional development.** All the developers provide significant training, seminars, and workshop opportunities for teachers. The content, frequency, and duration of these professional development programs depends, of course, on what is being taught. These opportunities vary in frequency and duration. Several also include such supports for principals and administrators.[5] Others also provide follow-up visits to provide on-site technical assistance to teachers.[6]
- **Structures.** Several developers provide master schedules of classes, schedules to ensure planning time for teachers, student assignment methods, or house structures as a way to ensure that

---

[1] Success For All (SFA, Chapter Seven), Different Ways of Knowing (Chapter Eight), High Schools That Work (HSTW, Chapter Twelve), America's Choice, Turning Points (Chapter Ten), Edison Schools (Chapter Thirteen), and the Institute for Learning (IFL, Chapter Fourteen).

[2] HSTW, SFA, Different Ways of Knowing, and IFL.

[3] DI, SFA, Project GRAD (Chapter Six), America's Choice, and Edison Schools.

[4] Co-nect (Chapter Nine), Different Ways of Knowing, Turning Points, NWP (Chapter Three), Cognitively Guided Instruction (CGI, Chapter Two), Talent Development High School (TDHS, Chapter Eleven), and HSTW.

[5] IFL, SFA, America's Choice, TDHS, HSTW, Edison Schools.

[6] Co-nect, NWP, SFA, HSTW, Edison Schools, and IFL.

schools and teachers create the infrastructure needed to support new curriculum and instruction.[7]

- **Facilitators and coaches.** Several developers require schools to provide facilitators to support implementation or provide such facilitators themselves to provide on-site assistance.[8]
- **Funding.** Some developers have recognized that sites need explicit support in gaining the funds needed for improvement and therefore provide services to help sites seek funding.[9]
- **Forums for exchanging information about new practices.** Several developers host annual forums or have developed Web sites, chat rooms, and newsletters to provide opportunities for teachers to exchange lessons on best practices or find solutions to problem they share.[10]

The real answer to the question of what works in supporting the implementation of school improvement programs is to use multiple, reinforcing approaches simultaneously. The contributors often pointed to the difficulties of changing practice and reported adding new forms of support and refining those already in place to ensure that school staff understood the reasons for change, understood why particular practices were being emphasized, understood and became adept at new practices, and felt supported in the long term in a professional network, by principals, and by administrators.

An overriding challenge in developing implementation strategies for scale-up is cost. The process of improving teaching and learning at any site is labor intensive and, therefore, expensive. Several authors noted that the (relatively) ample resources dedicated to implementation at demonstration sites, often made available through government or private grants, could not be sustained beyond the demonstration. Thus, in attempting to introduce the design in additional sites, they

---

[7] SFA, Project GRAD, America's Choice, Edison Schools, and the TDHS.

[8] SFA, Different Ways of Knowing, Turning Points, TDHS, HSTW, Edison Schools, and IFL.

[9] TDHS, Different Ways of Knowing, SFA, HSTW, and Edison Schools.

[10] NWP, CGI, Turning Points, SFA, TDHS, HSTW, and IFL.

faced the challenge of creating implementation supports that are affordable and useful to the average teacher or school adopter. To address this challenge, developers can use such "staff extenders" as videos, written texts, e-learning, and newsletters. From a school's point of view, it might appear to be far less expensive to adopt a developer's existing and documented curriculum, with associated support for implementation, than it is to pay for the teachers' time and effort to develop their own curriculum. Alternatively, if the developer's curriculum does not align well with the district's standards or assessments and does not entail adequate support for implementation, it will be too expensive at any price.

Implications. A major challenge that developers face in scaling up their designs is creating implementation supports for the adopters that are effective and economical. The intervention must be considered unfinished until the tools to implement it have been developed, have been tested, and have proven successful in ensuring that deep changes in practice occur at multiple sites. Thus, implementation approaches and tools need significant attention during research and development, not just during scale-up.

Funders should understand what financial commitments are involved in supporting implementation and should determine whether the developer has access to the expertise necessary for this function. Those interested in adopting designs, or in moving them from demonstration to scale, must understand that creating a new practice is not enough to ensure scale. The quality, cost, and usability of the implementation supports should be just as important as the design concepts. These supports need to match the capacity and skill levels of the teachers and administrators whose practice is the target of reform.

Ensure High-Quality Implementation at Each Site

As they grow, external assistance organizations must become increasingly concerned with ensuring that their services are of high quality and enable effective implementation at each site. RAND's past work has suggested that, at least for whole-school designs, school-level concerns about the quality of the assistance provided were frequently mentioned as reasons the design did not take hold (Bodilly et al., 1998).

Approaches to Ensuring Quality. While the staff members responsible for development might themselves provide services in the initial sites, they must hire others as scale increases, both to deliver services and to manage the people needed to deliver the services. The necessity to delegate these tasks might result in significant variation in the quality of implementation across sites (Berends, Bodilly, and Kirby, 2002). Several of the programs discussed in this volume provided examples of a quality assurance process for developer services:

- The national office of NWP chose a scale-up strategy of creating school-university partnerships to deliver the training, seminars, and services of the project. To address unevenness in the delivery of services, it created a peer-based quality-control process for evaluating partnerships in terms of the quality of their delivery. Continued membership in the network, and the associated funding, depends on the outcome of this evaluation. The national office continues to spend a high proportion of its time managing this process.
- America's Choice, Different Ways of Knowing, and SFA discussed the overwhelming importance of highly qualified staff to provide training, workshops, and seminars and their struggles to ensure this quality. The reforms met this challenge by developing their own training programs for trainers. For example, America's Choice developed its own national college to train regional delivery staff. In addition, SFA tried as much as possible to recruit trainers from schools that had successfully implemented the design. This trainer development, however, came at a cost. Investment had to be made in human-resource development before scale-up, implying the need for investment capital.

Several contributors discussed the processes they used to check the level of implementation at sites or with teachers and ensure positive outcomes. These clustered into several approaches, and developers often use several processes to gauge progress at sites:

- **Formal site visits.** The developer or peers from other schools implementing the designs visit the site to assess its progress and recommend ways to address remaining challenges. The developer can then work with the sites to help improve implementation.[11]
- **Direct observation.** Trainers or consultants observe the implementation and, based on the observations, help the trainers to recognize issues and remediate teacher practices. Some programs have created formal checklists for this process.[12]
- **Feedback from teachers or teacher self-reports and self-surveys.**[13] Turning Points, CGI, and NWP, for example, made quality the responsibility of the implementers themselves. In two of the examples Carpenter and Franke present in Chapter Two, no external agent was responsible for the quality of the advice provided.

The means of assessing the quality of implementation, however, were not always clear. The BASRC and IFL organizations continue to struggle with the quality and the manner in which their services were used or capitalized on in the subsequent operations of the districts or schools they work with and how to assess this use across sites.

Implications. Implementation quality assurance must be addressed if depth of implementation is a goal. If externally developed interventions are to contribute to the improvement of a school's performance, this function must become more prominent and more must be learned about how to achieve it. Funders need to emphasize the development of these supports. Adopters should be inquisitive about this process and understand the quality assurances the developers provide. None of these developers warrantied their products and services, at least as discussed in this volume. Future analyses of scale-up efforts could focus on the relative effectiveness of different

---

[11] America's Choice, Turning Points, Co-nect, and HSTW.

[12] For example, America's Choice, SFA, Edison Schools, and Different Ways of Knowing.

[13] For example, America's Choice, CGI, NWP, and Turning Points.

approaches to ensuring the quality of implementation, which would benefit the education community as a whole.

Evaluate and Improve the Intervention

Closely tied to quality assurance for implementation is the need to determine whether the intervention, once implemented, produces the desired or claimed effects on student performance.

Discussion in the chapters and within the group meetings indicated evaluation was essential for the following reasons:

- Developers need to know what effects they are achieving so that they can improve the product.
- Evaluation results are needed to support marketing of the program. Without such information, adopters will not show interest.
- Adopters should know the efficacy of the model during the selection process so that they can select a product that meets their performance needs.
- Funders deserve to know whether their money was well spent.

The Growing Challenge of Providing Evidence of Effectiveness. Carrying out high-quality evaluations has been a challenge for several reasons, not the least of which has been a shift in what constitutes evidence of effectiveness. Over several years, as more federal funds have been invested in implementing designs, the federal government has emphasized scientific evidence of effectiveness to gain funding. For example, the reauthorization of the Office of Educational Research and Improvement in 1994 required the office to assess the evidence of effectiveness of programs of wide interest to the education community.[14] The Comprehensive School Reform Demonstration (CSRD) program only supports implementation of "research-based" comprehensive school reform programs. The Reading Excellence Act of 1999 requires the implementation of "scientifically based reading research." The Department of Education's research and development

---

[14] This office has since become the Institute of Education Sciences.

arm, now known as the Institute of Education Sciences, established an online resource, the What Works Clearinghouse, which is intended to provide rigorous syntheses of evidence of the effectiveness of educational programs and practices. The idea behind current federal policy is that knowledge based on high-quality scientific research will allow development of better programs and that data on program performance will help districts and educators make better-informed decisions concerning programs to adopt and implement.

Most, but not all, of the chapters in this volume cite evidence that the programs have worked. We asked authors to confine proof of efficacy to references to evaluative studies published in journals, technical reports, or on Web sites.[15] Most of these programs, however, lack the sort of evidence that those arguing for scientific proof of program efficacy have imagined and will have great difficulty ever producing such evidence (see Berliner, 2002, for a similar perspective).

The reasons for this difficulty are straightforward and presented in several different chapters:

- Programs of such scope and complexity do not lend themselves to the tight scientific evaluation through field trials that is being advocated. The interventions described in this volume normally vary in relation to the specific context in which they are implemented.
- Many of the interventions advocate continuous refinement of concepts and practices that is based on implementation experiences over time. As the characteristics of the interventions change, measures of efficacy must also change, but such adaptations undermine the ability to assess program effectiveness over time and across sites.
- Most of the schoolwide interventions cited here require staff in schools considering the design to vote to participate in the implementation, thus making it impossible to conduct field tri-

---

[15] These sources are listed either in the references section at the end of each chapter or in Appendix B.

als involving random assignment, something advocates of scientific evaluation emphasize.

- Most interventions are intended to produce effects as a result of a significant implementation period (e.g., over the K–5 period) that a student will be in an elementary program. By the time the trial is completed, the intervention is likely to have changed as a result of implementation experience. Or, as Engelmann and Engelmann (Chapter Four) point out, districts may abandon or modify a reform before seeing its full effects, thus missing what the results might have been for a cohort of children who have been taught according to the original reform's principles for their entire elementary career.

Even though the methodologies considered most rigorous are not readily applicable, it is possible to develop evidence of effectiveness that will be valuable to educators or administrators who are attempting to evaluate and select interventions appropriate for their schools or teachers. Doing so would mean using several different classes of evidence to assess effectiveness and to help improve the product and services. The activities of the new What Works Clearinghouse can expose research based in these methods to public discussion and review. These classes of evidence include the following:

- **Evidence on design components.** Most of the programs described here are built on instructional components or organizational concepts for which there is research support.[16] If the nation continues to support more-rigorous research on learning and instruction, reviewing and documenting such evidence could contribute significantly to our knowledge of practices that help improve student achievement.
- **Evidence from research using quasi-experimental evaluation designs.** A significant number of evaluations using quasi-experimental methods (Campbell and Stanley, 1966; Cook and Payne, 2002) can be accessed for information of interest to

---

[16] See for example, SFA, America's Choice, Different Ways of Knowing, and CGI.

potential adopters and policymakers.[17] Data and conclusions from such evaluations can be useful, although attention must be devoted to potential alternative explanations of positive outcomes.

- **Evidence from clinical experience.** The experiences of the schools and individuals who have implemented or tried to implement the intervention or program should be useful to individuals, schools, and districts deciding to adopt or participate in such programs as those described in this volume. HSTW, for instance, uses a multifaceted assessment system that includes surveys of both teachers and students, the results of which would interest potential adopters.

- **Examination of failed sites.** It is important to understand threats to successful implementation. In this volume, the chapters on SFA, Project GRAD, and DI present examples of instances in which interventions have failed and analyze the reasons they failed. Other essays suggest that the authors could produce similar information that could affect adopters' decisions about whether to engage the developer organization or, at least, might prompt early discussions of adaptations needed to make the intervention successful at a particular site. In many cases, the developers have modified their designs or implementation strategies on the basis of their own analyses of the reasons for failures.

- **Evaluation of success at scale.** Reviewing the Web sites and evaluations mentioned above reveals that developers have been subjected to or have subjected themselves to evaluations of one or two of their sites during demonstration and during scale-up. These evaluations usually examine a few sites but not scale-up efforts as a whole or implementation at all sites. Thus, developers have seldom, if ever, demonstrated their success at scale-up to the public. While some developers have collected more-systematic evidence of effectiveness, we have yet to see a devel-

---

[17] Various chapters in this volume also offer such examples, including Chapters Five (SFA), Eight (Different Ways of Knowing), Seven (America's Choice), and Six (Project GRAD).

oper publish implementation levels and associated performance gains across all program sites. Only by collecting and analyzing the data needed to address these outcomes can the developer provide a potential adopter with an important piece of information: the probability of the design producing beneficial outcomes during the scale-up phase. That piece of information is also essential for improving the design and implementation assistance.

Implications. Assessing program effectiveness will require creativity and flexibility. Evaluation needs will grow over time but can be met using different types of analyses. Policymakers and funders should entertain notions other than randomized experimental designs to answer important questions about, for example, implementation quality. The accumulation of evidence should take precedence, rather than attempting one single definitive study, which is unlikely to produce sufficient clarity. Developers and funders who are serious about achieving scale-up will require systematic collection of implementation and outcome data across all the sites to measure scale-up effectiveness rather than effectiveness at a handful of sites. Potential adopters and funders should ask for (and, if need be, funders might provide) incentives to develop evidence of the probability that a teacher's or school's or district's assessed performance will improve by association with the developer.

Obtain the Financial Support Needed

As scaling goes forward, obtaining the financial resources needed to sustain the enterprise is probably the greatest preoccupation of most program leaders. Money is needed to pay for services and materials and building the capacity to provide them, as well as for continuing efforts to improve the intervention. Each developer was challenged to create an effective "business model" that permitted it to sustain the design organization and ensure high-quality implementation.

Current Approaches. In most cases, the organizations adopted a mixed funding model, allowing them to move from an emphasis on private and public funding to charging fees for services as the interventions moved from design to demonstration to scale-up and to take advantage of different sources that specify the uses of the funds. What is most clear from this review is that the sources of funding change over time and by purpose and that developers do not act alone. Obviously, some developers have had continued access to "angels," strongly committed philanthropic funders. Others have had to move more quickly to a fee-for-service business model because they lacked such a partner, which has implications for what they can provide. As indicated previously, developers can adjust the amount of services they provide depending on what consumers are willing to pay; but this, in turn, affects implementation and final outcomes. Bodilly (2001) covers this line of causality by describing how funding reductions affect design scope.

Operations. As scaling began, most programs began to operate on a fee-for-service basis. The shift from foundation or public funding has proven quite difficult for some of the older programs but is far more common today than it was a decade ago. Several federal programs have been instrumental in assisting schools or teachers to pay these fees. For example, schools can access Title 1 and CSRD funds to pay for the whole-school designs. CGI noted that schools accessed Eisenhower grants to pay for teacher training and time, and the U.S. Department of Education provides funding to schools and teachers to allow them to attend NWP seminars.

In a significantly different concept, HSTW is partially supported by membership fees paid by states that support the Southern Regional Education Board, HSTW's parent organization. In addition, because of HSTW's emphasis on career and technical education, federal funds are available to some schools and districts under the terms of the Carl D. Perkins Vocational Education Act. However, because these sources provide only a portion of the required resources, HSTW has also had to rely on foundation grants, CSR funds, and on other federal grants.

Several programs continued to rely on philanthropic funds, even for the scale-up operations that others have covered primarily through fees. For example, the Ford Foundation provided significant funding for Project GRAD's scale-up operations, and the program also requires a significant funding commitment from the local business community. Similarly, the Heinz and the Grable foundations supported Different Ways of Knowing's operations in western Pennsylvania, and the Hewlett and Annenberg foundations supported BASRC's operations. At various points in its history, HSTW has received operational funding from the Wallace, Charles Stewart Mott, Edna McConnell Clark, and Goldman Sachs foundations and from the Carnegie Corporation of New York. The program continues to seek support from such organizations but also provides some services on a fee-for-service basis.

Capital Investments. Perhaps the most difficult funding problem is finding the resources to build capacity in the developer's organization: training new staff, building back-office capabilities (e.g., accounting, information technology, human resource management), and improving the design and services over time. Funding for capital and improvement expenses has largely come from foundation or government grants or, in the cases of Edison Schools and Co-nect, from private investments. America's Choice noted that it pays for these functions through fees for services. Several authors cited the importance of continued government and foundation support for improving and extending their designs and for evaluating the effects of the designs as they evolve.

Capital for capacity-building in nonprofits has not traditionally been readily available, but new sources are emerging. Some foundations make funds available for this purpose or make program-related loans to nonprofits. In Chapter Sixteen, Millot forcefully argues for continued changes. The federal government has made a number of capacity-building grants for comprehensive school designs.[18] New American Schools has established a fund, which Millot briefly describes, to make loans to educational entrepreneurs for these purposes, and several venture funds are seeking opportunities to invest in potential profit-making educational reforms.

---

[18] See, for example, Johannesen's (Chapter Eight) discussion of the development of Different Ways of Knowing after 1998.

Working Capital. Finally, one contributor noted that schools and districts often do not pay their bills until long after services have been delivered, making it difficult to find the working capital needed to sustain the organization. Philanthropic and private venture funders provided grants and loans to SFA to establish a line of credit to operate in advance of payment.

Continuing Challenges. Finding funding sources remains challenging. In particular, the developers have remarked on the difficulties associated with finding venture capital and making the shift to a fee-for-service business model.

Venture Capitalists. Funding sources for venture development in education has recently begun to emerge. During the heady growth of the 1990s, a few venture-capital firms began serious consideration of investment in education. The Entrepreneurs Fund of New American Schools and the New Schools Venture Fund are examples. Letts, Ryan, and Grossman (1997) support this approach, arguing that philanthropic foundations should emphasize assistance to enterprises that they have helped to start, so that these organizations can effectively scale their work and become self-sufficient.

Millot (Chapter Sixteen) argued that access to venture funding and foundation funding should be associated with stricter attention to mutual accountability. Arguing from a venture capitalist's view, he noted that private funders might play a larger role in future ventures than they have in the past but that they will want to help shape the incentives for such ventures to market and scale up their programs. In particular, because such funders take equity interests in new designs, they might actively participate in program management or at least offer their expertise in business planning, financial management, and human-resource policies—which all new ventures need for success. In addition, expecting a profit in the long run, they are more likely to hold the developers accountable for the delivery of products than in the past. The more the market moves in this direction, the more developers will need to interact with this new group and be accountable for results.

Move to Fee-for-Service Financing. Teachers, schools, and districts have long bought services from vendors. They purchase textbooks and supplies and frequently pay university or freelance consultants for courses or training sessions. But as Millot (Chapter Sixteen) observes, the comprehensive improvement services described in this volume were, for many years, provided by organizations supported almost entirely by grants—organizations that, when working with school districts, schools, or teachers, often brought funding with them.

The shift to fee-for-service financing has been necessary for widespread scale-up of the interventions and expertise that external intermediaries or institutions have developed. Few, if any, funding agencies are willing to provide continuing funding for improvement activities in a school or school district. While such agencies might be interested in fostering educational innovation and might recognize a need for startup funding, they almost always view continued improvement to be the responsibility of the adopter. This volume is a product of the simultaneous, but potentially contradictory, desires of funders to limit the length of their investments in specific education improvement activities and to see the products of their investments used on a wide scale. To the degree that advice, training, materials, and coaching are needed to implement the models resulting from such investments, some form of fee-for-service funding is necessary.

However, as Tucker (Chapter Seven) and Millot (Chapter Sixteen) argue, moving to fee-for-service support for operations has profound effects for external providers, and these effects extend far beyond the revenues fees generate. The move shifts the entire basis of the relationship between the developer and the school or district with which it is working. If a district must find the financial resources to pay service fees, it is likely to make a greater effort to identify its needs and determine what the developer will provide for the fee. The district might require concessions from the developer to ensure that the district's investment in the work of the developer pays off. Similarly, if the developer depends on obtaining a fee for its services and materials, it has a strong incentive to see that its offerings meet the needs of potential adopters. Thus, fee-for-service operations can promote important forms of mutual accountability.

As several of the essays indicate, moving from grant support to fee-for-service operations significantly affected relationships between school improvement organizations and their customers—teachers, schools, and districts. A teacher, school, or district paying a fee can be expected to take the efforts of the developer seriously and to create the conditions needed for the efforts to bear fruit. A developer that depends on attracting paying business can be expected to provide services that satisfy the needs and interests of the teachers, schools, and districts.

While a fee-for-service market for educational improvement services can have very important positive effects, there is an important caveat: Teachers, schools, or districts that are reluctant to change existing practices might seek service providers that will modify these practices only marginally. The growth of standards-based systems, however, safeguards against such shortsighted approaches.

Implications. The challenges of funding will remain over the lifetime of the scale-up, but their nature will shift during that time. Funding markets for scale-up are shifting to encourage providers to be more responsive to funders' and customers' needs. The quality of designs and implementation supports, as well as the rates of spread and improvement, is highly dependent on capturing a stable funding stream for each of the developer's needs and creating a service structure that can operate within the resulting budget. Funders can help in this regard not just by providing such streams but also by being knowledgeable about the multiple streams available and helping developers, schools, and teachers access them effectively. While it might be tempting for a philanthropy to provide operational support to ensure progress, there is much to be said for leaving it to the teachers and schools to decide what they need and to determine how to access public funds to pay for it. As Tucker (Chapter Seven) and Millot (Chapter Sixteen) point out, free goods are seldom well used. Millot emphasized the usefulness of more-constructive accountability mechanisms among funders, adopters, and developers that will provide incentives for the developers to move toward self-sustainment and that will ensure proof of the effectiveness of the practices.

Build Organizational Capacity to Support Scale-up

As Millot (Chapter Sixteen) notes, it is rare that the individuals responsible for the development and initial implementation of interventions possess the skills (or stomachs) for the tasks of building and managing the larger organization needed to serve increasing numbers of sites. Transforming small organizations driven by the ideals and energy of their founders into stable entities capable of providing a consistent set of services in multiple sites is difficult. The overall impression of that process one gets from these essays probably understates most of the difficulties involved in the transition. In addition to the challenges of acquiring the resources for capacity-building discussed in the previous section, several of the developers noted the fundamental challenge they faced in expanding their services to many dispersed sites.

Approaches to Building Capacity. The challenge is to provide affordable services to a growing number of sites, while maintaining the quality of the services they provide. Several solutions have been attempted, each with its own strengths and weaknesses.

Building a High-Quality Staff. As noted previously, Different Ways of Knowing, SFA, and America's Choice discussed developing a set of highly skilled trainers before expansion to avoid expanding poorly. As Slavin and Madden (Chapter Five) note, "the most important limitation on the broad dissemination of SFA is our own capacity to provide high-quality professional development services to a very large number of schools." These developers eventually created their own training programs for trainers, and SFA recruits trainers from existing SFA schools. Taking a related approach, HSTW, which works extensively with state departments of education, has recruited state employees seeking a "second career" to serve as coaches and in other staff positions. As with the SFA trainers, these individuals have come to know the program by working with it in a professional capacity.

Economy by Regionalization. Economically, having a central national office provide labor-intensive services to sites across the nation is not only time-consuming but expensive. Thus, several of the developers have gone to a regional-center model.[19] Turning Points and NWP took great pains to discuss the challenges involved, particularly the need to control the quality of the services these centers provide. For NWP, this approach eventually required building a quality-assurance process for the regional centers and tying funding to meeting set provision standards.

Economy by Clustering. An alternative is for the developer, before committing to provide services, to insist that a cluster of schools or significant numbers of teachers in a small geographic area agree to use the services. DI, Co-nect, NWP, and TDHS particularly noted the need for such a geographic concentration approach. Others have used it more indirectly. For example, the support that America's Choice, HSTW, and SFA receive from states or districts has allowed them to capture economies of scale in providing services and thus allows more-efficient capacity building. Project GRAD also uses this strategy, but in this case, to ensure consistent delivery of sound curriculum and instruction.

Contracting or Partnerships. Slavin and Madden (Chapter Five) describe SFA's attempts to use existing institutions (universities, education labs, and a private organization) to build capacity, but these attempts often ended badly. In large part, these unhappy endings came about because the partner or contractors did not meet the service standards the developer felt were necessary to ensure implementation and improved outcomes. In contrast, Johannesen (Chapter Eight) notes that Different Ways of Knowing has successfully used contracting practices for its marketing functions.

Implications. Building capacity to serve new markets well is and continues to be a significant challenge. The developers discussed how they dealt with the internal challenges of growth, but its challenges will remain significant and are likely to recur as the organization serves more sites or provides more kinds of services. Becoming familiar with the pitfalls of capacity-building documented in this volume

---

[19] These are NWP, Turning Points, America's Choice, and SFA.

will help new developers avoid similarly painful discovery experiences. Funders could provide an important service not only by helping developers confront these issues and helping them work toward solutions but also by providing incentives for them to attend to these capacity-building issues and holding them accountable for a return on their investment (see Millot, Chapter Sixteen). Finally, in choosing among interventions, adopters might explore whether a given developer has the capacity to deliver the services it promises.

Market the Product

The most common way to achieve "spread" is what might be termed *marketing*. The purpose of marketing is usually to gain the interest of potential customers, but, in this field, developers also use the term to refer to the process through which the intervention is sold and teachers commit to trying it.

Approaches to Marketing. Most of the interventions described in the essays have relied on some combination of the following mechanisms to create interest among potential users:

- word of mouth, especially teacher to teacher
- presentations at professional associations, at state and local sponsored meetings or fairs, to district and school leaders, and to state education officials
- published descriptions and evaluations of interventions in professional journals or magazines
- distribution of promotional materials or public-access Web sites
- published third-party descriptions of reform options, including the What Works Clearinghouse
- special interest networks.

The chapters did not focus on this information-dissemination component of marketing. Perhaps because of the What Works Clearinghouse and CSR Web sites, third parties have become heavily involved in rating the effectiveness of these interventions and disseminating that and related important information. From a consumer's point of view, a great deal more information is available to provide a basis for informed decisionmaking than in the past.

Several authors did focus on the importance of the process of selecting or choosing to adopt the product. The major challenge they identified is recruiting informed and committed adopters but doing so at a reasonable cost. Several processes have been developed that appear to depend on the design and the focus of the intervention. More-formal selection processes might help ensure that adopting organizations understand the level of commitment required for full implementation, thus potentially avoiding partial implementation or "dropouts."

Individual Self-Selection. The developers who target teachers as the focus of intervention function on a word-of-mouth model, with teachers volunteering to undertake the professional development series because of what they have heard from colleagues.[20] While other types of designs might require considerably more work on the front end to ensure commitment, the opportunity cost here is lower if an individual teacher decides not to pursue more in-depth practice. Thus, interventions that focus on individual teachers did not rely heavily on formal selection processes (although, as noted previously, NWP does use formal selection and evaluation processes at the site level). The high rates of teacher return and the building of strong networks that our contributors report testify to the efficacy of the hands-off approach. In fact, group discussions surrounding these two interventions focused on their "stickiness," their ability to take hold of a teacher's motivation and imagination and ensure continued interest.

School Commitment. Other developers, requiring more-direct interactions among groups of teachers in schools, have developed a different process of selection and buy-in. During this process, those involved at the school formally learn about the intervention and how it compares with others and requires the teachers to vote on adoption. Several encourage potential adopters to visit demonstration sites and talk with teachers there to understand the level of change involved.[21]

---

[20] For example, CGI and NWP.

[21] These are Co-nect, SFA, and HSTW.

Planning Year. At least one of the interventions (TDHS) has developed a planning-year concept to enable teachers in schools to learn more about the interventions. In the planning year, elements of the TDHS model are taught and plans are made for implementing other parts of the design within individual schools. The planning year provides the opportunity to communicate the importance of key design elements—thus, in principle at least, reducing the tendency for designs to fragment during implementation.

Implications. Marketing by the developer and selection by the teacher or school are two sides of the same process: gaining thoughtful and committed implementers at an affordable cost. Much has been written about the need for better information for consumers, as well as better selection processes. But most of this literature appeared in the 1990s, when little information was available for consumers on the whole-school designs that emerged at that time. More recently, developers and the government have begun to establish significant marketing materials and processes. However, whether and how often these marketing and selection processes work is unknown, and consumers or adopters still have much work to do to find services that will provide the benefits they are seeking.

Create Approaches to Meet Local Context Needs

Developers must be able to adapt their interventions to contexts other than the ones in which they were first implemented.

Approaches to Local Needs. There must be an effective and "sellable" balance between standardization of the intervention and adaptation to the needs of individual intervention sites. Failure to pay attention to this could yield one of several unwanted outcomes:

- Potential users will reject the product because it does not fit their specific situation.
- After adopting the product and services, users will implement them poorly or shallowly, resulting in the intervention having little or no effect on practices or outcomes.

- Allowing significant adaptation requires additional labor-intensive, site-specific support, thereby increasing the cost to adopters.

Contrasting Approaches. Developers have focused on standardizing different parts of the designs because of different assumptions about teachers and what they need to improve practice.

Standardized Curriculum and Pedagogy. Several of the interventions provide curriculum and instructional plans to teachers, schools, or districts to adopt, including America's Choice, SFA, DI, Edison Schools, and Project GRAD. In using these designs, teachers are not expected to develop their own lesson plans but to benefit from the standardized products that the developers and their experts have created. The relationships schools adopting these designs will have with the developers will involve less interactive mutual development, at least around curriculum and pedagogy. While HSTW does not provide a specific set of lesson plans, it does push for a specific set of course offerings and graduation requirements. In recent years, the program has begun to work closely with schools and teachers to ensure that the courses it recommends do, in fact, teach the content students need to know to meet both the state's performance standards and HSTW's own performance standards. Thus, although teachers are free to choose books and create their own assignments, they are given clear guidance about what they should be teaching.

Standardized Process. Several of the interventions do not have standardized curriculum and instruction but instead standardize a process that should lead to improvements. One or two have both standardized curriculum and processes. TDHS, BASRC, HSTW, Co-nect, and Different Ways of Knowing each use standardized processes; these programs assume that an imposed curriculum will not be adopted and that teachers must learn by doing. The developers often, however, provide sample lessons or other helpful materials.

Customization. Several developers have created a different scheme to ensure high-quality implementation while meeting local needs. Co-nect (Chapter Nine) developed a customized set of three options that sites can choose from, suiting each to needs of specific types of sites. America's Choice noted instances of customizing the adoption process to fit the needs of specific classes of adopters. Similarly, Different Ways of Knowing (Chapter Eight) developed an entire package of assistance for schools with very high proportions of children from low-income backgrounds to address the specific development needs of their students. HSTW (Chapter Twelve) and Turning Points (Chapter Ten) took similar approaches to customization.

The Challenge of Standards-Based State Systems. One area appeared to be problematic for almost all the developers—or at least troubled them until they found solutions: alignment between the developer's and the adopter's standards, curriculum, and assessments. Many of the developers created their designs before the growth in standards-based state systems. At the time, states and districts not only lacked standards-based curriculum and assessments, they also lacked the standards. In such settings, some developers, such as DI, SFA, America's Choice, and Co-nect, took pains to create such systems, and other programs, such as Project GRAD and Edison Schools, adopted components of other designs that had done so.

With the growth of state standards and aligned curriculum and assessment, these developers have been forced either to align their concepts with the explicit or implicit accountability requirements for the specific sites implementing the interventions or to persuade site decisionmakers to permit the developers' requirements to supercede those of the site so that the developers could implement their ideas effectively. Such alignment is more challenging in some subject areas than others. Early reading and mathematics standards are similar in most states; history, social studies, and science standards appear to be more varied.

In some cases, conflicts between the requirements of districts and developers prompt developers to ask districts for waivers from their existing standards, curriculum, pedagogy, or assessment systems. In particular, Engelmann and Engelmann (Chapter Four) suggest that, in an "extensive requirements model," such as DI, the developer must seek waivers from district guidelines to implement the model successfully. In contrast, BASRC and IFL take the state's standards as given and works with instructional leaders throughout the district to build teaching and learning that meet those standards. Several others work with districts to show that the program curricula meet the content and performance standards or make adaptations to meet the state standards.[22]

The teacher-targeted interventions, such as NWP and CGI, face the same issue. In these programs, teachers have the right and the responsibility to examine the principles of the developers, reflect on their own practices, and choose the means of implementing the developer's principles. In effect, each teacher's changed practice becomes a "local adaptation." And, as with schools and districts, teachers must ensure that their students meet externally imposed standards. Thus, their choices about how to implement interventions must be guided by the need to fulfill the two goals of meeting standards and aligning their practice with the tenets of effective teaching, as derived from research and effective practice. In these two programs, the developer's role was to advise teachers as they attempted to implement the principles appropriately on the most local level of all—their own classrooms. These two interventions rely heavily on interaction among networks of teachers to adapt the interventions to local needs and circumstances, to provide mutual support for effective implementation, and to reduce friction between state and district standards and those of teachers in their respective subject areas.

The move to performance-based systems (i.e., accountability based on test scores) has reemphasized the importance of context to scale-up. Over the past five to seven years, however, a significant number of large districts have reasserted their responsibility for instructional programs. This shift has occurred, in part, because both the states and individual communities naturally look to the school district to deal with schools that are failing to perform adequately in the state accountability system, rather than to the schools. Second, powerful backing from civic and business leaders has encouraged forceful superintendents in such large districts as Los Angeles, San

---

[22] TDHS, Edison Schools, and Co-nect.

Diego, New York City, and Boston to ensure improvement through strong central-office management. In addition, given the move to high standards for all students, districts have focused on the issue of variable curriculum and instruction across schools and teachers and on how such variations affect the increasingly large portion of the urban student population that is highly mobile—changing schools several times if not more in their careers. Proponents of central-office control argue that a uniform curriculum and an instructional strategy geared to state assessments will help these mobile children stay on a consistent learning path.

Aligning Other Infrastructure. School systems are difficult to penetrate and change.[23] Accepting this, many programs, including some represented in this volume, initially devised scale-up strategies that largely bypassed the school district and went directly to individual schools or teachers. This was particularly true of comprehensive school designs (e.g., Turning Points, TDHS, SFA, and Different Ways of Knowing), which focus on individual schools. Often, efforts to engage the education systems in which implementation took place was minimal or poorly executed (Bodilly et al., 1998; Datnow, Hubbard, and Mehan, 2002).

In some cases, however, the lack of school and district policies and infrastructure—other than those on standards, curriculum, or assessments—to support the design concepts thwarted teacher attempts at implementation, whether inadvertently or consciously. Thus, developers have found that they must work with schools and districts to help ensure that infrastructure is better aligned. Several examples were covered:

- Developers have had to negotiate with districts over the needed professional development and ensure that other district mandates or lack of funding did not pose barriers to teacher attendance in developer-supported professional development. NWP solved this challenge by developing a professional education program jointly with the schools and the district. The TDHS

---

[23] See Elmore (2000) for a lively discussion of this issue.

developers arrange for the district to give teachers release time to attend the program's workshops in lieu of the district's.

- Several developers have translated their materials into other languages to support the appropriate school populations (SFA, TDHS). In another case, Edison School had to adopt the district's bilingual approach to education.
- TDHS had to realign its professional development schedule and the proposed master schedule for the schools to meet the needs of a district that had adopted year-round schooling.
- Edison Schools has created a high-level position for "relationship managers," who make sure that the needs of parents and teachers are met.
- The America's Choice design is based on the premise that the state, district, and school infrastructures must be aligned into coherent systems to meet the goal of improved performance for all students.

Implications. Developers and users must work together to understand the constructs of the design and must mutually adapt to promote the goal of improved student performance. The essays convey an important message: Successful implementation requires clear communication and mutual understanding. The developer and the school or district must agree about how the implementation will take place and whether the site and the developer will alter their policies and approaches. Even waivers involve a process of discovery and communication.

Sustain the Design

With some exceptions, our contributors devoted relatively little attention to explicit efforts to sustain reforms through time, which might simply reflect the relative novelty of many of these activities. The developers have concentrated on perfecting the intervention itself rather than on supporting its continuation once it is in place. Another important factor might be that, to the degree that scaling efforts have been funded by limited lifetime funds (e.g., CSRD grants have a three-year life span), the financial incentives for focusing on efforts to sustain a program over the long run are limited.

Approaches to Sustainability. The most common approach to sustaining reform efforts that the developers emphasize is creating networks that permit the teachers, principals, and administrators implementing the designs to meet, share experiences, and support one another. Most of our contributors cite regional and national meetings as ways to sustain and renew the efforts of those adopting their interventions. While there is little doubt that such networking engenders enthusiastic support among those who participate, we have seen no evidence on the effectiveness of this strategy and its relationship to sustaining interventions.

Strategies for sustaining innovative practices could be regarded as an important responsibility of the school district rather than the responsibility of the developer. If the district invests its own funds or grant money in outside support for instructional improvement—whether for school designs or professional improvements, such as NWP or CGI—it has an important reason to set up its own processes to provide the support necessary to sustain the intervention through time. Such support might include fostering networks within a district, developing capacity and plans to train new staff in content and pedagogy appropriate to the design, providing for professional development over time (including incentives for improved practice), and assigning principals who will support the instructional program that is in the school.

This lack of attention to the sustainability of the design overlaps with the important issue of transfer of ownership of the design. Perhaps because developing ownership has not traditionally been considered a responsibility of design and development groups, many of our contributors pay little explicit attention to this attribute of scaling in their essays.[24] Slavin and Madden (Chapter Five) mention the desirability of having teachers who have mastered the SFA requirements move beyond what SFA provides to make further improvements in

---

[24] This should in no way imply that the authors do not believe this is important—just that they tended not to emphasize it.

their instruction, but it is clear that they see helping teachers and schools improve their near-term performance as more important. CGI's approach, relying as it does on the initiative of practitioners, begins with the idea of ownership. The same might be said of NWP because most target participants have voluntarily decided to join, and the program emphasizes collective responsibility for the work. HSTW encourages ownership by conducting professional development workshops in which teachers and other school leaders are asked to generate ideas about how the organization's key practices could be implemented in their schools. This practice is based on the idea that there is more than one way to, say, establish high expectations and that local people will know best what works in their setting. HSTW and America's Choice also encourage ownership of their programs beyond the school level by working with state legislators and state departments of education, encouraging them to incorporate the elements of their designs into state policies.

Ownership can be seen as a central focus of the two programs that explicitly say their goal is to build capacity: BASRC and IFL. For much of its lifetime, BASRC has tried to foster the capacity of individual schools to assess their own strengths and weaknesses and to identify sources of expertise to address the weaknesses. The program has characterized its effort as building a "cycle of inquiry," a process of continued examination of performance and ways to improve performance, followed by changes in practice based on that analysis. While initially focused on schools, BASRC's recent program has moved to include districts as well.

Similarly, IFL has sought to foster ownership by districts, emphasizing its role as a partner in an effort to build districtwide capacity to improve instruction in all classrooms. However IFL's experience amply supports the idea that getting a large organization, such as a school system, that is subject to pervasive funding and policy uncertainty to take such ownership can be very difficult. When combined with cultural traditions of schools emphasizing individual autonomy for teachers, these uncertainties lead districts to emphasize compliance and responsiveness to outside pressures—not ownership of the problem and the means for its solution.

Implication. Sustainability and ownership appear to be less developed as concepts; many ideas are now being tested but need significant attention if they are to meet the goals of scale-up. Both in the essays and in our group discussions, these characteristics of scale-up remained underdeveloped, even though all the contributors thought the notion was very important. Support for research in this area is essential. Current evaluations of different interventions should focus on the percentage of schools or teachers that maintain improved practices over time, how context affects decisions to abandon specific interventions, and the characteristics of designs and implementation support that lead to site ownership. Funders should be especially interested in these concepts, urging developers to address them and to fund research that can unveil effective practices.

Conclusions

The efforts to develop, demonstrate, scale up, and evaluate new designs for education we have described are potentially a critical component of the changes needed to reform education practices. To achieve the goals that the nation espouses, teachers, schools, and districts must find ways to take ownership of the problem and its solution. They must find their way to cultures emphasizing continuing improvement. External organizations carrying out school improvement efforts, such as those our contributors describe, provide important sources of expertise, ideas, designs, and support. However, introducing these resources will produce the sought-after improvements in student performance only if the external organizations and their potential clients or associates in schools connect with one another, use the designs and expertise to change instruction and learning in meaningful ways, find ways to continue the efforts over time, and continue to improve on the efforts the introduction of the design and the assistance of the developers have prompted. These organizations and others like them are resources that hardly existed 20 years ago. If combined with a steady and stable demand for improvement in student performance, they might contribute significantly to achieving national goals—for all students, including those our schools have not, historically, served well.

As ambitious as the work is, it is not sufficient to accomplish this goal. Scaled research and development efforts need to be combined with coherent, robust, and stable systems of accountability; a human-resource development system that ensures an adequate supply of teachers and administrators with the requisite skills; and funding that is sufficient and so allocated that all children are assured the opportunity to achieve high standards.

Those seeking to support reform—whether developers, funders, teachers, schools, or districts—would do well to keep the observations we have made here about scale-up in mind as they consider the challenges and payoffs of improvement efforts. Especially, they should consider the extent to which the effort is likely to achieve the attributes of successful scale-up: spread, depth, sustainability, and ownership. By using this concept of scale-up and the set of core tasks specified here when evaluating proposals for improvement, both private and public organizations can increase the likelihood that their investments of time and money will help bring about real improvement in the performance of students in our schools. Participants in reform efforts must recognize and accept the inevitably of the "continuous improvement" approach to scaling up school reform. At the same time, they must recognize the importance of all the tasks enumerated and the need to determine how each one can be carried out effectively.

Thus, the major lesson of this volume is that, *no matter the target of reform or the design construct, the process is iterative, complex, and requires support by multiple actors.* This is likely to remain so for the foreseeable future. The next major lesson to come from this description is that *the actors must jointly address a set of known, interconnected tasks if scale-up is to succeed; especially, the actors must align policies and infrastructure to sustain practice.* How each group addresses them varies according to design, context, and resources. Actors should be aware of these tasks. Specifically, they must be aware of the following:

- Developers must create supports for the implementers that are effective and economical and meet the specific needs of the sites.
- Promoting depth of changed practice requires developing procedures and applying measures of implementation for ensuring implementation quality and applying these procedures consistently.
- Assessing program effectiveness will require creativity and flexibility to address the methodological challenges that flow from efforts that are complex, locally situated, adaptive, and iterative. A combination of methods and studies that develop evidence over time is likely to have high payoff.
- The challenges of funding remain over the lifetime of the scale-up, but their nature will change over that time. While funding markets are shifting to make providers potentially more responsive to customers' needs, much greater attention must be paid to the different types of funding needs, and when they occur, if scale-up is to be achieved.
- Increasing the capacity to serve new markets well posed a significant challenge and will continue to do so. This can partly be remedied by obtaining funding specifically for capacity-building investments, but developers and funders must also recognize specific capacity needs and create effective plans to address them.
- To increase the likelihood of creating and sustaining successful working relationships, developers must focus their efforts on thoughtful, committed customers, and customers must carefully review designs and implementation supports to ensure a good fit with their needs. All must pay attention to ensuring that this process takes place within an affordable cost structure.
- Developers and users must work together to understand the constructs of the design and mutually adapt to promote the goal of improved student performance. This process will be long and will involve complex change. The parties must be willing and prepared to work together to create a coherent system of supports.

- As yet, little is known about how to sustain changes and how to transfer ownership effectively. Achieving these ends is likely to involve all the previous activities, including creating a coherent support structure and promoting engagement at every level. These concepts must be addressed directly and must receive significant attention if they are to be achieved.

Those who seek to fund research, design, and development intended to foster improved performance in the nation's education systems can learn much from those who have been working on these problems. When planning their own programs, funders or investors should bear these common tasks in mind. Similarly, those who would use the designs and skills of these organizations should assure themselves that they understand both the capacities of the organizations and what they must undertake to utilize these capacities. The set of tasks we have identified can be used to develop questions about the characteristics and costs of interventions and about the orientation and capacities of developer organizations, teachers, schools, and districts seeking school improvement services. Their use can increase the likelihood of obtaining a good fit between their needs and capacities and the services they are purchasing.

References

Berends, M., S. J. Bodilly, S. N. Kirby, *Facing the Challenges of Whole-School Reform: New American Schools After a Decade*, Santa Monica, Calif.: RAND Corporation, MR-1498-EDU, 2002.

Berliner, D. C., "Educational Research: The Hardest Science of All," *Educational Research*, Vol. 31, No. 8, November 2002, pp. 18–20.

Bodilly, S. J., *New American Schools' Concept of Break the Mold Designs: How Designs Evolved and Why*, Santa Monica, Calif.: RAND Corporation, MR-1288-NAS, 2001.

Bodilly, S. J., B. Keltner, S. W. Purnell, R. E. Reichardt, and G. L. Schuyler, *Lessons from New American Schools' Scale-Up Phase: Prospects for*

Bringing Designs to Multiple Schools, Santa Monica, Calif.: RAND Corporation, MR-942-NAS. 1998.

Campbell, D. T., and J. C. Stanley, *Experimental and Quasi-Experimental Designs for Research*, Chicago: Rand McNally, 1966.

Coburn, C. E., "Rethinking Scale: Moving Beyond Numbers to Deep and Lasting Change," *Educational Researcher*, Vol. 32, No. 6, 2003, pp. 3–12.

Cook, T. D., and M. R. Payne, "Objecting to the Objections to Using Random Assignment in Educational Research," in F. Mosteller and R. Boruch, eds., *Evidence Matters: Randomized Trials in Education Research*, Washington, D.C.: Brookings Institution Press, 2002, pp. 150–178.

Datnow, A., L. Hubbard, and H. Mehan, *Extending Educational Reform: From One School to Many*, London: Routledge/Falmer, 2002.

Elmore, R. F., "Getting to Scale with Successful Educational Practices," *Harvard Educational Review*, Vol. 66, No. 1, 1996, pp. 1–26.

Elmore, R. F., *Building a New Structure for School Leadership*, Washington, D.C.: Albert Shanker Institute, 2000.

Fullan, M., *The New Meaning of Educational Change*, 3rd ed., New York: Teachers College Press, 2001.

Glennan, T. K., *New American Schools After Six Years*, Santa Monica, Calif.: RAND Corporation, MR-945-NAS, 1998.

Herman, R., D. Aladjem, P. McMahon, E. Masem, I. Mulligan, A. O'Malley, S. Quinones, A. Reeve, and D. Woodruff, *An Educator's Guide to Schoolwide Reform*, Arlington, Va.: Education Research Service, 1999.

Letts, C., W. Ryan, and A. Grossman, "Virtuous Capital: What Foundations Can Learn from Venture Capitalists," *Harvard Business Review*, Vol. 97, March–April 1997, pp. 36–44.

Sarason, S. B., *The Predictable Failure of Educational Reform: Can We Change Course Before It's Too Late?* San Francisco: Jossey-Bass Publishers, 1990.

_____, *Revisiting "The Culture of the School and the Problem of Change,"* New York: Teachers College Press, 1996.

Contributors

Cognitively Guided Instruction
Chapter Two

Thomas Carpenter is professor of curriculum and instruction (mathematics education) at the University of Wisconsin–Madison and is director of the National Center for Improving Student Learning and Achievement in Mathematics and Science. He is former editor of the *Journal for Research in Mathematics Education*. Together with Elizabeth Fennema, Megan Franke, and a number of research associates and teachers, he developed Cognitively Guided Instruction. He is currently studying how to extend this concept to include the development of algebraic reasoning throughout the elementary school.

    Megan Loef Franke is an associate professor in the Department of Education at the University of California, Los Angeles, and director of Center X: Where Research and Practice Intersect for Urban School Professionals. Her work focuses on understanding and supporting teacher learning through professional development.

National Writing Project
Chapter Three

Joseph P. McDonald is professor of teaching and learning at New York University, where his teaching and research focus on the policies and practices of school reform, in particular on the role of teacher learning. His experience in the National Writing Project dates to the early 1980s, when he became one of the first teacher-consultants of the Boston Writing Project. He is coauthor of *The Power of Protocols: Educator's Guide to Improving Practice* (2003). His other books include *School Reform Behind the Scenes* (1999), *Redesigning School* (1996), and *Teaching: Making Sense of an Uncertain Craft* (1992).

Judy Buchanan is the deputy director of the National Writing Project. Her experience with the National Writing Project dates to 1986, when, as a classroom teacher, she helped found the Philadelphia Writing Project. She joined the National Writing Project in 1999 after serving for four years as deputy director of the Philadelphia Education Fund. She has worked with a number of education organizations and currently serves on advisory boards for Research for Action and the MacArthur Learning Partnership.

Richard Sterling is the executive director of the National Writing Project at the University of California, Berkeley, Graduate School of Education, and adjunct professor in the Graduate School of Education's Language, Literacy, and Culture division. Prior to 1994, he was a member of the faculty at Lehman College at the City University of New York and the director and founder of the Institute for Literacy Studies and the New York City Writing Project. In 2003, he chaired the Advisory Board to the College Board's Commission on Writing in America's Schools and Colleges. The most recent publication of the National Writing Project, *Because Writing Matters* (2003), presents the case for the importance of writing for all students.

Direct Instruction

Chapter Four

Kurt E. Engelmann began his career in education in the early 1980s as a tutor working with a variety of learning-disabled students, ranging from adult remedial readers to severely language-delayed first graders. In the mid-1980s, Dr. Engelmann worked as a behavioral consultant for the Engelmann-Becker Corporation in cooperation with the Eugene "4J" School District and Lane Education Service District in Oregon. During that time, he also worked on the development of a behavioral research program for the Oregon Research Institute. From 1994 to 2000, Dr. Engelmann served as outreach coordinator in the Jackson School of International Studies at the University of Washington. Since July 2000, Dr. Engelmann has been the administrative director of the National Institute for Direct Instruction, where he is responsible for organizing administrative support for Direct Instruction implementations, serving as liaison between school district administrators and the institute and for coordinating medium and long-term planning of the institute's implementation efforts.

Siegfried E. Engelmann is a University of Oregon professor, researcher, and author of more than 85 instructional programs and test series, including developmental reading and corrective reading series; spelling series; math and corrective math modules; earth science, chemistry, and energy videos; and language arts programs. He is also the author or coauthor of 27 monographs and chapters of professional books and more than 65 professional books and articles including *Conceptual Learning* (1969), *Theory of Instruction: Principles and Applications* (1991), and *Theory of Mastery and Acceleration* (1997). His latest book, *Inferred Functions of Performance and Learning* (2004), is a theoretical text on the logic of learning and performance. He has authored several books on educational reform, including *War Against the Schools' Academic Child Abuse* (1992). Engelmann created the Direct Instruction model and has overseen more than a hundred implementations of Direct Instruction, beginning with the Brieter-Engelmann Preschool at the University of Illinois in 1964. He founded the National Institute for Direct Instruction in 1997 and currently serves as chairman of its board of directors. Engelmann received the Council of Scientific Society President's Award of Achievement in Education Research in December 2002.

Success For All

Chapter Five

Robert Slavin is currently codirector of the Center for Research on the Education of Students Placed at Risk at Johns Hopkins University and chairman of the Success For All Foundation. He received his BA in psychology from Reed College in 1972, and his PhD in social relations in 1975 from Johns Hopkins University. Dr. Slavin has authored or coauthored more than 200 articles and 18 books, including *Educational Psychology: Theory into Practice* (1986, 1988, 1991, 1994, 1997, 2000), *Effective Programs for Students at Risk* (1989), *Cooperative Learning: Theory, Research, and Practice* (1990, 1995), *Preventing Early School Failure* (1994), *Every Child, Every School: Success For All* (1996), *Show Me the Evidence: Proven and Promising Programs for America's Schools* (1998), and *Effective Programs for Latino Students* (2000). He received the American Educational Research Association's Raymond B. Cattell Early Career Award for Programmatic Research in 1986, the Palmer O. Johnson Award for the best article in an American Educational Research Association journal in 1988, the Charles A. Dana Award in 1994, the James Bryant Conant Award from the Education Commission of the States in 1998, the Outstanding Leadership in Education Award from the Horace Mann League in 1999, and the Distinguished Services Award from the Council of Chief State School Officers in 2000.

Nancy A. Madden is currently president of the Success For All Foundation. She received her BA in psychology from Reed College in 1973, and her PhD in clinical psychology from American University in 1980. From 1980 to 1998, she was a research scientist at the Center for Research on the Education of Students Placed at Risk at Johns Hopkins University, where she directed the development of the reading, writing, language arts, and mathematics elements of Success For All. Dr. Madden is the author or coauthor of many articles and books on cooperative learning, mainstreaming, Chapter 1, and students at risk, including *Effective Programs for Students at Risk* (1989) and *Every Child, Every School: Success For All* (1996).

Project GRAD

Chapter Six

James L. Ketelsen is the retired chairman of the board of Tenneco, Inc. He was born November 14, 1930, in Davenport, Iowa, and graduated from Northwestern University in 1952. He began his business career in 1955 as a certified public accountant in Chicago with the firm of Price Waterhouse. In 1959, he joined J. I. Case Company and became its president in 1967. Mr. Ketelsen moved to Houston in 1972 as an executive of Tenneco, Inc. He served as chairman and chief executive officer of Tenneco, Inc., from July 1, 1978, to January 1, 1992.

America's Choice

Chapter Seven

Marc S. Tucker is president of the National Center on Education and the Economy, a leader in the movement for standards-based school reform in the United States. Mr. Tucker authored the Carnegie Report, *A Nation Prepared: Teachers for the 21st Century* (1986), which called for a restructuring of America's schools based on standards; created the National Board for Professional Teaching Standards; created the Commission on the Skills of the American Workforce and coauthored its report, *America's Choice: High Skills or Low Wages!* (1990), which called for a new high school–leaving certificate based on standards; was instrumental in creating the National Skill Standards Board and chaired its committee on standards and assessment policy; and, with Lauren Resnick, created the New Standards consortium, which pioneered the development of performance standards in the United States and created a set of examinations matched to the standards. With Ray Marshall, Mr. Tucker coauthored *Thinking for a Living: Education and the Wealth of Nations* (1992), selected by *Business Week* as one of the 10 best business books of 1992; with Judy Codding, he coauthored *Standards for Our Schools: How to Set Them, Measure Them, and Reach Them,*

(1998); and with Judy Codding, he coedited *The Principal Challenge* (2002).

Different Ways of Knowing
Chapter Eight

Linda Johannesen has an MA in educational psychology from the University of Chicago and a BA in elementary and special education from Northeastern Illinois University. She is co–principal investigator and senior author of *Different Ways of Knowing K–6* and senior author of *Different Ways of Knowing Middle Grades Project*. She was formerly a teacher, researcher, and curriculum specialist with the Chicago Public Schools. She has also been a consultant to such educational publishers as Scholastic, Charlesbridge, The Wright Group, The Creative Edge, and Graphic Learning and to the Utah State Office of Education, the Connecticut State Department of Education, and several other states and districts. She is senior author of *Writing and Thinking: A Process Approach* (K–6 series); *Think and Write: An Audio-Visual Program*; and *Roadmap to Literacy*, a teacher training guide for introducing the California Framework in English and Language Arts. She is also the vice president of PEN, the international writers' organization.

Co-nect
Chapter Nine

Bruce Goldberg, founder and chief educational officer of Co-nect, holds a PhD in philosophy from the University of Colorado. Dr. Goldberg helped found Co-nect in 1992, while serving as a Division Scientist at BBN Systems and Technologies in Cambridge, Massachusetts. Prior to joining the Co-nect Schools project, he was codirector of the Center for Restructuring and associate director of the Educational Issues Department at the American Federation of Teachers in Washington, D.C. Dr. Goldberg has been a policy advisor on education to many organizations and has served on many advisory committees and boards, including the Gates Foundation's Education Initiative Advisory Committee, the U.S. Department of Education's Advisory Committee on High Intensity Technology Sites, and the Grammy Foundation's Education Advisory Committee.

Turning Points

Chapter Ten

Dan French is the executive director of the Center for Collaborative Education in Boston and the former director of instruction and curriculum for the Massachusetts Department of Education, where he was responsible for all agency school restructuring initiatives, state curriculum frameworks, and school improvement plans. He began his career as a special educator. French has an EdD from the University of Massachusetts, Amherst. He is 1993 winner of the Manuel Carballo Award for Outstanding State Service, Commonwealth of Massachusetts. French is author of numerous publications including a 1998 *Phi Delta Kappan* article, "The State's Role in Shaping a Progressive Vision of Public Education."

Leah Rugen, director of publications for National Turning Points, has worked at the Center for Collaborative Education since 1997 as writer, change coach, and program director of the National Turning Points Center. Previously, she worked for Expeditionary Learning Outward Bound and the New York City Outward Bound Center. She began her education career teaching English and writing in public school in New York. She has written and edited many education publications, including a 1997 *Phi Delta Kappan* article, "From the Inside Out: The Expeditionary Learning Process of Teacher Change." She received her master of arts in teaching (MAT) in English from Brown University.

Talent Development High School
Chapter Eleven

Nettie Legters is research scientist at the Johns Hopkins University Center for Social Organization of Schools and associate director of the Center for Research on the Education of Students Placed at Risk Talent Development High Schools program. Her primary research areas include high school restructuring, teachers' work, and equity in urban education. Dr. Legters is committed to translating research into policy and practice and has worked actively in urban high schools to support major restructuring efforts. She has been a key developer and organizational facilitator in Talent Development High School replication sites and has cowritten a Talent Development High School planning guide (1999) and a guide for creating a ninth-grade success academy (1998). She also has published articles and reports aimed at improving urban schools for teachers and students, including *Small Learning Communities Meet School-to-Work: Whole School Restructuring for Urban Comprehensive High Schools* (1999). Her book, *Comprehensive Reform for Urban High Schools: A Talent Development Approach* (2002), is now available through Teachers College Press.

James M. McPartland is research professor of sociology and director of the Center for Social Organization of Schools at Johns Hopkins University. He received his PhD in sociology from Johns Hopkins in 1968 and spent his early research years in Washington, D.C., as a coauthor of the influential Coleman Report: *Equality of Educational Opportunities* (1996). He was also a contributor to the U.S. Commission on Civil Rights study, *Racial Isolation in the Public Schools* (1967). His work has continued in the sociology of education on topics of effective schooling for students from poor and minority backgrounds, with more than 70 published articles, chapters and monographs. Since 1994, he has led the Johns Hopkins University team that is developing, evaluating, and scaling-up the Talent Development High School with Career Academies, a comprehensive research-based reform model.

Robert Balfanz is an associate research scientist and associate director of the Talent Development High School program. Dr. Balfanz has 15 years' experience in the research, development, design, and implementation of curricular and instructional reforms. A central focus of his research and development work is translating research findings into effective classroom interventions. He has contributed to *Everyday Mathematics*, a product of the University of Chicago School Mathematics Project, which is currently used by more than 2 million students nationwide. He leads the Talent Development High School curriculum and instruction research and development team and also is codeveloper of the program's Transition to Advanced Mathematics course. Dr. Balfanz has written widely on the implementation challenges that comprehensive school reform models face and the characteristics of secondary schooling in large urban school districts. He received his PhD in education from the University of Chicago.

High Schools That Work

Chapter Twelve

Gene Bottoms has been director of the Southern Regional Education Board's High Schools That Work initiative since 1987. In July 1997, Dr. Bottoms was promoted to senior vice president of the Southern Regional Education Board, reflecting his role in and the board's interest in and commitment to the High Schools That Work initiative. Before joining the Southern Regional Education Board, Dr. Bottoms was executive director of the American Vocational Association, where he emphasized academics as an integral part of vocational education at the secondary and postsecondary levels. He was director of educational improvement for the Georgia Department of Education for 13 years, overseeing improvement efforts in both vocational and academic education. In 1995, Secretary of Education Richard Riley appointed Dr. Bottoms to the National Educational Research Policy and Priorities Board, which is charged with forging a national consensus with respect to a long-term agenda for educational research, development, and dissemination. In September 1995, Dr.

Bottoms received the Harold W. McGraw, Jr., Prize in Education. This award is presented annually to individuals who have made significant contributions to the advancement of knowledge through education. In 2000, he was appointed to the National Commission on the Senior Year. Dr. Bottoms has also been a local school teacher, principal, and guidance counselor.

Edison Schools

Chapter Thirteen

John E. Chubb is a founding partner and chief education officer of Edison Schools Inc. He received his BA (*summa cum laude*) in 1974 from Washington University, St. Louis, and his PhD from the University of Minnesota in 1979, both in political science. Dr. Chubb joined the Edison Project in February 1992 as a member of the original core team. After a decade of research and writing on student achievement and education policy, he devoted his initial time with the Edison Project to school design. Since 1993, he has headed Edison's Curriculum Division. In 1998, he also headed Edison's Operating Schools Division, and in 1999 he was appointed chief education officer of Edison Schools. In addition to his work at Edison, Dr. Chubb is a nonresident senior fellow with the governmental studies program at the Brookings Institution. Prior to joining Brookings, Dr. Chubb was a member of the faculty at Stanford University. In recent years, he has been a visiting professor at Johns Hopkins University and Woodrow Wilson School of Public and International Affairs at Princeton University. Dr. Chubb has been awarded more than a dozen important fellowships and grants including the Hoover Institution National Fellowship (1983–84) and the Leonard D. White Award of the American Political Science Association (1980) and has written and edited several books and articles, including *A Lesson in School Reform from Great Britain*, with Terry M. Moe (1992) and *Politics, Markets and America's Schools*, with Terry M. Moe (1990). His areas of expertise include education, American politics, public policy, and statistics.

Institute for Learning

Chapter Fourteen

The late **Thomas K. Glennan, Jr.**, was a senior advisor for education policy in the Washington Office of the RAND Corporation. He received a PhD in economics from Stanford University in 1968. His research at RAND spanned a wide variety of policy planning issues in such diverse areas as education, manpower training, energy, environmental enforcement, demonstration program management in health and human services, and military research and development. Through 1997, he led RAND's analytic effort in support of the New American Schools Development Corporation. He also examined potential national and federal policies in support of the use of technology in elementary and secondary education. Most recently, he led an effort to develop plans for coherent, long-term programs of research and development in reading and mathematics education for the Office of Education Research and Improvement in the U.S. Department of Education. He was a member of the MacArthur Network on Teaching and Learning. He coauthored books on the management of research and development and the use of social experiments in policy planning. Dr. Glennan was director of research and acting assistant director of the Office of Economic Opportunity for Planning, Research, and Evaluation before becoming the first director of the National Institute of Education in 1972.

Lauren Resnick is an internationally known scholar in the cognitive science of learning and instruction. Her recent research has focused on socializing intelligence, the nature and development of thinking abilities, and the relation between school learning and everyday competence, with special attention to mathematics and literacy. Her current work lies at the intersection of cognitive science and policy for education. Dr. Resnick founded and directs the Institute for Learning, which focuses on professional development based on cognitive learning principles and effort-oriented education. She is cofounder and codirector of the New Standards Project, which has developed standards and assessments that have widely influenced state and school district practices. Resnick was a member of the Commission on the Skills of the American Workforce and chaired the assessment committee of the SCANS Commission and of the Resource Group on Student Achievement of the National Education Goals Panel. She has served on the Commission on Behavioral and Social Sciences and Education and on the Mathematical Sciences Education Board at the National Research Council. Her National Academy of Sciences monograph, *Education and Learning to Think* (1987), has been influential in school reform efforts, and her widely circulated Presidential Address to the American Educational Research Association, "Learning in School and Out," has shaped thinking about youth apprenticeship and school-to-work transition. Dr. Resnick is a professor of psychology at the University of Pittsburgh, where she directs the prestigious Learning Research and Development Center. Educated at Radcliffe and Harvard, she is a member of the Smithsonian Council and was the recipient of the 1998 E. L. Thorndike Award from the American Psychological Association and the 1999 *Oeuvre* Award from the European Association for Research on Learning and Instruction.

Bay Area School Reform Collaborative

Chapter Fifteen

Merrill Vargo is the executive director of the Bay Area School Reform Collaborative. Before founding and joining the collaborative in January 1995, Vargo spent nine years as a college faculty member, managed her own consulting firm, and served as executive director of the California Institute for School Improvement, a Sacramento-based nonprofit that provides staff development and policy analysis for educators. Vargo was director of regional programs and special programs and special projects for the California Department of Education, where she provided leadership to a number of key school reform efforts, including the SB 1274 School Restructuring Initiative, Charter Schools, Goals 2000, and the School Improvement Program. Vargo received her BA and PhD in English literature from Cornell University.

Funding the Scale-Up of Educational Improvement Programs

Chapter Sixteen

Marc Dean Millot is an independent consultant working with a range of clients to operate effectively in the emerging K–12 school improvement market. During the 1990s, he was part of the RAND Corporation team working with New American Schools on strategic planning and focused on the problem of taking its design teams programs to scale, writing the first memo on the problem of transitioning teams from grant to fee, and drafting the memoranda of understanding New American Schools used to bring its designs to scale in major urban districts around the country. In 1997, he joined New American Schools as its director of design team operations, in effect its grants program officer. In 1998, New American Schools stopped making grants, started making loans, and Mr. Millot became vice president for design team investment, something more like the lead partner in a venture capital firm. In 1999, Mr. Millot formed the $15 million Education Entrepreneurs Fund and became its first president.

Program Descriptions and Contact Information

Cognitively Guided Instruction

The Program

Cognitively Guided Instruction (CGI), developed in 1986 at the Wisconsin Center for Education Research, is a research-based professional development program that focuses on how children think about mathematics. CGI does not provide a curriculum for teachers to follow or specify explicit forms of teaching, grouping students, or interacting with them. Instead, teachers learn to use conceptual models of student thinking to engage in practical inquiry in their classrooms, so that student learning becomes generative. The focus on student thinking provides a context for deepening teacher's knowledge of essential mathematics and for reconceptualizing their practice.

CGI uses a fine-grained analysis of mathematics content to help teachers improve their understanding of how students think and, in the process, to provide a basis for teachers to learn related mathematics content. CGI is grounded in research-based knowledge about the development of children's mathematical thinking. Most children enter school with a rich store of informal knowledge and problem-solving strategies that can serve as the basis for developing much of the mathematics of the primary school curriculum. Within this framework, teachers are taught to relate types of mathematics problem situations to the strategies that children use to solve them and the evolution of children's strategies along predictable trajectories.

CGI is an outgrowth of a study that explored the effects of sharing research-based knowledge about the development of children's mathematical thinking with teachers and has grown through the grassroots efforts of teachers. The Comprehensive Center, Region VI, at the University of Wisconsin adopted the program as its primary effort for improving mathematics achievement and increasing teacher capacity to teach mathematics at the primary grade levels. Responding to teacher demand, additional institutes have been developed to train a cohort of experienced teachers who can provide training to additional teachers on a site-by-site basis.

Funding

Research on the development of cognitively guided instruction was supported primarily by a grant from the National Science Foundation. Additional support has been provided by a grant from the U.S. Department of Education Office of Educational Research and Improvement (now the Institute for Education Sciences) to the National Center for Improving Student Learning and Achievement in Mathematics and Science and the Wisconsin Center for Educational Research.

Effectiveness

Evaluations of CGI have shown improvements in students' math achievement and increases in teachers' understanding and sense of efficacy.

Contact Information

Thomas Carpenter
Wisconsin Center for Education Research
1025 West Johnson Street
Madison, WI 53706
(608) 263-4200
http://www.wcer.wisc.edu

National Writing Project

The Program

The National Writing Project (NWP) is a nationwide professional development program for teachers, begun in 1974 at the University of California, Berkeley. Its primary goal is improving student writing by improving the teaching of writing in the nation's schools. NWP receives federal funding, which it currently grants to 175 local sites in 50 states, the District of Columbia, Puerto Rico, and the U.S. Virgin Islands. Sites operate from university campuses and collaborate with surrounding schools and districts. Collectively, these sites serve approximately 100,000 teachers every year, from kindergarten through university and in all disciplines. The NWP model is based on the beliefs that teachers are the key to education reform, that teachers make the best teachers of other teachers, and that teachers benefit from studying and conducting research.

NWP sites operate on a teachers-teaching-teachers model. Successful teachers attend invitational summer institutes at their local writing project sites, where they examine their classroom practice, conduct research, and develop their own writing skills. During the school year, these teachers provide professional development workshops for other teachers in their schools and communities.

The national office develops, supports, and reviews the quality of its growing network of sites by awarding grants to each local site, providing technical assistance, conducting an annual review of every site, and sponsoring annual evaluation studies. In addition, the national office designs and supports targeted national learning networks and programs that enable teachers across the country to explore common issues, discuss the latest research, exchange classroom strategies, and collaborate on publishing and disseminating what they have learned.

Funding

NWP receives support from the U.S. Department of Education, foundations, corporations, universities, and K–12 schools. Sites must match all federal funds they receive from NWP.

Effectiveness

Ongoing evaluation studies are currently investigating the effects of the model. Studies have shown evidence that NWP professional development leads to improved student writing achievement. Evaluation data are online at http://www.writingproject.org/Publications/other/index.html (as of July 26, 2004).

Contact Information

National Writing Project
University of California
2105 Bancroft Way, #1042
Berkeley, CA 94720-1042
(510) 642-0963
http://www.writingproject.org/

Direct Instruction

The Program

Direct Instruction (DI) is a model for teaching that emphasizes well-developed and carefully planned lessons designed around small learning increments and clearly defined and prescribed teaching tasks. DI was developed in the late 1960s, and more than 10,000 schools use some form of it today. DI is based on the assumption that controlling the school setting can greatly accelerate children's rate of academic achievement. This acceleration is most seriously needed in failing schools, where children historically perform in the first quartile. The comprehensive DI model used for these schools controls teaching variables and setting variables. DI assumes that even very-low-performing children are capable of learning if the instruction is appropriate. The model further assumes that if specific learning has not occurred, adequate teaching has not been provided. Learning and teaching are verified only by the children's behavior.

The program's instructional sequences are designed to teach more than traditional programs do in the same amount of time. The efficiency is realized by scripting the teacher's presentation, grouping children homogeneously, collecting data on student performance, specifying schedules for subjects that provide sufficient daily exposure, providing extensive preservice and in-service training on specific skills and content, requiring all teachers to participate in the program, implementing schoolwide management and reinforcement procedures, and using a problem-identification and problem-solution approach.

Founded in 1997, the National Institute for Direct Instruction is a not-for-profit corporation dedicated to providing school districts with a solid training program and approach for implementing DI in districts, schools, and classrooms. Sites implementing DI that are in close geographic proximity often communicate with one another, and fully implementing schools may serve as models for other adopters.

Funding
Schools implementing DI may reallocate existing funds or use Title 1 funds to pay for services and materials.

Effectiveness
The basic DI model has been extensively evaluated and is judged by various meta-analyses to be one of the few models that has ample evidence of effectiveness—for all populations and socioeconomic levels. Studies show positive student achievement and affective outcomes. Evaluation data are available on the Web site.

Contact Information
National Institute for Direct Instruction
P.O. Box 11248
Eugene, OR 97440
(877) 485-1973
http://www.nifdi.org/

Success For All

The Program

Success For All (SFA) is a program designed for comprehensive restructuring of elementary schools that serve many children at risk of failure. It emphasizes prevention, early and intensive intervention, and tutoring for students with academic difficulties. SFA began in 1987 at Johns Hopkins University and currently serves about 1,500 schools in 48 states.

SFA's state-of-the-art curriculum and instructional methods emphasize the integration of phonics and meaning-focused instruction, cooperative learning, curriculum-based assessments, writing and language arts instruction emphasizing writer's workshops, preschool and kindergarten instruction with story-telling and language development, and adaptations for Spanish and English as a second language. The model also emphasizes a support program that engages parents, community members, and integrated services, as well as extensive professional development, to help schools start children with success and then build on that foundation throughout the elementary grades. Additional components of the model include math, science, and social studies curricular materials; eight-week assessments; tutors; early learning (preschool and kindergarten); a facilitator; and staff support teams.

The Success For All Foundation, the nonprofit organization formed to manage the development and implementation of SFA and its related programs, provides services to its extensive network of schools through employees located in 25 regional training programs throughout the United States. A major goal of the model is promoting communication among partner schools, thus decreasing the isolation of implementers, by creating a network of sites through national and local conferences, a newsletter, and local meetings.

Funding

Schools forming partnerships with SFA use Title 1 and/or Comprehensive School Reform funds to pay for services and materials. The foundation is funded largely by fees from schools for training and materials, supplemented by grants and loans from charitable foundations and government agencies.

Effectiveness

SFA has engaged in an extensive use of data to evaluate the effectiveness of the model, including rigorous experimental-control studies. Use of SFA is associated with positive effects on student reading achievement and on avoiding such outcomes as special education placements and retentions. Evaluation data are available on the Web site.

Contact Information

Success For All Foundation
200 West Towsontown Boulevard
Baltimore, MD 21204-5200
(800) 548-4998
http://www.successforall.net/

Project GRAD

The Program

Project GRAD is a nonprofit school-community collaborative successfully enhancing the instructional quality and culture of at-risk feeder systems in the nation's inner cities. A comprehensive yet cost-effective program, Project GRAD combines resources and expertise from school districts, universities, foundations, corporations, community and national nonprofit organizations, and federal and state government agencies to work in partnership with school feeder patterns (all the elementary and middle schools that feed students into a high school). Project GRAD's mission is to increase the high school graduation and college attendance rates of inner-city students across the nation, as well as to close the achievement gap between minority and nonminority students. The philosophy guiding the program is that all prekindergarten through 12th grade students can be effective learners, regardless of socioeconomic background. Infusing appropriate and timely programmatic interventions beginning in preschool and maintaining them consistently through high school ensures success. Since its founding in 1993, Project GRAD has partnered with nine school systems.

Project GRAD emphasizes a solid foundation of skills in reading, writing, and math, along with building self-discipline and providing resources to support at-risk children and their families. The model uses a number of curriculum models that have been widely and individually piloted and validated as effective innovative models, including MOVE IT Math; Communities in Schools; Success For All; and Consistency Management and Cooperative Discipline. Other program elements include scholarships for eligible students that can be used at any accredited college, university, or degree-granting institution; summer institutes for students; and family and community involvement through such components as a local governing board and not-for-profit organization.

Project GRAD is implemented within feeder patterns of schools, creating a consistency in school programs and reforms across grade levels and within school systems. Leaders from various partner systems communicate with one another at national directors' meetings.

Funding

To build and sustain community support within each adopting city, the model requires cities to form a not-for-profit 501(c)(3) as a governing and fundraising organization. Districts must provide a percentage of the funding for the cost of the program from public education money, while the remaining funds are raised from government and/or private sources. Research and development activities are supported by federal GEAR-UP grants and funds from the Ford Foundation.

Effectiveness

Studies have shown evidence of positive outcomes for students, including improved achievement and increased high school graduation, college entrance, and college graduation rates. Evaluation data are available by contacting the project's office.

Contact Information
Project GRAD USA
1100 Louisiana, Suite 450
Houston, TX 77002
(713) 986-0499
http://www.projectgradusa.org

America's Choice[1]

The Program

The America's Choice School Design specifies a comprehensive model of school organization, leadership, instruction, and curriculum based on extensive study of the best educational practices in the United States and abroad. The aim of the design is to ensure that every student is successful on state and local assessments and is prepared for college. The model works to achieve this through creating coherent educational systems focused on instruction and by building the capacity at all levels of the educational system to sustain widespread improvement. The design complies in every respect with the requirements of the federal No Child Left Behind Act of 2001. The design, in operation since 1998, currently works with 466 schools in 15 states and the District of Columbia.

The America's Choice program offers designs for elementary, K–8, middle, and high schools directly to the schools. Program developers also work closely with states and school districts interested in using the America's Choice design as the core of their statewide or districtwide strategies for raising student achievement. The design focuses on five key tasks in readying students for success in today's economy: (1) standards and assessments; (2) aligned instructional systems; (3) high-performance management, leadership, and organization; (4) professional learning communities; and (5) parent or guardian and community involvement.

---

[1] Note that contact information for other regions is available on the America's Choice Web site.

The America's Choice school design provides professional development and the delivery of services to partner schools through a decentralized model of six regional offices. Regional professional development and service delivery staff undergo a training and certification process at the America's Choice National College to ensure consistency in training and materials provided to sites. A network of partner schools and a national conference provide for the sharing of experiences and information among sites.

Funding
Research and development activities are supported by foundation and government funds. The organization uses a fee-for-service model to support its services to schools.

Effectiveness
Studies have shown improved academic achievement among students in America's Choice schools. Evaluation data are online at http://www.ncee.org/acsd/results/index.jsp (as of July 26, 2004).

Contact Information
America's Choice
Mid-Atlantic Regional Office
One Thomas Circle, NW, Suite 700
Washington, DC 20005
(202) 783-3668
http://www.ncee.org/acsd/index.jsp?setProtocol=true

Different Ways of Knowing

The Program
Different Ways of Knowing is an adaptable, research-based, field-validated school improvement partner for elementary, middle, and K–12 schools. Our strategies and tools improve student achievement by dramatically improving classroom practices. Started in 1989 as an initiative of the Galef Institute in Los Angeles, California, Different

Ways of Knowing has partnered with more than 600 schools in 24 states since its inception. During the 2002–03 school year, Different Ways of Knowing partnered with 101 schools throughout the United States.

Different Ways of Knowing works with schools to identify what their students are expected to learn and what state and district accountability measures require and to understand their current school improvement plans. Together with schools, model facilitators identify the Different Ways of Knowing strategies and tools that are most appropriate to the school setting and that will accelerate the school's improvement plan. Strategies combine coaching for results, a proven ability to develop student expertise in literacy, and the use of the arts to help every student learn reading, writing, mathematics, social studies, and science. The approach is customized to each school and district and is grounded in six practices of high-achieving schools. Different Ways of Knowing works with teachers to create standards-driven classrooms focused on student learning, guides site administrators to use data to drive and monitor school improvement, and partners with district officials to provide the resources and professional development that schools need to create effective, engaging learning environments.

The Different Ways of Knowing site network has expanded through several district partnerships and one state partnership, allowing the sharing of information and experiences across sites and the establishment of local teams of coaches to work with the national team.

Funding

Schools partnering with Different Ways of Knowing raise funds from public and private sources, such as federal Comprehensive School Reform funds, to pay for the cost of services and materials. Research and development activities are supported by grants from the U.S. Department of Education and various foundations.

Effectiveness

Studies have shown evidence of improved student achievement associated with each year of participation for students in Different Ways of Knowing sites. Evaluation data are available on the Web site.

Contact Information

The Galef Institute
5670 Wilshire Boulevard
20th Floor
Los Angeles, CA 90036-5623
(323) 525-0042, ext. 115
http://www.differentways.org/

Co-nect

The Program

Members of the Educational Technologies Group at Bolt, Beranek and Newman, a research and development firm in Cambridge, Massachusetts, founded Co-nect in 1992 in response to a call for proposals from the New American Schools Development Corporation (NASDC). Originally operating as a comprehensive school reform design, Co-nect acts as a professional development organization dedicated to helping educators and administrators build the capacity needed to improve and sustain achievement for all students. Today, Co-nect has grown from a small research and development project to a national organization providing school improvement services in more than 225 schools in 26 states.

Co-nect provides professional development and technology integration services that help K–12 districts and schools accelerate school improvement. Its resources include a nationwide staff of education professionals who work on site with faculty using a suite of online learning modules, diagnostic tools, and teacher resources. To account for different needs and priorities among schools and districts, Co-nect offers four models of services: (1) Co-nect Comprehensive, (2) Co-nect Tech, (3) Co-nect Literacy, and (4) Co-nect Dataflow.

Co-nect's educational consultants partner with districts and schools to tailor offerings according to performance, existing programs, and budget guidelines, focusing on the areas most likely to drive measurable improvements at each site.

Co-nect offers opportunities for sharing among participants at partner schools at its annual national conference.

Funding

Schools partnering with Co-nect can receive Title 1, Comprehensive School Reform, or other state or federal education funds to pay for services and materials. Research and development activities are funded by federal and state grants and by various foundations.

Effectiveness

Evaluation studies have found evidence of improved student achievement in Co-nect schools. Evaluation data are available on the Web site.

Contact Information

Co-nect
625 Mount Auburn Street
Cambridge, MA 02138
(617) 995-3100
http://www.co-nect.net/

Turning Points

The Program

Turning Points is a comprehensive education reform model for middle schools that focuses on improving student learning. Recognizing the need to both strengthen the academic core of middle schools and establish caring, supportive environments that value all young adolescents, Turning Points helps schools undergo dramatic change.

The Center for Collaborative Education, with the full endorsement of the Carnegie Corporation and New American Schools, coordinates Turning Points' assistance to middle schools using an intensive, whole-school reform designed to significantly improve teaching, student engagement, and learning. Started in 1999, Turning Points currently partners with 68 middle schools in 12 states.

With comprehensive support services from Turning Points staff, participating middle schools commit to a multiyear, systemic change process that is based on seven guiding principles: teach a curriculum grounded in standards; use instructional methods designed to prepare all students; prepare teachers for middle grades; organize relationships for learning; govern democratically by involving all staff members; provide a safe and healthy school environment; and involve parents and communities in supporting learning. These principles form a framework for creating middle schools that address the needs of young adolescents.

Turning Points operates through a network of independent regional centers linked to a national center. Using a system of shared governance and accountability, the centers work to provide consistency in training and principles while being adaptable to local conditions. Local, regional, and national networking activities promote communication among sites and regional center staff, including network meetings and conferences, regional summer institutes, and a national coaches' institute.

Funding

Schools partnering with Turning Points use Comprehensive School Reform or Title 1 funds to pay for services and materials. Foundation funds currently support the research and development activities of the parent organization.

Effectiveness

Ongoing evaluation studies point to positive achievement out comes for students in Turning Points schools. Evaluation data are online at http://www.turningpts.org/success.htm (as of July 26, 2004).

Contact Information
National Turning Points Center
Center for Collaborative Education
1135 Tremont Street, Suite 490
Boston, MA 02120
(617) 421-0134
http://www.turningpts.org/

Talent Development High Schools

The Program
The Talent Development High School (TDHS), featuring career academies, is a comprehensive reform model for large high schools that face serious problems with student attendance, discipline, achievement scores, and dropout rates. The model consists of specific changes in school organization and management to establish a strong, positive school climate for learning; curricular and instructional innovations to transition all students into advanced high school work in English and mathematics; parent and community involvement activities to encourage college awareness; and professional development systems to support the implementation of the recommended reforms.

TDHS was initiated in 1995 through a partnership of the Johns Hopkins University Center for Research on the Education of Students Placed At Risk and Patterson High School in Baltimore and has now expanded to 40 high schools in 11 states across the country. Providing more curricular and organizational structure than other high school reform models, this center strives to balance a commitment to the implementation of its core components with a reliance on school-based teachers and administrators to own and adapt the Talent Development model to meet the needs of their school. Key components of the Model include small learning community formulation, including a ninth-grade academy and upper-grade career academies; extended class periods; a focus on attendance and discipline; twilight school; parent and community involvement; a principals' network; and various curriculum modules.

TDHS serves its growing number of schools by relocating teams of facilitators to areas with member schools. Efforts are made to work with several schools within a "hub" district to facilitate training and the dissemination of ideas across sites. Networks of school leaders and annual meetings promote communication among adopters.

Funding

The federal Obey-Porter Comprehensive School Reform Demonstration legislation specifically recognized TDHS, and schools can use funding from that program, Small Learning Communities in High Schools, Title 1, or foundation funds to pay for the model. The developer organization receives its primary funding from the U.S. Department of Education and the Interagency Educational Research Initiative.

Effectiveness

Evaluation studies are currently investigating the effects of the model. Early studies have shown evidence of improved student achievement, attendance, and discipline outcomes in TDHS schools. Evaluation data are online at http://www.csos.jhu.edu/tdhs/results.htm (as of July 26, 2004).

Contact Information

Talent Development High School
Center for Social Organization of Schools
Johns Hopkins University
3003 North Charles Street, Suite 200
Baltimore, MD 21218
(410) 516-8800
http://www.csos.jhu.edu/tdhs/index.htm

High Schools That Work

The Program

The Southern Regional Education Board's High Schools That Work (HSTW) program is the nation's largest and fastest-growing effort to combine challenging academic courses and modern career and technical studies to raise the achievement of high school students. The initiative was established in 1987 by the SREB–State Vocational Education Consortium, a partnership of SREB, states, school systems, and school sites. The model is based on the belief that most students can master complex academic and technical concepts if schools create an environment that encourages students to make the effort to succeed. HSTW currently partners with more than 1,100 sites in 30 states.

The mission of schools in the HSTW network is to prepare high school students for both postsecondary education and a career by having them complete a solid academic core and either an academic, a career or technical, or a blended concentration. The major goals of HSTW are to (1) raise the mathematics, science, communication, problem-solving, and technical achievement of more students to the national average and above; (2) blend the essential content of traditional college-preparatory studies—mathematics, science, and language arts—with high-quality career and technical studies by creating conditions that support school leaders, teachers, and counselors in carrying out HSTW's key practices; and (3) advance state and local policies and leadership initiatives necessary to sustain a continuous school-improvement effort for both academic and career and technical studies.

SREB works with 30 states as part of a consortium around vocational education. SREB provides member states and sites with staff development, technical assistance, communications and publications, and assessment services, while member states assume certain responsibilities associated with maintaining and developing a state school-improvement network. In addition, consistency in training and communication among HSTW states and sites is promoted through national meetings, workshops, and conferences.

Funding

Schools working with HSTW receive school-improvement funds from the federal Comprehensive School Reform project, federal or local agencies, or private foundations. Research and development activities are supported by state consortia, the U.S. Department of Education, and various foundations.

Effectiveness

Studies have shown positive achievement and course completion outcomes for HSTW students. Evaluation data are online at http://www.sreb.org/programs/hstw/ResearchReports/researchindex.asp (as of July 26, 2004).

Contact Information

High Schools That Work
Southern Regional Education Board
592 10th Street NW
Atlanta, GA 30318-5790
(404) 875-9211
http://www.sreb.org/programs/hstw/hstwindex.asp

Edison Schools

The Program

Founded in 1992, Edison Schools, a private corporation that is the nation's leading partner with public schools and school districts, focuses on raising student achievement through its research-based school design, uniquely aligned assessment systems, interactive professional development, integrated use of technology, and other proven program features. After engaging in three years of intensive research and development to design innovative schools that could operate at public school spending levels, Edison opened its first four schools in August 1995 and has grown rapidly in every subsequent year. Edison has now implemented its school design in 150 public schools, including many charter schools, which it operates under management contracts with local school districts and charter school boards. Approximately 110,000 students currently attend Edison partnership schools.

Edison takes responsibility for implementing the educational program, technology plans, and management systems of each school and is accountable to a local authority for the performance of the school. Edison schools remain public schools, open to all students and funded with tax dollars. Edison's school design is the product of the thought, discussion, observations, and ideas of educators from all walks of school life. It is supported by volumes of research documenting successful education practices from this country and around the world. The ten fundamental principals guiding Edison's school design include: (1) schools organized for every student's success, (2) a better use of time, (3) a rich and challenging curriculum, (4) teaching methods that motivate, (5) assessments that provide accountability, (6) a professional environment for teachers, (7) technology for an information age, (8) a partnership with families, (9) schools tailored to the community, and (10) the advantages of system and scale.

Using a business model, Edison manages its network of partner schools with a matrix of divisions. Regional vice presidents of the school operations division supervise principals and schools, while other divisions provide regional and national support to schools in such areas as curriculum, assessment, and technology.

Funding

The initial development activities of Edison were funded by private capital, while ongoing research and development is funded through investors and additional venture capital. Edison receives funds from local educational agencies to manage schools.

Effectiveness

Ongoing evaluation studies have shown positive achievement outcomes for students attending Edison schools. Evaluation data are online at http://www.edisonschools.com/design/d23.html (as of July 26, 2004).

Contact Information
Edison Schools
521 Fifth Avenue, 11th Floor
New York, NY 10175
(212) 419-1600
http://www.edisonschools.com/

Institute for Learning

The Program

Since its inception in 1995, the Institute for Learning (IFL) has sought to develop relationships between the expertise of its parent institution, the Learning Research and Development Center of the University of Pittsburgh, and working educators in school systems nationwide. Its mission is to provide educators with the resources and training they need to enhance learning opportunities for all students. IFL serves as a think tank, a design center for innovative professional development systems in the schools, and an educator of core groups of school professionals. Its philosophy rests on the belief that all students with appropriate forms of effort are capable of high achievement and high-level thinking, regardless of their background. This focus on the importance of effort challenges the traditional assumption that the ability to learn depends on innate aptitude. IFL partners with school districts in an effort to bring about systemwide change in teaching and learning; currently, IFL is engaged with 12 school districts.

The core focus of the IFL intervention is improving the quality of instruction and learning in all classrooms within the district by working with the administrative and teaching leaders throughout the district to focus their efforts on instructional improvement. To do this, IFL works with actual and potential instructional leaders across a district to help them to understand the qualities of effective instruction and to develop ways to increase the quality of instruction across the district. These qualities of effective instruction are embodied in the IFL's principles of learning. Additionally, IFL provides professional development to member districts in such areas as Content-Focused Coaching^SM, instructional quality assessment, disciplinary literacy, the conduct of LearningWalks^SM, and the operation of nested learning communities.

IFL assigns one or more staff members to serve as liaisons to each of its partner districts. IFL staff members meet regularly to share and plan work and to reflect on what they have learned in that work. Staff members and leaders from partner districts periodically convene at regional and national meetings to receive training, discuss IFL 's theories and work, and learn from one another's experiences.

Funding

Districts working with IFL pay for the services and materials they receive, while research and development activities are supported by various government and foundation grants.

Effectiveness

Because the work of IFL is integrated with the work of the district, it is impossible to separate the affects of the program from other possible influences on student performance. However, many of the institute's district partners have begun to show improvement in core-subject test scores, particularly at the elementary school level, and, in the past four years, all the urban districts with which the institute has worked have chosen to continue their partnerships.

Contact Information

Institute for Learning
Learning Research and Development Center
3939 O'Hara Street, Room 310
Pittsburgh, PA 15260
(412) 624-7093
http://www.instituteforlearning.org/

Bay Area School Reform Collaborative

The Program

The Bay Area School Reform Collaborative (BASRC) is a nonprofit organization dedicated to raising student achievement and to narrowing the gap in performance between socially advantaged and socially disadvantaged students. BASRC does this by improving the quality of teaching and the ways that schools and school districts are led. Using its foundation funding, BASRC provides grants to schools in the San Francisco Bay Area in an effort to build organizational capacity for improvement in area schools. Currently, BASRC is engaged with 98 schools and 27 districts.

BASRC engages teams of educators in a data-driven continual-improvement process that is much like total quality management. Adaptations of this process are used by teachers working in grade-level, subject-matter, and schoolwide teams. Individual teachers and district-level management teams also use adaptations of this "inquiry" process. Schools have used their BASRC grants to enable teachers to attend BASRC workshops and network activities (often by paying substitute teachers to take over briefly in the classroom), to hire outside consultants with special expertise in data and assessment and specific areas of pedagogy and assessment (particularly literacy), and to pay the full- or part-time salary of a teacher to manage the school's reform effort.

BASRC promotes communication among partner schools and districts through regional learning networks for principals and district leaders. In addition, BASRC provides network meetings for local collaborative coaches, district members who serve as coaches by working with teachers in clusters of BASRC-member schools designated as a local collaborative.

Funding

BASRC was founded in 1995 thanks to substantial grants from the William and Flora Hewlett Foundation and the Annenberg Foundation. In 2001, both foundations provided additional grants to

BASRC to continue its work, which is currently expanding at the district level.

Effectiveness

Studies have found improvements in student achievement and changes in school culture in BASRC schools. Key areas of change included the way schools evaluate and adopt teaching methods and the ways they train teachers, involve parents, and manage the school. Evaluation data are available on the Web site.

Contact Information

Bay Area School Reform Collaborative
181 Fremont Street
Second Floor
San Francisco, CA 94105-2208
(415) 348-5500
http://www.basrc.org/